Peterson Reference Guide to

OWLS

OF NORTH AMERICA
AND THE CARIBBEAN

THE PETERSON REFERENCE GUIDE SERIES

OWLS
OF NORTH AMERICA AND THE CARIBBEAN

SCOTT WEIDENSAUL

HOUGHTON MIFFLIN HARCOURT
BOSTON   NEW YORK
2015

Sponsored by
the Roger Tory Peterson Institute
and the National Wildlife Federation

**AREA COVERED
BY THIS BOOK**

For information about permission to reproduce selections from this book,
write to Permissions, Houghton Mifflin Harcourt Publishing Company,
215 Park Avenue South, New York, New York 10003.

www.hmhco.com

PETERSON FIELD GUIDES and PETERSON FIELD GUIDE SERIES
are registered trademarks of Houghton Mifflin Harcourt Publishing Company.

Library of Congress Cataloging-in-Publication Data is available.

ISBN 978-0-547-84003-1

Book design by Eugenie S. Delaney

Printed in China
SCP 10 9 8 7 6 5 4 3 2 1

The legacy of America's greatest naturalist and creator of the field guide series, Roger Tory Peterson, is kept alive through the dedicated work of the Roger Tory Peterson Institute of Natural History (RTPI). Established in 1985, RTPI is located in Peterson's hometown of Jamestown, New York, near Chautauqua Institution in the southwestern part of the state.

Today RTPI is a national center for nature education that maintains, shares, and interprets Peterson's extraordinary archive of writings, art, and photography. The institute, housed in a landmark building by world-class architect Robert A. M. Stern, continues to transmit Peterson's zest for teaching about the natural world through leadership programs in teacher development as well as outstanding exhibits of contemporary nature art, natural history, and the Peterson Collection.

Your participation as a steward of the Peterson Collection and supporter of the Peterson legacy is needed. Please consider joining RTPI at an introductory rate of 50 percent of the regular membership fee for the first year. Simply call RTPI's membership department at (800) 758-6841 ext. 226, or e-mail membership@rtpi.org to take advantage of this special membership offered to purchasers of this book. For more information, please visit the Peterson Institute in person or virtually at www.rtpi.org.

For Amy, who puts up with a lot of
nights alone because of owls

And for Sandy Lockerman and Gary Shimmel,
for years of teamwork and friendship

Peterson Reference Guide to

OWLS

OF NORTH AMERICA
AND THE CARIBBEAN

CONTENTS

HOW TO USE
THIS BOOK

Muffled by velvety plumage and downy edges on its major flight feathers, an Eastern Screech-Owl makes remarkably little sound when it flies—an adaption to both hide its approach from sharp-eared prey and not interfere with its own ability to hear while hunting. Some owls that prey mostly on arthropods lack such adaptations for silent flight. *(Manitoba. Christian Artuso)*

WHAT IS AN OWL?

Owls are instantly identifiable, even by those who otherwise cannot tell a Mallard from a Bald Eagle. They are also endlessly fascinating—and have clearly intrigued us for as long as we've been fully human. One of the earliest expressions of human art, on the walls of the Chauvet Cave in France, is an owl, complete with ear tufts, drawn with a fingertip in the wet mud of the cavern wall some 30,000 years ago.

More technically, owls belong to the avian order Strigiformes. As a group, they have big heads, short tails, soft and cryptically patterned plumage, and enormous and forward-facing eyes that provide superb binocular vision at night. They have strong, sharp talons and sharp, hooked beaks, traits in common with diurnal raptors to which they are not closely related. Many owls have adaptations for enhanced hearing, including a highly developed facial disk on each side of the head, attached to muscular flaps that allow the owls to modify the shape of the disk to catch sounds. Some species have asymmetri-cal ear openings—either the structure of the external ear, or the bony openings themselves. Their soft plumage permits silent (or nearly silent) flight.

Owls are also still very much a mystery. For all that we have learned about them—and this book summarizes much of the ecology and natural history of all North American and Caribbean species—a reader will soon discover there is much that we simply do not know.

WHAT'S COVERED AND WHERE

The Peterson Reference Guide to Owls of North America and the Caribbean covers the 39 species of owls found north of Guatemala, including 5 endemic Caribbean species.

This volume covers North America and environs (Canada, including the Magdalen Islands, Saint Pierre, and Miquelon; the continental United States; Mexico; Bermuda; and the Bahamas) and the Greater and Lesser Antilles. It does not include Trinidad and Tobago, Curaçao, Bonaire, and the other small islands on the northern coast of South

America, whose avifauna is more decidedly continental than Caribbean.

Each species account provides the four-letter alpha code based on its English name; basic measurements (length, wingspan where known, and mass); longevity records and lifespan information based on banding returns; a review of the systematics and taxonomy of each species, and the etymology of its names; detailed distribution information and a range map, including an overview of migration for migratory species; descriptions and identification of adult and juvenal plumages, color morphs, and similar species; vocalizations; ecological information on habitat, niche, and diet; nesting and breeding; behavior; and status and conservation. Species-specific notes and a bibliography follow each account. Some citations in these references are in full, while others are cited by author and date (i.e., Smith 2001) when the full citations appear in either the specific bibliography or in the General Bibliography section at the back of the book.

MEASUREMENTS

All measurements are expressed in both English and metric. Where possible, measurements (especially mass) are given by subspecies and by gender, covering the regional and sexual variation in many species. Even for common, widespread species, however, there is often limited information on these basic measurements. Among Eastern Screech-Owls, for instance, the only significant weight samples that have been published are from northern Ohio in the 1970s, and Fred Gehlbach's extensive studies in Texas. Very few studies have tracked seasonal weight change in owls, which can be dramatic among nesting females. In some cases, multiple averages and ranges are given for the same species, subspecies, or region. Sources are cited in the endnotes of each species account.

REVERSED SEXUAL DIMORPHISM

Reversed sexual dimorphism by size—RSD, for short—is a common but not universal phenomenon among both diurnal and nocturnal raptors, in which females average larger than males.

Among owls in our area, the degree of RSD varies from nonexistent among Flammulated Owls, in which males and females are essentially the same size, to dramatic among Boreal Owls, Great Gray Owls, and Mottled Owls, in which females may be 20 or 30 percent larger than males. Only one species, the Burrowing Owl, exhibits standard size dimorphism, with males averaging fractionally larger than females in terms of overall measurements—

1. Aguascalientes
2. Baja California
3. Baja California Sur
4. Campeche
5. Chiapas
6. Chihuahua
7. Coahuila
8. Colima
9. Durango
10. Guanajuato
11. Guerrero
12. Hidalgo
13. Jalisco
14. México
15. Michoacán
16. Morelos
17. Nayarit
18. Nuevo Léon
19. Oaxaca
20. Puebla
21. Querétaro
22. Quintana Roo
23. San Luis Potosí
24. Sinaloa
25. Sonora
26. Tabasco
27. Tamaulipas
28. Tlaxcala
29. Veracruz
30. Yucatán
31. Zacatecas
DF. Federal District

STATES AND FEDERAL DISTRICT OF MEXICO

Reversed sexual dimorphism by size, in which females are larger than males, is common among owls, but the degree varies from species to species. The Great Gray Owl is one of the most highly size-dimorphic species. *(Washington. Paul Bannick/ VIREO)*

Most explanations for reversed sexual dimorphism (RSD) are drawn from observations of northern owls, but the Mottled Owl of the Neotropics—which has the most profound rate of RSD in the world—upends most of those theories. *(Chiapas. Christian Artuso)*

but even so, males are consistently, if only slightly, lighter in terms of weight.

There is an ever-growing number of hypotheses—more than 20, at last count—to explain RSD in raptors, none of them fully satisfying. Most fall into several broad categories.

Ecological hypotheses usually focus on the role that size differences play in allowing members of a pair to hunt different-size prey and thus expand their niche while not competing with each other. Larger females may be better able to withstand food shortages, especially at the start of wintry breeding seasons. Conversely, small males may not require as much food, allowing them to provide more of the prey they catch to their mates and chicks instead of eating it themselves.

Behavioral hypotheses generally credit the need for females to be larger than their potentially dangerous mates, or for males to be small enough to display effectively to females during courtship. Other variants hypothesize that small males are more efficient at territorial defense.

Reproductive-effort hypotheses focus on the roles each member of a pair plays—that larger females can easily carry more eggs and incubate a bigger clutch, while perhaps allowing the male to hunt with greater agility.

Sexual-selection hypotheses suggest that females compete for high-quality males that will invest a great deal of energy in raising their chicks—and thus constitute a scarce commodity.

Scientists have performed complex analyses of the habits, behavior, and ecology of many species of raptors, hoping to crack the RSD nut. Generally, they have concluded that RSD is most highly developed in species that hunt agile vertebrate prey, especially birds, and engage in active nest defense—except that such studies almost always focus exclusively on temperate and boreal species, which are the best-studied owls because they are found close to major population areas (and thus to universities).

Few tropical or island species have figured into RSD studies, and some of them, like the Mottled Owl of the Neotropics, really throw a wrench into these tidy conclusions. This dark-eyed forest owl, which has been studied to any degree only in Guatemala, exhibits the most profound RSD of any owl species in the world—and it is a hunter of beetles, grasshoppers, and a few small mammals, not agile birds. As a cavity nester, it would seem to have a limited need for nest defense, and the Mottled Owl defends a ridiculously small territory size for such a moderately large bird. Perhaps the long-sought grand, unifying theory of RSD awaits the closer study of such poorly known tropical raptors, and not just those that live in the north.

LONGEVITY

Band recovery data from the U.S. Bird Banding Lab, including longevity records and average age at re-encounter, are included but must be interpreted with caution. For example, longevity records are a "minimum maximum," so to speak; with time, such records will only get longer, not shorter.

Lifespan estimates are complicated by many variables, including the number of individuals that have been banded. The average lifespan calculated for the Northern Saw-whet Owl, shown here, among which 5,600 banded birds have been recovered, is more reliable than among Elf Owls, fewer than half a dozen of which have been recaptured. *(New York. Chris Wood)*

Average age at re-encounter is an even slipperier measure, since several factors come into play. One is the harsh fact that most young birds—by some estimates as many as 70 or 80 percent—die before their first birthday. Any attempt to assess average lifespan must start with the assumption that only a small minority will live more than a few months after fledging and many will die even before leaving the nest.

Another variable is the number of individuals banded and later found dead or recaptured. With nearly 6,000 band returns from Northern Saw-whet Owls, we can have greater faith in the average re-encounter age of 1.9 years for that species than we can for the average of 3.75 years for Elf Owls—because the latter is based on barely half a dozen band returns. Banders also tend to report only the oldest of retrapped birds, which can skew the averages.

Other factors affecting the accuracy of longevity averages include the manner in which most birds of that species are recovered (dead, or alive at banding stations), and the ecology of any particular species. For example, dead Barn Owls—large, obvious, and often lying along roads or in buildings—are far more likely to be discovered than small Boreal Owls living deep in remote forests. Finally, rarity can have an inverse effect on knowledge. We know more about the lifespan and demography of the federally threatened (and therefore intensely studied) Northern Spotted Owl than for most far more abundant and widespread owls.

In some cases, frequently cited extraordinary records prove on closer examination to be misleading, such as an allegedly 34-year-old Barn Owl. That band was found on a skeleton of unknown age—hardly a legitimate longevity record.

SYSTEMATICS AND TAXONOMY

Although often used interchangeably, systematics and taxonomy are allied but separate fields. Systematics examines the evolutionary relationships between organisms, while taxonomy is the science of classifying and naming them based on the latest understanding of those relationships. Both disciplines are especially intriguing when it comes to owls.

Superficially, owls appear closely tied to the diurnal birds of prey like hawks and eagles—the same hooked, tearing beaks, the same sharp, highly

Scientists have struggled for years with where to place owls, like this Snowy Owl, within the evolutionary framework of birds. DNA analysis initially suggested they were close relatives of the nightjars, but more extensive molecular work places them in a large clade of landbirds, closest to the African mousebirds. *(British Columbia. Gerrit Vyn)*

Barn Owls, along with Ashy-faced Owls, are the only representatives of the family Tytonidae in our region—long-legged, heart-faced, and distinct from the majority of the world's owls, which belong to the family Strigidae. *(Arizona. M. Hyett/VIREO)*

Most of the world's owls belong to the large, complex family Strigidae, including the Black-and-white Owl of the Neotropics. *(Costa Rica. Tom Johnson)*

Molecular analyses have opened new insights into the taxonomy and systematics of owls. Barred Owls north of the Rio Grande have traditionally been broken into three subspecies, based on physical attributes, but DNA suggests there are only two clades, probably based on Ice Age refugia. *(Florida. Luke Seitz)*

developed talons. In the eighteenth century, Carl Linnaeus classified all the raptors as one unified group, but as ornithologists looked more deeply, they soon suspected that those similarities were not the result of a close relationship, but of convergent evolution—the independent development of similar adaptations, under similar forces of natural selection, among unrelated lineages. Any bird that captures vertebrate prey with its feet and must dismember that prey in order to eat it is likely to evolve the same basic toolkit that we see in both owls and diurnal raptors.

The advent of DNA analysis initially supported this view, suggesting that owls were most closely related to the Caprimulgidae, the family of nocturnal birds that includes the nightjars, oilbird, potoos, frogmouths, and owlet-nightjars. But more-recent and far more extensive molecular studies, looking at multiple genes, have placed owls in a large clade of landbirds that includes motmots, trogons, woodpeckers, and toucans. This analysis suggests that owls are, in fact, most closely allied with the weird mousebirds of Sub-Saharan Africa.

In these classifications, owls are again relatively close to hawks, ospreys, and New World vultures (but not to falcons, which have proved to be more closely related to parrots), and quite distant, in evolutionary terms, from the caprimulgids, which group with hummingbirds and swifts. The only safe statement at this point is that the study of the deep evolutionary relationships among birds is rapidly evolving itself, and that further changes in our understanding are not just possible, but likely.

All these molecular studies, though, confirm the long-standing division of owls into two families—the Tytonidae (the barn and bay owls) and the Strigidae (the so-called typical owls). The tytonids are a fairly straightforward group, sharing a distinctive suite of characteristics, although the two species of Old World bay owls are odd enough to warrant their own subfamily.

The strigids are vastly more complex, however, and DNA analysis of both families has upended some long-standing assumptions about their internal relationships, just as it has with owls as a whole. The systematics and taxonomy of owls is, in some ways, still a fascinating muddle, with uncertainty and debate about classification at the genus and (especially) the species levels. Snowy Owls have been moved to the genus *Bubo,* with Great Horned Owls (to the consternation of some Snowy Owl experts, who believe they still warrant their own genus, *Nyctea*), while the tropical wood-owls of the genus *Ciccaba* are sometimes rolled into the larger genus *Strix.*

But if DNA has clarified some questions, it has raised others. In the case of Eastern Screech-Owls

The welter of subspecies now classified as the Northern Pygmy-Owl includes groups that differ significantly in vocalizations and appearance and may represent up to four distinct species. *(British Columbia. Glenn Bartley)*

and Barred Owls, for instance, the molecular divisions do not correspond neatly to long-recognized subspecies. Close attention to vocalizations is also revealing many previously cryptic forms hidden within what are now classified as wide-ranging, geographically diverse species—forms that may warrant their own species designations.

Experts are divided, for example, on whether to split the Western Hemisphere population of Barn Owls from the Old World race, and whether (and which) island subspecies of the Barn Owl deserve species rank themselves. The screech-owls and pygmy-owls are particularly ambiguous groups. In 1997, the "Least Pygmy-Owl" complex was carved into five species, three of which are in this book's region, based on differences of voice and appearance. Authorities currently disagree on just whether and how to divvy up taxa like the Vermiculated Screech-Owl (which has been split into as many as four species by some experts), the Northern Pygmy-Owl (up to four species), and the Ferruginous Pygmy-Owl (three or more species).

While conceding that some splits and shifts are all but certain, this book follows the classification used by the American Ornithologists' Union's *Check-list of North American Birds,* 7th edition (through the 55th supplement). Prospective or obsolete forms (both species or subspecies) that are not officially recognized by the AOU are shown in quotes (such as "American Barn Owl" or "Ridgway's Pygmy-Owl (*G. ridgwayi*)."

Even the most thoroughly studied owls still hold taxonomic surprises. A new subspecies of Great Horned Owl from the Great Basin and Rocky Mountains was described in 2008, and the tiny population of Great Gray Owls from the Sierra Nevada was recognized as a distinct subspecies only in 2014.

ETYMOLOGY, NAMES, AND CODES

Each species account includes a discussion of the origin of both the current English and scientific names, along with local names in Spanish, French, and some native languages, such as Náhuatl or Mayan in Mexico, and Iñupiatun or Inuit in the Arctic, where applicable.

The derivation of scientific names is drawn largely from *A Dictionary of Scientific Bird Names* (Jobling 1991) and *The Dictionary of American Bird Names,* rev. ed. (Choate 1985), as well as Elliott Coues's *Check List of North American Birds* (1882).

The list of Spanish names may be long, but it does not reflect "official" names; some of the names are highly localized, especially those from the Yucatán or Chiapas, and vary between Mexico and Spanish-speaking islands in the Caribbean. Spanish terms for owls include *búho, lechuza* (often but not always applied to the Barn Owl), and *mochuelo. Tecolote* and its diminutive, *tecololito,* were borrowed from *tecolotl* in the native language Náhuatl. In Cuba, the term *sijú* is used. In some cases, close variants of Spanish names are indicated with brackets: i.e., *Tecolote [tecolotito] flameado* are both used for Flammulated Owl.

Spanish names from Mexico are drawn primarily from *Native Names of Mexican Birds* (Birkenstein and Tomlinson 1981), along with other sources. Native names are also drawn from a variety of sources, including Hunn (1975), *Iñupiatun Eskimo Dictionary* (Seiler 2012), *Ahtna Noun Dictionary* (Smelcer, Kari, and Buck 2011), and the online *Inuktitut Living Dictionary.*

ALPHA CODES

Bird banders have long used four-letter abbreviations for bird names, and in recent years the practice has become widespread among birders—who do not always follow (or know) the guidelines under which these alpha codes are formulated.

Generally speaking, the banding codes from the federal Bird Banding Lab (BBL) use the first four letters of a single-word name; the first two letters of each part of a two-word name, and so forth. The trouble arises when two names would generate the same code: Barn Owl and Barred Owl, for example, would both be BAOW. To avoid such collisions, neither species is assigned that code; instead, under the Banding Lab system Barn Owl is BNOW, while Barred Owl is BDOW.

Unfortunately, BBL codes largely exclude nonmigratory species south of the Mexico border (where Spectacled Owl would have the same code as Spotted Owl), and have collided with each other increasingly as more and more North American species are split. An alternate system of codes was proposed in 2003 by Peter Pyle and David F. DeSante, with four-letter codes based on English names, and six-letter codes based on Latin names. Among owls in our region, there are only two species whose four-letter Pyle-DeSante codes vary from the BBL versions—Barn Owl (BNOW/BANO) and Barred Owl (BDOW/BADO). Where they exist for species covered in this book, BBL codes are used, while Pyle-DeSante codes are used for the remaining species.

DISTRIBUTION AND RANGE MAPS

The distribution of owls—or at least our understanding of their distribution—is in a surprisingly active state of flux. Because owls are generally nocturnal and often highly secretive, they are easily overlooked, even by avid birders.

In the 1960s, Boreal Owls were assumed to nest no farther south than southern Manitoba—but 20 years later, they had been found breeding down

Already beleaguered by clear-cutting of its old-growth forest habitat, Spotted Owls like this one now face competition from invading Barred Owls. *(Washington. Gerrit Vyn)*

the spine of the Rockies all the way to northern New Mexico, a range extension of some 1,100 mi. (1,700 km). Similarly, Stygian Owls have recently been discovered in central Tamaulipas, a dramatic northward extension of their mapped range—though a 1911 record suggests the owls have always been present in that area, just overlooked. And Fulvous Owls have recently been recorded hundreds of miles north and west of their previously known range in southern Mexico.

Other species have, in reality, been on the move. Barred Owls began expanding north and west in the late nineteenth and early twentieth centuries and haven't stopped since, colonizing an immense area from the Canadian prairies to southeastern Alaska and the southern Sierra Nevada Mountains in California. (This to the detriment of their threatened relative, the Northern Spotted Owl, whose habitat the Barred Owl now occupies.) Barred Owls are, to a lesser extent, also expanding north and east into Quebec and Labrador. Likewise, the Antillean race of the Short-eared Owl has been greatly expanding its presence in the Caribbean and now regularly wanders north into southern Florida and the Keys, where nesting may not be out of the question in the future.

Distribution descriptions and range maps are based on a wide variety of sources—published distributional lists, state and provincial breeding bird atlases, banding data, and other references. Mapped ranges in Mexico take into account potential distribution as mapped by Navarro and Peterson (2007).

Of tremendous and growing value are the millions of observations uploaded monthly by birders across the hemisphere to eBird (www.ebird.org), the cooperative online checklist program run by the Cornell Lab of Ornithology and the National Audubon Society. While a powerful tool for studying bird distribution, eBird is only as good as the data fed into it—and there is an unavoidable bias toward easily birded sites as well as easily observed species

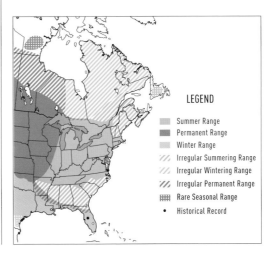

LEGEND

- Summer Range
- Permanent Range
- Winter Range
- Irregular Summering Range
- Irregular Wintering Range
- Irregular Permanent Range
- Rare Seasonal Range
- • Historical Record

The distribution of many owls, especially those in the tropics, is still very poorly understood, and new regional populations of species like the Stygian Owl are still being discovered. *(Sonora. Dean LaTray)*

(which usually do not include owls). Still, eBird is revolutionizing our ability to map and track birds.

Range maps are included for all 39 species, along with generalized subspecies maps for Eastern and Western Screech-Owls, Spotted Owls, and Great Horned Owls. Range maps are as accurate as the author can make them, within the constraints of the available information and the inherently challenging aspects of owls as a whole. The nomadic or irruptive nature of many owls obviously complicates matters, for example, as do tiny, disjunct populations of species like Barn Owls, Flammulated Owls, and Long-eared Owls. In some cases, the most honest map tool—and one used here—is a question mark, reflecting uncertainty about the true extent of a species's occurrence. In the end, range maps are the hardest element for an author to create and the easiest to fault; it was ever thus, and those presented here are not free of mistakes, compromises, or generalizations.

Migratory routes are not mapped, in part because they're essentially unknown for most migratory owls, and anything beyond a few vague arrows would be speculative at best. Where we do have migration data, it is based almost exclusively on banding captures and recoveries. While useful, such information is incomplete. For example, the most

frequently banded species, the Northern Saw-whet Owl, is monitored by a network of more than 125 collaborative banding stations (www.projectowl-net.org). But these stations are heavily clustered in southeastern Canada, the Northeast, Mid-Atlantic states, and upper Midwest, with far sparser coverage elsewhere. Any maps based on banding data would reflect that geographic bias.

VAGRANTS AND ACCIDENTAL SPECIES

Rates of vagrancy are quite low among owls, especially involving species from outside our coverage area; most rare or out-of-range owls are irruptive species crossing state or provincial lines, not oceans or international boundaries.

Only two Old World species have been accepted on the North American list, the Oriental Scops Owl and Northern Boobook, both of which breed in northeastern Asia, are highly migratory, and have been recorded in Alaska. A live scops owl was found on Amchitka Island in the central Aleutians in 1979, while a dismembered wing was found on Buldir Island in the western Aleutians in 1977.

Two individuals of the Northern Boobook (formerly known as the Brown Hawk-Owl, until that species was split in 2014) have also been documented in Alaska. One was a live bird on Saint Paul Island in the Pribilofs in 2007 (perched among huge stacks of crab traps, which may have been the closest thing to appropriate habitat that this forest-dwelling owl could find on that treeless island). The other was a carcass, recovered in 2008 on Kiska Island in the western Aleutians.

Two Neotropical species, Mottled Owl and Stygian Owl, have wandered north of the Mexico border into Texas. Details of those vagrants can be found in their respective species accounts.

DESCRIPTION AND IDENTIFICATION

TOPOGRAPHY OF AN OWL

Owls are distinctive-looking birds, and their appearance derives largely from a couple of shared elements that evolved because of a nocturnal, predatory lifestyle—their cryptic plumage, large and rounded heads, enormous eyes, semicircular facial disks, and, in some species, ear tufts. Topographic terms used in this book are shown on the accompanying photographs.

Ear tufts—as all but the newest of recruits to birding know—have nothing to do with hearing but are merely erectable clumps of feathers whose primary purpose seems to be one of camouflage. The Flammulated Owl, all screech-owls in our region, the Great Horned Owl, and most of the owls in the genus *Asio* carry ear tufts, which may or may not be visible, depending on the owl's mood. Pygmy-owls can create pseudo-tufts by compressing their facial

TOPOGRAPHY

CROWN
NAPE
BACK
SCAPULARS
TAIL

GREATER COVERTS
SECONDARIES
ALULA
CARPAL PATCH
PRIMARIES

FOREHEAD
FACIAL DISK
FACIAL RUFF
LESSER COVERTS
MEDIAN COVERTS
PRIMARY COVERTS

BACK

SCAPULARS

TERTIALS
PRIMARIES

FLANKS
GREATER COVERTS
SECONDARIES
TAIL

CROWN
FOREHEAD
EAR TUFT
EYEBROW
FACIAL DISK
FACIAL RUFF

RICTAL BRISTLES
BACK
SCAPULARS
MEDIAN AND LESSER COVERTS

CHIN
THROAT
UPPER CHEST
CHEST
ALULA
GREATER COVERTS
PRIMARY COVERTS

BELLY
FLANKS
SECONDARIES
PRIMARIES

TALONS

TAIL

feathers while leaving other feathers on their heads erect.

On a number of species, the outer webbing of the scapular feathers, which form the edge of the back overlapping the folded wings, is white or buffy. These spots often form a light stripe along the edge of the back on either side and look enough like a pair of suspenders that they are sometimes called "suspender bars" or "braces."

MORPHS, MOLTS, AND PLUMAGES

For the most part, owls exhibit few gender-based differences in plumage. In a number of species—Barn, Long-eared, and Short-eared Owls among them—males on average are paler and less richly colored on the underparts, but the differences are subtle and are complicated by regional and individual variations. Depending on the species, male and female pygmy-owls may average more or less rufous or more or less richly pigmented. Among Snowy Owls, males on average are less heavily marked than females, and adults are less so than juveniles, but here again, there is a confounding

Many species of small owls, most notably screech-owls and pygmy-owls, exhibit polymorphism—multiple plumage colors that are not connected to age or gender. The Eastern Screech-Owl's rufous morph is most common in warmer, more-humid hardwood forests in the Southeast and is increasingly replaced to the north and west by a gray morph that dominates in cooler, drier, more-coniferous areas. *(Pennsylvania. Tom Johnson)*

degree of variation. Burrowing Owl males are often noticeably lighter than females, if only because they spend more time in the sun and thus bleach more quickly.

Owls as a group show an unusually high degree of polymorphism—more than one color variant, like the rufous, gray, and brown forms of many screech-owls. Morphs are unrelated to gender or age and do not change with time. (Because of this, the old term "phase" is now frowned upon because it suggests a coloration that changes with time.*)

Recent research has thrown interesting new light on why polymorphism may have evolved among owls and several other groups of birds. Rufous-morph owls are more common in warmer, more-humid environments, and gray-morph birds are more common in cooler, drier climates. Rather than providing better camouflage, as once believed, the morphs may be an expression of genes that allow the owls to better handle different environmental conditions—gray-morph Eastern Screech-Owls appear to be better able to withstand cold tempera-

The whitish natal down of hatchling owls is quickly replaced by a second downy coat known as the mesoptile plumage, as in this juvenile Great Gray Owl. Barn Owls, on the other hand, transition directly from natal down to adultlike plumage. *(Manitoba. Christian Artuso)*

---

*Recently, age-related polymorphism has been documented in an Asian species, the Collared Pygmy-Owl, *Glaucidium brodiei*, which changes from rufous to gray after about 7 months of age, calling into question whether the New World pygmy-owls that are considered polymorphic actually are.

All of the larger owls, like this Great Gray, and some of the small species require at least 2 or 3 years to replace all of their flight feathers. *(Wyoming. Kevin Loughlin/Wildside Nature Tours)*

tures, for instance. Even more surprising, rufous-morph individuals may actually possess sharper hearing across a greater range of frequencies. For additonal information about polymorphism, see "Eastern Screech-Owl," p. 57.

Although morphs do not change with time, each owl must replace its feathers regularly, as the old ones fade and fray. Juvenile owls also undergo a sequence of molts from hatching to adulthood, which in some species involves dramatic changes in appearance.

Newly hatched nestlings are covered in a coat of natal down (known as neoptile plumage), which is almost invariably white or off-white. Barn Owls replace their natal down directly with adultlike juvenal plumage,* but strigid owl chicks develop a second downy coat known as mesoptile plumage. The flight feathers and an adultlike juvenal plumage emerge through it, often tipped for weeks thereafter by small tufts of down.

Most juvenal plumages resemble that of the adults, but in some species the juveniles are dramatically different. Young Boreal Owls are almost black, with stark white eyebrows and rictal bristles, while a juvenile Northern Saw-whet Owl is dark brown with a deep cinnamon belly. Spectacled Owls have perhaps the most eye-catching juvenal

---

* "Juvenal" refers to an immature bird's plumage, while "juvenile" is the term for the young bird itself. Yes, it's confusing.

plumage of all—a creamy white body with black facial disk and dark flight feathers, and large downy-tipped back feathers and coverts. Despite frequently cited claims that this unusual plumage is retained for 3 to 5 years, in captive-raised Spectacled Owls it is replaced by the adult plumage in 9 to 12 months, as the dark chest band and head feathers molt in.

Some small owls replace all of their flight feathers annually, while Barn Owls, some of the small strigid species (like Boreal, Northern Saw-whet, and Flammulated Owls), and almost all of the larger owls require 2 or 3 years to replace all of their feathers. Small owls—pygmy-owls, screech-owls, the *Aegolius* owls among them—all molt their tails simultaneously, and for several weeks they look even more than usual like flying fluff balls. (These generalizations apply to northern species, at least; very little if any work has been done on the molt of most tropical owls.)

ABERRANT PLUMAGES

Compared with some groups of birds, like diurnal raptors, aberrant plumages are quite rare overall in owls. Among North American species, white or partially white individuals have been reported in Barred, Spotted, Great Gray, Eastern and Western Screech-, Burrowing, Short-eared, Northern Hawk, and Northern Saw-whet Owls. Melanistic (unusually dark) individuals have been documented in Great Horned and Great Gray Owls. Sometimes owls exhibit a melanin reduction known as "pastel

Aberrant plumages in owls, including melanism and leucism, are uncommon. Among the rarest is a "pastel" melanin reduction, seen here in a Northern Saw-whet Owl, which results in a bleached appearance. *(Pennsylvania. Andrew McGann)*

dilution," in which the pattern is normal but the plumage appears bleached out. This condition is extremely rare; among Northern Saw-whet Owls, it was found in just 7 out of more than 30,000 owls caught for banding.

SIMILAR SPECIES

Because owls are, as a rule, a fairly sedentary group, the similar species included in each account are generally those that are likely to be found in the same range and similar elevations as the featured species—although with tropical owls, where distributional limits are poorly known, it is wise not to trust entirely in what we think is the "normal" range.

HYBRIDS

Unlike groups such as gulls, ducks, and hummingbirds, which seem to hybridize at the drop of a hat, owls have an extraordinarily low hybridization rate in the wild, although hybrid pairings are somewhat more common in captivity (including some strange intergeneric crosses, such as a Barn Owl × Striped Owl pair at the Saint Louis Zoo that produced fertile eggs).

The most common hybrids involve Western Screech-Owl × Eastern Screech-Owl crosses, where these two sister species overlap in the Great Plains from Colorado south; Western Screech-Owl × Whiskered Screech-Owl hybrids have also been reported from Arizona, but documentation is lacking. Barred × Spotted Owl hybrids, first detected in 1989, are increasingly common in the Pacific Northwest and Sierra Nevada, where Barred Owls are overrunning the latter species's range, yet even here, so-called "Sparred Owls" remain a relative rarity.

A clearly intermediate Long-eared Owl × Short-eared Owl hybrid was documented in Ontario in 1990—an injured bird that was euthanized by the rehabilitator and prepared as a specimen, then overlooked in a museum collection for almost two decades.

VOCALIZATIONS

Owls are a famously vocal group, and their calls are usually the best (and sometimes the only) way to locate and identify them. All species have multiple vocalizations. While the male's advertisement call is generally the most commonly heard and usually the most familiar, there may be a dozen or more adult vocalizations used in a variety of contexts, from territorial defense to copulation solicitation, agitation, nest defense, and pair contact. Juveniles give food-begging calls that are usually some version of a raspy, screechy cry so loud and annoying one doesn't have to be an adult owl to want to stuff a mouse into the chick to shut it up.

In addition to the text descriptions with each species account, there is a downloadable album of the following 86 representative vocalizations for each of the 39 species covered in *The Peterson Reference Guide to Owls of North America and the Caribbean*, drawn from the Macaulay Library of the Cornell Laboratory of Ornithology. The album can be downloaded, free, at hmhco.com/owls.

1. BARN OWL *(Tyto alba)*. Territorial scream or advertising call (California).

2. BARN OWL *(Tyto alba)*. Sustained defensive hiss by adult (New York).

3. BARN OWL *(Tyto alba)*. Fledgling begging snore (Florida).

4. ASHY-FACED OWL *(Tyto glaucops)*. Territorial scream (Dominican Republic).

5. FLAMMULATED OWL *(Psiloscops flammeolus)*. Male territorial hoot or advertising song (Oregon).

6. FLAMMULATED OWL *(Psiloscops flammeolus)*. Nestling begging snore and low amplitude hoot of adult delivering food (Oregon).

7. FLAMMULATED OWL *(Psiloscops flammeolus)*. Bark by alarmed female, and nestling begging snore (Oregon).

8. WESTERN SCREECH-OWL *(Megascops kennicottii)*. Bouncing ball and double-trill songs (Washington).

Vocalizations are usually the best way to find and identify owls in the wild, including the deep, resonant hoots of the Great Horned Owl, the most widely distributed species in the Western Hemisphere. *(Arizona. Tom Johnson)*

9. WESTERN SCREECH-OWL *(Megascops kennicottii)*. Duetting pair (Arizona).

10. WESTERN SCREECH-OWL *(Megascops kennicottii)*. *Te-te-do* call progressing into agitated double trill (Oregon).

11. EASTERN SCREECH-OWL *(Megascops asio)*. Descending trill (whinny) and monotone trill (New York).

12. EASTERN SCREECH-OWL *(Megascops asio)*. Begging rasps, chitter calls and chuckle rattle of nestlings (New York).

13. EASTERN SCREECH-OWL *(Megascops asio)*. "McCall's" Eastern Screech-Owl (Texas).

14. BALSAS SCREECH-OWL *(Megascops seductus)*. Bouncing ball call (Jalisco, Mexico).

15. BALSAS SCREECH-OWL *(Megascops seductus)*. Monotone trill (Jalisco, Mexico).

16. PACIFIC SCREECH-OWL *(Megascops cooperi)*. Territorial calls by pair (Costa Rica).

17. PACIFIC SCREECH-OWL *(Megascops cooperi)*. "Lamb's" Pacific Screech-Owl (Oaxaca, Mexico).

18. WHISKERED SCREECH-OWL *(Megascops trichopsis)*. Male short trill (New Mexico).

19. WHISKERED SCREECH-OWL *(Megascops trichopsis)*. Telegraphic trill by adult pair (Arizona).

20. BEARDED SCREECH-OWL *(Megascops barbarus)*. Trill call (Chiapas, Mexico).

21. VERMICULATED SCREECH-OWL *(Megascops guatemalae)*. Primary trill call (Quintana Roo, Mexico).

22. PUERTO RICAN SCREECH-OWL *(Megascops nudipes)*. Primary song (Puerto Rico).

23. PUERTO RICAN SCREECH-OWL *(Megascops nudipes)*. Duet by pair with chattering (Puerto Rico).

24. BARE-LEGGED OWL *(Margarobyas lawrencii)*. Primary song (Cuba).

25. CRESTED OWL *(Lophostrix cristata)*. Main growl vocalization (Costa Rica).

26. SPECTACLED OWL *(Pulsatrix perspicillata)*. Pair duetting (Peru).

27. GREAT HORNED OWL *(Bubo virginianus)*. Territorial hooting by pair (California).

28. GREAT HORNED OWL *(Bubo virginianus)*. Juvenile agitation calls, adult hoots (Maryland).

29. GREAT HORNED OWL *(Bubo virginianus)*. Juvenile begging calls (Washington).

30. GREAT HORNED OWL (*Bubo virginianus*). Chitter call (New York).

31. SNOWY OWL (*Bubo scandiacus*). Male territorial hoot or advertising song (Sweden).

32. SNOWY OWL (*Bubo scandiacus*). *Ca-cah-cah* nest defense call (Nunavut, Canada).

33. NORTHERN HAWK OWL (*Surnia ulula*). Male advertising call (Alaska).

34. NORTHERN HAWK OWL (*Surnia ulula*). *Scree*-yip and yelp calls (Alaska).

35. NORTHERN PYGMY-OWL (*Glaucidium gnoma*). Slow single-hooter (California).

36. NORTHERN PYGMY-OWL (*Glaucidium gnoma*). Slow double-hooter (Baja California Sur, Mexico).

37. NORTHERN PYGMY-OWL (*Glaucidium gnoma*). Fast single-hooter (Arizona).

38. NORTHERN PYGMY-OWL (*Glaucidium gnoma*). Fast double-hooter (Arizona).

39. NORTHERN PYGMY-OWL (*Glaucidium gnoma*). "Guatemalan" pygmy-owl (Guatemala).

40. COLIMA PYGMY-OWL (*Glaucidium palmarum*). Male advertisement call (Sinaloa, Mexico).

41. TAMAULIPAS PYGMY-OWL (*Glaucidium sanchezi*). 2- and 3-note male call (Tamaulipas, Mexico).

42. CENTRAL AMERICAN PYGMY-OWL (*Glaucidium griseiceps*). Male advertisement call (Belize).

43. FERRUGINOUS PYGMY-OWL (*Glaucidium brasilianum*). Male advertisement call (*G. b. ridgwayi*) (Texas).

44. FERRUGINOUS PYGMY-OWL (*Glaucidium brasilianum*). Male advertisement call (*G.b. cactorum*) (Sinaloa, Mexico).

45. CUBAN PYGMY-OWL (*Glaucidium siju*). Male territorial call (Cuba).

46. CUBAN PYGMY-OWL (*Glaucidium siju*). Long chatter call (Cuba).

47. ELF OWL (*Micrathene whitneyi*). Male chatter call and female station call (Arizona).

48. ELF OWL (*Micrathene whitneyi*). Bark call (Arizona).

49. BURROWING OWL (*Athene cunicularia*). Male primary call (California).

50. BURROWING OWL (*Athene cunicularia*). "Rattlesnake" call (Arizona).

51. MOTTLED OWL (*Ciccaba virgata*). Primary call (Veracruz, Mexico).

52. MOTTLED OWL (*Ciccaba virgata*). Bouncing ball call (Colima, Mexico).

53. BLACK-AND-WHITE OWL (*Ciccaba nigrolineata*). Primary call (Guatemala).

54. NORTHERN SPOTTED OWL (*Strix occidentalis caurina*). Male hoot, female contact call (Oregon).

55. NORTHERN SPOTTED OWL (*Strix occidentalis caurina*). Female contact call (Oregon).

56. MEXICAN SPOTTED OWL (*Strix occidentalis lucida*). Male four-note hoot (Arizona).

57. MEXICAN SPOTTED OWL (*Strix occidentalis lucida*). Bark series, both sexes (New Mexico).

58. SPOTTED OWL X BARRED OWL HYBRID, Advertisement hoot (Washington).

59. BARRED OWL (*Strix varia*). Two-phrase hoot (New York).

60. BARRED OWL (*Strix varia*). One-phrase hoot and wail (Oregon).

61. BARRED OWL (*Strix varia*). Inspection or *hoo-wa* call (Florida).

62. BARRED OWL (*Strix varia*). Duetting and caterwauling between pairs (Arkansas).

63. BARRED OWL (*Strix varia*). "Gurgle" call (Florida).

64. BARRED OWL (*Strix varia*). Fledgling begging call (Maryland).

65. FULVOUS OWL (*Strix fulvescens*). Advertisement hoot (Chiapas, Mexico).

66. GREAT GRAY OWL (*Strix nebulosa*). Male hoot (Alaska).

67. GREAT GRAY OWL (*Strix nebulosa*). Female "whoop" call (Oregon).

68. GREAT GRAY OWL (*Strix nebulosa*). Female chitter and juvenile food-begging calls (Oregon).

69. LONG-EARED OWL (*Asio otus*). Male advertisement call (Washington).

70. LONG-EARED OWL (*Asio otus*). Female "nest call" with wing snaps (Washington).

71. LONG-EARED OWL (*Asio otus*). Juvenile food-begging calls (Vermont).

72. LONG-EARED OWL (*Asio otus*). Female bark alarm (New Jersey).

73. STYGIAN OWL (*Asio stygius*). Advertisement hoots (Belize).

74. SHORT-EARED OWL (*Asio flammeus*). Male primary hoots and wing claps (Alaska).

75. SHORT-EARED OWL *(Asio flammeus)*. Bark calls at nest intruder (Manitoba, Canada).

76. SHORT-EARED OWL *(Asio flammeus)*. Fledgling begging calls (Manitoba, Canada).

77. STRIPED OWL *(Pseudoscops clamator)*. Adult hoot and juvenile begging calls (El Salvador).

78. JAMAICAN OWL *(Pseudoscops grammicus)*. Advertisement call (Jamaica).

79. JAMAICAN OWL *(Pseudoscops grammicus)*. Juvenile begging call (Jamaica).

80. BOREAL OWL *(Aegolius funereus)*. Male staccato song (Alaska).

81. BOREAL OWL *(Aegolius funereus)*. *Skiew* call (Germany).

82. NORTHERN SAW-WHET OWL *(Aegolius acadicus)*. Male advertisement call (Oregon).

83. NORTHERN SAW-WHET OWL *(Aegolius acadicus)*. Barks, whines, and *skiew* calls (Pennsylvania).

84. NORTHERN SAW-WHET OWL *(Aegolius acadicus)*. Food deliveries at nest (Pennsylvania).

85. UNSPOTTED SAW-WHET OWL *(Aegolius ridgwayi)*. Advertisement call (Chiapas, Mexico).

86. UNSPOTTED SAW-WHET OWL *(Aegolius ridgwayi)*. Whine calls and advertisement call (Chiapas, Mexico).

HABITAT, NICHE, BREEDING, AND BEHAVIOR

These sections cover the ecology and natural history of each species. In the past century we've learned much about how owls live, but the reader will quickly discover how much remains unknown. Many aspects of the lives of even the most common and widespread species are still largely a mystery, and for many of the island and tropical species in particular, the phrases "no information," "little data," and "largely unknown" recur throughout the book. Even the nest and eggs of one species, the Unspotted Saw-whet Owl, have yet to be convincingly described.

STATUS AND CONSERVATION

Owls suffered direct persecution for centuries, viewed with superstitious dread or as competitors for wild game and poultry. Such threats are largely a thing of the past in the United States and Canada but remain a vivid danger in parts of Mexico and the Caribbean. Especially in the latter, owls are still seen as ill omens or supernaturally dangerous and are frequently shot or stoned to death when encountered.

In the United States, all owls are protected by the Migratory Bird Treaty Act (MBTA), the bedrock federal law that covers all native wild birds; its Canadian counterpart, stemming from the same 1917 treaty, is the Migratory Birds Convention Act. When the U.S. legislation was passed, however, it pointedly excluded raptors, and for much of the twentieth century, owls were shielded only by a welter of state laws, until the MBTA was amended in 1972, in a treaty with Mexico, to include raptors.

Even today, Native and First Nations communities in both the United States and Canada are allowed to take owls for food, feathers, and body parts; the impact of such subsistence hunting is unknown, but in the case of Snowy Owls in Alaska, it is thought to be substantial.

Some species warrant additional federal, state, or provincial protection. In the United States, species are listed under the 1973 Endangered Species Act (ESA), while north of the border, federal listing decisions are made by the Committee on the Status of Endangered Wildlife in Canada (COSEWIC) under the Species at Risk Act (SARA). In Mexico, laws known as Norma Oficial Mexicana (Official Mexican Standard, or NOM) 059-ECOL-2001 and 059-SEMARNAT-2010 establish the list of rare, threatened, and endangered species protected

Because of land use changes and prairie dog eradication campaigns, Burrowing Owl populations have contracted significantly throughout the species's western range, especially along the eastern edge, in Canada, and in California. *(California. Tom Johnson)*

While not federally listed in the United States or Canada, the Short-eared Owl is given special conservation status in half the states and provinces, a measure of its declining population. *(Pennsylvania. Alan Richard)*

through the Secretariat of the Environment and Natural Resources. The degree of protection afforded by these federal listings varies, with the U.S. ESA considered among the toughest environmental statutes in the world.

States and provinces usually maintain their own lists of rare species, often using conservation rankings developed by the Nature Conservancy and maintained by NatureServe. Species may be listed globally (G), nationally (N), or subnationally (S) to reflect geographic scope, and ranked from 1 (critically imperiled) to 5 (secure). Distinctions are often made between breeding and nonbreeding populations. Thus, Flammulated Owls are ranked as S1B (critically imperiled breeding population) in South Dakota, while Short-eared Owls are ranked as S3N (vulnerable nonbreeding population) in Arkansas.

Official status designations, which often carry additional legal protections, are presented here in quotations (e.g., "endangered," "threatened," "species of special concern") to distinguish these formal designations from broader generalizations about the abundance or rarity of an owl.

The International Union for the Conservation of Nature (IUCN) maintains the Red List of Threatened Species, the most comprehensive global assessment of rare plants and animals. BirdLife International is the IUCN's official authority for birds; IUCN/BirdLife rankings range from "least concern" to "critically endangered."

Finally, the North American Bird Conservation Initiative (NABCI) ranks the U.S. species in greatest conservation need, using criteria from Partners in Flight to list them on its two Watch Lists—a Yellow Watch List for species at moderate vulnerability, and a Red Watch List for those at highest risk.

Roughly one-third of Watch List species already receive ESA protection: http://www.stateofthebirds.org/extinctions/watchlist.pdf. (This new Watch List replaces one maintained for many years by the National Audubon Society, a NABCI member, which in turn replaced Audubon's earlier "Blue List" of at-risk species.)

EXTINCT OWLS

At first glance, owls would seem to have avoided the worst of the extinction crisis that swept across the New World's avifauna in the eighteenth and nineteenth centuries. No formally described species of owl within our region is known to have gone extinct, although several island subspecies—the Socorro Island Elf Owl, the Marie-Galante and Antigua Burrowing Owls, and the Virgin Island race of Puerto Rican Screech-Owl, for example—have disappeared. These are discussed more fully in the respective species accounts.

But paleontology, particularly in the Caribbean, is telling a very different story. It's obvious that several unique species became extinct within (or very close to) historical times, when European colonization radically altered the landscape. But the biggest wave of owl extinctions appears to have occurred several thousand years earlier, presumably as a result of Amerindian settlement of what until then had been uninhabited islands, perhaps in concert with climate changes at the end of the last ice age.

Some of these owls were unlike anything else on Earth. There were several species of enormous barn owls in the Antilles, and Cuba was home to a variety of mega-owls. The biggest was *Ornimegalonyx*, a Cuban genus of one or more species of giant, long-legged, largely or completely flightless owls, whose remains were first discovered in 1954 and which do not appear to be closely related to any living owls.

These were impressive Pleistocene predators; *Ornimegalonyx* would have stood roughly waist-high to a human, and weighed an estimated 20 lbs. (9.1 kg). It had leg bones twice as long as a Eurasian Eagle Owl's, the largest modern owl, and three times those of a Snowy Owl. Its likely prey, experts believe, were juvenile ground sloths—meaning that *Ornimegalonyx* was one seriously capable predator. Nor was it alone. Fossil leg bones from *Bubo osvaldoi*, larger than the biggest modern eagle owls, have also been found in Pleistocene deposits in Cuba.

Why this gigantism in the Antilles? Island evolution often pushes organisms in unexpected directions—dwarf versions of very large animals, and giant versions of smaller ones. The Greater Antilles were home to an extraordinary variety of now-extinct mammals, including large rodents, solenodons, and ground sloths, but lacked large mammalian carnivores. Raptors bulked up to fill the niche.

Paleontologists like Storrs Olson have noted that barn owls in the Caribbean and Bahamas fell into three distinct size categories—those similar in build to surviving species, those significantly larger, and the truly immense, thick-legged species like *T. riveroi*—a situation seen millions of years earlier on the Gargano Peninsula of Italy, when it too was separated from the mainland and also lacked mammalian predators.

The extinct Caribbean barn owls, from smallest to largest, were:

Tyto cavatica: Puerto Rico. Between modern Barn Owls and Ashy-faced Owls in size, this species may have survived into the twentieth century, if sketchy reports are to be believed.

Tyto noeli: Cuba. Larger than modern Barn Owls.

Tyto neddi: Barbuda, probably Antigua. One of the larger extinct barn owls, and the only one described from the Lesser Antilles. Its short toes suggest a diet specializing in midsize mammals, like the extinct oryzomyine rodents, midway in size between a rat and a muskrat.

Tyto ostologa: Hispaniola. An extremely large barn owl, with leg bones as heavy as a Snowy Owl's, and long, powerful toes, perhaps for killing large prey like endemic (and now extinct) monkeys.

Tyto pollens: Great Exuma, New Providence, and Andros Islands, Bahamas. This 3-ft.-high (1 m) probably flightless barn owl also had very robust leg bones, an indication of its likely prey, large rodents like huitas. Folk legends of a magical creature called the "chickcharnie" may well be all that remains of this large owl and suggest that it too survived until the beginning of the historical period.

Tyto riveroi: Cuba. This barn owl, described by the paleontologist who discovered it as "truly gigantic," was nearly as large as *Ornimegalonyx,* and like it, possibly preyed on young ground sloths.

Other extinct Caribbean owls include:

Otus [Megascops] providentiae: New Providence Island, Bahamas. The only example of a screech-owl in the Bahamas. (Although described and named as an *Otus*, that genus is no longer valid for New World screech-owls, which are now classified as *Megascops*.)

Bubo osvaldoi: Cuba. Based on leg-bone measurements, this enormous eagle owl was larger than any surviving species of owl, although it (like a number of other island species) appears to have reduced wing size.

Burrowing Owl *(Athene cunicularia):* Bones have been found in caves in Barbuda, where no owls of any sort are currently found. *Athene* bones and a claw have been found on Jamaica, but not enough material to determine species. Remains of a small, as-yet-undescribed species of *Athene* have been found on Puerto Rico.

Pulsatrix arredondoi: Cuba. This is the only example of this genus in the Caribbean north of Trinidad. Its leg bones were much shorter and wider than those of the Spectacled Owl.

Glaucidium dickensoni: Bahamas. Apparently similar to the Cuban Pygmy-Owl, which is the only surviving member of the genus in the West Indies.

Aegolius graydi: Bermuda. Similar to the Northern Saw-whet Owl, from which it almost certainly was descended, it had more robust legs and possibly reduced wings. It may have specialized in preying on birds and skinks, given the absence of native mammals other than bats. It apparently was quickly extinguished by the first Europeans. In 1623, John Smith reported "a kinde of small Owles in great abundance, but they are all now slaine or fled" (Olson 2012).

SPECIES
ACCOUNTS

Barn Owls are among the most widespread raptors on the planet, with a single subspecies, *Tyto alba pratincola*, encompassing the mainland of North America through Mexico, as well as Bermuda, the Bahamas, and Hispaniola. *(Kansas. Gerrit Vyn)*

BARN OWL
Tyto alba
Alpha code: BNOW*

LENGTH: 12.5–16 in. (32–40 cm)

WINGSPAN: 33–42 in. (84–106 cm)

MASS: Exhibits moderate reversed size dimorphism. Average mass reported from New Jersey and Utah remarkably similar, but Pacific coastal birds average smaller than other regions. New Jersey: Average, male: 16.75 oz. (475 g); range 15–19.4 oz. (425–550 g). Average, female: 20.1 oz. (569 g); range 17.1–24.7 oz. (485–700 g).[1] Utah: Average, male: 16.9 oz. (479 g). Average, female: 20 oz. (568 g). No range given.[2] California: Average, male: 15.3 oz. (434 g); range 13.4–16.75 oz. (380–475 g). Average, female: 18.1 oz. (513 g); range 14.5–22.4 oz. (410–635 g).[3]

LONGEVITY: Second only to Northern Saw-whet Owl as the most frequently banded owl in North America, with more than 3,600 re-encounters. Average age at re-encounter, 1.8 years. Longevity record, 15 years 5 months, Ohio, banded as a chick in 1961

Year-round/
breeding (rare)

and shot in 1976. Other notable records: 12 years 10 months, California, banded as an immature and found dead on a highway; 12 years 5 months, New Jersey, banded as a chick, found dead of undetermined causes.

Big-headed, long-legged, and buoyant on the wing, the Barn Owl is one of the most distinctive owls in the world—and among the most widely distributed of all raptors, found from Canada to the cone of South America and across Europe, Africa, the Middle East, and southern Asia. (Its taxonomy

*BBL code; Pyle-DeSante code is BANO.

is uncertain, however, and many authorities split the New World races into a variety of species distinct from those in the Old World.)

Its strange appearance gave rise to the old name "monkey-faced owl," but even more folk names spoke of its attraction to human structures—"steeple owl," "church owl," and "belfry owl" among them. Although most closely associated with old buildings, up to half of Barn Owl nests may be in natural cavities, even in highly developed areas like the Mid-Atlantic region, and nest sites in caves, large mammal burrows, and cliff openings are common in the West. They readily adopt artificial nest boxes.

However lovely and ethereal this species appears, it has a truly hair-raising voice, and its vocal array is primarily a repertoire of screams and hisses. Given its taste for abandoned buildings, the Barn Owl's cry has undoubtedly fostered many a ghost story. It is also among the most resolutely nocturnal of all owls.

Although the details of its habitat choices vary by region, this is very much an owl of the open country, from pastures in the Northeast to desert arroyos in the Southwest, dryland wheat farms in the West, and sugarcane fields in the Caribbean. Once more widespread in urban areas (one pair famously nested in the "castle" of the Smithsonian Institution in Washington, DC), it is now rare in developed landscapes, perhaps because of pervasive rodenticide use, which recent research suggests is a limiting factor in much of its range.

While not federally listed in the United States, the Barn Owl is declining in many parts of its range and appears on special-concern lists in nearly half the states, second only to the Short-eared Owl by this measure. The population in eastern Canada is listed as "endangered" and that in western Canada as "threatened." Habitat loss (including changing agricultural practices), limited nest sites, chemical poisoning, and vehicular collisions may all be factors.

Harsh winter weather is also a real threat to this cold-sensitive species, and along the northern margins of its range it experiences periodic contractions and crashes after especially severe winters. Such losses are countered by its remarkably high reproductive potential; Barn Owls may breed any month of the year, even in northern areas, if prey is abundant.

SYSTEMATICS, TAXONOMY, AND ETYMOLOGY

There is much disagreement regarding the systematics of barn owls, especially the status of insular forms. As currently recognized by the AOU, the Barn Owl encompasses all 14 subspecies found in the Americas, but some authorities have elevated *T. a. pratincola* (along with several South American forms) to a distinct species, the "American Barn Owl," and the AOU's South American classification committee has solicited proposals to elevate the Galapagos Island race to species status.

The four generally recognized subspecies in our region are as follows:

T. a. pratincola: Canada to southern Mexico, including Bermuda, Hispaniola, and the Bahamas

T. a. furcata: Cuba, Cayman Islands, Jamaica

T. a. nigrescens: Dominca

T. a. insularis: Southern Lesser Antilles (St. Vincent to Grenada)

A barn is just one of the human structures Barn Owls will adopt, accounting for such folk names as "church owl," "steeple owl," and "belfry owl." *(New Jersey. S. Greer/VIREO)*

The island race of Barn Owl from Dominica, *T. a. nigrescens,* is sometimes lumped with the equally dark subspecies from the southern Lesser Antilles as a distinct species. *(Dominica. John Mittermeier)*

The largest subspecies of Barn Owl in the Americas, *T. a. furcata* is found in Cuba, Jamaica, and the Cayman Islands. Its almost completely white secondary feathers are a distinct field mark and unique among Barn Owls worldwide. *(Cuba. Christian Artuso)*

Two additional Caribbean races were described in 1978 and are not universally recognized: *T. a. bondi:* Isla de Roatán and Isla de Guanaja (Bay Islands) off Honduras, and *T. a. neveicauda:* Isla de la Juventud (Isle of Pines), Cuba.

Some authors have lumped *T. a. insularis* and *T. a. nigrescens* into a single, separate species, the "Lesser Antilles Barn Owl," while other authorities have folded them into the Ashy-faced Owl.

ETYMOLOGY: *Tyto* is Greek for "owl," while *alba* is Latin for "white." The name of the most widespread subspecies, *pratincola,* means "meadow-dweller." The English name needs little explanation, given this species's love of old structures.

> **SPANISH:** *Lechuza mono, lechuza común, lechuza de campanario* (Chiapas and Yucatán Peninsula), *lechuza sacristán* (Chiapas); *lechuza* (Cuba, Puerto Rico); *lechuza común, lechuza blanca* (Dominican Republic)
> **FRENCH:** *Fresaie* (Haiti)
> **NÁHUATL:** *Yohoaltecolotl*

DISTRIBUTION

The northern boundaries of the Barn Owl's range stretch from extreme southern New England south through the Piedmont, with small numbers in western New York and southern Ontario, and west (generally avoiding the Appalachian Mountains and Plateau) through Ohio, southern Indiana, and Illinois, Iowa, and Nebraska (rare along the Missouri River in South Dakota). Northernmost range extends through Wyoming into southern and western Montana, Idaho, Washington, and extreme southern British Columbia, though generally absent from mountainous regions south into New Mexico. South of these limits, the species is widespread (though sometimes uncommon) in a variety of open habitats; Neotropical populations may show more tolerance for forested areas (likely due to more nest sites and higher prey base) and are more common in towns and villages than those in the United States and Canada. Evidence suggests it colonized (or recolonized) the island of Hispaniola in the mid-twentieth century, where it now exists with the Ashy-faced Owl.

NONBREEDING SEASON: Generally nonmigratory across most of its range. Even along the northern margin, where some individuals may migrate, others remain year-round.

MIGRATION AND MOVEMENTS: Poorly studied. The degree to which the Barn Owl is migratory remains an open question, and most populations appear to be sedentary. What seems to be migratory behavior on the part of some northern populations may at least be partially explained by juvenile dispersal. The best evidence for regular migration comes from Cape May, NJ, where a 9-year banding study found that Barn Owl migration occurred primarily between Oct. 6 and Nov. 9 annually, with adults migrating on average a few days before immatures. A visual study using night-vision scopes showed Barn Owls departing the coast in loose groups of vocalizing birds, some circling with set wings as though using thermal air currents.

POST-FLEDGING DISPERSAL: Barn Owl juveniles disperse like buckshot from a gun when they fledge, scattering in all directions—and sometimes moving incredible distances. Chicks banded in Utah dispersed up to about 750 mi. (1,200 km) from their nests, while two siblings from the same Ohio nest traveled 1,120 mi. (1,800 km)—in opposite directions. Most young Barn Owls do not travel nearly so far; in a Utah study, the average dispersal distance was 9 mi. (15 km) for males and 36 mi. (57.5 km) for females.

DISTRIBUTION OUTSIDE THE COVERAGE AREA: The Barn Owl is among the most widely distributed landbirds in the world. Found throughout South America, including the Falkland Islands. The subspecies *T. a. pratincola* from Texas and California was introduced to Hawaii (1958–1963) in an attempt to control rats on sugarcane plantations; also introduced to Lord Howe Island, Australia. Old World subspecies found throughout the British Isles, Europe west to western Russia, the Azores and Canary islands, north Africa and the Middle East, all of Sub-Saharan Africa and Madagascar, South Asia to Indonesia. Australian and New Guinean races are sometimes split into distinct species.

DESCRIPTION AND IDENTIFICATION

A medium-size, long-legged, dark-eyed owl with no ear tufts. Above, it is the color of a perfectly baked biscuit dusted with campfire ash, and white or creamy below. Seen well, especially when perched, a Barn Owl is essentially unmistakable anywhere in its range. Its uniquely shaped face, leggy build, and milky gold plumage are diagnostic anywhere except Hispaniola, where it overlaps with the closely related Ashy-faced Owl. In flight, however, the Barn Owl may be confused with a Short-eared Owl, sharing with pale (mostly male) individuals of that species a ghostly appearance and light, buoyant flight (see "Similar Species," p. 26).

BASIC (ADULT) PLUMAGE: Plumage descriptions apply to *T. a. pratincola*. Sexes similar, but males average paler and less heavily spotted than females, which usually exhibit darker buff underparts and

Barn Owls are somewhat dimorphic, with males averaging whiter and less heavily marked, and females more heavily spotted and more richly colored below. *(California. Gerrit Vyn)*

dusky facial disk, compared with male's white facial disk. Both sexes are golden brown above, with each feather tipped with ash gray vermiculations and a white, black-rimmed spot. Underparts white to buff, varying from unmarked to heavily spotted with black. White or grayish feathering extends halfway or more down the tarsi, which are bare and gray below. *T. a. furcata* of Jamaica, Cuba, and the Cayman Islands has white (not gold) secondary and tail feathers.

Adult Barn Owls develop (usually by age 2) a pectinate middle claw—a talon marked by comb-like flanges on the inner margin. Such structures are found on the claws of 17 orders of birds, including owls, and while these modified talons have long been assumed to play a role in grooming and parasite control, only recently has evidence supporting a connection been published. The pectinate claw is believed to be especially useful in controlling lice on the owl's head, where it is unable to preen with its bill.

JUVENAL PLUMAGE: Unlike typical (strigid) owls, which have a juvenal plumage intermediate between natal down and adult basic, chicks of tytonid owls like the Barn Owl have two down coats during the nestling phase. The first, largely white coat is replaced between 10 and 15 days of age with a grayer, more lank coat, through which the golden adult basic plumage emerges; a few wisps of natal down may be retained for months.

Requires up to three molt cycles (between ages 2 and 4) to replace all juvenal flight feathers, although this sequence may be accelerated in some tropical populations. Dark barring on the tail and flight feathers are helpful in determining the age of Barn Owls; young birds exhibit more (and more closely spaced) bars, which align evenly across the wings and tail. As feathers are replaced, the spacing and alignment of the barring may become noticeably uneven, allowing an observer to age the owl as an adult.

SIMILAR SPECIES: Ashy-faced Owl is smaller and markedly darker than the Barn Owl subspecies (*T. a. pratincola*) living on Hispaniola, with grayish facial disk and yellowish body plumage. Elsewhere, Short-eared Owl can be confusing in flight; note Short-eared's dark primary tips and carpal patch on underwing; from above, note pale patch on primary feathers contrasting with dark tips and large dark carpal patch.

VOCALIZATIONS

The Barn Owl makes a variety of screams, screeches, and hisses, almost all of them more or less thoroughly hair-raising. If you have a pulse, a Barn

The central talon on Barn Owls is pectinate, with a serrated, comblike structure along one edge that appears to aid the owl in controlling feather lice. *(Pennsylvania. Scott Weidensaul)*

Its facial disk feathers just emerging, a young Barn Owl shows the long, almost vulturine shape of the head on tytonid owls, usually masked by the dense feathers. *(Texas. Greg Lasley)*

Owl's scream is guaranteed to increase it. Authors have described from 4 to 15 different vocalizations, the most common of which is a harsh, high-pitched, rasping scream lasting a second or two. Both sexes make this call (the female's is somewhat lower), although males make it repeatedly while in flight, perhaps for territorial purposes. Nestlings and some females give a "snore" call, heard most often during prey deliveries to the nest, or as a solicitation call by the female before copulation.

When threatened, Barn Owls give a longer, shriller distress call and may, like a number of tytonid owls, perform a dramatic "toe-dusting" display, accompanied by loud hissing that builds in intensity to a piercing, often explosive scream. Initially the bird sways, wings open and drooped, while giving short hisses and bill-pops. As the owl's agitation increases, the wings are spread completely and tilted toward the intruder, while the owl leans forward and rapidly shakes its head, often rattling its beak across its toes and talons while still screaming.

HABITAT AND NICHE

As their wide geographic range suggests, Barn Owls have a fairly plastic notion of what constitutes the right habitat and niche. "Open country" is a term usually used to describe their habitat, but that may include the Chihuahuan Desert in north-central Mexico, rice fields in Cuba, the sandplains and moorlands of Nantucket Island in Massachusetts, tidal marshes along the Gulf Coast, hayfields in California, or a normally busy highway slicing through the Vancouver suburbs in the predawn hours, when traffic is absent and rodents may venture into the open. The one universal is that they avoid dense forests, although Barn Owls may venture into forest margins and will hunt in open woodlands, especially in their tropical and Caribbean range. A habitat mosaic—grasslands, wetlands, riparian zones, or agricultural lands—seems to support the most robust populations.

Nesting and roosting are often done in human structures, and the list is long and eccentric: besides the usual barns, steeples, and silos, the list includes baseball stadiums, duck blinds, bridge superstructures, construction scaffolding, derelict vehicles, abandoned railway cars—essentially anything that may provide walls and a roof. In California, they often nest in the dead fronds of ornamental palm trees. Where large digging mammals like badgers are present, Barn Owls will use natural burrows in steep bluffs, along with natural crevices and tree cavities.

DIET: The Barn Owl is justly famous as a rodent specialist. Although the range of prey taken varies dramatically depending on region and habitat, mammals often make up more than 90 percent of a Barn Owl's diet, whether it's hunting pocket gophers in the Central Valley of California, cotton rats in a Louisiana cane field, or meadow voles in a Virginia pasture. Farmers who expect nesting pairs to control the rats in their barns, however, are liable to be disappointed: large rodents like Norway rats are only rarely taken (and then generally only the smaller individuals), and the owls tend to do little or no hunting in the barns where they nest.

Barn Owls are opportunistic and appear to favor the most abundant small mammal in a roughly .9 to 4.4 oz. (25 to 125 g) weight range, regardless of species, although some studies have found a preference for microtine voles over deer mice (*Peromyscus*) where both occur.

Barn Owls are built for hunting low and slow, flying fairly close to the ground where they can deploy their extraordinary hearing to greatest effect. After dark they leave their roosts and begin coursing over fields, meadows, and wetlands, often following fencerows and ditches, listening for the rustle of small mammals in the undergrowth. Their wide, broad wings in relation to their relatively light mass give them very low wing-loading (among the lowest of any North American owl), allowing them to drift and glide easily with languid wingbeats. They are surprisingly agile when pivoting in flight to drop on prey, however, and their long, bare legs allow them to snatch animals hidden deep within vegetation or under the snow.

While they may not do much to control rats in a barn, Barn Owls have proven to be fairly effective control agents in some agricultural landscapes—generally where the pest species happens to be one on which the owls naturally prey. Erecting Barn

Three Barn Owl siblings roost together inside a silo. *(Pennsylvania. Scott Weidensaul)*

A solid, weathered mat of old pellets and rodent bones lies under a Barn Owl nest, testament to this species's taste for small mammals. *(Pennsylvania. Scott Weidensaul)*

Owl nest boxes and reducing the use of rodenticides is a form of integrated pest management increasingly practiced, for example, among California vineyards where voles and pocket gophers are the primary concern. Although popular, research supporting the efficacy of the practice is still fairly sparse and comes mostly from the Old World. One study in Israel, for instance, found that encouraging Barn Owls to nest near alfalfa fields increased annual crop yields by the equivalent of $30 per hectare by reducing vole damage.

Like all predators, Barn Owls are to some degree opportunistic, and their pellets may yield the chitinous remains of insects, scorpions, and centipedes, the bones of reptiles and amphibians, and, even more rarely, fish. Birds are usually a minor part of the Barn Owl's diet, but one Texas study found that birds made up 13 percent of prey remains, with blackbirds and cowbirds the most common; the researchers believed the owls switched to birds as a buffer during periods when rodent populations were low. On islands in the Gulf of California, Barn Owls prey on two species of native storm-petrels in almost exactly the same proportion as the seabirds' abundance, but they take black rats much more often than the rodents' abundance would suggest—incidental hunting of the birds, but targeted hunting of the rats.

NESTING AND BREEDING

Barn Owls are cavity-nesting obligates, although the definition of "cavity" can be pretty broad; open-ings in house-size stacks of hay bales are common nest sites in parts of the West, for example. It's likely that in presettlement days Barn Owls nested mostly in tree cavities, caves, and on cliffs, and natural nest sites may still account for up to half of all locations, even in heavily developed areas like New Jersey. Silos, barns, abandoned houses and factories, haylofts, church steeples, old military bunkers, duck blinds, and all manner of other structures provide Barn Owls with a roof over their head.

The only actual nest-building activity described for Barn Owls are several occasions when they have been observed scratching out nest cavities in dry soil with their talons, requiring 4 to 9 nights to dig a tunnel and chamber up to 6 ft. deep. Otherwise, the eggs are simply laid on the substrate of an existing cavity, which in the case of a nest site used by generations of owls means a thick, densely matted felt of fur, bones, dried feces, and the mummified remains of unlucky chicks. Getting a close whiff of an active Barn Owl nest is a memorable olfactory experience.

Barn Owls readily accept artificial nest boxes, which, unlike typical nest boxes, usually feature a horizontal design with a long, rectangular floor. Boxes mounted on the inside of a building, with the

Although willing to accept almost any manmade structure for nesting, from silos and old barns to duck blinds and haystacks, Barn Owls will also use natural sites like caves or hollow trees. *(Colorado. Bill Schmoker)*

An adult stands stoic guard on two half-grown chicks when a researcher opens a Barn Owl nest box to band the family. *(Pennsylvania. Scott Weidensaul)*

access hole cut through the outer wall, can provide excellent security from climbing predators such as cats, raccoons, and rats.

Primarily monogamous, although polygyny is known. Loose colonies may form, with the pairs defending little more than the immediate area around the nest; one colony observed in Utah numbered 38 owls (including a few fledged young) at its peak.

Clutch size averages range from 4 to 6 eggs in most studies, but Barn Owls have a highly flexible approach to egg-laying. Clutches may be as small as 2 or as large as 11 eggs, the latter usually associated with prey explosions. Eggs are laid at 2- or 3-day intervals, and, as with most owls, the adults begin incubation when the first egg is laid, producing staggered hatch times and widely disparate ages among the chicks. Competition for food between large, older chicks and their smaller, younger siblings tends to limit fledging success in large broods, however, except when conditions are exceptionally favorable.

Multiple broods occur, depending on local climate and prey abundance, and while nesting is most common in Mar. through June in temperate

A Barn Owl delivers a mouse, food for an ever-voracious brood, to one of its fast-growing chicks. *(Oregon. K. Smith/VIREO)*

areas, if food is abundant, Barn Owls may breed at almost any point in the year, even near the northern edges of their range. There is one midwinter breeding record (downy chicks in Feb.) in Oaxaca, and a gravid female was collected in mid-Oct. in Yucatán. While a new nest site is sometimes chosen, the second clutch may be laid in the same cavity as the nearly fledged first brood. The incubation period is 29 to 34 days, with the chicks fledging between 50 and 64 days of age.

BEHAVIOR

Despite its wide range and long history of scientific study, there are still large gaps in our understanding of Barn Owl behavior and ecology. Much of what is known comes from studies in Europe, which may not apply to Western Hemisphere populations (especially in tropical regions). And while pellet studies give a broad picture of dietary preferences, we know relatively little about the night-to-night life of this intensely nocturnal owl. The details—like the owls themselves—remain cloaked in darkness.

Researchers have noted the inordinate amount of time this owl spends doing essentially nothing, though its long periods of inactivity may be more a reflection of highly refined (and highly effective) hunting skills than a lack of motivation. If you're as good at finding food in the dark as the Barn Owl appears to be, you might not have to work that hard either.

Barn Owls live and die by their ears, and there has been ample exploration of the pinpoint accuracy of this species's hearing. Both the location of the Barn Owl's ear openings and the shape of the muscular, moveable preaural flaps that cover them are asymmetrical, with the left ear being slightly higher (and the flap slightly smaller and rounder) than the right. This asymmetry permits the owl to more quickly and accurately distinguish the source of a sound, while the facial disk, which forms a parabola on each side of the head, concentrates sound waves. The experimental removal of the facial ruff resulted in the owl being unable to localize sound on a vertical axis.

Barn Owls mature fast, breed hard, and die young. At an evolutionary level, they have traded a long life with low reproductive potential for a lifestyle that has more than a little in common with the rodents on which they prey. Band recoveries suggest a short average lifespan (the average age at re-encounter is just 1.8 years), and studies from Europe suggest a similar lifespan for Old World subspecies, with harsh winter weather a prime killer. Deep snow provides a safe blanket for the owls' prey, while the Barn Owl's relatively small body mass doesn't provide much of a hedge against prolonged cold temperatures. A published longevity

record of 34 years for a wild Barn Owl appears to refer to the 1975 discovery in New Jersey of a Barn Owl leg bone with a band dating to 1942 (which is actually 33 years). Because there is no way of determining when the owl died, this age record is speculative at best, and should be discounted.

Winter weather may also drive the owls into a secondary danger: vehicle collisions. Plowed regularly and blown clear of snow by traffic, highway margins may become favored hunting sites in snowy landscapes—and if these conditions occur after several successful nesting seasons, when the Barn Owl population is high, the results can be horrific.

Vehicles are a danger to Barn Owls regardless of the season, however, in part because the birds forage at roughly the height of a car or tractor-trailer. A study in Idaho, for instance, found dead Barn Owls at a rate of six per kilometer of road—a rate higher than all other species of birds and mammals combined, and one that led the researchers to question whether the local population was sustainable.

Offsetting that short lifespan and high mortality is the Barn Owl's ability to breed early in life and, when prey is abundant, to produce large numbers of chicks. Studies in Utah found that, on average, female Barn Owls began breeding at about 1 year of age, and nested an average of just 1.3 times in their lives, producing a lifetime average of 5.6 fledglings.

They will sometimes roost communally. From a single immense, hole-ridden tree in Pennsylvania, one late-nineteenth-century naturalist counted 14 Barn Owls emerging at dusk—and promptly shot 5 of them for his collection.

STATUS

The Barn Owl is a species of conservation concern across much of its U.S. range and is listed as "endangered" in eastern Canada, where it occurs only in very limited numbers in extreme southern Ontario; it also occurs in British Columbia around Vancouver and on Vancouver Island and is listed as "special concern" in that province. Nationally in Canada it is listed as "endangered" under COSEWIC and "special concern" under SARA.* Its status in Latin America is unclear, although it appears to be both widespread and relatively common in appropriate habitat, and Barn Owls are common to locally uncommon in most of the Caribbean, where they are routinely persecuted.

Barn Owls are a listed species (endangered, threatened, or some other special-concern designation) in 23 states, particularly near the northern limits of their range. Breeding bird atlases have documented significant declines in some border regions. In Massachusetts, Barn Owls disappeared

---

*For an explanation of conservation acronyms, see page 17.

Barn Owls are creatures of open country, hunting at night—and sometimes, as here, at sunrise—over meadows, deserts, or marshes. *(Florida. Tom Johnson)*

from all mainland sites between the late 1970s and 2007, remaining only on Martha's Vineyard and Nantucket, while in New York, the species experienced a 78 percent decline between the 1980–1985 and 2000–2005 atlases. Maryland's second atlas, ending in 2007, showed a similar (72 percent) decrease, while Pennsylvania experienced a 53 percent decline, with a statewide population estimate of 100 pairs, despite a major nest-box program. The species now appears extirpated from Michigan, where it was fairly common in the 1940s. One exception to this trend was Ohio, where atlas detections rose dramatically between the mid-1980s and the late 2000s.

Although there have been many studies showing the link between Barn Owl survival and rodent populations, there has been little work exploring the impact of agricultural practices on this species. A study in Florida found that nests surrounded by unharvested sugarcane fields enjoyed almost complete fledging success, while those whose neighboring fields had been harvested had only about 50 percent fledging survival, and surviving chicks weighed less, probably because harvest severely reduced rodent numbers.

NOTES

1. B. A. Colvin. 1984. "Barn owl foraging behavior and secondary poisoning hazard from rodenticide use on farms." PhD diss., Bowling Green State University.

2. C. D. Marti. 1990. Sex and age dimorphism in the barn owl and a test of mate choice. *Auk* 107:246–254.

3. G. M. Santolo. 2014. Weights and measurements for American kestrels, barn owls, and loggerhead shrikes in California. *North American Bird Bander* 38:161–162.

BIBLIOGRAPHY

American Ornithologists' Union. 2013. Classification of bird species of South America, pt. 3, http://www.museum.lsu.edu/~Remsen/SACCBaseline03.htm.

Boves, T. J., and J. R. Belthoff. 2012. Roadway mortality of barn owls in Idaho. *Journal of Wildlife Management* 76:1381–1392.

Bush, S. E., S. M. Villa, T. J. Boves, D. Brewer, and J. R. Belthoff. 2011. Influence of bill and foot morphology on the ectoparasites of barn owls. *Journal of Parasitology* 98 (2): 256–261.

Colvin, B. A. 1985. Common barn-owl population decline in Ohio and the relationship to agricultural trends. *Journal of Field Ornithology* 56:224–235.

Duffy, K., and P. Kerlinger. 1992. Autumn owl migration at Cape May Point, New Jersey. *Wilson Bulletin* 4:312–320.

Keran, D. 1981. The incidence of man-caused and natural mortalities to raptors. *Journal of Raptor Research* 15 (4): 108–112.

Knudsen, E. I., and M. Konishi. 1979. Mechanisms of sound localization in the barn owl (*Tyto alba*). *Journal of Comparative Physiology* 133:13–21.

Lever 2005.

Marti, C. D., A. F. Poole, and L. R. Bevier. 2005. Barn owl (*Tyto alba*). In The Birds of North America Online, no. 1, ed. A. Poole. Ithaca, NY: Cornell Lab of Ornithology, http://bna.birds.cornell.edu.bnaproxy.birds.cornell.edu/bna/species/001doi:10.2173/bna.1.

———. 1999. Natal and breeding dispersal in barn owls. *Journal of Raptor Research* 33:181–189.

———. 1997. Lifetime reproductive success in barn owls near the limit of the species' range. *Auk* 114 (4): 581–592.

Martin, D. J. 1973. Burrow digging by barn owls. *Bird-Banding* 44:59–60.

Meyrom, K., Y. Motro, Y. Leshem, S. Aviel, I. Izhaki, F. Argyle, and M. Charter. 2003. Nest-box use by the barn owl *Tyto alba* in a biological pest control program in the Beit She'an valley, Israel. *Ardea* 97:463–467.

Millsap, B. A., and P. A. Millsap. 1987. Burrow nesting by common barn-owls in north central Colorado. *Condor* 89:668–670.

Otteni, L. C. 1971. "Predator-prey relationships and reproduction of the barn owl in southern Texas." MS thesis, Texas Tech University.

Paynter 1955.

Reed, J. H. 1897. Notes on the American barn owl in eastern Pennsylvania. *Auk* 14:374–383.

Russell, R. W., P. Dunne, C. Sutton, and P. Kerlinger. 1991. A visual study of migrating owls at Cape May Point, New Jersey. *Condor* 93:55–61.

Smith, D. G., C. R. Wilson, and H. H. Frost. 1974. History and ecology of a colony of barn owls in Utah. *Condor* 76:131–136.

Velarde, E., R. Avila-Flores, and R. A. Medellín. 2007. Endemic and introduced vertebrates in the diet of the barn owl (*Tyto alba*) on two islands in the Gulf of California, Mexico. *Southwestern Naturalist* 52:284–290.

Darker and duskier than the Barn Owl, the Ashy-faced Owl is endemic to the island of Hispaniola, where its status is unclear, although it appears to be more common in the Dominican Republic than in Haiti. *(Dominican Republic. Dax M. Román)*

ASHY-FACED OWL
Tyto glaucops
Alpha code: AFOW

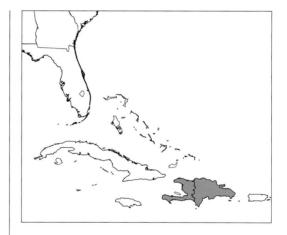

LENGTH: 13–14 in. (33–35 cm)

WINGSPAN: 33 in. (85 cm)

MASS: Based on limited data, strong reversed size dimorphism. Male, range 9.2–12.2 oz. (260–346 g). Female, range 16.4–18.9 oz. (465–535 g).[1]

LONGEVITY: Unknown

Like a duskier, darker version of the Barn Owl, the Ashy-faced Owl is named for its distinctive, silvery gray facial disk. Inhabiting the more-open woodlands of the island of Hispaniola, it hunts birds, bats, rodents, reptiles, and amphibians. Initially described as a distinct species, it was reclassified as a subspecies of the cosmopolitan Barn Owl, then re-elevated to full species status in the 1980s.

The Ashy-faced Owl was long thought to be the only native *Tyto* on the island of Hispaniola. Barn Owls were believed to have colonized the island only in the mid-twentieth century, and the fact that both species appear to coexist without interbreeding—a condition biologists call sympatry—was considered powerful evidence that these two similar owls are, in fact, distinct species.

However, the recent excavation of a fossil deposit in a sinkhole cavern in Haiti revealed the bones of both Ashy-faced and Barn Owls, which apparently occupied this high-elevation region roughly 1,000 years ago, after several millennia of Amerindian occupation but before European and African contact.

While it is possible Barn Owls on Hispaniola were overlooked by early ornithologists, it seems likely that they were extirpated at some point in the past millennia, until their recent recolonization.

SYSTEMATICS, TAXONOMY, AND ETYMOLOGY

First described in 1853 as the "Hispaniolan Barn Owl" but later considered a small, dark subspecies of the Barn Owl, the Ashy-faced Owl was officially split as a distinct, monotypic species (initially called "Ashy-faced Barn-owl") in 1983. The *insularis* and *nigrescens* races of the Barn Owl are sometimes lumped with the Ashy-faced Owl as the "Lesser Antilles Barn Owl."

ETYMOLOGY: For the genus name, see the "Barn Owl" account. The species name comes from the Greek *glaukopis,* "bright-eyed," or "with gleaming eyes." *Glaukopis* was a common Homeric epithet for Athena, goddess of wisdom, who was in turn closely associated with owls. The common name refers to the plumage coloration.

> **SPANISH (DOMINICAN REPUBLIC):** *Lechuza, lechuza cara ceniza*
> **FRENCH (HAITI):** *Frize figi gri*

DISTRIBUTION

Year-round endemic resident on the island of Hispaniola and Île de la Tortue (Tortuga), more common in Dominican Republic than in Haiti. Sedentary. Little known about juvenile dispersal.

DISTRIBUTION OUTSIDE THE COVERAGE AREA: None

DESCRIPTION AND IDENTIFICATION

With the build and posture typical of *Tytos*—long legs, outsize rounded head, and a pronounced, heart-shaped facial disk—the Ashy-faced Owl looks like a small, yellowish Barn Owl that's been dusted in soot.

BASIC (ADULT) PLUMAGE: The facial disk is silvery gray, smudged with black around the eyes and rimmed with an orange-chestnut ruff. The underparts have a yellowish buff or reddish cast, with heavy vermiculations that form horizontal, zigzagging barring. The upperparts are darker and grayer than in the West Indian subspecies of Barn Owl, densely vermiculated, and appearing largely gray from a distance. The feathers of the upperparts lack any white flecks or spots.

Wetmore and Swales (1931) stated that the Ashy-faced Owl had two color morphs, "one being light with light buffy and grayish tints predominating and the other very dark with the buff very deep and the color of the back much darker." But they also noted that individual variation was so broad that

"the two phases merge imperceptibly" between specimens. Whether these differences represent true morphs or simply individual or sexual variation is unclear.

JUVENAL PLUMAGE: "[C]overed with long soft down, in color somewhat duller than light buff."[2]

SIMILAR SPECIES: The Barn Owl is larger and paler, lacking the sooty gray face of the Ashy-faced Owl, with white or light buff underparts that are spotted to varying degrees, lacking the overall dark yellow-buff cast and fine, dark horizontal vermiculations.

VOCALIZATIONS

Harsh scream similar to Barn Owl, lasting .5 to 2 seconds, "prefaced by a series of high-pitched, ratcheting clicks."[3]

HABITAT AND NICHE

Hispaniola is the only place in the Western Hemisphere where two species of *Tyto* owls coexist. The Ashy-faced Owl prefers somewhat more wooded habitats than the Barn Owl, and is found in open country, dry, and semi-deciduous forests on Hispaniola.

The Ashy-faced Owl sticks to more wooded habitat than does the Barn Owl on Hispaniola and takes a wider selection of prey, including many birds, bats, reptiles, and amphibians. *(Dominican Republic. Dax M. Román)*

Balancing for support, a male Ashy-faced Owl mounts his mate to copulate. Little is known about the breeding ecology of Ashy-faced Owls, which nest most frequently in caves and sinkholes and on cliff ledges. (Dominican Republic. Dax M. Román)

It is normally said to inhabit forests below about 6,560 ft. (2,000 m), avoiding higher-elevation cloud forests and dense woodlands, but Bond reported in the 1920s that it occurred at the top of Morne La Selle (Pic la Selle) in Haiti, at 8,790 ft. (2,680 m). It appears to avoid agricultural and urban areas, where Barn Owls are the more common *Tyto*, although to what extent this may reflect competitive exclusion or habitat preference is unclear. Pellet studies suggest the Ashy-faced Owl has a broad ecological niche (see "Diet," below).

DIET: Like many tropical species, the Ashy-faced Owl has been poorly studied. Wetmore and Swales published the details of several pellet analyses in the 1930s, but the subject was left largely fallow until a detailed comparison of the diets of Ashy-faced and Barn Owls on Hispaniola was recently published.

That study found that both species fed heavily on small mammals, but these comprised only about half of the Ashy-faced Owl's diet, versus more than 76 percent of the Barn Owl's; the proportion of mammals in the Ashy-faced's diet was also lower than reported in the 1930s. Rodents (especially exotic brown rats and house mice) made up 40 percent of the Ashy-faced Owl's diet in the most recent study, followed by birds (29 percent, of 78 species), bats (11 percent), and reptiles and amphibians (19 percent). Rats accounted for almost three-quarters of the biomass consumed.

Although both *Tyto* species took a variety of prey, the Ashy-faced Owl preyed on a wider diversity of species than the recently colonizing Barn Owl and seemed to occupy a broader ecological niche. Ashy-faced Owls were found to take prey as small as frogs weighing just .002 oz. (0.6 g) and as heavy as Cattle Egrets and Limpkins, which might exceed the owl's own weight.

NESTING AND BREEDING

Poorly described. The Ashy-faced Owl nests most frequently in caves, limestone sinkholes, or cliffs,

Owls face entrenched persecution in many parts of the Caribbean thanks to superstition, as well as the hostility many rural inhabitants feel toward raptors. The degree to which this remains a threat to the Ashy-faced Owl is unclear. *(Dominican Republic. Tom Johnson)*

only occasionally in buildings, making no nest but laying 3 to 7 eggs directly on the ground. Main breeding season Jan. to June.

BEHAVIOR

Little information. Nocturnal, roosting by day in caves, tree cavities, and cliff ledges. Wetmore and Swales, citing early accounts, suggested it was previously more common in towns and villages.

STATUS

The Ashy-faced Owl is assumed to be secure—although this is more by way of absence of any evidence of declines, rather than any hard data regarding its population numbers or trends. IUCN/BirdLife ranks it as "least concern" but notes an unknown number of mature individuals. The Ashy-faced Owl faces persecution in both Haiti and the Dominican Republic—not only that facing almost any bird of prey in a developing country, but because of superstitions and mistrust surrounding owls in particular. The limited work on ecological overlap between the Barn Owl and this species suggests the two can coexist, using somewhat differing prey bases and habitats, but much more research remains to be done.

NOTES

1. König and Weick 2008.

2. Wetmore and Swales 1931.

3. Raffaele et al. 1998.

BIBLIOGRAPHY

BirdLife International. 2015. Species factsheet: *Tyto glaucops,* http://www.birdlife.org/datazone/species/factsheet/22688511.

Bond 1928.

Latta et al. 2006.

Steadman, D. W., and O. M. Takano. 2013. A late-Holocene bird community from Hispaniola: Refining the chronology of vertebrate extinction in the West Indies. *Holocene* 23 (7): 936–944.

Wetmore and Swales 1931.

Wiley, J. W. 2010. Food habits of the endemic ashy-faced owl (*Tyto glaucops*) and recently arrived barn owl (*T. alba*) on Hispaniola. *J. Raptor Research* 44 (2): 87–100.

FLAMMULATED OWL
Psiloscops flammeolus
Alpha code: FLOW

LENGTH: 6–6.5 in. (15–17 cm)

WINGSPAN: 16 in. (40.5 cm)

MASS: Essentially no size dimorphism. Average, male: 2 oz. (57.2 g); range 1.6–2.2 oz. (45–63 g). Average, female: 1.9 oz. (53.9 g); range 1.8–2.2 oz. (51–63 g).[1] Nesting females may increase their weight by 50 percent, reaching 3.4 oz. (96 g). Immature owls on their first migration average slightly less (1.9 oz., 54 g) than adults (2.1 oz., 60 g).[2]

LONGEVITY: Limited information. The average age at re-encounter for a small number (15) of banded Flammulated Owls was 3.2 years, but research suggests this is an unusually long-lived species for so small a raptor. Studies in Colorado documented survival to age 14 for a male and to age 8 for a female.[3]

The Flammulated Owl is a bird of paradoxes. It is a tiny owl with a big voice, widespread but largely unknown, even to scientists. Aspects of its biology, like its longevity and reproductive rate, turn conventional wisdom on its head. It looks vaguely like a small screech-owl but occupies its own genus and exhibits a radically different ecology and behavior— as well as possessing striking dark eyes that give it an otherworldly appearance.

Almost wholly insectivorous, "Flams" inhabit cool, fairly open mountain forests from British Columbia to northern Mexico, where conifers like ponderosa pine mix with aspen and oak. Built for

Both the English and Latin names for the Flammulated Owl mean "flame-colored" or "fiery," a reference to the rufous tones that overlay this small owl's cryptic, grayish plumage. Its small ear tufts often lie flat against the head. *(Washington. Paul Bannick/VIREO)*

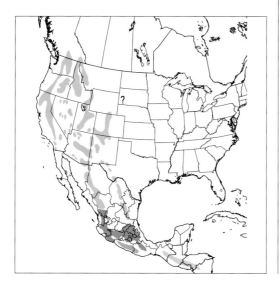

travel, with unusually long, pointed wings, they are the most highly migratory of North American owls, moving rapidly out of the northern mountains during early autumn and essentially disappearing into southern Mexico and Central America, where virtually nothing is known about their distribution or ecology. Even among a group as poorly studied as owls, the Flammulated Owl remains a genuine mystery.

SYSTEMATICS, TAXONOMY, AND ETYMOLOGY

Up to six subspecies have been described, but most authors now treat the Flammulated Owl as monotypic, with weak, clinal regional differences masked by individual variation. Mitochondrial DNA studies support this, finding high gene flow and few regional

Although it looks superficially like a screech-owl, the Flammulated Owl is the sole member of its genus. This small, almost completely insectivorous owl breeds as far north as British Columbia and migrates to Mexico and Central America. *(Nevada. Rob Lowry)*

differences among widespread Flammulated populations, both migratory and resident. The exception was the northeastern Mexico (Nuevo León) population, which appears to be isolated. The sedentary southwestern Mexico population may be the result of geologically recent southward expansion.

Perhaps fittingly for a bird cloaked in so much mystery, the taxonomic relationship between the Flammulated Owl and other small "eared" owls has long been a puzzle. Initially classified as *Megascops*, for most of the twentieth century it was placed in the genus *Otus* with Old World scops owls and the New World screech-owls, although it differs from both in significant ways. Although superficially like screech-owls, it has a single, simple song instead of two song variants, and its deep, hooting vocalization is markedly different from the trilling calls of the screech-owls. At times some authorities considered it part of a superspecies with the Eurasian Scops Owl, *Otus scops*.

After the screech-owls were split into *Megascops*, based on vocalizations and DNA, the Flammulated Owl was retained in *Otus* because of vocal similarities with the scops owls. However, fresh DNA analyses showed that the Flammulated Owl is actually more closely related to New World screech-owls, and in 2013 it was reassigned to the genus *Psi-*

loscops, a name originally bestowed on it in 1899 by Elliott Coues and resurrected by the AOU for this monotypic species.

ETYMOLOGY: The genus name comes from *psilo-*, Greek for "bare," while *scops* is from the Greek *skōps*, meaning "an owl." Both the common and species name derive from the Latin *flammeus*, "flame-colored" or "fiery."

SPANISH: *Tecolote [tecolotito] flameado, tecolote [tecolotito] de flámulas, tecolote ojo-oscuro*
NÁHUATL: *Tlalquepacle*

DISTRIBUTION

The breeding distribution of the Flammulated Owl is an archipelago of disjunct pockets, some large and some quite small and isolated, that trace the higher elevations of the western mountain ranges from southern British Columbia into Mexico and that largely reflect the distribution of ponderosa and Jeffrey pine. Wintering areas in Central America are so poorly known as to be based on little more than guesswork.

BREEDING SEASON: Found from southern interior British Columbia south through Washington, Oregon, Idaho, and western Montana; in California in the Klamath and North Coast ranges, Sierra Nevada, and (more widely scattered) in the mountains of southern California. Occurs in isolated pockets at higher elevations in Nevada and western Utah and more contiguously in the remainder of Utah, central and southern Colorado, western New Mexico, and the mountains of Arizona. Presumably breeds in the Guadalupe, Davis, and Chisos Mountains in Texas, although evidence is scant. One detection in the Black Hills of South Dakota suggests possible rare breeding there. In Mexico it breeds in the Sierra Madre Occidental as far as Oaxaca, where there are records of specimens in breeding condition, and in the eastern Sierra Madre in Chihuahua and Coahuila. The Flammulated Owl appears to be a year-round resident in the southern portion of its Mexican range.

NONBREEDING SEASON: Very poorly known; southern Mexico, Guatemala, and El Salvador. The degree to which wintering migrants may overlap with breeding residents in southern Mexico is unclear.

MIGRATION AND MOVEMENTS: A long-distance migrant, the Flammulated Owl appears to make a rapid, compressed migratory push south in early autumn—presumably clearing out of the high, chilly mountains before cold weather numbs the insects on which it depends and before temperatures drop to levels dangerously low for this tiny raptor.

During migration it may be found at lower elevations than during the breeding season, and it occasionally wanders far out of range, to the Gulf Coast or oil rigs in the Gulf of Mexico. As late as the 1960s, some ornithologists argued that this species was a permanent resident, simply overlooked during the nonbreeding season instead of migratory. While it is now clear that Flammulated Owls migrate, much of what we think we know about their movements is still fairly speculative.

AUTUMN MIGRATION:

Poorly studied until recently, the advent of the use of mist nets and audiolures playing a Flammulated Owl call have shed new light on the timing and intensity of migration. The autumn migration appears to begin in mid-Aug., to peak in mid-Sept. in Idaho and Nevada, and to be essentially over by the end of Oct.; timing may not be substantially different in more southerly areas, given evidence that the main movement south is rapid and fairly compressed, occurring within a few weeks.

Young Flammulateds appear to migrate slightly ahead of adults, but the timing difference isn't significant. Unlike the breeding season, when Flams are restricted to higher-elevation conifer forests, during migration they are of necessity sometimes found in lower elevations and in a wider variety of habitats, including riparian corridors.

A study in Idaho found significant annual swings in capture rates, presumably reflecting dramatic differences in the number of migrating Flammulated Owls from year to year. The researchers found that the owls increased their body condition (measured in mass and fat) as the migration season progressed—something expected in long-distance migrants, and in contrast with Northern Saw-whet Owls migrating through the same locations, which are much shorter distance, more-languid travelers.

SPRING MIGRATION:

The timing of spring migration is less well understood. A few birds are returning through the Mexican borderlands by Mar., with the bulk of the northbound migration in mid- to late Apr. and May.

The six described subspecies of Flammulated Owl are weakly differentiated, and most experts consider the species monotypic. *(Colorado. Bill Schmoker)*

POST-FLEDGING DISPERSAL: The male and female each take roughly half the chicks after fledging, caring for them over the course of about a month as the young become independent and range farther and farther from the nest. Owls banded as chicks were recaptured as territorial adults up to 8.7 mi. (14 km) from their nests, but the high rate of gene flow across the species's range suggests Flammulated Owl chicks must disperse widely, since adults are tenaciously loyal to their breeding sites.

DISTRIBUTION OUTSIDE THE COVERAGE AREA: Winters in Central America to El Salvador. Only a handful of specimens and sight records for winter months north of the Mexico border.

DESCRIPTION AND IDENTIFICATION

A tiny, "eared" owl with gray-red plumage, short tail, and dark eyes, the Flammulated Owl weighs little more than a thrush and has unusually small, delicate feet. Exhibiting one of the lowest rates of sexual size dimorphism among North American owls, the sexes are, for all practical purposes, equal in size. The short ear tufts are erectile but raised only when a bird is agitated or alarmed; when relaxed, the Flammulated's head looks rounded and proportionally large and the dark eyes seem especially prominent.

The mottled, heavily vermiculated plumage is primarily gray, with rufous overtones in the facial disk and throat, and bold rufous markings on the scapulars, which form distinct rusty "suspenders" framing the back. Rufous appears in varying degrees on the feet and legs, flanks and breast, and upperparts, including the nape. Some individuals are more heavily rufous than others, and some authorities have claimed there are distinct gray and reddish morphs. Birds from the northern Rockies and Great Basin tend to be darker and grayer, while those in the southern extent of the breeding range may average redder. Whether these differences in coloration rise to the level of true morphs, however, or simply represent slight regional forms amplified by individual variation, is unknown. Old reports of a brown morph appear to be based on faded specimens.

The wings are longer and more pointed than in most small owls and extend past the tip of the tail when perched. The outermost primary (P10) is the longest of the flight feathers, unlike in most owls, in which P9 is the longest; this is presumably an adaptation for long-distance migration. One notable aspect of Flammulated Owl wing topography is the reduction in comblike structures on the leading edges of the outer primary feather, which in most owls helps to deaden the noise of flight. Because Flammulated Owls do not hunt vertebrates, such soundproofing is probably unnecessary.

BASIC (ADULT) PLUMAGE: No sexual differences. Crown, head, and upperparts gray-brown or cinnamon brown and heavily vermiculated, with a partial collar of light spots across the base of the neck, and bold rufous scapular tips forming a light chestnut band along the upper edge of the folded wings. Upperwing coverts densely vermiculated and lightly spotted with white. Flight feathers dark gray-brown with four to six buffy spots (outer primaries) or buffy gray mottled bars (inner primaries and secondaries).

Facial disk rufous and lightly speckled with black, rimmed with dark brown, and with fairly intense rufous around the eyes, bill, and throat.

Eyebrows light gray with fine vermiculations, ending in short gray-brown ear tufts. Underparts whitish gray (washed with rufous, especially on the lower belly, in some birds), heavily streaked with fine, irregular crossbarring, and occasional small splashes of cinnamon. Pink to white eyeshine, usually visible only at a distance or with low illumination.

JUVENAL PLUMAGE: Grayish white, finely barred horizontally with dark gray on the undersides, back, and head. Fledglings have short ear tufts and generally exhibit chestnut tones to the face and throat but initially lack the rufous scapulars of basic plumage. Their appearance is essentially like that of adults by the fourth week after fledging, and preformative molt is complete by Oct.

SIMILAR SPECIES: Most easily distinguished from larger screech-owls by dark eyes, a trait shared only with the Balsas Screech-Owl in southwestern Mexico, which is gray-brown and has white, not rufous, scapular markings. Brown morph of Western Screech-Owl is heavily washed in rufous but has white scapular markings and yellow eyes. Whiskered Screech-Owl is about one-third larger, has yellow-orange eyes, and gray morph lacks all rufous tones; rufous morph, most common in Mexican Transvolcanic Belt, is more russet overall. Bearded Screech-Owl, similar in size, has yellow eyes. Similar in size to Northern Pygmy-Owl, but heavily vermiculated plumage and dark eyes of the Flammulated Owl are starkly different, and the latter lacks the pygmy-owl's black-and-white eyespot markings on the back of the head.

VOCALIZATIONS

For a tiny bird, the male Flammulated Owl has an extraordinarily deep, resonant voice—notes as low as, or lower than, those from owls that outweigh it several times over.

The secret lies in the structure of the male's syrinx, the avian equivalent of a human larynx. The Flam's syrinx is proportionally much larger and

The mesoptile plumage of a young Flammulated Owl, as with screech-owls, is grayish with dusky barring and incipient ear tufts, through which the adult plumage emerges. *(Colorado. Scott Rashid)*

often coming in a two/one sequence, which early ornithologists creatively transcribed as *bootle-oop, boot . . . bootle-oop, boot.* When two notes are given, there may be an emphasis on the second.

The female's hoot, usually single, is higher-pitched, slightly more drawn out, and raspier. Both sexes give a high bark lasting about 1.5 seconds when agitated, as at the nest, and which may climb into an ascending shriek accompanied by bill-claps if the intrusion continues.

The male's song is famously quiet and ventriloquial, but there is evidence that the owl reduces the volume when intruders like humans are present, evidently to mask his location. Early in the breeding season, singing males can show extraordinary tenacity, continuing without interruption for hours. Brian Linkhart, who has studied the species extensively in Colorado, found that as the nestlings grew in size, the male's singing shifted to later at night, after the chicks had been fed.

HABITAT AND NICHE

Flammulated Owls have specialized habitat requirements, being closely tied to open, dry conifer forests at cool, midrange elevations, usually on east- or south-facing slopes. This probably reflects both their small body size, which makes them vulnerable to colder temperatures at higher elevations and latitudes, and their reliance on night-flying insects like moths, which make up almost their entire diet.

Flams are most closely associated with forests of ponderosa pine, probably the most widespread conifer in the West, as well as Douglas-fir, trees whose ecology depend on frequent, low-intensity wildfires. Such periodic blazes create an open, park-like woodland with large, fire-scarred trees, especially mature aspen that establish themselves in the wake of fire, and a rich understory of grasses and wildflowers. Fire-killed trees attract woodpeckers, especially Northern Flickers and Pileated Woodpeckers, which in turn provide the cavities that Flammulateds require for nesting; oaks may also be particularly important as roost and nest sites. The understory provides the habitat for the insects on which the owl depends.

Where ponderosa pine and Douglas-fir are not found, Flammulated Owls are to a lesser extent associated with forests of Jeffrey pine, Washoe pine, limber pine, white fir, or subalpine fir, among others. In all cases, however, the structure of the forest remains fairly constant—open and semiarid with rather widely spaced, mature conifers, some hardwoods, a grassy and herbaceous understory, and dense pockets of deciduous cover.

Ideal habitat is much harder for Flams to find these days, however. Old-growth ponderosa pine and Douglas-fir has largely been timbered, and a

more heavily muscled than one would expect in such a tiny owl—comparable to that of one of the screech-owls, which weigh more than twice what a Flammulated male weighs.

Not only is the syrinx unusually large, the membranes that line it are thick, corrugated, and covered in places with small protrusions, all of which further reduce the rate of vibration when the owl calls. The researcher who first noted this unusual structure in 1947 likened it to a person with a swollen larynx, whose voice may drop considerably as a result.

The low, flat hoot of the male Flammulated is one of several characteristics that early on set it apart from the superficially similar screech-owls. The quality is hollow and slightly hoarse: *boot* or *boo-ot,* usually at a rate of one every 2 or 3 seconds, and

Beetles, moths, crickets, grasshoppers, and other insects, in proportions that vary with the season, make up virtually all of the Flammulated Owl's diet. (Colorado. Scott Rashid)

century of fire suppression in the West has shifted forest structure in many areas from open, mature stands with little understory to densely vegetated tracts of close-packed pole-timber. In addition to being less useful to Flammulated Owls, such forests are much more vulnerable to devastating, high-intensity fires. Remaining mature or old-growth ponderosa pine has also been further reduced by exurban housing development in the mountains, where lots among the scenic ponderosa forests fetch a high price. What effect all this has had on Flammulated Owl populations is unclear, but forest management techniques, such as prescribed burns and thinning treatments, may benefit the owl.

The Flammulated Owl's habitat preferences in Mexico and Central America are essentially unknown, but presumably it uses high-elevation pine-oak forests similar in structure to those found farther north.

DIET: Early ornithologists like Charles Bendire assumed that, like other most small owls, the Flammulated was a mammal hunter, but it appears to be strictly insectivorous. In fact, studies have found that the ponderosa pine and Douglas-fir forests favored by Flammulated Owls support up to four times the moth diversity found in other western forest types, which may be particularly important to the owls early in spring and during autumn migration, when many cold-hardy moth species are flying.

Grasshoppers and crickets comprised more than 60 percent of the diet of Flammulated Owls studied in Oregon, while beetles and moths together made up almost 60 percent of the diet in Arizona and Mexico. The raptors appear to be opportunistic, taking whatever prey is most readily available; in the Oregon study, the variety and proportions of insects brought to the nests closely mirrored what the researcher was catching in her insect traps.

NESTING AND BREEDING

Secondary cavity nesters, Flammulated Owls depend on nest sites created by woodpeckers. Where available, the larger holes of Pileated Woodpeckers appear to be preferred, but across most of the owl's range, cavities made by Northern Flickers may be most commonly used, along with those made by Acorn Woodpeckers and the three western species of sapsuckers.

As with most cavity-nesting owls, the Flammulated adds nothing to the hole, simply laying up to 4 (usually 2 or 3) white eggs on the damp wood of the cavity. The female alone incubates for 21 to 24 days and continues to brood the chicks until they are about 12 days old, by which time their juvenal plumage is emerging from the natal down. Thereafter she joins the male in foraging for the chicks. After fledging, the pair roughly divides the brood for care (see "Post-Fledging Dispersal," p. 40).

Flams take an unusual approach to breeding. Many small owls are short-lived species, compensating with a frenzied reproduction rate when conditions permit—a condition known to ecologists as *r*-selection. Northern Saw-whet Owls are a good example of this; that species rarely lives much longer than 3 or 4 years, but when rodent populations are high, a female saw-whet may lay two clutches of eggs in a single season, with up to 7 or more eggs in each clutch, thus maximizing her reproductive potential.

Flammulated Owls are examples of the reverse strategy, known as *K*-selection. They are exceptionally long-lived, and their reproductive output is both modest (usually only 2 or 3 eggs per year) and remarkably consistent from year to year. *K*-selection is most frequently seen in larger animals, making its presence in this very small raptor all the more unusual. One puzzle for owl researchers remains: how to square this reproductive approach, which normally limits significant annual changes in populations, with large swings in annual catch rates reported by banding stations in the Flammulated Owl's northern range.

Flammulated Owls have been reported to nest semi-colonially, based on a number of males singing in a restricted area surrounded by empty but seemingly appropriate habitat. McCallum (1994) argued that these clusters may represent several males facing off aggressively against one another in song duels at the edges of adjacent territories.

Alternately, he suggested, clusters could also result from a past collapse in Flammulated Owl populations, in which Flams became restricted to scattered pockets of habitat and from which, given their low reproductive rate, they have not yet spread. However, recent DNA work shows limited genetic differences between widely separated mountain ranges in New Mexico and Utah, suggesting that young Flammulated Owls disperse very widely.

One case of polygyny—a male caring for chicks in two nests with different females—has recently been documented in Flammulated Owls. The second nest lay some 550 yds. (500 m) from the first and was started about 2 weeks later; the male delivered fewer prey items to the second nest, which fledged only one young, versus three from the primary nest.

In New Mexico, researchers discovered three Flammulated Owl nests infested with colonies of stinging, biting ants, which swarmed the scientists painfully but left the owls and their chicks undisturbed. The researchers speculated this was a symbiotic relationship and noted that similar situations have been recorded with Eastern and Western Screech-Owls.

There is one extraordinary recent record of a pair of Flammulated Owls in Montana nesting in a hollow in the ground, in an area that had been burned the previous year in a wildfire. Two chicks hatched but apparently were killed by Great Horned Owls just before fledging. The researchers, noting the presence of Flammulated Owls in the area prior to the fire—and the species's tremendous site fidelity—theorized that a resident pair may have used the ground hole in desperation, rather than abandon their territory. It appears to be the first record of an obligate cavity-nesting owl using such a strategy.

BEHAVIOR

Camouflaged against the russet, flaky bark of a ponderosa pine, its dark eyes watching for movement, a Flammulated Owl is impossible to see in the dusk of a mountain evening—until it drops to the ground on a cricket or flashes through the air to snag a moth in mid-flight.

Flammulated Owls appear to be largely perch hunters, waiting and watching for prey, sallying

Researchers have found that mated Flammulated Owls show tremendous fidelity to their nesting sites and to each other, remaining together for years. They usually adopt cavities made by Pileated Woodpeckers and Northern Flickers for nesting. *(Colorado. Scott Rashid)*

out to capture it, and then returning to their perch. They often hover-glean, a foraging technique more typical of songbirds like kinglets and some warblers than owls, hovering near the end of a branch or shrub to pluck an insect without landing.

Strictly nocturnal, Flammulated Owls hunt most actively just after dusk and again before dawn, foraging in the open, cathedral-like spaces beneath the canopies of mature pines, as well as more open grasslands and burn scars that border the forests. Home ranges, based on studies in Colorado and Oregon, varied from 13 to 59 acres (5.5 to 24 hectares). Singing males are easy to detect using playback early in the nesting season; in one study, the detection rate was 100 percent during courtship and incubation periods, although this dropped drastically after the chicks fledged. Conversely, unmated males will sing longer and more strenuously later in the breeding season than mated males, making nesting population estimates difficult. The male usually sings from a hidden spot, tucked back in the branches of a pine or fir.

Pair bonds persist over the years, and adult owls show very strong fidelity to their breeding sites; whether the pair remains together through the winter is unknown.

STATUS

Given its dependence on old-growth ponderosa pine forest—a natural community that has been severely impacted by a century of timbering and fire suppression—Flammulated Owls are assumed to have suffered population declines in the late nineteenth and twentieth centuries, but the extent of these declines and any subsequent recoveries are unknown. Despite this, they are widespread and fairly common in appropriate habitat and far less rare than once believed.

Even where mature conifer forests with the right structure exist, a lack of suitable nest cavities may be a limiting factor for this species. Firewood cutting often targets exactly the standing dead snags in which woodpeckers (and thus Flammulated Owls) often nest, and this has been identified as a particular threat. The probable extinction of the Imperial Woodpecker in Mexico, which shared the owl's high-elevation conifer habitat, may also limit nesting opportunities in that portion of the Flam's range. The other large woodpeckers in Mexico, the Pale-billed and Linneated, are generally found at lower elevations, leaving Northern Flickers as the most common cavity maker in the Mexican range.

Being insectivorous, Flammulated Owls may be affected both directly and indirectly by aerial spraying for forest pests, like Douglas-fir tussock moth and western spruce budworm. Even where biological controls are used instead of synthetic insecticides, the reduction in nontarget moth populations, on which the owls depend for much of their diet, may have a negative impact.

The Flammulated Owl is not listed under the federal Endangered Species Act, but the U.S. Forest Service and federal Bureau of Land Management—on whose lands much of the population depends—classify it as "sensitive." In Canada the Flammulated Owl is restricted to a small area of southern interior British Columbia, and that population is listed as "special concern" by COSEWIC. It was included on the 2014 Yellow Watch List because of limited range and declining population trends.

Globally, the species is ranked as "least concern" by IUCN/BirdLife, which notes a declining population trend that does not appear rapid enough to warrant listing as "vulnerable." Total population estimate by Partners in Flight is 20,000 individuals.

Flammulated Owls are listed as "vulnerable" in Idaho and Montana, are a candidate species in Washington, and are considered of "potential concern" in Wyoming. The species is listed as "critically imperiled" in South Dakota, east of the main breeding range, where in 2002 a single individual was located in the Black Hills during targeted surveys.

NOTES

1. Earhart and Johnson 1970.

2. J. P. DeLong. 2006. Pre-migratory fattening and mass gain in flammulated owls in central New Mexico. *Wilson Journal of Ornithology* 118 (2): 187–193.

3. B. D. Linkhart and D. A. Mccallum. 2013. Flammulated Owl (*Psiloscops flammeolus*). In The Birds of North America Online, ed. A. Poole. Ithaca: Cornell Lab of Ornithology, http://bna.birds.cornell.edu.bnaproxy.birds.cornell.edu/bna/species/093doi:10.2173/bna.93.

BIBLIOGRAPHY

Arsenault, D. P., P. B. Stacey, and G. A. Hoelzer. 2005. Mark-recapture and DNA fingerprinting data reveal high breeding-site fidelity, low natal philopatry, and low levels of genetic population differentiation in flammulated owls (*Otus flammeolus*). *Auk* 122 (1): 329–337.

Balda, R. P., B. Clark McKight, and C. D. Johnson. 1975. Flammulated owl migration in the southwestern United States. *Wilson Bulletin* 87 (4): 520–533.

Barnes, K. P., and J. R. Belthoff. 2008. Probability of detection of flammulated owls using nocturnal broadcast surveys. *Journal of Field Ornithology* 79 (3): 321–328.

Blancher et al. 2013.

Browning, M. R. 1990. Taxa of North American birds described from 1957 to 1987. *Proceedings of the Biological Society of Washington* 103 (2): 432–451.

Given 2004.

Johnson, N. K. 1963. The supposed migratory status of the flammulated owl. *Wilson Bulletin* 75 (2): 174–178.

Linkhart, B. D., E. M. Evers, J. D. Megler, E. C. Palm, C. M. Salipante, and S. W. Yanco. 2008. First observed instance of polygyny in flammulated owls. *Wilson Journal of Ornithology* 120 (3): 645–648.

Linkhart, B. D., and R. T. Reynolds. 2007. Return rate, fidelity, and dispersal in a breeding population of flammulated owls (*Otus flammeolus*). *Auk* 124 (1): 264–275.

———. 2004. Longevity of flammulated owls: Additional records and comparisons to other North American strigiforms. *Journal of Field Ornithology* 75 (2): 192–195.

Mayr, E., and L. L. Short. 1970. *Species Taxa of North American Birds: A Contribution to Comparative Systematics*, no. 9. Cambridge, MA: Nuttall Ornithological Club.

McCallum, D. A. 1994. Review of technical knowledge: Flammulated owl. In *Flammulated, Boreal, and Great Gray Owls in the United States*, ed. G. D. Hayward and J. Verner, Gen. Tech. Rep. RM-253. Fort Collins, CO: U.S. Department of Agriculture, U.S. Forest Service.

———. 1994. Conservation status of flammulated owls in the United States. In ibid.

———. 1994. Information needs: Flammulated owls. In ibid.

McCallum, D.A., F. R. Gehlbach, and S. W. Webb. 1995. Life history and ecology of flammulated owls in a marginal New Mexico population. *Wilson Bulletin* 107 (3): 530–537.

Mika, M. 2010. "Phylogeography and landscape genetics of the flammulated owl: Evolutionary history reconstruction and metapopulation dynamics." PhD diss., University of Nevada Las Vegas.

Miller, A. H. 1947. The structural basis for the voice of the flammulated owl. *Auk* 64:133–135.

Morgan, P. 1994. Dynamics of ponderosa and Jeffery pine forests, in *Flammulated, Boreal and Great Gray Owls in the United States,* ed. G. D. Hayward and J. Verner. Gen. Tech. Rep. RM-253. Fort Collins, CO: U.S. Department of Agriculture, U.S. Forest Service.

Navarro-Sigüenza, A. G., and A. T. Peterson. 2007. *Otus flammeolus* (tecolote ojo-oscuro) invierno distribución potencial. In *Mapas de las Aves de México Basados en WWW,* ed. A. G. Navarro and A. T. Peterson. Final report, SNIB-CONABIO project no. CE015. México DF.

Nelson, M. D., D. H. Johnson, B. D. Linkhart, and P. D. Miles. 2008. Flammulated owl (*Otus flammeolus*) breeding habitat abundance in ponderosa pine forests of the United States, in *Proceedings of the 4th International Partners in Flight Conference,* ed. T. D. Rich, C. Arizmendi, D. Demarest, and C. Thompson. McAllen, TX: Partners in Flight, pp. 71–81.

Phillips, A. R. 1942. Notes in the migrations of the elf and flammulated screech owls. *Wilson Bulletin* 54 (2): 132–137.

Proudfoot, Gehlbach, and Honeycutt 2007.

Rashid 2009.

Rosenberg et al. 2014.

Scholer, M. N., M. Leu, and J. R. Belthoff. 2014. Factors associated with flammulated owl and northern saw-whet owl occupancy in southern Idaho. *Journal of Raptor Research* 48:128–141.

Smucker, K. M. 2013. Flammulated owls nest in hollow in ground. *Journal of Raptor Research* 47 (4): 421–422.

Stock, S. L., P. J. Heglund, G. S. Kaltenecker, J. D. Carlisle, and L. Leppert. 2006. Comparative ecology of the flammulated owl and northern saw-whet owl during fall migration. *Journal of Raptor Research* 40 (2): 120–129.

Williams, S. O. III. 2007. A January specimen of the flammulated owl from northern New Mexico. *Journal of Field Ornithology* 119 (4): 764–766.

The Western Screech-Owl forms a species pair with the very similar Eastern Screech-Owl, but unlike the eastern species rarely has a rufous morph, with most individuals gray or gray-brown. *(California. Tom Johnson)*

WESTERN SCREECH-OWL
Megascops kennicottii
Alpha code: WESO

LENGTH: 7.5–9.5 in. (19–24 cm)

WINGSPAN: 18–22 in. (45–55 cm)

MASS: Weak to moderate reversed size dimorphism; clinal variation in mass and dimorphism from north (larger, more dimorphic races) to south (smaller and less dimorphic) and from higher to lower elevations. Mass for all subspecies ranges from just 3.1 oz. (89 g) in the smallest males to 10.6 oz. (300 g) in largest females. Average weights for selected subspecies are as follows:

M. k. kennicottii: Averages, male: 5.75 oz. (163 g);[1] 4.4 oz. (123 g);[2] 5.4 oz. (152 g).[3] Averages, female: 6.5 oz. (183 g);[1] 5.1 oz. (145 g);[2] 6.6 oz. (186 g).[3]

M. k. macfarlanei (Idaho): Average, male: 6.75 oz. (191 g); range 5–8.1 oz. (143–230 g). Average, female: 8.3 oz. (235 g); range 5.6–10.75 oz. (166–305 g).[1] Heaviest female weights in winter.[2]

M. k. bendirei: Averages, male: 5 oz. (141 g);[3] 5.1 oz. (143 g).[2] Averages, female: 5.5 oz. (157 g and 155 g).[3, 2]

M. k. aikeni: Average, male: 4.2 oz. (119 g). Average, female: 5.1 oz. (145 g).[2]

M. k. suttoni: Averages, male: 3.8 oz. (108 g);[3] 4 oz. (113 g).[2] Averages, female: 4.5 oz. (127 g and 129 g).[3, 2]

M. k. yumanensis: Average, male: 3.9 oz. (110 g). Average, female: 4.3 oz. (123 g).[2]

M. k. vinaceus: Average, male: 3.75 oz. (106 g). Average, female: 4.3 oz. (123 g).[1]

M. k. xantusi: Average, male: 3.1 oz. (89 g). Average, female: 4 oz. (114 g).[4]

LONGEVITY: Average age at re-encounter, for more than 300 banding records, 2.1 years, a bit longer than pairs studied in Idaho, in which average lifespans were 1.7 years (females) and 1.8 years for males.[1] Two longevity records of individuals 13 years or older, both from California in the 1930s. One, banded as a juvenile in 1926, was 13 years old when found dead; the other, banded at an unknown age in 1924, was killed by a vehicle 13 years 4 months later. The long-standing nature of these records suggests that it is exceptional for a Western Screech-Owl to reach such an advanced age, and

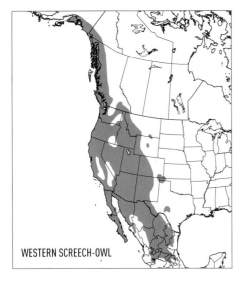

WESTERN SCREECH-OWL

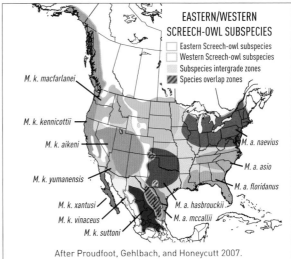

EASTERN/WESTERN SCREECH-OWL SUBSPECIES

- Eastern Screech-owl subspecies
- Western Screech-owl subspecies
- Subspecies intergrade zones
- Species overlap zones

M. k. macfarlanei
M. k. kennicottii
M. k. aikeni
M. k. yumanensis
M. k. xantusi
M. k. vinaceus
M. k. suttoni
M. a. naevius
M. a. asio
M. a. floridanus
M. a. hasbrouckii
M. a. mccallii

After Proudfoot, Gehlbach, and Honeycutt 2007.

only seven other banding records are of birds that exceeded 7 years.

The "bouncing ball" song of the Western Screech-Owl is a familiar sound from the rain forests of southeastern Alaska to lush riparian woods in California, saguaro stands in Arizona, and pine-oak plateaus in Mexico. Adaptable in its habitat requirements and open-minded when it comes to food, this species can thrive under an extraordinary range of conditions. This, in turn, is reflected by a welter of geographic forms, varying in coloration and size, which have confused ornithologists for more than a century but which genetics may finally be sorting out.

Commonplace as it is, the Western Screech-Owl was not recognized as a separate species until 1983, when it was split from the Eastern Screech-Owl, with which it occasionally hybridizes in the few areas where the two species overlap. In this, they are similar to a number of other "species pairs" of birds that diverged on either side of the Great Plains—Bullock's and Baltimore Orioles, Lazuli and Indigo Buntings, Black-headed and Rose-breasted Grosbeaks, and Western and Eastern Wood-Pewees among them.

The primary distinction between the Western and Eastern Screech-Owls lies in their voices. The Western's accelerating, single-pitch song is strikingly different from the descending whinny or monotone trill of the Eastern, though early ornithologists simply characterized the former as "slightly different and more prolonged" than the eastern bird's. Ralph Hoffmann, a transplanted easterner who became one of the leading lights of western ornithology, first described the Western Screech-Owl's call as sounding like "a ball bouncing more and more rapidly over a frozen surface."[5] Vo-

cal differences like this may seem like a thin reason to split a species, but DNA work has confirmed that even slight vocal differences among owls may indicate a wide genetic divergence between seemingly similar forms.

SYSTEMATICS, TAXONOMY, AND ETYMOLOGY

Until 1983, the Western and Eastern Screech-Owls were considered a single species, and were that year split based primarily on vocal differences. Hybrids between the two have been documented in overlap zones in Texas, Oklahoma, Colorado, and Coahuila, Mexico, but DNA analysis suggests the two species diverged about 4 million years ago.

Nine subspecies of the Western Screech-Owl have generally been recognized, ranging from the extremely large, gray-brown birds of the Great Basin and the dark nominate form of the Pacific Northwest and Alaska, to the small races of Baja, the lower Colorado basin, and Mexico:

- *M. k. kennicottii*: Coastal Oregon north to southeastern Alaska. Large and dark, with coarse markings. Variable coloration, most brownish gray, with rare rufous morph.
- *M. k. bendirei*: Coastal southern Oregon to southern California and northern Baja. Brownish gray, no rufous morph.
- *M. k. cardonensis*: Northern Baja. Small, blackish subspecies, toes bristled, not feathered.
- *M. k. macfarlanei*: Great Basin from Wyoming to southern British Columbia and northern Nevada. Largest race.
- *M. k. aikeni*: Eastern California and Nevada to western Colorado, south to Arizona and West Texas. Pale gray, no rufous morph.
- *M. k. suttoni*: West Texas and Madrean Sky-Island mountains to central Mexico. Coarse black markings on upperparts.

M. k. xantusi: Southern Baja. Smallest subspecies.

M. k. vinaceus: Northwestern Mexico (Sonora and Chihuahua to northern Sinaloa). Dark gray, underparts washed with russet-buff.

M. k. yumanensis: Lower Colorado River basin. Small, pale gray tinged with pink, no rufous morph.

The validity of *M. k. cardonensis* is questioned by some authorities, and Proudfoot, Gehlbach, and Honeycutt (2007) did not recognize it in their analysis of mitochondrial DNA in the Western Screech-Owl, concluding it was simply a transitional form. Nor did they recognize *M. k. bendirei*, finding no genetic difference between it and *kennicottii*, into which they subsumed it.

The AOU has recognized two subspecies groups: "Vinaceous Screech-Owl," which includes only *M. k. vinaceus*, and "Western/Kennicott's Screech-Owl," which includes all the rest. Proudfoot, Gehlbach, and Honeycutt's DNA analysis, on the other hand, found three genetically supported subdivisions, which they believe should be considered subspecies and whose roots probably lay in geographic separation by mountains and deserts: *M. k. kennicottii/bendirei* west of the Sierra Nevadas and Cascades; *M. k. macfarlanei* in the Great Basin; and *M. k. aikeni* and *suttoni × yumanensis* from Nevada and Utah south into Mexico. (Because of limited specimens, the status of Mexican subspecies was assessed by morphology and not DNA, and requires further research.)

ETYMOLOGY: The name "screech-owl" has always been a misnomer for this group of small New World owls, whose calls are generally trills and which screech only in extremis, usually when the nest is being disturbed. Folk names like "whickering owl," "whinnerying owl," and "shivering owl" (applied to both Western and Eastern Screech-Owls) were more appropriate.

The genus name *Megascops,* first applied to screech-owls in 1848 and resurrected in 2003, derives from *mega-,* from the Greek for "great or large," and *scops,* from the Greek *skōps,* meaning "an owl."

The specific (originally subspecific) name *kennicottii* honors Robert Kennicott, who as a teenager began collecting for the Smithsonian Institution. Kennicott died in 1866 at age 30 during his second expedition to Alaska, surveying a telegraph route to Europe for Western Union. "Kennicott's Screech-Owl," the large, dark form found from Alaska to northern California, was named for him the following year by D. G. Elliot. "In bestowing on this owl the name which I trust it is ever destined to bear,

The largest and most heavily marked subspecies of the Western Screech-Owl, *M. k. macfarlanei* is found in the Great Basin. *(Washington. Michael Woodruff)*

I simply express the desire," Elliot wrote, "to render honor to him who, combining the intrepidity of the explorer with the enthusiasm of the naturalist, twice penetrated the forbidding, cheerless districts of the far north."[6]

SPANISH: *Tecolote occidental*

DISTRIBUTION

BREEDING SEASON: Widely distributed across lower, forested elevations of western North America from southern Alaska to south-central Mexico.

Resident from southeastern Alaska (rare west to Kenai Peninsula) through coastal British Columbia (absent from Queen Charlotte Islands / Haida Gwaii) and southern interior British Columbia. South through Washington, Idaho, and western Montana and Wyoming, western and central Colorado, and southeast along upper Arkansas River system. A few records from the Cimarron River in extreme southwestern Kansas; somewhat more regularly along the Cimarron in extreme western Oklahoma. Found in most of Oregon and California (largely absent from Central Valley and Mojave Desert) to southern Baja. Patchy distribution in much of intermountain West, including Utah, Nevada, and Arizona. Common in western and central

New Mexico and the trans-Pecos region of West Texas, more rarely east to the Stockton and western Edwards Plateaus, and south through north-central and southwestern Mexico to the Transvolcanic Belt.

MIGRATION AND MOVEMENTS: Nonmigratory. Some populations may exhibit limited, fairly local seasonal movements, including altitudinal shifts, but more study is needed.

POST-FLEDGING DISPERSAL: Young birds disperse about 2 months after fledging, with females moving farther from the nest site than males; radio-tagged females in Idaho dispersed an average of about 9 mi. (15 km), versus about 3 mi. (5 km) for males, and the movements were fairly rapid, taking place in 2 weeks or less. Banded immatures have been found up to 186 mi. (300 km) from their nest sites.

DISTRIBUTION OUTSIDE THE COVERAGE AREA: None. Because the Western Screech-Owl is nonmigratory, it almost never appears as a vagrant outside its breeding range.

DESCRIPTION AND IDENTIFICATION

A small "eared" owl with yellow eyes, whose overall color ranges from gray to brownish, but with significant geographic variation in size and coloration.

Size decreases from north to south across the species's range, and locally within at least some regions from higher to lower elevations. Ear tuft length is similarly shorter in the southern subspecies. Northern or coastal populations are larger, especially the brownish *kennicottii* and the even bigger, paler gray *macfarlanei*. *M. k. suttoni* from central Mexico is smaller but especially dark and contrasting.

In more arid areas of the American Southwest and Mexico, Western Screech-Owls average grayer, with less brown or buff; "grays are lighter and whitish areas purer in the most arid regions, as in the Colorado River valley, the Owens Valley, and the southern part of Baja California. Darker grays with even less tawny or brown hues prevail eastward in the less severely arid regions both at low elevations and in the mountains."[4] *M. k. aikeni* from southwest California through northern Mexico and *xantusi* from the lower Baja are the smallest races.

The degree to which this species exhibits color morphs is muddied by geographic variation and fading, which may shift a bird's color to brown, but brownish birds are more common in the coastal Northwest; about 7 percent of *kennicottii* are reddish. *M. k. vinaceus* of northwestern Mexico, the reddest of the subspecies, can approach what in other screech-owls would be considered a rufous morph, but other southwestern and Mexican races are entirely gray.

Brownish morph Western Screech-Owls are most common among the Pacific Northwest subspecies, *M. k. kennicottii*. (Washington. J. Fuhrman/VIREO)

BASIC (ADULT) PLUMAGE: No sexual differences. Ground color overall brown, gray-brown, or gray (rarely rufous). Crown, back, and upperwing covert feathers heavily streaked with black, with narrow crossbars (less coarsely vermiculated on back and coverts). Outer half of scapular feathers white, forming "suspenders" along upper edge of folded wings. Primary covert tips white.

Facial disk generally grayish, with dusky concentric rings and bordered in black (narrowly bordered at top). Eyebrows gray; ear tufts short and erectile, gray with dark central streaks. Rictal bristles and chin grayish or gray-buff. Underparts whitish or grayish with heavy, dark vertical streaks and much finer horizontal barring. Eyes yellow, bill blackish (greenish in northwestern Great Plains).

JUVENAL PLUMAGE: Typical of screech-owls; white natal down replaced by grayish mesoptile down with dark, indistinct barring. Bill gray, becoming dark after fledging.

SIMILAR SPECIES: Most easily distinguished from Eastern Screech-Owl by voice. Western's bill is blackish versus yellowish in Eastern, although both species have greenish bills in overlapping zones of the western Great Plains. Eastern Screech-Owl's underparts show heavier, more-irregular horizontal barring, in contrast to the narrow and more precise crossbars of the Western. Whiskered Screech-Owl is smaller, has noticeably more-delicate feet, and its bill averages paler than Western; its plumage

Screech-owl juveniles, regardless of species, are cut from the same general cloth—grayish with dusky horizontal barring, like these Western Screech-Owl chicks. *(Washington. Paul Bannick/VIREO)*

is more coarsely and heavily marked, especially on the chest. Call and elevation are more useful for identification. Slightly larger Balsas Screech-Owl, with which it may overlap a bit, has brown eyes.

VOCALIZATIONS

The characteristic "bouncing ball" song is the male's advertisement and territorial defense call, although both sexes make it. It consists of 8 to 20 rapid *toot*s (fewer notes, occasionally as few as 4, among *suttoni* and possibly *vinaceus*) on a single pitch, accelerating quickly at the end and lasting 1.5 to 2 seconds. The male's voice is pitched about 30 percent lower than the larger female's.

The double-trill call consists of a short, then longer trill, sometimes with preliminary notes; used as contact call between mates, with longer pauses between introductory notes for females. Male and female may duet, sometimes as a preliminary to copulation, and neighboring pairs may sing in chorus, especially on moonlit nights. *Te-te-do* call is higher and whinier than the bounce call, a two- or three-note vocalization in which the first note is higher and the third is sometimes stretched or down-slurred.

Males call from an exposed perch close to the nest site. Calling intensity is highest in late winter and early spring (generally Dec. through Feb. in

The Western Screech-Owl's diagnostic vocalization is the "bouncing ball" call, given by both sexes, but primarily the male in territorial defense and mate attraction. This is the coastal subspecies, *M. k. kennicottii. (California. Tom Johnson)*

California, Feb. through Apr. in much of range, and into May in northern extremes). Response to recorded calls during a study in southeastern Alaska peaked in mid- to late Apr. and increased progressively after sundown each night, presumably because the male was hunting for the female or chicks. Response rates to playback in general have been

A bird of deciduous forests or shrublands, the Western Screech-Owl is rarely found in conifers. Across much of its range, it is especially common in riparian habitat. *(Arizona. Tom Johnson)*

found to rise again in late summer and autumn, when parents are tending fledglings.

Researchers have found that it is possible to identify individual Western Screech-Owls by their calls, measuring such variables as bout length and internote distance by using spectrographic analysis. Perhaps not surprisingly, the screech-owls themselves can discriminate between the calls of neighboring birds they have come to know (and which they largely ignore) and recordings of strange individuals, to which they respond aggressively—and they do it all without a spectrograph.

HABITAT AND NICHE

Not surprising for a species found across such a huge swath of western North America, the Western Screech-Owl uses a multitude of habitats, but there are a few constants. They are most often associated with deciduous forests or shrubland and only rarely use conifer stands; riparian zones are a particular favorite, to the extent that the presence of these screech-owls is sometimes used as an indicator of healthy riparian corridors; and they are restricted to lower elevations—from sea level up to about 3,280 ft. (1,000 m) in the northern portions of their range, to 7,545 ft. (2,300 m) in New Mexico, and up to 7,875 ft. (2,400 m) in the mountains and plateaus of central Mexico.

This is not a fussy bird, however; it will use palms in California, farmyard cottonwoods in Utah, saguaros in the Sonoran Desert, shade trees in city parks in Colorado, oak-juniper hillsides in New Mexico, moss-draped Sitka spruce in coastal Alaska, and dense oak-pine and pine forests or desert scrub

in Mexico. Recent research suggests that, outside the breeding season, it may not be as restricted to riparian forests as once thought, and requires a much larger territory than once believed (see "Behavior," p. 53). Its adaptability to the West's seemingly endless array of wooded habitats is one reason it has such an expansive range.

The Western Screech-Owl shares at least some of that range with 9 or 10 other species of owls roughly its size or smaller. Some, like Eastern Screech-Owl and Balsas Screech-Owl, barely touch its range, while others—Flammulated Owl, Whiskered Screech-Owl, Northern Pygmy-Owl, and Northern Saw-whet among them—have broad overlap with this species. Many of them feed largely or exclusively on arthropods, intensifying competition with the heavily insectivorous Western Screech-Owl.

Biologists have observed a number of ways—behavioral, ecological, and physiological—that these owls avoid directly competing with one another. Where they overlap with Whiskered Screech-Owls,

The subspecies *M. k. aikeni* is found across much of the Southwest, where it may be found as high as 7,500 ft. (2,300 m) in mountain forests. Where they overlap with Eastern Screech-Owls in the western Plains, Western Screech-Owls tend to occupy higher, drier forested habitat. *(Arizona. Greg Lasley)*

Although small mammals and, to a lesser extent, birds make up the bulk of the Western Screech-Owl's diet, it depends more on arthropods than its eastern cousin, as with this large centipede. *(Texas. Greg Lasley)*

for instance, the latter tend to occupy higher, more densely wooded sites.

Eastern Screech-Owls have a longer bill, on average, than the Western, perhaps because their diet depends more heavily on vertebrates. But in areas where western and eastern species coexist, that difference is accentuated, especially in southern contact zones. The generally larger eastern birds also tend to inhabit lower, wetter sites than the westerns, and each species may mimic the calls of the other as a way of protecting their territories from closely related cousins.

Despite its abundance and range, the Western Screech-Owl is still relatively poorly studied, and much of its behavior and ecology is based on a relative handful of detailed studies.

DIET: The Western Screech-Owl's diet is even more catholic than its habitat preferences; essentially anything small enough to grab and swallow will fall prey somewhere, sometime. Diet varies with region and season, with mammalian prey (primarily small to midsize rodents) and, to a lesser extent, small birds more common in the north and in colder weather. It is more insectivorous than the Eastern Screech-Owl, a reflection of a general trend among small western owls to depend more heavily on arthropods than eastern species do; prey includes crickets, grasshoppers, moths, scorpions, centipedes, and ants.

One early naturalist shot a Western Screech-Owl hanging around the eaves of a barn where Cliff Swallows were nesting. "But I did the bird an injustice, I think, for when I skinned it I found its stomach and gullet packed with ants," he wrote. "The owl was so full of the insects that a few of them hung from the corners of its mouth, and its stomach was hard to the touch, so tightly packed was it with ants."[7]

Nineteenth-century ornithologist Charles Bendire found trout and whitefish up to 8 in. long in nest cavities in Washington. "It still puzzles me to know just how they manage to catch such active fish, but [I] believe that, where obtainable, these as well as frogs form no inconsiderable portion of their daily fare, while the smaller rodents and grasshoppers supply the remainder," he concluded.[8]

In coastal areas this species (like the Queen Charlotte Island subspecies of the Northern Saw-whet Owl) forages in intertidal pools for marine invertebrates and small fish; it will take crayfish in freshwater streams. Earthworms may be an important prey item in some parts of its range, especially the Northwest. Overall, the greater dependence on vertebrate prey in the north may explain why northern subspecies are more dimorphic in size than the southern races.

Screech-owls are not shy about punching above their weight. They have been known to feed on Mallards, Ring-necked Pheasants, feral pigeons, and adult cottontails, though such large prey (which in the case of the duck would have outweighed the owl seven- or eightfold) must be considered exceptional. Whether or not the prey was killed by the owl is also a question in some cases: this species has been observed feeding on the carcass of a road-killed opossum in California, and scavenging may be more common than once realized. But attacks on domestic ducks, chickens, and pheasants make clear that they will tackle unreasonably large prey at times.

NESTING AND BREEDING

Courtship begins in mid- to late winter (limited information about timing in Mexico). Western Screech-Owls appear to be monogamous, although how stable pair bonds are from year to year isn't known. The male solicits the female with advertisement calls near potential nest sites, leading her from cavity to cavity, sometimes offering prey items; they may duet and preen each other.

A secondary cavity nester, it depends, like other small owls, on natural cavities or those made by other birds. In much of its range, cottonwoods provide the majority of nest sites, although they will use a variety of hardwoods (occasionally conifers) and treelike cacti such as saguaros and cardóns. The owls will use naturally occurring cavities (which in the mountains of southeastern Arizona comprised almost 60 percent of nest sites studied), while in

other areas, cavities cut by Northern Flickers and Pileated Woodpeckers are the most important nest locations.

In the Sonoran Desert of Arizona, 10 of 12 Western Screech-Owl nests found by researchers were in saguaros, the remaining 2 in mesquite trees. Thick and fleshy, the large saguaros (and related cardóns in Baja) may offer better insulation for a cavity nest than trees do—an important consideration in an environment with blistering summer temperatures. Holes cut by Gilded Flickers, and in larger-than-average cacti, were most often chosen; the flickers cut slightly bigger holes than those of Gila Woodpeckers, the other common large woodpecker in the region. As with territories in woodlands, desert nest sites tended to be fairly open and to average less understory and shrub cover, suggesting that regardless of the environment, the owls like a clear flight zone around the nest.

As with other small cavity-nesting owls like Eastern Screech-Owl and Ferruginous Pygmy-Owl, a Western Screech-Owl pair requires multiple cavities within its territory, which serve as alternate nest sites, roosts, and food caches. Nest sites are often reused. They will accept artificial nest boxes with an entrance hole diameter of 3 in. (7.6 cm); see "Eastern Screech-Owl" for more information, as box dimensions for the two species are similar.

The average clutch size is 3 or 4 eggs (rarely 2 to 7), laid a day or two apart. Incubation begins with the first or second egg, so that hatching is similarly staggered. Incubation lasts 26 to 30 days, and the chicks fledge around 35 days of age. They remain at least somewhat dependent on the parents for about 5 weeks, after which they disperse, females traveling farther than males (see "Post-fledgling Dispersal," p. 49).

BEHAVIOR

Western Screech-Owls are nocturnal, although telemetry studies suggest they may be crepuscular hunters, most active at dusk and dawn. Like most screech-owls, they are perch hunters, but little is known about their nocturnal behavior. They return to habitual daytime roosts shortly after daybreak, with the male often perching near the nest hole, perfectly camouflaged against the rough bark of a cottonwood, oak, or mesquite tree.

Where prey is abundant and nest sites limited, Western Screech-Owls can breed in surprising densities; a researcher in California found 14 pairs along 4 mi. (6.4 km) of riverine forest. But while most research suggests that Western Screech-Owl home ranges are relatively small, usually 6 to 25 acres (2.5 to 10 hectares), a study in southern British Columbia found that average range size was 160 acres (65 hectares). Part of the discrepancy may be

Ear tufts, like all feathers, can be controlled by muscles, so a Western Screech-Owl can raise and lower them at will—especially when trying to camouflage itself, as this bird is doing. *(Arizona. Greg Lasley)*

explained by the fact that most studies took place in the breeding season. The British Columbia research found that the owls had fairly small activity areas (about 50 acres / 20 hectares) in summer, but much larger ranges (averaging almost 222 acres / 90 hectares) in winter. Furthermore, there was very little overlap between the winter ranges used by members of a mated pair, although their territories overlapped widely in summer. Nor was there much overlap between the summer and winter areas used by any one owl.

Among the biggest dangers to a small owl are larger owls, and Western Screech-Owls have been known to be killed by Barred, Spotted, and Great Horned Owls. Mammalian predation of nests seems to be fairly limited. More bizarrely, an adult in Arizona was found entangled in the stems of Coulter's spiderling (*Boerhavia coulteri*), a weedy annual wildflower with resinous glands at the base of its leaves. The owl, presumably chasing prey, was so enmeshed in the sticky stems that it had damaged or lost a number of flight feathers and had to be taken to a rehabilitator.

STATUS

Common to fairly common across most of its range, the Western Screech-Owl is listed as being of "potential concern" in Wyoming. The *macfarlanei* subspecies is listed as "endangered" under the Canadian Species at Risk Act and Red-Listed by British Columbia. Under COSEWIC it and the *kennicottii* race are listed as "threatened" in Canada. Little is known about populations in Mexico, or about long-term trends in most of its range.

In the Pacific Northwest, Western Screech-Owls may be significantly affected by predation from expanding populations of Barred Owls, which use much the same habitat. A 15-year study on Bainbridge Island, Washington, in concert with Christmas Bird Count data, found a strong link between steeply declining screech-owl numbers and growing Barred Owl detections. Western Screech-Owls, once common on the island, now appear to be extirpated there. The Pacific Northwest population is listed on the Red Watch List of distinct population units at risk.

Of more than 50 Western Screech-Owls checked in California for West Nile virus, 23 percent tested positive, a higher rate than was found for Barn and Great Horned Owls, suggesting this species was at moderate risk from this exotic avian disease. Surveys using playback in southern Baja found that Western Screech-Owls were progressively less common in altered habitats, and essentially absent from populated areas, and may be less able to cope with habitat loss than other screech-owls.

Partners in Flight estimated the range-wide population of the Western Screech-Owl at 740,000 individuals but acknowledged this was little more than a guesstimate based on limited data and might be off by an order of magnitude.

NOTES

1. R. J. Cannings and T. Angell. 2001. Western screech-owl (*Otus kennicottii*). In *The Birds of North America*, no. 597, ed. A. Poole and F. Gill. Philadelphia, PA: Birds of North America.

2. F. R. Gehlbach. 2003. Body size variation and evolutionary ecology of eastern and western screech-owls. *Southwestern Naturalist* 48 (1): 70–80.

3. Earhart and Johnson 1970.

4. A. H. Miller and L. Miller. 1951. Geographic variation of the screech owls of the deserts of western North America. *Condor* 53 (4): 161–177.

5. R. Hoffmann. 1927. *Birds of the Pacific States*. Boston: Houghton Mifflin, p. 66.

6. Elliott 1867.

7. S. F. Rathbun, quoted in A. C. Bent. 1937. *Life Histories of North American Birds of Prey*, pt. 2. Washington, DC: Smithsonian Institution, Bulletin 167, pp. 269–270.

8. C. Bendire. 1892. *Life Histories of North American Birds*. Washington, DC: National Museum Special Bulletin 1, p. 372.

BIBLIOGRAPHY

Acker, J. 2012. Recent trends in western screech-owl and barred owl abundances on Bainbridge Island, Washington. *Northwestern Naturalist* 93:133–137.

Allen, M. L., and A. P. Taylor. 2013. First record of scavenging by a western screech-owl (*Megascops kennicottii*). *Wilson Journal of Ornithology* 125 (2): 417–419.

Cannings, R. J., and H. Davis. 2007. The status of the western screech owl (*macfarlanei* subspecies) *Megascops kennicottii macfarlanei* in British Columbia. Naramata and Armstrong, BC: Canning Holm Consulting and Artemis Wildlife Consultants.

Davis, H., and R. D. Weir. 2010. Home ranges and spatial organization of western screech-owls in southern British Columbia. *Northwestern Naturalist* 91:157–164.

Earhart and Johnson 1970.

Elliot, D. G. 1867. Description of an apparently new species of owl, of the genus *Scops*. *Proceedings of the Academy of Natural Sciences of Philadelphia* 19:99–100.

Gehlbach, F. R., and S. H. Stoleson. 2010. Western screech-owl (*Megascops kennicottii*). In *Raptors of New Mexico*, ed. J. Cartron. Albuquerque, NM: University of New Mexico Press, pp. 511–523.

Hardy, P. C., and M. L. Morrison. 2003. Nest-site selection by western screech-owls in the Sonoran Desert, Arizona. *Western North American Naturalist* 63 (4): 533–537.

Herting, B. L., and J. R. Belthoff. 2001. Bounce and double trill songs of male and female western screech-owls: Characterization and usefulness for classification of sex. *Auk* 118 (4): 1095–1101.

Kissling, M. L., S. B. Lewis, and G. Pendleton. 2010. Factors influencing the detectability of forest owls in southeastern Alaska. *Condor* 112 (3): 539–548.

Navarro-Sigüenza, A. G., and A. T. Peterson. 2007. *Megascops kennicottii* (tecolote occidental) residencia permanente distribución potencial. In *Mapas de las Aves de México Basados en WWW*, ed. A. G. Navarro and A. T. Peterson. Final report, SNIB-CONABIO project no. CE015. México DF.

Palmer, G. H., R. N. Gwinn, and J. E. Gwinn. 2009. Entanglement of a western screech-owl (*Megascops kennicottii*) in Coulter spiderling (*Boerhavia coulteri*). *Southwestern Naturalist* 54 (4): 523–524.

Proudfoot, Gehlbach, and Honeycutt 2007.

Pyle 1997.

Rodríguez-Estrella, R., and A. Peláez-Careaga. 2003. The western screech owl and habitat alteration in Baja California: A gradient from urban to rural landscapes to natural habitat. *Canadian Journal of Zoology* 81 (5): 916–922.

Rosenberg et al. 2014.

Tripp, T. M. 2004. "Use of bioacoustics for population monitoring in the western screech-owl (*Megascops kennicottii*)." M.S. thesis, University of Northern British Columbia.

Tripp, T. M., and K. A. Otter. 2006. Vocal individuality as a potential long-term monitoring tool for Western Screech-owls, *Megascops kennicottii. Canadian Journal of Zoology* 84 (5): 744–753.

Wheeler, S. S., C. M. Barker, Y. Fang, M. V. Armijos, B. D. Carroll, S. Husted, W. O. Johnston, and W. K. Reisen. 2009. Differential impact of West Nile virus on California birds. *Condor* 111 (1): 1–20.

EASTERN SCREECH-OWL
Megascops asio
Alpha code: EASO

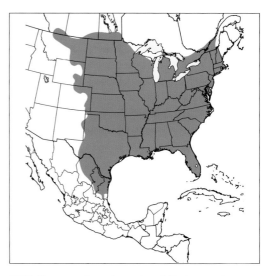

LENGTH: Overall length, range-wide 6–10 in. (16–25 cm). Averages by subspecies (male and female): *asio* 8.1 and 8.5 in. (20.7, 21.5 cm); *maxwelliae* 8.9 and 9.4 in. (22.7, 23.8 cm); *hasbrouckii* 8.4 and 8.7 in. (21.4, 22.2 cm); *mccallii* 8.4 and 8.7 in. (21.4, 22.2 cm); *floridanus* 7.8 and 7.9 in. (19.8, 20 cm).[1]

WINGSPAN: 18–22 in. (45–55 cm)

MASS: Significant regional variation, with increasing dimorphism to the north (the southeastern subspecies *floridanus* is an exception). Mass ranges from 3.3 oz. (94 g) for the smallest males to 8.9 oz. (252 g) for the largest females. Range-wide averages in two studies were males: 5.6 and 5.9 oz. (159 and 167 g); females: 5.8 and 6.25 oz. (166 and 177 g).[2, 3] Individual weights vary seasonally and peak Oct.–Dec.

Mass by selected subspecies:

M. a. "*naevius*" (northern portion of *asio*): Northern Ohio: Average, male: 5.9 oz. (167 g); range 4.9–7.4 oz. (140–210 g). Average, female: 6.8 oz.; range 5.3–8.3 oz. (150–235 g).[4] No source locations given: Average, male: 6.6 oz. (188 g). Average, female: 7 oz. (198 g);[2] Average, male: 5.6 oz. (160 g); range 3.5–8.0 oz. (99–229 g). Average, female: 6.5 oz. (184 g); range 4.4–8.9 oz. (126–252 g).[5]

M. a. *asio* (southern portion of *asio*): Average, male: 4.8 oz. (135 g). Average, female: 5.4 oz. (153 g).[2] Average, male: 5.9 oz. (167 g). Average, female: 6.8 oz. (194 g).[6]

M. a. *maxwelliae*: Manitoba (small sample): Average, male: 4.5 oz. (127 g). Average, female: 4.8 oz. (136 g).[7]

M. a. *hasbrouckii*: Average, male: 5.4 oz. (153 g). Average, female: 5.8 oz. (166 g).[2]

M. a. *mccallii*: Average, male: 4.2 oz. (119 g). Average, female: 4.5 oz. (128 g).[2]

LONGEVITY: Of 1,084 Eastern Screech-Owls banded and re-encountered in the United States and Canada, the average age at encounter was 2.1 years; 10 percent exceeded 5 years of age. The oldest wild Eastern Screech-Owl on record was banded in 1955 in Ontario as an adult, and found dead in 1968, for a minimum age of 14 years 6 months. Other notable records include ages of at least 12 years 7 months (two individuals), 13 years 2 months, and 13 years 6 months. A Canadian record of 27 years

NOTE: See map for subspecies of Eastern and Western Screech-Owls in Western Screech-Owl account, on page 47.

10 months is sometimes cited, but the band was found on a bone and the age at death cannot be determined.

Perhaps the most common owl east of the Rocky Mountains, the Eastern Screech-Owl is also the quintessential backyard raptor for many people—assuming, that is, they even realize what is making that eerie, quavering, decidedly unhootlike trill in the nighttime darkness.

The screech-owl's call has always carried a tinge of the melancholy; Thoreau called it "a most solemn graveyard ditty, the mutual consolations of suicide lovers."[8] But this so-called "whinny," one of two common vocalizations, is actually the sound of lively courtship, a solid relationship, or the bond between parent and offspring. It is also, as any good birder knows, one of the best ways to stir up some interesting trouble. A whistled imitation of a screech-owl's trill, with some excited pishing tossed in, will bring a mob of angry songbirds on the attack. Given that at some times of the year a screech-owl's diet may be three-quarters avian, the outrage is certainly justified.

Eastern Screech-Owls are found from the Florida Keys to the prairies of Manitoba and the mountains of eastern Mexico, and they have shown a remarkable ability to adapt to an increasingly urbanized landscape. They also represent one of the best examples of polymorphism in the bird world, with rufous, brown, and gray individuals. Research now suggests these color morphs are more than mere genetic happenstance: they appear to confer significant advantages and disadvantages in terms of climate tolerance and even auditory sensitivity.

A dimorphic pair of the southeastern-most subspecies of the Eastern Screech-Owl, *M. a. floridanus*. Recent molecular work suggests that, except for "McCall's Screech-Owl" in Texas and Mexico, which may warrant species status, the rest of the races should be lumped into one subspecies, *M. a. asio*. (Florida. Paul Bannick/ VIREO)

"Maxwell's Screech-Owl," *M. a. maxwelliae,* is the most northwesterly of the described subspecies of the Eastern Screech-Owl and also the palest and most lightly marked. *(Manitoba. Christian Artuso)*

SYSTEMATICS, TAXONOMY, AND ETYMOLOGY

The Eastern Screech-Owl was split from the Western Screech-Owl in 1983, based on vocal and morphological differences. The Eastern is larger, longer-billed, and shorter-winged than Western Screech-Owl. Limited hybridization occurs between the species in overlap zones; see "Western Screech-Owl."

Five or six subspecies in two groups are generally recognized, increasing in size from south to north, in color intensity from west to east, and in density of ventral markings from north to south. Red morphs are more common to the south, and gray morphs to the north. The eastern group includes *M. a. asio* from northern Georgia to northern Mississippi and Missouri north to Minnesota and southern New England (including *M. a "naevius"* in the northern portion of this area); and the smallest subspecies, *M. a. floridanus,* from southern Georgia to Louisiana and Florida.

The western group includes the largest and most overwhelmingly gray race, *M. a. maxwelliae,* in the northern Great Plains from Oklahoma, eastern Colorado, and Kansas to southern Manitoba and southeastern Saskatchewan; *M. a. hasbrouckii* in the southern Great Plains from southern Kansas to northern and central Texas; and *M. a. mccallii* from South Texas into northeastern Mexico.

The subspecies of the southern Plains, *M. a. hasbrouckii*, has coarse, heavy blackish markings and closely resembles Western Screech-Owls of the *aikeni* race, with which it sometimes overlaps. Recent genetic work suggests all Eastern Screech-Owls, except those in South Texas and Mexico, are best classified as a single subspecies. (Oklahoma. Steve Metz)

"McCall's Screech-Owl," *M. a. mccallii*, from South Texas and northeastern Mexico, is considerably smaller than other races of the Eastern Screech-Owl and has a faster, longer, higher-pitched monotone trill. Coupled with genetic differences, this may mean it deserves full species status. Rufous morphs are unknown in Texas but more common in Mexico. (Texas. Marshall Iliff)

A mitochondrial DNA study of screech-owls found essentially no genetic differences among four of the five traditional subspecies, however, and recommended lumping *asio, floridanus, maxwelliae,* and *hasbrouckii* into a single subspecies, *M. a. asio.* On the other hand, the researchers found that *M. a. mccallii* had a unique haplotype (DNA variations), and coupled with its markedly smaller size (about 25 percent smaller than *hasbrouckii* to the north) and faster, longer, higher-pitched monotone trill, concluded that it warrants subspecific—and possibly full species—status.[9]

ETYMOLOGY: See "Western Screech-Owl" for discussion of genus and common name. The specific name *asio* is Latin, from the writings of Pliny, meaning "a horned owl," and is sometimes translated as "little horned owl."

SPANISH: *Tecolote oriental, tecolote [tecolotito] chillón*

FRENCH: *Petit-duc maculé*

DISTRIBUTION

BREEDING SEASON: Resident across its range. Found from the eastern slope of the Sierra Madre Oriental in extreme northern Veracruz and southeastern San Luís Potosí, north through western Texas and Coahuila to Montana, extreme southeastern Saskatchewan, and southern Manitoba; east through central Wisconsin and the lower peninsula of Michigan to southeastern Ontario, southern Quebec, and possibly southwestern New Brunswick; from southern Maine south across the eastern United States to the Florida Keys.

The western edge of its range is complex and patchy, following forested corridors along major river systems like the Platte, Missouri, and Yellowstone in Colorado and Montana. Recent scattered reports in New Brunswick, Nova Scotia, and Prince Edward Island may represent a population expanding east along the Saint Lawrence lowlands, although confusion with nocturnal calls of migrating Black Scoters may account for many spring records; documented sight records remain very rare. The species is still quite rare in southern Maine (fewer than 15 records since 2000, now 1 to 3 annually), despite a thriving population just to the west in New Hampshire. In Southeast, absent or rare only in Everglades and large cane-producing areas in Florida.

A gray-morph Eastern Screech-Owl blends almost seamlessly with tree bark—an example of the cryptic plumage many owls depend upon. *(Manitoba. Christian Artuso)*

MIGRATION AND MOVEMENTS: Nonmigratory, other than some limited, local movements under severe winter or food stress.

POST-FLEDGING DISPERSAL: Average juvenile dispersal distances ranged from 1 to 1.7 sq. mi. (2.7 to 4.4 km).[1]

DISTRIBUTION OUTSIDE THE COVERAGE AREA: None

DESCRIPTION AND IDENTIFICATION

A small, "eared" owl with yellow eyes and two main color morphs—reddish most common in warmer, more humid hardwood forests; gray in cooler, drier, or more heavily coniferous regions to the north and west; and an uncommon intermediate brown morph.

The Eastern Screech-Owl shows more pronounced size dimorphism than the western species, especially in northern populations and in the subspecies *floridanus,* presumably because it is more dependent on vertebrate prey than the fairly insectivorous Western Screech-Owl. This is reflected as well in its somewhat larger feet and longer bill than the Western Screech-Owl has.

Color morphs: Eastern Screech-Owls are famously polymorphic, with distinct rufous and gray morphs and an intermediate brownish form, which are not directly tied to age or gender but which vary fairly predictably with region and climate.

Gray-morph owls dominate in colder, drier, more coniferous habitats to the north and west. Rufous screech-owls are most common in more

A female Eastern Screech-Owl delivers food to her chicks, which are days away from fledging. Like most cavity-nesting owls, Eastern Screech-Owls require multiple cavities for nesting, roosting, and food storage and benefit from artificial nest boxes, especially if they are clustered in a small area. *(Manitoba. Christian Artuso)*

southerly and eastern regions and in humid deciduous forests. In the mid-South and Mid-Atlantic regions, half to three-quarters of all screech-owls are rufous, as are nearly 80 percent in southern Illinois and eastern Tennessee. From North Dakota to Mich-

Eastern Screech-Owls are dramatically polymorphic. The rufous (red) morph is most common in southerly and eastern regions, in predominantly hardwood forests. The gray morph is most common in colder, drier areas in the north and west of the species's range. The intermediate brown morph (right) is generally rare but somewhat more common in the north as well as Florida and the Gulf Coast. *(Pennsylvania. Alan Richard, Tom Johnson, Howard Eskin)*

igan, the percentage of red birds ranges from 17 to 22 percent, and at the northern extreme of their range in Manitoba, rufous morphs comprise fewer than 1 percent of the very pale *maxwelliae* race.

Intermediate brownish birds are found in relatively low numbers but are more common in the north as well as in Florida and along the Gulf Coast, where they replace many of the rufous individuals in the population. The frequency of rufous-morph owls in Mexico requires more study; *M. a. mccalli* apparently has no rufous morph in South Texas, but Marshall (1967) indicated reddish birds again become more frequent south of the Rio Grande, comprising 13 percent of the population in Tamaulipas and San Luís Potosí.

In this polymorphism, Eastern Screech-Owls are not unique; a number of gallinaceous birds like Ruffed Grouse, and nightjars like Eastern Whippoor-wills, exhibit the same north/south, humid/dry, hardwood/conifer dichotomy between rufous and gray morphs. The screech-owl group as a whole, along with Old World scops owls and pygmy-owls, also show this tendency, which is genetically based and appears linked to a dominant rufous gene.

But if the root cause is obviously genetic, just why two dramatically different morphs should persist in these birds has long puzzled scientists, who have unearthed some intriguing lines of evidence that the color variations are driven by more than simple camouflage.

Speculation that rufous feathers were more susceptible to wear has not been shown to be true, but gray-morph birds do have a lower metabolic rate than red-morph owls, which may give them an advantage in colder climates and during extreme weather. It may also influence an owl's choice of territories; a study in Pennsylvania, where both morphs occur, found that reddish owls chose winter territories with higher mouse populations than did gray individuals, perhaps to compensate for higher caloric demands. Greater winter mortality has been documented in rufous Eastern Screech-Owls as well as in reddish-morph Tawny Owls (*Strix aluco*) in Europe.

On the other hand, researchers found that rufous-morph Eastern Screech-Owls appear to have more sensitive hearing, across a greater range of frequencies, than do gray-morph birds. And studies linking the intensity of spotting in Barn Owls with resistance to parasites suggest that plumage coloration may be linked to immunological benefits in some birds. Females also make up a majority of rufous-morph Eastern Screech-Owls.

In a study in Iowa, 58 percent of female Eastern Screech-Owls were rufous, as were 45 percent of males, and the percentage of rufous morphs decreased from east to west in tandem with average precipitation, but not temperature. Looking back at records to the 1880s, the author concluded that the percentage of rufous birds had decreased since the early twentieth century.

Given these apparent links to temperature and precipitation, one aspect that has yet to be explored is how climate change may be altering the distribution of color morphs in Eastern Screech-Owls. Scientists in Europe, examining skin collections spanning a 137-year period, found a significant increase in the red morph of the Scops Owl (*Otus scops*) that corresponded to an increase in rainfall, temperature, and humidity over that time. Gehlbach (1994,

2012) found rufous-morph Eastern Screech-Owls more common in warm, humid suburban areas of Texas than in the surrounding countryside, and potentially benefiting from a warming climate over a three-decade period.

BASIC (ADULT) PLUMAGE: No sexual differences. Erectile ear tufts, bright yellow eyes, yellowish bill. Toes feathered in northern races, bare and bristled in southern forms.

Gray morph: Upperparts gray, sometimes tinged with brown, moderately vermiculated and with black streaks along most feather shafts. Broad blackish streaks on forehead. Outer half of scapular feathers white, forming "suspenders" along the upper edges of the folded wings. White patches at bend of folded wings from white-edged coverts. Facial disk gray, with fine, dusky concentric barring, broadly bordered with black or dark brown. Broad vertical black streaks on upper chest, with distinct, widely spaced crossbarring (see "Similar Species," p. 63); finer vertical streaks with crossbarring on breast and flanks. Northern Plains race *M. a. maxwelliae* paler overall, more lightly marked, and with more white below.

Rufous morph: Upperparts bright orange-brown, lightly marked with dark streaks along the feather shafts, but exhibiting little horizontal barring or vermiculation on the head, back, or upperwing coverts. Streaks heaviest on forehead and scapulars; scapular feathers broadly tipped with white, forming "suspenders" as in gray morph. White patches at bend of folded wings from white-edged coverts. Facial disk light rufous, largely unmarked, and broadly edged in black. Underparts heavily marked with blackish teardrop streaks and rufous crossbarring, creating a mottled effect. Upper chest suffused with rufous, fading to white ground color on belly and flanks. Rufous morph exceedingly rare in *M. a. maxwelliae*, unknown in *mccalli* in Texas but moderately common in eastern Mexico.

Intermediate (brown) morph: Similar to gray morph, but suffused with warm brown overall.

JUVENAL PLUMAGE: White neoptile down at hatching, replaced by grayish or slightly rufous juvenal plumage with dusky, indistinct horizontal barring, similar to all juvenile screech-owls. Ear tufts are erectile and prominent on nestlings and fledglings. Color morphs are obvious before fledging.

SIMILAR SPECIES: Distinguished from Western Screech-Owl by voice; yellowish, not blackish bill (but use caution in western Great Plains, where

Three fledgling Eastern Screech-Owls, freshly out of the nest, wear the grayish, dusky-barred juvenal plumage typical of all screech-owls—and eye up a human intruder with surprise and suspicion. *(Manitoba. Christian Artuso)*

both species may have greenish bills); coarser, more-irregular crossbarring on breast feathers. Degree of overlap with Western Screech-Owl in eastern Mexico unknown. In eastern Sierra Madre distinguished from Whiskered Screech-Owl by voice and larger size (nearly 40 percent), bright yellow versus orangish eyes, and elevation: Eastern Screech-Owl inhabits lower forests, usually below 4,920 ft. (1,500 m), and range overlap may be limited.

VOCALIZATIONS

Two main vocalizations, including the well-known "whinny" call and a monotone trill, are familiar night sounds across much of North America. Both sexes produce these calls, although the female tends to have a higher-pitched voice. As with its western congener, none of the Eastern Screech-Owl's typical calls can remotely be termed a "screech," although a defensive scream often given by chicks, or by adults before attacking a nest intruder, certainly qualifies.

The whinny call is used primarily for territorial defense, and the monotone trill between members of a pair or by adults with their chicks. The whinny is a slurred, descending trill that generally lasts 1.5 to 2 seconds and may be repeated every few seconds for long periods. The monotone trill may be fairly short (1.5 to 3 seconds) but may last 8 seconds or longer, and the cadence may be smooth and even or somewhat staccato. The monotone may have a slight crescendo and may rise or fall subtly in pitch at the end.

Gehlbach (1994) tracked the average frequency that these two call types were heard at a site in Texas and found that the monotone trill peaked in Feb. at roughly 10 singing bouts an hour, dropped to just twice hourly in May, but rose to 6 per hour again in June, when the young fledged. The monotone call largely ceased in autumn, but after the young fledged in July the whinny call rose sharply in frequency. Its use then declined at a slow rate through autumn, a time when young owls are attempting to set up their own territories and trespass on established pairs. Members of a pair may trill antiphonally, which he believes is also territorial defense against dispersing juveniles.

Males advertise in spring by calling from potential nest holes using the monotone trill, often singing persistently. At this time of year a slower version of the trill may be given. Pairs may duet using the monotone trill.

The South Texas and Mexican race, *M. a. mccallii*, is generally thought to lack a whinny call, although Gehlbach (1995) says it has a shortened version. It also gives a higher, faster monotone trill than other subspecies, often with a modest crescendo in the middle and a slightly accelerating pace at the end. Given DNA evidence that *mccallii*

may constitute a separate species, its vocalizations deserve more study.

Eastern Screech-Owls may also make low, insistent hoots when disturbed, which can transition into increasingly strident, querulous barks. Older chicks give a rattling, raspy food-begging call, often with dogged repetition in the weeks following fledging, and females being offered food by a courting male will sometimes produce this vocalization as well.

As with a number of species of owls, calling may increase in frequency on moonlit nights.

HABITAT AND NICHE

Able to thrive in a variety of wooded habitats—including fragmented landscapes, suburban, and even urban environments—and capable of taking an enormous range of prey, it's no surprise that the Eastern Screech-Owl is ubiquitous across most of the eastern half of North America.

Eastern Screech-Owls are tightly bound to hardwood or mixed forests (as well as pine forests in the South), but they tend to avoid extensive tracts of unbroken forest, as well as elevations above about 2,000 ft. (600 m) in the north and 5,000 ft. (1,500 m) in Mexico. Instead, they do best in fragmented, patchy lowland habitat that mixes forested areas with brushland, field edges, wooded backyards, and riparian corridors—in other words, exactly the kind of conditions found in much of densely populated eastern North America.

"The screech owl's lifestyle is geared to environmental flux," noted screech-owl researcher Frederick R. Gehlbach has written.[10] In his landmark study in Texas, Gehlbach found evidence that the owls do better in suburbia than in the countryside, with higher survival and longevity compared with rural sites. Included among the factors favoring suburban sites are more-mature hardwoods in open, parklike settings that facilitate hunting and provide nest cavities, dense evergreens for roosting, a more stable climate, abundant open water, and lower densities of at least some predators.

Similarly, a study of screech-owls at the northern limit of their range in Winnipeg, Manitoba, found an even stronger association with suburban subdivisions, especially in riparian areas. The researcher, Christian Artuso, detected almost two-thirds of all Eastern Screech-Owls in moderate- to high-density suburban areas (which he defined as more than 20 people per hectare / 2.5 acres), fewer in inhabited rural areas, and none at all in a variety of wild habitats—perhaps because that's where Great Horned Owls were most common. One recent study in suburban Connecticut and New York found that even highly urbanized areas with as little as 20 percent forest cover could support screech-owls.

In summer, Eastern Screech-Owls often roost amid the concealing foliage of hardwood trees, but once the leaves drop, they usually switch to cavities—sometimes taking advantage of warm sunshine on a cold day. *(New York. Tom Johnson)*

But most screech-owls do not live in subdivisions; rather, they inhabit patchy woodlands across the East. In Pennsylvania, for example, they are most common in the low ridge-and-valley country and Piedmont, and are considerably rarer in the dense, contiguous forests north and west of the Allegheny Front. In New York, they are common in a belt across the middle of the state but are much less abundant in the Catskills and Adirondacks, as well as the Allegany hills. Forest type plays as much a role as elevation in their distribution. For instance, the northern edge of their breeding range in Michigan also marks the extent of the more southerly oak-hickory and beech-maple forests, and the beginning of the boreal conifer forest.

DIET: "The screech owl enjoys a varied bill of fare including almost every class of animal life," Arthur Cleveland Bent wrote in 1938.[11] Less insectivorous and more dependent on vertebrate prey than its western counterpart, the Eastern Screech-Owl nevertheless consumes an extraordinary range of prey, from small insects to birds and mammals considerably larger than itself. Fish and crayfish are surprisingly regular menu items. An alligator researcher in the Big Cypress Swamp of Florida watched one repeatedly wade into shallow water to catch small fish with quick grabs of its feet.

Small mammals (primarily rodents) and birds

Legs outstretched and talons poised, an Eastern Screech-Owl pounces on a meal. Less insectivorous and more dependent on small mammals and birds than the Western Screech-Owl, it nevertheless feeds on an extraordinary variety of prey. *(Manitoba. Christian Artuso)*

make up the bulk of the screech-owl's diet in the northern areas of its range, however, with invertebrates, reptiles, and amphibians increasingly important to the south. Proportions vary seasonally; in both Ohio and Tennessee, birds made up almost exactly the same percentage of the diet during the breeding season (68 and 65 percent, respectively), but while rodents comprised 60 percent of the winter diet in Ohio, in Tennessee the proportion of birds rose further, to 73 percent.

By contrast, in Texas, invertebrates made up half the breeding-season diet in some areas. Examination of the stomachs of roadkilled screech-owls in Tennessee showed a heavy dependence on insects during spring, and studies that rely on tabulating prey brought back to the nest box, or cached for later use, may underestimate the importance of invertebrates, even in the north.

Vertebrate prey are generally fairly small: mice and voles dominate the mammalian roster, and most birds taken are songbirds. Increasing house sparrow populations in southern Manitoba may have assisted the expanding urban screech-owl population there. The farther north they are found, the more limited the menu; in Manitoba, Eastern Screech-Owls took only 8 species of small mammals and 26 kinds of small birds. But like their western cousins, Eastern Screech-Owls are not averse to occasionally tackling outsize prey like Ruffed Grouse and adult cottontails, not to mention smaller owls like Northern Saw-whets and occasionally even other screech-owls.

NESTING AND BREEDING

Courtship begins in late winter with males singing, and pairs often duet together. The male advertises using the monotone trill near (or in) potential nest cavities, although the decision on the final location appears to be the female's. Pairs may be checking nest sites as early as the beginning of Feb. in Ohio.

Mates (especially in successful pairs) will stay together between years, often for life, but the high mortality rate among screech-owls leads to a lot of annual turnover, and in one study, half the nesting females each spring were less than a year old. Eastern Screech-Owls show strong fidelity to their nest sites, especially if they were successful the previous year. One of the most surprising findings from Gehlbach's long-term study of Eastern Screech-Owls in Texas was that only barely more than a quarter of all females ever reproduced successfully, and that half the fledglings in his study area were produced by only about 16 percent of the females.

Secondary cavity nesters, screech-owls depend on natural tree cavities formed by injury or rot, or former woodpecker nests, especially those of Pileated Woodpeckers and Northern Flickers, the larg-

A brown-morph adult Eastern Screech-Owl delivers a mouse to its brood of four chicks. *(North Carolina. Paul Bannick/VIREO)*

est species in most of their range. Squirrels and starlings are among the most serious competitors for available cavities. One female screech-owl hatched an American Kestrel egg laid in her box, although the chick soon disappeared, while another hatched five Wood Duck chicks and tended them until they jumped from the nest 2 days later.

Eastern Screech-Owls readily accept artificial nest boxes with an entrance hole of 3 in. (7.6 cm) and a depth below the entrance of about 12 in. (30.5 cm), although they will use larger boxes, like those designed for Wood Ducks. A box with somewhat larger than normal internal dimensions, roughly 8 to 10 in. (20 to 25 cm) square, prevents crowding and premature fledging in large broods. Add an inch or so of coarse wood shavings, and hang the box facing east or south (away from the prevailing winds) 10 to 20 ft. (3 to 6 m) high in a well-shaded location.

Because each mated pair requires multiple cavities for nesting, male and female roost sites, and food cache sites, hanging a number of nest boxes in a fairly small area may significantly increase the chance of attracting Eastern Screech-Owls. In fact, this trick seems to work with most cavity-nesting owls and probably reflects the general scarcity of suitable natural nest sites.

The nesting period is fairly compressed and uniform across the species's wide range, with egg-laying beginning in late Mar. and lasting through early May. In most pairs, laying takes place in Apr., with only a week separating the average onset among Florida owls and those in the Northeast and Midwest. (One Ohio study, however, found average egg-laying fell in mid-Mar.) A typical clutch is 4 eggs (3 in *floridanus*), but the number can range from 3 to 7. Incubation lasts 27 to 34 days, with hatching occurring in roughly the order in which the eggs were laid. (Incubation often begins with the second egg laid.)

The female broods for about 2 weeks while the male does all the hunting, usually bringing the prey to a nearby perch, where he transfers it to the female. Once the older chicks can maintain a safe body temperature, the female spends increasing amounts of time away from the nest, assisting with the hunting, although the male continues to bring in the bulk of the chicks' food.

Because the chicks regurgitate pellets and defecate in the nest, the smell, accentuated by prey remains, can be atrocious by the time the chicks begin to fledge at about 28 to 32 days of age. Driven by hunger—their parents often hold back food as an incentive—the chicks launch from the cavity over the course of several nights, oldest to youngest. They remain dependent on the adults for about 2 months, and Eastern Screech-Owls are famously aggressive in defending both nest and fledged chicks, often strafing and striking passersby if the nest is in a park or neighborhood.

BEHAVIOR

Eastern Screech-Owls are opportunistic wait-and-see hunters, nocturnal but, like many owls, especially active at dusk and dawn. The Northern Cardinal—a species that habitually feeds much earlier and later than most songbirds—is a frequent screech-owl victim.

The owl typically leaves its roost about 20 minutes after sunset (earlier on cloudy evenings) and returns to its roost about half an hour before daylight. The birds often roost among concealing foliage in a hardwood or conifer, usually tight against the trunk, where their plumage masks their outline. Once the foliage drops in autumn, they will switch to cavities or nest boxes, and on cold, sunny days, they frequently sunbathe at the entrance, where gray- and brown-morph birds are particularly well camouflaged.

The ear tufts play an important role in both concealment and expressing the owl's mental state.

Found out despite its camouflage, an Eastern Screech-Owl reacts to a scolding Blue Jay, whose alarm calls may draw in a large mob of harassing songbirds. *(Manitoba. Christian Artuso)*

Although Eastern Screech-Owls have proven highly susceptible to West Nile virus, females that have survived the exotic disease can pass on a degree of immunity through their eggs to their chicks. (*Pennsylvania. Alan Richard*)

When relaxed, the tufts lie flat on the head, but a screech-owl that is alarmed will draw itself tightly erect and raise its tufts, often half-closing its easily noticeable yellow eyes and turning side-on to the intruder—the "broken stick" pose that allows it to all but vanish from casual sight.

In the hand, Eastern Screech-Owls employ one of two tactics. They may bite and use their talons, but more often they play possum, going rigid, with their eyes closed, feigning death. A nesting female may employ the trick when a nest box is opened. (One researcher used this habit to his advantage, weighing the motionless screech-owl by hanging it by the tip of its bill from a spring scale.) This charade does not stop the owl from defecating often and copiously when handled, however, releasing a viscous, brown fluid that certainly smells bad enough to thwart a predator.

Home range estimates for this species vary dramatically with season. When nesting, activity areas of 10 to 22 acres (4 to 9 hectares) are typical, but telemetry research in suburban Connecticut found that Eastern Screech-Owl home ranges expanded during the summer to more than 250 acres (100 hectares). They contracted dramatically to about 22 acres (9 hectares) in midwinter, then expanded again at the onset of nesting. (This is effectively the opposite of what has been documented in some Western Screech-Owls.) Yet nightly activity ranges—the area an individual screech-owl was using on a particular night—were largest in this study from Nov. through Feb., and smallest in June. The explanation for this paradox is that in summer, the birds ranged over shorter distances each night but hunted new locations night after night, cumulatively covering more ground on a monthly basis.

One of the Eastern Screech-Owl's most bizarre behaviors was first documented by Gehlbach (who has spent his career studying this bird)—a symbiotic relationship with Texas blind snakes, which are up to 8 in. long and resemble earthworms. Nesting adult owls catch the slender, burrowing reptiles alive, carefully carrying them back to the cavity in their bills (not their talons, like normal prey). Released in the hole or box, the snakes burrow into the matted refuse at the bottom, where they presumably feed on parasitic fly larvae and ants that would otherwise attack the chicks.

The benefit for the owls is clear: Gehlbach's research shows that nests hosting blind snakes have a significantly higher fledging and chick survival rate than those without snakes. The behavior has not been documented in Western Screech-Owls, even though other species of blind snakes occur in at least part of that owl's range. Gehlbach found the snake-catching behavior more common in suburban habitats, perhaps because regular lawn-watering brings the snakes to the surface more frequently than in wild locations.

STATUS

The Eastern Screech-Owl is widespread and generally secure, listed only at the extremes of its range—as "threatened" in Mexico, as "special concern" in Maine, and as being of "potential concern" in Wyoming. Breeding Bird Survey results show a slight long-term decline between 1966 and 2010 across its range, with an even smaller increase between 2000 and 2010, but the survey does a poor job of censusing nocturnal birds with low population density, like owls, and those results should be taken with a grain of salt. In 1981 the Eastern Screech-Owl was added to the National Audubon Society's "Blue List" of potentially declining species, but is not included on the current Watch List of birds of conservation concern.

Vehicle collisions are clearly an important source of mortality, since this species often hunts along roads, taking advantage of the easy pickings when prey tries to cross. The toll of rodenticides has likely been underestimated in this and other nocturnal raptors, although the subject has received heightened attention in recent years. Tests found that Eastern Screech-Owls were far more sensitive to one commonly used anticoagulant than were Mallards and Northern Bobwhites, the two species normally used in toxicology testing.

After West Nile virus first appeared in the Western Hemisphere in 1999, it quickly became clear that some owls were susceptible to this novel, mosquito-borne disease. Eastern Screech-Owls have been shown to be especially sensitive to it, and while pinning down a single cause is difficult, the virus may be at least partially responsible, for example, for up to 50 percent declines in screech-owl populations in some parts of Pennsylvania between the mid-1980s and mid-2000s. It appears, though, that female screech-owls are able to pass antibodies to the disease through the eggs to their chicks, providing at least a degree of immunity.

Although this species can show great tolerance for fragmentation and suburban development, intense urbanization eventually drives it out. Fairly common in New York City's boroughs in the late nineteenth and early twentieth centuries, it was essentially extirpated by the 1990s. Attempts to reintroduce Eastern Screech-Owls into Central Park began in 1998 with the eventual release of 32 chicks. Limited nesting was documented in subsequent years, but the population again declined and had apparently disappeared after 2011.

After studying Eastern Screech-Owls in Texas for nearly 30 years, Fred Gehlbach found that the dramatically warming climate had advanced the nesting season in suburban areas by an average of 4.5 days. Fledging success—already high in the suburbs—had risen even further, perhaps in part because insect prey was available earlier in the year. The owls were also preying more heavily on birds, which were probably attracted by feeders and water.

NOTES

1. F. R. Gehlbach. 1995. Eastern screech-owl (*Otus asio*). In *The Birds of North America*, no. 165, ed. A. Poole and F. Gill. Philadelphia: Academy of Natural Sciences, and Washington, DC: American Ornithologists' Union.

2. F. R. Gehlbach. 2003. Body size variation and evolutionary ecology of eastern and western screech-owls. *Southwestern Naturalist* 48 (1): 70–80.

3. Craighead and Craighead 1956.

4. C. J. Henny and L. F. VanCamp. 1979. Annual weight cycle in wild screech owls. *Auk* 96:795–786.

5. Earhart and Johnson 1970.

6. L. F. VanCamp and C. J. Henny. 1975. The screech owl: Its life history and population ecology in northern Ohio. In *North American Fauna*, no. 71. Washington, DC: U.S. Fish and Wildlife Service.

7. C. Artuso, pers. comm.

8. H. D. Thoreau. 1854. *Walden; or, Life in the Woods*. Boston: Ticknor and Fields, p. 135.

9. Proudfoot, Gehlbach, and Honeycutt 2007.

10. F. R. Gehlbach. 1994. *The Eastern Screech Owl*. College Station, TX: Texas A&M University Press, p. 186.

11. Bent 1938, Bulletin 167, p. 250.

BIBLIOGRAPHY

Artuso, C. 2009. Breeding and population density of the eastern screech owl (*Megascops asio*) at the northern periphery of its range. *Ardea* 97 (4): 525–533.

———. 2009. "Life on the edge: the eastern screech-owl in Winnipeg." PhD diss., University of Manitoba.

———. 2007. Eastern screech-owl hatches wood duck eggs. *Wilson Journal of Ornithology* 119 (1): 110–112.

Breen, T. F., and J. W. Parrish Jr. 1996. Eastern screech-owl hatches an American kestrel. *Journal of Field Ornithology* 67 (4): 612–613.

Brittan-Powell, E. F., B. Lohr, D. C. Hahn, and R. J. Dooling. 2005. Auditory brainstem responses in the eastern screech owl: An estimate of auditory thresholds. *Journal of the Acoustic Society of America* 118 (1): 314–321.

Brommer, J. E., K. Ahola, and T. Karstinen. 2005. The colour of fitness: Plumage coloration and lifetime reproductive success in the tawny owl. *Proceedings of the Royal Society,* B 272 (1566): 935–940.

Campbell, G. 2012. *Atlantic Canada Nocturnal Owl Survey.* Port Rowan, ON: Bird Studies Canada.

Carpenter, T. 2011. Eastern Screech-owl (*Otus asio*). In *Second Michigan Breeding Bird Atlas, 2002–2008,* ed. A. T. Chartier, J. J. Baldy, and J. M. Brenneman. Kalamazoo MI: Kalamazoo Nature Center, accessed online at http://www.mibirdatlas.org/Portals/12/MBA2010/EASOaccount.pdf.

DeCandido, R. 2005. History of the eastern screech-owl (*Megascops asio*) in New York City, 1867–2005. *Urban Habitats* 3 (1): 117–133.

Deuser, W. G. 2011. Evening nest-box departure times of eastern screech-owls. *Wilson Journal of Ornithology* 123 (3): 641–646.

Dinets, V. 2011. Eastern screech-owl catches fish by wading. *Wilson Journal of Ornithology* 123 (4): 846–847.

Galeotti, P., D. Rubolino, R. Sacchi, and M. Fasola. 2009. Global changes and animal phenotypic responses: Melanin-based plumage redness of scops owls increased with temperature and rainfall during the last century. *Biology Letters* 5 (4): 532–534.

Gehlbach, F. R. 1994. *The Eastern Screech Owl.* College Station, TX: Texas A&M University Press, p. 186.

———. 1995. Eastern screech-owl (*Otus asio*). In *The Birds of North America,* no. 165, ed. A. Poole and F. Gill. Philadelphia: Academy of Natural Sciences, and Washington, DC: American Ornithologists' Union.

———. 2012. Eastern screech-owl responses to suburban sprawl, warmer climate, and additional avian food in central Texas. *Wilson Journal of Ornithology* 124 (3): 630–633.

Gorrie, S., J. Duncan, C. Foster, S. Faber, and J. Hildebrand. 2003. *Manitoba's Nocturnal Owl Survey.* Winnipeg, MB: Manitoba Conservation.

Hahn, D. C., N. M. Nemeth, E. Edwards, P. R. Bright, and N. Komar. 2006. Passive West Nile virus antibody transfer from maternal eastern screech-owls (*Megascops asio*) to progeny. *Avian Diseases* 50 (3): 454–455.

Hayward, G. D., and E. O. Garton. 1984. Roost habitat selection by three small forest owls. *Wilson Bulletin* 96 (4): 690–692.

Mosher, J. A., and C. J. Henny. 1976. Thermal adaptiveness of plumage color in screech owls. *Auk* 93:614–619.

Nagy, C., K. Bardwell, R. F. Rockwell, R. Christie, and M. Weckel. 2012. Validation of a citizen-science-based model of site occupancy for eastern screech owls with systematic data in suburban New York and Connecticut. *Northeastern Naturalist* 19 (6): 143–158.

Navarro-Sigüenza, A. G., and A. T. Peterson. 2007. *Megascops asio* (tecolote oriental) residencia permanente distribución potencial. In *Mapas de las Aves de México Basados en WWW,* ed. A. G. Navarro and A. T. Peterson. Final report, SNIB-CONABIO project no. CE015. México DF.

Nemeth, N. M., D. C. Hahn, D. H. Gould, and R. A. Bowen. 2006. Experimental West Nile virus infection in eastern screech-owls (*Megascops asio*). *Avian Diseases* 50:252–258.

Olsen, B., and P. Mooney. 2001. Effect of colour phase on winter habitat characteristics of the eastern screech owl, *Otus asio,* in central Pennsylvania. *Journal of Ecological Research at Juniata College* 2:53–61.

Owen, D. F. 1963. Polymorphism in the screech owl in eastern North America. *Wilson Bulletin* 75 (2): 183–190.

———. 1963. Variation in North American screech owls and the subspecies concept. *Systematic Zoology* 12 (1): 8–14.

Pannkuk, E. L., L. M. Siefferman, and J. A. Butts. 2010. Colour phases of the eastern screech owl: A comparison of biomechanical variables of body contour feathers. *Functional Ecology* 24:347–353.

Proudfoot 2007.

Richards, N. L., P. Mineau, D. N. Bird, P. Wery, J. Larivée, and J. Duffe. 2006. First observations of an eastern screech-owl (*Megascops asio*) population in an apple-producing region of southern Quebec. *Canadian Field Naturalist* 120:289–297.

Roulin, A. 2004. The evolution, maintenance and adaptive function of genetic colour polymorphism in birds. *Biological Reviews* 79 (4): 815–848.

Roulin, A., C. Riols, C. Dijkstra, and A. L. Ducrest. 2001. Female plumage spottiness signals parasite resistance in the barn owl (*Tyto alba*). *Behavioral Ecology* 12 (1): 103–110.

Sordahl, T. A. 2014. Distribution of color-morphs of the eastern screech-owl in Iowa. *Wilson Journal of Ornithology* 126:321–332.

Sparks, E. T., J. R. Belthoff, and G. Ritchison. 1994. Habitat use by eastern screech-owls in central Kentucky. *Journal of Field Ornithology* 65 (1): 83–95.

Turner, L. J., and R. W. Dimmick. 1981. Seasonal prey capture by the screech owl in Tennessee. *Journal of the Tennessee Academy of Science* 56 (2): 56–59.

Weidensaul, S. 2012. Eastern screech owl (*Megascops asio*). In *Second Atlas of Breeding Birds in Pennsylvania,* ed. A. M. Wilson, D. W. Brauning, and R. S. Mulvihill. University Park, PA: Pennsylvania University Press.

Larger than other Mexican screech-owls, and with dramatically dark brown eyes, the Balsas Screech-Owl was not described for science until 1941 nor elevated to species status until 1983. It remains poorly known within its restricted range in Mexico. *(Colima. Pete Morris)*

BALSAS SCREECH-OWL
Megascops seductus
Alpha code: BASO

LENGTH: 9.5–10.5 in. (24–26.5 cm)

WINGSPAN: No information

MASS: Overall 5.3–6.2 oz. (150–175g).[1] Two males weighed 5.6 and 5.7 oz. (158 and 161g).[2]

LONGEVITY: Unknown

Not described for science until 1941, and only recognized as a separate species in 1983, the Balsas Screech-Owl is endemic to southwestern Mexico, where it inhabits tropical dry forests, thorn scrub, farm edges, and stands of giant cardón cactus. Considerably larger than neighboring species of screech-owls, it is best distinguished by its dark brown eyes and rough, bouncing-ball song. Habitat loss within its restricted range may pose a risk to this poorly understood owl, but much of what has been published about its ecology and life history amounts to little more than informed speculation.

SYSTEMATICS, TAXONOMY, AND ETYMOLOGY

First described in 1941 from a specimen collected in Michoacán, the Balsas Screech-Owl was originally classified as the "Michoacán Screech Owl," a subspecies of *Otus vinaceus*—which itself is now considered a subspecies of the Western Screech-Owl, *Megascops kennicottii vinaceus*. Robert T. Moore, who first described it, noted the Balsas Screech-Owl's much larger size when compared with *M. k. vinaceus* to the north and the Pacific and Vermiculated Screech-Owls to the south and east.

The Balsas Screech-Owl was split as a distinct species in 1983 by the AOU and is considered monotypic. A subspecies, *M. s. colimensis*, described from Colima in 1958, is said to average larger and buffier and with more heavily feathered toes, but this race is not recognized by most authors.

ETYMOLOGY: For the genus name, see "Western Screech-Owl." The specific name, *seductus,* is usually translated from the Latin adjective as "distant," "retired," or "secluded," but in this case, Moore translated it as "remote, referring to the great extension of the habitat of the species into southern Mexico."[3] The common name comes from the Río Balsas, the lower drainage of which encompasses the southern extent of the bird's range.

SPANISH: *Tecolote de Balsas, autillo de Balsas*

DISTRIBUTION

Year-round resident of the arid Pacific slope in southwestern Mexico, inland of the coast. From southern Jalisco and Colima south through Michoacán, western Guerrero, and southern Morelos in the Río Balsas drainage, from about 2,000 ft. (600 m) up to 4,000 to 5,000 ft. (roughly 1,200 to 1,500 m) in elevation. However, one major review of Mexican owl distribution[4] put its elevational range as sea level to 4,000 ft. (1,200 m).

MIGRATION AND MOVEMENTS: Presumably resident. No information about post-fledging dispersal, but increased vocal response to playback in Oct. and Nov. may reflect greater activity by fledglings.

DISTRIBUTION OUTSIDE THE COVERAGE AREA: None

DESCRIPTION AND IDENTIFICATION

Typical screech-owl but with dark brown, not yellow, eyes and fairly short, erectile ear tufts. Proportionately large feet. No rufous morph is known.

BASIC (ADULT) PLUMAGE: No sexual differences known. Gray-brown overall, lightly suffused with

Balsas Screech-Owls inhabit dry tropical forests up to at least 4,000 ft. (about 1,200 m) in the Río Balsas drainage of southwestern Mexico. Most of their natural history and ecology are a mystery. *(Colima. Pete Morris)*

a faint wine red tone that is more distinct in some individuals. Broad blackish streaks on the forehead and crown framed by grayish eyebrows. Gray-brown (sometimes predominantly brown) facial disk with dusky, concentric markings. Upperparts heavily vermiculated, often with small white spots (ocelli) on either side of each feather shaft. Scapular feathers edged in white or off-white to form moderate white "suspenders" line along upper edge of the folded wings. Underparts have a gray-white base color with prominent dark shaft streaks and much finer horizontal crossbarring; often with heavy, dark, vertical streaks or spots framing the upper breast. Bill greenish. Eyes generally dark brown, but a few individuals with golden brown and yellowish irises have been reported.

JUVENAL PLUMAGE: Apparently undescribed, but presumably similar to other screech-owls, with grayish ground color and dusky horizontal barring.

SIMILAR SPECIES: The degree to which the Balsas Screech-Owl overlaps with other *Megascops* is unclear. Dark eyes and rougher voice are the best characteristics to distinguish from Western Screech-Owl, whose *vinaceus* race to the north is more lightly marked on the upperparts. The Vermiculated Screech-Owl is restricted to lower, moister tropical forests closer to the coast.

VOCALIZATIONS

Similar to the accelerating, bouncing-call of Western Screech-Owl, but hoarser in tone, usually lasting 2.5 to 3.5 seconds. Marshall described the vocalizations as "the same as those of the [Western Screech-Owl] but much louder and of an ominous, gruff, threatening quality, never sounding pure or mellow except at a distance."[5] Sometimes gives a monotone trill lasting 9 or 10 seconds, descending slightly at the end.

HABITAT AND NICHE

Restricted to a variety of dry, open tropical forest communities, including acacias, mesquite thickets, woodlands dominated by giant columnar cacti like organ pipe cactus and *Pachycereus,* and brushy second-growth among small-scale farm plots.

The only significant study of this species to date, conducted in the Sierra de Huautla Biosphere Reserve in Morelos, found that the Balsas Screech-Owl used all major vegetation types in the reserve, including dry forest dominated by columnar cacti; patchy acacia forest grazed by cattle; and agricultural areas where corn, sorghum, and beans were grown. The owls were detected significantly less often in *Gliricidia-Caesalpinia* plantations than in other habitat types.

Marshall said the owls were "abundant" in Colima in open woods with columnar cacti, and they "abounded at the edges of milpas and perched in mesquites far out in the fields. We could find none in denser or steeper growth along the coast."[5] In steeper, denser forests Balsas Screech-Owl was replaced by Vermiculated Screech-Owl. Schaldach (1963) found them in thorn forests but not thorn scrub in Colima.

DIET: Said to feed primarily on arthropods and some small vertebrates, but no serious study of its diet has been undertaken.

NESTING AND BREEDING

Essentially unknown. Marshall (1967) indicated that he found them nesting in June in Michoacán, which appears to be the only reference to breeding season. It is assumed to use cavities in trees and large cacti, like other *Megascops.*

BEHAVIOR

As with almost every other aspect of its ecology and life history, the behavior of the Balsas Screech-Owl is basically unknown. The Sierra de Huautla study found an average of 6.7 owls per square kilometer of dry tropical forest, suggesting it was moderately common within appropriate habitat. Peak calling intensity was in Oct. and Nov., when up to 12 owls per square kilometer were heard. The lowest detection rate was in Feb., which may reflect poor resources during the dry season, minimal vegetation cover, and a lack of breeding-season urgency.

STATUS

Because of habitat loss within its restricted range, the Balsas Screech-Owl is of conservation concern. It is listed as "threatened" by Mexico, while IUCN/BirdLife lists it as "near-threatened," with a declining population trend—although there is little solid data. Stotz et al. (1996) considered it to be of both high conservation and research priority because of habitat destruction. The lone population density study found it to be moderately common in the right habitat, but cattle ranching and citrus cultivation are destroying tropical dry forests in the region.

NOTES

1. A. Alba-Zúñiga, P. L. Enríquez, and J. L. Rangel-Salazar. 2009. Population density and habitat use of the threatened Balsas screech owl in the Sierra de Huautla Biosphere Reserve, Mexico. *Endangered Species Research* 9:61–66.

2. Dunning 2007.

3. R. T. Moore. 1941. Three new races in the genus *Otus* from central Mexico. *Proceedings of the Biological Society of Washington* 54:156.

4. Enríquez-Rocha, Rangel-Salazar, and Holt 1993.

5. Marshall 1967, p. 16.

BIBLIOGRAPHY

BirdLife International. 2014. *Megascops seductus.* In IUCN Red List of Threatened Species, version 2014.3. http://www.iucnredlist.org/details/22724664/0.

Hekstra 1982.

Howell and Webb 1995.

Navarro-Sigüenza, A. G., and A. T. Peterson. 2007. *Megascops seductus* (tecolote del Balsas) residencia permanente distribución potencial. In *Mapas de las Aves de México Basados en WWW,* ed. A. G. Navarro and A. T. Peterson. Final report, SNIB-CONABIO project no. CE015. México DF.

Schaldach, W. J. 1963.

Stotz et al. 1996.

PACIFIC SCREECH-OWL
Megascops cooperi
Alpha code: PASO

LENGTH: 8–9.5 in. (20–25 cm)

WINGSPAN: 19–22 in. (45.75–56 cm)

MASS: Limited data. Three males of *M. c. cooperi* average 5.25 oz. (149 g); range 5.1–5.4 oz. (145–153 g), and a single female weighed 6.4 oz. (181 g).[1] *M. c. lambi* males averaged 4.4 oz. (125 g);[2] another source cites a single, unsexed specimen as also weighing 4.4 oz. (125 g).[1]

LONGEVITY: No information

One of the Spanish names for the Pacific Screech-Owl is *tecolote manglero,* the "mangrove owl." Living in a narrow band along the Pacific from Oaxaca to Costa Rica, it is often found in mangrove swamps, palm groves, and thickets, as well as in more open and arid cardón-dominated landscapes of the coastal lowlands. A subspecies endemic to southwestern Mexico, *M. c. lambi,* is sometimes classified as a separate species, the "Oaxaca Screech-Owl." Like most of the tropical members of this genus, the Pacific Screech-Owl's behavior, ecology, and breeding biology are largely a blank slate.

SYSTEMATICS, TAXONOMY, AND ETYMOLOGY

As with many of the *Megascops,* the taxonomy of the Pacific Screech-Owl is a bit of a jumble. Described in 1878 from specimens collected in Costa Rica, it was originally classified as a full species, *Scops cooperi,* and later as a subspecies of both the western (*kennicottii*) and eastern (*asio*) groups of screech-owls. When the AOU reordered the New World screech-owls in 1983, it was again elevated to full species status, along with a number of other taxa, including the Balsas Screech-Owl.

Three subspecies have been described. The nominate race, *M. c. cooperi,* is found from southern Chiapas to Costa Rica. *M. c. lambi* was described in 1959 from the Pacific slope of Oaxaca, and while the AOU considers it a subspecies of Pacific Screech-Owl, a few authors have granted it species rank as the "Oaxaca Screech-Owl." DNA work to clarify the relationships among the Mesoamerican screech-owls is badly needed.

A third subspecies, *M. c. chiapensis,* was described in 1947, based on two specimens from southeastern Mexico, but the differentiation is slight and most authorities do not recognize it.

ETYMOLOGY: For derivation of genus name, see "Western Screech-Owl." The specific name, *cooperi,* was given in 1878 by Smithsonian ornithologist Robert Ridgway in honor of Juan Cooper of Costa Rica, a friend of the man who collected the type specimens, Jose Castulo Zeledón. The subspecies *chiapensis* was named for the type locality in Chiapas, while *lambi* was named for C. C. Lamb, who first collected it in Oaxaca.

SPANISH: *Tecolote [tecolotito] manglero, tecolote [tecolotito] de Cooper*

DISTRIBUTION

Resident in a narrow belt along the Pacific slope from southeastern Oaxaca and coastal Chiapas east to Costa Rica, from sea level to about 3,200 ft. (1,000 m).

MIGRATION AND MOVEMENTS: None known

DISTRIBUTION OUTSIDE THE COVERAGE AREA: Pacific slope from Honduras to northwestern Costa Rica.

DESCRIPTION AND IDENTIFICATION

A fairly large screech-owl with moderately long ear tufts and bristled, not feathered, toes. Eyes yellow, sometimes tinged with orange; overall color gray-brown (wine-colored in *M. c. lambi*). No rufous morph known.

BASIC (ADULT) PLUMAGE: No sexual differences known. Nominate race overall gray tinged with brown, upperparts very finely marked with narrow streaks and very narrow vermiculations. As with most screech-owls, the scapulars are edged in white and form a white bar above the folded wings. Underparts with narrow, blackish, vertical shaft streaks and "a chaos of little freckled dots"[2] that

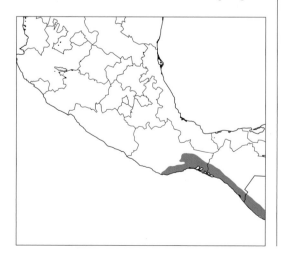

Inhabiting the Pacific lowlands from Oaxaca to Costa Rica, the Pacific Screech-Owl is a common raptor, but as with many tropical screech-owls, little is known about its life history. *(Costa Rica. Steve Easley)*

Pacific Screech-Owls of the nominate subspecies, like this one, have a rough trill that rises in pitch before stuttering to a stop. Those of *M. c. lambi*, from Oaxaca, have a strikingly different call and are considered by some experts to be a distinct species. *(Costa Rica. Tom Johnson)*

form the horizontal crossbarring. Bill greenish.

M. c. lambi, "Oaxaca Screech-Owl," averages about 15 percent smaller than the nominate subspecies, with smaller, more delicate feet. It is ruddier overall and more coarsely marked, with darker crown streaks giving it a dark-capped appearance that contrasts with the back and "frosty" area on the hind neck. The underparts have more-distinct dark vertical streaks, with the horizontal barring comprised of neat, narrow lines of rusty dots, accentuating the overall foxier coloration. As with *M. c. cooperi,* the facial disk is cool gray rimmed by a narrow brownish ruff. Bill greenish.

JUVENAL PLUMAGE: Buffy gray, paler below, with indistinct grayish barring.

SIMILAR SPECIES: Vermiculated Screech-Owl inhabits denser forests, voice a softer trill. Whiskered Screech-Owl is smaller, restricted to higher-elevation montane forests above 5,000 ft. (1,600 m); often exhibits red morph unknown in Pacific Screech-Owl. Pacific's range lies well south of Western Screech-Owl's.

VOCALIZATIONS

For nominate subspecies, rough trilled notes begin in close succession, then slow and rise in pitch before stuttering to a finish, usually lasting about 2 or 3 seconds, although aggressive response to an intruder (or playback) can be longer. *M. c. lambi* is said to have a descending whinny call, and primary song "a guttural *croarrr* followed by a staccato *gogogogogogok*";[3] these vocal differences are one of the arguments for considering *lambi* a separate species.

HABITAT AND NICHE

The habitat preferences for this species seem to vary across its relatively small coastal range and perhaps between subspecies. Marshall (1967) found *M. c. lambi* mostly in tall tropical forests with cardón cacti, in mangrove swamps, and in freshwater marshes with palms and mesquite in Oaxaca, while *cooperi* was found close to the coast in Oaxaca and

The nominate subspecies of the Pacific Screech-Owl, *M. c. cooperi*, found from Chiapas south, is gray with a brown wash and has fine vermiculations on the upperparts. No rufous morph is known in this species. *(Chiapas. Greg Lasley)*

Chiapas, almost always in mangrove stands. Elsewhere it is found in more-arid and semi-arid locations, evergreen forest edges, gallery forests, and in uplands to about 1,000 ft. (330 m), although recorded to 3,000 ft. (1,000 m). In Costa Rica, at the southern extent of its range, it is most commonly associated with tropical dry forests. Its habitat preference is said to be more open and not as dense as Vermiculated Screech-Owl's.

DIET: Little information. Arthropods, including large insects and scorpions, are presumed to make up a significant portion of the diet, but its relatively large, strong feet suggest at least some dependence on small vertebrates.

NESTING AND BREEDING
Nesting and breeding are poorly described. The Pacific Screech-Owl, in typical fashion for the genus, uses natural cavities and old woodpecker holes and apparently lays 3 or 4 eggs. Breeding takes place primarily in the spring dry season. Among the few published records was a nest with two half-grown young in Oaxaca at the end of Mar. In Costa Rica

Pacific Screech-Owl chicks peer from their nest hole. Like all screech-owls, the Pacific is dependent on old woodpecker cavities for most of its nest sites, breeding primarily in the dry season. *(Costa Rica. Chris Jimenez)*

3 or 4 eggs are laid in the dry season, with families remaining together until the rainy season begins.

BEHAVIOR

Very little known; presumably similar to its close relatives.

STATUS

Although the Pacific Screech-Owl is considered fairly common across its range, and is ranked as "least concern" by IUCN/BirdLife, the status of the endemic Oaxacan subspecies *lambi* merits further study. Given its very limited range, that race would probably receive a higher degree of protection and concern were it elevated to species rank, as some suggest.

NOTES

1. Dunning 2007.

2. Marshall 1967.

3. Mikkola 2012.

BIBLIOGRAPHY

Binford 1989.

BirdLife International. 2015. Species factsheet: *Megascops cooperi*, http://www.birdlife.org/datazone/speciesfactsheet.php?id=30134.

Moore, R. T., and J. T. Marshall Jr. 1959. A new race of screech-owl from Oaxaca. *Condor* 61:224–225.

Navarro-Sigüenza, A. G., and A. T. Peterson. 2007. *Megascops cooperi* (tecolote de Cooper) residencia permanente distribución potencial. In *Mapas de las Aves de México Basados en WWW*, ed. A. G. Navarro and A. T. Peterson. Final report, SNIB-CONABIO project no. CE015. México DF.

———. 2004. An alternative species taxonomy of the birds of Mexico. *Biota Neotropica* 4 (1), http://www.biotaneotropica.org.br/v4n2/pt/abstract?taxonomic-review+BN03504022004.

Ridgway, R. 1878. A review of the American species of the genus *Scops*, Savigny. *Proceedings of the United States National Museum* 1:85–117.

Stiles and Skutch 1989.

The Whiskered Screech-Owl gets its name from the long, fine extensions of the facial disk feathers, which frame the head—and which are almost impossible to see in the wild, making this a poor field mark. The Whiskered's distinctive "telegraphic trill" call is a better identification clue. *(Arizona. Tom Johnson)*

WHISKERED SCREECH-OWL
Megascops trichopsis
Alpha code: WHSO

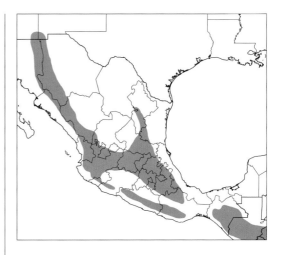

LENGTH: 7.25 in. (18 cm)

WINGSPAN: 18 in. (45 cm)

MASS: Weakly reversed size dimorphism, with females averaging 14 percent heavier than males.
  M. t. asperus: Average, male: 2.9 oz. (83.6g). Average, female: 3.4 oz. (96.3g).[1]
  M. t. trichopsis: Two studies. 1: Average, male: 2.9 oz. (83.7 g). Average, female: 3.4 oz. (96.6 g).[1] 2: Average, male: 3 oz. (84.5 g); range 2.5–3.7 oz. (70–104 g). Average, female: 3.25 oz. (92.2 g); range 2.8–4.3 oz. (79–121 g).[2]
  M. t. mesamericanus: Average, male: 3.3 oz. (92.9 g). Average, female: 3.6 oz. (102.7 g).[1]

LONGEVITY: Little data. One female lived to 4 years, but maximum age is likely longer, as with other screech-owls.

Although common across much of its Mexican range, the Whiskered Screech-Owl is poorly known, and almost all of the research on its ecology and behavior comes from the small population that barely crosses the United States–Mexico border into the Madrean Sky Island mountains of New Mexico and Arizona.

Small and highly insectivorous, the "Spotted Screech Owl" (as it was once known) inhabits dense

The most southerly subspecies, *M. t. mesamericanus,* which is found from Chiapas to Nicaragua, is also the ruddiest, especially in the rufous morph, shown here. *(Guatemala. Knut Eisermann)*

Despite their similarity in appearance, the Whiskered Screech-Owl is not a close cousin to the Western or Eastern Screech-Owl but appears to be more closely related to two primarily South American species. *(Arizona. Gerrit Vyn)*

forests of evergreen oak and pine as well as mountain canyons with an abundance of cavity-rich sycamores. Farther south in Mexico and northern Central America it expands into dry tropical forests, including shade-coffee farms.

SYSTEMATICS, TAXONOMY, AND ETYMOLOGY

Looks can be deceiving. The Whiskered Screech-Owl is extremely similar to Western and Eastern Screech-Owls in appearance (including yellow eyes, feathered toes, and dimorphic plumage colors) and somewhat so in voice. Its range also overlaps broadly with Western Screech-Owl (with which it has apparently hybridized) as well as the Flammulated Owl. But a mitochondrial DNA review found that it is more closely related to two primarily South American species, the Tropical Screech-Owl (*M. choliba*) and the White-throated Screech-Owl (*M. albogularis*), which differ substantially from it in appearance and vocalizations.

Up to eight subspecies have been described, but three are generally recognized:

M. t. aspersus: from the Sky Island ranges of southeastern Arizona and southwestern New Mexico, south in the Sierra Madre Occidental through Sonora and Chihuahua; and in the Sierra Madre Oriental from southern Nuevo León into San Luis Potosí. (Includes the races *pinosus, ridgwayi,* and *guerrerensis,* which are no longer recognized.)

M. t. trichopsis: from Durango to Querétaro, and Jalisco southeast to Oaxaca.

M. t. mesamericanus: from Chiapas to Nicaragua; includes the obsolete subspecies *pumilus.*

ETYMOLOGY: For the derivation of the genus name, see "Western Screech-Owl." The common name and scientific names both refer to the unusually long, wispy bristles at the end of this owl's facial disk feathers, which when backlit give it a whiskered appearance. The specific name, *trichopsis,* is from the Greek *thrix* (*trikhos*), "hair," and *opsis,* "seeing" or "sight," alluding to its appearance.

SPANISH: Tecolote [tecolotito] manchado, tecolote [tecolotito] rítmico, tecolote [autillo] bigotudo; zumaya (Chiapas)

NÁHUATL: Tlalquipatl

MAYAN: Ah-coo-akab, kulte' (Yucatec); ch'urukinkuj (Ch'ol)

DISTRIBUTION

BREEDING SEASON: Dense montane oak and oak-pine forests. Madrean Sky Island region from southeastern Arizona (from the Galiuro and possibly Winchester mountain ranges south to the border and west to Baboquivari Mountains) and southwestern New Mexico (the Peloncillo and, historically, the Animas Mountains). Its occurrence in less accessible mountain ranges is poorly documented and may be wider than realized. Found down the Sierra

Madre Occidental from northeastern Sonora and Chihuahua through mountainous portions of Sinaloa and Durango, Nayarit, Jalisco, and Colima through Michoacán to Puebla (a few records) on the Mexican Plateau. North through Hidalgo (rare) and western Veracruz along the Sierra Madre Oriental to San Luis Potosí, southeastern Tamaulipas, and southern Nuevo León. Disjunct range in coastal mountains of Guerrero and Oaxaca, and again in Chiapas.

Typically 5,000–7,500 ft. (1,524–2,286 m) in Arizona and New Mexico, but occasionally down to 3,800 ft. (1,160 m) in canyons. In Mexico, generally 4,000–9,800 ft. (1,200–3,000 m), but reportedly as low as 2,460 ft. (750 m).

MIGRATION AND MOVEMENTS: Permanent resident. Fledgling dispersal apparently occurs Aug. through Oct. in the American Southwest, but no data on timing or distance.

DISTRIBUTION OUTSIDE THE COVERAGE AREA: High-elevation forests south to north-central Nicaragua.

DESCRIPTION AND IDENTIFICATION

A smallish screech-owl with yellow-orange eyes, erectile ear tufts, somewhat dainty feet, and coarse markings. "Whiskers" (long, fine extensions of facial disk feathers) are difficult to see in the field. Red morph is essentially absent in the extreme northern extent of its range, including the small U.S. population, but it may comprise a third of all Whiskered Screech-Owls in Jalisco and Michoacán.

BASIC (ADULT) PLUMAGE: Females average darker than males, but no distinct sexual differences. Dimorphic plumage in most of its range, but grayest "normal" morph birds are *asperus* in the north, where red morph is all but absent, with blackish cast, to *trichopsis* from the southern Mexican Plateau, and progressively ruddier plumage farther south in *mesamericanus,* which lessens contrast with the rufous morph. There is an overall darkening (regardless of base color) from north to south, with browner upperparts and more intense cinnamon on the throat.

In *asperus* the base color is cool gray (fading to brownish with wear), coarsely marked above, with wide black shaft streaks on the crown, nape, and back. Facial disk gray with concentric dark gray barring; dark facial ruff becoming smudged and indistinct along upper rim, with long, soft, black extensions of the facial disk feathers creating "whiskered" effect, especially around upper half of the disk. Supercilium mottled gray, contrasting little with the facial disk. Throat often lightly cinnamon, sometimes extending up along the head outside the facial ruff.

White edges of scapulars somewhat reduced, creating a less distinct white line above the folded wings than in most screech-owls. Underparts pale gray with heavy, distinct vertical streaks along

Whiskered Screech-Owls are dimorphic, as this pair in the mountains of Mexico show. The rufous morph is almost nonexistent in the northernmost subspecies, *M. t. asperus,* but among this race, *M. t. trichopsis,* red individuals may comprise a third of the population. *(Colima. Pete Morris)*

breast feather shafts, and narrow, fairly regular horizontal crossbarring (heavier and coarser in *trichopsis,* forming a checkerboard pattern, much more brown-red in *mesamericanus*). Females average darker than males, but with much overlap in tone. Eyes yellow to yellow-orange; bill variable, usually greenish yellow with a pale tip.

Rufous morph occurs from Sinaloa south. As with the Eastern Screech-Owl, the rufous morph is most common in warm, moist forests, while gray-morph birds may enjoy a metabolic advantage in the colder, northern mountains.

JUVENAL PLUMAGE: Grayish with dusky or rufous crossbarring, depending on morph.

SIMILAR SPECIES: Range overlaps with several similar small "eared" owls. Flammulated is smaller, with prominent rusty markings and dark eyes. Western Screech-Owl is larger; bill is blackish with pale tip, versus yellowish green; eyes clear yellow, versus yellow-orange or gold; and finer, more-muted markings on the upperparts and undersides. Western's feet are larger, but this is rarely a useful field mark. While some vocalizations are very similar to Western Screech-Owl's, the Whiskered's "telegraphic trill" is distinctive.

In Mexico, voice distinguishes it from Vermiculated Screech-Owl, which has fine, narrow breast markings and (in a good view) bristled toes; and from Bearded Screech-Owl, which has prominent whitish eyebrows, naked pink toes, and scalloped underparts.

VOCALIZATIONS

"As soon as it becomes dark this little bird begins to bark its four, evenly pitched notes, which are more doglike than those of the [western] Screech Owl," pioneering Arizona ornithologist Herbert Brandt wrote in 1937, listening to what in those days was known as the "Spotted Screech Owl." "It is tireless in its refrain, which may continue uninterrupted for an hour or more. . . . The voice is gentle yet has far-reaching power and somewhat resembles the sound produced by blowing across the opening of a bottle."[3]

The Whiskered Screech-Owl often gives more than the four notes Brandt heard, actually. Its usual song is a series of 4 to 10 notes reaching a shallow crescendo and dropping off slightly at the end, and similar enough to a Western Screech-Owl's that one must listen closely. The "telegraphic trill," an erratic series of fast and slow notes that sound like someone tapping out Morse code, is common and far more recognizable—often two fast notes followed by three slower ones but occurring in a variety of combinations. As with many owls, the

A hunter of arthropods, the Whiskered Screech-Owl is closely linked with the pine-oak or cloud forests across much of its range, although at lower elevations it can be found in dry tropical forests. *(Colima. Pete Morris)*

slightly larger female has a higher-pitched voice. Mated pairs often duet. Evenly spaced notes may resemble the call of the Unspotted Saw-whet Owl or "Guatemalan" form of the Northern Pygmy-Owl but are lower-pitched than either.

As with other screech-owls, the Whiskered gives hoots, barks, and screeches in the presence of intruders, generally in that sequence as the intensity of the disturbance increases.

HABITAT AND NICHE

A largely insectivorous predator, the Whiskered Screech-Owl is tightly bound to the Madrean oak-pine forest, a biome that barely crosses the United States border but flourishes through the mountains, deep canyons, and high plateaus of Mexico—forests of Chihuahuan and Apache pines, evergreen oaks of a number of species, grading to juniper-oak, oak, and riparian forests at the lower elevations. The owl is especially fond of steep slopes and canyons with dense vegetation—much denser than would attract other screech-owls.

Volunteers for the Arizona Breeding Bird Atlas project recorded 40 percent of all Whiskered Screech-Owl detections in extensive areas of live oaks, and another 33 percent in riparian forests of Arizona sycamore, oak, Arizona cypress, and juniper, with sycamores making up a significant

Territorial and courtship calling by male Whiskered Screech-Owls begins in midwinter. Egg-laying begins in March in Mexico, and by mid-April to early May in Arizona and New Mexico. This is the northern race, *M. t. asperus*. *(Arizona. Tom Johnson)*

portion of the forest. In New Mexico, on the other hand, sycamores are scarce in Whiskered Screech-Owl territories. In southern Mexico and northern Central America, the owls are also found in dry tropical forests at the lower margins of their elevational range, and in pine and cloud forests at the upper reaches. Marshall (1967) found them "in considerable numbers" in traditional shade-coffee farms in El Salvador.[4]

DIET: Almost entirely arthropods, including beetles, large moths and caterpillars, grasshoppers, crickets, centipedes, scorpions, and spiders. Prey selection may shift seasonally to track local abundance, from moths in spring to beetles in summer. "Centipedes are taken more frequently during the winter," one early naturalist wrote. "Practically every stomach examined during the colder months contained one or more small centipedes."[5]

Lizards, small snakes, and small rodents are less common but account for a significant portion of the biomass brought to the nest. Scientists in the Chiricahua Mountains of Arizona were surprised to find Whiskered Screech-Owls delivering two species of normally diurnal lizards to their nests—evidence that these lizards had an unknown period of activity at dusk.

NESTING AND BREEDING

A secondary cavity nester, the Whiskered Screech-Owl appears to be much more dependent on natural cavities, rather than woodpecker holes, than are other small owls in its range. One study found that 93 percent of Whiskered Screech-Owl nests were in natural cavities, like those formed by fallen limbs and rotted trunks, while almost 90 percent of Flammulated Owl nests in the same region were in woodpecker holes. The area around the nest, especially in front of the cavity, tends to be fairly open, and the nest cavities are often rather high off the ground—up to 33 ft. (11 m).

Most information comes from Arizona and New Mexico; the Whiskered Screech-Owl's breeding ecology has been essentially unstudied in the rest of its range, where Gehlbach and Gehlbach (2000) listed only three nests that had been found.[1]

Male calling (to defend a territory or attract a female) begins in midwinter and increases through Jan. and Feb., with a shift from short trills to longer trills as male–male territorial encounters grow. Courtship begins in Mar. in Arizona and New Mexico, with egg-laying as early as mid-Apr., but more typically through early May; in southern Mexico, egg-laying may occur by mid-Mar.

The typical clutch, as with most screech-owls, appears to be 3 or 4 eggs.

BEHAVIOR

There is a surprising dichotomy to the Whiskered Screech-Owl. In the appropriate habitat in the Madrean mountains it is one of the easiest owls to hear, especially if one uses a recording. (At times a little *too* easy; see "Status.") But learning the secrets of their behavior and ecology—*that* has proven a real challenge for researchers. Whiskered Screech-Owls live at fairly high elevations, often in remote and inaccessible areas, and they spend much of their lives high in the canopy of dense oak and pine forest. Most of what we know comes from a handful of dedicated scientists observing them near their nest sites in Arizona and New Mexico.

So far as is known, the Whiskered's behavior mirrors that of most other screech-owls, though as a primarily insectivorous species, it does most of its hunting in the canopy, snagging moths, beetles, caterpillars, and other prey from the foliage, much as do Flammulated Owls.

While it uses cavities for nesting, the adults roost among dense foliage, often in or near the nest tree during the breeding season. Detected during the day, it assumes a typical screech-owl "broken branch" pose—eyes closed, ear tufts erect, and plumage compressed. But at night it takes a very different approach. "It fluffs out its feathers and leans forward in such a manner that it looks very much like a bulge on the limb," ornithologist E. C. Jacot wrote in 1931. "Occasionally, one will be seen perched near the end of the branch and closely resembles a cluster of leaves."[5]

Unlike most small owls, which depend largely on old woodpecker holes, Whiskered Screech-Owls have been found to use almost nothing but old rot holes and other natural cavities. Nests tend to be fairly high off the ground and surrounded by open forest. *(Arizona. Greg Lasley/VIREO)*

The males sing most commonly after dusk and before dawn and on moonlit nights, often calling from in or near multiple cavities in their territories. In Chiapas, the Ch'ol Maya believe the call of the Whiskered Screech-Owl, or *ch'urukinkuj,* means that the weather will clear up.

Densities of more than 10 pairs per square kilometer have been reported from Arizona.

STATUS

Although it is one of the most common (sometimes the most common) small owl in its mountain habitat, the Whiskered Screech-Owl is listed as a "special concern" species in Arizona and "threatened" by the state of New Mexico; Partners in Flight gives it a high vulnerability score because of its limited range. It has no federal listing in the United States, nor in Mexico where it is fairly common in the right habitat, but it was included on the 2014 Yellow Watch List because of limited range and declining population trends.

Habitat destruction, especially unregulated logging, is the biggest threat in its Mexican range, and changing fire regimes there and in the American Southwest—with climate change and persistent drought producing bigger, hotter, more damaging fires—may pose an increasing risk in the future.

Partners in Flight estimates the global population at 200,000 individuals, although that estimate is not underpinned by a high degree of confidence. The New Mexico population is believed to be stable or increasing, perhaps as a result of recolonization from Mexico. Conservation objectives recommended by the New Mexico Partners in Flight include avoiding disturbance to known nesting areas, avoiding prescribed burns in canyon bottoms within its range, and discouraging the construction of new roads in the Peloncillo Mountains.

But because it is a highly sought specialty bird in the Sky Island region, the Whiskered Screech-Owl is one of the few species for which the impact of birding figures into the conservation equation. Overuse of recordings, banging on nest trees to flush the birds, and other boorish behavior has led some reserves, parks, and national forests to strictly regulate how birders can operate. Conservationists suggest that birders focus on finding roosting males in the daytime during the breeding season, rather than using recordings at night, and to use whistled imitations rather than recordings.

Although they are widespread in the Mexican mountains, almost everything known about Whiskered Screech-Owls has come from a handful of researchers in Arizona and New Mexico. *(Arizona. Gerrit Vyn)*

NOTES

1. F. R. Gehlbach and N. Y. Gehlbach. 2000. Whiskered screech-owl (*Otus trichopsis*). In *The Birds of North America*, no. 507, ed. A. Poole and F. Gill. Philadelphia: Birds of North America.

2. Earhart and Johnson 1970.

3. Brandt, H. 1937. Some Arizona bird studies. *Auk* 54 (1): 62–64.

4. Marshall 1967.

5. E. C. Jacot. 1931. Notes on the spotted and flammulated screech owls in Arizona. *Condor* 33 (1): 8–11.

BIBLIOGRAPHY

Brown, D. E., ed. 1994. *Biotic Communities: Southwestern United States and Northwestern Mexico.* Salt Lake City, UT: University of Utah Press.

Corman and Wise-Gervais 2005.

Duncan, W. W., F. R. Gehlbach, and G. A. Middendorf III. 2003. Nocturnal activity by diurnal lizards (*Sceloporus jarrovi, S. virgatus*) eaten by small owls (*Glaucidium gnoma, Otus trichopsis*). *Southwestern Naturalist* 48 (2): 218–222.

Enríquez-Rocha, Rangel-Salazar, and Holt 1993.

Flesch, A. D. 2008. Distribution and status of breeding landbirds in northern Sonora Mexico. *Studies in Avian Biology* 37:28–45.

Flesch, A. D., R. Stone, and R. L. Hutto. 2010. Distribution and status of breeding birds in the Sky Islands of northern Sonora. Missoula, MT: University of Montana.

Howell, T. R. 2010. Thomas R. Howell's checklist of the birds of Nicaragua as of 1993. *Ornithological Monographs* no. 68:1–108. Washington, DC: American Ornithologists' Union.

Howell and Webb 1995.

Hull, K., and R. Fergus. 2011. Ethno-ornithological perspectives on the Ch'ol Maya. *Reitaku Review* 17:42–92.

Monson, G. 1998. Whiskered screech-owl. In *Raptors of Arizona*, ed. R. L. Glinski. Tucson, AZ: University of Arizona Press.

Navarro-Sigüenza, A. G., and A. T. Peterson. 2007. *Megascops trichopsis* (tecolote rítmico) residencia permanente distribución potencial. In *Mapas de las Aves de México Basados en WWW*, ed. A. G. Navarro and A. T. Peterson. Final report, SNIB-CONABIO project no. CE015. México DF.

New Mexico Partners in Flight. 2007. New Mexico Bird Conservation Plan Version 2.1. C. Rustay and S. Norris, compilers. Albuquerque, NM, http://www.nmpartnersin-flight.org/bcp.html.

Proudfoot, Gehlbach, and Honeycutt 2007.

Rosenberg et al. 2014.

Found only in the montane forests of Chiapas and Guatemala, the Bearded Screech-Owl has the smallest distribution of any screech-owl in the region—a range that is increasingly threatened by logging and fragmentation. *(Chiapas. Nick Athanas)*

BEARDED SCREECH-OWL
Megascops barbarus
Alpha code: BESO

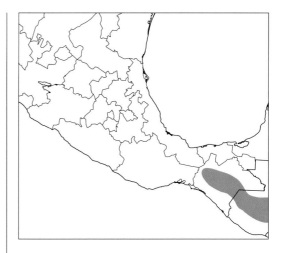

LENGTH: 6–7.5 in. (16–20 cm)

WINGSPAN: Undocumented

MASS: Moderate reversed size dimorphism. Average, male: 2.2 oz. (63 g); range 2–2.4 oz. (58–69.5 g). Average, female: 2.5 oz. (72 g); range 2.2–2.8 oz. (62.5–79 g).[1] Two females from Chiapas each 2.4 oz. (69 g).[2]

LONGEVITY: Very limited banding data. One female, banded as an adult, was recaptured at more than 4 years of age.

The smallest and rarest screech-owl in North America, the Bearded Screech-Owl certainly has the most restricted range in that group (smaller even than that of the island-bound Puerto Rican Screech-Owl), being found only in the high-elevation oak and pine forests of Chiapas and neighboring Guatemala. Although said to be common in places, its habitat has been badly fragmented and significantly degraded; consequently, the Bearded Screech-Owl is listed as "threatened" by Mexico, and as "vulnerable" by IUCN/BirdLife. Much of what is known about this rare owl comes from the research of a single scientist, and there are still enormous gaps in our knowledge of even the most basic aspects of its life history.

SYSTEMATICS, TAXONOMY, AND ETYMOLOGY

First described in 1868 from Santa Barbara, Guatemala. One of two early specimens from 1861, a rufous morph, was initially misidentified as a Flammulated Owl. The Bearded Screech-Owl was not included in any of the recent DNA analyses of owl taxonomy, and so its exact relationship to other members of *Megascops* is unclear.

ETYMOLOGY: Obsolete English names include "Bridled Screech Owl" and "Santa Barbara Screech Owl," the latter after the type locality. For etymology of the genus name, see "Western Screech-Owl." The specific name, *barbarus,* means "foreign" or "strange," not "bearded," as is sometimes claimed (that would be *barbatus*). There is nothing especially "bearded" about this species, and the English and Spanish names may be little more than a mistake.

SPANISH: *Tecolote barbudo, tecolote grillo, tecolotito ocotero, tecolotito bigotón* (Chiapas)

DISTRIBUTION

Found only in humid montane forests from the central highlands of Chiapas to the Atlantic slope highlands of western and central Guatemala, generally above 5,900 ft. (1,800 m).

MIGRATION AND MOVEMENTS: Year-round resident. No information on juvenile dispersal distances.

DISTRIBUTION OUTSIDE THE COVERAGE AREA: Highlands of Guatemala, possibly including the Sierra de las Minas.

DESCRIPTION AND IDENTIFICATION

A small, fairly dark "eared" owl with heavily marked plumage creating a mottled effect, especially on the underparts, and most striking in gray-brown morphs. Tail is noticeably short, with wings projecting well beyond the tip.

BASIC (ADULT) PLUMAGE: Polymorphic. Most owls are either gray-brown or rufous, although an intermediate form that mixes gray and red does occur. No known sexual differences, but a limited sample of known-sex live birds examined by Enríquez (2007) showed that five of eight females were red morphs, but only one of six males. Two unknown-sex birds from Guatemala were intermediate-morph.

Gray-brown morph: Crown heavily streaked with black and lightly spotted, contrasting moderately with grayish, speckled eyebrows. Facial disk grayish brown, sometimes tinged with rufous, with indistinct concentric barring and rimmed in blackish brown, with heavy dark rictal bristles around the bill. Upperparts gray-brown, spotted with whitish gray (forming a light band across the nape), and whitish-edged scapulars forming a distinct light "suspender" bar above each folded wing. Underparts heavily marked with rounded crossbars, producing an ocellated effect on the upper breast,

Polymorphic, most Bearded Screech-Owls are gray-brown, but rufous morphs are common, while the intermediate brown morph (left) is much rarer. (Guatemala. Knut Eisermann)

more lightly marked on belly and flanks. Tarsi feathered to the toes. Eye yellow, bill greenish. Rufous morph's markings generally less intense and distinct, and dark red-brown rather than blackish.

JUVENAL PLUMAGE: A single juvenile, approximately 3 weeks old, was photographed but not otherwise described beyond having gray-morph plumage and a gray beak. The photograph shows the barred juvenile plumage typical of screech-owls.

SIMILAR SPECIES: Whiskered Screech-Owl is roughly similar in size but has a longer tail, reaching to the tips of the wings, more prominent ear tufts when erect, and lacks heavy scalloping on the underparts.

VOCALIZATIONS

Primary call is a high, quiet, toadlike trill lasting 4 to 6 seconds.

HABITAT AND NICHE

Almost everything known about the life history of the Bearded Screech-Owl comes from doctoral fieldwork conducted in the humid, high-elevation oak and cloud forests of Chiapas by Paula L. Enríquez.

She found the species in landscapes dominated

Bearded Screech-Owls appear to be dependent on old-growth forests of oak, but small clearings may be important for this almost entirely insectivorous owl—at least, based on the single study to date of its ecology. (Guatemala. Knut Eisermann)

by old-growth forest, particularly moist oak woodlands, but also concluded that forest edges were important to Bearded Screech-Owls for hunting and roosting. Using playback, she found them at an average density of 1.65 owls per kilometer of forest trail surveyed, well below the 2.5 owls per kilometer recorded for Balsas Screech-Owl but similar to rates reported for Flammulated Owls. Curiously, some areas that appeared to offer suitable habitat had no owls. Daytime roosts were found on four occasions, twice in broadleaf trees and twice in pines.

DIET: Limited information, although the species appears to be largely (perhaps almost completely) insectivorous, with beetles the most common prey, especially scarab and ground beetles; crickets were also important prey items and with scarab beetles comprised almost three-quarters of the biomass eaten. Remains of roaches and moths were also found in the single nest site examined. The species does not appear to produce pellets, forcing researchers to rely on fecal examinations. An analysis of stable isotopes in feathers, from which scientists can determine diet, found carbon and nitrogen isotopic signatures similar to those of insectivorous bats.

So little is known about the Bearded Screech-Owl that only a single nest of this species has been described—yet it is fairly common in parts of its limited range. (Chiapas. Christian Artuso)

NESTING AND BREEDING

Females with brood patches were found in Apr., and Enríquez believes egg-laying begins in Mar. or Apr., at the end of the dry season. Only a single nest has been described, in a natural cavity in an oak, in which a single nestling was brooded by an adult female. Like the Western Screech-Owl, the Bearded Screech-Owl appears to avoid soiling the nest cavity.

BEHAVIOR

Little information. Enríquez observed Bearded Screech-Owls at night, perched in the understory and dropping to the ground to pick up arthropod prey. Home range size, determined by radiotelemetry, varied considerably, from 10 to 91 acres (4.1 to 36.8 hectares), with a mean size of 56 acres (22.4 hectares).

STATUS

The Bearded Screech-Owl is listed as "threatened" by Mexico, and in 2012 IUCN/BirdLife uplisted it to "vulnerable," with a decreasing population trend.

A recent reexamination of the species's known and potential range in Mexico and Guatemala found that it comprised, at most, 3,776 sq. mi. (9,780 sq. km), barely a fourth the size of previous estimates. Even that figure may overstate the available area, since much of the pine-oak and cloud forest in the region has been badly fragmented by logging and human activity, degraded by pine-bark beetle infestations, and subjected to the effects of civil war. The owl's use of forest edges, however, suggests it may be somewhat resilient to fragmentation.

Between 1975 and 2000, roughly 25 percent of the forest in the Chiapas highlands was logged or converted to farming. The Bearded Screech-Owl has been recorded from relatively young pine plantations, but whether such habitat (which would lack much in the way of nest cavities) can actually support the species is unclear. The owls use forest edges for hunting and roosting, which may place them at greater risk from people hunting with slingshots.

NOTES

1. P. L. Enríquez and K. M. Cheng. 2008. Natural history of the threatened bearded screech-owl (*Megascops barbarus*) in Chiapas, Mexico. *Journal of Raptor Research* 42 (3): 180–187.

2. Dunning 2007.

BIBLIOGRAPHY

BirdLife International. 2015 *Megascops barbarus*. In IUCN 2014. IUCN Red List of Threatened Species, version 2014.3, http://www.iucnredlist.org/details/22688807/0.

Cayuela, L., J. M. Benayas, and C. Echeverría. 2006. Clearance and fragmentation of tropical montane forests in the highlands of Chiapas, Mexico (1975–2000). *Forest Ecology and Management* 226:208–218.

Eisermann, K. 2011. Conservation status of bearded screech-owl *Megascops barbarus* 2011. Cobán, Guatemala: Proeval Raxmu Bird Monitoring Program.

Enríquez, P. L. 2007. "Ecology of the bearded screech owl (*Megascops barbarus*) in the central highlands of Chiapas, Mexico." PhD diss., University of British Columbia.

Enríquez, P. L., K. M. Cheng, and J. E. Elliott. 2010. The "near threatened" bearded screech-owl *Megascops barbarus:* Diet pattern and trophic assessment using δ^{13}C and δ^{15}N stable-isotopes. *Bird Conservation International* 20 (1): 25–33.

Hernández-Baños, B. E., A. T. Peterson, A. G. Navarro-Sigüenza, and B. P. Escalante-Pliego. 1995. Bird faunas of the humid montane forests of Mesoamerica: Biogeographic patterns and priorities for conservation. *Bird Conservation International* 5:251–277.

Moore and Peters 1939.

Navarro-Sigüenza, A. G., and A. T. Peterson. 2007. *Megascops barbarus* (tecolote barburdo) residencia permanente distribución potencial. In *Mapas de las Aves de México Basados en WWW*, ed. A. G. Navarro and A. T. Peterson. Final report, SNIB-CONABIO project no. CE015. México DF.

Sclater, P. L., and O. Salvin. 1868. Descriptions of new species of birds of the families Dendrocolaptidae, Strigidae, and Columbidae. In *Proceedings of the Scientific Meetings of the Zoological Society of London.* London: Longmans, Green, Reader and Dyer, pp. 53–60.

VERMICULATED SCREECH-OWL
Megascops guatemalae
Alpha code: VESO

LENGTH: 8–9 in. (20–25 cm); size increases from smallest *M. g. cassini* in north to largest *M. g. guatemalae* in south.

WINGSPAN: Unknown

MASS: Degree of sexual dimorphism unknown. An unsexed range of 3.2–4.5 oz. (91–128 g) has been cited but appears to represent the South American *roraimae* form, while eight birds averaging 4.2 oz. (118 g) were from Peru and Ecuador.[1] Other published weights (3.5 oz. / 100 g;[2] 5.3 oz. / 150 g[3]) are for birds in the Central American *vermiculatus* group.

LONGEVITY: No information

Widespread and fairly common, the Vermiculated Screech-Owl is a mystery at almost every turn. Its taxonomy is cloudy and confusing, and remarkably little has been documented of its life history and ecology, especially when compared with a threatened, range-restricted species like the Bearded Screech-Owl. There are compelling reasons to consider the form found in our area as a distinct species, the "Guatemalan Screech-Owl," although the AOU has not yet made that split.

SYSTEMATICS, TAXONOMY, AND ETYMOLOGY

"In this very confusing genus," an AOU taxonomy committee has observed, "this species complex may have the most complicated taxonomic and nomenclatural problems."[4] What has been treated as a single, wide-ranging species by the AOU, as well as by

What is today known as the Vermiculated Screech-Owl—named for its delicate gray or rufous markings—may actually include several distinct species. The races found in Mexico and northern Central America are sometimes classified as the "Guatemalan Screech-Owl." *(Nayarit. Rick and Nora Bowers/VIREO)*

Dickinson and Remsen (2013), has been split into up to four species by various authorities, largely on the basis of vocal differences.

The most common split is a two-way divide:

The polytypic "Guatemalan Screech-Owl," including *M. g. hastatus* from southern Sonora to Oaxaca; *M. g. cassini* from Tamaulipas to northern Veracruz; *M. g. guatemalae* from southern Veracruz to Nicaragua, including the Yucatán Peninsula; and *M. g. dacrysistactus,* which some authorities combine with *guatemalae,* in the highlands of southern Honduras and northern Nicaragua.

The "Vermiculated Screech-Owl," including *M. [vermiculatus] vermiculatus* from Costa Rica and Panama, *M. [v.] roraimae* from northeastern South America, and *M. [v.] napensis* from Colombia and Ecuador.

A number of authors elevate *roraimae* and *napensis* to species status.[5, 6, 7, 8, 9] On the other hand, Marshall, Behrstock, and König (1991) lumped the disjunct populations from Mexico and northern South America with *M. atricapilla* as a superspecies, calling it the "Variable Screech-Owl," with the form in our area becoming *M. a. guatemalae*.

To further complicate matters, some have argued that the Puerto Rican Screech-Owl (*M. nudipes*) is conspecific with the *guatemalae* group.[10] It should be clear from all this that here is a taxon badly in need of a careful reexamination with current molecular tools to compliment morphological and auditory evidence. The single study that addressed the phylogeny of these related screech-owls[11] included only one sample of Vermiculated Screech-Owl, and that was a bird from South America.

ETYMOLOGY: For the derivation of *Megascops*, see "Western Screech-Owl." The specific name comes from the type specimen, collected in Guatemala and described in 1875 as *Scops guatemalae*. The common name comes from the coarsely vermiculated pattern of the plumage.

> **SPANISH:** *Tecolote vermiculado, tecolote crescendo, autillo [tecolotito] guatemalteco, tecolotito maullador* (Chiapas), *guia de León* (Chiapas)
> **MAYAN:** *Kulte'* (Yucatec)

DISTRIBUTION

Dense humid and semiarid forests from sea level to about 5,000 ft. (1,500 m). Pacific slope from southern Sonora and Chihuahua south in a narrow coastal band to Oaxaca, and the Atlantic slope from southern Tamaulipas and Veracruz, across the Isthmus of Tehuantepec into Chiapas, and north into the Yucatán (including Cozumel).

MIGRATION AND MOVEMENTS: Year-round resident. No information on juvenile dispersal distances.

DISTRIBUTION OUTSIDE THE COVERAGE AREA: Southern Central America to Colombia and Ecuador.

DESCRIPTION AND IDENTIFICATION

BASIC (ADULT) PLUMAGE: No sexual differences known. Dimorphic, with a gray-brown morph that predominates and a rufous morph in some areas. A small, generally gray-brown screech-owl with short ear tufts, contrasting whitish eyebrows, and gray-brown facial disk moderately edged in dark brown (the dark disk edging is absent in *vermiculatus* birds to the south). Marshall (1967) described the spearlike markings on the dorsal feathers as resembling small pagodas. Typical screech-owl "suspenders" formed by white-edged scapular feathers. Owls from some areas (Yucatán, Sonora) have more

The subspecies *M. g. guatemalae*, found from southern Veracruz to Nicaragua, including the Yucatán Peninsula, is part of the group sometimes split into the "Guatemalan Screech-Owl." *(Belize. Steve Easley)*

evident rusty tones in upperparts. Rufous morph shows reduced markings on the upperparts and less overall contrast.

Coloration in brown morph grades from north to south, with the smallest northern race, *cassini*, the darkest, having distinctly black dorsal markings, especially on the crown, nape, and back, and heavy crossbarring on the breast feathers. The putative *dacrysistactus* race of northern Central America has very light, fine breast vermiculations and paler dorsal coloration, while *hastatus* is intermediate in coloration and marking intensity. Toes are long and naked. Eyes yellow, bill greenish.

JUVENAL PLUMAGE: Typical screech-owl pattern of dusky barring on grayish (or rufous) ground color.

SIMILAR SPECIES: Overlaps locally with Pacific Screech-Owl and, in pine-oak forests, with Whiskered Screech-Owl. Voice is the best characteristic; distinguished from somewhat larger Pacific by naked (not bristled) toes, and from smaller Whiskered by larger feet and finer markings.

VOCALIZATIONS

The primary song of the *guatemalae* group is a striking monotone trill typically lasting 4 to 10 seconds, which starts quietly but builds steadily to a strong, piercing climax and an abrupt end. The male's call is noticeably lower than the female's, although the basic structure is similar in both. A secondary song is shorter (4 to 6 seconds) and faster in tempo, accelerating in a bouncing-ball fashion.

HABITAT AND NICHE

An inhabitant of woodlands from sea-level tropical forests and mangroves up into higher-elevation, oak-dominated stands, the Vermiculated Screech-Owl likes its habitat thick and dense, more so than any other screech-owl in the region. For such a widespread and generally common bird, almost nothing has been published about its life history or ecology. Ranging up to about 5,000 ft. (1,500 m) in Mexico, it is found at somewhat lower elevations farther south and east.

Marshall (1967) described its preferred habitat as "dense, tall, continuous, broadleaved woods (and rain forests?) from tropical deciduous woods and thorn forests of lowlands and foothills up into oak woodlands," noting that it tends to be found in denser forests than other screech-owls.

DIET: Reported to be primarily insectivorous, taking occasional vertebrates.

NESTING AND BREEDING

Limited data, and much of that refers to birds of the *vermiculatus* group from southern Central or South America. A female in breeding condition was

A pair of Vermiculated Screech-Owls roosts together in the shade of dense forest; this owl prefers thicker woodland cover than any other Mesoamerican screech-owl. The gray-brown morph is most common overall, but rufous-morph individuals are found in some areas. *(Honduras. Kevin Loughlin/Wildside Nature Tours)*

collected at her nest entrance in early Apr. in Tamaulipas, but the contents of the nest were not determined. In Oaxaca, three chicks ("prejuvenile") were collected June 20. Males make advertising calls in Feb. in the Yucatán, with incubation in June. Central American races reportedly lay 2 to 5 (usually 3) eggs in cavities, incubating 26 to 37 days.

BEHAVIOR

What little information has been published paints a picture of a perch hunter similar to other *Megascops,* foraging in the subcanopy and on the ground or snatching flying insects.

STATUS

Given its wide range and apparently stable population, BirdLife/IUCN classifies the Vermiculated Screech-Owl as "least concern," although there is essentially no hard information on populations or trends. Deforestation and fragmentation may be a concern, at least locally.

NOTES

1. Dunning 2007.

2. W. D. Robinson, J. D. Brawn, and S. K. Robinson. 2000. Forest bird community structure in central Panama: Influence of spatial scale and biogeography. *Ecological Monographs* 70:209–235.

3. Stiles and Skutch 1989.

4. M. B. Robbins. 2001. Continue to recognize a broad *Otus guatemalae* (namely, to include *O. vermiculatus, O. napensis, O. roraimae*). American Ornithologists' Union South American Classification Committee, http://www.museum.lsu.edu/~Remsen/SACCprop12.html.

5. Hardy, Coffey, and Reynard 1999.

6. Ridgely and Greenfield 2001.

7. Weick 2006.

8. König and Weick 2008.

9. Mikkola 2012.

10. van der Weyden 1975.

11. Heidrich, König, and Wink 1995.

BIBLIOGRAPHY

BirdLife International. 2015. *Megascops guatemalae.* In IUCN Red List of Threatened Species, v. 2014.3. http://www.iucnredlist.org/details/61767847/0.

Hardy, J. W., B. B. Coffey Jr., and G. B. Reynard. 1999. *Voices of the New World Owls,* rev. ed. Gainesville, FL: ARA Records.

Heidrich, P., C. König, and M. Wink. 1995. Molecular phylogeny of South American screech owls of the *Otus atricapillus* complex (Aves: Strigidae) inferred from nucleotide sequences of the mitochondrial cytochrome *b* gene. *Zeitschrift fur Naturforschung C-Journal of Biosciences* 50 (3): 294–302.

Marshall, J. T., R. A. Behrstock, and C. König. 1991. Frontispiece: Variable screech-owl (*Otus atricapillus*) and its relatives. *Wilson Bulletin* 103 (2): 314–315.

Navarro-Sigüenza, A. G., and A. T. Peterson. 2007. *Megascops guatemalae* (tecolote vermiculado) residencia permanente distribución potencial. In *Mapas de las Aves de México Basados en WWW,* ed. A. G. Navarro and A. T. Peterson. Final report, SNIB-CONABIO project no. CE015. México DF.

Ridgely, R. S., and P. J. Greenfield. 2001. *Birds of Ecuador,* vol. 1. Ithaca, NY: Cornell University Press.

Sharpe, E. B. 1875. *Catalogue of the Birds of the British Museum,* vol. 2. London: British Museum, pp. 112–114.

Sutton, G. M., and O. S. Pettingill Jr. 1942. Birds of the Gomez Farias region, southwestern Tamaulipas. *Auk* 59 (1): 1–34.

With its dark eyes, lack of ear tufts, and mostly featherless legs, the Puerto Rican Screech-Owl resembles the Bare-legged Owl of Cuba and has sometimes been classified with it. While the nominate race is common on Puerto Rico, a subspecies once found in the Virgin Islands is presumed to be extinct. *(Puerto Rico. Alberto López)*

PUERTO RICAN SCREECH-OWL
Megascops nudipes
Alpha code: PRSO

LENGTH: 9–10 in. (23–25 cm)

WINGSPAN: About 18–22 in. (45–55 cm)

MASS: Slight reversed size dimorphism. Average, both sexes: 5 oz. (143 g).[1] Average, nine males: 4.6 oz. (131 g); range 3.6–5.1 oz. (103–146 g). Average, 14 females: 5.1 oz. (144 g); range 3.6–6 oz. (103–169 g).[2]

LONGEVITY: No information

More similar, at first glance, to the Bare-legged Owl of Cuba than with its own relatives in *Megascops,* the Puerto Rican Screech-Owl is common but little understood, from both ecological and taxonomic perspectives. The Virgin Islands race, which may not be a valid subspecies, hasn't been documented persuasively since the early twentieth century and appears to be extinct.

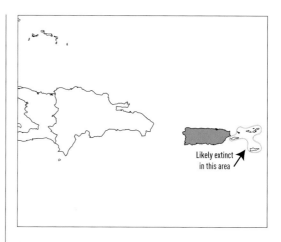

Likely extinct in this area

SYSTEMATICS, TAXONOMY, AND ETYMOLOGY

The taxonomic relationship between the Puerto Rican Screech-Owl and other small Neotropical owls, especially the similar Bare-legged Owl of Cuba, has been unsettled almost since the species was first described in 1800 as *Strix nudipes*. Because the Puerto Rican and Cuban owls share a lack of ear tufts and mostly (in the latter's case, completely) bare tarsi, subsequent ornithologists lumped them into one species in the genus *Gymnoglaux,* although the Virgin Islands race was, for a time, considered distinct.

Finally in 1868, the British scientists Philip Sclater and Osbert Salvin—who for the first time had specimens from all three island areas to compare—assigned the Puerto Rican and Virgin Islands owls to one species, *Gymnoglaux nudipes,* and the Cuban birds to *G. lawrencii.*

The genus name changed to *Gymnasio* in 1875, and both the Puerto Rican and Cuban species were at one point placed in *Otus.* The Bare-legged Owl has more recently been placed in its own genus, *Margarobyas,* mostly because of vocal differences, but the Puerto Rican Screech-Owl remains in what is now *Megascops.*

Two subspecies are recognized: *M. nudipes nudipes* on Puerto Rico, and *M. n. newtoni* in the Virgin Islands and possibly Vieques and Culebra (see "Distribution," below). The Virgin Islands race was said to be grayer and less vividly marked, but Moreno (1998) has pointed out that the plumage differences on which *newtoni* was described may fall within the range of variation shown by *nudipes,* suggesting the subspecific designations may not be valid.

ETYMOLOGY: For the derivation of the genus name, see "Western Screech-Owl." The specific name *nudipes* comes from the Latin *nudus,* "nude" or "bare," and *pedis,* "foot," referring to the bird's naked lower tarsi. The common name stems from the type locality in Puerto Rico; previously also called the "Puerto Rican Bare-legged Owl." A folk name for the Virgin Islands subspecies was "cuckoo-bird."

> **SPANISH:** *Mucáro de Puerto Rico, autillo de Puerto Rico, mucáro común, mucarito, mucarito Puertorriqueño*

DISTRIBUTION

Endemic to Puerto Rico, Vieques, and the Virgin Islands, although its historical presence on Vieques, Culebra, Tortola, and Virgin Gorda seems to rest on thin evidence. Further, any owls that did occur on Vieques and possibly Culebra are more likely to have been *M. n. nudipes* rather than *newtoni.* Year-round resident. No information on juvenile dispersal distances.

DISTRIBUTION OUTSIDE THE COVERAGE AREA: None

DESCRIPTION AND IDENTIFICATION

Small reddish or grayish brown (very rarely gray) owl that lacks true erectile ear tufts.

BASIC (ADULT) PLUMAGE: No sexual differences known. Polymorphic, although red-brown morph predominates. Gray-brown with varying degrees of rusty overtones above, scapulars with limited whitish edging producing a much thinner, less distinct pale bar above each folded wing than is typical in most screech-owls, and absent entirely in some individuals. Facial disk dark rufous with a limited dark brown rim, heavily edged with white along lower margins, which merges with a broad, white chin strap, forming a distinctive field mark. Contrasting whitish eyebrows. Upper chest heavily marked with rufous-brown vermiculation, merging with vertical brownish streaks and crossbarring (varying in intensity) on whitish belly and flanks. Lower tarsi bare. Eyes yellow to yellow-orange or yellow-brown; bill greenish yellow. Intensely rufous individuals show less contrast and vividness in markings. Gray morph very rare, restricted to dry forests.

JUVENAL PLUMAGE: Gray-brown or rufous base color with dusky, indistinct barring, typical of nestling screech-owls.

SIMILAR SPECIES: The only small owl within its range. Most similar to Cuban Bare-legged Owl, but has partially feathered (instead of completely naked) tarsi.

VOCALIZATIONS

Basic song is a low, growling trill, often rising slightly midway, and lasting 2 to 4 seconds. Call sometimes breaks into higher-pitched trills, chatters, or cackles, often part of a duet between mates. The folk name "cuckoo-bird" comes from a two-noted *coo-coo* vocalization.

HABITAT AND NICHE

Dependent on woodlands, like all its relatives, the Puerto Rican Screech-Owl may have passed through an ecological keyhole in the late nineteenth and early twentieth centuries, when much of the island of Puerto Rico was stripped of its tropical forest. As little as 3 percent of intact forest cover remained in 1949, much of that in the form of shade-coffee farms. This traditional form of agriculture may have provided a refuge for this and other forest species, despite a folk belief that the owls eat coffee beans, and for which they were long persecuted. (The almost total loss of forest on the Virgin Islands during this same period appears to have wiped out the species there.)

Beyond requiring woods, Puerto Rican Screech-Owls do not appear to be fussy about habitat. They are generally found in thick forests, but surveys using tape playback detected them almost as frequently in fragmented forests as in large, unbroken tracts in the Luquillo Mountains. They are fairly

A drooped-wing posture is typical of the Puerto Rican Screech-Owl when it is agitated or frightened. *(Puerto Rico. Alberto López)*

common in forest edges, suburbanized areas, and agricultural zones, including modest forest patches (as small as 23 acres [9.2 hectares]) in the San Juan metropolitan area. They can be found right to sea level, occurring in small, isolated pockets of trees that provide cover, food, and cavities for roosting and nesting.

Limited radiotelemetry suggests an unusually small home range for this species, with one adult using 11 acres (4.5 hectares), and a juvenile 5.6 acres (2.3 hectares), over the course of a month. The territories were adjacent but showed almost no overlap. Detectability in roadside counts peaked sharply in Nov. and Dec.

DIET: Like most tropical screech-owls, this species feeds heavily on insects and other arthropods, although coqui frogs may comprise up to a third of their diet, and lizards and songbirds are also taken.

NESTING AND BREEDING

Secondary cavity nester. Breeding occurs from Apr. through June, with 1 to 4 (more typically 2) eggs. Despite the species's abundance, little is known about the details of its nesting ecology.

Egg predation by the Pearly-eyed Thrasher (*Margarops fuscatus*) has been reported, but the owl also kills nesting thrashers and takes over their nest holes or boxes. The owl may also be affected by competition with introduced European honeybees, which have been known to evict owls from nest cavities.

BEHAVIOR

Strictly nocturnal, roosting in dense foliage, cavities, and caves. When agitated, it may partially open and droop its wings and—while not possessing normal ear tufts—raise the ends of its eyebrows to create small feather bumps. As with its breeding ecology, the life history and behavior of this screech-owl remain largely unexplored.

STATUS

Having recovered from widespread deforestation in the late nineteenth and early twentieth centuries, the Puerto Rican Screech-Owl is common in forested areas throughout Puerto Rico, especially lowland woodlands but also in mountainous and karst regions. Surveys in the 1990s found it to be the third most abundant raptor in moist and wet habitat on the island. It is listed as stable and of "least concern" by IUCN/BirdLife. The folklore blaming it for eating coffee beans, or a belief that eating its heart would cure asthma, is thankfully fading.

The Virgin Islands subspecies, *M. n. newtoni*, on the other hand, has not been documented on several islands since the 1800s, and the latest sighting appears to be 1972 on Saint Croix. (Screech-owls heard in 1976 and 1977 on Culebra may have been the nominate race.) Attempts to relocate *newtoni* in 1995 in the largest remaining forest tracts in the U.S. Virgin Islands failed, and a report of owl pellets on Guana Island in the British Virgin Islands is the only evidence suggesting this race is not already extinct. In 1984, a petition to list the Virgin Islands population under the federal Endangered Species Act was ruled "warranted but precluded," and the subspecies received no additional federal protection.

NOTES

1. W. J. Arendt, J. Faaborg, G. E. Wallace, and O. H. Garrido. 2004. Biometrics of birds throughout the Greater Caribbean Basin. *Proceedings of the Western Foundation of Vertebrate Zoology* 8:1–33.

2. Dunning 2007.

BIBLIOGRAPHY

Arendt, W. J. 2006. Adaptations of an avian supertramp: Distribution, ecology, and life history of the pearly-eyed thrasher (*Margarops fuscatus*). U.S. Forest Service Gen. Tech. Report IITF-GTR-27.

BirdLife International. 2015. *Megascops nudipes*. In IUCN Red List of Threatened Species, v. 2014.3. http://www.iucnredlist.org/details/22688891/0.

Federal Register, Jan. 20, 1984. Proposed rules. Vol. 49 (14): 2485–2488.

Gannon, M. R., K. Pardieck, M. R. Willig, and R. B. Waide. 1993. Movement and home range of the Puerto Rican screech-owl (*Otus nudipes*) in the Luquillo Experimental Forest. *Caribbean Journal of Science* 29 (3-4): 174–178.

Goodson, Chloe. 2014. Puerto Rican Screech-Owl (*Megascops nudipes*). In Neotropical Birds Online, ed. T. S. Schulenberg. Ithaca, NY: Cornell Lab of Ornithology, http://neotropical.birds.cornell.edu/portal/species/overview?p_p_spp=209016.

Hume and Walters 2012.

Moreno, J. A. 1998. Status of the Virgin Islands screech-owl. *Journal of Field Ornithology* 69 (4): 557–562.

Nellis, D. W. 1979. Record of Puerto Rican screech owl, turkey vulture and osprey from Saint Croix, U.S. Virgin Islands. *Wilson Bulletin* 91 (1): 148–149.

Pardieck, K. L., J. M. Meyers, and M. Pagán. 1996. Surveys of Puerto Rican screech-owl populations in large-tract and fragmented habitats. *Wilson Bulletin* 108 (4): 776–782.

A forest raptor, the Puerto Rican Screech-Owl may have hit a nadir in the mid-twentieth century, when an estimated 97 percent of the island's tropical woodlands had been cleared. But as forest cover has expanded, so has the owl's range and numbers. (*Puerto Rico. Alberto López*)

Rivera-Milán, F. F. 1995. Distribution and abundance of raptors in Puerto Rico. *Wilson Bulletin* 107 (3): 452–462.

Suarez-Rubio, M., and J. R. Thomlinson. 2009. Landscape and patch-level factors influence bird communities in an urbanized tropical island. *Biological Conservation* 142:1311–1321.

Wiley 1986a.

Wiley 1986b.

Wunderle, J. M. Jr., and W. Arendt. 2011. Avian studies and research opportunities in the Luquillo Experimental Forest: A tropical rain forest in Puerto Rico. *Forest Ecology and Management* 262:33–48.

Zelick, R. D., and P. M. Narins. 1982. Analysis of acoustically evoked call suppression behaviour in a neotropical treefrog. *Animal Behavior* 30:728–733.

BARE-LEGGED OWL
Margarobyas lawrencii
Alpha code: BLOW

LENGTH: 8–9 in. (20–23 cm)

WINGSPAN: Not documented

MASS: Degree of size dimorphism unknown. Average, 10 birds of both sexes: 3.3 oz. (95.2 g); range 2.8–3.9 oz. (80–111 g).[1]

LONGEVITY: Little information

Although long considered a screech-owl—or at least a close relative—the Bare-legged Owl differs significantly enough in physical structure and vocalizations to warrant its own genus today. Common throughout Cuba and the Isla de Juventud / Isle of Pines in wooded habitat, it is nevertheless very poorly known, and only the outlines of its life history and ecology have been described.

SYSTEMATICS, TAXONOMY, AND ETYMOLOGY
Initially lumped with the Puerto Rican Screech-Owl (which see), the Bare-legged Owl was split from it in 1868. Like the Puerto Rican species, the Cuban owl has been shuffled through genera—from *Noctua* to *Gymnoglaux* to *Gymnasio* and back to *Gymnoglaux*. In 1998 the AOU merged *Gymnoglaux* with *Otus* but then reversed course in 2003, noting the vocal and physical differences between the Bare-legged Owl and typical screech-owls. Because *Gymnasio* and *Gymnoglaux* are synonyms, in 2013 they renamed the monotypic genus *Margarobyas*.

A subspecies, *M. l. exsul,* has been described from western Cuba and the Isla de Juventud / Isle of Pines. Said to be browner and with larger, more

The only member of its genus, the Bare-legged Owl is common throughout Cuba wherever there are thickets or woodlands, especially stands of palms. (Cuba. Doug Wechsler/VIREO)

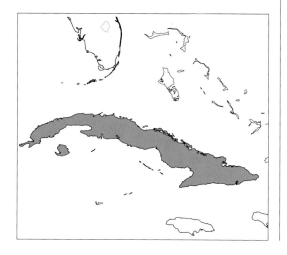

numerous spots than birds from eastern and central Cuba, it is not generally recognized.

ETYMOLOGY: The genus name comes from the Greek *margarites,* "a pearl," and *byas,* "an owl," "in allusion to Cuba, Pearl of the Antilles."[2] The specific name honors New York businessman and ornithologist George N. Lawrence, who in 1862 differentiated this species from the Puerto Rican Screech-Owl. The English name refers to the long, unfeathered tarsi.

　　SPANISH: *Sijú contunto, autillo Cubano*

DISTRIBUTION
Cuba and the Isla de Juventud / Isle of Pines. Year-round resident.

DISTRIBUTION OUTSIDE THE COVERAGE AREA: None

DESCRIPTION AND IDENTIFICATION

A small, "earless" owl with long, bare legs and brown eyes.

BASIC (ADULT) PLUMAGE: No morphs or known sexual differences. Crown brown with dark streaking, contrasting with whitish or cream-colored eyebrows and facial disk; prominent dark rictal bristles. No ear tufts. Upperparts brown to somewhat rufous, with prominent white spots in the scapulars and coverts and white barring on flight feathers. Underparts gray-white or yellow-white with a brownish wash at the throat; sparse brown streaking (with some light and limited crossbarring) on the upper breast and sides. Eyes dark brown, bill greenish, legs greenish yellow.

JUVENAL PLUMAGE: Similar to adult, with fewer white dorsal spots.

SIMILAR SPECIES: Burrowing Owl is slightly larger, with yellow eyes, heavily barred underparts, and longer, partially feathered gray legs. Cuban Pygmy-Owl is smaller, has feathered legs and distinct eye-spot markings on the nape.

VOCALIZATIONS

An accelerating *hu-hu-hu-hutututututu,* dropping slightly in pitch at the end, lasting 2 to 4 seconds. No secondary song, one of the factors distinguishing it from *Megascops.*

HABITAT AND NICHE

The conversion of Cuba's original forest to a fragmented, highly modified landscape was probably a boon for the Bare-legged Owl, which is fairly common throughout the island wherever thickets and woodlands are found, especially those with palm stands, and in somewhat more open habitat in limestone regions.

DIET: Primarily insects and other arthropods, although small vertebrates (amphibians, reptiles, and rarely birds) are sometimes taken.

NESTING AND BREEDING

Secondary cavity nester, reliant on natural openings and old woodpecker holes (especially in palms) as well as small caves and rock crevices. Little published on nesting ecology beyond average clutch size (said to be 2 eggs) with incubation by the female. Breeding Jan. to June.

BEHAVIOR

Poorly studied. Frequently forages on the ground, leading some authors to speculate it partially filled the niche of the rarer Burrowing Owl in Cuba.

Little is known about the ecology of the Bare-legged Owl. Its diet is heavily insectivorous, although it does take some small vertebrates, including reptiles, amphibians, and an occasional bird. *(Cuba. Christian Artuso)*

Bare-legged Owls are, like many small owls, dependent on old woodpecker cavities for their nest sites—which, in the case of this species, are generally in palm trees, like this nest. *(Cuba. Rick Collins)*

Strictly nocturnal, roosting in cavities and caves by day.

STATUS

The Bare-legged Owl is common in appropriate habitat throughout Cuba and is listed as "least concern" by IUCN/BirdLife.

NOTES

1. Dunning 2007.

2. S. L. Olson and W. Suárez. 2008. A new generic name for the Cuban Bare-legged Owl *Gymnoglaux lawrencii* Sclater and Salvin. *Zootaxa* 1960:67–68.

BIBLIOGRAPHY

Bangs, O. 1913. New birds from Cuba and the Isle of Pines. *Proceedings of the New England Zöological Club* 4:89–92.

BirdLife International. 2015. *Gymnoglaux lawrencii*. In IUCN Red List of Threatened Species, version 2014.3 http://www.iucnredlist.org/details/22688883/0.

Cicero, C. 2013. Recognize a new generic name for *Gymnoglaux lawrencii*. AOU North and Middle America Classification Committee, http://checklist.aou.org/nacc/proposals/PDF/2013-A.pdf.

Lawrence, G. N. 1878. On the members of the genus *Gymnoglaux*. *Ibis*, ser. 4, 2:184–187.

Raffaele et al. 1998.

Ridgway 1914.

CRESTED OWL
Lophostrix cristata
Alpha code: CROW

Stunning and unmistakable, the Crested Owl is found across much of the New World tropics, but almost nothing is known about its biology, ecology, or behavior. *(Costa Rica. Steve Easley)*

LENGTH: 14–17 in. (36–43 cm)

WINGSPAN: Not documented

MASS: Limited data. Reverse size dimorphism, but degree uncertain. Two males averaged 16.5 oz. (468 g); range 15–18 oz. (425–510 g), and a single female 21.9 oz. (620 g), but samples included birds from Mexico and Peru.[1] Weight for Costa Rica given as 14.1 oz. (400 g), but no information on sex or sample size.[2] Weight for Panama given as 18 oz. (510 g), but source unclear.[3]

LONGEVITY: Little information

Unforgettable when seen, but still largely an enigma to science, the Crested Owl has a wide range in the Neotropics, with the subspecies found in Mexico and northern Central America distinct enough that it may warrant species status. Coming face-to-face with a Crested Owl on its daytime roost—with those extraordinary white eyebrows and long ear tufts, stark against the blackish head and rufous facial disk—or seeing one briefly in the beam of a flashlight at night can be the highlight of any tropical birding trip.

SYSTEMATICS, TAXONOMY, AND ETYMOLOGY

The Crested Owl occupies its own genus, *Lophostrix,* which has traditionally been placed near (and sometimes with) the African Maned Owl, *Jubula lettii,* which it somewhat resembles. Limited DNA work, however, suggests it is most closely allied with the New World genus *Pulsatrix,* perhaps

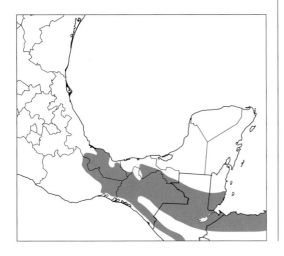

forming their own tribe, the Pulsatrigini. Juvenal plumages of *Lophostrix* and *Pulsatrix,* and certain skeletal details, are also similar.

Three subspecies are generally recognized, of which one is in our coverage area: *L. c. stricklandi,* from southern Veracruz and northern Oaxaca to western Panama. *L. c. wedeli* is found from eastern Panama to extreme northwestern South America northwest of the Andes, and *L. c. cristata* east and south of the cordillera across the remainder of northern South America. Given its differences in plumage and vocalization, some authors have argued that *stricklandi* deserves full species rank.

ETYMOLOGY: The genus name comes from the Greek *lophos,* "a crest," and the Latin *strix* and the Greek

A pair of Crested Owls roosts together in a palm—typical behavior for this species, which often roosts in pairs and often surprisingly close to the ground, although at night they call from the forest canopy. *(Costa Rica. Nick Athanas)*

strigx, "a screech owl." The specific name is Latin, meaning "crested." The common name refers, naturally, to the large, striking white ear tufts.

SPANISH: *Búho corniblanco [cuerno blanco], tecolote crestado, búho penachudo; búho cuerniblanco* (Chiapas)

DISTRIBUTION

Southern Veracruz and northern Oaxaca through central and southern Chiapas on both Atlantic and Pacific slopes, to at least 5,250 ft. (1,600 m). Year-round resident; no seasonal movements known. Juvenile dispersal distances unknown.

DISTRIBUTION OUTSIDE THE COVERAGE AREA: Guatemala and southern Belize through extreme northwestern South America, and disjunct distribution from western and southern Amazonia through the Guianas and southern Venezuela.

DESCRIPTION AND IDENTIFICATION

A stunning owl of medium size, with striking contrast between its long, white ear tufts and dark face. Difficult to confuse with any other species.

BASIC (ADULT) PLUMAGE: No sexual differences known. Weakly dimorphic. The subspecies *stricklandi,* in our coverage area, is distinct in its blackish head and dark chestnut facial disk, and its starkly contrasting pale bill and long, white, tapered ear tufts. Wide band of sooty gray-brown across the upper chest; belly and flanks gray-brown or somewhat rufous, finely speckled and vermiculated. Upperparts brown, with white spots on wing coverts

and white-edged scapulars. Eyes yellow to yellow-orange. Wings extend to the end of the indistinctly barred tail.

JUVENAL PLUMAGE: Long, lax, snow-white plumage through which adult feathers emerge; facial disk rufous and strongly contrasting. Fledglings may

The juvenal plumage of the Crested Owl is as striking as that of the adult—and completely its opposite, with long, lax, snow-white plumage through which the dark adult contour feathers emerge. *(Costa Rica. Chris Jimenez)*

The northern subspecies of Crested Owl, *L. c. stricklandi,* found from Veracruz to western Panama, has a dark chestnut facial disk and blackish head and is darker overall than those found from Panama south. These differences in plumage, along with differences in vocalizations, have led some authorities to split *stricklandi* into a separate species. *(Costa Rica. Chris Jimenez)*

show entirely dark, adultlike wings contrasting with a white body. Rounded ear tufts of down soon replaced by longer adult tufts. Bill dark.

SIMILAR SPECIES: The adult is unmistakable; no other owl in its range has its long, white ear tufts. Juveniles are largely white with dark facial patches and shorter ear tufts, and while molting into adult plumage may be confused with Spectacled Owl, especially if showing a dark chest band.

VOCALIZATIONS

Low, throaty growl, *whooooaaAAARRRrr,* lasting 1 to 1.5 seconds, rising steadily and falling off slightly at the end, repeated every 9 to 20 seconds. At close range, a few quiet, staccato introductory notes can be heard. Calls of *stricklandi* appear to be longer than those of the other two subspecies, with longer intervals between growls.

HABITAT AND NICHE

A bird of dense tropical broadleaf forest, the Crested Owl occupies a surprisingly wide range of elevations and habitat types, from lowland tropical and swamp forests at sea level, to cloud forests at elevations of at least 3,300 ft. (1,000 m), although some authorities give maximum elevations of 5,250 ft. (1,600 m) and

6,500 ft. (1,980 m), the latter in Honduras. Found in primary forests in Chiapas, and reported in tropical evergreen, semi-deciduous and swamp forests in Oaxaca. Often encountered in riverine and gallery forests, and reportedly in secondary woodlands, forest edges, and small clearings.

Poorly studied, so relatively little is known about this species's ecology, habitat preferences, or behavior.

DIET: Primarily large insects and arthropods; perhaps some small vertebrates. Essentially unknown.

NESTING AND BREEDING

No information on clutch size, and little is known about nest site selection other than the use of tree cavities (along with one report of a nest in a house loft in South America). Breeding period said to be the end of the dry season and beginning of the wet season.

BEHAVIOR

Like most of this owl's life history, its behavior is largely a mystery. Active at night, it roosts in dense foliage during the day, often in pairs, and often surprisingly close to the ground.

Researchers in Costa Rica found that Crested

Owls were more likely to respond vocally to recordings of other species than to their own calls—something not found in any of the other species of owls studied there. They responded especially strongly to Mottled Owl recordings, perhaps because both species use the same habitat at the study site. Although Crested Owls roosted primarily in the midcanopy, they called from the high canopy.

STATUS

The Crested Owl is listed as "threatened" in Mexico, although the true status of so poorly studied a species is uncertain. Howell and Webb (1995) considered it uncommon to fairly common, while other authors have called it rare in Chiapas and Oaxaca. Listed range-wide as "least concern" by IUCN/BirdLife, despite a projected loss of 19 to 22 percent of its habitat over three generations (17 years), based on Amazonian deforestation rates. Certainly, the importance of dense, intact tropical woodland to this owl suggests that continuing deforestation in southern Mexico poses a threat.

NOTES

1. Dunning 2007.

2. Stiles and Skutch 1989.

3. W. D. Robinson, J. D. Brawn, and S. K. Robinson. 2000. Forest bird community structure in central Panama: Influence of spatial scale and biogeography. *Ecological Monographs* 70 (2): 209–235.

BIBLIOGRAPHY

Binford 1989.

BirdLife International. 2015. Species factsheet: *Lophostrix cristata*, http://www.birdlife.org/datazone/speciesfactsheet.php?id=2256.

Enríquez-Rocha, Eisermann, and Mikkola 1993.

Enríquez, P. L., and J. L. R. Salazar. 1997. Intra- and interspecific calling in a tropical owl community. In *Biology and Conservation of Owls of the Northern Hemisphere*, ed. J. R. Duncan, D. H. Johnson, and T. H. Nicholls. 2nd International Symposium. Gen. Tech. Rep. NC-190. Saint Paul, MN: U.S. Department of Agriculture, Forest Service, North Central Forest Experiment Station, pp. 525–532.

Howell 2010.

Monroe 1968.

Navarro-Sigüenza, A. G., and A. T. Peterson. 2007. *Lophostrix cristata* (búho cuerno blanco) residencia permanente distribución potencial. In *Mapas de las Aves de México Basados en WWW*, ed. A. G. Navarro and A. T. Peterson. Final report, SNIB-CONABIO project no. CE015. México DF.

Patten et al. 2011.

Storer, R. W. 1972. The juvenile plumage and relationships of *Lophostrix cristata*. *Auk* 89 (2): 452–455.

Wink et al. 2009.

SPECTACLED OWL
Pulsatrix perspicillata
Alpha code: SPEO

LENGTH: 17–20 in. (42–53 cm)

WINGSPAN: 30–36 in. (76–91 cm)

MASS: Moderate reversed size dimorphism; females of *P. p. saturata* average 14 percent larger than males. Average, male: 25.7 oz. (729 g); range 23.1–28.2 oz. (655–800 g). Average, female: 29.4 oz. (834 g); range 17.6–34.6 oz. (500–982g).[1]

LONGEVITY: Little information. In captivity it may live up to 25 years.

Large, strong, and stunningly plumaged, the Spectacled Owl is one of the handsomest raptors in the world. Widespread in primarily moist lowland forests from southern Mexico across much of South America, it is a generalist hunter, taking prey that ranges from insects and large spiders to mammals the size of agoutis, opossums, and, on rare occasions, three-toed sloths, but its diet is mostly composed of rodents and birds, including smaller owls. Its juvenal plumage is especially striking, but despite many claims to the contrary, it does not require up to 5 years to develop.

SYSTEMATICS, TAXONOMY, AND ETYMOLOGY

The Spectacled Owl has two (or three, depending on classification) close relatives in the genus *Pulsatrix,* all sharing the same large-headed, tuftless build with prominent facial markings and similarly powerful feet. *Pulsatrix*'s place in owl taxonomy was unresolved by a recent molecular phylogenetic analysis, but the study did suggest it lay somewhere

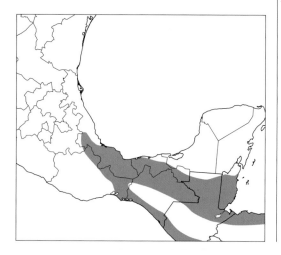

Large and unmistakable, the Spectacled Owl inhabits lowland forests in Middle and South America. The subspecies found in southern Mexico, *P. p. saturata,* has a black head and dark buff undersides, often with fine, dark barring. *(Costa Rica. Glenn Bartley)*

between *Megascops* and *Strix.* The authors recommended moving *Pulsatrix* from its traditional place in the tribe Strigini and placing it in a newly designated tribe, Pulsatrigini, along with the poorly examined genus *Lophostrix,* with which it shares skeletal features and juvenal plumage characteristics.

Up to six subspecies have been described, although only three are widely recognized. Of these, only one, *P. p. saturata,* the "Sooty Spectacled Owl," is found in our coverage area, ranging from Veracruz and northern Oaxaca south to the Pacific coast of southwestern Panama. It differs from other subspecies in being slightly larger, having a black (not brownish) head and bib, and more richly buff underparts with fine, dark barring. One subspecies, *P. p. pulsatrix* from southeastern South America, is sometimes elevated to species status.

ETYMOLOGY: *Pulsa-* comes from the Latin *pulsator* or *pulsare,* "to pulsate," referring to its rhythmic vocalization, while *-trix* is the feminizing form of otherwise masculine nouns ending in *-tor.* The common name refers to the white facial markings, as does the specific name, *perspicillata,* which is Latin for "spectacled."

SPANISH: *Búho de anteojos, lechuza de anteojos*

DISTRIBUTION

BREEDING SEASON: Uncommon to fairly common resident in wooded habitat (though locally rare thanks to deforestation, despite an alleged higher tolerance for fragmentation than some large woodland owls, but see "Habitat and Niche"). Found in swamp forests, evergreen tropical forests, and semideciduous forests from sea level to 1,500 ft. (457 m) in Oaxaca. Northernmost historical record from Sierra de Tuxtla, Veracruz, but more regularly from southern Veracruz and northern Oaxaca south and east through central Chiapas; rarer along Pacific coast of Oaxaca and Chiapas. A handful of sight records from northern Guatemala suggest it may be present but rare in the Mexican Yucatán.

MIGRATION AND MOVEMENTS: No evidence of migratory behavior or elevational movements. No information on juvenile dispersal.

DISTRIBUTION OUTSIDE THE COVERAGE AREA: Widespread tropical forest owl, found south through Panama and into South America along the Pacific coast to northwestern Peru, as well as everywhere east of the Andes south to southern Bolivia and northern Argentina.

DESCRIPTION AND IDENTIFICATION

Large and spectacularly marked, the Spectacled Owl is one of the most recognizable raptors in the Neotropics, and the subspecies found in southern Mexico, *P. p. saturata,* is especially attractive, with dramatic contrast between its black head, white facial markings, and finely barred, more richly cinnamon belly.

BASIC (ADULT) PLUMAGE: No sexual differences. Head blackish with bright, white eyebrows and rictal bristles, and a broad creamy band encircling the lower half of the black facial disk. Back and upperparts dark brown, with somewhat paler, indistinct graybrown markings on the back and wings, including the coverts, which vary in intensity between individuals. Flight feathers and tail are dark blackish brown, narrowly barred with paler brown above and grayish below.

A broad, blackish brown bib crosses the chest, below which the undersides are suffused with pale cinnamon, often with fine horizontal barring on the flanks or extending into the belly. Bill yellowish or greenish; irises yellow to yellow-orange; toes buffy white.

JUVENAL PLUMAGE: The juvenile Spectacled Owl undergoes one of the most dramatic plumage transitions of any raptor, nocturnal or diurnal—but despite an oft-repeated claim that this progression requires up to 5 years, observations of captive-reared chicks suggest adult plumage is attained in a much more normal 9 to 12 months.[2]

The nestling's gray-white natal down is replaced by a long, silky coat of pure white feathers, contrasting with the black facial disk and chin. The dark flight feathers resemble those of the adult and contrast with juvenal greater wing coverts that are fringed with long wisps of down and broadly tipped and barred with white. The lesser coverts are similarly lax and downy.

The call of a Spectacled Owl is one of the weirder sounds of the Neotropical rain forest—a throbbing call like someone shaking a long saw blade. *(Costa Rica. Kevin Schafer/VIREO)*

The juvenile Spectacled Owl starts with a coat of long, pure white feathers similar to the plumage of the young Crested Owl. With time, the adult feathers emerge, eventually leaving only a ruff of white around the head, as in this immature bird. Despite claims that the transition requires up to 5 years, most Spectacled Owls acquire adult plumage by about 9 months of age. *(Costa Rica. Steve Easley)*

Adult body plumage begins to appear on the belly and chest. In the final stages, the bird retains a white head with black mask, in contrast with adult body plumage, including a partial dark bib. Emerging adult head feathers gradually replace much of the remaining white on the head, leaving the white eyebrows and lower facial disk rim; at the same time, long, white rictal bristles emerge to complete the facial markings.

SIMILAR SPECIES: None in our region for the adult Spectacled Owl. The adult Crested Owl's white eyebrows extend to the tip of the long ear tufts, while the Spectacled Owl's end at the edge of the facial disk. The juvenal plumage of the Crested Owl, however, is remarkably similar to that of an immature

Spectacled Owl. The young Crested Owl has short, rather inconspicuous white ear tufts that are lacking in the juvenile Spectacled Owl, and which give the head a squarer appearance; its facial disk is also more noticeably rusty instead of black.

VOCALIZATIONS

The fast-throbbing call of the Spectacled Owl, consisting of 7 to 15 notes, is often described as a knocking sound, but it is softer, more muffled and otherworldly than that description might suggest. Rather, the call sounds like someone rapidly shaking a long metal saw blade or similar piece of sheet metal: *wuup-WUU-WUU-WUU-WUU-WUU-wuu-wuu,* falling off a bit at the end. Pairs often duet, the male's lower voice and the female's higher calls sometimes overlapping in no particular order, or one seamlessly finishing the other's call to form an especially long, single vocalization.

Females also give a higher, harsher two-syllable *huEEe-oooo* that falls off in pitch and is similar to the even higher-pitched juvenile begging call.

HABITAT AND NICHE

A large and powerful species with a generalist's diet, the Spectacled Owl is second in size in its range only to the Great Horned Owl and is usually the largest owl of any species in the moist lowland forests it inhabits. It is most common in thick, tropical, semi-deciduous and riparian forests (including tidal swamps), and can occur in densely wooded traditional coffee farms, large forest patches, gallery forests in savannahs, and other more-open or disturbed areas. Found from sea level to about 1,500 ft. (457 m), higher in Central American mountains, where it may occur up to 4,900 ft. (1,500 m).

The Spectacled Owl is said to be more tolerant of forest openings and clearings than some large owls (especially the Crested Owl), and in Costa Rica it reportedly often hunts along such openings. But an examination of a limited number of pellets from Oaxaca, collected from a roost only 430 yds. (400 m) from the forest edge, found no prey species common to fields—only those routinely found in forests (see "Diet," below). Research from Costa Rica also suggests it may not be as tolerant of fragmentation as previously believed, and a study of habitat use in Chiapas found a strong correlation between the presence of mature trees and Spectacled Owls.

DIET: Wide-ranging, from insects, large spiders, and crustaceans to reptiles and amphibians, birds, and mammals—including some that weigh considerably more than the owl. Thorough dietary studies are lacking, however. Pellets from a Oaxaca roost were dominated by the remains of naked-tail

Big and powerful, second only to the Great Horned Owl in size in its region, the Spectacled Owl takes prey as small as insects and spiders and as large as agoutis and sloths that may weigh up to 10 lbs. (4.5 kg). *(Honduras. Kevin Loughlin/Wildside Nature Tours)*

climbing rats, an arboreal forest species weighing 10–11 oz. (280–360 g), or roughly half the weight of the owls that were preying on them; Spectacled Owls in Panama are also known to take this rodent, which may be too heavy for other rain forest owls to tackle.

Other mammalian prey includes mouse opossums (and large Neotropical opossums), rice rats, agoutis and acouchis, skunks, and rabbits. They sometimes take bats, and researchers in Brazil observed greater spear-nosed bats mobbing a roosting Spectacled Owl near a bat roost—the first time bats of any species have been seen mobbing a predator.

Agoutis generally weigh 3–9 lbs. (1.3–4 kg), and even at the smaller end of the scale, that is a substantial target for an owl that weighs no more than about 2 lbs. (1 kg) itself. But biologists in Panama documented what they believe was predation by a Spectacled Owl on an adult female three-toed sloth

estimated to weigh 7.7–10 lb. (3.5–4.5 kg), basing that conclusion on patterns of puncture wounds and consumption. If true, this is by far the heaviest prey species known for this species of owl. The sloth was apparently attacked on the ground while the mammal was defecating—a risky and evolutionarily inexplicable weekly event in the life of this otherwise arboreal mammal.

Spectacled Owls take a fair number of medium-size birds, including jays, motmots, smaller owls, and young oropendolas snatched from their long, oriole-like nests. Arthropods taken include large spiders, katydids, and click, scarab, and darkling beetles.

NESTING AND BREEDING

Cavity nesters about which relatively little is known in the wild, Spectacled Owls have long been bred in captivity and are common in zoo and aviary collections.

In the wild, the Spectacled Owl is a secondary cavity nester dependent on large woodpecker excavations and naturally occurring rot holes. Nesting usually coincides with the dry season or the start of the wet. Most records are for Apr. through June (a female collected in 1961 in late June in Oaxaca was sitting on 2 eggs), but nesting may be later in the year in Central American populations.

The Spectacled Owl usually lays 2 or 3 eggs, which hatch after about 35 days of incubation. The young are said to fledge in 5 to 6 weeks, leaving the nest before they're able to fly, although a captive chick left its nest box for the first time at 7 weeks, abandoning the cavity entirely by 10 weeks of age. Chicks may remain dependent on the adults for up to a year. Reportedly only one chick usually survives to independence, but whether this is the result of siblicide is not clear.

BEHAVIOR

Nocturnal. Daytime roosts are usually in thick cover, often in riparian forests; birds roost singly or in pairs, and fledglings may roost with their parents until independent. Little is known about its ecology and behavior in the wild, though it is presumed to be a perch hunter. In Amazonian forests its density has been estimated at .5 to .75 pairs per 247 acres (100 hectares), but similar estimates are lacking for its Mexican range.

STATUS

Although widespread and uncommon to fairly common farther south, the Spectacled Owl is listed as "endangered" in Mexico, where it is restricted to three states and possibly a fourth. It is considered rare in primary lowland forests at Palenque, Chiapas. Little is known about population trends and threats, although deforestation and fragmentation likely pose the most serious hazard to its conservation. Range-wide, it is listed as "least concern" by IUCN/BirdLife, and Partners in Flight estimates the global population in the 500,000 to 4.9 million range.

NOTES

1. Whitacre 2012.

2. G. Morgan, pers. comm.

BIBLIOGRAPHY

Beavers, R. A. 1992. *The Birds of Tikal.* College Station, TX: Texas A&M University Press.

BirdLife International. 2015. *Pulsatrix perspicillata.* In IUCN Red List of Threatened Species, version 2014.3, http://www.iucnredlist.org/details/22689180/0.

Kelso, L. 1934. A key to the owls of the genus *Pulsatrix* Kaup. *Auk* 51:234–236.

Knörnschild, M., and M. Tschapka. 2012. Predator mobbing behaviour in the greater spear-nosed bat. *Chiroptera Neotropical* 18:1132–1135.

Navarro-Sigüenza, A. G., and A. T. Peterson. 2007. *Pulsatrix perspicillata* (búho anteojos) residencia permanente distribución potencial. In *Mapas de las Aves de México Basados en WWW,* ed. A. G. Navarro and A. T. Peterson. Final report, SNIB-CONABIO project no. CE015. México DF.

Rivera-Rivera, E., P. L. Enríquez, A. Flamenco-Sandoval, and J. L. Rangel-Salazar. 2012. Occupancy and abundance of nocturnal raptors (Strigidae) in the Selva El Ocote Biosphere Reserve, Chiapas, Mexico. *Revista Mexicana de Biodiveridad* 83:742–752.

Thiollay, J.-M. 1994. Structure, density and rarity in an Amazonian rainforest bird community. *Journal of Tropical Ecology* 10:449–481.

Voirin, J. B., R. Kays, M. D. Lowman, and M. Wikelski. 2009. Evidence for three-toed sloth (*Bradypus variegatus*) predation by spectacled owl (*Pulsatrix perspicillata*). *Edentata* 8–10:15–20.

Wilkins, L. 2005. Breeding the spectacled owl (*Pulsatrix perspicillata*) at Drayton Manor Zoo. *World Owl Trust Newsletter* 30:9–10.

Wink et al. 2009.

The Great Horned Owl has the widest range of any owl in the Western Hemisphere and one of the widest distributions of any bird of prey in the world. *(Alberta. Gerrit Vyn)*

GREAT HORNED OWL
Bubo virginianus
Alpha code: GHOW

LENGTH: 18–26 in. (46–63 cm)

WINGSPAN: 49–62 in. (124–157 cm)

MASS: Moderate reversed dimorphism. Overall (three studies, multiple subspecies combined): Average, male: 2.9 lbs. (1,304 g).[1] Average, male: 2.5 lbs. (1,142 g). Average, female: 3.4 lbs. (1,509 g).[2] Average, male: 3.2 lbs. (1,449 g); range 3–3.7 lbs. (1,384–1,692 g). Average, female: 3.5 lbs. (1,597 g); range 3.2–4.1 lbs. (1,454–1,876 g).[3]

Mass by selected subspecies:

virginianus: Average, male: 2.7 lbs. (1,237 g); range 2.2–3.5 lbs. (985–1,588 g). Average, female: 3.9 lbs. (1,768 g); range 3.1–5.5 lbs. (1,417–2,503 g).[4]

subarcticus (*"wapacuthu"*): Average, male: 2.7 lbs. (1,237 g); range 2.3–3.1 lbs. (1,035–1,389 g). Average, female: 3.4 lbs. (1,556 g); range 3–4.4 lbs. (1,357–2,000 g).[4]

pallescens: Average, male: 2 lbs. (914 g); range 1.6–2.8 lbs. (724–1,257 g). Average, female: 2.5 lbs. (1,142 g); range 1.8–3.4 lbs. (801–1,550 g).[4]

"occidentalis": (*pinorum* and *pallescens*, in part): Average, male: 2.5 lbs. (1,154 g); range 1.9–3.2 lbs. (865–1,460 g). Average, female: 3.4 lbs. (1,555g); range 2.4–4.5 lbs. (1,112–2,046 g).[4]

pacificus: Average, male: 2.2 lbs. (992 g); range 1.5–2.8 lbs. (680–1,272 g). Average, female: 2.9 lbs. (1,312 g); range 1.8–3.7 lbs. (825–1,668 g).[4]

LONGEVITY: The average age at re-encounter for banded Great Horned Owls is 2.35 years, while for those more than a year old at re-encounter, the average age is 4 years. The longevity record for a wild Great Horned Owl is one banded in Ohio in 1977 and captured 28 years later because of an injury and placed in captivity. About two dozen other banded Great Horned Owls of 20 years or more have been documented. In captivity they routinely live to 25 or 30 years, and a female at the San Francisco Zoo died in 2012 shortly after turning 50, which appears to be a record for the species.

Big, powerful, and ubiquitous, the Great Horned Owl must rank as one of the most successful raptors in the world, at least when judged by the sheer area it encompasses and the breadth of habitats it calls home.

From the Brooks Range in Alaska and subarctic Labrador in the East, all the way to the southern cone of South America, this opportunistic hunter is at home in woodlands, boreal bogs, deserts, farmlands, cloud forests, coastal mangrove swamps, arid scrub, riparian corridors, prairie shelterbelts, and city parks, to name but a few habitats. Only a handful of other birds of prey—and arguably no other owl—exceeds it in both geographic and ecological span.

Famously open-minded when it comes to food, capable of tackling prey as large as geese or as small as crickets, the Great Horned Owl is on average very much a hunter of mammals. Dietary studies have shown a particular focus on lagomorphs (rabbits and hares) and small and midsize rodents like rats, mice, and voles. But more often than not, a hungry Great Horned is prepared to take a chance on anything unwary that comes within range of its large, strong talons.

SYSTEMATICS, TAXONOMY, AND ETYMOLOGY

Until the Snowy Owl was recently moved from *Nyctea* to *Bubo*—a change not all specialists accept—the Great Horned was considered the only Western Hemisphere example of the highly successful eagle-owl group from the Old World, where some 16 species occupy Africa and Eurasia.

Given its enormous range both geographically and ecologically, it is no wonder that the Great Horned Owl shows complex regional variation.

Great Horned Owls are a species of enormous regional variation in size and plumage. This bird, perched on a spruce in Churchill, Manitoba, is the huge, pale race *B. v. subarcticus*. (Manitoba. Tom Johnson)

The number of generally recognized subspecies (up to 16) is second only to the 19 named races of the Burrowing Owl—and may exceed the latter, since scientists suspect a number of the Burrowing Owl forms are not valid. Subspecies vary by size, with the largest individuals in the most northerly regions and the Midwest, and the smallest in Mesoamerica, and by coloration, with the darkest in humid environments and the palest in dry or subarctic habitats. While subspecies at their extremes can be quite

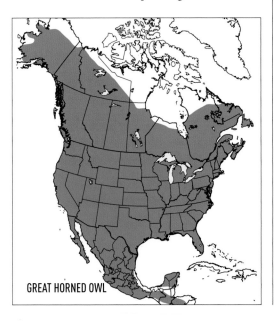

GREAT HORNED OWL

GREAT HORNED OWL
SUBSPECIES

Uncertain affinities

B. v. lagophonus
B. v. subarcticus
B. v. saturatus
B. v. heterocnemis
B. v. pinorum
B. v. virginianus
B. v. pacificus
B. v. elachistus
B. v. pallescens
B. v. mayensis
B. v. mesembrinus

distinct, clinal variation makes the lines of demarcation especially fuzzy, and there is a great deal of uncertainty about the status of some named races, one of which was described as recently as 2008.

The subspecies below, from our coverage area, generally follow Artuso et al. (2014) and Dickerman and Johnson (2008).

B. v. heterocnemis: Breeding range Newfoundland, Labrador, and northern Quebec; irregular in winter as far south as southern Ontario and southern New England. Sooty and dark, with a dark gray-brown facial disk and heavy, blackish breast markings.

B. v. virginianus: Breeding range Canadian Maritimes west to Minnesota (expanding into North Dakota) and southeastern South Dakota, south through the eastern Great Plains to oak/pine-forested areas of central and southern Texas (overlapping with *pallescens,* which is in xeric habitat), and along the eastern seaboard to Florida. Richly colored with strong rusty tones, sharply distinct barring on the underparts, and buffy rust feet, sometimes with fine barring.

B. v. subarcticus: The palest subspecies and among the largest. Breeds from northern Ontario (Hudson Bay) west to the Mackenzie River in the Northwest Territories and south along the eastern front of the Rockies to at least Montana, Wyoming, and North Dakota; southern and eastern extent of range unclear. Can occur in winter as far south as New Jersey. Pale, with tawny tones reduced or essentially absent in some birds, some of which may appear almost as bleached as a Snowy Owl. The obsolete and erroneous name "*wapacuthu*" was once applied to this subspecies. Birds from northern Ontario, which are more heavily barred below with black, have been described as a separate form, "*B. v. scalariventris,*" but this race is not widely recognized.

B. v. pallescens: Southern and western Texas west to southeastern and central California, north to western Kansas (possibly Nebraska?), and south through Mexico to western Veracruz and Guerrero. Smaller and paler than the nominate race, with bleached, sandy coloration (mixed with rufous tones on the crown and upper back) and white, unmarked feet. Darker individuals inhabit the higher elevations of Mexico, approaching *mesembrinus* in color. Overlaps with *virginianus* in Texas, inhabiting drier habitat, and with *pinorum* in Arizona and New Mexico, inhabiting lowland areas.

Not described for science until 2008, the subspecies *B. v. pinorum* is found from the Mexico border north to at least central Washington in dry coniferous forests at high elevations. *(Colorado. Scott Rashid)*

B. v. pinorum: Breeds in dry coniferous (especially ponderosa pine) forests from at least Washington and the Snake River basin in Idaho to northeastern California, Nevada, Utah, western Colorado, northeastern Arizona, and northern New Mexico; south disjunctly at high elevations in Sky Island ranges to at least the Chiricahua Mountains (Arizona) and Guadalupe Mountains (Texas), possibly into northern Mexico. Some elevational migration in winter. Medium gray overall. Paler and more lightly barred below than *lagophonus,* with white or lightly mottled feet; more heavily barred below than *pallescens,* with blacker crown and back feathers. Described in 2008.

B. v. lagophonus, found from central Idaho through the Yukon and Alaska, is notable for the heavy black markings on its head and upperparts. This pair was nesting in a cliff on the Columbia Plateau. *(Washington. Paul Bannick/VIREO)*

B. v. lagophonus: Breeds in the Rocky Mountains north of the Snake River, west to eastern Oregon and north through montane forests in British Columbia and northern Yukon to the Yukon River drainage of west-central Alaska. To New Mexico and Texas in winter. Gray to brownish gray with heavy black markings on the crown and back; Alaskan birds average larger. Paler than *saturatus* but more heavily barred than *pacificus,* with a rustier facial disk. (Includes "*B. v. algistus*" along Alaskan coast of Bristol Bay and Bering Sea to Seward Peninsula, likely an invalid subspecies; little or no breeding habitat in that area.)

B. v. saturatus: Resident in coastal forests from northern California to southeastern Alaska. Large. The darkest of the subspecies in our area, its plumage is suffused with sooty tones, the underparts heavily barred and blotched, and the legs and feet mottled. Losing ground to *pinorum* as old-growth forests are logged.

B. v. pacificus: Resident from inland northern California to northwestern Baja. Intermediate in degree of barring between the heavily marked *saturatus* and the indistinctly barred *pallescens,* and shows more rufous tones in the facial disk than the latter. Smaller than *saturatus.*

B. v. elachistus: Resident in southern Baja California. Similar to *pacificus* but markedly smaller.

B. v. mayensis: Resident in arid and coastal scrub on Yucatán Peninsula from north-

The coastal rain-forest race of the Great Horned Owl, *B. v. saturatus,* is among the darkest subspecies and depends on mature forests to an unusual degree for a Great Horned Owl. Logging is fragmenting its habitat, and subspecies from the east are pushing into its range. *(British Columbia. Glenn Bartley/VIREO)*

ern Campeche across Yucatán and south to southern Quintana Roo. Small, with a notably short wing. Pale; coloration similar to *pallescens,* but with sides, flanks, and undertail coverts more neatly barred, and upperparts with less gray and more dull tawny tones. Paler than *mesembrinus.*

- *B. v. mesembrinus:* Resident in a variety of forested habitat from the Isthmus of Tehuantepec east to western Panama. Larger, darker, and with more rufous or tawny tones than *mayensis;* much smaller, blacker above, and more heavily and coarsely barred below than *pallescens.*

ETYMOLOGY: The genus name is from the Latin *bubo,* "a horned owl" or "owl of ill omen" (referring to the Eurasian Eagle-Owl) and was first applied to the genus in 1806 by the French zoologist André Marie Constant Duméril, replacing *Strix.* The species name refers to Virginia, from which J. F. Gmelin described the type specimen in 1788, although the specific location is unknown. The common name refers to both the large size of this raptor and its prominent ear tufts.

SPANISH: *Búho cornudo, tecolote cornudo, tecolotón* (Chiapas), *búho real* (Chiapas), *búho grande* (Yucatán Peninsula)
FRENCH: *Grand-duc d'Amerique*
INUKITUT: *Unnuasiuti*
IÑUPIATUN: *Nukisuǧaq*
YUCATEC MAYAN: (*B. v. mayensis*): *Tunkuluchuj*

DISTRIBUTION

BREEDING SEASON: Found in virtually all forested, scrub, or desert habitats from subarctic timberline south to tropical lowlands, this is one of the most adaptable raptors in the Western Hemisphere. It's hard to find a place without a resident pair of Great Horned Owls.

The northern extent of the breeding range stretches from Newfoundland across northern Labrador and Quebec (not including the Labrador and Ungava Peninsulas), including most of James Bay; northwest inland of Hudson Bay and along the northern edges of Great Slave and Great Bear Lakes to the lower Mackenzie River; west through the Brooks Range and south to the lower Yukon/Kuskokwim drainages to the Alaska Peninsula. Absent from Kodiak Island and the Queen Charlotte Islands (Haida Gwaii).

In Mexico, rare or absent from Gulf tropical lowlands (except subspecies *mayensis* in northern Yucatán) and the Pacific coastal plain in Chiapas.

NONBREEDING SEASON: Some irruptive or migratory movement from northern populations occurs but

With a wingspan of up to 5 ft. (1.5 m) and weighing up to 5.5 lbs. (2,500 g), the Great Horned Owl is eclipsed by only the Snowy Owl as the heaviest and most powerful owl in the Western Hemisphere. This subspecies, *B. v. pallescens,* is found in arid regions from the western Great Plains through most of Mexico. (Arizona. Tom Johnson)

remains within the overall breeding range of the species (see "Migration and Movements," below).

MIGRATION AND MOVEMENTS: Generally resident, although northern populations undergo irruptive (and perhaps even predictably migratory) movements that are largely masked by the ubiquity of Great Horned Owls throughout North America. Such movements are most noticeable and well documented among the northern subspecies like *subarcticus* and *lagophonus,* which tend to differ visibly from resident populations to the south. But one specimen of the darkly marked, supposedly resident Pacific Northwest race *saturatus* has been documented in New Mexico—with a desert cottontail in its stomach to strongly suggest it was living there naturally before its death.

Great Horned Owl irruptions appear primarily tied to declines in snowshoe hare population cycles and coincide with the more-visible irruptions of Northern Goshawks that similarly depend on the hares. In low-hare years significant numbers of banded Great Horned Owls from the Canadian prairies make irruptive flights with a strong southeasterly direction as far south as Minnesota, Nebraska, Kansas, and Iowa—and in one exceptional event, almost 1,300 mi. (2,092 km) from Alberta to Illinois. (An even longer record in the banding database—1,995 mi. / 3,210 km, from New York to Oregon—should be considered suspect, because the band number was read in the field with a scope rather than in the hand.)

POST-FLEDGING DISPERSAL: Great Horned Owls have a long period of post-fledging dependence on the adults, with the parents supplying food well into late summer and early autumn. Juveniles in southwestern Yukon dispersed from their parents' territories in Sept. and Oct., while in more southerly populations such dispersal peaks in Nov. and Dec. Dispersal distance in northern populations appears to be tied to snowshoe hare abundance, with young owls moving shorter distances in years with high hare numbers (averaging 26 mi. / 43 km), than those with few hares (averaging 35 mi. / 57 km).

DISTRIBUTION OUTSIDE THE COVERAGE AREA: South through Central America (very rare) to South America, generally avoiding humid lowland forests; absent or rare from much of the Amazon and Orinoco drainages. Found at moderate and high elevations in the northern Andes and in lowlands in southeastern South America. The form found in arid and semiarid forests and scrub along the Pacific coast from Peru to Tierra del Fuego, *B. v. magellanicus,* is often elevated to species status, the "Magellanic Horned Owl."

Introduced in 1927 from California to Hiva Oa in the Marquesa Islands (French Polynesia) for rat control, where instead the owls may have contributed to the decline and disappearance of native birds, especially fruit pigeons.

DESCRIPTION AND IDENTIFICATION

The Great Horned Owl is everyone's mental archetype of owl, with its imposing size, prominent ear tufts, and large yellow eyes. Regional differences are reflected primarily in the intensity of blackish markings and the degree of rusty or tawny tones in the plumage, especially the facial disk, head, and chest and coloration of the feet. There is no evidence for color morphs, and occasional abnormally light or dark specimens often prove on closer inspection to be irruptive birds from other regional populations.

BASIC (ADULT) PLUMAGE: Sexes alike, although females may average darker overall, with heavier barring on the underwing coverts and thinner barring on the secondaries. The description that follows applies to the nominate race, *B. v. virginianus.*

Overall dark brown, suffused with rich cinnamon tones on the head, face, and chest. Crown brown-rust, heavily marked with blackish mottling, nape with bright rufous. Ear tufts moderately long and black, with rusty inner margins. Eyebrows narrow and white, rictal bristles grayish. Upperparts dark brown mottled with black and suffused with tawny.

For generations, the Great Horned Owl has been known as the "hoot owl," for its deep, resonant hoots. The female's call is longer but higher-pitched despite her bigger size. *(Florida. Arthur Morris/VIREO)*

Greater upperwing coverts grayer, primary coverts dark brown and indistinctly marked. Underwing coverts creamy and rust with heavy dark barring. Primaries and secondaries dark brown with indistinct dark bars above, buff with narrow blackish bars (wider on outer primaries) below. Tail medium brown above, buff below, with five or six dark bars.

Facial disk bright chestnut, sharply rimmed in black, with a narrow white chin mark extending along the lower rim of the disk. Throat mottled black and rust. Upper chest with a broad white bib that tapers to the central chest and bordered below by an uneven band of large black blotches. Underparts washed with rich cinnamon, especially on the upper breast, and heavily barred and blotched with black. Feet tawny or buff, often with fine dark spotting or barring. Talons and bill black, irises clear yellow.

JUVENAL PLUMAGE: Natal down pure white tinged with gray on the back and wings, replaced between 1 and 3 weeks of age with the long, soft gray-tawny mesoptile down. Flight feathers begin to emerge from their sheaths at a month of age and are fully grown by 8 or 9 weeks, when mesoptile plumage has been replaced by juvenal body plumage. Underparts are grayish washed in rusty tones and narrowly barred; upperparts grayer with wider, more distinct barring. Ear tufts small and indistinct, facial disk bright rufous. By about 5 months, juvenal

Great Horned Owls do not exhibit strong reversed size dimorphism, but when the pair is perched together, the size difference between the male and female becomes apparent. *(Manitoba, Christian Artuso)*

plumage has been replaced by first basic plumage, which resembles that of adult. However, the central tail feathers tend to show wide, dark bars (versus more and narrower bars or mottling on adult tail feathers), and the wing feathers show fewer and relatively wider bars (versus narrower, more closely spaced bars on adults).

SIMILAR SPECIES: Any of the eared owls may be mistaken for this species by inexperienced observers, and screech-owls of any species are often assumed to be "baby horned owls." A more legitimate ID challenge is posed by the Long-eared Owl, which resembles the Great Horned in general coloration and shape but is only two-thirds the size of the bigger species and more noticeably slender, especially when it stretches upright and compresses its plumage in alarm.

VOCALIZATIONS

The Great Horned Owl is the quintessential "hoot owl," the territorial call of both sexes being a string of five to seven deep, resonant hoots, given with the mouth closed and gular sac inflated, greatly expanding the white chest bib. One naturalist likened the quality of the call to "the sound of a distant foghorn, the far-away whistle of a locomotive, or the barking of a large dog in the distance. . . . The ordinary note, when the owl is not excited, is a prolonged, soft, somewhat tremulous, and subdued hoot, with little or no accent, *whoo-hoo-ho-o-o,* or, longer, *who-ho-o-o, whoo-hoo-o-o, whoo.*"[5]

Like many owls, Great Horned Owl chicks often leave the nest weeks before they can fly. These "branchers" often wind up on the ground, but thanks to attentive parents, most survive to fledge and fly. *(Alberta. Gerrit Vyn)*

Great Horned Owls thrive in the kinds of fragmented habitats humans create, and generally avoid the interiors of large, mature forests. *(Washington. Gerrit Vyn)*

Territorial hooting is most common in autumn and winter, in the run-up to courtship. Paired birds often call antiphonally, the larger female with a higher-pitched voice despite her size (and because of her smaller syrinx). The female gives a longer call of six to nine notes versus four to six for the male. The number of notes, and the intervals between them, are individually distinct and uniform and can allow identification of individuals (by use of spectrograms, not by ear).

Researchers have categorized several other hoot variants. Females may drop the last note of the hoot string, which may be an indication of sexual arousal, while the staccato hoot, given by males and females alike and which may end with a territorial hoot, seems to indicate excitement and may precede copulation.

Nestlings and fledglings give a harsh, repeated shriek, lasting about a second and sometimes slightly bisyllabic, as a food-begging call and a similarly grating call when threatened. Adult owls give squawk or double-squawk calls, which may serve as contact calls between mates or with chicks.

Like most owls, Great Horneds make a rapid, high-pitched chittering call when in pain or distress, and sometimes in less dire straits of agitation. They also hiss and make loud bill snaps when frightened or distressed.

HABITAT AND NICHE

This is by far the most adaptable owl in the Western Hemisphere, to such an extent that it might be simpler to list the habitats and situations where Great Horned Owls are generally *not* found than to list those where they *are*. It's a short list—Arctic and subarctic tundra well beyond the edge of tree lines

(and alpine zones above timberline, including the Andes above about 14,500 ft. / 4,400 m), extensive areas of completely treeless prairie, and dense lowland rain forest. That's about it.

Almost everywhere else, Great Horned Owls may be found in varying degrees of abundance and are often the most common (or next most common) species of owl. They thrive in the kinds of fragmented habitat that humans have created. Great Horned Owls, which tend to avoid the interiors of large, mature forests, benefited when those tracts were cut into countless smaller pieces by roads, utility lines, developments, logging, and agriculture. Similarly, they were likely much rarer in parts of the Great Plains in presettlement days but have followed the expansion of shelterbelts, fencerows, and tree-lined ranch houses and small-town backyards into every corner of grasslands that once offered little in the way of wooded habitat.

A variety of studies confirm the Great Horned Owl's preference for habitat with a mix of forest and open country. In southern California, they were found most often in oak-sycamore woodlands and disturbed grasslands, while in high-elevation conifer forests in Wyoming, researchers found Great Horned Owls most commonly in mature lodgepole pine stands, but usually close to natural openings, and in tracts that were less dense, with a more open canopy. Wet meadows, though rare landscape features overall in the Wyoming forests, were present in almost 40 percent of Great Horned Owl territories.

In Manitoba, Great Horneds tended to avoid forested muskeg, with a preference for study plots that included clear-cuts or old burns, and were frequently found near agricultural areas. In Alberta, they were most often found in agricultural areas with moderate amounts (roughly one-third to two-thirds) of forest cover, and the highest populations were in areas with a diverse mix of habitats and more edge habitat; they were least common in either unbroken forest or open fields. And in northern New Jersey, a study in a forested wilderness area abutting urbanized landscapes showed that Great Horned Owls gravitated to the more fragmented and disturbed habitats, avoiding the deep, unbroken interior where Barred Owls were the more common large owl. A study of nest sites in the Northeast also found Great Horned Owls using sites closer to roads, buildings, and forest edges.

DIET: Along with its ability to adapt to a wide variety of habitats, the Great Horned Owl has an extraordinarily plastic approach to dining. Mammals make up the bulk of its diet, followed by birds. But reptiles, amphibians, fish, crustaceans, large insects, arachnids, earthworms, carrion—all end up in a Great Horned's stomach to greater or lesser degrees.

Prey selection seems to depend on whatever is most readily available. Great Horned Owls hunting urban parks in Seattle depend—perhaps not surprisingly—on Norway and black rats, almost to the exclusion of anything else, while voles and deer mice make up almost 95 percent of the diet of those nesting on cliffs next to farmland in northern California. In the boreal forest of Alaska and Canada, the large northern subspecies may prey on little else but snowshoe hares when those animals are near the peak of their 10-year population cycle, then switch to a more diverse diet when the hare numbers crash.

Researchers who combined studies from a number of areas in North America looked at average Great Horned Owl diets in terms of biomass, rather than the number of individual animals eaten—a single heavy animal, after all, is worth more, nutritionally, than a number of much smaller ones. They found that mammals made up 90 to 94 percent of the biomass of Great Horned Owl diets, whether in the hardwood forests of Pennsylvania or Oklahoma, the grasslands of Montana or Wisconsin, the dry foothills of California, or the spruce forests of Canada.

More specifically, hares and rabbits comprised 47 percent of the species's diet in temperate forests and roughly 55 percent in grasslands and arid shrublands; in boreal forests, where snowshoe hares are abundant, they were more than 70 percent of the total. Large rodents made up almost 40 percent of the biomass eaten by Great Horned Owls in temperate forests, about 25 percent in arid shrublands, and 12 percent or less in boreal forests and grasslands. Birds ranged from 5 to 11 percent, especially

Although they show a particular fondness for mammals, especially rabbits and hares, Great Horned Owls will eat almost any vertebrate (and some invertebrate) prey—like this one, pausing in messy mid-meal as it consumes an American Coot. (Arizona. Kevin Loughlin/Wildside Nature Tours)

waterfowl, grouse, and pheasants. In a study in the prairie pothole region of North Dakota, however, birds—especially ducks and grebes—formed up to 90 percent of some nesting owls' diet, while other wetland species like waterbirds, muskrats, and tiger salamanders were commonly taken.

One bizarre pellet, found in Pennsylvania, included an entire, intact primary wing feather from a male Ring-necked Pheasant, more than 7.5 in. (19 cm) long, around the lower quill of which was wadded a more traditional pellet of matted feathers and fur. Such finds aside, the intense gastric juices in the owl's stomach, combined with the delicacy of bird bones, may lead ornithologists to underestimate the frequency with which birds are eaten, if judging simply from bony remains in Great Horned Owl pellets.

Given their size and strength, Great Horned Owls are capable of taking birds as large as Canada Geese and Great Blue Herons, and nocturnal attacks on incubating herons have been documented in recent years thanks to automatic nest cameras.

The owls also pose a significant predation threat to other raptors, from smaller owls to large diurnal species like Red-tailed and Red-shouldered Hawks and Ospreys, especially incautious young birds that pick an exposed roost site after dark. Cannibalism by adults has been reported on rare occasions.

Insects and other arthropods made up a fraction of the biomass, which isn't surprising. But there are times when it pays even for a large raptor like a Great Horned Owl to feed on tiny prey, if they are abundant enough and easily enough captured. One Great Horned Owl in Texas was observed feeding for hours on hordes of field crickets swarming on the ground below a security light.

Fish show up sporadically in Great Horned Owl nests and pellets. In northeastern California, tui chub and Tahoe sucker bones and scales were found in owl pellets—possibly scavenged from nearby shorelines where dead fish often washed up. But in Pennsylvania, discarded heads of brown bullhead catfish were found below the nest and "butcher block" perch (where the male often dismembers and hands off prey to his mate) of a pair of Great Horned Owls, along with skull plates and the sharp pectoral spines of the catfish in a number of their pellets. Many bullheads were spawning in shallow water in a nearby pond, suggesting these fish were taken alive.

Great Horned Owls are famous for preying on skunks, although dietary studies suggest skunks are fairly infrequent prey items—but the olfactory reminder of a single encounter may linger for weeks.

While skunks are smelly, they don't pose much of a danger to an owl—especially compared with other, often surprisingly small, hazards. Other raptors are obviously dangerous; a Great Horned Owl that attacked an adult Red-shouldered Hawk in Georgia died, along with its prey, when the hawk's talons pierced the owl's jugular. Similarly, Great Horned Owls have been killed or incapacitated on a number of occasions by large snakes they tried to catch, like the 61-in. (1.5 m) black racer that strangled an attacking owl in Arkansas before succumbing to its own wounds. Great Horned Owls perforated by porcupine quills—from which they sometimes recovered—have been recorded on a number of occasions, including one from which more than 60 quills were removed.

Perhaps the strangest turnabout by an unlikely prey species, though, involved the case of an adult female Great Horned Owl found dead on the campus of the University of California at Berkeley. When she was necropsied, a California newt was found in her stomach. Such newts secrete tetrodotoxin from their skin, a potent neurotoxin capable of killing a large bird in minutes, and are considered the most toxic salamanders in the world. Hunting at night, the owl may have missed the newt's bright warning coloration, which usually scares off hungry birds.

Great Horned Owls and Red-tailed Hawks—both generalist, opportunistic predators that thrive in much the same fragmented, human-disturbed habitats—are often described as ecological analogs, diurnal and nocturnal mirrors of each other. When researchers have closely examined their diets, they have found broad overlap in general terms—but also significant differences in the particular species each raptor hunts in a given area, especially in the West. This suggests that they are not such close analogs as had been assumed.

NESTING AND BREEDING

Great Horned Owls are, with Bald Eagles, the earliest-nesting birds in North America, especially in the northern portions of their range, where they often settle on eggs months before the snow melts. Courtship and pair-bonding begin in autumn with increased territorial hooting, often initiated by the female, which intensifies in early winter. The pair bond is long-term and possibly for life, but there is little hard data on this aspect of the owl's breeding biology.

Although they don't use structures as frequently as Barn Owls, Great Horned Owls will take advantage of manmade nest sites, especially in a place like the Canadian prairies, where tree nests may be hard to find. (Manitoba. Christian Artuso)

Any large nest, from a magpie's, squirrel's or crow's up to a Bald Eagle's, may be appropriated by a Great Horned Owl—after which the original owner, even an eagle, finds it difficult to dislodge the powerful interloper. (Washington. Gerrit Vyn)

Great Horned Owls are secondary nest users, taking over existing raptor, corvid, heron, or mammal (primarily gray and fox squirrel) nests. Those built by Red-tailed Hawks, which are similar in size and occupy many of the same habitats as the owls, are an especially common target. But Great Horneds will use almost every "nest" imaginable, including cliff and quarry ledges, shallow caves, large cavities, snag hollows in old trees (which comprised more than 35 percent of nest sites in one Ohio study), abandoned buildings and barns, bridges, "witches' brooms" (infestations of dwarf mistletoe or several species of rust fungi in conifers), and rarely ground nests like hollow logs, clumps of vegetation, and old waterfowl nests.

Although not normally associated with artificial nest sites, Great Horned Owls readily accepted manmade platforms, ranging from old tires mounted just above the water's surface for Canada Geese, to larger, higher platforms built for Ospreys and Bald Eagles. While it's rare for anyone to build a nest platform especially for Great Horned Owls, they will adopt them easily, as a researcher in Ohio showed, attracting 53 nesting pairs over the years. Young owls sometimes make poor decisions in their first nesting season, such as one that occupied an old Blue Jay nest that quickly collapsed under the weight of the massive incubating raptor.

One advantage to the Great Horned Owl's extremely early nesting schedule may be having the pick of available nest sites; even large, aggressive raptors like Northern Goshawks have little chance of displacing an incubating female Great Horned Owl from an occupied nest, and few try. But nest sites can change hands: Arthur Cleveland Bent recounted a nest in Massachusetts in the early twentieth century that alternated for several years among Red-shouldered Hawks, Barred Owls, and Great Horned Owls, and another in Connecticut that was used by Great Horneds, Red-tailed and Cooper's Hawks, and Barred Owls in just 4 years.

Egg-laying begins by Nov. or Dec. in Florida and Alabama, but even in southern Ohio more than a third of clutches were initiated the last 10 days of Jan., and a quarter in the first week of Feb. If that seems incredibly early in a cold climate, consider that the earliest nests in this study—which may have involved older, more experienced parents—raised more chicks than those from later nests. Incubation begins with the first egg and averages 33 days. Typical clutch size is 2, but ranges from 1 to 5 eggs. Siblicide is rare but can occur when prey is scarce.

Breeding information for the Mexican subspecies is scanty. A fledgling of *B. v. mayensis,* capable of flying a short distance, was collected in Apr. 1949 in Quintana Roo from a nest containing two chicks, in "a large, exposed tree at the edge of a *cocal* [coconut plantation]."[6]

By about 5 or 6 weeks of age, the young—still clad in mesoptile down but with their flight feathers emerging—routinely leave the nest, clambering around the branches of the nest tree and not infrequently winding up on the ground. This so-called "jumper" or "brancher" stage may occur weeks before the owlets are capable of even partial flight, but their survival rate is high, thanks to the close attention of the adults. Fledging takes place about 9 weeks of age, and the young owls remain in the adults' territory and dependent on their parents through autumn (see "Post-Fledging Dispersal," p. 116).

BEHAVIOR

In behavior, as in most aspects of its life, the Great Horned Owl is flexible. Though primarily nocturnal, it often hunts at dusk and dawn and, while not as routinely diurnal as the Barred Owl, can at times be found actively hunting in daylight, especially on cloudy days and in midwinter. Generally it spends the day roosting in a concealed location, often in thick cover high in a tree and close to the trunk, its eyes closed and (if an intruder is detected) its plumage sleeked and ear tufts erect, heightening its camouflage.

Other birds often harass Great Horned Owls if they're found in daylight, but no other birds mob them with the tenacity and sheer hell-for-leather passion as crows. The owl will usually try to wait out the harassers for a while, then rapidly fly to a succession of new roosts until the posse becomes distracted or bored. It's not unusual for several dozen crows to mob a Great Horned Owl, and one observer counted a remarkable 136 in a single, loud frenzy. And with justification, because Great Horned Owls are a significant threat to nesting and roosting crows—one reason why crows often roost in large numbers in lighted, urban parks, where the threat of an attack from the dark is somewhat lessened.

Mated pairs may roost together out of the breeding season, and the male roosts within sight of the nest tree when his mate is on eggs or tending chicks. Siblings will roost together when they first leave the nest, but become solitary, and even mated owls will roost alone at times. Communal roosts were unknown until a recent report of up to six Great Horned Owls roosting within a few yards of one another in a tree belt in Utah during the winter. The birds made no response to recorded territorial hoots, leading the scientists to conclude they were not a pair with the previous summer's young.

In the North, where black flies transmit avian malaria, Great Horned Owls have been seen to shift from well-hidden roosts averaging 16 ft. (5 m) off the ground in early spring to open, nearly ground-level roosts in late summer, when black flies are at their worst—locations where the insects are far less abundant.

For the most part, Great Horned Owls are perch hunters, although they will sometimes course low

Nestled in a cavity in an immense sycamore tree, a female Great Horned Owl feeds a tidbit to her chick. This is the richly colored eastern subspecies, *B. v. virginianus.* (Pennsylvania. Alan Richard)

over suitable habitat, hoping to flush prey, more in the habit of a Barn Owl or Northern Harrier. Individual owls may learn (probably by accident) particular hunting techniques, which they employ with increasing frequency and success. At one nest in Pennsylvania, the remains of woodpeckers of several species were surprisingly common, suggesting that one of the adults had learned to reach into tree cavities at night and snag the roosting woodpeckers.

Home range size varies with prey density and probably with the overall density of other Great Horned Owls in the area. In southern California, home ranges for females averaged 445 acres (180 hectares) and for males, 1,050 acres (425 hectares). The largest female range was more than three times the smallest (217 versus 697 acres / 88 versus 282 hectares). Male territory size ranged from 363 to 2,755 acres (147 to 1,115 hectares), a more than seven-fold difference, but each owl used only about 20 percent of its territory on any night. In the Yukon, territory size for nesting pairs averaged 1,193 acres (483 hectares).

Intensive research on territorial pairs and "floaters" (unmated individuals) in the Yukon found that pairs showed extraordinary fidelity to their territories. Movements of more than 1.8 mi. (3 km) were very unusual, and they never showed any overlap with neighboring territories. Floaters, which do not advertise their presence by hooting, moved much more widely, overlapping many established territories and the ranges of other floaters.

STATUS

Widespread and common in most of its range, the Great Horned Owl is considered to be of "least concern" by IUCN/BirdLife and is not listed as a special concern species anywhere in the United States or Canada. The lone exception is the Yucatán subspecies *B. v. mayensis,* which is listed as "threatened" in Mexico.

Among the last native raptors to suffer sanctioned persecution, Great Horned Owls finally received federal protection in the United States in 1972, ending decades during which they had been subjected to bounty payments and other ill-conceived "control" measures.

But while still common, Great Horned Owl populations have declined in some areas, and one likely culprit is an exotic disease, West Nile virus, which was introduced to the New York area in 1999 and quickly spread across the country. While not as susceptible to infection as some birds (especially their traditional nemesis, the crows), Great Horned Owls frequently suffer damage to the central nervous system, heart, and eyes as a result of West Nile virus, which is spread by mosquitoes. An affected bird often holds its head tilted, is unable to fly well, and suffers paralysis or tremors.

An analysis of Christmas Bird Count data a few years after the epidemic began showed declines in Great Horned Owl counts in the Northeast that were "highly consistent"[7] with the expected effect of the disease. But evidence for such declines is inconsistent. Researchers in Wisconsin found no evidence of nesting declines in Great Horned Owls there, despite many adult owls testing positive for antibodies of the disease.

Breeding bird atlases in the Northeast, on the other hand, found evidence of broad declines a full decade or more after West Nile hit. In Pennsylvania, for example, Great Horned Owls were found in 28 percent fewer blocks in 2004–2009 than had been the case 20 years earlier; in some parts of the state the decline between atlases exceeded 40 percent. In New York, the species was found in 18 percent fewer blocks in the 2000–2005 atlas than two decades earlier.

But even so, the Great Horned Owl remains one of the most common raptors across this region, and evidence that nesting females can pass acquired antibodies through the egg to their chicks (as has also been shown for Eastern Screech-Owls) suggests the owls and the virus will come to a natural balance.

NOTES

1. Craighead and Craighead 1956.

2. Snyder and Wiley 1976.

3. Eckert and Karalus 1973.

4. Earhart and Johnson 1970.

5. Bent 1938.

6. Paynter 1955.

7. C. Caffery and C. C. Peterson. 2003. Christmas Bird Count data suggest West Nile virus may not be a conservation issue in northeastern United States. *American Birds* 57:14–21.

BIBLIOGRAPHY

Anderson and Clark 2002.

Artuso, C., C. S. Houston, D. G. Smith, and C. Rohner. 2014. Great horned owl (*Bubo virginianus*). In The Birds of North America Online, ed. A. Poole. Ithaca, NY: Cornell Lab of Ornithology, http://bna.birds.cornell.edu. bnaproxy.birds.cornell.edu/bna/species/372 doi:10.2173/bna.372.

Bennett, J. R., and P. H. Bloom. 2005. Home range and habitat use by great horned owls (*Bubo virginianus*) in southern California. *Journal of Raptor Research* 39:119–126.

Bogiatto, R. J., B. A. Sardella, and J. J. Essex. 2003. Food habits of great horned owls in northeastern California with notes on seasonal diet shifts. *Western North American Naturalist* 63:258–263.

Bolgiano, N. C. 2012. Great horned owl, *Bubo virginianus.* In *Second Atlas of Breeding Birds in Pennsylvania,* ed. A. M. Wilson, D. W. Brauning, and R. S. Mulvihill. University Park, PA: Pennsylvania State University Press, pp. 206–207.

Boone, S., R. W. Gerhold, and K. Keel. 2010. Aerial attack produces reciprocal fatal trauma between great horned owl and red-shouldered hawk. *Southeastern Naturalist* 9:179–180.

Bosakowski and Smith 1997.

Dickerman, R. W. 2013. The distribution of *Bubo virginianus pinorum* north and west to Washington. *Western Birds* 44:309–311.

——. 2004a. Notes on the type of *Bubo virginianus sclariventris. Bulletin of the British Ornithological Club* 124:5–6.

——. 2004b. Distribution of the subspecies of great horned owls in Texas. *Bulletin of the Texas Ornithological Society* 37:1–16.

——. 2002. The subarctic great horned owl (*Bubo virginianus subarcticus*) nesting in the United States. *American Midland Naturalist* 148:198–199.

Dickerman, R.W., and A. B. Johnson. 2008. Notes on great horned owls nesting in the Rocky Mountains, with a description of a new subspecies. *Journal of Raptor Research* 42:20–28.

Fitzgerald, S. D., J. S. Patterson, M. Kiupel, H. A. Simmons, S. D. Grimes, C. F. Sarver, R. M. Fulton, B. A. Steficek, T. M. Cooley, J. P. Massey, and J. G. Sikarskie. 2003. Clinical and pathologic features of West Nile virus infection in native North American owls (family Strigidae). *Avian Diseases* 47:602–610.

Grossman, S. R., S. J. Hannon, and A. Sánchez-Azofeifa. 2008. Responses of great horned owls (*Bubo virginianus*), barred owls (*Strix varia*), and northern saw-whet owl (*Aegolius acadicus*) to forest cover and configuration in an agricultural landscape in Alberta, Canada. *Canadian Journal of Zoology* 86:1165–1172.

Hinam and Duncan 2002.

Holt, J. B. Jr. 1996. A banding study of Cincinnati area great horned owls. *Journal of Raptor Research* 30:194–197.

Houston, C. S. 1978. Recoveries of Saskatchewan-banded great horned owls. *Canadian Field-Naturalist* 92:61–66.

Kinstler, K. A. 2009. Great horned owl *Bubo virginianus* vocalizations and associated behaviours. In *Proceedings of the Fourth World Owl Conference*, ed. D. H. Johnson, D. Van Nieuwenhuyse, and J. R. Duncan. *Ardea* 97:413–420.

Lambert, A. 1981. Presence and food preferences of the great horned owl in the urban parks of Seattle. *Murrelet* 62:2–5.

Marti, C. D., and M. N. Kochert. 1995. Are red-tailed hawks and great horned owls diurnal-nocturnal dietary counterparts? *Wilson Bulletin* 107:615–628.

Millard, J. B., T. H. Craig, and O. D. Markham. Cannibalism by an adult great horned owl. *Wilson Bulletin* 90:449.

Mobley, J.A., and T. A. Stidham. 2000. Great horned owl death from predation of a toxic California newt. *Wilson Bulletin* 112:563–564.

Murphy, R. K. 1997. Importance of prairie wetlands and avian prey to breeding great horned owls (*Bubo virginianus*) in northwestern North Dakota. In *Biology and Conservation of Owls of the Northern Hemisphere*, ed. J. R. Duncan, D. H. Johnson, and T. H. Nicholls. United States Department of Agriculture Forest Service Gen. Tech. Report NC 1997: 286–298.

Navarro-Sigüenza, A. G., and A. T. Peterson. 2007. *Bubo virginianus* (búho cornudo) residencia permanente distribución potencial. In *Mapas de las Aves de México Basados en WWW*, ed. A. G. Navarro and A. T. Peterson. Final report, SNIB-CONABIO project no. CE015. México DF.

Nelson, E. W. 1901. Descriptions of a new genus and eleven new species and subspecies of birds from Mexico. *Proceedings of the Biological Society of Washington* 15:169–175.

Odom, K. J., J. C. Slaght, and R. J. Gutiérrez. 2013. Distinctiveness in the territorial calls of great horned owls within and between years. *Journal of Raptor Research* 47:21–30.

Parkes, K. C. 1950. Great horned owl versus porcupine. *Wilson Bulletin* 62:213–214.

Perry, R. W., R. E. Brown, and D. C. Rudolph. 2001. Mutual mortality of great horned owl and southern black racer: A potential risk of raptors preying on snakes. *Wilson Bulletin* 113:345–347.

Pittaway, R. 1993. Subspecies of great horned owl in Ontario. *Ontario Birds* 11:64–69.

Robinson, B. 2014. A communal roosting of the great horned owl (*Bubo virginianus*). *Journal of Raptor Research* 48:88–89.

Rohner, C. 1996. The numerical response of great horned owls to the snowshoe hare cycle: Consequences of non-territorial "floaters" on demography. *Journal of Animal Ecology* 65:359–370.

———. 1994. "The Numerical Response of Great Horned Owls to the Snowshoe Hare Cycle in the Boreal Forest." PhD diss., University of British Columbia, Vancouver.

Rohner, C., C. J. Krebs, D. B. Hunter, and D. C. Curie. 2000. Roost site selection of great horned owls in relation to black fly activity: An anti-parasite behavior? *Condor* 102:950–955.

Rudolph, S. G. 1978. Predation ecology of coexisting great horned and barn owls. *Wilson Bulletin* 90:134–137.

Schwertner, T. W. 2002. An observation of the foraging behavior of a great horned owl (*Bubo virginianus*) feeding on field crickets (*Gryllus*). *Southwestern Naturalist* 47:117–118.

Seidensticker, J. C. IV. 1968. Notes on the food habits of the great horned owl in Montana. *Murrelet* 49:1–3.

Skoruppa, M. K., M. C. Woodin, and G. Blacklock. 2009. Species richness, relative abundance, and habitat associations of nocturnal birds along the Rio Grande in southern Texas. *Southwestern Naturalist* 54:317–323.

Snyder, L. L. 1961. *On an Unnamed Population of the Great Horned Owl*. Contribution No. 54. Toronto: Royal Ontario Museum.

Stout, W. E., A. G. Cassini, J. K. Meece, J. M. Papp, R. N. Rosenfield, and K. D. Reed. 2005. Serologic evidence of West Nile virus infection in three wild raptor populations. *Avian Diseases* 49:371–375.

Webster, J. D., and R. T. Orr. 1958. Variation in the great horned owls of Middle America. *Auk* 75:134–142.

Woodman, N., C. J. Dove, and S. C. Peurach. 2005. A curious pellet from a great horned owl (*Bubo virginianus*). *Northeastern Naturalist* 12:127–132.

Snowy Owls display strong reverse size dimorphism, despite early studies to the contrary. Males average about 3.5 to 4.5 pounds (1,600 to 2,050 g), and females 4.6 to 6.5 pounds (2,100 to 2,950 g). *(British Columbia. Gerrit Vyn)*

SNOWY OWL
Bubo scandiacus
Alpha code: SNOW

LENGTH: 23.5 in. (60 cm)

WINGSPAN: Males, 56 in. (142 cm); females, 61 in. (155 cm)

MASS: Strong reversed size dimorphism, despite early studies to the contrary; females average 22–26 percent heavier than males. Published body masses from North America average heavier than published weights from Russia, but this may reflect seasonal differences. Average mass for males banded in New York about 3.5 lbs. (1,600 g), for females about 4.6 lbs. (2,100 g).[1] In salvaged, live-trapped, and museum specimens from Canadian prairies, average weight for males 3.9 lbs. (1,806 g); range 3.5–4.5 lbs. (1,606–2,043 g) and females 5 lbs. (2,279 g); range 4–6.5 lbs. (1,838–2,951 g).[2] Adults in that study averaged heavier (with more fat) than immatures.

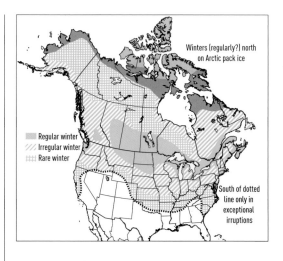

Winters (regularly?) north on Arctic pack ice

Regular winter
Irregular winter
Rare winter

South of dotted line only in exceptional irruptions

LONGEVITY: Of more than 400 Snowy Owls banded in North America (91 percent on the wintering grounds) and re-encountered, the average age at encounter was 2 years. Longevity record, a bird recaptured by a bander and released, is 19 years 7 months. Other notable records include nine individuals between 10 years 7 months and 16 years 8 months of age.

Perhaps the most recognizable owl in the world, the Snowy Owl has also been one of the most thoroughly misunderstood. Assumptions about almost every aspect of its life—its breeding and wintering ecology, the driving forces behind its dramatic irruptions, how to distinguish different age and sex classes in the field, even something as basic as how many there are in the world—have undergone a tectonic shift in the past 15 years, upending much that we thought we knew about this beautiful Arctic raptor.

Much of this new knowledge has come from the use of high-tech tracking devices, which have allowed scientists to finally follow what may well be the world's most nomadic bird—one that may move hundreds of miles between breeding sites, and thousands of miles between wintering areas, from one year to the next. It is a species so supremely adapted to the Arctic that some Snowy Owls actually migrate *north* in winter, hunting the desolate surface of the pack ice in the perpetual gloom of the Arctic winter—a behavior that was also only recently uncovered.

Restricted as a breeding species to a narrow rim of Arctic coastal tundra on the most northerly land areas on the planet—and dependent there on lemmings, whose population cycles are in turn threatened by changes to temperature and precipitation—the Snowy Owl may also be among the world's species most immediately at risk from climate change. Although populations appear stable, the recent recognition that global Snowy Owl numbers are but a fraction of what scientists had long believed makes this vulnerability even more worrisome.

SYSTEMATICS, TAXONOMY, AND ETYMOLOGY

The Snowy Owl was among the first birds classified by Linnaeus, although he initially described the male and female as separate species, *Strix scandiaca* and *S. nyctea*. The genus was changed to *Nyctea* in 1809, and for the next century or more, the owl was known as *Nyctea scandiaca*.

Beginning in the 1990s, however, the taxonomic status of the Snowy Owl came into question. Although morphological similarities had long suggested a relationship between the Snowy Owl and the eagle-owls of the genus *Bubo,* early DNA work hinted at a more direct link, leading some researchers to recommend nesting the species within *Bubo.* The AOU accepted this approach in 2003, renaming it *Bubo scandiacus.* (The specific name changed because the gender of a species name, if an adjective, must match that of its genus. *Bubo* is masculine—hence the change from the feminine *scandiaca* to the masculine form *scandiacus.*)

Not all owl experts accept the change in genus. Potapov and Sale (2012) made a spirited defense for retaining the Snowy Owl in *Nyctea* as a monotypic genus, citing weakness in the genetic studies and a litany of morphological differences between the Snowy Owl and eagle-owls, including disparities in skeletal structure, plumage, size and shape of the sclerotic ring in the eye, absence or presence of ear tufts, mating systems, and clutch size.

Regardless of its placement in or near *Bubo,* it's clear that the Snowy Owl is derived from the same ancestral stock as eagle-owls (and, less closely, the Asian fish owls of *Ketupa*). Molecular studies suggest the two lines diverged about 4 million years ago and that Snowy Owls may be most closely related to Great Horned Owls.

There are no known regional differences, nor have any subspecies been described. Genetic analyses suggest considerable gene flow throughout the circumpolar breeding range, which is in line with recent revelations about the highly nomadic behavior of this species, which may move extraordinary distances between breeding seasons.

ETYMOLOGY: For the genus name, see "Great Horned Owl"; the former genus name *Nyctea* comes from the Greek *nycteus,* "nocturnal." The specific names *scandiaca* and *scandiacus* both derive from *scandia,* usually referring to southern Sweden, but also a term used in classical times to refer to the unknown islands of northern Europe. The common name is as self-explanatory as any in ornithology.

FRENCH: *Harfang des neiges*
INUIT: *Uppik*
IÑUPIATUN: *Ukpik*

DISTRIBUTION

BREEDING SEASON: Limited to Arctic and subarctic tundra zones in northern Canada, extending south to extreme northern Labrador and Quebec, Cape Churchill in Manitoba, and northwest across Nunavut and the northern Northwest Territories, along the Beaufort Sea coastal plain of Yukon and Alaska, and south along the Chukchi and Bering Sea coasts of Alaska to Hooper Bay. There are historic breeding records from the western Aleutians as well as Saint Matthew, Saint Lawrence, and Hall Islands in Alaska, but these areas cannot be considered part of the species's normal breeding range.

Most range maps probably overstate the normal breeding distribution of Snowy Owls. Given their highly nomadic nature and their habit of concentrating where lemming populations are at cyclic peaks, much of the breeding range may have few or no Snowy Owls in any given nesting season. The most consistent areas for breeding appear to be extreme northern Alaska around the Point Barrow Peninsula, and the islands of the Canadian High Arctic. Breeding in the more southerly areas of "normal" summer distribution, in regions like the Ungava and Labrador Peninsulas, may be much less frequent than originally believed.

NONBREEDING SEASON: Regular winter resident in northern Alberta and Saskatchewan (most reliably), the northern New England coast south to Cape Cod, the Saint Lawrence River valley, and parts of the northern Great Lakes. Irregular winter visitor along the coast to Long Island and New Jersey, the upper Midwest, northern Great Plains, and the coast of southern British Columbia, Washington, and Oregon.

In major irruptions, Snowy Owls have been found as far south as Florida, Mississippi, and Texas, although the normal southern boundary even in major flight years is more typically the Mid-Atlantic coast through the central Great Plains, north to Wyoming and Montana and west to Oregon and the northern Central Valley in California.

MIGRATION AND MOVEMENTS: Irruptive, although a regular winter migrant into the northern Great Plains, and even outside of this area lesser or greater numbers of Snowy Owls appear every winter in southern Canada and the northern United States (see "Nonbreeding Season," p. 128; "Autumn Migration," below; and "Spring Migration," p. 130).

AUTUMN MIGRATION:

Generally irregular and irruptive in nature, although Snowy Owls are regular southward migrants to a few areas (see "Nonbreeding Season," p. 128). Satellite tracking has shown that many adults remain in the Arctic for the winter or even migrate north from their breeding areas (see "Behavior," p. 138).

Although most people assume that hunger drives irrupting owls south, in major Snowy Owl invasions the cause is usually extraordinary plenty, not privation. Major irruptions are usually the result of extremely high chick production the previous summer—which in turn is the result of a cyclical peak in the population of lemmings on which nesting owls feed. Such irruptions are largely (at times almost exclusively) comprised of young birds making their first migration, and these birds tend to be in excellent physical condition, contradicting the long-standing assumption that irrupting Snowy Owls languish and starve on the wintering grounds. (More rarely, smaller flights, made up primarily of

Clad in their thick, gray mesoptile down, Snowy Owl chicks are well enough insulated to allow the female to leave the nest for long periods to help hunt. *(Nunavut. Meggie Desnoyers)*

The Snowy Owl has no subspecies, with almost uninterrupted gene flow through its circumpolar breeding area, thanks to its highly nomadic behavior. *(Pennsylvania. Alan Richard)*

Snowy Owls have a complex and still poorly understood migration strategy that—depending on the year, region, and even the individual—combines highly nomadic behavior with predictable migration. They are generally irruptive but are regular winter residents in some places, such as the Canadian prairies. (New Jersey. Tom Johnson)

adults, may occur; these irruptions may in fact be driven by prey scarcity in the Arctic, and such birds tend to be in poorer physical condition.)

Many factors may determine what triggers a large irruption. While a bountiful breeding season is an obvious requirement, other elements are believed to play a role. These may include early and heavy snow in the Arctic, the availability of alternate prey, like Willow Ptarmigan and hares, and weather patterns in late autumn and early winter that may push the owls into the northern edge of the boreal forest, prompting a rapid transit south until they reach more suitable habitat.

The earliest migrants into southern Canada and the northernmost United States rarely appear before late Oct., with the bulk of both irruptive and nonirruptive migrants arriving in Nov. and Dec. to the north, and into early Jan. to the south. In the Northeast, young males tend to arrive first (and perhaps average the farthest penetration south), with immature females appearing later in the winter and possibly displacing males. However, Keith (1960) found the opposite in Manitoba, with females arriving first, usually in Nov. Telemetry studies have shown that some individuals move extensively through the winter, making significant (>150 mi. / 390 km) flights in a few days, while others remain in very limited (1 sq. mi. / 2.6 sq. km) winter territories for months.

SPRING MIGRATION:

Northward movement may begin as early as Feb., though some individuals linger until May, and a handful of over-summering records usually follow a major irruption. Earlier departure dates (late Feb. through early Mar.) were reported from the Great Plains among predominantly adult owls than among predominantly juvenile birds in the Northeast (late Mar. and early Apr.). Because Snowy Owls are not thought to breed until their second full summer, the adults likely feel a greater urgency to return to the breeding grounds.

Eleven of 17 satellite-tagged owls in coastal Massachusetts began their spring migration between Mar. 21 and Apr. 11, with the latest remaining until Apr. 27. Telemetry tracks showed that the Saint Lawrence River valley was an important stopover site in both spring and fall. By contrast, 3 GPS-tagged owls from inland Pennsylvania departed Mar. 15 to 19 in concert with mild temperatures and south winds, moving north and west to Lakes Erie and Ontario. Some owls made rapid, moderately long movements of several hundred miles in a night or two. One owl, which remained in western

Quebec at a large open-pit gold mine, died in late June of undetermined causes.

POST-FLEDGING DISPERSAL: Poorly studied, but one famous example likely represents a record for any owl species. Out of a single nest of seven chicks banded in 1960 on Victoria Island in the Canadian Arctic, one was subsequently shot on James Bay, one in southern Ontario near Ottawa—and one on Sakhalin Island in extreme eastern Russia, then part of the USSR, roughly 4,000 mi. (6,100 km) from its birthplace.

DISTRIBUTION OUTSIDE THE COVERAGE AREA: Circumpolar in distribution, breeding from eastern Siberia across the northern extent of tundra to Franz Josef Land and Svalbard, the Norwegian mainland, and Greenland, although areas of regular breeding are much more localized within this range. Winters irregularly across northern Europe and Eurasia.

DESCRIPTION AND IDENTIFICATION

Huge, all-white, with varying intensity of black and brownish markings, tiny and generally hidden ear tufts, and yellow eyes. If you can't identify this owl, you aren't trying. Sexing Snowy Owls by plumage is, however, considerably more complex and difficult than birders generally believe, and many previous assumptions about sex- and age-related plum-age differences have proven to be unfounded or simplistic. There are no known regional differences, probably reflecting the species's highly nomadic behavior and significant gene flow. Snowy Owls exhibit marked reversed sexual dimorphism by size, with females averaging 22 percent heavier than males. They also have unusually high wing-loading for an owl—the ratio of body weight to wing area—to a degree more typical of hawks and falcons, to which their fast, powerful flight is often compared, and the opposite of light, buoyant owls like Barn or Short-eared Owls.

BASIC (ADULT) PLUMAGE: Females average more heavily marked with black than males, but there is considerable overlap. Similarly, older Snowy Owls probably average whiter than younger individuals of the same gender, but there is considerable variation here as well; furthermore, some owls may darken, then lighten again with subsequent molts, or vice versa, perhaps because of environmental conditions. A study in Saskatchewan, where Snowy Owls return regularly each winter, found that a third of males showed fewer wing spots with age, a third showed more, and a third remained the same.

Base color is clear white, marked with black that quickly fades to brownish, especially on the scapulars and inner secondaries most heavily exposed to sunlight. Adult males (3 years or older) may have

Aging and sexing Snowy Owls is not as straightforward as many birders believe. While females like this one average more heavily marked than males, and adults average whiter than juveniles of the same gender, there can be considerable overlap in plumage. *(Washington. Gerrit Vyn)*

In juvenile Snowy Owls, males and females can be distinguished by the pattern on their wings and tail feathers. Young males like this one show spots (instead of bars) on their middle secondary feathers and have three or fewer tail bars, which do not reach to the edge of the feather. *(Pennsylvania. Alan Richard)*

few to no black markings, but even among adult males there are more heavily marked individuals that approach the appearance of the lightest females. Sexual differences in the intensity of black and white colors, subtle to the human eye but presumably more evident to Snowy Owls, have been reported through the use of spectrophotometers.

The overall degree of dark markings on the head and body is suggestive of gender, but not definitive, with females averaging darker. However, first-year birds may be sexed in the hand (or with clear photographs) using wing and tail markings. Immature females show bars (either complete or irregular in shape and reaching the feather shaft) on the middle secondary feathers. Immature males have spots instead of bars on the same feathers, and the markings do not touch the quills. In addition, males generally have three or fewer bars on the upper surface of the tail, while females have three or more. The bars on a female's tail extend completely to the edge of the feather, while on a male the bars are narrowly edged with white—a characteristic readily visible only in the hand.

The wing coverts and tertials are extensively mottled in immature Snowy Owls, but because some of these feathers may be retained for up to 3 years, the presence of mottling alone should not be used as an aging characteristic.

Flight feather molt is still incompletely under-stood. It seems similar to, but faster than, that of the Eurasian Eagle-Owl, requiring three annual molt cycles for the complete replacement of all primaries and secondaries. Older flight feathers become dingy and yellowish, and a bird in the hand (or photographed clearly with open wings) may thus be aged up to the fourth calendar year in autumn and fifth calendar year in the spring.

The feet and toes are feathered more extensively than on any other species of owl, and the rictal bristles surrounding the beak are unusually long and

Juvenile female Snowy Owls show wide or irregular bars on the middle secondary feathers, and three or more tail bars that reach the outer edge of the feathers. *(British Columbia. Glenn Bartley/VIREO)*

dense, trapping and warming air in frigid environments during respiration. The face, including the facial disk and throat, are pure white regardless of the degree of body marking. The ear tufts are small and rarely seen except when agitated, especially by the presence of other Snowy Owls, but, curiously, they are visible on most incubating females. The eyes are yellow or yellow-gold, and the bill and talons are black.

JUVENAL PLUMAGE: Newly hatched chicks are covered in gray-white natal down, which is replaced by thicker and dark gray mesoptile plumage about the time the eyes open, roughly around 10 days of age. Flight feathers begin to emerge at about 17 days of age, and at roughly a month old, the chick's white juvenal plumage begins to show, most noticeably in the face, creating the so-called "white-mask" stage. The wings and back are by this point almost fully feathered, and the owlet has a striking piebald look. Its first full juvenal plumage is complete by about 2 months of age, by which time the chick is becoming independent. Despite considerable variation, most young Snowy Owls in their first basic plumage average more heavily marked than adults of their gender.

SIMILAR SPECIES: It is difficult to imagine anyone misidentifying a Snowy Owl; this is one of the most immediately distinctive birds of any type in the world. That said, a variety of raptors are often mistakenly identified as Snowy Owls, especially by nonbirders. Barn Owls seen in flight account for some mistaken identifications, and some subarctic races of the Great Horned Owl are almost as pale as a heavily marked Snowy Owl. But, surprisingly, the majority of bad IDs involve light-bellied buteos, especially Red-tailed Hawks. Viewed from a distance with their chest feathers fluffed and illuminated by the sun, and their dark heads blending with the background, such hawks can appear to be all-white birds to a casual observer.

VOCALIZATIONS

Largely silent except on the breeding grounds, where in addition to courtship hoots the adults (especially males) are vocal during nest defense.

The male, and rarely the female, gives a flat, rough hoot that may be heard up to 2 mi. away. The male may call while perched on a low rise or, less often, a manmade structure like a utility pole or building, raising his tail and inflating his throat while bowing with each low, booming call. Neighboring males may answer, and Sutton (1932) reported a hooting bout involving 10 male Snowy Owls. What some researchers have termed "threat hooting," in response to an intruding human, involves a more upright

Wings held high, a juvenile male Snowy Owl tries to fend off the swooping attacks of a Peregrine Falcon. *(New Jersey. Tom Johnson)*

posture; Snowy Owls in flight may also hoot, although more quietly than when perched. Hoots are frequently paired but may occur in a string of half a dozen or more.

Males defending the nest often give three to six barking, slightly descending calls, *cah-cah-cah-cah;* females have been known to give similar vocalizations during nest defense, but they attack intruders far less frequently than the males and call less vigorously. Adults defending the nest may also give low hoots and loud, rapid bill snaps along with barks. Females make a high, reedy, piercing call during courtship feeding and after copulation, which Potapov and Sale (2012) have characterized as a begging call.

As with many owls, Snowies may make a rapid, high-pitched twittering, sometimes when in physical discomfort, but sometimes in reaction to simply being handled. The call may also be given along with barks and bill snaps during nest defense.

HABITAT AND NICHE

In its breeding range, the Snowy Owl inhabits open, shrub-free tundra, usually picking a higher, drier spot for its ground nest. Although Snowy Owls have been reported nesting on alpine plateau tundra in Norway, in North America they are restricted in summer to elevations below 660 ft. (200 m), generally along coastal plains and Arctic islands.

In winter, those owls moving south of the boreal forest belt gravitate to a variety of open-country situations, ranging from coastlines and beaches (perhaps the most common winter habitat in the East, upper Great Lakes, and Pacific Northwest) to farm fields, grasslands, bogs, industrial zones, and even urban centers, where an abundance of flat-topped buildings provide the unbroken sightlines

Once south of the Arctic, Snowy Owls gravitate to open habitats that look vaguely like the flat, treeless expanses of the tundra—beaches and shorelines, frozen lakes, airports, and, as in this case, farmland. *(Ontario. Gerrit Vyn)*

they prefer. The more open, the better; in irruption years, for example, Snowy Owls in Pennsylvania are found most often in farming areas with large Amish and Mennonite communities, whose farms tend to be heavily cropped, with a minimum of trees and fencerows—creating the kind of expansive, uncluttered horizon that makes a Snowy Owl feel at home.

Human activity—especially vehicular activity—is rarely much of a deterrent. Whizzing traffic doesn't faze them, and busy metropolitan airports are dangerously attractive to migrants, posing a hazard both to the owls and the planes that may strike them. In the mega-irruption of 2013–2014, more than 150 owls were trapped and relocated from Logan Airport in Boston alone.

Recent satellite tracking has found that some adult Snowy Owls winter on the Arctic pack ice, spending up to 3 months at a time in this seemingly inhospitable, perpetually dark environment. The owls appeared to focus on open-water polynyas, where they presumably prey on concentrations of wintering waterbirds, especially eiders, Long-tailed Ducks, and small alcids. GPS tracking of juvenile Snowy Owls showed that some of these birds pursued a similar course on the ice-bound Great Lakes, spending weeks at a time among giant, wind-driven ice sheets on Lakes Erie and Ontario and presumably hunting waterfowl or gulls in the constantly shifting leads of open water.

DIET: Famous for their reliance on lemmings during the breeding season, Snowy Owls are actually very flexible in their dietary habits outside the nesting season, eating almost anything with fur or feathers (and a few things with neither) that they can wrestle into submission with their bulk and large, immensely powerful feet. The feet are, in fact, a dead giveaway to this all-embracing diet: unlike the delicate toes and talons of a Rough-legged Hawk, which is a true small-mammal specialist, those of a Snowy Owl are built to handle whatever opportunity presents, from the smallest shrew to geese and herons.

During the breeding season, though, the Snowy Owl's dietary world revolves around small mammals, especially collared (or varying) lemmings and brown lemmings. Lemmings experience extraordinary population swings on a roughly 4-year cycle, and Snowy Owls rarely breed anywhere in numbers without a corresponding lemming boom to underpin their nesting efforts. Satellite tracking has shown that the owls are highly nomadic, moving hundreds of miles from one year to the next to take advantage of a lemming explosion.

Ornithologists have calculated that a Snowy Owl would need to consume between 1,600 and 2,400 lemmings annually—but Snowy Owls eat much more than just lemmings. Even during the breeding season they will take a variety of other prey, including other rodents, ptarmigan, snowshoe and Arctic hares, songbirds, and waterfowl. The proportion of alternate prey goes up as the lemming population goes down in any given area, and nesting owls may also switch to other prey once the average body weight of the lemmings drops below a certain

An almost completely white adult male Snowy Owl delivers a lemming to its nest as his mate feeds one of their chicks. The cyclical explosions of lemming numbers drive Snowy Owl reproduction, setting the stage for some of the largest irruptions of these Arctic raptors. *(Nunavut. Gerrit Vyn)*

Small-mammal specialists in the summer, Snowy Owls take an enormous range of prey in the winter, from farmland rodents to rabbits, muskrats, songbirds, waterfowl as large as geese, and even fish. *(Pennsylvania. Alan Richard)*

threshold in late summer. In those few areas where Snowy Owls breed in the absence of lemmings, they may specialize in unusual prey, like the pair nesting in the Aleutian Islands that fed almost entirely on waterbirds, especially Ancient Murrelets.

It is in winter, though, that Snowy Owls really show their predatory flexibility. Those moving south of the Arctic appear to focus their energies on whatever prey is most abundant and easily available—voles and mice in agricultural fields, muskrats and ducks in tidal wetlands, rats and Rock Pigeons in urban areas, gulls and other waterbirds along the coast.

There have been surprisingly few studies of Snowy Owl winter food habits, but each has confirmed the inclusive nature of their diet. Those conducted at inland sites have tended to find a high percentage of rodents, while in coastal locations, waterbirds such as ducks, gulls, and grebes dominate. One of the largest studies, ongoing work by Norman Smith in Massachusetts, found, based on more than five thousand pellets, that Norway rats, meadow voles, and American Black Ducks were the predominant prey, but Smith has documented the owls taking more than 30 species of birds and mammals, including Canada Goose, Great Blue Heron, Short-eared Owl, and Peregrine Falcon, as well as small, agile songbirds like Snow Buntings

and Horned Larks. A study in the 1940s near Toronto, Canada, found that meadow voles made up 85 to 98 percent of the owls' diet in farmland and grassland, while birds (particularly Long-tailed Ducks) comprised 45 percent along the city waterfront, followed by 35 percent Norway rats. In west-central Montana, more than 90 percent of the diet of more than 40 Snowy Owls over the course of one winter was montane and meadow voles.

A number of accounts on both the breeding and wintering grounds suggest Snowy Owls occasionally take fish. Audubon described watching Snowy Owls lying on rocks beside open water in the Ohio River, snagging fish with one foot—and while he was not always the most reliable correspondent, fish, frogs, and some aquatic invertebrates have been recorded in Snowy Owl diets by less impeachable sources. Snowy Owls will scavenge, including feeding on whale carcasses in the Arctic, and have been observed feeding on dead dolphins (and in one case even defending a carcass from a Turkey Vulture) on the Atlantic Coast.

NESTING AND BREEDING

Pair bonds are thought to last only a single season, given the nomadic nature of the Snowy Owl's movements. By some means still unknown, adult owls are able to locate areas of high lemming abun-

One wingtip leaving a fine trail in the sand, a Snowy Owl launches itself on the attack, aiming for a group of ducks along the Atlantic Coast. *(New Jersey. Tom Johnson)*

dance while the rodents are still hidden beneath late-winter snow, and the owls gather in breeding concentrations where and when the rodents are near their cyclical peak, usually by May or early June. In addition to hooting, the male performs a striking courtship display with deep, exaggerated wingbeats and an undulating flight pattern, visible from miles, while carrying a lemming in its beak; this may be followed by a ground display in which the male bows low, wings and tail partially spread, with the lemming on the ground in front of him.

Lemmings are the key to Snowy Owl breeding success. Researchers have found a sharp increase in the number of nesting pairs when lemming density reaches about 4 per acre (10 per hectare), and nest-

ing density peaks when lemmings exceed 8 per acre (20 per hectare). Owl densities of 15 to 25 pairs per 38 sq. mi. (100 sq. km) seem typical for such concentrations, although up to 47 pairs per 38 sq. mi. (100 sq. km) in the same area have been reported from northern Canada.

The nest is an unlined ground scrape made by the female, usually placed on a hillock or other prominent rise with good visibility in all directions; the female may methodically nip off any surrounding vegetation that interferes with her line of vision. The number of eggs is in part determined

Collared lemmings litter a Snowy Owl nest in the Arctic, where three chicks have hatched and three eggs remain. The age difference between the oldest chick, in the rear, and the youngest, in the front, is evident. *(Nunavut. Gerrit Vyn)*

Found across the polar regions in North America, Greenland, and Eurasia, Snowy Owls nest most consistently and predictably in only the very highest latitudes—in North America, the Point Barrow peninsula in Alaska, and the islands of the Canadian High Arctic. Farther south in the breeding range, nesting may be far less frequent than once thought. *(Nunavut. Pierre-Yves L'Hérault)*

A female Snowy Owl glides into her nest, her brood patch—a naked, highly vascularized patch of skin with which she incubates her eggs—sagging from her belly feathers. *(Nunavut. Gerrit Vyn)*

by the female's condition and the number of lemmings the male supplies. A nest photographed in northern Quebec had 4 eggs (possibly an incomplete clutch) surrounded by 78 dead lemmings and voles, brought in by the male. In lean times, the clutch may be as few as 3 eggs (5 to 7 is average) but clutches as high as 14 eggs have been reported. Such high productivity accounts for the population booms that can (if other conditions are right) result in a large winter irruption.

As is typical with raptors, incubation begins with the first egg, and hatching is asynchronous after a roughly 33-day incubation period, during which the female rarely leaves the nest. In large clutches there is extreme size difference between the youngest and oldest chicks, but siblicide—which is common among many raptors—is rarer among Snowy Owls because the chicks quickly scatter from the nest scrape. By the time they are 2 or 3 weeks old, and weeks before they are capable of flight, the chicks leave the nest and hide among the low tundra vegetation, fed and ferociously defended by the adults. A human that ventures near the nest risks a slashing, bloody attack to the head, and researchers have seen Snowy Owls rout moose, caribou, and wolves that came too close.

The male also provisions the female and chicks with most of their food, especially during the first weeks of the nestling period. During a lemming ex-

Their flight feathers emerging from their mesoptile down, three young Snowy Owls crouch near their nest, old enough to instinctively react when an intruding human approaches, even if the tundra offers few places to hide. *(Nunavut. Cassandra Cameron)*

plosion this may be a relatively simple task to accomplish, however. One ornithologist observed a male on Baffin Island tending two nests (one of the few examples of polygyny in this species). Despite hunting for himself, two adult females, and their 13 chicks, the owl still managed to spend roughly 19 hours a day sleeping.

A Snowy Owl chick grows quickly, from a 1.5-oz.

(45 g) hatchling to a 4-lb. (1,800 g) fledgling that is beginning to fly, in less than a month and a half. The chicks remain dependent on their parents for food for several more weeks, after which they drift away from the nest site and into independence.

BEHAVIOR

Snowy Owls are enigmas—birds that in many respects turn normal avian convention on its head but that are also in some regards more "typical" an owl than they are given credit for.

Virtually every species of bird exhibits what ornithologists call "site fidelity"—a drive to return, often with astonishing precision and regularity, to the same nesting and wintering location every year. Snowy Owls stand in stark contrast to this almost universal rule. They are perhaps the most completely nomadic bird in the world, rarely showing any attachment not only to a particular nest site or wintering location, but even to a general region of the circumpolar north. A Snowy Owl that breeds in Alaska one year may be nesting in Siberia the next and northern Canada the year after that; its wintering grounds may shift by a thousand miles or more from season to season. A study of Snowy Owls in Nunavut found that the average distance between breeding sites was almost 500 mi. (800 km), and was as great as 763 mi. (1,228 km).

There are exceptions, however. Snowy Owls regularly winter in the northern Canadian prairies, with band returns suggesting that some birds return annually or near annually and defend winter territories. Satellite tracking of Snowy Owls tagged in Massachusetts showed that many of the marked birds made return flights south in subsequent years into southeastern Canada and New England, and none of the tagged birds left eastern North America. Further study may explain why fidelity and nomadism seem to coexist in this species.

The Snowy Owl's daily activity pattern is also badly misunderstood. Most published references to this raptor—not only those written for a general audience, but many scientific publications as well—refer to it as diurnal. And it's true that Snowy Owls are active in the broad daylight of an Arctic midsummer day—though they have little choice in this, given that the sun doesn't set there for months on end. Any Arctic organism is, by simple default, diurnal for at least part of the year.

So while it's true that Snowy Owls are more active in daytime than many owls, when they have a choice—at a time or place where darkness falls—they are clearly nocturnal, like most owls. And of course they are fully nocturnal if they winter, as many do, north of the Arctic Circle, where the sun barely lightens the sky to a dim gloom in the middle of winter. The cold is no obstacle: laboratory ex-

Although birders often consider Snowy Owls diurnal, they are most active—and do most of their serious hunting—at night in the winter. In the perpetual daylight of the Arctic summer, of course, they have no choice but to be diurnal. *(Pennsylvania. Alan Richard)*

periments have shown that Snowy Owls can survive temperatures below −90°F (−67.7°C), the lowest reading ever recorded in the Northern Hemisphere, and captive Snowy Owls survived 5 hours at −135°F (−93°C) with no sign of tissue damage or frostbite.

Snowy Owls wintering south of the boreal forest make full use of long winter nights for travel and hunting. During the day, an owl generally finds the most open, treeless spot it can, usually perching on or very close to the ground and often huddled against a concealing object—a fencepost, a pile of snow or ice, an airport taxiway sign, a driftwood log, or clump of grass on the beach. If undisturbed by humans, it may not stir all day—and while it may take advantage of an easy meal if prey presents itself, serious hunting usually takes place after dark.

As the sun settles, the owl becomes more active, ruffling and preening, stretching its wings, and sometimes regurgitating a pellet. As twilight gathers, it will fly up to a high perch—a dune or old post, a utility pole, barn roof, any position with a commanding view of the neighborhood. If potential prey is in view, the owl may go through exaggerated head-bobbing and craning before launching itself on the attack. With full darkness, the owl heads off for the night, sometimes flying miles from its daytime roost to search for prey before returning in the morning.

One revelation from GPS tracking is the degree to which some Snowy Owls hunt over open water. Several immature owls, tracked along the Mid-Atlantic and New England coasts, made repeated flights of a third to half a mi. (.5 to .75 km) out over open water of bays and the Atlantic Ocean after dark, often using the same channel markers and buoys as perches, presumably hunting for waterfowl. Interestingly, other Snowy Owls wintering in the same areas restricted their hunting to beaches and salt marsh habitat, rarely venturing over open water. More than one observer has noted their falconlike flight; Snowy Owls are capable of easily overtaking fast-flying prey, like ducks and alcids, and picking off agile songbirds, like larks and buntings.

One of the most striking characteristics of Snowy Owls is their naiveté toward humans; it's often possible to approach them so closely that casual observers may conclude the owl is sick or exhausted, instead of merely disinterested. Especially outside their typical winter range, where a single Snowy Owl may attract large crowds, repeated disturbance from birders and photographers has sometimes prompted authorities to post guards.

Off the breeding grounds, Snowy Owls may be highly aggressive toward one another (with females usually dominating smaller males), but they may also gather in small groups in apparent peace. Perhaps the largest concentration recorded in North America was at Cape Race, Newfoundland, at the beginning of the 2013–2014 irruption, when an extraordinary 306 owls were counted on the peninsula, 75 of them visible from one spot. Many of the owls in this group displayed erect ear tufts, likely a sign of unease and agitation in the presence of so many others owls.

The 2013–2014 irruption involved thousands of Snowy Owls, although exact numbers were impossible to determine. An estimated 400 owls were believed to have been in Massachusetts, and an estimated 300 in Pennsylvania—the latter a state where more than 1 or 2 is a rarity. Thirty-three Snowies tallied on the Nantucket Island, MA, Christmas Bird Count was more than eight times the previous record, 4, which was reached just twice in the previous century.

STATUS

The status of the Snowy Owl is undergoing a major reassessment as new information about its extreme nomadism is being taken into account.

The Snowy Owl is ranked as "least concern" by IUCN/BirdLife, with a decreasing population trend. In Canada it is listed as "not at risk" under COSEWIC and SARA, although it is a priority species in two bird conservation regions (Arctic Plains and Mountains, and Quebec Arctic Plains). Alaska's Wildlife Action Plan lists it as a "species of greatest conservation need," and further assessments in the state have ranked the Snowy Owl as category V (orange), because of "unknown status and either high biological vulnerability or high action needed."

Feathers fly as two immature Snowy Owls tussle over territory in a Pennsylvania farm field. These are both males; the larger females tend to dominate such encounters. *(Pennsylvania. Alan Richard)*

The Snowy Owl may be one of the species at most immediate risk from climate change. Winter weather pattern changes in parts of Greenland and the Norwegian Arctic have caused a collapse of the lemming cycle, and with it, breeding Snowy Owl populations. In parts of Canada and Russia, the 4-year lemming cycle has lengthened to up to 8 years, with unknown consequences for the owls. *(Ontario. Scott Linstead/VIREO)*

Partners in Flight estimates the global population at 200,000 birds, with half that number in North America. These population totals were arrived at, however, by simply adding up peak breeding numbers˝ around the circumpolar region. As satellite telemetry data have now shown, Snowy Owls may move widely between breeding sites, meaning that conservationists have likely been overestimating Snowy Owl populations, perhaps by more than an order of magnitude.

Using this new understanding of Snowy Owl ecology, Potapov and Sale (2102) calculated that the global Snowy Owl population may fluctuate between a high of just 14,000 pairs following an especially productive breeding season, to only 5,000 pairs when lemming "lows" synchronize across wide areas of the Arctic, as they often do. Regardless of the actual total, authorities agree that roughly half the world population lives in the Canadian Arctic.

Snowy Owls may also be among the species at most immediate risk from climate change. This may take the form of habitat loss, as woody shrubs like alder and willow invade open tundra with the advancing tree line, rendering it unsuitable for the lemmings on which breeding Snowy Owls depend. Changes in weather and precipitation may also have profound effects on lemmings, which rely on an insulating blanket of snow to thrive and even breed through the Arctic winter.

Changes in winter temperature and humidity, which affect not only the depth but also the density of the snowpack, have been blamed for the breakdown of lemming cycles in alpine tundra regions of Norway, where the rodents have failed to peak since 1994. The same thing has occurred since 1998 in parts of northeastern Greenland, where in the wake of the lemming collapse Snowy Owl fledging success dropped 98 percent and the species essentially abandoned the study areas.

Such dramatic changes have not yet been observed in other parts of the Arctic, although the regularity of lemming cycles may be eroding; the average period between cycle peaks on Banks Island in the Canadian Arctic has increased from 4 to 5 years since the late 1990s, while in sections of Siberia it has grown dramatically from 4 years to 8 since the early 2000s. Anecdotal evidence suggests similar changes to lemming cycles have taken place in northern Alaska.

The kind of freeze-thaw cycles and ground-level icing that appear to have driven lemming collapses in Norway and Greenland haven't been documented in Canada, and recent local trends toward deeper snow suggest conditions there may actually improve for lemmings, at least in some places and in the near term. But researchers warn they have little hard information about how climate change is altering the Arctic and the complex interaction between keystone prey species, like lemmings and their predators, including the Snowy Owls. Furthermore, some climate models suggest collared lemmings could lose 60 percent of their habitat in the Canadian Arctic as the region warms.

Although Snowy Owls nest in some of the most remote locations on the planet, human intrusion is increasing. Oil and gas development has degraded habitat in some areas, especially on the North Slope in Alaska, and the accelerating loss of summer sea ice will open more and more areas of the High Arctic to extractive industries. Disturbance from hunting and use of off-road vehicles is an issue near villages such as Barrow, AK.

As noted earlier, threats to individual birds in winter run the gamut of human hazards, from rodenticides and environmental contaminants to vehicular collisions (including plane strikes) and electrocution. Direct persecution is less of a problem than it was in the nineteenth and early twentieth centuries, when hundreds of Snowy Owls might be shot during a single irruption, but it does still occur: of 20 Snowy Owls tagged with satellite transmitters in Massachusetts between 1999 and 2011, three were shot and killed in that state. Trapping with leghold traps and exposed bait for Arctic foxes has, at least in the past, caused the deaths of uncounted numbers of Snowy Owls in Siberia—which, given the Holarctic nature of the owl's movements, may have an impact on North American numbers.

Snowy Owls are still subject to largely unregulated subsistence hunting in Alaska and Canada among Native communities, for food and traditional uses of feathers and skins. The Alaskan harvest is unquantified and essentially unmonitored, but has been characterized as "substantial,"[3] while Canadian management plans call for more rigorous monitoring of subsistence hunting to determine its impact on this species.

NOTES

1. T. McDonald, pers. comm.

2. P. Kerlinger and M. R. Lein. 1988. Causes of mortality, fat condition, and weights of wintering snowy owls. *Journal of Field Ornithology* 59:7–12.

3. K. Walton, T. Gotthardt, and T. Fields. 2013. Alaska species ranking system summary report: Snowy owl. Alaska Natural Heritage Program, University of Alaska.

BIBLIOGRAPHY

Alaska Department of Fish and Game. 2006. *Our Wealth Maintained: A Strategy for Conserving Alaska's Diverse Wildlife and Fish Resources.* Juneau, AK: Alaska Department of Fish and Game.

Audubon, J. J. 1856. *The Birds of America,* vol. 1. New York: V. G. Audubon.

Bilodeau, F., G. Gauthier, and D. Berteaux. 2013. The effect of snow cover on lemming population cycles in the Canadian High Arctic. *Oecologia* 172:1007–1016.

BirdLife International. 2015. Species factsheet: *Bubo scandiacus,* http://www.birdlife.org/datazone/species-factsheet.php?id=2236.

Bortolotti, G. R., and M. Stoffel. 2012. The coloration of snowy owls is not so black and white. In *The Snowy Owl,* E. Potapov and R. Sale. London: T & A D Poyser, pp. 22–24.

Detienne, J. C., D. Holt, M. T. Seidensticker, and T. Pitz. 2008. Diet of snowy owls wintering in west-central Montana, with comparisons to other North American studies. *Journal of Raptor Research* 42:172–179.

Fuller, M., D. Holt, and L. Schueck. 2003. Snowy owl movements: Variation on the migration theme. In *Avian Migrations,* ed. P. Berthold, E. Gwinner, and E. Sohnnenschein. Berlin: Springer-Verlag, pp. 359–366.

Gessaman, J. A. 1972. Bioenergetics of the snowy owl. *Arctic and Alpine Research* 4:223–238.

James, R. D. 1980. Snowy owl food in different habitats in the Toronto region, in the winter of 1945–46. *Ontario Field Biologist* 34:11–16.

Josephson, B. 1980. Aging and sexing snowy owls. *Journal of Field Ornithology* 51:149–160.

Kausrud, K. L., A. Mysterud, H. Steen, J. O. Vik, E. Østbye, B. Cazelles, E. Framstad, A. M. Eikeset, I. Mysterud, T. Solhøy, and N. C. Stenseth. 2008. Linking climate change to lemming cycles. *Nature* 456:93–98.

Keith, L. B. 1960. Observations on snowy owls at Delta, Manitoba. *Canadian Field-Naturalist* 74:106–112.

Kerlinger, P., and M. R. Lein. 1985. Population ecology of snowy owls during winter on the Great Plains of North America. *Condor* 90:866–874.

Kerlinger, P., M. R. Lein, and B. J. Sevick. 1985. Distribution and population fluctuations of wintering snowy owls (*Nyctea scandiaca*) in North America. *Canadian Journal of Zoology* 63:1829–1834.

Kerr, J., and L. Parker. 1998. The impact of climate change on mammal diversity in Canada. *Environmental Monitoring and Assessment* 49:263–270.

Parmalee, D. F. 1992. Snowy owl. In *The Birds of North America,* no. 10, ed. A. Poole, P. Stettenheim, and F. Gill. Philadelphia: Academy of Natural Sciences, and Washington, DC: American Ornithologists' Union.

———. 1972. Canada's incredible Arctic owls. *The Beaver* 52:30–41.

Potapov, E. and R. Sale. 2012. *The Snowy Owl.* London: T & A D Poyser.

Reid, D. G., R. A. Imes, N. M. Schmidt, G. Gauthier, and D. Ehrich. 2012. Lemmings (*Lemmus* and *Dicrostonyx* spp.). In Arctic Report Card: Update for 2012, http://www.arctic.noaa.gov/report12/lemmings.htm.

Seidensticker, M. T., D. W. Holt, J. Detienne, S. Talbot, and K. Gray. 2011. Sexing young snowy owls. *Journal of Raptor Research* 45:281–289.

Schmidt, N. M., R. A. Ims, T. T. Høye, O. Gilg, L. H. Hansen, J. Hansen, M. Lund, E. Fuglei, M. C. Forchhammer, and B. Sittler. 2012. Response of an arctic predator guild to collapsing lemming cycles. In *Proceedings of the Royal Society B: Biological Sciences* 279:4417–4422.

Solheim, R. 2012. Wing feather moult and age determination of snowy owls, *Bubo scandiacus. Ornis Norvegica* 35:48–67.

Sutton, G. M. 1932. *The Birds of Southampton Island*, part 2 sec. 2. Pittsburgh, PA: Memoirs of the Carnegie Museum.

Taylor, P. S. 1973. Breeding behavior of the snowy owl. *Living Bird* 12:137–154.

Therrien, J.-F., G. Gauthier, and J. Bêty. 2011. An avian terrestrial predator of the Arctic relies on the marine ecosystem during winter. *Journal of Avian Biology* 42:363–369.

Therrien, J.-F., G. Gauthier, J. Bêty, and G. Mouland. 2008. Long-distance migratory movements and habitat selection of snowy owls in Nunavut. Report to Nunavut Wildlife Management Board.

Watson, A. 1957. The behaviour, breeding, and food ecology of the snowy owl *Nyctea scandiaca. Ibis* 99:419–462.

Wink et al. 2009.

NORTHERN HAWK OWL
Surnia ulula
Alpha code: NHOW

LENGTH: 13.5–17.5 in. (33.5–44.4 cm). Males average 16.5 in. (42 cm), and females 17 in. (43 cm)

WINGSPAN: 30–35 in. (76–89 cm)

MASS: Weak reversed size dimorphism. Three pooled studies varied (in one case, widely) in averages and ranges for this species: Average, male: 10.5 oz. (299 g); range 9.6–11.5 oz. (273–326 g). Average, female: 12.2 oz. (345 g); range 10.8–13.8 oz. (306–392 g).[1] Average, male: 10.6 oz. (301 g); range 8.5–13.2 oz. (242–375 g). Average, female: 12 oz. (340 g); range 8.8–16 oz. (250–454 g).[2] Average, male: 8 oz. (226 g); range 6.8–9.4 oz. (194–266 g). Average, female: 8.9 oz. (252 g); range 7.1–9.6 oz. (202–273 g).[3]

LONGEVITY: Limited data; fewer than 30 band recoveries from North American birds. Oldest record is an 8-year-old owl banded as a chick in Minnesota in 1987 and recaptured in Manitoba; other notable records include one banded as an immature in Alberta in 2004 and found dead there at 5 years 11 months of age. Published report of "several banded specimens" over 10 years old[3] are not reflected in Banding Lab records. Average age on re-encounter, 1.6 years.

Built like a plump falcon, fast and nimble in flight, primarily diurnal—there is little that is stereotypically owlish about the Northern Hawk Owl, a species with an immense range but a spotty, unpredictable distribution and highly nomadic lifestyle. An inhabitant of the more-northerly sections

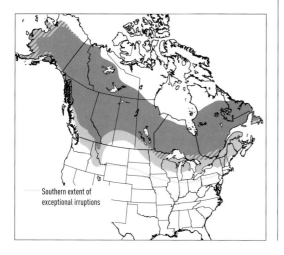

Southern extent of exceptional irruptions

The Northern Hawk Owl has an enormous range across the boreal forest zone of North America, but its abundance is spotty and it is common nowhere. *(Quebec. Gerrit Vyn)*

of the boreal forest, it makes erratic irruptive flights south when the populations of voles and other small mammals on which it depends crash, showing up as far south as New Jersey and Washington State on rare occasions, and sometimes lingering to breed in places like northern Minnesota. While widespread, it is nowhere common, and expanding logging, mineral extraction, and oil and gas development pose threats—as does climate change, which may severely limit its habitat in the century ahead.

SYSTEMATICS, TAXONOMY, AND ETYMOLOGY

Worldwide, this circumboreal species is divided into three subspecies, one of which, *S. u. caparoch,* occupies its entire North American range. The nominate race, *S. u. ulula,* from Eurasia to Siberia, has been recorded in extreme western Alaska. The New World birds are somewhat larger and darker than the nominate subspecies, although the differences are slight enough that some have questioned the validity of the forms.

ETYMOLOGY: The common name is readily apparent to anyone who has been struck by the hawklike appearance and behavior of this owl. The genus name, *Surnia,* is more of a mystery. It seems to have no basis in classical Greek or Latin, although Elliot Coues (1903) linked it to a putative modern Greek word, *surnion,* meaning "owl." The specific name *ulula* comes from the Latin *ululare,* "to howl, yell, or shriek," and may have referred to the Eurasian Tawny Owl. The subspecific name, *caparoch,* was coined by the German zoologist Phillip Ludwig Statius Muller, in a 1776 supplement to Linnaeus's taxonomic work. The word *caparoch* was said to be based on an indigenous name for the Hawk Owl around Hudson Bay, rendered as *caparacoch* or *coparacoch.*

Oddly, the hyphen-mad American Ornithologists' Union, whose checklist committee has given us such awkward constructions as "night-heron," "ground-dove," and, of course, "screech-owl," has chosen not to hyphenate the English name of this owl. The reasoning is that, unlike the Old World Hawk-Owls of the genus *Ninox,* which includes many species, *Surnia* is a monotypic genus and there is no risk of confusion.

> **FRENCH:** *Chouette érpervière*
> **INUIT:** *Niaqortuarajuh*
> **IÑUPIATUN:** *Niaquǧruaǧruk*

DISTRIBUTION

Generally resident (with irruptive movements south) throughout the boreal forest zone in Canada and Alaska north to the tree line. The limit of breeding shifts south after major irruptions, but it generally lies north of about latitude 48.

BREEDING SEASON: Nests from northern Newfoundland across Labrador and Quebec (not including the Ungava and Labrador Peninsulas); west across central and northern Ontario, including most of James Bay, then northwest to Cape Churchill (skirting the southern coast of Hudson Bay), across extreme southern Nunavut, then east and north of Great Slave and Great Bear Lakes to the lower Mackenzie Valley, and along the southern fringe of the Brooks Range to western Alaska. Normal southern extent from central British Columbia east across the boreal zone of central Alberta and Saskatchewan, southern Manitoba to Ontario and Quebec. Following major irruptions, may nest as far south as New Brunswick, southern Quebec and Ontario, and northern Minnesota (seven Minnesota counties since 1970). Since at least the early 1990s, a small population has bred in northwestern Montana, and the species has nested in northern Idaho and Washington.

NONBREEDING SEASON: Regularly irruptive south to southern New England and northern New York;

The subspecies of Northern Hawk Owl found in North America, *S. u. caparoch,* is somewhat larger and darker than the nominate race in Eurasia, which has been recorded in extreme western Alaska. *(Ontario. Glenn Bartley)*

Hawk Owl irruptions have been noted by naturalists since the mid-nineteenth century and appear to be driven by scarcity of prey on the breeding grounds. These irruptions are large-scale movements south that often occur in tandem with Great Gray Owls and Boreal Owls. *(Manitoba. Christian Artuso)*

northern Michigan, Wisconsin, and Minnesota; the northern Rockies south to Idaho and northern Washington. Much more rarely and unpredictably south of this band to New Jersey and Pennsylvania, Illinois, Iowa, Nebraska, Wyoming, and Oregon.

MIGRATION AND MOVEMENTS: Highly nomadic, irruptive, and unpredictable, although there is almost no hard information about between-season movements in either summer or winter among the North American population (and relatively little in Eurasia, where the Hawk Owl has been studied far more extensively). Assumed to show no fidelity to its nesting site, although this needs further study.

Unlike the largest irruptions of Snowy Owls, and the cyclically heavy autumn migrations of Northern Saw-whet Owls—which are driven by high prey density, and which follow a highly productive breeding season—the irruptions of Northern Hawk Owls are provoked by hardship and hunger. Often occurring in tandem with flights of Boreal Owls and Great Gray Owls, they take place after rodent populations on the breeding grounds collapse. In eastern Canada, for example, the flights of all three owls are tied to crashes in red-backed vole numbers, although Hawk Owl irruptions are less predictable than the punctual, 4-year timing of Boreal Owls.

Following an irruption from Scandinavia into continental Europe in the 1980s, the age and sex of nearly 80 dead Hawk Owls was determined. Researchers found that adult females showed the greatest propensity to move away from the breeding grounds, followed by immature males, with adult males and immature females most likely to stay north.

As with Boreal Owls (and probably Northern Saw-whets), this may reflect a tension between two fundamental pressures. Scarcity of prey may drive adult females south, where they can find more food and enter the next breeding season in the best possible condition. A scarcity of quality nest cavities in the scrubby forests of the boreal zone, on the other hand, may force the males to stay north and risk starvation in order to defend their territories. How this hypothesis squares with assumptions about nomadic behavior remains to be determined, however.

Hawk Owl irruptions have been noted by naturalists since the mid-nineteenth century, although only in more recent decades have there been enough observers to allow rough attempts to quantify and compare irruptions. In Minnesota, 11 invasions were documented between the winters of 1962–1963 and 2005–2006, with statewide counts ranging from 9 to 475 owls; several of these have been 2-year events, occurring in consecutive winters.

In the record-breaking 2004–2005 irruption,

Just because Northern Hawk Owl irruptions are usually triggered by prey scarcity in the north, the birds themselves aren't necessarily starving. In one record irruption in 2004–2005, most of the Hawk Owls banded that winter were healthy and well-fed, and their average weights increased as the winter went on. *(Manitoba. Christian Artuso)*

Active and agile hunters, Northern Hawk Owls fly with crisp wingbeats, resembling a kestrel in flight or an accipiter when gliding. *(Michigan. Tom Johnson)*

Although they appear to use sound far less for hunting than many owls do, Northern Hawk Owls will sometimes plunge through deep snow for mice that they could have detected only by sound. *(Maine. Luke Seitz)*

Hawk Owls were seen from Ontario to the Canadian prairies, but in fairly modest numbers, with a few exceptional individuals in Oregon and Washington. The epicenter of the flight was northeastern Minnesota, however, where up to 233 were counted in a single county, and 42 on a single Christmas Bird Count. The Hawk Owl flight coincided with even more staggering numbers of Great Gray Owls (see that species account, p. 238, for details) and a significant flight of Boreal Owls into much the same region.

Fall movements in irruptive years may begin as early as late Sept. or early Oct., although most migrants appear in Nov. or Dec., with additional movement through the first half of winter; how much of this represents new birds coming south, or owls shuffling among wintering locations, isn't entirely clear. Despite assumptions that irrupting owls are starving and food-stressed, of the nearly 150 Hawk Owls banded in Minnesota in 2004–2005 (two-thirds of them adults), most were reported to be healthy and well-fed. Their average weights increased through the winter, suggesting that the owls

may have arrived in diminished condition because of prey shortages farther north, but soon made up the difference.

POST-FLEDGING DISPERSAL: Little information. Long-distance band recoveries from Eurasia include movements of up to 1,200 mi. (1,900 km).

DISTRIBUTION OUTSIDE THE COVERAGE AREA: Circumboreal. The nominate subspecies breeds from Kamchatka and Sakhalin Island north to the Siberian tree line and west across northern Russia to Fennoscandia and (rarely) Estonia; extinct in Latvia. *S. u. tianschanica* is restricted to the Tian Shan and Dzungarian Alatau Mountains in northern China, the Kazakhstan borderlands, and possibly Mongolia. Vagrants from the New World subspecies *caparoch* have been recorded in Bermuda, Britain, and the Canary Islands.

DESCRIPTION AND IDENTIFICATION

More likely to be initially mistaken for an accipiter or small falcon than an owl, the Northern Hawk Owl is sleek and tapered, with a long, narrow tail that when perched extends well beyond the pointed wings, which reflect its active hunting style. The eyes are proportionately small for an owl. The large, squarish head bracketed by bold black and white markings, and the neatly and distinctly barred breast, are obvious field characteristics on a perched bird.

Flight is rapid, with crisp wingbeats; in powered flight it most resembles a kestrel, but when it pauses to glide, the impression is that of an accipiter. It often perches at the tip of a tree or snag, swooping up from below in the manner of a shrike, and will pump its tail like an American Kestrel, especially when preparing to launch an attack.

On those seen from above or behind, the black-and-white nape pattern is obvious and distinctive. Viewed from below in flight, virtually the entire owl—body, wings, coverts, flanks, and tail—appears closely patterned with fine, distinct, blackish barring. The Hawk Owl's plumage is less downy and velvety than on most owls, since silent flight is less of a necessity in this primarily diurnal hunter.

BASIC (ADULT) PLUMAGE: Sexes essentially identical. Crown and nape black, heavily speckled with white; large dark area with little white spotting in central nape. Facial disk broadly edged with black, which along the lower rim forms a partial collar. A secondary black "sideburn" mark is on each side of the head, separated from the disk rim by a large patch of white. Eyebrows narrow, indistinct, and gray-white. No ear tufts, although black upper corners of the facial disk rim can give the impression of

First-winter Northern Hawk Owls like this one have more extensive tail barring than adults do, and reduced back spotting increases the contrast with the white "suspender" bars on the scapulars. (Quebec. Tom Johnson)

small tufts when the owl is agitated and its feathers are erect. Facial disk and rictal bristles grayish, chin indistinctly and variably marked with darker gray. Narrow white collar at the top of the breast, and undersides including undertail coverts densely patterned in narrow, sharply marked black horizontal barring. Irises bright yellow, bill pale yellowish, feet densely feathered to the toes.

Ground color of upperparts is subject to fading; freshly molted owls are dark blackish brown, fading to chocolate brown by spring or summer. Large white tips on the scapulars, which form distinct "suspender" bands along the upper edge of the folded wings and merge with abundant white spotting, especially on the lower back. Upperwing coverts dark brown with gray-white spots on greater and primary coverts. Flight feathers gray-brown above and dark gray below with neat, narrow bars, white below and above on outer primaries, pale brown above on inner primaries and secondaries.

Tail dark brown above with white terminal band; six to eight narrow, gray-white to light brown bands.

JUVENAL PLUMAGE: Natal down white, replaced by grayish to gray-white mesoptile plumage, indistinctly barred with darker gray or gray-brown. The upper chest is darker gray. The facial disk is blackish, with a wide black rim enclosing large areas of white on the lower face, divided by a blackish chin. Upperparts gray-brown and downy, with large white spots on the scapulars and coverts. First-winter plumage is similar to the adult's but has reduced white spotting on the tertials and back, creating greater contrast with the white "suspender" bands on the scapulars. The tail barring is more extensive and more distinct on first-winter birds than on adults, although in the hand, the white tip of the central tail feather is narrower on immature Hawk Owls.

SIMILAR SPECIES: More likely to be mistaken for a hawk or falcon than an owl, both when perched and in flight. The Boreal Owl has a pronounced black rim around the facial disk reminiscent of the Hawk Owl's pattern, but the Boreal is smaller and plumper, has markedly shorter wings and tail, and rarely perches in the conspicuous locations favored by the Hawk Owl. The Northern Pygmy-Owl is partially diurnal, somewhat similar in shape, and has

A juvenile Northern Hawk Owl. Like a number of irruptive species, Hawk Owls have a habit of breeding well south of their normal range following major irruptions. (Manitoba. Christian Artuso)

dark eyespots on the nape but is less than half the size of the Hawk Owl and barely overlaps with the Hawk Owl in southwestern Canada.

VOCALIZATIONS

The advertisement call is a long, fairly sweet, bubbling trill, *ululululululululululululululululu,* lasting 5 to 15 seconds, typically 7 to 10 seconds, given from a prominent perch in morning or evening. The intensity and pitch may vary unevenly through the call, and there is some indication that this is especially true of the female's shorter version The similar Boreal Owl song is more uniform in pitch, less musical, and more decidedly "hollow" in tone than the Hawk Owl's. The Hawk Owl also gives an even faster, higher trill as a contact call and when the nest is disturbed.

Alarm calls include a flickerlike series of *reek-reek-reek-reek-reek* notes, and a harsh, two-part call lasting about 1.5 to 2 seconds that begins with a grating screech and ends abruptly with a short, high syllable: *screeeeeeeee-YIP!* Such screech calls may start with a short burst of the advertisement trill. When defending the nest or young, adults may give a *kwit-witit* or *whit-it, kwhit-whit-it* call.

HABITAT AND NICHE

A denizen of open, broken boreal forests, the Hawk Owl is most commonly found where spruce woods are liberally interspersed with bogs, old burns, marshes, muskeg, and other openings—habitat that covers vast expanses of the boreal zone, especially on its northern fringe where the dense, closed-canopy forest begins to break up into more of a mosaic.

Wildfire burns appear to be an especially important—and previously underappreciated—factor in maintaining Hawk Owl habitat and could be one reason this species is so nomadic in its movements. A study in Alberta—one of the few in North America on habitat choice in this species—found the greatest number of nesting Hawk Owls in areas that had burned 3 years previously, and none in forests that had burned more than 8 years prior. The owls likewise were completely absent from unburned tracts, and contrary to studies in Europe, they avoided clear-cuts as well.

Fires not only create a mosaic of mixed habitat, interweaving open land with older, mature forests; freshly burned areas also experience population booms of voles and other small mammals, while the shrub cover is still thin enough for sight hunters like Hawk Owls to find prey. And unlike a clear-cut, where most of the trees are removed, a fresh burn has many standing snags for hunting perches. Neighboring areas of unburned forest provide woodpecker holes, rot cavities, and large, snapped-off hollowed snags for nest sites—rare commodi-

ties in a region where trees grow slowly and remain fairly stunted.

The Hawk Owl's winter habitat tends to be very similar to its breeding habitat, with a greater use of field edges and other manmade openings, as well as deciduous and mixed forest edges. Summer or winter, the Hawk Owl is a perch hunter, using its sharp eyes (and most likely relying less on its hearing than other owls) to locate prey, which is captured in a fast, agile attack.

DIET: Most of what's known about the diet of the Northern Hawk Owl comes from Eurasia, where voles of various species make up the great bulk of the prey during the summer—from 93 to 98 percent, depending on the study, dropping significantly over the winter, when birds (especially ptarmigan) and hares played a bigger role. Birds may be critical for those owls that remain on the breeding grounds through winter, and this dietary flexibility may give them a survival edge that other irruptive northern owls like Great Grays lack.

The sparse North American research bears out this heavy dependence on voles, though with some interesting departures. Overall, a summary of eight studies from Minnesota to Alaska, summer and winter, found that voles made up almost 90 percent of the individual prey items in Hawk Owl pellets. In Denali National Park in Alaska, voles comprised more than 70 percent of the biomass in summer, but juvenile snowshoe hares and red

Voles comprised up to 98 percent of the Northern Hawk Owl's diet in summer, though in winter birds and young hares make up a significant part of their diet. *(Manitoba. Christian Artuso)*

squirrels together made up another 20 percent, and Gray Jays—especially young birds that had recently fledged—were common prey in early summer. Opportunistic, a hungry Hawk Owl will tackle almost any small or midsize mammal or bird, including smaller owls and birds up to the size of Willow Ptarmigan and Spruce Grouse.

NESTING AND BREEDING

Secondary cavity adopters, Northern Hawk Owls will use old woodpecker holes (especially those of Northern Flickers) and natural rot cavities, but more than half of the nests in one study were in the hollowed-out tops of broken snags. They will also use old stick nests from hawks or corvids and will nest on the dense growths known as "witches' brooms" that form (as a result of fungal infection or parasitic dwarf mistletoe) on the branches of spruce and fir. They will accept artificial nest boxes if provided, a practice that is more common in Europe than in North America. No nesting material is added.

Hawk Owls are believed to show no fidelity to their nesting sites, instead moving widely from year to year depending on vole populations; those in areas with poor vole numbers may not even attempt to breed. Whether they remain paired from breeding season to breeding season isn't known, but given their nomadism, it is unlikely.

The male begins courtship calling by Feb., and egg-laying usually occurs from late Apr. to early May across most of its range. As with many northern owls, the number of eggs depends on the abundance of prey, and clutch size may be as small as 3 or as large as 13, with 6 or 7 the normal size. An egg is laid every day or two until the clutch is complete. Incubation lasts 25 to 30 days and begins (as in most owls) with laying the first egg, so hatching is staggered. The chicks grow exceptionally fast— three times the rate of Boreal Owls in Europe— and branch out or jump to the ground as early as 3 weeks of age, well before they can fly.

Hawk Owls, like a number of irruptive species, have a habit of breeding well south of their normal nesting range following invasion winters. In northern Minnesota, Hawk Owls nested following six of eleven irruptions between the 1960s and mid-2000s.

BEHAVIOR

Although the Northern Hawk Owl is considered primarily diurnal, little is known about the degree to which it is also active at night. Certainly its physical adaptations seem geared toward a diurnal lifestyle. Its eyes are proportionately small compared with most owls, and its ear openings lack the asymmetry common in highly nocturnal species.

An adult Northern Hawk Owl delivers half a rodent to its fledgling in Glacier National Park. *(Montana. Paul Bannick/VIREO)*

But those Hawk Owls that winter in the northern reaches of the breeding grounds and experience almost endless winter nights are nocturnal by necessity, and as with Snowy Owls, we may have an exaggerated sense of how diurnal they are when given a choice.

Birders are invariably struck by the Northern Hawk Owl's naiveté around humans, a characteristic shared with several other North Woods owls, including the Boreal, Northern Saw-whet, and Great Gray. But they are trusting only to a point. Get too close to the nest or recently fledged young, and you may be sent scurrying with a bloody scalp, for Hawk Owls are known for their spirited defense— as one egg-collector in 1919 discovered. The female, he said, was "with the exception of one Goshawk the most warlike of any I have had to deal with. As I climbed the stub she charged and knocked my heavy Stetson hat off and struck me several times on top of the head and quite hard."[4] (Unfortunately, the female's attack failed to stop him from taking her 7 eggs.)

Hawk Owls have a decidedly falconish flair—in silhouette when perched, in rapid flight, or when hovering (as they sometimes do) they can look remarkably like Merlins or chunky American Kestrels. The usual hunting approach is to perch at the tip of a tree or snag for long periods, scanning the surroundings, then swoop down rapidly on prey that reveals itself for an instant; an excited Hawk Owl may rhythmically pump its tail before launching it-

Built like a plump falcon instead of a typical owl, the Northern Hawk Owl is an active daytime hunter, although, because little research has been done with this species, no one knows the extent to which it may be nocturnally active as well. *(Manitoba. Christian Artuso)*

self after prey. If it's chasing a small bird or a young hare through dense cover, it can maneuver as nimbly as a Sharp-shinned Hawk, its long tail providing the rudder for snap turns and split-second twists.

Although the Hawk Owl would seem poorly suited for locating prey under deep snow, there are examples of it snow-plunging for voles, suggesting that it uses its ears as well as its eyes, sometimes diving completely out of sight in soft snow. Banding suggests that once they settle in at a wintering site with sufficient prey, Hawk Owls may move relatively little, at least in areas with good prey numbers: several dozen banded and re-encountered in Minnesota generally moved less than 5 mi. from where they were first banded.

STATUS

Widespread but uncommon across most of its breeding range. Nesting in some of the most remote parts of North America, Northern Hawk Owls have been largely shielded from human encroachment; although until at least the mid–twentieth century they were badly persecuted when they came south. At one time, the slaughter of irrupting Hawk Owls was tremendous. "Hawk Owls came three weeks ago in greater numbers than ever seen before. Farmers' sons have been killing them all over the country," one New Hampshire resident wrote in 1884.[5] That

same winter, a taxidermist in Maine received 28 in just a few weeks, and "for every one preserved a dozen were probably thrown away," said ornithologist William Brewster, who was busily shooting as many as he could for his own collection.[6]

Today the owls are safer in winter but facing potentially much more serious challenges in their breeding range. As with many northern boreal species, there is little hard information about numbers and trends; one estimate placed the North American population at a fairly stable 10,000 to 50,000 pairs, while Partners in Flight estimated the global population at 120,000 individuals, with half in North America. But bird surveys are scanty in that part of the world, and the data on which these estimates are based are fairly thin. No one knows if the increasing frequency and magnitude of irruptions in the upper Midwest since the early 1990s indicates an increasing owl population to the north, or if it simply reflects a temporary coincidence of factors like prey abundance and weather.

One concern is the rapid development in parts of the boreal forest—large-scale timbering that may eliminate nesting habitat, and increasing exploration and extraction of minerals, natural gas, and tar sands. Changes in wildfire regimes, and timbering practices (such as salvage logging) that eliminate dead standing timber following burns, may also have negative effects. Alberta has at times listed the species as "sensitive" in recognition of the potential risk from timber harvests. Montana, where the most southerly population nests, lists the Hawk Owl as "vulnerable."

Climate change is another serious concern for northern boreal birds. While research from North America is lacking, researchers in Finland found that Northern Hawk Owls there had shifted their breeding range significantly to the north between the periods 1979–1984 and 2006–2010—in fact, the owl showed the second-greatest shift of any species in the study. Based on climate models, researchers concluded that the Hawk Owl could lose between 60 and 90 percent of its habitat in Finland by 2080.

NOTES

1. Earhart and Johnson 1970.

2. J. R. Duncan and P. A. Duncan. 1998. Northern hawk owl (*Surnia ulula*). In *The Birds of North America,* no. 356, ed. A. Poole and F. Gill. Philadelphia, PA: Birds of North America.

3. Eckert and Karalus 1973.

4. A. D. Henderson. 1919. Nesting of the American hawk owl. *Oölogist* 35:59–64; quote p. 63.

5. N. Norton, quoted in W. Brewster. 1885. Hawk owls in New England. *Auk* 2:108–109.

6. W. Brewster, ibid.

BIBLIOGRAPHY

Byrkjedal, I., and G. Langhelle. 1986. Sex and age biased mobility in hawk owls *Surnia ulula. Ornis Scandinavica* 17:306–308.

Chevaeu et al. 2004.

Coues, E. 1903. *Key to North American Birds*, vol. 2., 5th ed. Boston: Dana Estes.

Duncan, P. A., and W. C. Harris. 1997. Northern hawk owls (*Surnia ulula caparoch*) and forest management: A review. *Journal of Raptor Research* 31:187–190.

Eckert 2005.

Gill, F. B., M. T. Wright III, S. B. Conyne, and R. Kirk. 2009. On hyphens and phylogeny. *Wilson Journal of Ornithology* 121:652–655.

Grosshuesch, D. 2008. Presence of breeding northern hawk owls (*Surnia ulula*) in Minnesota, 2006. *Loon* 80:180–187.

Hannah, K. C., and J. S. Hoyt. 2004. Northern hawk owls and recent burns: Does burn age matter? *Condor* 106:420–423.

Kertell, K. 1986. Reproductive biology of northern hawk-owls in Denali National Park, Alaska. *Journal of Raptor Research* 20:91–101.

Nicoletti, F. J., R. Brady, and D. Alexander. 2005. The winter 2004–2005 influx of northern owls, part III: Northern hawk owl banding. *Loon* 77:209–219.

Smith, C. Y., I. G. Warkentin, and M. T. Moroni. 2008. Snag availability for cavity nesters across a chronosequence of post-harvest landscapes in western Newfoundland. *Forest Ecology and Management* 256:641–647.

Sonerud, G. A. 1997. Hawk owls in Fennoscandia: Population fluctuations, effects of modern forestry, and recommendations on improving foraging habitats. *Journal of Raptor Research* 31:167–174.

Svingen, P. H., and F. J. Nicholetti. 2005. The 2004–2005 influx of northern owls, part 1: Northern hawk owl. *Loon* 77:132–140.

Virkkala, R., R. K. Heikkinen, A. Lehikoinen, and J. Valkama. 2014. Matching trends between recent distributional changes of northern-boreal birds and species-climate model predictions. *Biological Conservation* 172:124–127.

Virkkala, R., R. K. Heikkinen, N. Leikola, and M. Luoto. 2008. Projected large-scale range reductions of northern-boreal land bird species due to climate change. *Biological Conservation* 141:1343–1353.

NORTHERN PYGMY-OWL
Glaucidium gnoma
Alpha code: NOPO

LENGTH: 6.5–7.3 in. (16.5–18.5 cm)

WINGSPAN: 15 in. (38 cm)

MASS: Weak reversed size dimorphism. Information on most subspecies is limited. Body mass of females, but not males, decreases through the nesting season.

- *G. g. californicum*: Average, male: 2.2 oz. (61.9 g); range 1.9–2.6 oz. (54–74 g). Average, female: 2.6 oz. (73 g); range 2.25–3 oz. (64–87 g).[1] Average for eight males: 2.2 oz. (62.8 g); range 2–2.4 oz. (57.3–68 g).[2] Average, combined sexes: 2.2 oz. (61.5 g); range 1.9–2.25 oz. (54–64 g).[3]
- *G. g. "pinicola"*: Average, male: 1.4 oz. (40.8 g); range 1.2–1.6 oz. (34.6–46.8 g). Average, female: 1.6 oz. (44.8 g); range 1.3–1.8 oz. (36.9–50.7 g).[4]
- *G. g. gnoma*: One female, 1.9 oz. (54.3 g).[5] Average for four males: 1.9 oz. (52.9 g); range 1.8–2 oz. (50.3–57.5 g). One female, 2.1 oz. (60 g).[6]

LONGEVITY: Very limited information. Relatively few Northern Pygmy-Owls have been banded, and only three have been re-encountered, the oldest at 3 years 11 months. In captivity they can live up to 10 years.

A century ago, little was known about the life history and biology of the Northern Pygmy-Owl—and to a surprising degree that hasn't changed a great deal, despite this tiny raptor's wide range, relative abundance, partially diurnal activity, and outsize reputation for ferocity.

One of the smallest owls in North America, the Northern Pygmy-Owl is found in mountain forests from Alaska to Central America, where it hunts rodents, birds, and other small—and at times not-so-small—prey, up to squirrels and quail that may weigh several times its own mass. It's also a fascinating taxonomic puzzle, with a complex of subspecies, vocalization patterns, and plumage differences that may mask up to four distinct species.

In the past, scientists have assumed the Northern Pygmy-Owl's ecology, vocal repertoire, and behavior would be similar to the much better studied Eurasian Pygmy-Owl (*G. passerinum*), on the presumption that these two such similar-looking species must be closely related. But appearances aside,

This Northern Pygmy-Owl, its bill and feet stained with blood from a recent meal, belongs to the "mountain" group, two subspecies found from the Southwestern Sky Island ranges to Honduras. *(Arizona. Glenn Bartley)*

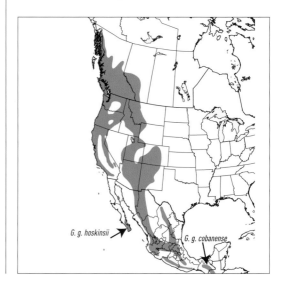

Northern Pygmy-Owls are taxonomically complex, with six or seven subspecies divided into three broad groups, but which show five basic vocal distinctions suggestive of species-level divisions. There are also regional color variations, along with color morphs. Those from the Pacific Northwest, like this one, are the darkest and brownest. *(British Columbia. Glenn Bartley)*

The "Cape Pygmy-Owl," the subspecies *G. g. hoskinsii*, is restricted to the mountains of extreme southern Baja Sur and is sometimes treated as a separate species. *(Baja. Pete Morris)*

DNA analysis suggests the New World and Old World pygmy-owls aren't close cousins.

SYSTEMATICS, TAXONOMY, AND ETYMOLOGY

Taxonomically complex, the Northern Pygmy-Owl has half a dozen or so subspecies lumped into three major groups. While the AOU has not yet split them, waiting for more detailed genetic information, a number of other authorities have already divided them into as many as four species, and such a move by the AOU seems likely.

Plumage differences are slight, with size and coloration varying clinally with latitude, elevation, and humidity. While initial genetic testing seems to indicate fairly limited divergence among the groups, they have regionally distinct song types (see "Vocalizations," p. 157). A proposal to split the "Guatemalan Pygmy-Owl," *G. g. cobanense,* was apparently rejected in part because the AOU would prefer not to carve up the Northern Pygmy-Owl piecemeal, but make a single, comprehensive job of it once enough information is in hand.

On top of that, both genetic and morphological evidence suggest that the New World pygmy-owls are distinct enough from the Old World forms to warrant their own genus—although the suggested name, *Phalaenopsis* (first applied by Charles Lucien Bonaparte in 1854), had been bestowed 29 years earlier on a genus of what are now popular ornamental orchids. While it is technically acceptable for plants and animals to share a genus name, the practice is usually avoided, and should be in this case.

At the moment, six or seven subspecies in three groups are usually recognized.

"Northern Pygmy-Owl" group: *G. g. grinnelli:* Coastal; southeast Alaska south to southern California. *G. g. swarthi:* Vancouver Island and nearby Gulf Islands. *G. g. californicum:* Interior British Columbia east to western Alberta, south to southern California, Arizona, and New Mexico. (Rocky Mountain birds, from northwestern Wyoming and Utah south, are sometimes classified as a fourth subspecies in this group, *G. g. pinicola.*) Coastal birds are darker and browner or redder, while interior individuals are grayer. These subspecies are sometimes considered a single distinct species.

"Mountain Pygmy-Owl" group: *G. g. gnoma:* Southern Arizona and New Mexico, and the Sierra Madres north of Oaxaca and Puebla. *G. g. cobanense:* Chiapas south to Honduras. *G. g. cobanense* has been proposed for species status as the "Guatemalan Pygmy-Owl," while other authorities lump both races into the "Northern Pygmy-Owl."

"Cape Pygmy-Owl": *G. g. hoskinsii:* Restricted to the mountains of extreme southern Baja. It is sometimes treated as a separate species, sometimes lumped with the "mountain" group.

ETYMOLOGY: The genus name comes from the Greek *glaukidion*, "glaring," and *glaukos* or *glaux*, a reference to "a small owl." The species name, *gnoma*, is Latin, from the Greek *gnome*, "thought" or "intelligence," referring to the assumption of intelligence in owls and their association with Athena, goddess of wisdom. The English name reflects its northernmost distribution within the New World pygmy-owls.

SPANISH: *Tecolote [tecolotito] serrano, tecolote [tecolotito] norteño, picametate* (also for Ferruginous Pygmy-Owl); *tecolotillo duende* (Chiapas)
NÁHUATL: *Tlalquepacle*

DISTRIBUTION

BREEDING SEASON: Essentially resident in western mountains from Alaska to Chiapas, with some elevational movements (see "Migration and Movements," p. 155). Nonbreeders north to Yakutat and possibly Prince William Sound, Alaska. Breeds north to Admiralty Islands in southeastern Alaska (rarely), east across central British Columbia to southwestern Alberta. South through the Rockies in Idaho and western Montana, northwestern Wyoming, Utah, Colorado, Arizona, and western New Mexico; in Cascades, Coast Ranges and Sierra Nevada south through Washington and Oregon to southern California, and in the mountains of eastern and central Nevada. Isolated population (*G. g. hoskinsii*) in extreme southern Baja. Sky Island mountains of Arizona and New Mexico, south through the Sierra Madre Occidental to Colima, east to Oaxaca and Puebla, and north through the Sierra Madre Oriental to Coahuila. Disjunct *G. g. cobanense* in highlands of Chiapas south to Honduras.

Elevational zones range from near sea level to 4,000 ft. (1,200 m) in Alaska and British Columbia; 4,000–7,300 ft. (1,220–2,225 m; upper range "exceptionally high")[2] in northeast California; 5,600–9,800 ft. (1,700–3,000 m), sometimes higher, in central and southern Rockies. Generally between 5,900 and 12,100 ft. (1,800 and 3,700 m) in Mexico, but as low as 4,000 ft. (1,220 m) along the Pacific slope and up to 13,000 ft. (3,960 m) on the highest volcanic peaks. Between 6,600 and 10,000 ft. (2,210 and 3,050 m) in Oaxaca.

MIGRATION AND MOVEMENTS: Altitudinal migrant in the Rockies, moving to lower areas in winter, although the degree and frequency of such movements are poorly understood. No evidence for latitudinal migration, but this species has been little studied. There are a handful of accepted records from the Chisos Mountains in West Texas.

POST-FLEDGING DISPERSAL: Adults tend fledged chicks for 30 to 34 days, after which the young dis-

A rufous morph is fairly common among the "Guatemalan Pygmy-Owl," *G. g. cobanense*, found from Chiapas to Honduras, and which has been split as a distinct species by some experts. *(Guatemala. Knut Eisermann)*

perse from the breeding territory. No information about dispersal distances.

DISTRIBUTION OUTSIDE THE COVERAGE AREA: Range extends into Guatemala and Honduras.

DESCRIPTION AND IDENTIFICATION

Diminutive and round-headed, long-tailed and short-winged, the Northern Pygmy-Owl is distinctive in its proportions, plumage, and behavior. The flight is undulating and woodpecker-like. Females are said to be richer and rustier-brown by subspecies, but this remains to be confirmed. The exact status of color morphs in the "northern" subspecies group is also confused by feather wear and regional variation—ranging from darkest and brownest in humid coastal forests (especially Vancouver Island) to palest and grayest in higher-elevation Rocky Mountain locations—and likewise needs further study. A distinct rufous morph does occur in the "mountain" group from northern Mexico south, including *G. g. cobanense*, among which such red

The eyespots on the nape of the neck on pygmy-owls, once thought to deter larger predators, may in fact be a defense against smaller annoyances—the angry songbirds that noisily mob pygmy-owls when they discover the small raptors. *(Washington. Greg Lasley)*

morphs are fairly common. The "Cape Pygmy-Owl" (*G. g. hoskinsii*), on the other hand, is monomorphic.

BASIC (ADULT) PLUMAGE: Sexes generally alike (see "Description and Identification," p. 155). Crown and upperparts brown, rufous-brown, or gray-brown, with small white dots on the forehead and the crown. Nape marked by large, black, inverted teardrop "eyespots" rimmed in white. Scapular tips white, forming a series of large white dots above each folded wing; back feathers sparsely tipped in small triangular white spots. Wing coverts tipped in white, and buff-white barring on flight feathers visible on folded wing. Tail dark brown with five or six narrow, incomplete whitish bars.

No ear tufts, per se, but can flare feathers on the side of the head while compressing the face to create a similar effect (see "Behavior," p. 160). Facial disk poorly developed, with ground color matching crown, marked with concentric rows of fine, light streaks. Eyebrows narrow and gray-white; rictal bristles grayish. Upper chest and sides brown to rufous-brown, spotted with white; breast white with crisp, vertical rufous-brown streaks. Iris yellow, bill pale yellow. Feet sparsely feathered, toes yellow.

JUVENAL PLUMAGE: Natal down white. Juvenile plumage resembles that of the adult, but the grayish, rela-

Though lacking ear tufts, pygmy-owls can nonetheless create a similar impression by compressing their facial disks and flaring the feathers at the upper corners—a concealment posture that helps to break up their outline. *(Colorado. Scott Rashid)*

tively unspotted head contrasts with browner back and wings, especially marked in coastal populations.

SIMILAR SPECIES: Range overlaps slightly with very similar Ferruginous Pygmy-Owl in Mexico and southern Arizona, but elevation and habitat usually separate them—Northern Pygmy-Owl in the mountainous conifer forests, Ferruginous usually at lower elevations below about 4,200 ft. (1,300 m) in thorn scrub, cactus, and desert riparian zones. Ferruginous is noticeably more rufous, especially on tail. Elf Owl is smaller, with a very short tail, and lacks eyespots; generally at lower elevations.

Vocally, the songs of Northern Saw-whet Owls resemble those of single-hoot populations of Northern Pygmy-Owls, but the former more rarely

An adult of the "northern" subspecies group feeds its chick part of a freshly killed junco. Juvenile Northern Pygmy-Owls show contrast between the gray, unspotted head and browner back, but this is less pronounced in interior populations. *(Colorado. Scott Rashid)*

call in daylight and often call continuously for long stretches. Ferruginous Pygmy-Owl calls are higher-pitched, faster, and less consistent in rhythm.

VOCALIZATIONS

There are five basic vocal divisions within the Northern Pygmy-Owl complex, which in the opinion of many experts reflect species-level distinctions. However, vocal differences, DNA, and morphology do not divide neatly and consistently, and the AOU has been waiting for more information before making any official splits.

The territorial song is a series of clear *toot* notes, but depending on region, they may be single or paired, and slow or fast; single-noted calls may also become two-noted with excitement. Howell and Webb (1995) described the basic song types as "slow single-hooters" on the coast from Alaska and British Columbia to California (*G. g. swarthi* and *grinelli*); "slow double-hooters" in southern Baja (*G. g. hoskinsii*); "fast single-hooters" in the interior from British Columbia south to Arizona (*G. g. californicum*/"*pinicola*"); and "fast double-hooters" from southern Arizona to Oaxaca (*G. g. gnoma*).

The "Guatemalan" Pygmy-Owl, *G. g. cobanense,* has a faster call rate of single or paired notes in the territorial song while the female's call when duetting is a rapid *whiwhiwhi*. The single-noted version is very similar to the territorial call of the Unspot-

ted Saw-whet Owl, but it is slightly higher and less nasal. During long singing bouts, the "Guatemalan" Pygmy-Owl usually lapses into multiple-noted calls, but short *toot* series can be confusing.

Vocalizations tend to peak just after sunset and again around and just after sunrise. When singing, the owl distends its white throat patch with each *toot*. As with many owls, the smaller male has a slightly deeper voice. The juvenile begging call is a high, rapid trill very much like a cricket.

HABITAT AND NICHE

This is a forest owl, with a general preference (though not an absolute requirement) for conifers or mixed coniferous-deciduous woods at higher elevations—since it is also found in temperate rain forests near sea level at the northern edge of its range, in dense montane oak forests and sycamore canyons in Arizona and northern Mexico, oak savannahs in California, and cloud forests in southern Mexico. The subspecies (or, perhaps, species) show their own habitat and elevation preferences. In the Madrean Sky Island ranges of Arizona, for example, "Northern" race birds are found in high,

Across its wide range, the Northern Pygmy-Owl shows a preference for conifer or mixed conifer-hardwood forests. Those of the "mountain" group in Mexico, like this bird, tend to inhabit pine-oak and pine forests at lower elevations than those from the "northern" group. *(Colima. Pete Morris)*

Northern Pygmy-Owls rarely hesitate to tackle prey that weighs as much as or more than themselves—as this chipmunk, caught by a grayish interior bird from the "northern" group, learned too late. (Colorado. Scott Rashid)

cool conifer forests, while "Mountain Pygmy-Owls" are found at lower, warmer, oak-dominated elevations. In Mexico, found in humid pine-oak and more arid pine forests.

As with many aspects of the Northern Pygmy-Owl's ecology, relatively little is known about its habitat requirements at a finer scale. Since the early twentieth century, observers have claimed the owls like to hunt the edges of forest openings and clearings, but more recent research—especially that involving radiotelemetry—has cast doubt on this assumption. It may be simply that these small, somewhat secretive owls are more easily spotted in edge habitat.

One study in western Wyoming found that Northern Pygmy-Owls preferred to nest in spruce and fir forests where the trees were significantly larger and taller than average. This finding was echoed by research across the mountains of Oregon, where the pygmy-owls were fairly common in almost all conifer and mixed conifer–hardwood forest types, but increased in number with the average diameter of the biggest trees. In both Alberta and the Olympic Peninsula of Washington they favored older, taller, more structurally complex stands.

The Washington study, which used radio transmitters to track owls in an area fragmented by logging, found clear-cut edges were used least of all. The authors concluded that such openings were of little value to pygmy-owls, which gravitated to structurally diverse habitats. In northern California, the removal of snags from a giant sequoia forest led to the complete extirpation of this owl over a 50-year period. The only exception to this general preference for older forests was found on Vancouver Island, where one study of the *G. g. swarthi* race reported a preference for lower, younger, more open forests near lakes and wetlands.

DIET: Northern Pygmy-Owls rather famously lack a sense of proportion when it comes to picking their prey. Feeding mostly on small rodents, insects, reptiles (especially lizards), and small birds (this last especially in winter), they will on occasion wrestle into submission animals considerably—sometimes almost insanely—bigger and heavier than themselves. That's a risky proposition for any predator, much less a bird with hollow, fairly delicate bones, for whom a fracture or sprain may mean a slow, lingering death.

Such concerns do not stop Northern Pygmy-Owls, however. Only about as big as a large thrush, this small hunter has been known to kill Gambel's and California Quail more than two and a half times its weight. Flickers and other large woodpeckers, Mourning Doves, Robins, even red squirrels have been recorded as prey.

In 1874, pioneering ornithologist and cavalry officer Charles Bendire described how a pygmy-owl latched on to a gopher, which carried the apparently unruffled owl for some distance before finally being dispatched. Pygmy-owls have occasionally been caught by hand when they were unwilling to relinquish prey that was too heavy to carry off. One scientist in California, seeing a pygmy-owl latch on to a young quail, scooped up both of them. "When I picked them up, the owl seemed unconcerned and continued to grip and bite the head of the quail during the 45-minute ride home."[7]

"Its powers can not be measured by its size," one early naturalist observed with respect.[8] Another, stuck between admiration and scorn, said, "Its friends would call it courageous and determined; its enemies, ferocious and blood thirsty."[9] Ornithologists today, of course, would call it none of those things—just a potent and effective predator, doing what it's supposed to do.

While discussions of pygmy-owl diet tend to focus on exceptionally large prey, its bread and butter is much smaller quarry—though even a vole or mouse is substantial for so small a predator.

One reason the Northern Pygmy-Owl has managed to succeed across such a wide geographic and ecological range is its ability to take an equally wide variety of food. With a few exceptions, though, the sort of detailed dietary studies common for other wide-ranging owls are missing for this species.

In one (based on an examination of stomach contents of 70 Northern Pygmy-Owls), mice, voles, and shrews were found to make up more than a third of the diet of males and more than half that of females, perhaps because the latter are heavier and better able to grapple down a mammal. Males took more birds and lizards (the latter seasonally in spring and summer), while insects (Jerusalem crickets, cicadas, grasshoppers, and beetles) comprised between 27 and 38 percent of their diet. Birds are more important in winter for both sexes.

In another study, this one in coastal Oregon, mammals and birds made up roughly equal parts of the diet when averaged over time, but varied dramatically from year to year. Mammals comprised almost 70 percent of the diet one year, for example, but just 15 percent the next year, while birds made up 82 percent of the prey brought to nests. Insects were taken only in the year when mammal numbers were lowest.

How an owl's diet is studied can also make a big difference in the results. Researchers on the Olympic Peninsula used three methods to assess what male Northern Pygmy-Owls ate—direct observation, pellet analysis, and an examination of prey remains. Compared with direct observation, pellets substantially underestimated the percentage of birds in the diet: birds made up more than half the diet by direct observation, but only 18 percent according to pellet analysis. This may be because bird bones are more completely digested than mammal bones, especially mandibles. On the other hand, pellets seemed to give a fuller picture of insect consumption than either other approach.

NESTING AND BREEDING

A secondary cavity nester, the Northern Pygmy-Owl is dependent on woodpecker holes (especially those cut by Northern Flickers, and Hairy and Pileated Woodpeckers) as well as natural openings. Territorial calling and duetting begin in late winter and peak during Mar. and Apr. across much of its range, when territories are being established, and the males sing from inside prospective cavities; a few observations suggest the male may also carry prey in and out of potential nest sites, or leave it inside, to entice the female.

Pygmy-owls often return to the same territory year after year but appear to reuse nest holes infrequently. In one of the few studies of nesting success in this species, researchers in Oregon found that Northern Pygmy-Owls were highly successful parents, laying 4 to 7 eggs (with an average of about 6) and fledging more than 90 percent of their chicks. Incubation lasted 29 to 33 days, with the chicks leaving the nest over the course of 2 days at about 27 days of age. It's unclear if—in contrast to most owls—Northern Pygmy-Owls wait until the last egg of the clutch is laid to begin incubation, as is the case with Old World species.

The Oregon study also revealed an unexpected twist. Northern Pygmy-Owls are among the smallest owls to begin with, but the tiniest females in the study area were found to breed earliest and—in years when small mammals were scarcest and hunting was presumably hardest—to also lay the most eggs and fledge the most young. Why? It may be that a smaller mother needs less food for herself and can devote more of what she and her mate catch to feeding their offspring. In a lean year, that may make the difference between success and failure.

In Montana and Idaho, chicks fledged between mid-June and early Aug., and in coastal Washington, between mid-June and mid-July. In all three cases, fledging generally occurred within a few hours, lending weight to the suspicion that the eggs are incubated as a full clutch and hatch synchronously. The chicks in the Rocky Mountains remained together, tended at first by both adults, but the females abandoned the family group in as few as 9 days, leaving care of the young to the males alone. The young owls begin to try their hand at hunting, making their own kills about 2 weeks after leaving the nest. In the weeks after fledging, the families used areas ranging from 99 to 227 acres (40 to 92 hectares), until the male, too, abandoned the youngsters about a month after they'd fledged. Not long thereafter, the siblings went their separate ways.

BEHAVIOR

This is the only owl you're likely to see at a bird feeder—though it's not there for the seeds and suet. Especially in winter, they're not above picking off small birds at a feeding station. Most active just after daybreak and again at dusk, the Northern Pygmy-Owl may hunt at any time of day, especially in cloudy weather. (Exactly how active they may be at night, if at all, remains essentially unstudied.)

Most of this pygmy-owl's hunting consists of patient waiting and a quick ambush from a perch, often signaling its rising excitement as the attack grows more imminent with a catlike, side-to-side twitch of its tail. But it will make short, rapid chases when circumstances demand, using its long tail

A Northern Pygmy-Owl chick peers from its nest, an old woodpecker hole in an aspen in the Rocky Mountains. Chicks usually fledge at about 27 days of age. *(Colorado. Scott Rashid)*

Active hunters, Northern Pygmy-Owls take a wide variety of prey—rodents, small birds, lizards, and insects. Although most of their hunting is done at dawn and dusk, they may be active throughout the day, especially in cloudy weather. *(Washington. Gerrit Vyn)*

and short wings to great effect, weaving through the undergrowth like a small accipiter. It lacks the silent-flight adaptations of most owls (in fact, its flapping flight is quite noisy), and it has a poorly developed facial disk, which, with its symmetrical ear openings, are indications that sound is of less importance than sight in hunting. In direct flight it alternates flaps and short, stalling glides, creating a woodpecker-like undulation.

One of the easiest ways to find a pygmy-owl is to listen for the frantic, scolding alarm calls of chickadees, sparrows, wrens, and other songbirds, which relentlessly mob any pygmy-owl they find in day-light. The prominent eyespots on the owl's nape, which naturalists long assumed were meant to startle and deter larger predators, may also be a way of minimizing the harassment and threat of physical harm from a mobbing horde by directing attacks away from the owl's blind spot at the rear.

(Interestingly, scientists have found that Black-capped Chickadees, which often lead the mobbing efforts, employ slightly different calls to announce the presence of small, maneuverable raptors that pose the greatest hazard—including Northern Pygmy-Owls—and thus elicit the most intense response from smaller birds.)

STATUS

Because of its wide range, the Northern Pygmy-Owl is ranked as "least concern" by the IUCN/Bird-Life, but some populations at the edge of its range (Alaska, Wyoming) are of concern because of limited numbers or a lack of information.

The endemic Vancouver Island subspecies, *G. g. swarthi,* is on a provincial "blue list" of vulnerable species in British Columbia owing to its small population size, a possible declining trend, negative impacts from logging, and increasing predation from Barred Owls, which have increased significantly in the Pacific Northwest.

Although Mexico does not list the species as a whole, the endemic Baja California Sur subspecies *G. g. hoskinsii* is of potential concern because of its limited range and population size. The status of the "Guatemalan" Pygmy-Owl, *G. g. cobanense,* is also uncertain because of deforestation in its fairly small range.

Although there has been an uptick in research efforts directed at this species, the Northern Pygmy-Owl remains one of the most under-studied common owls in our area. The limited work on habitat use and nest sites suggests it may be sensitive to logging that reduces forest complexity, while the rise in Barred Owls in the Northwest may be putting pressure on pygmy-owls, as with several other small owl species in the region.

NOTES

1. Earhart and Johnson 1970.

2. N. K. Johnson and W. C. Russell. 1962. Distributional data on certain owls in the western Great Basin. *Condor* 64:513–514.

3. D. W. Holt and J. L. Petersen. 2000. Northern pygmy-owl (*Glaucidium gnoma*). In *The Birds of North America*, no. 494, ed. A. Poole and F. Gill. Philadelphia: Birds of North America.

4. Eckert and Karalus 1973.

5. L. Paynter. 1952. Birds from Popocatépetl and Ixtac-cíhuatl, Mexico. *Auk* 69:293–301.

6. Binford 1989.

7. T. G. Balyoogen. 1969. Pygmy owl attacks California quail. *Auk* 86:358.

8. E. A. Preble 1930. Quoted in Bent 1938, p. 403.

9. P. A. Taverner 1926. Quoted in Bent 1938, p. 406.

BIBLIOGRAPHY

Cooper, J., and S. M. Beauchesne. 2004. "Vancouver Island" northern pygmy-owl. In *Accounts and Measures for Managing Identified Wildlife*, v. 2004. Victoria, BC: Ministry of Water, Land and Air Protection.

Darling, L. M. 2003. Status of the Vancouver Island northern pygmy-owl (*Glaucidium gnoma swarthi*) in British Columbia. Victoria, BC: Ministry of Water, Land and Air Protection and Ministry of Sustainable Resource Management.

Deppe, C., D. Holt, J. Tewksbury, L. Broberg, J. Petersen, and K. Wood. 2003. Effect of northern pygmy-owl (*Glaucidium gnoma*) eyespots on avian mobbing. *Auk* 120:765–771.

Deschler, J. F., and M. T. Murphy. 2012. The breeding biology of the northern pygmy-owl: Do the smallest of the small have an advantage? *Condor* 114:314–322.

Eisermann 2013.

Eisermann, K., and S. N. G. Howell. 2011. Vocalizations of the Guatemalan pygmy-owl (*Glaucidium cobanense*). *Journal of Raptor Research* 45:304–314.

Enríque-Rocha, Rangel-Salazar, and Holt 1993.

Friedman, Griscom, and Moore 1950.

Frye, G. G., and H. R. Jageman. 2012. Post-fledging ecology of northern pygmy-owls in the Rocky Mountains. *Wilson Journal of Ornithology* 124:199–207.

Giese, A. R., and E. D. Forsman. 2003. Breeding season habitat use and ecology of male northern pygmy-owls. *Journal of Raptor Research* 37:117–124.

Howell, S. N. G., and K. Eisermann. 2011. Guatemalan pygmy-owl *Glaucidium cobanense* is a good species. *Neotropical Birding* 9:74–76.

Howell and Webb 1995.

Kessell, B., and D. D. Gibson. 1978. *Status and Distribution of Alaska Birds*. Lawrence, KS: Cooper Ornithological Society and Allen Press.

Marshall, J. T. 1988. Birds lost from a giant sequoia forest during fifty years. *Condor* 90:359–372.

Navarro-Sigüenza, A. G., and A. T. Peterson. 2007. *Glaucidium gnoma* (tecolote serrano) residencia permanente distribución potencial. In *Mapas de las Aves de México Basados en WWW*, ed. A. G. Navarro and A. T. Peterson. Final report, SNIB-CONABIO project no. CE015. México DF.

Piorecky, M. D., and D. R. C. Prescott. 2006. Multiple spatial scale logistic and autologistic habitat selection models for northern pygmy owls, along the eastern slopes of Alberta's Rocky Mountains. *Biological Conservation* 129:360–371.

Sater, D. M., E. D. Forsman, F. L. Ramsey, and E. M. Glenn. 2006. Distribution and habitat associations of northern pygmy-owls. *Journal of Raptor Research* 40:89–97.

Scott, L. 2007. Northern pygmy-owl preys on mourning doves at Creston, British Columbia. *Wildlife Afield* 4:76–78.

Templeton, C. N., E. Greene, and K. Davis. 2005. Allometry of alarm calls: Black-capped chickadees encode information about predator size. *Science* 308:1934–1937.

Walton, K., T. Gotthardt, and T. Fields. 2013. Alaska species ranking system—northern pygmy-owl. Anchorage, AK: Alaska Natural Heritage Program.

Originally part of the "Least Pygmy-Owl" complex, the Colima Pygmy-Owl was split in 1997, along with the Tamaulipas and Central American Pygmy-Owls. *(Sinaloa. Cody Conway)*

COLIMA PYGMY-OWL
Glaucidium palmarum
Alpha code: CPYO

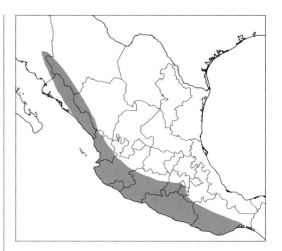

LENGTH: 5.5–6 in. (14–15.2 cm)

WINGSPAN: Undocumented

MASS: Moderate reversed size dimorphism, although data are more complete for wing chord and tail length than weight. Average, male: 1.6 oz. (44.9 g).[1] Average, two males: 1.6 oz. (45.7 g); range 1.5–1.7 oz. (42.4–49 g).[2] Average, female: 1.8 oz. (50 g).[3]

LONGEVITY: No information

A pale, grayish brown little raptor from the Pacific Coast in Mexico—in fact, one of the smallest owls in the world, with males only slightly heavier than Elf Owls—the Colima Pygmy-Owl was one of three species in Mexico and Central America that were split in the 1990s, mostly based on their distinctive vocalizations. Fairly common in parts of its range, it has scarcely been studied, and most of

what we think we know about its ecology is inferred from other species.

SYSTEMATICS, TAXONOMY, AND ETYMOLOGY

Beginning in the 1980s, with the realization that vocalizations are a critical clue to species limits in some groups of birds, ornithologists began reassessing the "Least Pygmy-Owl," a complex of what was then eight subspecies stretching from Mexico to Brazil. While physical and plumage differences within this group were fairly slight, their vocalizations differed in often rather stark ways. In 1997, the AOU formally split off the Colima, Tamaulipas, and Central American Pygmy-Owls, which, in addition to their distinctive calls, also lack color morphs.

There are three described subspecies of the Colima Pygmy-Owl: *G. p. oberholseri* (which is often lumped with *palmarum*) from southern Sonora to southern Sinaloa; the nominate *G. p. palmarum* from Nayarit to Oaxaca; and the somewhat larger *G. p. griscomi* in the Río Balsas drainage in Morelos and Guerrero. Some authors believe the differences are so slight that they consider the Colima Pygmy-Owl monotypic, while others have suggested further splitting the Colima Pygmy-Owl,[4] with the smaller races *palmarum* and *oberholseri* forming one species, and the slightly larger *griscomi* another.

ETYMOLOGY: For the origin of the genus name, see "Northern Pygmy-Owl." The specific name *palmarum* comes from the Latin meaning "of the palms"; the type specimen was collected in a palm forest near San Blas, Nayarit, in 1897. The common name refers to the Mexican state of Colima, which lies within its range.

> **SPANISH:** *Tecolote [tecolotito] colimense, tecolotillo minimo, tecolotillo pinto*
> **NÁHUATL:** *Tlatlancapacle*

DISTRIBUTION

BREEDING SEASON: Permanent resident. Central Sonora to Oaxaca and inland along the Río Balsas basin, from sea level to 4,900 ft. (1,500 m).

MIGRATION AND MOVEMENTS: None known, but elevational movements are at least possible.

POST-FLEDGING DISPERSAL: No information

DISTRIBUTION OUTSIDE THE COVERAGE AREA: None

DESCRIPTION AND IDENTIFICATION

The pygmy-owls are all remarkably similar in appearance, and the Colima Pygmy-Owl is cut from the common cloth—large-headed, tuftless, with large eyespots on the nape of the neck, though even tinier than most. There are no true color morphs; this owl is paler and more grayish brown in comparison to other members of the former "Least Pygmy-Owl" complex.

BASIC (ADULT) PLUMAGE: Sexes similar. Crown and nape grayish brown, evenly marked with fine whitish spots. Eyebrows narrow, indistinct, and gray, not extending past middle of eye. Poorly developed facial disk; face same ground color as crown, lightly flecked in concentric circles with gray-white. Chin gray, throat brownish.

Upperparts grayish brown, with a rufous-tinged collar below the nape; indistinct pale brownish spots on the scapulars. Back largely unmarked. More distinct buffy bars on the folded primaries. Tail dark gray-brown with four narrow, incomplete whitish bars generally visible (six or seven bars present, but upper two generally concealed by coverts). Underparts white with broad, chestnut streaks that merge to form solid rufous band on either side of the breast. Feet large, sparsely feathered, and yellow. Bill yellowish, iris yellow.

JUVENAL PLUMAGE: Natal down whitish gray. Juvenile has a grayer head than adult, with fewer white flecks.

SIMILAR SPECIES: At higher elevations may overlap with Northern Pygmy-Owl, which is larger, has more extensive white spotting on upperparts, and a longer tail. Ferruginous Pygmy-Owl, generally restricted to lower forests, is also larger and longer-tailed, brighter rufous, and with more prominent white scapular spots. Does not overlap in range with Tamaulipas or Central American Pygmy-Owls.

VOCALIZATIONS

Primary call a steady, rhythmic series of whistled *toot*s, roughly two per second. Initial songs are short (two or three notes) and build to longer whistled sequences; the owl may give a soft trill as an introduction. The notes have "a hollow, wooden to slightly plaintive quality that suggests the Ferruginous Pygmy-owl."[1]

HABITAT AND NICHE

As with all pygmy-owls, this is a forest-dweller with fairly flexible tastes. Found in thorn scrub and coastal palm forests, dry tropical forests, shade-coffee farms, and, at higher elevations, oak and pine-oak woodlands.

In Sonora, found on steeper slopes and in denser vegetation than Ferruginous Pygmy-Owls. In Colima, reported to be most abundant in gullies and arroyos with tropical deciduous forest. In Sinaloa, *G .p. palmarum* is found in lower humid tropical forests, and *G. p. oberholseri* in higher, more-arid tropical forests from 1,000 to 3,000 ft. (304 to 914 m). In Oaxaca "very common . . . in tropical deciduous forest and Pacific swamp forests up to 1,050 ft." (320 m).[5] Most information comes from regional bird surveys, with little or no in-depth research into this owl's habitat requirements or ecology.

DIET: Poorly known. Small vertebrates (especially birds and reptiles) taken along with insects.

One of the smallest raptors in the world, only slightly heavier than the Elf Owl, the Colima Pygmy-Owl is found only in lowland forests in western Mexico. *(Sinaloa. Pete Morris)*

NESTING AND BREEDING

Little information; generally similar to that of other close relatives, laying 2 to 4 eggs in old woodpecker holes. A female of *G. p. griscomi* was collected in May with 2 large eggs in her oviduct.

BEHAVIOR

Essentially unstudied, although likely to be similar to its close relatives. Crepuscular and at least partially diurnal, like all New World pygmy-owls; calling peaks just before sunrise and after sunset.

STATUS

Usually described as fairly common to common, but apparently rare and local in some parts of its range. The Colima Pygmy-Owl is considered "least concern" by IUCN/BirdLife. Computer modeling suggests, however, that future climate change could rob the Colima Pygmy-Owl of almost 20 percent of its already fairly limited current range, and the species is listed as "threatened" by Mexico.

NOTES

1. Howell and Robbins 1995.

2. Dunning 2007.

3. Marks, Cannings, and Mikkola 1999.

4. Navarro-Sigüenza and Peterson 2004.

5. Binford 1989.

BIBLIOGRAPHY

Almazán-Núñez, R. C, and A. G. Navarro-Sigüenza. 2006. Avifauna de la subcuenca del río San Juan, Guerrero, México. *Revista Mexicana Biodiversidad* 77:103–114.

BirdLife International 2015 *Glaucidium palmarum*. In IUCN Red List of Threatened Species, version 2014.3. http://www.iucnredlist.org/details/22729012/0.

Buchanan 1964.

Enríquez-Rocha, P., and J. L. Rangel. 2008. Ficha técnica de *Glaucidium palmarum*. In *Fichas Sobre las Especies de Aves Incluidas en el Proyecto de Norma Oficial Mexicana PROY-NOM-ECOL-2000*, part 2, ed. P. Escalante-Pliego. México DF: Instituto de Biología, Universidad Nacional Autónoma de México.

Flesch, Beardmore, and Mesta 2008.

Moore, R. T. 1947. New owls of the genera *Otus* and *Glaucidium*. *Proceedings of the Biological Society of Washington* 60:31–38.

———. 1937. Two new owls from Sinaloa, Mexico. *Proceedings of the Biological Society of Washington* 50:103–106.

Navarro-Sigüenza, A. G., and A. T. Peterson. 2007. *Glaucidium palmarum* (tecolote colimense) residencia permanente distribución potencial. In *Mapas de las Aves de México Basados en WWW*, ed. A. G. Navarro and A. T. Peterson. Final report, SNIB-CONABIO project no. CE015. México DF.

———. 2004. An alternative taxonomy of the birds of Mexico. *Biota Neotropica* 4:1–32.

Peterson, A. T., A. G. Navarro-Sigüenza, and X. Li. 2010. Joint effects of marine intrusion and climate change on the Mexican avifauna. *Annals of the Association of American Geographers* 100:908–916.

The Tamaulipas Pygmy-Owl, an inhabitant of cloud forests in the eastern Sierra Madre, has the smallest range of any mainland owl in the region. *(Tamaulipas. Jeffrey Gordon)*

TAMAULIPAS PYGMY-OWL
Glaucidium sanchezi
Alpha code: TAPO

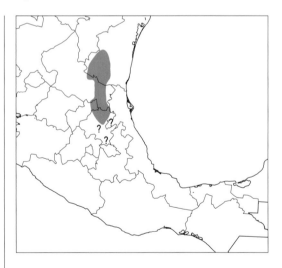

LENGTH: 5.5–6 in. (14–15.2 cm)

WINGSPAN: Undocumented

MASS: Weak reversed size dimorphism, although data are more complete for wing chord and tail length than weight. Average, two males: 1.9 oz. (53.5 g).[1] One male: 1.9 oz. (55 g).[2] Unsexed ranges: 1.8–1.9 oz. (51–55 g)[3] and 1.8–2 oz. (52–56 g).[4]

LONGEVITY: No information

Endemic to the cloud forests of the eastern Sierra Madre, this small, dark pygmy-owl is unique in several respects. It has the smallest range of any mainland owl species in our region (and smaller than a number of island owls). And alone among all the pygmy-owls, it is sexually dimorphic, with the females much redder than the slightly smaller males. Yet beyond these few facts, almost nothing is known about the Tamaulipas Pygmy-Owl, including its conservation status.

SYSTEMATICS, TAXONOMY, AND ETYMOLOGY

See "Colima Pygmy-Owl," p. 163, for discussion of general taxonomy of the former "Least Pygmy-Owl" complex in Mexico. The Tamaulipas Pygmy-Owl is monotypic.

ETYMOLOGY: For the etymology of the genus name, see "Northern Pygmy-Owl." The species name, given in 1949 when this owl was thought to be a race of the "Least Pygmy-Owl," honors Carlos Sánchez Mejorada, an early Mexican birder and ornithologist. The common name refers to the Mexican state of Tamaulipas, in which the bulk of its range lies.

SPANISH: *Tecolote [tecolotito] tamaulipeco, tecolotillo minimo, tecolotillo pinto*

DISTRIBUTION

BREEDING SEASON: Resident in cloud forests in the Sierra Madre Oriental in southern Tamaulipas, southeastern San Luis Potosí, northern Hidalgo, and northeastern Querétaro, between 2,900 and 6,900 ft. (900 and 2,100 m). Speculation that its range may extend into central Veracruz remains unconfirmed; habitat modeling also suggests it could potentially range south to Puebla in appropriate habitat.

MIGRATION AND MOVEMENTS: None known, although elevational movements are at least possible.

POST-FLEDGING DISPERSAL: No information

DISTRIBUTION OUTSIDE THE COVERAGE AREA: None

DESCRIPTION AND IDENTIFICATION

Typical of pygmy-owls in our region in general appearance, but unique among them in that the sexes are dimorphic, with female's head and upperparts washed in rufous, while the male's are duller brown.

BASIC (ADULT) PLUMAGE: Male has crown and nape gray-brown, contrasting with olive-brown upperparts. Very fine whitish spots on crown; eyebrows whitish, moderately pronounced. Facial disk matches ground color of head, with irregular whitish flecks. Back largely unmarked, with a few indistinct spots on the scapulars. Tail dark brown, with whitish, incomplete tail bars. Central underparts white with broad, dark rusty vertical streaks; solid dark rusty sides. Female's head, nape, and upperparts "overall fairly uniform and distinctly redder than male. . . . The chest sides and underpart streaks are dark rufous-brown."[1] Spotting on head and back is cinnamon in female.

JUVENAL PLUMAGE: Similar to adult, with grayer, largely unspotted head.

SIMILAR SPECIES: Overlaps in range and elevation only with Northern Pygmy-Owl, which is larger and longer-tailed, with complete (versus broken) and broader white tail bars. Adult Northern Pygmy-Owl has distinctly spotted back, but this feature is lacking in the juvenile, which more closely resembles the Tamaulipas Pygmy-Owl.

VOCALIZATIONS

Unlike the long, rhythmic series of notes that the other *Glaucidium* give, the Tamaulipas Pygmy-Owl generally sings two or three slow whistled *toot*s (three notes in about 2 seconds). "Strikingly different [from Colima and Central American Pygmy-Owls] . . . by virtue of its long notes and inter-note intervals, and number of notes."[1] Those in Tamaulipas sing a slightly slower song than those in San Luis Potosí.

HABITAT AND NICHE

An inhabitant of eastern Sierra Madrean cloud forests and old second-growth of Douglas-fir, cypress, sweetgum, and pines, the Tamaulipas Pygmy-Owl apparently has some tolerance for fragmentation, as long as at least half the canopy cover is intact. Limited surveys in its habitat have found it to be quite scarce (.5 individuals per 100-point counts).[5]

DIET: Essentially unknown, beyond a few observations, although presumably similar to other *Glaucidium,* including small vertebrates (especially lizards) and insects.

NESTING AND BREEDING

No information; presumably similar to other Neotropical pygmy-owls.

BEHAVIOR

Essentially unstudied. Crepuscular and at least partially diurnal; calling peaks just before sunrise and after sunset.

STATUS

As noted, the Tamaulipas Pygmy-Owl has the smallest range of any mainland owl in our area—by contrast, the Balsas Screech-Owl's estimated range is almost five times larger. Birders have found it to be fairly reliable (when lured with recordings) near the birding hotspots of Gómez Farías and El Cielo in Tamaulipas, and El Naranjo in San Luis Potosí, but overall it seems to be less common and more localized within its range than are most other pygmy-owls. Worse, it appears to be sensitive to forest fragmentation, which is rampant in the eastern Sierra Madre.

Mexico has upgraded its status to "endangered," because of the owl's small range and habitat loss. IUCN/BirdLife, on the other hand, has listed the Tamaulipas Pygmy-Owl as "least concern," citing an apparently stable population and a lack of evidence for serious habitat fragmentation. However, BirdLife reduced its estimate of this pygmy-owl's range from 10,500 sq. mi. (27,200 sq. km) to 7,450 sq. mi. (19,300 sq. km), and is reassessing the owl's status to consider a change to "near threatened." Its range does include several significant protected areas, including the El Cielo and Sierra Gorda biosphere reserves.

NOTES

1. Howell and Robbins 1995.

2. Dunning 2007.

3. König and Weick 2008.

4. Mikkola 2012.

5. Escalante and Néquiz 2004.

BIBLIOGRAPHY

BirdLife International. 2015 Species factsheet: *Glaucidium sanchezi*, http://www.birdlife.org/datazone/speciesfactsheet.php?id=9788.

Buchanan 1964.

Escalante, P., and V. Néquiz. 2004. The Mexican bird red list and changes needed at the global level. *Biologia Neotropica* 15:175–181.

Gomes de Silva, H., and E. Alvarado-Reyes. 2010. Breve historia de la observación de aves en México en el siglo XX y pricipios del siglo XXI. *Huitzil* 11:9–20.

Lowery, G. H. Jr., and R. J. Newman. 1949. New birds from the state of San Luis Potosí and the Tuxtla Mountains of Veracruz, Mexico. *Occasional Papers of the Museum of Zoology, Louisiana State University*, no. 22.

Martínez-Morales, M. 2008. Ficha técnica de *Glaucidium sanchezi*. In *Fichas Sobre las Especies de Aves Incluidas en el Proyecto de Norma Oficial Mexicana PROY-NOM-ECOL-2000*, part 2, ed. P. Escalante-Pliego. México DF: Instituto de Biología, Universidad Nacional Autónoma de México.

Navarro-Sigüenza, A. G., and A. T. Peterson. 2007. *Glaucidium sanchezi* (tecolote tamaulipeco) residencia permanente distribución potencial. In *Mapas de las Aves de México Basados en WWW*, ed. A. G. Navarro and A. T. Peterson. Final report, SNIB-CONABIO project no. CE015. México DF.

Rojas-Soto, O. R., L. A. Sánchez-González, and S. López de Aquino. 2002. New information on the birds of northern Hidalgo, Mexico. *Southwestern Naturalist* 47:471–475.

Taylor, J. 2013. Tamaulipas pygmy-owl (*Glaucidium sanchezi*): Eligible for uplisting? BirdLife's Globally Threatened Bird Forums, http://www.birdlife.org/globally-threatened-bird-forums/2014/08/tamaulipas-pygmy-owl-glaucidium-sanchezi-eligible-for-uplisting/.

So little is known about the Central American Pygmy-Owl—one of three species split in 1997 from the "Least Pygmy-Owl" complex—that its distribution is still unclear. *(Costa Rica. Mary Ann Smith)*

CENTRAL AMERICAN PYGMY-OWL
Glaucidium griseiceps
Alpha code: CAPO

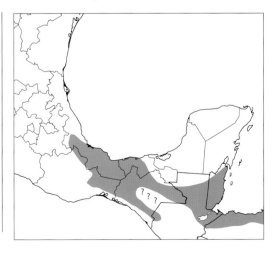

LENGTH: 5.5–6 in. (14–15.25 cm)

WINGSPAN: Undocumented

MASS: No hard data on degree of reversed size dimorphism; believed to be weak. Average, male: 1.8 oz. (50.6 g); no range given.[1] Males, range 1.75–1.8 oz. (49.5–51.7 g); no average given.[2] Unsexed range

1.8–2 oz. (50–57 g); no average given.[3] Female mass estimated at 10 percent larger than male, approx. 2 oz. (approx. 56 g).[4]

LONGEVITY: No information

A pygmy-owl of humid forests from southern Mexico to northwestern South America, the Central American Pygmy-Owl is as much a cipher as its other close relatives that were once lumped together as the "Least Pygmy-Owl." Little is known about its life history, breeding ecology—even how much it weighs. But its forested habitat has suffered fragmentation and destruction, and there are indications its population may be decreasing, at least in some areas.

SYSTEMATICS, TAXONOMY, AND ETYMOLOGY

See "Colima Pygmy-Owl," p. 163, for discussion of general taxonomy of the former "Least Pygmy-Owl" complex in Mexico. Three subspecies have been described, only one of which, *G. g. occultum,* occurs in our area. Some specialists, noting that the subspecies are weakly differentiated based on the limited number of specimens available for examination, consider the Central American Pygmy-Owl monotypic.

ETYMOLOGY: For the origin of the genus name, see "Northern Pygmy-Owl." The species name comes from the Latin *griseues,* "gray," and *-ceps,* "headed," referring to the contrasting coloration of the head. The English name refers to the core of its distribution.

> SPANISH: *Tecolote [tecolotito] mesoamericano, tecolotito centroamericano, tecolotillo minimo, tecolotillo pinto*
> NÁHUATL: *Tlatlancapacle*

DISTRIBUTION

BREEDING SEASON: Resident. Distribution still somewhat poorly known. Central Veracruz (Orizaba) and eastern Oaxaca east along Atlantic slope to northern Chiapas and Tabasco; also reported from the Pacific slope in southeastern Chiapas (El Triunfo, Volcán Tacaná). Sea level to about 4,300 ft. (1,300 m).

MIGRATION AND MOVEMENTS: None known, although elevational movements are at least possible.

POST-FLEDGING DISPERSAL: No information

DISTRIBUTION OUTSIDE THE COVERAGE AREA: Poorly known. Guatemala to Panama (recently confirmed in Nicaragua), and in Colombia and Ecuador, where new records have significantly extended its range southward.

DESCRIPTION AND IDENTIFICATION

A short-tailed pygmy-owl whose gray-brown head contrasts with the more rufous back and wings. This contrast is less noticeable in the Mexican subspecies *occultum.*

BASIC (ADULT) PLUMAGE: Sexes similar. Crown and nape gray-brown with even white spotting. Eyebrows very narrow, grayish, and indistinct, extending only midway past eye. Black false eyespots on nape rimmed in grayish white. Upperparts chestnut brown, with limited and indistinct whitish spots on scapulars. Upper wings chestnut brown with paler chestnut barring. Tail short, with two visible white, incomplete bars.

Facial disk same ground color as head, with very fine white flecks. Rictal bristles gray. Throat, upper chest, and sides bright chestnut; broad chestnut streaks on white underparts.

JUVENAL PLUMAGE: Head grayer and less heavily spotted; tail bars may be buff or pale rusty rather than white.

SIMILAR SPECIES: Range overlaps with Ferruginous Pygmy-Owl's, which is normally in more-open habitats. Ferruginous is larger, longer-tailed, more brightly rufous overall, with more distinct scapular spots, and has five to seven tail bars above versus two on Central American Pygmy-Owl. Not known to overlap in range with Tamaulipas Pygmy-Owl; see "Vocalizations," below, for song differences.

VOCALIZATIONS

Most commonly, a repeated burst of 4 to 10 steady hoots, roughly 3 to 3.5 notes per second, but occasionally up to 20 notes and varying in length. Lower-pitched but faster than Tamaulipas Pygmy-Owl, which sings shorter (1 to 3 notes) songs. Those from Mexico and eastern Guatemala sing slightly shorter songs than those farther east and south. Ferruginous Pygmy-Owl's call faster, slightly higher, with a rising inflection to each note, and usually in more consistently longer singing bouts.

HABITAT AND NICHE

Humid rain forests and forest edges. Buchanan (1964) said the "typical habitat is the ever-damp cloud forests, and the humid pine-oak forests above," and indicated it was most common above 3,000 ft. (915 m), although it is found to sea level. Sometimes seen in secondary forests and old plantations, but whether it nests in such habitat is unknown.

DIET: Typical of pygmy-owls in general; large insects, lizards, small birds up to the size of tanagers.

NESTING AND BREEDING

Secondary cavity adopter; most nests known were in old woodpecker holes. Little information; in Costa Rica it is believed to breed in the dry and early rainy seasons. Clutch size 2 to 4 eggs.

BEHAVIOR

Behavior and ecology are essentially unknown. Crepuscular and at least partially diurnal, but to what degree (if any) it is active at night has not been studied. The Central American Pygmy-Owl calls most frequently at dawn and dusk, like other pygmy-owls.

STATUS

The Central American Pygmy-Owl is the most widespread but perhaps the least common of the three former "Least Pygmy-Owl" species, although to what extent it is simply overlooked is unclear. Howell and Webb (1995) describe it as uncommon to fairly common, but more recently it was described as rare in the Atlantic lowlands and mountains of eastern Oaxaca, and rare as well in primary and mature secondary forests in Palenque, Chiapas. Owl surveys at La Selva Biological Station in Costa Rica suggest that the Central American Pygmy-Owl steadily declined there—from common to uncommon to rare—between 1960 and 1995.

Although IUCN/BirdLife considers the Central American Pygmy Owl "least concern" with a stable population trend, it is listed as "threatened" in Mexico. Habitat loss is undoubtedly the biggest threat to this pygmy-owl, as to its other close Neotropical relatives.

NOTES

1. Howell and Robbins 1995.

2. Dunning 2007.

3. Mikkola 2012.

4. Marks, Canning, and Mikkola 1999.

BIBLIOGRAPHY

Buchanan 1964.

Enríquez-Rocha, P., and J. L. Rangel-Salazar. 2008. Ficha técnica de *Glaucidium griseiceps*. In *Fichas Sobre las Especies de Aves Incluidas en el Proyecto de Norma Oficial Mexicana PROY-NOM-ECOL-2000*, part 2, ed. P. Escalante-Pliego. México, DF: Instituto de Biología, Universidad Nacional Autónoma de México.

Enríquez-Rocha and Rangel-Salazar 1995.

Freile, J. F., and D. F. Castro. 2013. New records of rare screech owls (*Megascops*) and pygmy owls (*Glaucidium*), with taxonomic notes and a conservation assessment of two globally imperilled species in Ecuador. *Cotinga* 35:5–10.

Múnera-Roldán, C., M. L. Cody, R. H. Schiele-Zavala, B. J. Sigel, S. Woltmann, and J. P. Kjeldsen. 2007. New and noteworthy records of birds from south-eastern Nicaragua. *Bulletin of the British Ornithologists' Club* 127:152–161.

Navarro-Sigüenza, A. G., and A. T. Peterson. 2007. *Glaucidium griseiceps* (tecolote mesoamericano) residencia permanente distribución potencial. In *Mapas de las Aves de México Basados en WWW*, ed. A. G. Navarro and A. T. Peterson. Final report, SNIB-CONABIO project no. CE015. México DF.

Patten et al. 2011.

Petersen et al. 2003.

Stiles and Skutch 1989.

FERRUGINOUS PYGMY-OWL
Glaucidium brasilianum
Alpha code: FEPO

LENGTH: 6.75–7.5 in. (17–19 cm)

WINGSPAN: 12–15 in. (30.5–38 cm)

MASS: Moderate to strong reversed size dimorphism, although only partially reflected by weight.

> *G. b. cactorum:* Average, male: 2.3 oz. (66.3 g); range 1.9–2.7 oz. (54–77 g). Average, female: 2.6 oz. (73 g); range 2.2–3.0 oz. (62–84 g).[1]

> *G. b. ridgwayi:* Average, male: 2.16 oz. (61.4 g); range 1.6–2.6 oz. (46–74 g). Average, female: 2.6 oz. (75.1 g); range 2.2–3.3 oz. (62–95 g).[2] Texas population only: Average, male: 2.25 oz. (64.3 g); range 1.9–2.8 oz. (53–79 g). Average, female: 2.7 oz. (77.2 g); range 2.3–3.6 oz. (66–102 g).[3]

> *G. b. intermedium:* Range, two males, one female: 2.2 oz. (62.25–63.1 g).[4]

LONGEVITY: Normal first-year mortality about 65 percent. Longevity record 9 years (three individuals).[5]

Small, fierce, and largely diurnal, the Ferruginous Pygmy-Owl's steady, seemingly endless *toots* are one of the signature sounds of daybreak in the tropical lowlands of Mexico and Central America. But while it is common throughout Mesoamerica, this is the rarest owl in the United States, where tiny populations exist only in southern Arizona and Texas. The Arizona birds in particular have been in frightening decline for decades, the victims of sprawling urban subdivisions and poor land management, and their status has been the focus of a fractious legal battle for more than 20 years.

Some authorities advocate splitting the North and Central American forms of the Ferruginous Pygmy-Owl from those in South America, and molecular studies seem to support this approach, with those from Panama north comprising "Ridgway's Pygmy-Owl." *(Costa Rica. Glenn Bartley)*

SYSTEMATICS, TAXONOMY, AND ETYMOLOGY

The taxonomy of the Ferruginous Pygmy-Owl is no less messy and confusing than with the other members of this genus. At the moment, the AOU recognizes some 15 races of a single species, stretching from the United States to Tierra del Fuego, but mitochondrial DNA analysis shows divisions within this complex that probably warrant species-level splits.

Four subspecies, all weakly differentiated by appearance and voice, have been described from our area. Coloration varies somewhat with habitat—darker in humid zones, paler in arid areas.

> *G. b. cactorum:* Southern Arizona south to Nayarit along the Pacific slope. Originally,

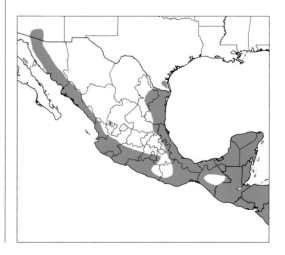

birds from South Texas, Nuevo León, and Tamaulipas were also assigned to *cactorum*, but should be considered *ridgwayi* based on DNA evidence that shows almost no gene flow between the two areas. Grayer, paler, shorter-winged, and longer-tailed than *ridgwayi*.

G. b. ridgwayi: Now includes populations from South Texas and the Atlantic slope in Mexico, south to extreme northwestern Colombia.

G. b. intermedium: Pacific Coast from southern Nayarit to southern Oaxaca, possibly into Chiapas. Darker above than *cactorum* and paler and larger than *ridgwayi*.

G. b. saturatum: Humid Pacific lowlands in Chiapas and Guatemala. Darker and larger than both *ridgwayi* and *intermedium*.

Several authorities have proposed splitting the North and Central American forms from those in South America, and molecular analyses (including Proudfoot, Honeycutt, and Slack[6]) seems to support this approach, with those subspecies from Panama north comprising "Ridgway's Pygmy-Owl (*G. ridgwayi*)." Thus far, however, the AOU has not taken up this potential split, awaiting more information.

ETYMOLOGY: For the origin of the genus name, see "Northern Pygmy-Owl." The common name refers to the bright orangish coloration of some rufous-morph individuals (rare in the United States). The species names refers to Brazil, from which the type specimen came in the eighteenth century.

SPANISH: *Tecolote [tecolotito] bajeño, tecolotillo [tecolotito] rayado, tecolotito comoún; tecolotillo cuatrojos; maclovio, aurorita* (Chiapas); *vieja* (Yucatán Peninsula)

PIMA (ARIZONA): *Koo-ah-kohld*

MAYAN: *Toj-caj-xnuk* (Yucatec)

DISTRIBUTION

BREEDING SEASON: Resident. Southern Arizona (now rarely north to Tucson) south through Sonora and southwestern Chihuahua along the Pacific Coast to Michoacán and Guerrero, and inland in the Rió Balsas drainage; along the coast in Oaxaca to Chiapas. Also from coastal South Texas (including the lower Rio Grande Valley, where now rare) along the Atlantic slope east of the Sierra Madre Oriental to Chiapas and Yucatán.

Elevational range 1,300–3,900 ft. (400–1,200 m) in Arizona, but records as low as 450 ft. (137 m) and as high as 4,200 ft. (1,280 m). Sea level to 4,600–5,000 ft. (1,400–1,525 m) in Mexico.

G. b. intermedium, the subspecies of Ferruginous Pygmy-Owl found along the Pacific Coast, is darker than *G. b. cactorum* to the north. *(Oaxaca. Dominic Sherony)*

Ferruginous Pygmy-Owls overlap to a degree with several other *Glaucidium* species, but all have spotted, not streaked, crowns. *(Mexico. Luke Seitz)*

MIGRATION AND MOVEMENTS: None known. Speculation of seasonal movements in parts of northwestern Mexico now generally discounted. One vagrant record from western Texas may have been *G. b. cactorum.*

POST-FLEDGING DISPERSAL: Fledglings disperse at about 7 or 8 weeks of age. Fledglings followed with radio transmitters in Texas and Arizona moved 5 to 19 mi. (8 to 31 km) from nest site within first 2 months of fledging, but one Arizona female moved 66 mi. (106 km), a record for this species.[7]

DISTRIBUTION OUTSIDE THE COVERAGE AREA: South and east through Belize and Guatemala to extreme northwestern Colombia. Other subspecies (perhaps distinct from "Ridgway's Pygmy-Owl") from northern Colombia south to central Argentina and southern Uruguay.

DESCRIPTION AND IDENTIFICATION

A fairly rusty-colored pygmy-owl, although with a complex suite of plumage forms that include multiple morphs, one of which—unique among North American owls—has two different tail patterns. The rufous morph, the most truly "ferruginous" of the bunch, is rare in the United States. Like all pygmy-owls it lacks ear tufts, but a concealment posture creates the appearance of tufts by accentuating

The Ferruginous Pygmy-Owl has one of the most complex plumage variations of any raptor. It occurs in gray-brown, rufous, and intermediate morphs, and the gray-brown morph has two forms—one with a blackish tail with narrow, incomplete white bars, the other with a browner tail and broader, usually complete rufous barring, shown here. *(Tamaulipas. Greg Lasley)*

The rufous morph, the most truly "ferruginous" of the Ferruginous Pygmy-Owl plumages, is rare in the United States but more common farther south. *(Honduras. Kevin Loughlin/Wildside Nature Tours)*

long facial feathers on the sides of the head, which remain erect when the rest of the owl's plumage is compressed in alarm.

BASIC (ADULT) PLUMAGE: Sexes similar, although males may average darker brown and have less contrast between the back and tail, while females have more rufous (in grayer morphs) than males on upperparts. Polymorphic, with gray-brown, rufous, and intermediate morphs. Gray-brown morph, in turn, has two forms—one with a blackish tail with fairly narrow, incomplete white tail bars broken at the shaft, the other with a browner tail and broader, usually complete rufous barring. Rufous morph may lack dark bars on tail.

Gray-brown morph: Crown, nape, and upperparts rusty brown to gray-brown; crown and nape finely streaked with white. Black eyespots rimmed with whitish gray on nape. Large whitish or buffy spots on the scapulars, smaller white spots on greater coverts. Folded wings show light edges to tertials, and pale cinnamon barring on secondaries and primaries. Tail as noted above.

Poorly defined facial disk same ground color as head, with light to moderately dense, fine white flecks. Eyebrows whitish gray, rictal bristles and throat grayish. Upper chest and sides rusty brown; belly white with rusty-brown vertical streaks. Iris pale yellow, bill gray-yellow or greenish yellow, toes yellow or yellow-green and sparsely bristled.

JUVENAL PLUMAGE: Natal down white. Juvenal plumage similar to adult (but varies by morph), with eyespots fully developed by 12 weeks of age, but juvenile lacks all streaking on crown, while scapular spots are more distinct.

SIMILAR SPECIES: Overlaps to a degree (though usually not in habitat or elevation) with members of the "Least Pygmy-Owl" complex. Colima Pygmy-Owl (with which it overlaps in southern Nayarit) and Central American Pygmy-Owl are smaller and shorter-tailed, not as rufous, with fewer visible tail bars. Northern Pygmy-Owl grayer, usually at higher elevations. All have spotted, not streaked, crowns. Voice is the best clue. Colima Pygmy-Owl's tone suggests Ferruginous, but is slower and generally sings in much shorter bouts. Central American call slightly slower, usually in shorter singing bouts. Northern Pygmy-Owl's call is slower and lower-pitched, often (depending on subspecies) with paired notes.

Elf owl is smaller, lacks eyespots, and has long wings that extend past the tip of the very short tail when perched.

VOCALIZATIONS

The territorial call is a series of up to 50 (but more typically 20 to 30) whistled notes, 3 to 3.5 per second, with a clean, slightly explosive quality due to the rising inflection of each note. Female call is generally higher-pitched, and the notes can be more distinctly bisyllabic.

Juveniles produce a cricketlike food-begging call, sometimes mixed with lower chitter notes. Adults chitter, sometimes mixed with territorial call (male) or given during courtship food-begging (female). Female gives a two-syllable alarm call, *chee-chee,* and a higher, squeakier version as an aggression call.

Calls most often around daybreak and in early morning. Using recorded playback, scientists have found that Ferruginous Pygmy-Owls call more aggressively to intruders during nesting season, but while the response from males remains steady through the period, that of females dropped to almost nothing by the time the chicks were hatched and being brooded.

The steady *tooti*ng call of the Ferruginous Pygmy-Owl is one of the signature sounds of Neotropical deserts, scrub, and lowland forests. Although the owls may call at any time, they are most vocal at daybreak and in the cool hours immediately thereafter. *(Arizona. Tom Johnson)*

Ferruginous Pygmy-Owls show great latitude in habitat and are found in saguaro cactus stands, swamps, arid scrub, rain forest, and pine savannah, among other habitats. *(Texas. Gerrit Vyn)*

HABITAT AND NICHE

A bird of lowland forest edges but with cosmopolitan tastes, the Ferruginous Pygmy-Owl is as comfortable in desert scrub and giant saguaro stands in the northern Sonoran Desert of Arizona, honey mesquite and live-oak thickets in South Texas, and tropical deciduous woods in southern Sonora as it is in Pacific-slope swamp forests and arid scrubs in Oaxaca, lowland rain forests and shade-coffee farms in Chiapas, or low cloud forests and pine savannah in Central America.

Regardless of the habitat type, the Ferruginous Pygmy-Owl sticks to the margins and borders and is often encountered along the edges of jungles, roadsides, and small farm plots rather than deep in undisturbed forests, like some of the members of the smaller "Least Pygmy-Owl" complex found at higher elevations. Ferruginous Pygmy-Owls rarely stray much above about 4,200 ft. (1,300 m), though they range somewhat higher in the southern parts of their range.

At the northern edge, in Texas, it is associated with moderate to dense thornbrush understory in otherwise open forests with trees large enough for cavities. In Arizona, it is associated with riparian forests of cottonwoods and willows, in foothills and desert scrub with saguaro cacti. Ironically, low-density housing developments intruding into desert may provide some of the best remaining habitat, since residential irrigation creates a somewhat denser, lusher native plant community than in natural areas, mimicking the high-quality habitat found in riparian zones.

Like all the members of this genus, Ferruginous Pygmy-Owls are pugnacious hunters, and anything that can be wrestled into submission is fair game. This one has taken a Least Sandpiper—hardly typical prey. *(Costa Rica. Steve Easley)*

Ferruginous Pygmy-Owls are faithful to their mates and homes: a male in Mexico remained on the same territory for 8 years, and pairs have stayed together for up to 6 years. *(Tamaulipas. Greg Lasley)*

DIET: Opportunistic hunters of large arthropods and small vertebrates. Outside of its limited U.S. range, the species has been relatively poorly studied.

An examination of stomach contents in Veracruz found scorpions and insects, especially grasshoppers, while in Arizona lizards form the largest part of the diet. In Texas, nestling diets were 58 percent insects, followed by reptiles (22 percent, largely lizards), birds (10 percent), and small mammals (9 percent). But because this did not take biomass into account, and because some of the vertebrates were as large as Eastern Meadowlarks and cotton rats, simply focusing on the number of insects may give a skewed view of the species's diet. Furthermore, the owl's diet varies year to year with the availability of prey.

In Arizona, the few observations of nesting owls that have been published showed year-to-year variations in diet, with reptiles comprising 35 to 56 percent, birds 8 to 38 percent, mammals 2 to 7 percent, and insects 2 to 5 percent, depending on the year. (Between 15 and 26 percent of prey items brought to the five nests observed couldn't be identified.)

As with the Northern Pygmy-Owl, the Ferruginous has been known to tackle birds as large as or larger than itself, including Northern Cardinals, Northern Mockingbirds, Mourning Doves, and quail. Most of their avian prey are sparrow-size, however. In Texas they have been found to prey on several species of bats, presumably taken from tree roosts rather than on the wing.

Like other pygmy-owls, Ferruginous Pygmy-Owls adopt old woodpecker holes and naturally occurring rot cavities for their nests. *(Tamaulipas. Greg Lasley)*

NESTING AND BREEDING

A secondary cavity adopter, the Ferruginous Pygmy-Owl is dependent on woodpecker holes and natural rot cavities. While it once nested primarily in riparian cottonwoods in Arizona, that tiny population now depends entirely on woodpecker excavations in saguaro cacti. In Texas, most nest sites are in live oak and mesquite. There is at least one record of a nest in a hole in an earthen bank.

Pairs have remained together and on territory for up to 6 years, and a male in Mexico remained on territory for 8 years. Courtship singing begins in midwinter in the northern population, peaking around the time egg-laying begins. Clutches range from 3 to 7 eggs, averaging 5, in Texas, where the earliest egg-laying date is Mar. 29, and the latest (an unsuccessful nest) in late June. Most are laid from late Apr. to mid-May in the United States and Mexico; there are records from Oaxaca, for example, of nests with eggs from early Apr. to mid-May. In Central America, it breeds in dry to early wet season.

This is the only pygmy-owl whose incubation has been well studied, and the findings are intriguing. While some females begin to incubate with the first egg—in the manner typical of owls, and resulting in asynchronous hatching—others wait until the clutch is nearly complete. The timing at the other end of the incubation period is therefore predictably complex. Glenn A. Proudfoot's study of Ferruginous Pygmy-Owls in Texas found that in some nests the eggs hatched at 20- to 26-hour intervals, while in others, 4 or 5 eggs might hatch at once, followed several days later by the remainder. Whether or not other pygmy-owls exhibit this same mixed incubation strategy—which Proudfoot believes is tied to weather, precipitation, and prey supplies—remains to be seen.

The nestlings fledge at 3 to 4 weeks of age, and the siblings remain close together for the first week or so thereafter, as they begin to experiment (not very successfully) with hunting. With time the siblings begin to go their own ways, although they remain dependent on the adults for about 2 months after fledging. Adults can be aggressive in nest defense, even against an intruding human.

Ferruginous Pygmy-Owls readily accept artificial nest boxes with an entrance hole with a 2-in. (5 cm) diameter and depth of about 14 in. (35.5 cm). As with many cavity-nesting owls, the provision of multiple boxes within each territory increases the chance of overall occupancy, since each pair needs separate cavities for nesting, roosting, and cache sites.

BEHAVIOR

"Their monotonous whistle is heard regularly in the early morning, just at dawn, and in the evening, and may be noted occasionally at almost any hour of the day," American ornithologists George Lowery Jr. and Walter Dalquest wrote of the Ferruginous Pygmy-Owl in Veracruz in 1951. "At almost any thicket or the edge of almost any jungle, at any time of day, an imitation of their almost intermina-ble short, whistled notes would cause one or more birds to answer."[8]

Crepuscular and partially diurnal, pygmy-owl activity in Texas is tied to moon phase. From about 10 days before the full moon to about 4 days after, the owls are most active at night. There is also some indication that Ferruginous Pygmy-Owls in more humid habitats may be more nocturnal (or at least more decidedly crepuscular) than those in desert or semiarid environments. This tiny raptor is a perch hunter with lightning reflexes, dropping on a lizard or grasshopper, but also pursuing small birds like a miniature accipiter, weaving through dense cover and battening on to large prey, simply grappling it into submission.

Because of their taste for small birds, they are routinely mobbed by passerines (and a whistled imitation of a pygmy-owl call, anywhere in the range of any *Glaucidium* species, is a great way to attract an agitated, angry flock of songbirds). Ferruginous Pygmy-Owls have a rapid flight, without the pronounced undulating pattern of a Northern Pygmy-Owl, and like the other members of the genus, lack the typical owl adaptations for silent flight, such as velvety feather edges. Like the Northern Pygmy-Owl, the Ferruginous wags its tail side to side or cocks it up when agitated by the presence of humans, when preparing to fly, or when its mate approaches, though normally the tail is held down.

Breeding-season territories used by adults and chicks in Texas ranged from 22 to 146 acres (9 to 59 hectares), while an unmated male used 272 acres (110 hectares). Territory size remains constant, but the daily use area varies seasonally, contracting to a small core around the nest during incubation, and gradually expanding as the chicks grow and become independent. The area used by radio-tagged males increased more than threefold after the nesting season ended. Territory size may also increase dramatically during droughts, presumably because prey become harder to find. And even when not actively used in summer, the larger, overall territory is defended.

STATUS

Range-wide, the Ferruginous Pygmy-Owl is one of the most ubiquitous and widespread Neotropical raptors, common or abundant in most appropriate habitat from central Mexico south. It is listed as "least concern" by IUCN/BirdLife, though with a decreasing population trend.

At the northernmost limits of its range, however, this pygmy-owl has suffered significant declines. In Texas, the eastern subspecies, *G. b. ridgwayi*, is restricted to an area of large, private cattle ranches along the coastal plain in Kenedy, Brooks, and Willacy Counties, as well as a few along the lower Rio

The Cactus Ferruginous Pygmy-Owl, *G. b. cactorum,* has been the focus of decades of legal and regulatory conflict in Arizona. Listed as federally "endangered" in 1997, it was delisted in 2006 after a lawsuit challenging aspects of the initial decision. *(Arizona. Tom Johnson)*

Grande in Hidalgo and Cameron Counties, where construction of a border wall has further damaged the already degraded riverine ecosystem.

The western race, *G. b. cactorum,* is increasingly rare in northern Sonora, where changing rainfall patterns (which in turn drive prey abundance) may be to blame. In Arizona, *cactorum* was originally described as common along rivers and streams but suffered major declines in the twentieth century, caused largely by sprawl development, overgrazing, and the destruction of riparian woodlands that were once its major habitat. It disappeared from Yuma County in extreme southwestern Arizona by the 1950s, and from Maricopa County (Phoenix) in the early 1970s. By the mid-2000s the last nesting pairs had disappeared from around Tucson. Some federal sources have estimated the Ferruginous Pygmy-Owl population in the state at fewer than 30 adults, but a full, statewide survey for this species has never been conducted, and no one really knows what the actual population may be.

The owl has been the center of a bitter legal dispute lasting more than 20 years. In 1997, the U.S. Fish and Wildlife Service listed the Ferruginous Pygmy-Owl as "endangered" in Arizona. A lawsuit by home builders, challenging aspects of the ESA listing, prompted the agency to delist the Arizona owls in 2006 over the objections of conservationists. Legal efforts continue to force restoration of ESA protection for the Arizona birds and to list the Sonoran population for the first time. A captive breeding program for Arizona *cactorum* pygmy-owls has been underway since 2007.

Federal protections aside, the state of Arizona lists the Ferruginous Pygmy-Owl as "critically imperiled," and Texas lists its population as "threatened."

NOTES

1. G. A. Proudfoot. 1996. "Natural history of the cactus ferruginous pygmy-owl." MS thesis, Texas A&M University–Kingsville.

2. Earhart and Johnson 1970.

3. G. A. Proudfoot and R. R. Johnson. 2000. Ferruginous pygmy-owl (*Glaucidium brasilianum*). In *The Birds of North America*, no. 498, ed. A. Poole and F. Gill. Philadelphia: Birds of North America.

4. A. R. Phillips. 1965. Further systematic notes on Mexican birds. *Bulletin of the British Ornithologists' Club* 86:86–94.

5. G. A. Proudfoot, pers. comm.

6. Proudfoot, Honeycutt, and Slack 2006a.

7. D. Abbate, Arizona Game and Fish Department, pers. comm.

8. Lowery and Dahlquest 1951, quote p. 575.

BIBLIOGRAPHY

American Ornithologists' Union North and Middle America Classification Committee. 2008. Proposals 2008-C: Split *Glaucidium ridgwayi* from *G. brasilianum,* http://www.aou.org/committees/nacc/proposals/2008-C.pdf.

Binford 1989.

BirdLife International. 2015. *Glaucidium brasilianum.* In IUCN Red List of Threatened Species, v. 2014.3. http://www.iucnredlist.org/details/61815999/0.

Brodkorb, P. 1941. The pygmy owl of the district of Soconusco, Chiapas. *Occasional Papers of the Museum of Zoology, University of Michigan* 450:1–4.

Cartron, J-L. E., S. H. Stoleson, S. M. Russell, G. A. Proudfoot, and W. S. Richardson. 2000. The ferruginous pygmy-owl in the tropics and at the northern end of its range: Habitat relations and requirements. In *Ecology and Conservation of the Cactus Ferruginous Pygmy-owl in Arizona,* ed. J.-L. E. Cartron and D. M. Finch. USDA Gen. Tech. Rep. RMRS-GTR-43, pp. 47–55.

Cartron, J-L. E., W. S. Richardson, and G. A. Proudfoot. 2000. The cactus ferruginous pygmy-owl: Taxonomy, distribution, and natural history. In *Ecology and Conservation of the Cactus Ferruginous Pygmy-owl in Arizona,* ed. J.-L. E. Cartron and D. M. Finch. USDA Gen. Tech. Rep. RMRS-GTR-43, pp. 5–15.

Corman and Wise-Gervais 2005.

Flesch, A. D., and R. J. Steidl. 2007. Detectability and response rates of ferruginous pygmy-owls. *Journal of Wildlife Management* 71:981–990.

———. 2006. Population trends and implications for monitoring cactus ferruginous pygmy owls in northern Mexico. *Journal of Wildlife Management* 70:867–871.

Johnson, R. R., J.-L. E. Cartron, L. T. Haight, R. B. Duncan, and K. J. Kingsley. 2003. The cactus ferruginous pygmy-owl in Arizona, 1872–1971. *Southwestern Naturalist* 48:389–401.

———. 2000. A historical perspective on the population decline of the cactus ferruginous pygmy-owl. In *Ecology and Conservation of the Cactus Ferruginous Pygmy-owl in Arizona,* ed. J.-L. E. Cartron and D. M. Finch. USDA Gen. Tech. Rep. RMRS-GTR-43, pp.17–26.

Navarro-Sigüenza, A. G., and A. T. Peterson. 2007. *Glaucidium brasilianum* (tecolote bajeño) residencia permanente distribución potencial. In *Mapas de las Aves de México Basados en WWW,* ed. A. G. Navarro and A. T. Peterson. Final report, SNIB-CONABIO project no. CE015. México DF.

Proudfoot, G.A. 2005. "Mitochondrial and nuclear assessment of ferruginous pygmy-owl (*Glaucidium brasilianum*) phylogeography." PhD diss., Texas A&M University.

Proudfoot, G. A., R. L. Honeycutt, and R. D. Slack. 2006a. Mitochondrial DNA variation and phylogeography of the ferruginous pygmy-owl (*Glaucidium brasilianum*). *Conservation Genetics* 7:1–12.

———. 2006b. Variation in DNA microsatellites of the ferruginous pygmy-owl (*Glaucidium brasilianum*). *Conservation Genetics* 7:945–956.

Proudfoot, G. A., and S. L. Beasom. 1997. Food habits of nesting ferruginous pygmy-owls in southern Texas. *Wilson Bulletin* 109:741–748.

Richardson, W. S., J.-L. E. Cartron, D. J. Krueper, L. Turner, and T. H. Skinner. 2000. The status of the cactus ferruginous pygmy-owl in Arizona: Population surveys and habitat assessment. In *Ecology and Conservation of the Cactus Ferruginous Pygmy-owl in Arizona,* ed. J.-L. E. Cartron and D. M. Finch. USDA Gen. Tech. Rep. RMRS-GTR-43, pp. 27–39.

Santillan, M. A., J. H. Sarasola, and M. Dolsan. 2008. Ear tufts in ferruginous pygmy-owl (*Glaucidium brasilianum*). *Journal of Raptor Research* 42:153–154.

Schaldach, Escalante, and Winker 1997.

Stiles and Skutch 1989.

U.S. Fish and Wildlife Service. 2006. Final rule to remove the Arizona distinct population segment of the cactus ferruginous pygmy-owl (*Glaucidium brasilianum cactorum*) from the federal list of endangered and threatened wildlife. *Federal Register* 72:19452–19458.

———. 2003. Cactus ferruginous pygmy-owl (*Glaucidium brasilianum cactorum*) draft recovery plan. Albuquerque, NM: Region 2, U.S. Fish and Wildlife Service.

Isolated on its island home, the Cuban Pygmy-Owl has evolved a decidedly un–pygmy-owl–like song, a fast, squeaky, rising call that sounds more like a flycatcher. *(Cuba. Christian Artuso)*

CUBAN PYGMY-OWL
Glaucidium siju
Alpha code: CUPO

LENGTH: 7 in. (17.5 cm)

WINGSPAN: Undocumented; approx. 12–15 in. (30.5–38 cm)

MASS: Slight reversed size dimorphism.
  G. s. siju: Average, male: 2 oz. (57.1 g); range 1.8–2.3 oz. (50–64.4 g). Average, female: 2.3 oz. (64.7 g); range 2.2–2.4 oz. (62–67 g). Guanahacabibes Peninsula: Average, male: 2.1 oz. (60 g); range 1.9–2.3 oz. (54–65 g). Average, female: 2.7 oz. (76.5 g); range 2.5–3 oz. (72–84 g).[1]
  G. s. vittatum: Average, male: 3.1 oz. (87.1); range 3–3.25 oz. (84–92 g). Female, no data.[1]
  G. s. turquinense: No data.

LONGEVITY: Little information; presumably similar to other pygmy-owls.

A common and widespread endemic, the Cuban Pygmy-Owl's unusual vocalizations—including a fast, squeaky, ascending song that sounds more like a flycatcher than an owl—are heard throughout the island. Little is known about its ecology, however, beyond the bare bones of its natural history.

SYSTEMATICS, TAXONOMY, AND ETYMOLOGY

There are three subspecies, one only recently described. *G. s. siju* is found on almost all of Cuba except for the highlands around Pico Turquino, while *G. s. vittatum* is restricted to the Isla de la Juventud (Isle of Pines); it is larger, grayer, and more heavily barred above than the nominate race. Individuals of *siju* from the Guanahacabibes Peninsula in extreme western Cuba are larger than those on the rest of the island, and are sometimes placed in *G. s. vittatum.*

A third subspecies, *G. s. turquinense,* inhabits the highlands of Pico Turquino in southeastern Cuba, the island's highest point, where it replaces *G. s. siju.* This montane race—darker than the nominate, and brownish gray instead of brown—was first collected

The Cuban Pygmy-Owl may be more nocturnal than its relatives, calling frequently at night—but little is known about its behavior, ecology, or diet. (Cuba. Rick Collins)

DESCRIPTION AND IDENTIFICATION

The smallest owl in Cuba, with a typical pygmy-owl build and eyespots on the nape of the neck. Two color morphs, gray-brown, described below, and an uncommon rufous form.

BASIC (ADULT) PLUMAGE: Sexes similar, but females average more rufous-brown, contrasting with generally grayer males (although some males exhibit hints of rufous). Head and upperparts gray-brown, with a pale cinnamon collar below the nape, and black eyespots edged with white along the upper margins. Forehead and crown finely spotted with white. Back and folded wings barred with white or light cinnamon. Tail gray-brown with four (sometimes five) visible whitish, narrow, and complete bars.

Facial disk matches ground color of crown, with well-defined concentric rings of fine white streaks, but contrasts with more rufous nape. Eyebrows gray-white and narrow. Rictal bristles and throat grayish. Upper chest, sides, and flanks broadly marked with pale chestnut and darker brown barring, and rufous-brown barring and scalloping on white central chest and belly. Legs feathered, whitish gray; toes yellowish. Eyes bright yellow, bill gray- or green-yellow.

JUVENAL PLUMAGE: Similar to adults but downier, with a mostly unstreaked, gray-brown crown, unmarked back, streakier underparts. Eye color may be less bright yellow compared with adults.

SIMILAR SPECIES: The Bare-legged Owl is slightly larger and has dark eyes, long legs, and a tail that barely extends beyond the folded wings. The Burrowing Owl, which is rarely in trees, is markedly larger, with very long legs and a very short tail.

VOCALIZATIONS

Distinctive and unlike any other pygmy-owl in our region. "The call was a loud, rather high pitched *ts-weep*, a most un-owl-like sound which had me baffled for a while until I saw the bird," one ornithologist admitted in the 1920s.[2]

Male territorial song is a slow series of unexpressive *huee* notes, spaced every 2 to 8 seconds apart (most commonly every 4 to 6 seconds). Both sexes give a series of 15 to 30 wheezy, squeaky notes, starting with 2.5 notes per second, smoothly accelerating and rising in pitch and intensity, *wee-wee-*

in 1917 by the American ornithologist Rollo Beck, but it lay unrecognized in museum collections until Cuban biologists described it in 2002 from Beck's specimens.

ETYMOLOGY: For the genus name, see "Northern Pygmy-Owl." The species name is of local Caribbean origin, *sijú*, a general name for small owls including the Pygmy-, Burrowing, and Bare-legged Owls. The origin of the common name for this Cuban endemic is obvious.

SPANISH: *Sijú platanero, sijú sijucito*

DISTRIBUTION

BREEDING SEASON: Permanent resident. *G. s. turquinense* is found above 5,250 ft. (1,600 m) on Pico Turquino.

wee-wee-wee-wee-weep-weep-weep-WEEP-WEEP-WEEPWEEPWEEP, sometimes ending in a high, squeaky chatter.

HABITAT AND NICHE

Common in almost any semiopen wooded habitat, including residential areas, especially where there are stands of palms.

DIET: Not well studied; large insects (especially grasshoppers, crickets, beetles, and moths), lizards, small snakes, some birds, frogs, and small mammals. One early naturalist reported seeing a Cuban Pygmy-Owl tackle and kill an Eastern Meadowlark, "only to be in its turn attacked and driven off by half a dozen of the latter."[3]

NESTING AND BREEDING

A secondary cavity adopter, the Cuban Pygmy-Owl uses old woodpecker holes and natural rot cavities, especially in palm trees. Breeding begins in Dec., but egg-laying peaks in Mar. and Apr., with 3 or 4 eggs being a typical clutch size and the female doing all the incubation.

BEHAVIOR

"This little owl . . . is one of the first birds to attract the attention of a newcomer," American ornithologist Walter E. C. Todd wrote in 1916, "coming boldly as it does into gardens and the vicinity of houses, and showing little fear of man."[3] The Cuban Pygmy-Owl remains common and confiding, even by the approachable standards of its relatives—although when agitated it will jerkily twitch its tail from side to side, often while steadily cocking it upward.

Although most vocal at dawn and dusk, it is often active in full day, like other pygmy-owls. In contrast to most *Glaucidiums,* however, the Cuban Pygmy-Owl often calls at night and may be more nocturnal than its relatives, especially during the breeding season.

STATUS

The Cuban Pygmy-Owl is common on most of Cuba, and is listed by IUCN/BirdLife as "least concern" with a stable population trend. The population and status of the recently described *G. s. turquinense* are unknown.

Cuban Pygmy-Owls are dimorphic, with this gray-brown form most common, and the rufous morph rarer. *(Cuba. Christian Artuso)*

3. W. E. C. Todd. 1916. Birds of the Isle of Pines. *Annals of the Carnegie Museum* 10:146–296, quote p. 233.

BIBLIOGRAPHY

Bangs, O., and W. R. Zappey. 1905. Birds of the Isle of Pines. *American Naturalist* 39:179–215.

BirdLife International. 2015. *Glaucidium siju.* In IUCN Red List of Threatened Species, v. 2014.3. http://www.iucnredlist.org/details/22689262/0.

Kirwan, G. M. 2010. Cuban pygmy-owl (*Glaucidium siju*). Neotropical Birds, ed. T. S. Schulenberg. Ithaca, NY: Cornell Lab of Ornithology, http://neotropical.birds.cornell.edu/portal/species/overview?p_p_spp=212536.

Pyle, P., A. Andrews, P. Veléz, R. L. Wilkerson, R. B. Siegel, and D. F. DeSante. 2004. Molt patterns and age and sex determination of selected southeastern Cuban landbirds. *Journal of Field Ornithology* 75:136–145.

Raffaele et al. 1998.

Roberts, E. A. 2014. *A Comprehensive Etymological Dictionary of the Spanish Language,* vol. 2. Bloomington, IN: Xlibris.

Walkinshaw, L. H., and B. W. Baker. 1946. Notes on the birds of the Isle of Pines, Cuba. *Wilson Bulletin* 58:133–142.

NOTES

1. O. H. Garrido. 2002. Subespecie nueva de sijú platanero (*Glaucidium siju*) para Cuba (Aves: Strigidae), con comentarioes sobre otras especies de la familia. *Solenodon* 2:45–52.

2. S. T. Danforth. 1928. Birds observed in the vicinity of Santiago de Cuba. *Wilson Bulletin* 40:178–182, quote p. 180.

Of two widespread subspecies, *M. w. whitneyi*, shown here, is found from West Texas and the Southwest borderlands into Sonora and Sinaloa, and is brown above and distinctly cinnamon below. *M. w. idonea*, from the lower Rio Grande into northeastern Mexico, is grayer and lacks the rusty wash. *(Arizona. Tom Johnson)*

ELF OWL
Micrathene whitneyi
Alpha code: ELOW

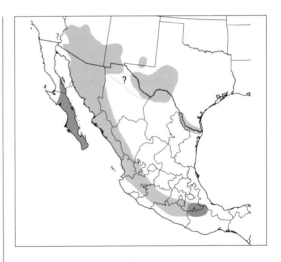

LENGTH: 5.25–5.75 in. (13.3–14.5 cm)

WINGSPAN: 12–14 in. (30.5–35.5 cm)

MASS: In addition to being the smallest owl in the world, the Elf Owl exhibits one of the lowest degrees of reversed size dimorphism among North American owls.

  M. w. whitneyi: Average weight of unsexed adults in two studies in southeastern Arizona: 1.4 oz. (41 g); range 1.3–1.5 oz. (35.9–44.1 g),[1] and 1.3 oz. (37.5 g); range 1.25–1.4 oz. (35.4–39.8 g).[2]

  M. w. idonea: Average weight of unsexed adults in South Texas: 1.5 oz. (44 g); range 1.4–1.7 oz. (41–49 g). Average, male: 1.5 oz. (43 g); range 1.4–1.6 oz. (41–46 g). Average, female: 1.6 oz. (46 g); range 1.6–1.7 oz. (45–47 g). Limited data from nonmigratory Mexican population; one male from Puebla 1.5 oz. (43 g).[3]

LONGEVITY: Little information; fewer than half a dozen band returns for the species, with an average age at encounter of 3.75 years. Longevity record 5 years 10 months, an owl banded in Big Bend National Park in Texas and knocked unconscious in Apr. 1984 when the utility pole in which it was nesting was taken down. (Fortunately, after a brief recovery period, the owl was released.) Other notable longevity record 4 years 11 months, but has lived to 14 years in captivity.

A tiny bird with an outsize voice, the Elf Owl is the smallest owl in the world, weighing only as much as a small thrush. The male's so-called "chatter song," often likened to the yipping of an excited

Less than 6 in. (16 cm) long and weighing only about as much as a thrush, the Elf Owl is one of the smallest raptors of any kind in the world. *(West Texas. Greg Lasley)*

puppy, is a common dusk sound in the borderland deserts from southern and western Texas to Arizona, where it is often the most common owl. Closely associated—at least in birders' minds—with saguaro stands in the Sonoran Desert, it actually occupies one of the widest variety of habitats of any bird (owl or otherwise) in the region. Almost entirely insectivorous, northern populations are highly migratory, and the species has a peculiar, disjunct distribution in Mexico that cries out for closer study.

SYSTEMATICS, TAXONOMY, AND ETYMOLOGY

The validity of and the relationships among the four described subspecies are in need of detailed examination and are clouded by the close proximity of migratory and resident populations, uncertainty regarding the extent of breeding and wintering ranges, and one race's oddly disjunct distribution, which may mask an undescribed subspecies.

M. w. whitneyi: Breeds from western Texas and northern Coahuila through southern New Mexico and Arizona, south to northwestern Chihuahua, into Sonora and northern Sinaloa. Extirpated from southern Nevada and northern Baja, and nearly or completely so from lower Colorado River in southeastern California. More distinctly brown above and cinnamon below than *M. w. idonea.*

M. w. idonea: Migratory population breeds in the lower Rio Grande Valley of Texas and neighboring Tamaulipas and Nuevo León. Resident population in Puebla and adjacent areas of northern Oaxaca (perhaps north to Guanajuato) is ascribed to this subspecies, but such a disjunct distribution separated by some 500 mi. (800 km) would be remarkable. *M. w. idonea* has sometimes been lumped with the nominate race. Gray above with little or no brown overtones and no cinnamon wash on the face or underparts.

M. w. sandfordi: Resident in southern Baja. Smaller and grayer than *whitneyi,* although not as gray as *idonea.*

M. w. grayson: Endemic to Isla Socorro in the Revillagigedo Archipelago off Mexico's Pacific Coast. Sometimes elevated to species status. Almost certainly extinct (see "Status," p. 190). Rich olive-brown above, cinnamon below, lacking any gray tones; eyebrows cinnamon instead of white.

Elf Owls are highly migratory at the northern edge of their breeding range, but some Mexican populations are sedentary, and the extent of the nonmigratory range is unclear. *(Arizona. Greg Lasley)*

ETYMOLOGY: Originally assigned to the genus *Athene,* which is named for the Greek goddess of wisdom; *Micrathene* translates roughly to "little goddess of wisdom." The species name honors Josiah Dwight Whitney, chief of the Geographical Survey of California, and was conferred by Joseph Cooper, the survey ornithologist who first described the species in 1866. The common name refers to the elfin size of this smallest of all owls.

SPANISH: *Tecolotito [tecolote] enano, tecolotito colicorto*

DISTRIBUTION

BREEDING SEASON: Several disjunct migratory populations occur from southern Texas and northern Mexico west to Arizona—although more intensive surveys may show that these apparently discrete populations are contiguous—and south through Sonora and Sinaloa. Disjunct resident populations are also found in southern Baja and central Mexico. (See "Systematics, Taxonomy, and Etymology," p. 186, for detailed range descriptions by subspecies.)

NONBREEDING SEASON: Southern Sinaloa to Puebla and northern Oaxaca; exact extent and boundaries of the resident population in central Mexico unclear. Rare winter resident in southern Texas.

MIGRATION AND MOVEMENTS: Highly migratory at the northern extent of its range, although essentially nothing is known about the routes taken by this tiny raptor. As with many migrants, the males appear to arrive first on the breeding grounds in spring.

Spring arrival occurs in mid-Feb. (rarely) or early Mar. in southern Arizona, New Mexico, and northern Sonora, progressively later (to mid-Apr.) at higher and cooler elevations. Arrives in early to mid-Mar. in lower Rio Grande Valley of Texas and northeastern Mexico. In the Big Bend region of Texas, it arrives by late Mar. or early Apr. at low elevations, reaching 5,600 ft. (1,700 m) by mid- to late Apr.

Fall departure is generally from late Aug. through mid- to late Sept. (rarely into Oct.) among most migratory populations, but lack of vocalization after the breeding season makes departure detection more difficult than arrival in spring.

Although most migratory owls are presumed to be solitary, there are intriguing hints that Elf Owls may travel in flocks. In 1918, pioneering biologist J. S. Ligon encountered "numbers" of Elf Owls along the Gila River in New Mexico, "sitting on the ground or on rocks beneath thick scrub bushes. . . . This concentration probably preceded the southward migration."[4] Another collector reported, without details, a "large" flock of roosting Elf Owls in Sonora in Mar.[5]

Elf Owls are monomorphic, although females average somewhat redder than males, within regional populations. *(Arizona. Tom Johnson)*

POST-FLEDGING DISPERSAL: Unstudied

DISTRIBUTION OUTSIDE THE COVERAGE AREA: None

DESCRIPTION AND IDENTIFICATION

Almost comically diminutive, the Elf Owl is a tiny, bare-legged, tuftless owl with a piercing yellow-eyed glare. Hunting insects and other arthropods, it lacks fluffy plumage and other adaptations for silent flight—and while not apparent in the field, it also lacks the normal complement of tail feathers, with 10 instead of 12, as in all other owls.

BASIC (ADULT) PLUMAGE: Monomorphic, although females average slightly redder. Description applies to nominate race *whitneyi.* Upperparts brown-gray, lightly freckled with pale buffy cinnamon spots. Scapular edges whitish, forming narrow white "suspender" bars along the tops of the folded wings. Flight feathers dark brown with buffy white to pale cinnamon barring above and whitish barring below; outer greater and median coverts tipped with white or buffy white spots. Tail shorter than folded wings, dark brown with two or three narrow whitish bars visible.

Facial disk gray tinged with rufous, facial ruff indistinct or absent. Eyes narrowly but distinctly rimmed with black, accentuating the iris color, like heavy mascara. Eyebrows narrow and white. Throat pale rufous to rufous-gray. Underparts heavily mottled with gray and rufous-brown on upper chest, forming wide vertical streaks below against the white belly. Legs and feet buffy or yellowish and heavily bristled. Iris bright yellow, bill greenish yellow.

JUVENAL PLUMAGE: Nestling down white. Juvenal plumage grayer than adult, with less distinct markings and very fine, indistinct grayish barring overall. Central tail feathers may have more distinct white barring than on adults.

SIMILAR SPECIES: Smaller and daintier than all other owls but can be confused with Northern and Ferruginous Pygmy-Owls, which have much longer tails (extending well beyond the folded wings), and Flammulated Owl, which has dark eyes. Voice is dramatically different from any of these.

VOCALIZATIONS

The primary male advertisement call is a rapid series of six or seven squeaky, nasal yips that peak in intensity in the middle. Each burst lasts a bit longer than a second, with a short but distinct pause after the first, quieter note in each. This "chatter call," as it is known, is usually repeated every 2 to 4 seconds. The male trying to entice a female will call nearly continuously from inside the nest cavity.

Agitated adults of both sexes defending a nest may give a constant stream of rapid barks. Contact

From the rear, a very short tail and the absence of eye spots instantly distinguish an Elf Owl from any of the pygmy-owls—as does its squeaky vocalization, which sounds like a yipping puppy. (Arizona. Tom Johnson)

A newly fledged Elf Owl stares down an intruding human. Adult Elf Owls are extraordinarily good parents; one study documented a 90 percent nesting success rate, the highest of any owl in the world. (Arizona. Tom Johnson)

call between mates or adults and chicks is a quick, soft, whistled *weeuu* that falls off toward the end.

HABITAT AND NICHE

An inhabitant of a wide range of desert and thornscrub habitats—perhaps the widest range of any southwestern bird—the Elf Owl may be encountered in humid mesquite thickets near sea level along the lower Rio Grande River; in riparian woods along desert washes; in Sonoran saguaro stands; in sycamore-lined canyons; and in cool montane forests of oak above 5,000 ft. (1,525 m), and sometimes in pine-oak up to 7,000 ft. (2,130 m) high. Elf Owls can even do surprisingly well in the suburban fringe, where—as with the much rarer Ferruginous Pygmy-Owl—they are attracted to the lusher vegetation of irrigated yards and seem unperturbed by human activity. But dense urbanization is a major threat to this species.

In the Sonoran Desert, one study found that large, multibranched saguaro cacti with an overstory of mature mesquite held the densest numbers of Elf Owls—the cacti and trees providing roosts and nesting sites, the mesquite likely important because of insect prey they provide.

Although they are closely tied to saguaro cacti in the Sonoran Desert, Elf Owls occupy one of the widest ecological ranges of any bird in North America, from mesquite thickets near sea level in Texas to chilly pine-oak forests high in the mountains. *(West Texas. Greg Lasley)*

Elf Owls are almost completely insectivorous, taking whatever's most easily available. Crickets and moths dominate the diet in early summer, with beetles more common when the late-summer monsoons begin. *(Arizona. Paul Bannick/VIREO)*

Far less is known about their habitat needs on the Mexican wintering grounds, although they are encountered most often in dry, open forests. Their dependence on large cacti in Mexico is unclear, but nesting territories in Puebla appeared to be tied to the presence of large organ-pipe cacti.

DIET: Elliott Coues, the nineteenth-century ornithologist, said the Elf Owl's talons "are so small and weak as to be hardly more than insessorial rather than raptorial in character"[6]—meaning better adapted for perching, not hunting.

On the other hand, Coues never observed an Elf Owl in the wild, or he might have reconsidered such a dismissive comment. While the Elf Owl hunts primarily small insects and similar arthropods, it doesn't hesitate to tackle quarry that could be dangerous for a sparrow-size hunter, including large scorpions and venomous centipedes—often snipping off the stinger from the tail of a scorpion before eating it.

Prey varies seasonally; in Arizona, moths and crickets are most commonly caught in early summer, replaced by scarab beetles later in the season when the monsoon rains begin. Vertebrates—including lizards, small snakes, and rodents—are rare enough in their diet to usually merit special mention by scientists studying Elf Owls.

NESTING AND BREEDING

Males set up their territories and locate multiple potential nest sites right after returning in spring.

Male Elf Owls set up territories right after they arrive in the spring, often singing from inside the entrance to potential nest cavities—holes made, invariably, by woodpeckers. *(Arizona. Greg Lasley)*

Once the females arrive on the breeding grounds, the males begin to sing, often from the entrance to a hole. As the female approaches, the male sinks into the cavity, continuing to call (for up to 32 minutes without pause, according to one researcher timing the action). Courtship is believed to be rapid-fire, perhaps taking just a single night. An adult may return to the same nest site for at least 3 years, but the pair bond appears to last only a single season.

A secondary cavity nester, the Elf Owl depends—apparently without exception—on old woodpecker holes, including those of Gilded Flicker and Gila, Acorn, and Golden-fronted Woodpeckers. In the Chihuahuan Desert, Ladder-backed Woodpecker holes are of primary importance, and fenceposts, agave stalks, and utility poles serve where trees are scarce.

Although birders tend to associate this owl most closely with saguaros, it may be restricted to such nest sites only in Sonoran Desert uplands, where the thick, fleshy cacti provide insulation against extreme heat. In higher and cooler areas, Elf Owls will use nest cavities in whatever large trees are available. Nest height averages 20 to 30 ft. (6 to 10 m), a reflection of where woodpecker cavities can be found, although in the Sonoran Desert Elf Owls were found to prefer north-facing cavities, again perhaps for protection from the heat. Elf Owls will accept nest boxes with an entrance hole diameter similar to the 2 in. (5 cm) opening of most natural woodpecker excavations.

Typically of owls, no material is added to the nest, and the eggs are laid directly on the cavity floor. Clutch sizes ranges from 1 to 5 eggs, with 3 being typical; clutches of 4 are more common in low desert habitat. Incubation, by the female only, lasts about 24 days, usually beginning with the second egg, and hatching is asynchronous—the first 2 eggs together, the third a day or more later.

The nestling period lasts at least 28 days, with the adults using a soft, single-noted call to lure the young birds from the nest, and withholding food to encourage them to take the leap.

J. David Ligon, studying Elf Owls in the canyons of southeastern Arizona, documented an astounding 90 percent nesting success rate in the 1960s—the highest of any owl in the world. Other researchers have found equally impressive rates in this species. They may be small, but Elf Owls are extraordinarily good parents.

BEHAVIOR

Elf Owls are largely crepuscular, foraging most actively at dusk and dawn, which is also when the male's song is most frequently heard. They hunt primarily on the wing, coursing low over open ground, grabbing insects in flight or snatching them from the outer branches of trees, hovering and swerving like large moths. Observers have seen them knock beetles, moths, and other night-feeding insects from the nectar-rich blossoms of agaves.

Roost cavities in saguaros and other large cacti may provide the thermal insulation needed during the most brutal periods of summer heat. Once the cooling monsoon rains begin, Elf Owls often shift to roost sites in thickets and shrubs, and they appear to use similar sites on the nonbreeding grounds in Mexico.

Small and insectivorous, Elf Owls don't need much space if food is plentiful, and they sometimes defend remarkably small territories—as scant as three-quarters of an acre (.3 hectare). Nests have been found as close as 30 ft. (9 m) apart.

STATUS

Although locally common and even abundant in many areas, especially Sonoran Desert uplands, the status of the Elf Owl overall is unclear, and the species faces several significant threats. Little information on population trends exists, and the owls are poorly monitored by long-term efforts like the Breeding Bird Survey. Its presumed absence along much of the Rio Grande may reflect inadequate surveys rather than actual gaps in distribution.

There is evidence of some northward expansion of its range in West Texas, New Mexico, and Arizona,

An Elf Owl ferries a cricket to its chicks, hidden in a saguaro. In the Sonoran Desert the cactus, whose thick, fleshy walls provide protection against the summer desert heat, is a favorite nesting site. *(Arizona. Rick and Nora Bowers/VIREO)*

although this may in part be thanks to more active, thorough searches. Elf Owls have declined in urbanized areas of Arizona from rampant habitat loss and may face further declines from increasing frequency and intensity of wildfires, exacerbated by drought.

The population along the lower Colorado River between Arizona and California, the westernmost extent of the Elf Owl's range, suffered dramatic declines in the twentieth century because of water diversions and habitat loss. The historic cottonwood-willow forest along the river, watered by seasonal snowmelt floods, was all but eliminated, and the remaining scraps of habitat are now dominated by exotic tamarisk.

The Elf Owl appears almost or entirely extirpated from the California side of this much-reduced waterway and is listed as "endangered" by that state. There are relatively few pairs remaining on the Arizona side of the Colorado, notably in riparian forests in Bill Williams River National Wildlife Refuge. Restoration of floodplain forests along the lower Colorado River—a priority for many imperiled species in this battered ecosystem—and erection of nest boxes should help the Elf Owl.

The Socorro Island (Mexico) subspecies, *M. w. graysoni*, is considered probably extinct, doomed by feral cats and sheep and perhaps by avian malaria, similarly introduced to the island. The last specimen was collected in 1932, although it was said to still be common in the 1950s, when military personnel brought cats. The last report of this subspecies was 1970, and field searches for it in the 1980s and 1990s were fruitless. Elimination of sheep and the planned eradication of cats, which will benefit the other endemic species on the island, will likely come too late for this unique owl.

NOTES

1. P. M. Walters. 1981. Notes on the body weight and molt of the elf owl (*Micrathene whitneyi*) in southeastern Arizona. *North American Bird Bander* 6:104–105.

2. P. M. Walters. 1983. Notes on the mist-netting of seven elf owls (*Micrathene whitneyi*) and two western screech-owls (*Otus kennecotti*) on 15 July 1982. *North American Bird Bander* 8:13.

3. S. G. Henry and F. R. Gehlbach. 1999. Elf owl (*Micrathene whitneyi*). In *The Birds of North America*, no. 413, ed. A. Poole and F. Gill. Philadelphia: Birds of North America.

4. J. S. Ligon. 1961. *New Mexico Birds and Where to Find Them*. Albuquerque, NM: University of New Mexico Press, p. 147.

5. J. D. Ligon. 1968. The biology of the elf owl, *Micrathene*

whitneyi. Ann Arbor, MI: University of Michigan, Misc. Pub. no. 136.

6. E. Coues. 1866. List of the birds of Fort Whipple, Arizona. *Proceedings of the Academy of Natural Sciences of Philadelphia*. Philadelphia: Academy of Natural Sciences, p. 51.

BIBLIOGRAPHY

Aguirre-Muñoz, A., A. Samaniego-Herrera, L. Lunda-Mendoza, A. Ortiz-Alcaraz, M. Rodriguez-Malagón, F. Méndez-Sánchez, M. Félix-Lizárraga, J. C. Hernández-Montoya, R. González-Gómez, F. Torres-Garcia, J. M. Barredo-Barberena, and M. Latofski-Robles. 2011. Island restoration in Mexico: Ecological outcomes after systematic eradications of invasive mammals. In *Island Invasives: Eradication and Management,* ed. C. R. Veitch, M. N. Clout, and D. R. Towns. Gland, Switzerland: IUCN, pp. 250–258.

Carlson, J. S., J. E. Martínez-Gómez, A. Cornel, C. Loiseau, and R. N. M. Sehgal. 2011. Implications of *Plasmodium* parasite infected mosquitoes on an insular avifauna: The case of Socorro Island, Mexico. *Journal of Vector Biology* 36:213–220.

Great Basin Bird Observatory. 2012. *Final Project Report: Elf Owl Detectability Study 2010–2011*. Boulder City, NV: Lower Colorado River Multi-Species Conservation Program.

Hardy, P. C., and M. L. Morrison. 2001. Nest site selection by elf owls in the Sonoran Desert. *Wilson Bulletin* 113:23–32.

Hardy, P. C., M. L. Morrison, and R. X. Barry. 1999. Abundance and habitat associations of elf owls and western screech-owls in the Sonoran Desert. *Southwestern Naturalist* 44:311–323.

Hume and Walters 2012.

Jehl, J. R. Jr., and K. C. Parkes. 1982. The status of the avifauna of the Revillagigedo Islands, Mexico. *Wilson Bulletin* 94:1–19.

Navarro-Sigüenza, A. G., and A. T. Peterson. 2007. *Micrathene whitneyi* (tecolote enano) verano distribución potencial. In *Mapas de las Aves de México Basados en WWW,* ed. A. G. Navarro and A. T. Peterson. Final report, SNIB-CONABIO project no. CE015. México DF.

Ortiz-Alcaraz, A., J. M. Barredo-Barberena, A. Aguirre-Muñoz, F. Pérez-Castro, and F. A. Méndez-Sánchez. 2012. *Feral Cat Eradication Plan for Socorro Island, Revillagigedo Archipelago, Mexico.* Enenada, MX: Grupo de Ecología y Conservación de Islas.

Phillips, A. R. 1942. Notes on the migrations of the elf and flammulated screech owls. *Wilson Bulletin* 54:132–137.

Santaella, L., and A. M. Sada. 1991. The avifauna of the Revillagigedo Islands, Mexico: Additional data and observations. *Wilson Bulletin* 4:668–675.

Skoruppa, M. K., M. C. Woodin, and G. Blacklock. 2009. Species richness, relative abundance, and habitat associations of nocturnal birds along the Rio Grande in southern Texas. *Southwestern Naturalist* 54:317–323.

Wehtje, W., H. S. Walter, R. Rodriguez-Estrella, J. Llinas, and A. Caste-Llanos Vera. 1993. An annotated checklist of the birds of Isla Socorro, Mexico. *Western Birds* 24:1–16.

DNA analysis suggests that the disjunct Florida subspecies split off from the more widely distributed western race of Burrowing Owl some 350,000 years ago, with significant genetic differences between them. *(Florida. Kevin Loughlin/Wildside Nature Tours)*

BURROWING OWL
Athene cunicularia
Alpha code: BUOW

LENGTH: 9–10 in. (22.9–25.5 cm)

WINGSPAN: 22–24 in. (56–61 cm)

MASS: The only North American owl to exhibit non-reversed size dimorphism, with males slightly larger than females in overall measurements (though consistently still slightly lighter than females in terms of mass). Weights cited in Eckert and Karalus (1973) are 28–42 percent heavier than any other published sources and are not included here.

A. c. hypugaea (four studies): Colorado: Average, male: 5.2 oz. (146 g). Average, female: 5.5 oz. (156 g).[1] California: Unsexed adults, average summer weight: 5.2 oz. (147 g); average winter weights: 6.6 oz. (186 g).[2] California: Average, male: 6.1 oz. (172 g). Average, female: 5.9 oz. (168 g).[3] No origin specified: Average, male: 5.6 oz. (158.6 g); range 4.25–8 oz. (120–228 g). Average, female: 5.3 oz. (151 g); range 4.6–6.5 oz. (129–185 g).[4]

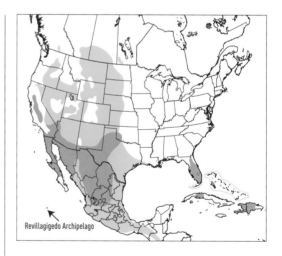

Revillagigedo Archipelago

A. c. floridana (three studies): Florida: Average, male: 5.25 oz. (149 g). Average, female: 5.3 oz. (150 g).[5] Florida: Average, male: 5.5 oz. (155 g). Average, female: 5.4 oz. (152 g).[6] Florida: Average, three unsexed adults: 6.4 oz. (182 g); range 6.3–6.5 oz. (179–185 g).[7]

LONGEVITY: Average age on re-encounter of more than 540 banded birds, 1.4 years. Longevity records 9 years 2 months, and 8 years 8 months.

Well studied because of its diurnal habits, its close association with humans, and—with increasing urgency—its rapid and almost range-wide declines, the Burrowing Owl is an engaging resident of open grasslands from the Canadian border through South America, with a disjunct population in Florida and parts of the Caribbean. Most closely associated with prairie-dog towns in its western range, the Burrowing Owl's habit of bobbing up and down gained it the folk name "howdy owl" in parts of the West—but the behavior is a sign of nervous agitation, not welcome.

SYSTEMATICS, TAXONOMY, AND ETYMOLOGY

Once placed in its own genus, *Speotyto*, the Burrowing Owl is now classified with the Little Owl of Eurasia and Africa as a member of *Athene*, which in turn appears to be closely aligned with the pygmy-owls in *Glaucidium* and the Northern Hawk Owl in *Surnia*. The Burrowing Owl's relationship with the Elf Owl has not been studied using DNA but may well be close.

Not surprising, given its immense geographic range, the Burrowing Owl shows a great deal of regional variation, with some 25 subspecies named at various times. This account follows Poulin et al. (2011), which recognizes 15 races, of which 7 (2 presumably extinct) are in our area. In addition, 2 as-yet-undescribed subspecies are said to exist in Cuba, 1 in white-sand savannas on Isla de la Juventud (Isle of Pines), and 1 in western Cuba.[8]

DNA microsatellite analysis found significant genetic differences between the *floridana* and *hypugaea* forms, suggesting they diverged an estimated 350,000 years ago. The same study found that within each subspecies, genetic differentiation was low, suggesting good gene flow within each race despite the sedentary habits of some populations.

A. c. hypugaea: Breeding range from southern Canadian prairies and Dakotas (originally east to Minnesota and Iowa), south to California and Baja, eastern Texas, and central Mexico. Winter range extends south into Guatemala and Honduras, casually to western Panama. Largest race in our area; paler brown than *floridana*, with buffy spotting above, and tarsi feathered more than halfway to feet. Eyebrows form wide white band across forehead. Juveniles show wide pale upperwing coverts.

A. c. floridana: Resident in Florida and the Bahamas. Smaller and more heavily marked below than *hypugaea*, darker brown overall in fresh plumage, but many individuals fade quickly from sun. Whitish (versus buffy) spotting above, tarsi feathered less than halfway to feet. Eyebrows narrow and gray-white. Juveniles have spotted upperwing coverts, lacking wide pale bar, and whitish (not buffy) underparts with irregular, diffuse dark blotches.

Because they are more active throughout the day, and thus spend more time in the sun, male Burrowing Owls become especially bleached and sandy-colored. *(Washington. Gerrit Vyn)*

A. c. rostrata: Resident in Revillagigedo Archipelago, Mexico, notably Isla Clarión. Distinguished from *hypugaea* by larger beak and feet, shorter wings and tail, narrower tail barring, and less-distinct head markings.

A. c. troglodytes: Resident on Hispaniola, including Isla Beata and Île de la Gonâve. Less heavily marked below than *floridana.*

A. c. guantanamensis: Resident in southeastern Cuba.

A. c. amaura: Antigua, Nevis, and possibly Saint Kitts, Lesser Antilles. Extinct since late nineteenth century.

A. c. guadeloupensis: Marie-Galante Island, Lesser Antilles. Despite published references (and its subspecific name), it probably never occurred on neighboring Guadeloupe. Extinct since late nineteenth century.

ETYMOLOGY: The genus name refers to Athena, the Greek goddess of wisdom, and was first applied to the Little Owl of Eurasia, which was associated with Athena in ancient Greece. The species name derives from the Latin *cunicularius,* a "miner" or "burrower." The common name refers to this species's unique habit of nesting belowground.

SPANISH: *Búho [lechuza, tecolote] llanero/llanera, lecuza de hojo* (Mexico); *el sijú de sabana* (Cuba)

FRENCH: *Chouette [chevêche] à terrier, cou-couterre* (Haiti)

NÁHUATL: *Zacatecólotl*

DISTRIBUTION

BREEDING SEASON: Migratory *hypugaea* population breeds from extreme southern British Columbia (reintroduced) and central Washington through western Oregon to eastern California, east across Arizona, New Mexico, and northern Texas to western half of Oklahoma, Nebraska, South Dakota, and southwestern North Dakota, into southwestern Saskatchewan and southeastern Alberta. Small remnant population in southwestern Manitoba. Absent from mountainous areas of Nevada, Utah, Colorado, Wyoming, Montana, and Idaho.

Resident or partially migratory *hypugaea* population from Central Valley and southern California south to southern Baja and northern Sinaloa (absent from western Sierra Madre), west to central Mexico and north through western Nuevo León to the Trans-Pecos and high plains of western Texas, and west across borderland regions of New Mexico and Arizona. Some resident individuals among otherwise migratory population in northern Great Basin and Pacific Northwest.

Resident *floridana* population in Florida, including Keys (rare) and one small disjunct population in Florida panhandle. *A. c. floridana* resident on Bahamas. Additional subspecies (two undescribed; see "Systematics, Taxonomy, and Etymology," p. 194–95) resident in Cuba; race *troglodytes* resident on Hispaniola.

NONBREEDING SEASON: Migratory and partially migratory *A. c. hypugaea* overlaps broadly with resident population (see "Breeding Season," p. 195), and extends in winter east through Texas and southern Louisiana (rarely farther east along Gulf Coast), and south through Mexico to Honduras and Guatemala, rarely to Costa Rica and western Panama.

MIGRATION AND MOVEMENTS: The Burrowing Owl exhibits a complex mix of migratory, partially migratory, and sedentary populations (and in some cases, differences among age or sex classes, such as adult males in parts of the Southwest that do not migrate, although adult females and immatures from the same areas do). Many in the northern population appear to make a leapfrog migration, passing over and to the south of generally resident populations.

Spring arrival on the breeding grounds generally occurs mid- to late Mar. in latitudes like northern Arizona and New Mexico, and by late Apr. and

Northern populations of Burrowing Owls are migratory, while those from the Southwest borderlands and California south, as well as Florida and the Caribbean, are resident. *(Florida. Gerrit Vyn)*

early May in the northern edge of the range in Manitoba and Saskatchewan. Autumn migration range-wide appears to occur in Sept. and Oct.

Limited tracking data suggest that owls from the northernmost breeding grounds spread out across a remarkably wide area in winter. Researchers laboriously flying aerial transects on the wintering grounds tracked down Burrowing Owls originally radio-tagged on the southern Canadian prairies. They found that while birds from British Columbia wintered from Washington to California, those from Alberta and Saskatchewan migrated to a wide swath from Michoacán and Veracruz in Mexico, and north to eastern Texas.

POST-FLEDGING DISPERSAL: Most fledglings disperse from their parents' territory by late summer (late July or Aug. in well-studied Canadian populations). Dispersal distances ranged from .2 mi. (.3 km) to 19 mi. (30 km) in Canada, while Florida birds averaged .7 mi. (1.1 km) for female fledglings and .2 mi. (.3 km) for males. Up to a third of male chicks in Florida took over their parents' territory, perhaps because of high adult male mortality. In a nonmigratory population in California, males dispersed an average of .25 mi. (.4 km) and females 1.1 mi. (1.8 km). Females remained near the nest much longer than males, and dispersal behavior was also influenced by the gender of siblings: mixed-sex siblings tended to remain closer to each other after fledging.

DISTRIBUTION OUTSIDE THE COVERAGE AREA: Widely distributed throughout South America.

DESCRIPTION AND IDENTIFICATION

A small, long-legged, short-tailed owl with horizontal barring on the underparts and no ear tufts. Brown with whitish or buff mottling and spots above. Its plumage quickly fades, so that even nominally darker races can bleach to a paler, sandy brown ground color. Active in the daytime and generally approachable. The following plumage descriptions refer to the western race, *A. c. hypugaea; A. c. floridana* averages darker and more heavily marked.

BASIC (ADULT) PLUMAGE: Sexes similar. Head and upperparts brown, often faded from exposure to the sun, especially males exposed to more sunlight than incubating females. Crown and nape liberally speckled with buffy spots and streaks. Back and upper surfaces of wings spotted with buffy white. Tail short, dark brown with narrow, buffy bars.

Facial disk limited in size, gray-brown, with broad white lower margins. Eyebrows wide, white. Chin buffy. Dark brown band separates chin from white upper chest. Underparts white, heavily mottled with brown on upper chest that becomes

The Florida race of the Burrowing Owl, *A. c. floridana*, is darker and more heavily marked than the western subspecies, *A. c. hypugaea*. Although they are open-country ground-dwellers, Burrowing Owls will occasionally perch in trees. *(Florida. Kevin Loughlin/Wildside Nature Tours)*

distinct horizontal brown bars, lighter and more diffuse toward the belly. Legs long, tarsi slightly feathered in white more than halfway to bristled, gray-buff feet. Bill greenish.

Iris normally yellow to pale yellow, but in southwest Florida (Cape Coral area) a small percentage of juveniles have dark brown or olive eyes, which transition as adults to either green-yellow or to a bizarre, kaleidoscope mosaic of large brown and golden flecks. Juveniles with mottled dark eyes generally transition to adults with normal yellow eyes, but with a few flecks of brown.[9]

JUVENAL PLUMAGE: Brown above, largely unmarked on crown and nape, more sparsely spotted on the back and upperparts than are adults. Pale greater and median coverts form pale bar on folded wings. Upper chest brown and unmottled, midchest and belly buffy and unmarked.

SIMILAR SPECIES: No other owl is likely to be active in daytime in open country, sitting on the ground or using low perches. All other small owls (such as pygmy-owls) have vertical breast markings, not horizontal barring.

VOCALIZATIONS

The primary song of the male is a two- or three-noted *wa-WAAH-oo*, lasting about .8 seconds and typically spaced 2.5 to 4 seconds apart. The female responds with an *eep* call.

Burrowing Owls' eyes are normally yellow, but in southwest Florida a few juveniles have dark brown or olive eyes, which may transition as adults to this otherworldly mosaic of brown and gold. *(Florida. Stan Bentley)*

Burrowing Owls can be semi-colonial, and old reports described immense colonies stretching for miles in both the West and central Florida. *(Kansas. Gerrit Vyn)*

One alarm call, most often given by nestlings and nesting females, is the famous "rattlesnake rasp," an explosive, staticlike hiss (usually 4 to 10 seconds, fading and faltering slightly toward the end) that sounds convincingly like the buzz of an angry rattlesnake—and not just to the human ear; spectrographic comparisons of the owl call and actual prairie rattlesnake rattles show a close similarity in frequency and energy signature. The juvenile food-begging call is essentially a short (.25 to .5 second) version of this rasp.

Adults defending the nest give an alarm chatter, typically 5 to 7 (but sometimes 3 to 15) sharp notes, *WEET-whit-whit-whit-whit-whit-whit,* in a rapid burst roughly 1 second long. Single *chick* notes sometimes precede the alarm chatter.

HABITAT AND NICHE

Active by both day and night, especially during the demanding nesting season, Burrowing Owls are hunters of insects and small invertebrates. They are raptors of open places—rangeland and roadsides, prairies, and deserts in the West and Mexico; sand plains, pastures, and coastlines in Florida; pine savannahs and open scrub in the Caribbean; and golf courses, airports, vacant lots, and housing developments almost everywhere they are found.

Early ornithologists described large colonies in the prairies, sagebrush, and desert grasslands of the West, usually in association with prairie-dog towns. Intensive agriculture and extermination of prairie dogs initially reduced those numbers, and the species's range and abundance have further contracted in recent decades (see "Status," p. 201).

Burrowing Owls are rather confiding birds and have both benefited and suffered from their often close association with humans. Nowhere has that tie been closer or the paradox more evident than in Florida. Burrowing Owls were once primarily restricted to widely scattered sand-scrub plains and seasonally flooded prairies in the center of the state—although sometimes in dense concentrations. One naturalist in the 1890s described "a continuous colony, three miles long . . . [that] formed the breeding grounds of several hundred pairs of Owls."[10]

As Florida's forests were cut and more land was placed in agriculture, especially grazing, the eastern Burrowing Owl's range expanded north and toward the Atlantic and Gulf Coasts. But researchers have found a complex relationship between the owls and development.

Homebuilding—with the clearing it brings and the high density of prey, like insects and small lizards, that lushly planted, irrigated yards produce—have worked in the owls' favor. Researchers studying Burrowing Owls at Cape Coral, on Florida's Gulf Coast, found that owl density was highest when homes occupied 55 to 60 percent of the lots; chick survival was also highest when home density was around the same level or a bit less.

But adult survival rates, especially for adult males, dropped as housing density increased, and once about 70 percent or more of the lots were built on, owl populations tumbled—one reason the Florida subspecies has experienced major declines.

DIET: Undemanding about their diet, Burrowing Owls will take any prey they can easily handle, from beetles and grasshoppers to rodents, small birds, snakes, lizards, and frogs. Numerically, insects comprise by far the largest portion of the diet, while the fewer but heavier vertebrates that are taken make up most of the biomass—between 80 and 90 percent, in some studies.

While most of their vertebrate prey is small—mice, voles, pocket gophers, and the like—Burrowing Owls will sometimes kill bigger prey, including young prairie dogs, muskrats, jackrabbits, and cottontails. A number of observers dating back to the nineteenth century have noted one avian specialty in the owl's diet—the Horned Lark, a grassland bird that often nests in the same sparsely vegetated grasslands as the western subspecies.

NESTING AND BREEDING

The Burrowing Owl is the only owl in the world that nests exclusively underground. Its congener, the Little Owl of the Old World, occasionally uses mammal burrows, and there are one or two cases of Barn Owls excavating cavities in the soft dirt of arroyo walls, but only the Burrowing Owl makes an ironclad habit of nesting belowground.

The western population appears almost completely dependent on existing burrows—a strategy that worked well in presettlement days, when the prairies were blanketed with millions of busy, burrow-digging prairie dogs. The disjunct *floridana* race, on the other hand, had no such advantages; except for gopher tortoises and armadillos, there are few large burrowing animals in that area, and most nesting pairs dig their own burrows, as do those in the Caribbean.

Prairie-dog towns provide two key ingredients for a nest-hunting Burrowing Owl—plenty of unoccupied burrows from which to choose, and sparse, close-cropped grass, which gives the birds a good view of larger predators. Studies in South Dakota found that lack of tree cover—on which avian predators might perch—was a critical factor in nest site selection, while a study in Montana found that the bigger the prairie-dog colony, the more likely it was to be used by owls.

The well-developed social network of the colonial rodents, which have hundreds or thousands of pairs

Though Burrowing Owls usually use natural burrows, they are not above using manmade substitutes when the opportunity arises. *(Texas. Greg Lasley)*

Unique among the world's owls, the Burrowing Owl is the only species to nest exclusively underground. The western subspecies almost invariably uses rodent burrows, while those in Florida often dig their own nests. *(Florida. Tom Johnson)*

of eyes constantly scanning for danger, is a further advantage. So closely are Burrowing Owls tied to prairie-dog towns that in the Oklahoma panhandle, two-thirds of all Burrowing Owls were found in dog towns, even though such colonies made up only 0.1 percent of the landscape.

Burrowing Owls are semi-colonial, and while the immense colonies described in both populations a century ago are gone, they often breed in smaller aggregations. In northern Arizona, scientists found an average of three nests for every 250 acres (100

Burrowing Owls can lay extremely large clutches—up to 14 eggs on rare occasions, although 7 to 9 is more typical. *(Kansas. Paul Bannick/VIREO)*

hectares) of prairie-dog town, while in Wyoming it was less than one nest for the same area. In one Oklahoma town, as many as 10 pairs were nesting in 1.5 acres (.6 hectare), while in the Mojave Desert, researchers found one owl territory for every 2.4 to 4.5 sq. mi. (6.3 to 11.5 sq. km).

In Florida, Burrowing Owls show a striking degree of fidelity both to their mates and to their nest sites. Migratory western populations are substantially less faithful to either, and nonmigratory western owls seem to split the difference. A few cases of polygyny (one male and two females) have been suspected or confirmed.

Burrowing Owl clutches can be large—up to 14 eggs, in one exceptional case, although 7 to 9 is more typical among western populations, and 4 to 6 eggs in Florida. Some females begin incubating with the first egg, while in the Canadian prairies females appear to wait until the clutch is half laid to start. Incubation lasts about a month, and the chicks first come aboveground when they're 2 weeks old. Fledging occurs at about 6 or 7 weeks of age.

Nonmigratory and, to a more limited extent, mi-gratory populations continue to use the burrows for roosting after the breeding season is over.

BEHAVIOR

The most diurnal owl in our region, Burrowing Owls nevertheless reserve their most serious hunting for dawn and dusk. A study in Oregon and Washington found that 90 percent of the prey brought to Burrowing Owl nests, both invertebrate and vertebrate, were nocturnal species.

Males do most of the foraging while the female remains in or near the burrow. The appearance of an intruder will elicit an alarm call from the female and a sometimes scorching attack from the male, as both adults bark and give their chatter calls. The male's primary role as the defender of the nest has been given as an explanation for why, in this one species, the normal rule among owls is upended, and the male is the slightly larger of the two.

One striking feature of Burrowing Owl nests is the amount of trash festooned around the entrance. Florence Merriam Bailey, one of the first female ornithologists in the West, described a burrow in New

Land-use changes, like farming and ranching—and especially the destruction of once-vast prairie-dog towns—have dramatically reduced Burrowing Owl numbers in the West, with especially acute declines in the Pacific Northwest and California. *(California. B. Shaw/VIREO)*

Young Burrowing Owls disperse from their parents' territory by late summer. Western owls usually move only a few miles, and Florida birds far less, yet genetic studies suggest there is good gene flow among the many, increasingly isolated local populations. *(Manitoba. Christian Artuso)*

Mexico as having "a great abundance of dry horse manure, some corn cobs, charcoal, tufts of cow hair, bits of hide, pieces of bone, a child's woolen mitten, a piece of calico and other rags, shore lark [Horned Lark] and other bird feathers, and bits of insects."[11]

Dried manure is an especially common ornament and burrow lining; it was once thought to serve as a defense against sharp-nosed mammalian predators, while other scientists speculated that it might attract beetles and other insects on which the owls feed. But Burrowing Owls collect many other items, including grass, plastic, aluminum foil, and pieces of carpet, which neither mask scent nor attract insects, and the reason for this behavior remains a mystery.

There is a perennial myth that Burrowing Owls live in some sort of symbiotic harmony with prairie dogs and rattlesnakes, each respecting the other in a grassland "kumbaya." The truth is that owls will kill and eat young prairie dogs, but both species mostly just ignore each other—and both avoid rattlesnakes.

STATUS

Although it lists Burrowing Owls as "least concern," IUCN/BirdLife notes their decreasing population trend, including a significant contraction from the eastern and northern margins of their North American breeding range, and an erosion of their population in many regions. On the state and provincial level, only Barn Owls are as widely considered threatened, endangered, or of special concern as this species.

Burrowing Owls are listed as "endangered" in Canada under COSEWIC, and are considered "endangered" or Red-Listed in the four provinces in which they occur. While not listed under the U.S. Endangered Species Act, they are a listed species in 15 of the 19 states in which they occur. (Designation as a candidate species under the federal ESA was dropped in 1996.)

Mate fidelity runs the gamut among Burrowing Owls. Florida birds are the most faithful to both their mates and nest sites, while migratory populations are the least. Western resident populations, like this pair in Texas, fall in between. *(Texas. Greg Lasley)*

Especially during the demanding chick-rearing season, Burrowing Owls are active both day and night, hunting for insects and small vertebrates for their offspring. *(California. B. Shaw/VIREO)*

Two island subspecies in our region, one on Antigua (and possibly Nevis and Saint Kitts), and another on Marie-Galante, are considered extinct, both presumably owing to the introduction of Asian mongooses to the Caribbean in the late nineteenth century—a bit of biological tinkering that had devastating effects on many ground-nesting birds.

Across most of its North American range, the biggest loss for Burrowing Owls probably occurred in the late nineteenth and early twentieth centuries, when "pest" eradication campaigns killed prairie dogs by the millions. Intensive farming removed millions of acres of grassland habitat as well, relegating Burrowing Owls to the margins.

Once common on the prairies of western Minnesota and western Iowa, they eventually disappeared from both states. In the three Canadian prairie provinces, annual declines of up to 20 percent were documented in the 1990s, with near-extirpation from British Columbia and Manitoba, where only occasional reports suggest some persistence. Attempts to reintroduce Burrowing Owls to Minnesota in the 1980s failed.

Significant declines have occurred in California, especially along the central and southern coasts, and in the Pacific Northwest, but even within the heart of the Burrowing Owl's range, the continued destruction of prairie-dog colonies (and colony collapses from sylvatic plague) appear to be a major factor in the decline of the owl. Interestingly, an examination of DNA shows no signs of inbreeding among the increasingly isolated western populations.

The status of Burrowing Owl populations in the Caribbean is unclear. After enjoying a range expansion in the nineteenth and twentieth centuries in Florida, because of expanding agriculture and development, numbers of Burrowing Owls in that state appear to have contracted significantly. A 2001 survey of current and historic sites in Florida found fewer than roughly 1,800 adult owls, well below the 3,000 to 10,000 estimated in the mid-1990s. The largest populations are in southwest Florida, where increasingly intensive development poses a risk. Other threats include invasive fire ants, as well as an increasing number of exotic reptiles, including Nile monitor lizards that can reach lengths of 6 ft. (1.8 m) and prey on adults and nests alike.

NOTES

1. D. L. Plumpton. 1992. "Aspects of nest site selection and habitat use by burrowing owls at the Rocky Mountain Arsenal, Colorado." MS thesis, Texas Tech University, Lubbock.

2. H. N. Coulombe. 1970. Physiological and physical aspects of temperature regulation in the burrowing owl *Speotyto cunicularia. Comparative Biochemical Physiology* 35:307–337.

3. L. Thomsen. 1971. Behavior and ecology of burrowing owls on the Oakland Municipal Airport. *Condor* 73:177–192.

4. Earhart and Johnson 1970.

5. Poulin et al. 2011.

6. Hartman 1955.

7. H. D. Prange, J. F. Anderson, and H. Rahn. 1979. Scaling of skeletal mass to body mass in birds and mammals. *American Naturalist* 113:103–122.

8. Garrido 2001.

9. B. Millsap, pers. comm.

10. C. S. L. Rhoads. 1892. Quoted in Bent 1938, p. 398.

11. F. M. Bailey. 1928. Quoted in Bent 1938, p. 387.

BIBLIOGRAPHY

Alverson, K. M., and S. J. Dinsmore. 2014. Factors affecting burrowing owl occupancy of prairie dog colonies. *Condor* 116:242–250.

Barclay, J. H., and S. Menzel. 2011. Apparent polygynous nesting by burrowing owls. *Journal of Raptor Research* 45:98–100.

Bayless, T. A., and P. Beier. 2011. Occurrence and habitat characteristics of burrowing owl nests in Gunnison's prairie dog colonies in northeastern Arizona. *Journal of the Arizona-Nevada Academy of Science* 42:65–74.

Butts, K. O., and J. C. Lewis. 1982. The importance of prairie dog towns to burrowing owls in Oklahoma. *Proceedings of the Oklahoma Academy of Science* 62:46–52.

Catlin, D. H., and D. K. Rosenberg. 2014. Association of sex, fledging date, and sibling relationships with post-fledging movements of burrowing owls in a nonmigratory population in the Imperial Valley, California. *Journal of Raptor Research* 48:106–117.

Crowe, D. E., and K. M. Longshore. 2010. Estimates of density, detection probability, and factors influencing detection of burrowing owls in the Mojave Desert. *Journal of Raptor Research* 44:1–11.

Florida Fish and Wildlife Conservation Commission. 2011. *Florida Burrowing Owl Biological Status Review Report.* Tallahassee, FL.

Garrido, O. H. 2001. Una nueva subespecie del Sijú de Sabana *Speotyto cunicularia* para Cuba. *Cotinga* 16:75–78.

Gervais, J. A., D. K. Rosenberg, and L. A. Comrack. 2008. Burrowing owl (*Athene cunicularia*). In *California Bird Species of Special Concern,* ed. W. D. Shuford and T. Gardali. Studies of Western Birds No. 1. Camarillo and Sacramento, CA: Western Field Ornithologists and California Department of Fish and Game.

Holroyd, G. L., H. E. Trefry, and J. M. Duxbury. 2010. Winter destinations and habitats of Canadian burrowing owls. *Journal of Raptor Research* 44:294–299.

Hume and Walters 2012.

Korfanta, N. M., D. B. McDonald, and T. C. Glenn. 2005. Burrowing owl (*Athene cunicularia*) population genetics: A comparison of North American forms and migratory habits. *Auk* 122:464–478.

Lantz, S. J., H. Smith, and D. A. Keinath. 2004. Species assessment for western burrowing owl (*Athene cunciularia hypugaea*) in Wyoming. Cheyenne, WY: Bureau of Land Management.

Leupin, E. E. 2006. Burrowing Owl (*Athene cunicularia*). Accounts and Measures for Managing Identified Wildlife. Vancouver, BC: British Columbia Ministry of Environment, http://www.env.gov.bc.ca/wld/frpa/iwms/documents/Birds/b_burrowingowl.pdf.

Martell, M. S., J. Schladweiler, and F. Cuthbert. 2001. Status and attempted reintroduction of burrowing owls in Minnesota, U.S.A. *Journal of Raptor Research* 35:331–336.

Martin, D. J. 1973. Spectrographic analysis of burrowing owl vocalizations. *Auk* 90:564–578.

Millsap, B. A. 2002. Survival of Florida burrowing owls along an urban-development gradient. *Journal of Raptor Research* 36:3–10.

Navarro-Sigüenza, A. G., and A. T. Peterson. 2007. *Athene cunicularia* (tecolote llanero) invierno permanente distribución potencial. In *Mapas de las Aves de México Basados en WWW,* ed. A. G. Navarro and A. T. Peterson. Final report, SNIB-CONABIO project no. CE015. México DF.

Poulin, R., L. D. Todd, E. A. Haug, B. A. Millsap, and M. S. Martell. 2011. Burrowing Owl (*Athene cunicularia*). In The Birds of North America Online, ed. A. Poole. Ithaca, NY: Cornell Lab of Ornithology, http://bna.birds.cornell.edu.bnaproxy.birds.cornell.edu/bna/species/061.

Smith, M. D., and C. J. Conway. 2011. Collection of mammal manure and other debris by nesting burrowing owls. *Journal of Raptor Research* 45:220–228.

Thiele, J. P., K. K. Bakker, and C. D. Dieter. 2013. Multiscale nest site selection by burrowing owls in western South Dakota. *Wilson Journal of Ornithology* 125:763–774.

Townsend, C. H. 1890. Scientific results of explorations by the U.S. Fish Commission steamer *Albatross,* no. XIV. *Proceedings of the United States National Museum* 13:131–142.

Wellicome, T. I., and G. L. Holroyd. 2001. Second international burrowing owl symposium: Background and context. *Journal of Raptor Research* 35:269–273.

Wetmore and Swales 1931.

MOTTLED OWL
Ciccaba virgata
Alpha code: MOOW

LENGTH: 11.5–13 in. (29–33 cm)

WINGSPAN: 33–36 in. (84–91 cm)

MASS: With females averaging almost 30 percent heavier than males, Mottled Owls are the most highly reversed dimorphic owls in the world, possibly exceeded only by the European race of Boreal Owl (Tengmalm's Owl). In terms of linear measurements, Mottled Owls rank third behind Boreal and Snowy Owls. See "Habitat and Niche," p. 206.

> *C. v. centralis:* Guatemala: Average, male: 8.5 oz. (240 g); range 7.8–9 oz. (220–256 g). Average, female: 11.8 oz. (335 g); range 10.9–13.6 oz. (308–385 g). Veracruz to Nicaragua: Average, male: 9.1 oz. (258 g); range 8.1–10.5 oz. (230–298 g). Average, female: 11.8 oz. (335 g); range 8.8–14.3 oz. (251–405 g).[1]

From the Yucatán, one male weighed 8.3 oz. (236 g), and a "nonbreeding" female reportedly weighed 6.6 oz. (187 g), exceptionally light for that gender.[2]

LONGEVITY: No information

One of the most abundant forest owls in Middle America, the Mottled Owl has been largely ignored by scientists, and almost everything known about the breeding biology and ecology comes from a single, long-term study by the Peregrine Fund at Tikal National Park in Guatemala, in which 21 pairs were followed over the course of 3 years.[3]

But what is known about this unusual owl is in-

Among the most common owls in Mesoamerica, the Mottled Owl is paradoxically one of the least well understood, with almost everything known about its ecology based on a single study. *(Guatemala. Knut Eisermann)*

triguing. It shows the greatest disparity between male and female size of any owl in the world, and yet despite its moderately large build, it inhabits breeding territories among the smallest of any North American owl. Its taxonomic position is unclear, and many specialists have divided those subspecies in our region into a separate species, the "Mexican Wood Owl."

SYSTEMATICS, TAXONOMY, AND ETYMOLOGY

The taxonomic affinities of the Neotropical owls traditionally placed in the genus *Ciccaba* are foggy, at both the generic and species levels, and are overdue for authoritative clarification.

That they are closely aligned with *Strix* in an overarching "wood owl" group has long been obvious, but whether the Mottled Owl and Black-and-white Owl should remain within *Ciccaba* or

be subsumed into *Strix* is contested. Differences in the structure (especially the degree of asymmetry) in the outer ear were the main reasons for splitting the genera, while DNA work suggests they belong in one genus. The majority of authors fold them into *Strix,* but the AOU has retained *Ciccaba,* in part because the actual science on either side of the argument has been pretty thin. The AOU appears to be waiting for a more thorough assessment of the entire family Strigidae before making a change.

At the species level, there is also disagreement about how to handle the Mottled Owl. As usually recognized, it encompasses seven subspecies from northern Mexico to northern Argentina, but many recent authors have split it into the "Mexican Wood Owl (*C. squamulata*)" ranging south to Colombia and Ecuador, and the "Mottled Owl (*C. virgata*)" in the remainder of South America.

The subspecies of the Mottled Owl within our coverage area, all in the putative "*squamulata*" group, are as follows:

C. v. squamulata: Southern Sonora to Guerrero and Morelos. Upperparts paler than *centralis,* spotted with white; base color of underparts buffy white with little mottling.

C. v. tamaulipensis: Tamaulipas and Nuevo León. Paler and grayer than *squamulata.* Upperparts spotted and marked with pale buffy brown.

C. v. centralis: Veracruz and Oaxaca to Yucatán and southeast to Panama. Larger and darker than *squamulata.* Upperparts more heavily barred, underparts pale buff or cin-

The western Mexican subspecies, *C. v. squamulata,* found from Sonora to Guerrero, is smaller and paler below, with limited mottling. *(Nayarit. Rick and Nora Bowers/VIREO)*

Mottled Owls are found from northwestern Mexico to Argentina, but many authors have split the northern "*squamulata*" group of subspecies into a separate species, the "Mexican Wood Owl." *(Chiapas. Christian Artuso)*

namon, sides of breast mottled with dusky brown. Legs heavily mottled.

ETYMOLOGY: The genus name comes from the Greek *kikkabe,* an owl mentioned in classical texts (and probably referring to the Little Owl), while the species name *virgata* derives from the Latin *virgatus,* "made of twigs," and *virga,* "twig or stalk," a reference to its striped belly pattern. The common name also refers to the plumage pattern.

SPANISH: *Búho [mochuelo, lechuza] café, mochuelo llanero, lechuza parda; mochuelo rayado* (Chiapas)

DISTRIBUTION

BREEDING SEASON: Resident, with a wide distribution in lowland forests across Mexico, except for Baja and the north-central region. Pacific slope and western Sierra Madre foothills from southern Sonora south to Guerrero, Morelos, Oaxaca, and southern Chiapas. Also from Tamaulipas and Nuevo León south along the Atlantic slope and foothills of the Sierra Madre Oriental through Veracruz, Tabasco, northern Oaxaca, and Chiapas through the Yucatán. Found from sea level up to about 6,900 ft. (2,100 m). Two records from Hidalgo County, TX, along the lower Rio Grande in 1983 and 2006, the first a roadkilled specimen.

POST-FLEDGING DISPERSAL: Fledglings remain near the nest, being fed by the adults, for up to 3 months and disperse about a month after that. No information on dispersal distance.

DISTRIBUTION OUTSIDE THE COVERAGE AREA: The "*virgata*" group (or species, depending on classification) extends to southeastern Brazil and northeastern Argentina.

DESCRIPTION AND IDENTIFICATION

The Mottled Owl is a medium-size, dark-eyed, round-headed owl. Many, especially dark individuals, have a distinct "hangman's hood" appearance, thanks to the dark head and upper chest that contrast with the paler, vertically streaked belly.

BASIC (ADULT) PLUMAGE: Sexes similar. Usually described as dimorphic, with lighter birds predominating in drier habitats, and darker morphs in humid forests, but high individual variability and regional differences confuse the issue. Very dark individuals can be almost blackish above and deep buff below.

Crown and head brown or gray-brown, lightly freckled with whitish or buffy spots and incomplete bars. Upperparts brown or gray-brown and mot-

---

Mottled Owls shows the greatest degree of reversed size dimorphism of any owl in the world—overturning most of the assumptions about the evolutionary underpinnings for this phenomenon. *(Chiapas. Christian Artuso)*

tled, with the outer webbing of the scapulars white, creating a distinct white band along each folded wing. Flight feathers and tail dark brown barred with light brown or cinnamon-brown; barring gray below.

Facial disk and rictal bristles gray-brown or brown, edged with a whitish or cinnamon ruff; eyebrows gray-white or buffy, moderately large but poorly defined. Underparts white or buffy with neat, vertical brown streaks, contrasting with the mottled brown upper chest, sometimes infused with rust and which may form a complete collar. Iris dark brown, bill yellowish or yellow-green, legs feathered, feet bare and yellow. Bright, purplish eyeshine when illuminated at night.

JUVENAL PLUMAGE: White natal down is replaced in *C. v. squamulata* with unmarked whitish gray to buff juvenal down, while that of *centralis* is "peach or golden hue."[4] In all races the head (later, just the facial disk) is white, flight feathers similar to those of adult. Legs white. By 4 months of age juveniles have molted into adult plumage.

SIMILAR SPECIES: In build and shape similar to Barred, Spotted, and Fulvous Owls, but all are significantly larger and restricted to upland forests.

VOCALIZATIONS

Highly vocal. Main vocalization for both sexes (female's higher-pitched) is a short series of whooping hoots (usually 3 or 4) usually preceded or followed by several muffled, introductory notes: *wu, wu, whOOo, whOOo, whOOo, wu*. Calls in Guatemala were individually recognizable. Mottled Owls also give a more rapid series of 12 to 18 short, monotone hoots that crescendo in pitch and cadence ("bouncing ball" call): *wu-wu-wu-WUU-WUU-WUU-WUU-WUU-WUU-WUU-wu-wuwuwu*, and a harsh scream that is likely a female food-begging call. There appear to be regional variations in Mottled Owl vocalizations that require further investigation, as they may shed light on possible species differences within this complex.

HABITAT AND NICHE

A raptor of lowland and foothill forests, the Mottled Owl occurs in a wide variety of woodlands, from humid to more-arid zones, including tropical evergreen and deciduous forests, coastal swamps, and palm stands. They appear to show a great deal of adaptability to human disturbance, and in Chiapas this species is said to be most common in second growth and forest edges, and less so in primary forests. Those studied in Guatemala, on the other hand, generally used dense, mature rain forests.

Mottled Owls—at least those from the well-stud-

The darkest and most heavily mottled of the subspecies in our region, *C. v. centralis* is found from Veracruz and Oaxaca to the Yucatán and east to Panama. *(Guatemala. Knut Eisermann)*

ied *centralis* race in Guatemala—exhibit some of the strongest reversed sexual dimorphism (RSD) in size of any owl in the world, with females weighing up to 30 percent more than males (see "Mass," p. 204). This is striking enough—but in the process, they upend many of the hypotheses that attempt to explain this puzzling phenomenon among raptors.

Reversed size dimorphism has generally been associated with raptors that feed on vertebrates, especially birds, and is thought to be least developed in insectivorous species. RSD is also said to be minimal among birds that use cavity nests, supposedly because active nest defense is less critical. But as a few researchers have pointed out, such assumptions are based largely on studies involving boreal and temperate species. That the Mottled Owl—a highly insectivorous cavity nester—shows the greatest RSD among all owls makes clear that we still do not understand the driving force behind this phenomenon.

DIET: As with much else about the Mottled Owl, the only real information comes from the Tikal study in Guatemala, where Richard and Dawn Gerhardt found that insects and rodents made up the bulk of the owl's diet. By their calculations, insects comprised about 60 percent of the biomass eaten, notably beetles and grasshoppers, while rice rats and cotton rats (*Oryzomys* and *Sigmodon*) were the most common vertebrates.

(The Gerhardts noted the difficulty in assessing diet strictly from pellets, since soft-bodied insects may be underrepresented. And they encountered further difficulties. Few pellets reached the ground intact, and those that did had a "half-life . . . measured in minutes, not days, as ants, termites, and reduviid bugs carried [them] off piece by piece.")[5]

NESTING AND BREEDING

Mottled Owls in the Guatemala study were obligate cavity nesters, depending on rot holes and other large openings in live trees and sometimes the crotch of large limbs overhung with vegetation. Nests were never reused in subsequent years. The population showed remarkable synchronization, with most eggs laid in late Mar. and fledging occurring just at the start of the rainy season in late May.

Most clutches were 2 or 3 eggs, with an asynchronous incubation period of 28 to 30 days that begins with the first egg. Fledging occurred at 27 to 29 days of age, with a prolonged (3-month) dependency period before dispersal.

Breeding information elsewhere in the species's

An inhabitant of lowland forests, swamps, and foothill woodlands, the Mottled Owl feeds mostly on beetles, grasshoppers, and small rodents. Daytime roosts, like this one, are usually in dense cover. *(Belize. Kevin Loughlin/Wildside Nature Tours)*

Mottled Owls, despite their fairly large size, have the second-smallest average territory size of any North American owl: at about 50 acres (about 20 hectares), only the tiny Flammulated Owl's is smaller. *(Costa Rica. Steve Easley)*

range is sparse. In Oaxaca, a male with enlarged testes was collected in mid-Mar., and a nest with two of what were described as "prejuveniles" was found May 6; another nest with 1 egg, cold and possibly abandoned, was found June 25. In the Yucatán, a female with an egg in the oviduct was collected in Feb.

BEHAVIOR

Strictly nocturnal. Daytime roosts in Veracruz were in "dense jungle, usually in the branches of trees about ten feet from the ground. A few were found in hollow trees."[6] In Guatemala, however, radio-tagged owls never used cavities for roosting, but instead they perched in dense vegetation averaging 16 ft. (5 m) from the ground. Two apparent adults were flushed from a ledge in a sinkhole cavern in Querétaro, below which lay a large number of old pellets and thousands of small mammal bones.

In Tikal, the estimated home ranges of six breeding males averaged just 53.6 acres (21.7 hectares), second only to the Flammulated Owl's as the smallest typical breeding range size in North American owls. (And this for a bird that is roughly five times the mass of a Flammulated.) Mottled Owls also exhibited very high nesting density when compared with temperate-zone owls, and they appeared to defend the entire territory from other Mottled Owls, physically attacking intruders on occasion.

Most pairs remained stable through the 3-year study and maintained the same territorial boundaries even when one of the pair was replaced.

STATUS

The Mottled Owl is usually ranked as common to fairly common across most of its wide range in Mexico and is probably the most abundant forest owl in Mesoamerica. It is listed as "least concern" by IUCN/BirdLife, although with a slowly decreasing population trend due to deforestation.

NOTES

1. Whitacre 2012, p. 376.

2. Paynter 1955, p. 136.

3. R. P. Gerhart and D. A. Gerhardt. 2012. Mexican wood owl. In *Neotropical Birds of Prey*, ed. D. F. Whitacre. Ithaca, NY: Cornell University Press.

4. Ibid., p. 316.

5. Ibid., p. 314.

6. Lowery and Dalquest 1951, p. 576.

BIBLIOGRAPHY

Cory, C. B. 1918. *Catalogue of Birds of the Americas*, pt. 2, no. 197. Chicago: Field Museum of Natural History.

Gerhart, R. P., and D. A. Gerhardt. 1997. Size, dimorphism, and related characteristics of *Ciccaba* owls from Guatemala. In *Biology and Conservation of Owls of the Northern Hemisphere*, ed. J. R. Duncan, D. H. Johnson, and T. H. Nicholls. Saint Paul, MN: U.S. Forest Gen. Tech. Rep. NC-190.

Gerhardt et al. 1994a.

Gerhardt et al. 1994b.

Griscom, L. 1929. A collection of birds from Cana, Darien. *Bulletin of the Museum of Comparative Zoology* 69:149–190.

Kelso, L. 1932. *Synopsis of the American Wood Owls of the Genus* Ciccaba. Lancaster, PA: Intelligencer Printing.

Navarro-Sigüenza, A. G., and A. T. Peterson. 2007. *Ciccaba virgata* (búho café) residencia permanente distribución potencial. In *Mapas de las Aves de México Basados en WWW*, ed. A. G. Navarro and A. T. Peterson. Final report, SNIB-CONABIO project no. CE015. México DF.

Peters, J. L. 1938. Systematic position of the genus *Ciccaba* Wagler. *Auk* 55:179–186.

Phillips, J. C. 1911. A year's collecting in the state of Tamaulipas, Mexico. *Auk* 28:67–89.

Ridgway 1914.

Voous, K. H. 1964. Wood owls of the genera *Strix* and *Ciccaba*. *Zoologische Mededelingen* 39:471–478.

BLACK-AND-WHITE OWL
Ciccaba nigrolineata
Alpha code: BLWO

Rare almost everywhere, and a blank slate where most of its life history is concerned, the Black-and-white Owl is essentially unmistakable and certainly unforgettable. *(Costa Rica. Tom Johnson)*

LENGTH: 15–16 in. (38–41 cm)

WINGSPAN: No information

MASS: Moderate to strong reversed size dimorphism, based on fairly limited data. Averages based on seven individuals from Mexico to Panama: Male: 14.7 oz. (418 g); range 14.2–15.3 oz. (403–435 g). Female: 17.2 oz. (487 g); range 15.6–18.9 oz. (443–536 g).[1]

LONGEVITY: No information, although the low reproductive rate documented in Guatemala suggests a long-lived species.

Among the least-studied owls in the Americas, the Black-and-white Owl is also one of the most striking of New World raptors, with its inky black head and back and closely barred undersides. Rare across most of its range, it remains poorly known but appears to be one of the few raptors to specialize, at least to an extent, in hunting bats. As with the Mottled Owl, the only serious research of this species's ecology and behavior was conducted by the Peregrine Fund in northern Guatemala, as part of its long-running Maya Project, in which just four nesting attempts by two pairs were documented.

SYSTEMATICS, TAXONOMY, AND ETYMOLOGY

Monotypic. For a discussion of the genus *Ciccaba,* see "Mottled Owl." A South American subspecies, "*C. n. spilonota,*" is no longer recognized. The Black-and-white Owl and the Black-banded Owl (*C. huhula*) of South America form a superspecies,

and some have argued they should be lumped together. The "San Isidro Owl" from Ecuador may be an undescribed subspecies of this or the Black-banded Owl or a hybrid form of the two.

ETYMOLOGY: For the derivation of the genus name, see "Mottled Owl." The specific name, *nigrolineata,* means "black-lined."
> **SPANISH:** *Búho blancquinegro, mochuelo zarado; lechuza listada* (Yucatán Peninsula)

DISTRIBUTION

BREEDING SEASON: Resident from San Luis Potosí and northwestern Veracruz south along Atlantic slope to the southern and central Yucatán, and from eastern Oaxaca along the Pacific slope through southern Chiapas. Found from sea level to 3,900 ft. (1,200 m).

MIGRATION AND MOVEMENTS: None known

POST-FLEDGING DISPERSAL: No information

DISTRIBUTION OUTSIDE THE COVERAGE AREA: Central America to Venezuela, Colombia, Ecuador, and northern Peru.

DESCRIPTION AND IDENTIFICATION

A moderately large, strikingly patterned bird, the Black-and-white Owl is elegant and virtually unmistakable. Seen in the field, a quick first impression is usually of a black, tuftless head contrasting with the white but finely barred body.

BASIC (ADULT) PLUMAGE: Sexes similar. Crown and facial disk sooty black, with white flecks forming diffuse eyebrows. Limited white edging to the facial disk ruff, merging with black-barred white on sides of neck and nape. Back and upper surface of wings black and unmarked, except for limited, very narrow gray-white barring on the flight feathers. Underwings gray-white and densely barred; flight feathers sooty gray to black with narrow white barring. Tail black with five or six narrow white bars. Underparts, including undertail coverts, pearly white with neat, black horizontal barring. Legs feathered to the toes, more densely barred black than belly. Iris dark brown, bill and feet yellow. Red-purple eyeshine.

JUVENAL PLUMAGE: Natal down white. Juvenal plumage light gray and uniformly marked with fine blackish barring, through which blackish adult flight feathers emerge; facial disk black, feet and bill initially pink, becoming yellow-orange.

SIMILAR SPECIES: The neatly barred body and black head and face make the Black-and-white Owl difficult to confuse with any other species in our area. Heavily marked individuals of the Spectacled Owl can have sparse barring on the belly, but the ground color of the underparts in such owls is a rich buffy cinnamon, and the birds show extensive white in the face.

VOCALIZATIONS

Typical call is a rising series of 4 to 11 emphatic, whooping hoots, lasting 1.5 to 2.5 seconds, with a short pause before the final one (sometimes two) more-protracted notes: *wu-wu-Wu-Wu, WUU!* or *wu-wu-Wu-Wu-Wu-WU WUU! WUU!* Female call is higher-pitched than the male's.

Sometimes a single hoot, rising in the middle and

Along with the Mottled Owl, the Black-and-white Owl is placed in the genus *Ciccaba* by the AOU, while many authors assign them both to the larger wood-owl genus *Strix*, to which they are closely allied. *(Costa Rica. Glenn Bartley)*

falling off in pitch, is given. A raspy, hissing call is believed to be the juvenile food-begging call

HABITAT AND NICHE

The Black-and-white Owl is an inhabitant of mature, lowland forests, with the limited information available suggesting an affinity for habitats near water, such as swamps, riparian areas, and coastal mangroves, especially during the nesting season.

In Chiapas, it is found more commonly in primary forests than are Mottled Owls. Roost sites in Guatemala were more often in upland forest zones, while nests were in *bajos* (swamp forest), and one radio-tagged male invariably included several small *bajo* ponds in his nightly hunting excursions. In Veracruz, shade-coffee farms (*cafetales*) are used.

DIET: The limited research into this owl's ecology suggests a heavy dependence on insects and bats, making it one of the few raptors anywhere to rely on bats for a significant portion of its diet.

An analysis of pellets from Guatemala found

beetle or grasshopper remains in every pellet examined, while nearly three-quarters of the pellets also contained bat bones. The researchers there cautioned that the pellets reflected only the diet during the breeding season, and that the remains of some common insects like cicadas and katydids, which would be logical prey for an insectivorous owl, might have been absent because their thinner shells were more easily digested.

Pellets from a nesting pair in Venezuela contained the remains of 14 species of bats, along with bones from house mice and black rats, a variety of songbirds, frogs, beetles, and grasshoppers. In that case, bats comprised almost a third the number of prey found in pellets, and more than two-thirds of the biomass. A Black-and-white Owl in Costa Rica was observed bringing a Barn Swallow to what may have been its mate.

NESTING AND BREEDING

In the Guatemalan study, just four nests by two pairs were found. It did show that the Black-and-white Owl may have the smallest average clutch size

Only a handful of Black-and-white Owl nests have been found, but each contained a single egg—the smallest average clutch size, so far as known, for any species of owl in the world. *(Belize. Christian Artuso)*

Black-and-white Owls are strictly nocturnal and feed most heavily on large insects like cicadas and katydids, as well as bats, making it one of the few raptors of any sort to depend heavily on bats for food. *(Costa Rica. R. Goodell/VIREO)*

of any owl known—just a single egg in each nesting attempt. Unlike earlier reports that this species used tree cavities or old stick nests, in all four cases the egg was laid among the thicket of epiphytic orchid or bromeliad vegetation on the branches of large, emergent canopy trees, averaging 67 ft. (20.5 m) above the ground.

Incubation, lasting approximately 30 to 35 days, was by the female only. None of the nests successfully fledged young, but the researchers estimated fledging would normally take place at about a month of age.

Eggs in the Guatemalan nests hatched in late Apr. Elsewhere, two "prejuveniles" (ages unclear) were reported in early and mid-May in Oaxaca.

BEHAVIOR

Strictly nocturnal. Black-and-white Owls apparently take much of their prey, both insect and mammal, in flight and have been observed snatching bats emerging from large cave roosts, and insects from around artificial lights. They may also hunt for fruit bats as the mammals forage at fruiting trees, and the Peregrine Fund team observed one male chasing a bat through the forest.

Daytime roosts in Guatemala averaged 46 ft. high (14 m), usually with overhanging vegetation. This is considerably higher than roosts of the closely related Mottled Owl in the same area, and the contrast between these near-relatives was even more pronounced when scientists radio-tagged them to look at home range size. The lone male Black-and-white Owl they tagged in the breeding season hunted a territory of about 1.7 sq. mi. (4.4 sq. km)—more than 20 times the territorial size of the Mottled Owls there. Distances between nesting pairs suggest a density of about one pair per 4.6 sq. mi. (12 sq. km).

Adults are monogamous and, in one case, the pair bond lasted at least 3 years.

STATUS

The Black-and-white Owl appears to be rare or uncommon across virtually all of its range, but it is not listed as "threatened" or "endangered" in Mexico. IUCN/BirdLife considers it "least concern," given its wide range and apparently stable population trend. The owl's apparent preference for primary or mature secondary forests, however, means it could be sensitive to continuing deforestation, and its increasing rarity in Veracruz has been ascribed to habitat loss.

NOTE

1. Whitacre 2012.

BIBLIOGRPAHY

Binford 1989.

BirdLife International. 2015. *Ciccaba nigrolineata*. IUCN Red List of Threatened Species, version 2014.3. http://www.iucnredlist.org/details/22689133/0.

Enríque-Rocha, Rangel-Salazar, and Holt 1993.

Friedman, Griscom, and Moore 1950.

Gerhardt, R. P., D. M. Gerhardt, N. Bonilla, and C. J. Flatten. 2012. Black-and-white owl. In *Neotropical Birds of Prey*, ed. D. F. Whitacre. Ithaca, NY: Cornell University Press.

Gerhardt et al. 1994a.

Gerhardt et al. 1994b.

Ibañez, C., C. Ramo, and B. Busto. 1992. Notes on food habits of the black and white owl. *Condor* 94:529–531.

Navarro-Sigüenza, A. G., and A. T. Peterson. 2007. *Ciccaba nigrolineata* (búho blancquinegro) residencia permanente distribución potencial. In *Mapas de las Aves de México Basados en WWW*, ed. A. G. Navarro and A. T. Peterson. Final report, SNIB-CONABIO project no. CE015. México DF.

Patten et al. 2011.

Sandoval, L., E. Biamonte, and A. Solano-Ugalde. 2008. Previously unknown food items in the diet of six Neotropical bird species. *Wilson Journal of Ornithology* 120:214–216.

Schaldach 2003.

The Northern Spotted Owl, the northernmost of three subspecies, has been a lightning rod for political controversy ever since it was listed as "threatened" under the U.S. Endangered Species Act—the only owl, along with the Mexican subspecies, so designated. *(Washington. Gerrit Vyn)*

SPOTTED OWL
Strix occidentalis
Alpha code: SPOW

LENGTH: 17–19 in. (43–48 cm)

WINGSPAN: 42–44.5 in. (107–113 cm)

MASS: Weak reversed size dimorphism and a clinal reduction in size from north to south, including within subspecies. Mass by subspecies:
  S. o. caurina: Average, male: 20.4 oz. (579 g). Average, female: 23.4 oz. (663 g).[1]
  S. o. occidentalis: Average, male: 20 oz. (566 g). Average, female: 22.8 oz. (646 g).[2]
  S. o. lucida: New Mexico and Arizona: Average, male: 18 oz. (509 g). Average, female: 20.1 oz. (569 g).[2] Chihuahua: Average, male: 17 oz. (483 g). Average, female: 18.3 oz. (518 g).[3]

LONGEVITY: Average age at re-encounter, based on banding records, was 3.6 years. Longevity record is a female Northern Spotted Owl from Oregon banded in 1988 and seen alive in 2006 at 21 years of age; other notable longevity records include owls that were 18 years 11 months old and 18 years 2

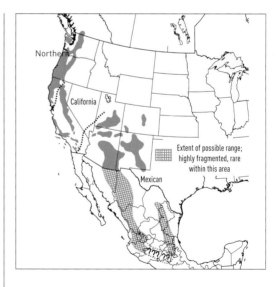

months old. Most records reflect the northern subspecies, the most intensively studied.

After decades of acrimony, lawsuits, protests, and vitriol, the Spotted Owl remains a political lightning rod, thanks to the listing of its northern subspecies as a federally threatened species and to that move's spillover effects on the Northwest forest industry. No other decision involving the U.S.

Still clad mostly in its brownish mesoptile down, a Mexican Spotted Owl fledgling explores the world under the watchful eye of one of its parents. *(Arizona. J. Cancalosi/VIREO)*

Endangered Species Act has engendered such raw and long-lasting emotion.

At the core of that debate was, and is, a disarmingly tame and approachable owl that, like many species in the Northwest, evolved to depend on the region's immense old-growth forests—a habitat that has suffered cataclysmic declines since the late nineteenth century. Although the ESA listing brought strong protections to remaining old-growth stands on federal land, Northern Spotted Owls have continued to decline in the face of further losses of mature forests on private land, as well as the growing intensity of major wildfires and competition from invading Barred Owls, which are larger and more aggressive.

While the Northern Spotted Owl is arguably the most thoroughly studied raptor in the world, much less is known about the Mexican Spotted Owl (also listed as federally threatened) and the California Spotted Owl, which enjoys no ESA protection. The Mexican population of this species is especially poorly known but appears to be rare and occurring in highly fragmented, isolated patches, beset by continuing (often illegal) logging.

SYSTEMATICS, TAXONOMY, AND ETYMOLOGY

The Spotted Owl and Barred Owl are closely related members of *Strix*—so closely related, in fact, that hybridization by invading Barred Owls is a significant conservation threat to some populations of Spotted Owl (see "Status," p. 221). There are three generally recognized subspecies:

S. o. caurina (Northern Spotted Owl): Southwestern British Columbia south in Coast and Cascade Ranges to central California coast. Largest and darkest of the three subspecies, with finer spotting than those to the south.

S. o. occidentalis (California Spotted Owl): Extreme southeastern Cascades in northern California south along Sierra Nevada, and disjunctly in mountains of southern California; reported (rarely) in northern Baja. Intermediate in size, coloration, and spotting between the Northern and Mexican races.

S. o. lucida (Mexican Spotted Owl): Colorado and Utah south through Arizona and New Mexico, and in the western Sierra Madre from the borderlands to Michoacán; in the eastern Sierra Madre from Coahuila to San Luis Potosí. Smallest and palest of the three commonly recognized subspecies, with large, coarse spotting.

What appears to be a stable intergrade zone between Northern and California Spotted Owls exists in the Klamath region of southern Oregon. Generally speaking, *S. o. caurina* is found north and west of the Pit River in Shasta County, CA, and *S. o. occidentalis* south and east of the river. DNA work has shown that the Spotted Owls along the coast as far north as Monterey County are the California subspecies, not the Northern.

Genetic analysis suggests that Northern Spotted Owls diverged roughly 115,000 to 125,000 years ago, while the Mexican and California subspecies split from each other only about 15,000 years ago, and the latter two races are at best weakly differentiated. Southern California owls in particular were found to have low genetic diversity.

In 1997, Dickerman published a review of specimens from the American Southwest and Mexico, and in addition to resurrecting an obsolete subspecies first described in 1910 (*S. o. huachucae,* the "Southwestern Spotted Owl"), he described a new race from central Mexico that he named *S. o. juanaphillipsae,* the "Volcano Spotted Owl." Both races are in the range generally ascribed to the Mexican Spotted Owl, with *huachucae* encompassing all Spotted Owls from Colorado to southern Arizona and New Mexico, West Texas, and adjacent areas of Chihuahua and Sonora, and *juanaphillipsae* limited to the mountains of central Mexico. Neither of these two putative subspecies has been widely accepted, however.

ETYMOLOGY: The genus name *Strix,* coined in 1766 by Linnaeus, is Latin, and is translated by most sources as "a screech owl." It derives from the earlier Greek, *strigx,* however, and both words refer not to a real owl, but to witches thought to take the form of night-flying birds and drink the blood of infants through their golden bills. The specific name *occidentalis* means "western," and refers to the species's range. The common name refers to the spotted plumage, especially that of the undersides.

SPANISH: *Búho [tecolote] manchado, tecolote moteado*

DISTRIBUTION

BREEDING SEASON: Northern Spotted Owl: Extreme southwestern British Columbia south along both slopes of the Cascades through Washington and Oregon; isolated population on the Olympic Peninsula. South along Coast and Cascade Ranges to northern California just north of San Francisco Bay, and in extreme southeastern Cascades to near Mount Shasta. Found near sea level to about 4,500 ft. (1,370 m) in British Columbia, up to about 7,500 ft. (2,300 m) in the south.

California Spotted Owl: Found from the extreme southeastern Cascades (Lassen Peak) south through the Sierra Nevada to northern Kern County, CA, and in disjunct populations in the Coast, Transverse, and Peninsular Ranges of southern California from the Carmel River to San Diego County. A few sight records indicate its range extends, at least rarely and historically, into northern Baja, although there are no known specimens. Found from 1,000 to 7,900 ft. (304 to 2,410 m) in the Sierra Nevada and from sea level to 8,500 ft. (2,600 m) along the coast and in the southern mountains, but most common at the southern extent of its range between 4,000 and 6,000 ft. (1,200 and 1,830 m).

Mexican Spotted Owl: Highly disjunct and fragmented distribution on mountain ranges, plateaus, and rocky canyons. Found from central Colorado and southern Utah through New Mexico and Arizona (rare in Guadalupe and Davis Mountains of West Texas), then south through the western Sierra Madre from Chihuahua and eastern Sonora to Michoacán, and from Coahuila to San Luis Potosí in the eastern Sierra Madre. Mexican distribution very poorly known, but appears to be even more widely scattered and insular than in the United States, with a relatively small number of recent records.

In Arizona, found in canyons as low as 3,700 ft. (1,130 m), but more commonly between 5,000 and 9,500 ft. (1,524 and 2,900 m); in wooded canyons at 7,000 to 8,500 ft. (2,130 to 2,590 m) in West Texas. In Mexico, generally between 3,900 and 8,200 ft. (1,200 and 2,500 m), sometimes to 8,530 ft. (2,600 m).

NONBREEDING SEASON: Northern subspecies nonmigratory. California race exhibits some altitudinal migration, while northern population of Mexican Spotted Owl can show both elevational and short-distance (12 to 31 mi. / 20 to 50 km) latitudinal migration.

MIGRATION AND MOVEMENTS: See "Nonbreeding Season," above.

POST-FLEDGING DISPERSAL: Among Northern Spotted Owls, average juvenile dispersal dates were mid-Sept. in Oregon and late Sept. in Washington, with no difference between genders. A second pulse of dispersal occurs in late winter and spring, and some individuals move multiple times between ages two and five. Average dispersal distance was 8.4 to 9.1 mi. (13.5 to 14.6 km) for males and 14.3 to 15.2 mi.

Rejected twice for the federal protection offered the other two subspecies, the California Spotted Owl is experiencing declining populations and poor genetic diversity. *(California. J. Fuhrman/VIREO)*

(23 to 24.5 km) for females. The maximum distance was 64 mi. (103 km).

Dispersal among California owls generally occurs in Oct. Juveniles in southern California moved an average of 6.2 to 7.5 mi. (10 to 12 km), with no significant difference between males and females, and more than half became territorial within a year. Juvenile Mexican Spotted Owls in Arizona disperse from natal territories in Sept. (primarily) and Oct., moving an average of 10.5 mi. (17 km), with some dispersing up to 46 mi. (73 km).

DISTRIBUTION OUTSIDE THE COVERAGE AREA: None

DESCRIPTION AND IDENTIFICATION

A medium-size and dark, round-headed owl with brown eyes and white spots on the undersides and back. Descriptions that follow apply to Northern (*S. o. caurina*) race. The base color becomes progressively paler, and the size of spots larger, in the California and Mexican subspecies, but differences are clinal and fairly slight. There is also a north-to-south size gradient from larger to smaller, which continues within subspecies.

BASIC (ADULT) PLUMAGE: Sexes similar, although head and face average darker in females. Head and upperparts dark chocolate brown with small white spots on the crown and nape, whitish barring on the neck, and larger, irregular white spots and bars on the back and upper wing coverts. Upper surface of flight feathers dark brown with four to six narrow, buffy white bars; underwing surfaces paler brown with wider, buffy bars.

Spotted Owls at the northern end of their range are largest and darkest, with the finest spotting, while the Mexican subspecies (roosting here in a canyon forest) is the smallest and brownest race, with large, coarse spots. *(Arizona. Tom Johnson)*

With some juvenal down still peeking through their adult feathers, two young Mexican Spotted Owls roost in the cool shade of a canyon in Arizona's Huachuca Mountains. *(Arizona. Tom Johnson)*

Facial disk brown to gray-brown with indistinct concentric rings and a dark ruff completely circling the face. Rictal bristles, throat, and eyebrows grayish to buffy gray. Upper chest mottled with dark brown; otherwise, undersides feature heavy barring that forms large, irregular whitish or buffy spots. Iris dark brown, bill yellow-green, feet fully feathered. Eyeshine bright orange-red.

JUVENAL PLUMAGE: White natal down replaced by light brown mesoptile plumage with diffuse dark transverse barring, heaviest on back, through which adultlike flight feathers emerge. Tail feathers tipped with large, white triangular spot, with a small downy tuft. Basic plumage complete by 22 weeks of age.

SIMILAR SPECIES: Barred Owl is very similar, but slightly larger and paler, ashy gray overall, with distinct vertical streaks on the whitish belly and flanks instead of the Spotted Owl's heavy crossbarring that forms irregular spots. Beware of hybrids, which are increasingly common in overlap zones in the Pacific Northwest and are intermediate in plumage characteristics. Mottled Owl significantly smaller, with darker facial disk, and in lowlands, with little or no overlap in habitat.

VOCALIZATIONS

Both sexes give a diagnostic four-hoot location call that has a variety of roles, including territorial defense. It begins with a muffled, introductory hoot, a short pause, two emphatic hoots, another brief pause, and a final, somewhat protracted and descending (occasionally two-noted) hoot: *wuu . . . WUU! WUU! . . . WUUhh.* The female's voice is higher.

Contact call, usually given by the female, is a slurred, ascending whine lasting 1 or 2 seconds and becoming shorter, higher-pitched, more insistent and frequent with increasing agitation: *wuuee-EEEP! wuuee-EEEP!* Juvenile food-begging call is a raspier version of the contact call. Adults also give a series of nasal barks, usually three to seven notes at a rate of about three per second.

An analysis of vocalizations from across the Spotted Owl's range found that the location calls of the three subspecies could be distinguished by slight differences in overall length and inter-note timing, with California Spotted Owls producing the longest location calls, and Mexican Owls the shortest. Viewed from a habitat perspective, owls from more densely forested locations produced slightly longer calls. Other researchers have found that Spotted Owls can recognize the calls of individual owls, and they react more strongly to strangers than to the calls of known neighbors.

HABITAT AND NICHE

Although Spotted Owls are most closely associated, at least in the popular imagination, with ancient, moss-draped forests in the Northwest, the species as a whole occupies a startlingly wide range of habitats, some of which have only recently been studied in any detail.

The Northern Spotted Owl's dependence on mature (often old-growth) conifer forests for nesting and hunting is well documented—in fact, the habitat requirements of this subspecies have been studied more thoroughly than for any other raptor in the world, given its place at the center of enormous political and economic controversy. They can be found from sea level to the edge of the subalpine forest zone, in a variety of evergreen forest communities, all of which share a few common traits—a high, closed canopy, and structural complexity in the middle layers of the forest, including fallen trees and dead snags, of the sort that usually takes 150 to 200 years of growth to achieve. By some estimates, that habitat has declined by almost 90 percent since the 1880s.

California Spotted Owls are likewise tied to mature conifer forests in some areas, especially the eastern Cascades and Sierra Nevada, in mixed conifer or fir forests at high elevations, and ponderosa pine or pine-oak forests in the foothills. But in coastal regions they use oak forests, redwood stands, and pine-juniper forests, often with no conifer component at all, and oak and bigcone Douglas-fir forests in the mountains. Wherever they are found, however, they consistently choose territories with large, mature trees and structural complexity, and there is often at least a portion of the original old-growth forest remaining within their home range.

For Mexican Spotted Owls, soaring cliffs and narrow canyons in the Southwest fill the habitat niche of the structurally complex old-growth forests that the Northern and California subspecies inhabit. *(Texas. Greg Lasley)*

A Northern Spotted Owl would likely curl up and die if dropped into the kind of landscapes that many Mexican Spotted Owls inhabit. Across much of its range, the Mexican subspecies is found largely in steep-walled canyons. Some, like Garden Canyon in the Huachuca Mountains of southeastern Arizona (where countless birders have gotten their life Spotted Owl), feel like an oasis, with fast-flowing creeks beneath the cool shade of sycamores, oaks, and cypresses. But in the Colorado Plateau, Spotted Owls do well in narrow, twisting tributary canyons whose sparse vegetation forms a meager green ribbon in the blisteringly hot, red-baked landscape. Spotted Owls may be found in patches of scrubby wooded habitat, mostly pinyon-juniper or desert scrub, only a few acres in size and isolated in a sea of desert.

In the Grand Canyon, Spotted Owls use wooded canyons, often staying in pinyon-juniper woods with an understory of Mormon tea and greasebush, and roosting in redbud, pine, acacia, and ash, moving as necessary to stay in the shade during the midday heat. In the Guadalupe Mountains of New Mexico and West Texas, the owls choose deep, well-shaded canyons with stands of bigtooth maple, hop hornbeam, chinkapin oak, and mixed conifers. Researchers have found that roosts and nest sites both tend to occur where the ground is thick with rock rubble—perhaps because such places are also good habitat for woodrats, the owl's primary food in the Southwest.

Little is known about the habitat requirements for the Spotted Owl in Mexico. Oak, pine-oak, juniper, and mixed-conifer forests in rugged canyons and isolated mountain ranges are the most common habitat associations.

In Chihuahua, scientists found Mexican Spotted Owls at roughly half the density at which they occur in Arizona and New Mexico, but three times the density seen in some Utah canyonlands. Roosts were in pines, oaks, and Douglas-firs, as well as cave walls, between 6,800 and 8,500 ft. (2,072 and 2,600 m). The owls in Chihuahua weren't as dependent on old-growth forest as some Northern populations—perhaps, the researchers speculated, because there is little such habitat left there.

DIET: Spotted Owls are mammal specialists, although the dominant prey guilds vary with habitat, season, and region. In northern and higher-elevation areas, both California and Northern Spotted Owls depend heavily on flying squirrels, *Peromyscus* mice, and voles, while those in lower and more southerly areas prey more heavily on woodrats.

Among Mexican Spotted Owls, woodrats consistently make up a high proportion of the diet almost regardless of where the study has been conducted. In southeastern Arizona, they made up almost 80 percent of Spotted Owl diets in canyon habitat, with white-footed mice and cottontails making up almost all of the rest; the woodrats' share fell to roughly half in forested habitat, with pocket gophers and rabbits making up the remainder.

In Utah, as well as the Grand Canyon in Arizona, woodrats and white-footed mice were the primary prey, while in the Guadalupe Mountains of New Mexico and Texas, woodrats accounted for 40 percent of the biomass consumed. In Chihuahua and Aguascalientes, Mexico, woodrats, mice, and cottontails also comprised almost all of the biomass.

In all regions, the owls prey to a lesser and opportunistic extent on a wide variety of other small mammals, along with amphibians, birds, and insects.

NESTING AND BREEDING

In Oregon and Washington, roughly a quarter of males and half of females were paired by 1 year of age, but many did not breed until they were several years older. Spotted Owls are monogamous,

and pair bonds last for years, if not for life. Pairs do not necessarily breed every year, however; among Northern Spotted Owls in Oregon, an average of only about 60 percent of pairs nested in any given year.

Northern and California Spotted Owls nest in large cavities, on wide forked limbs, the broken tops of snags, old raptor and squirrel nests, and the dense "witches' broom" growth in conifers that results from dwarf mistletoe infestations. Research has shown that both Northern and California Spotted Owls pick nest trees away from forest edges—the latter despite some claims that the owls prefer edge habitat, like that created by timbering, for nesting.

California Spotted Owls occasionally use caves, but Mexican Spotted Owls commonly use them, as well as cliff ledges, and in some areas they appear to use such nest sites almost exclusively. In the Grand Canyon, for example, all nests in one study were on rockfaces or caves, mostly in the Redwall limestone strata, which forms immense cliffs in the canyon—and which may fill the structural role that a tall, complex forest does elsewhere in the Spotted Owl's range.

Regardless of the substrate or location, the owl makes no addition to the nest before laying its eggs. Normal clutch size is 2, with 1 egg being rare (often the result of a young female in her first breeding season) and 4 exceptional. Incubation lasts about a month. The chicks fledge at about 35 days of age but often become branchers a week or more before they can fly. The siblings hang together after fledging, remaining near the nest (and roosting close to one another) for up to 3 months after fledging.

Among California Spotted Owls, siblings that fledged in pairs had a much greater survival rate than those that were single chicks or triplets—and that advantage stretched all the way into adulthood. Nests with single chicks, researchers speculate, may be the result of years when food is scarce, while triplets may simply strain the ability of the adults to provide enough resources, even in bountiful years.

BEHAVIOR

Tame and easily approachable, the Spotted Owl has made it easy for both researchers and birders who need (or want) to get a closer look at this attractive owl—at times, a little too close, which is why the use of recordings is banned in many popular birding locations that host this species.

Spotted Owls are primarily nocturnal, most active just after dusk (sometimes earlier, especially on overcast days) and just before dawn. Primarily perch hunters, they take up posts in areas where prey is abundant and wait for what fate and opportunity present. For Northern and California Spotted

Spotted Owls are paragons of monogamy, with pair bonds lasting for years, if not life. But pairs do not necessarily breed every year, and among Northern Spotted Owls, 4 in 10 pairs may not nest in any given year. (*Arizona. Glenn Bartley*)

Owls, those areas are usually in the oldest, most mature forest stands available. Mexican Spotted Owls living in forested habitat do much the same, while those in canyon habitat generally stay within the canyons themselves, rarely venturing onto the adjacent mesas. Males and females may forage in different habitats, perhaps because the larger females find it easier to maneuver in more open, less densely vegetated environments.

Mexican Spotted Owls show more short-distance and altitudinal migration than the other two subspecies, and while the need for milder temperatures may drive these movements, they also seem to seek out locations—like those that have recently burned—where prey is more common. In New Mexico, radio-tagged owls moved up to 9 mi. (14 km), remaining in roughly the same elevational zone, to hunt old wildfire burns, where biologists found that prey density was up to six times greater than on the birds' breeding territories. One female in Utah moved 22 mi. (35 km) between her breeding location and a wintering site in a higher-elevation fir forest, then returned in the spring.

Apparently heat sensitive, Spotted Owls tend to pick roost sites that provide a cool refuge during midday heat, often moving from roost to roost to stay in the shade (or, conversely, in the sun on a cold winter's day). In western Washington, Northern Spotted Owls consistently picked roost sites that were lower in elevation, with fewer but much larger trees and greater canopy cover than random sites. In the upper elevations of the Rincon Mountains

Spotted Owls tend to pick roost sites where they can enjoy some protection from the midday sun. *(Washington. Gerrit Vyn)*

Victims of a century of logging that reduced much of their old-growth forest habitat to stumps, the Northern and California Spotted Owls face a new threat—competition from invading Barred Owls. *(Washington. Paul Bannick/VIREO)*

894 hectares). Several studies have found that male territories are a bit larger than those of females.

Home ranges among Mexican Spotted Owls studied in the Southwest average smaller. In the canyonlands of Utah, the median size was 1,350 acres (545 hectares); in northern Arizona 2,200 acres (895 hectares); and in the Rincon Mountains of southeastern Arizona 798 acres (323 hectares) for individuals, and 1,181 acres (478 hectares) for mated pairs. Home range size in the Rincon Mountains varied tremendously, from as small as 84 acres (34 hectares) to as large as 1,610 acres (652 hectares).

STATUS

One recent estimate put the total Spotted Owl population at about 18,000 individuals—roughly 12,000 Northern Spotted Owls (*S. o. caurina*); 4,000 California Spotted Owls (*S. o. occidentalis*), with just 300 to 350 pairs in southern California; and 1,500 Mexican Spotted Owls (*S. o. lucida*), a figure that primarily represents the U.S. population, given the lack of data from Mexico. IUCN/BirdLife lists the Spotted Owl as "near-threatened" with a declining population trend.

Both the Northern and the Mexican subspecies are listed as "threatened" under the U.S. Endangered Species Act. They are the only owls so listed, and in the case of the Northern subspecies, the result was a political firestorm over the collision between conservation and the Northwest's already flagging timber industry. That fight continues to this day. The California Spotted Owl has been rejected twice for similar federal listing, and it is listed only as "special concern" by the state of California. Molecular studies suggest that the California race (especially the coastal population) has poor genetic diversity, with low numbers and a declining population trend. The Mexican subspecies is listed as "threatened" in Mexico.

In 1994, the Northwest Forest Plan laid out new management practices on some 24 million acres of federal land, designed to slow the decline in Northern Spotted Owl populations, as well as those of federally listed Marbled Murrelets, salmon, steelhead, and other species that depend on old-growth forests in the region. After 15 years, scientists estimated that while old-growth cover on federal lands had remained fairly steady, and should increase as younger forests mature, about 13 percent of late-successional and old-growth stands on private land had been timbered. Catastrophic wildfires, which destroy habitat and displace owls, were also a growing concern.

Northern Spotted Owls are in increasingly dire straits. From 1992 to 2006, their population dropped at almost 3 percent a year overall, and almost 6 percent annually in the northern portions

in Saguaro National Park in Arizona, Mexican Spotted Owls roosted almost exclusively in mixed-conifer forests, mostly using Douglas-fir, ponderosa and white pine, Gambel oak, and locust trees. No roosts were found below 7,021 ft. (2,140 m).

As with most aspects of Spotted Owl biology, home range size has been most closely studied in the Northern subspecies. In the Olympic Peninsula of Washington, the median home range size was roughly 5,900 acres (2,400 hectares), and some annual ranges encompassed 37,000 acres (15,000 hectares). These were considerably larger than home ranges among Northern Spotted Owls in Oregon or western Washington and may have been the result of a low density of flying squirrels, their main prey, which in turn may be tied to reduced old-growth forest cover that the squirrels need. In fire-prone habitat in southwestern Oregon, on the other hand, mean home range size was 1,420 acres (576 hectares), but varied from 467 to 2,209 acres (189 to

The Mexican Spotted Owl has a highly fragmented range across the American Southwest and Mexico and is threatened by habitat loss from increasingly intense wildfires and uncontrolled logging in Mexico. *(Arizona. Tom Johnson)*

of their range. In 2015, the U.S. Fish and Wildlife Service announced it was considering reclassifying the Northern Spotted Owl as "endangered," the highest level of federal protection and a reflection of the bird's continuing decline. In British Columbia, Spotted Owl numbers dropped from an estimated 100 in the late 1990s to only 14 known individuals in 2014. Another 17 were in a captive breeding program designed to bolster the wild population.

Along with habitat loss from timbering and fire, a new threat has emerged for the Northern Spotted Owl—competition and hybridization with larger Barred Owls, which invaded the latter's range beginning in the 1970s. The invasion may have been a result of habitat changes from large-scale logging, but more likely from natural expansion. Barred Owls now occupy essentially all of the Northern subspecies's range, and parts of the Sierra Nevada range of the California Spotted Owl, with records as far south as Mariposa and Tulare Counties, CA. In many places they significantly outnumber their smaller cousins, occupying similar habitat and feeding on similar prey.

While hybridization has been uncommon, scientists have found that Spotted Owls avoid Barred Owl territories; meanwhile, Barred Owls have significantly higher survival rates and produce up to six times the number of young as Spotted Owls. The threat from Barred Owl competition was con-

sidered great enough that federal officials in 2013 authorized a controversial experiment to kill or remove up to 3,600 Barred Owls in parts of Washington, Oregon, and northern California in a last-ditch attempt to bolster Spotted Owl numbers.

Until recently, much less attention had been paid to the ecology and status of the Mexican Spotted Owl, in part because its listing did have the same incendiary political and economic impact as the Northern Spotted Owl's. By one estimate, between 1976 and 2000 more than 214,000 acres (86,000 hectares) of habitat in Mexico was lost annually, and only half the remaining habitat is considered well conserved. In 2004, roughly 8.6 million acres (3.5 million hectares) of federal land in Colorado, Utah, New Mexico, and Arizona were designated as critical habitat, requiring special management. But where indiscriminant logging was originally the main threat, massive wildfires (fueled by drought, climate change, and bark beetle infestations in the Southwest) may be the biggest danger in its U.S. range today.

In Mexico, uncontrolled and frequently illegal logging may well still be the prime threat, although wildfires have destroyed much owl habitat here, too. While more than 1,300 Mexican Spotted Owl locations are known within the subspecies's U.S. range, only 34 sites are known from Mexico, 27 of them within the northern Sierra Madre Occidental.

NOTES

1. J. A. Blakesley, A. B. Franklin, and R. J. Guitiérrez. 1990. Sexual dimorphism in northern spotted owls from northwest California. *Journal of Field Ornithology* 61:320–327.

2. R. J. Guitiérrez, A. B. Franklin, and W. S. LaHaye. 1995. Spotted owl (*Strix occidentalis*). In *The Birds of North America*, no. 179, ed. A. Poole and F. Gill. Philadelphia: Academy of Natural Sciences, and Washington, DC: American Ornithologists' Union.

3. R. J. Gutiérrez, M. Cody, S. Courtney, and A. B. Franklin. 2007. The invasion of barred owls and its potential effect on the spotted owl: A conservation conundrum. *Biological Invasions* 9:181–196.

BIBLIOGRAPHY

BirdLife International. 2015. *Strix occidentalis*. The IUCN Red List of Threatened Species, Version 2014.3. http://www.iucnredlist.org/details/22689089/0.

Bowden, T. S. 2008. "Mexican spotted owl reproduction, home range, and habitat associations in Grand Canyon National Park." MA thesis, Montana State University.

Courtney, S. P., J. A. Blakesley, R. E. Bigley, M. L. Cody, J. P. Dumbacher, R. C. Fleischer, A. B. Franklin, J. F. Franklin, R. J. Gutiérrez, J. M. Marzluff, and L. Sztukowski. 2004. *Scientific Evaluation of the Status of the Northern Spotted Owl*. Portland, OR: Sustainable Ecosystems Institute.

Davis, J. N., and G. I. Gould Jr. 2008. California spotted owl (*Strix occidentalis occidentalis*). In *California Bird Species of Special Concern,* ed. W. D. Shuford and T. Gardali. Studies of Western Birds no. 1. Camarillo and Sacramento, CA: Western Field Ornithologists and California Department of Fish and Game.

Davis, R., G. Falxa, E. Grinspoon, G. Harris, S. Lanigan, M. Moeur, and S. Mohoric. 2011. *Northwest Forest Plan— The First 15 years (1994-2008): Summary of Key Findings.* Technical Paper R6-RPM-TP-03-2011. Portland, OR: U.S. Department of Agriculture Forest Service, Pacific Northwest Region.

Dickerman, R. W. 1997. Geographic variation in southwestern United States and Mexican spotted owls, with the description of a new subspecies. In *The Era of Allan R. Phillips: A Festschrift,* ed. R. W. Dickerman. Albuquerque, NM: Horizon Communications.

Forsman, E. D., R. G. Anthony, K. M. Dugger, E. M. Glenn, A. B. Franklin, G. C. White, C. J. Schwarz, K. P. Burnham, D. R. Anderson, J. D. Nichols, J. E. Hines, J. B. Lint, R. J. Davis, S. H. Ackers, L. S. Andrews, B. L. Biswell, P. C. Carlson, L. V. Diller, S. A. Gremel, D. R. Herter, J. M. Higley, R. B. Horn, J. A. Reid, J. Rockweit, J. P. Schaberl, T. J. Snetsinger, and S. G. Sovern. 2011. *Population Demography of Northern Spotted Owls.* Berkeley and Los Angeles: University of California Press.

Forsman, E. D., T. J. Kaminski, J. C. Lewis, K. J. Maurice, S. G. Sovern, C. Ferland, and E. M. Glenn. 2005. Home range and habitat use of northern spotted owls on the Olympic Peninsula, Washington. *Journal of Raptor Research* 39:365–377.

Forsman, E. D., R. G. Anthony, J. A. Reid, P. J. Loschl, S. G. Sovern, M. Taylor, B. L. Biswell, A. Ellingson, E. C. Meslow, G. S. Miller, K. A. Swindle, J. A. Thrailkill, F. F. Wagner, and D. E. Seaman. 2002. Natal and breeding dispersal of northern spotted owls. *Wildlife Monographs* 149:1–35.

Ganey, J. L., S. C. Kyle, T. D. Rawlinson, D. L. Apprill, and J. P. Ward Jr. 2014. Relative abundance of small mammals in nest core areas and burned wintering areas of Mexican spotted owls in the Sacramento Mountains, New Mexico. *Wilson Journal of Ornithology* 126:47–52.

Ganey, J. L., W. M. Block, J. K. Dwyer, B. E. Strohmeyer, and J. S. Jenness. 1998. Dispersal movements and survival rates of juvenile Mexican spotted owls in northern Arizona. *Wilson Bulletin* 110:206–217.

Gutiérrez, R. J., and G. F. Barrowclough. 2005. Redefining the distributional boundaries of the northern and California spotted owls: Implications for conservation. *Condor* 107:182–187.

Haas, W. E. 2004. Spotted owl *Strix occidentalis.* In *San Diego County Bird Atlas,* ed. P. Unitt. El Cajon, CA: Sunbelt Publications.

Haig, S. M., T. D. Mullins, and E. D. Forsman. 2004. Subspecific relationships and genetic structure in the spotted owl. *Conservation Genetics* 5:683–705.

Hamer, Forsman, and Glenn 2007.

Kelly, E. G., and E. D. Forsman. 2004. Recent records of hybridization between barred owls (*Strix varia*) and northern spotted owls (*Strix occidentalis caurina*). *Auk* 121:806–810.

LaHaye, W. S., R. J. Guitiérrez, and J. R. Dunk. 2001. Natal dispersal of the spotted owl in southern California: Dispersal profile of an insular population. *Condor* 103:691–700.

Livezey, K. B. 2010. Killing barred owls to help spotted owls: A global perspective. *Northwestern Naturalist* 91:107–133.

Mullet, T. C., and J. P. Ward Jr. 2010. Microhabitat features at Mexican spotted owl nest and roost sites in the Guadalupe Mountains. *Journal of Raptor Research* 44:277–285.

Navarro-Sigüenza, A. G., and A. T. Peterson. 2007. *Strix occidentalus* (búho manchado) residencia permanente distribución potencial. In *Mapas de las Aves de México Basados en WWW,* ed. A. G. Navarro and A. T. Peterson. Final report, SNIB-CONABIO project no. CE015. México DF.

Peery, M. Z., and R. J. Gutiérrez. 2013. Life-history tradeoffs in spotted owls (*Strix occidentalis*): Implications for assessment of territory quality. *Auk* 130:132–140.

Phillips, C. E., D. J. Tempel, and R. J. Gutiérrez. 2010. Do California spotted owls select nest trees close to forest edges? *Journal of Raptor Research* 44:311–314.

Schilling, J. W., K. M. Dugger, and R. G. Anthony. 2013. Survival and home-range size of northern spotted owls in southwestern Oregon. *Journal of Raptor Research* 47:1–14.

U.S. Fish and Wildlife Service. 2012. *Recovery Plan for the Mexican Spotted Owl, First Revision.* Albuquerque, NM: U.S. Fish and Wildlife Service.

———. 2011. *Revised Recovery Plan for the Northern Spotted Owl (Strix occidentalis caurina).* Portland, OR: U.S. Fish and Wildlife Service.

Van Gelder, J. J. 2003. "Variation in four-note location calls of male spotted owls (*Strix occidentalis*)." MA thesis, Humboldt State University.

Weins 2012.

Willey, D. W. 2013. Diet of Mexican spotted owls in Utah and Arizona. *Wilson Journal of Ornithology* 125:775–781.

Willey, D. W., and C. van Riper III. 2014. Home range characteristics of Mexican spotted owls in the Rincon Mountains, Arizona. *Wilson Journal of Ornithology* 126:53–59.

Willey, D. W., and M. Zambon. 2014. Predicting occurrence of Mexican spotted owls in arid canyonlands of southern Utah. *Journal of Raptor Research* 48:118–127.

Young, K. E., R. Valdez, P. J. Zwank, and W. R. Gould. 1998. Density and roost site characteristics of spotted owls in the Sierra Madre Occidental, Chihuahua, Mexico. *Condor* 100:732–736.

Young, K. E., P. J. Zwank, R. Valdez, J. L. Dye, and L. A. Tarango. 1997. Diet of Mexican spotted owls in Chihuahua and Aguascalientes, Mexico. *Journal of Raptor Research* 31:376–380.

BARRED OWL
Strix varia
Alpha code: BDOW*

LENGTH: 19–22 in. (48.25–56 cm)

WINGSPAN: 42.5–44 in. (108–112 cm)

MASS: Moderate to strong reversed size dimorphism.

S. v. varia: No locations specified: Average, male: 22 oz. (622 g), range 17–28.7 oz. (483–812 g). Average, female: 30.8 oz. (873g), range 22.9–36 oz. (650–1,020 g).[1] Average, male: 22.3 oz. (632 g), range 16.5–27.3 oz. (468–774 g). Average, female: 28.2 oz. (801 g), range 21.2–37 oz. (610–1,051 g).[2] Average, females only: 22 oz. (625 g).[3]

S. v. varia: North Carolina: Average, male: 24 oz. (681 g); range 20.1–27.1 oz. (570–770 g). Average, female: 32.1 oz. (909.5 g); range 30.3–40.6 oz. (860–1,150 g).[4]

S. v. georgica: Florida: Average, male: 24.25 oz. (744 g); range 24–28.2 oz. (681–800g). One female: 30.9 oz. (875 g).[5] Average, male: 25.3 oz. (718 g). Two females: 30, 30.9 oz. (850, 875 g).[6]

LONGEVITY: Average age at re-encounter for banded birds, 2.5 years. The longevity record in the wild is 24 years 1 month, a Minnesota Barred Owl that died after becoming entangled in fishing gear. Other exceptional records include two individuals 19 years or older, and six others 15 years or older.

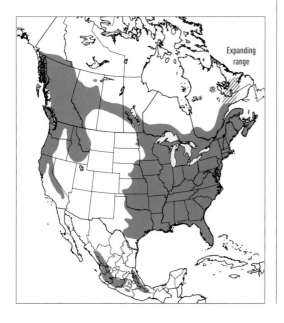

Expanding range

One of the most familiar owls in North America, with a loud, raucous voice that even an amateur birder can easily identify (and just as easily imitate), the Barred Owl is a fixture of mature forests, from the hardwood hammocks of the Everglades to the coastal rain forests of the Pacific Northwest, and from leafy suburbs in the Mid-Atlantic to shelter-belt thickets at the edge of the Great Plains. And no other North American owl has exploded in range and numbers like this large, round-headed species, having colonized an enormous swath of the West in the past century—to the detriment of its smaller and rarer cousin the Spotted Owl, with which it directly competes.

SYSTEMATICS, TAXONOMY, AND ETYMOLOGY

Four subspecies are generally recognized, based on fairly subtle plumage differences, the degree of feathering on the toes, and relative size of feet and bill.

S. v. varia: The most widespread subspecies, from the Canadian Maritimes west to southeastern Yukon, and south to northern Georgia and Oklahoma; in the west, south to California. Dark brown ground color; toes feathered at the base, bristled elsewhere.

S. v. georgica: Central Georgia and Florida west to eastern and north-central Texas. Dark brown ground color, toes largely naked.

S. v. helveola: South-central Texas. Paler brown above, with toes largely naked.

S. v. sartorii: Highlands and mountain forests of southern and central Mexico (see "Distribution," p. 226, for cautions). Largest and darkest of the subspecies. Sooty brown upperparts with contrasting white barring, more distinctly blackish markings on the underparts, and less distinct markings on the face. Toes feathered.

A molecular study by Barrowclough et al. (2011) found little support for the standard subspecies divisions, however. Instead, it identified two clades north of the Rio Grande, with little relation to the traditionally recognized subspecies—one centered along the Atlantic seaboard and the other in the south-central United States. These may correspond with two refugia during the peak of the last glaciation. There is a very wide overlap zone from the Gulf Coast to the upper Midwest, and across all of the Barred Owl's Canadian and western U.S. range.

The authors also found a significant genetic division between the northern groups and the Mexican Barred Owl, *S. v. sartorii,* suggesting the latter

---

*Bird Banding Lab alpha code; Pyle and DeSante (2003) use "BADO."

Although primarily nocturnal, Barred Owls are more active by day than most large owls, often hunting after dawn and before dusk, especially on gloomy, overcast days. *(Pennsylvania. Alan Richard)*

The most widespread of the traditional Barred Owl subspecies is *S. v. varia*, found from the Canadian Maritimes west to the Pacific, and south to northern Georgia and Oklahoma. *(Ontario. Gerrit Vyn)*

should be considered a distinct species. This potential split has not yet been taken up by the AOU.

ETYMOLOGY: For the genus name, see "Spotted Owl." The specific name is from the Latin *varius*, or "variegated," a reference to the barred and streaked plumage, which is also the derivation of the common name.

> SPANISH: *Búho [tecolote] listado, búho barrado, búho serrano, búho serrano vientrirrayado*
> FRENCH: *Chouette rayeé*

DISTRIBUTION

BREEDING SEASON: Resident. Northern group (*S. v. varia, georgica,* and *helveola*): Eastern North America from southern Ontario (north shore of Lake Superior) east to Cape Breton and Prince Edward Island, and south throughout the East to Florida. Evidence of expanding range in central Quebec; one recent record from Goose Bay, Labrador. Extirpated from Long Island, New York, by the early twentieth century; one recent breeding bird atlas record from the northeast tip of the island hints at possible recolonization across Long Island Sound, as Barred Owls have recently colonized Cape Cod in Massachusetts.

Western range limits, usually corresponding to riparian corridors in eastern Great Plains, stretch north from the Nueces River and Edwards Plateau in Texas through western Oklahoma, central Kansas, eastern Nebraska, southeastern South Dakota, extreme eastern North Dakota to Minne-sota. Found in a narrow band west across southern Manitoba and central Saskatchewan to central and western Alberta, as far north as the lower Peace River (rare), extreme southwestern Northwest Territories, and southern Yukon. South through southeastern Alaska and British Columbia (absent from the Queen Charlotte Islands / Haida Gwaii) to Washington and Oregon. Expanding in California; found along the coast south to San Francisco Bay, and in the Sierra Nevada south to Mariposa and Tulare Counties.

Generally found in lowland forests, but occurs at elevations to 6,000 ft. (1,800 m) in parts of the West.

Mexican Barred Owl (*S. v. sartorii*): Range disjunct; Durango to Michoacán, Mexico, and Guerrero along the Pacific slope and interior mountains, and on Atlantic slope from Oaxaca and Veracruz. Reported historically from Puebla. Exact distribution unclear, given potential confusion both in sight records and museum skins with Fulvous Owl, and the latter's previously unrecognized presence well north of the Isthmus of Tehuantepec. Found in montane pine and pine-oak forests, generally between 4,900 and 9,850 ft. (1,500 and 3,000 m).

Barred Owls made a dramatic—and continuing—range expansion in western North America, with serious conservation consequences for the federally threatened Spotted Owl, with which it com-

Three subspecies of Barred Owls have been recognized north of Mexico, differing in coloration and toe feathering. This is *S. v. georgica*, found from central Georgia through Florida. Recent DNA studies, however, suggest there are really just two genetic groups that don't align with traditional subspecies limits. *(Florida. John Sherman/VIREO)*

Barred Owls have been on a roll for much of the last century, breaching the Great Plains and expanding their range dramatically across the West and, to a lesser extent, into eastern Canada—and in the process jeopardizing the already threatened Spotted Owl. *(Ontario. Gerrit Vyn)*

petes. (See "Spotted Owl" species account, p. 213.) The Great Plains appear to have been a historical barrier to their westward movement, but in the late nineteenth century Barred Owls started moving up forested river corridors, reaching southeastern Montana by 1873.

The species never permanently established itself along those river courses but did in southwestern Montana. From this stronghold Barred Owls spread in several directions during the first decades of the twentieth century—northeast into the Canadian prairie provinces, meeting a second wave coming northwest from Minnesota through Manitoba; and northwest into Alberta and northern British Columbia, reaching Alaska in 1967 and the southern Northwest Territories by 1977. By the 1960s, Barred Owls were colonizing south through the Pacific Northwest, reaching northern California by 1976. They have now been found in that state as far south as Marin County on the coast, and as far as the southern end of the Sierra Nevada in Tulare County. See Livezey (2009a) for a detailed chronology; see "Habitat and Niche," p. 229, for a discussion of what may have triggered the expansion.

MIGRATION AND MOVEMENTS: Essentially nonmigratory, although some northern populations are suspected of making modest movements south during harsh winters, and individuals in the West may show some altitudinal migration. Old accounts speak vaguely of "great flights"[7] in harsh winters, but such large-scale movements have not been documented in the past century. Large numbers (about 50) of Barred Owls are sometimes noted in Minnesota during major northern owl irruptions like that of 2004–2005.

POST-FLEDGING DISPERSAL: Limited information for such a common species. Banded chicks in Nova Scotia were recovered up to 40 mi. (64 km) from their nest, and one individual moved 994 mi. (1,600 km) west to Ontario. In North Carolina, chicks fledging from rural nests dispersed an average of 2.6 mi. (4.1 km), compared with 1.7 mi. (2.7 km) from suburban nests, suggesting better habitat quality in more urbanized sites (see "Habitat and Niche," p. 229).

DISTRIBUTION OUTSIDE THE COVERAGE AREA: None

In all of its eastern range, the Barred Owl is unmistakable: no other owl combines its large size, round head, and dark eyes. *(Florida. Kevin Loughlin/ Wildside Nature Tours)*

DESCRIPTION AND IDENTIFICATION

A large, tuftless, round-headed owl with dark eyes, barred back, and pale, distinctly streaked belly. Active (and therefore encountered) somewhat more often in daytime than many other owls.

BASIC (ADULT) PLUMAGE: Sexes similar. Ground color of head and upperparts brown to brown-gray. Narrow, tightly concentric whitish or buffy barring on crown, nape, and neck; wider white or pale buffy barring on the back and upperwing coverts. Flight feathers dark brown, distinctly barred with buffy white. Tail moderately long, dark brown, with four or five narrow, gray-white bars.

Facial disk grayish or gray-brown with indistinct darker concentric rings and dark brown-black ruff; eyebrows and rictal bristles match ground color of the facial disk and are obscure. A wide collar,

horizontally barred, separates the throat and upper chest. Undersides white to pale buff, with distinct, vertical dark brown streaks. Underwing coverts pale buff to grayish, lightly spotted; undersides of flight feathers dark gray-brown with wide grayish bars. Bill yellowish, irises dark brown. Eyeshine bright orange-red.

JUVENAL PLUMAGE: Natal down is white, replaced at 2 or 3 weeks of age by gray mesoptile plumage with narrow, diffuse gray barring, through which adult-like flight feathers emerge. Juvenal contour feathers, which replace the mesoptile down, more closely resemble adult pattern but are loosely constructed and have downy tips, especially evident on the wings and back. Plumage resembles that of adults by about 4 months of age.

SIMILAR SPECIES: In the East and most of Canada, no other large owl combines dark eyes, round head, and brownish plumage. Great Gray Owl is considerably larger, with darkly mottled underparts and yellow eyes. Spotted Owl is smaller and (especially Northern Spotted Owl) darker, with transverse barring on the belly that creates a pattern of large, irregular spots. Rare Barred × Spotted hybrids are intermediate in size and markings. In Mexico, Mottled Owl is smaller and darker overall, especially in the facial disk. Very similar Fulvous Owl is smaller than Barred, with browner (versus grayer) upperparts and buff underparts. Bill bright, not dull, yellow.

VOCALIZATIONS

Famously and uproariously vocal, Barred Owls give one of the most instantly recognizable calls of any owl—the whooping *who-cooks-for-you, who-cooks-for-you-aaaaallllll,* which is made by both sexes. But they have a complex suite of 13 vocalizations that has only recently been studied in any depth.[8] As with the vocalizations of many owls, the female's calls are higher-pitched than those of the male and may be slower in pace.

The main call is known as the two-phrased hoot, and also reflects sexual differences, with the female's version having longer final notes (the *-aaaaallllll*) and more vibrato than that of a male Barred Owl. It appears this call has a variety of purposes, including territorial defense and contact between mated adults.

Both sexes also give a one-phrase hoot and an ascending hoot, the latter a series of 6 to 10 evenly spaced, ascending notes that ends in a falling, drawn-out wail: *hu-hu-hu-HU-HU-HU-HU-HUUUWaaaaaa;* the ascending hoot appears to be primarily an aggressive vocalization aimed at intruding owls. Barred Owls also give an "inspection," or contact, call, a single, drawn-out note that falls off at the end, which is among the most common vocalizations by both sexes.

Barred Owls are one of the few owls—and among the only temperate birds of any sort—to perform intricate vocal duets, creating layers of hooting and caterwauling, an activity most often associated with territorial defense. One component of duets—and perhaps the most astonishing (and, to someone unfamiliar with owls, easily the most alarming) of all Barred Owl calls—is the "gurgle" call, a raucous, maniacal laugh that can go on for minutes.

Female and juvenile begging calls are similar, a thin, weird, rising whistle (raspier in juveniles), lasting about 1.5 seconds (juveniles). Under duress, Barred Owls give a similar but longer and more intense alarm scream, lasting about 2.5 seconds.

Like most owls, Barred Owls of all ages will snap their bills when agitated. Adults also create loud wing-snaps by clapping the wings against the body, usually when trying to intimidate an intruder.

Although Barred Owl vocalizations are individually recognizable, there are no clear geographic patterns, at least within the range of *S. v. varia* and *S. v. georgica* in the southeastern United States. The vocal array of the Mexican subspecies, which could shed light on its potential species status, appears to be essentially unstudied; in fact, at this writing, no recordings of this owl are archived with either the Macaulay Library at the Cornell Lab of Ornithology, or at xeno-canto.com.

HABITAT AND NICHE

Ask birders where to find a Barred Owl, and they'll usually point you to a damp, dim, old forest. As A. C. Bent observed in the 1930s, this species lives "mainly in the deep, dark woods, heavily wooded swamps, gloomy hemlock forests, or the thick growths of tall, dense pines."[9]

But Barred Owls are actually quite flexible in their habitat requirements, inhabiting cottonwood, elm, and willow stands in the grasslands of Oklahoma, mixed boreal forests in western Canada, Douglas-fir–pine forests in the Rockies and Cascades, and fir forests as high as 6,000 ft. (1,800 m) in California. Good Barred Owl habitat usually includes a mix of conifer and hardwood species, with lots of big old trees in which this large cavity-dependent bird can find nest sites, and often proximity to water. Across their range, Barred Owls are most often found in older, structurally complex forests with closed canopies.

Older suburban neighborhoods, with their immense shade trees, have proven to be a very good habitat for Barred Owls in many areas, perhaps because such neighborhoods replicate many of those same qualities of mature forests—plenty of large cavities for nesting, and lots of open ground below

The main vocalization of the Barred Owl is one of the most instantly recognizable bird calls in North America—the whooping, wailing, *who-cooks-for-you-aaaaalllll,* which can become a caterwauling duet between mates. *[New York. Chris Wood]*

the expansive forest canopy where a large owl can easily maneuver. Although one study in Connecticut found that Barred Owls avoided areas with human habitation, other research in Ohio and North Carolina found that older suburban areas were favored habitat, with Barred Owls nesting within a stone's toss from occupied homes.

Winter studies in Montana suggest that some Barred Owls may move seasonally out of continuous forest and into more open country, roosting in shelterbelts and wooded streamsides and foraging along the edges of grasslands.

Relatively little is known about the ecology of the Mexican subspecies. It inhabits pine, pine-oak, and fir forests from 4,900 to 9,850 ft. (1,500 to 3,000 m).

Just why the Barred Owl made such an explosive range expansion into the West remains a topic of debate. While some experts credit the owl's natural adaptability, other scientists think the owl has been exploiting changes in the environment—first the growth of forest corridors along Great Plains rivers in the late 1800s, and then industrial logging that dramatically altered forest environments across the West. Others have suggested that the warming climate allowed Barred Owls to survive more easily in northerly areas. Regardless of the reason, Barred Owls have roughly doubled their range in the past century or so.

DIET: Barred Owls are opportunistic eaters, taking prey as large as Ring-necked Pheasants and as small as earthworms, and even snatching fish from the surface of the water. Although the bulk of their diet is mammalian, birds are often a surprisingly close second, and depending on season and location,

Barred Owls can thrive in a host of wooded environments, from lowland swamp forests to fir and pine woods 6,000 ft. (1,800 m) high in the Rockies. Older suburban neighborhoods, with immense old shade trees, make surprisingly good habitat. *(Ontario. Tom Johnson)*

they may take large numbers of reptiles, amphibians, crustaceans, and other invertebrates.

Mice, rats, voles, and shrews are the most commonly taken prey, usually making up between a third and two-thirds of the dietary total in most studies—and sometimes much more. In Montana, just two species of voles made up almost 94 percent of all the prey remains found in winter Barred Owl pellets. In western Oregon, mammals made up almost 90 percent of the biomass Barred Owls consumed, with flying squirrels comprising almost a quarter of that, followed by rabbits and moles.

Those same Oregon owls, however, took a total of 95 different species, including mountain beavers, woodrats, muskrats, ermine, birds, frogs, salamanders, insects, millipedes, springtails, crayfish, snails, and small fish. A different study in Oregon found that beetles, shrews, and flying squirrels were the common prey, but that the owls took 33 species of mammals, 25 birds, 4 reptiles, 4 amphibians, 12 insects, 3 snails, and 1 species each of fish, millipede, springtail, and crustacean. But across the Pacific Northwest, researchers have found that flying squirrels are the most important prey item, making up 25 to 41 percent of the biomass Barred Owls consume.

Because most studies depend on picking apart regurgitated pellets, it's likely that smaller (especially invertebrate) prey is underreported. Barred Owls have been seen catching moths in Florida, grasshoppers in Louisiana, and have often been observed wading in shallow water to catch crayfish. In the

Pacific Northwest, Barred Owls have been seen actively hunting for slugs and earthworms by flipping over leaves and vegetation. This is not only an interesting observation but also a cautionary note, because the remains of such prey (as well as small vertebrates like frogs and salamanders) will not show up in pellet analysis, the method by which most owl dietary studies are conducted.

Barred Owls have a penchant for taking birds and may well be the most serious threat to smaller owls like saw-whets, screech-owls, and pygmy-owls—and not-so-small owls too, including Long-eareds, which are almost half the Barred Owl's size. Barreds have also been known to take small hawks, grouse, and a variety of passerines. Birds comprised more than 50 percent of Barred Owl diets in suburban North Carolina, while those in nearby rural areas fed most heavily on reptiles, amphibians, and insects. In both cases, mammals made up less than 15 percent of the owls' diet.

And while there is little evidence for carrion-feeding among owls—perhaps because such behavior is hard to infer from pellet remains—Barred Owls in North Carolina were photographed feeding on a dead squirrel and the badly rotten rib cage of a road-killed deer at camera-trap sites set up for mammals.

NESTING AND BREEDING

Pair formation (and rebonding in existing pairs) begins in late winter, and the southerly populations may be laying eggs by Dec. or Jan. in Florida, and Feb. in Texas. Farther north, typical egg dates are

Pair formation among Barred Owls begins in late winter, with egg-laying as early as December in Florida and as late as May in parts of Canada. (Manitoba. Christian Artuso)

Too large for woodpecker holes, Barred Owls depend on natural rot cavities, broken snags, and the stick nests of raptors and crows for their nest sites. Here, two Barred Owl chicks huddle in the feather-strewn interior of their nest. (North Carolina. Rob Bierregaard)

Mar. and early Apr. in the Mid-Atlantic and Midwest, mid-Apr. in southern New England, and late Apr. or May in the Canadian Maritimes.

Too large for even the biggest woodpecker hole, nesting Barred Owls are dependent on large cavities—rot holes, broken snags, and the like—along with old stick nests from hawks, crows, and other large birds. (Unlike Great Horned Owls, which start nesting early enough to have their pick of still-empty nests, Barred Owls must sometimes evict the original occupants, like those found in Red-shouldered Hawk nests in Ohio, which still had

fresh greenery brought in by the hawks.) In suburban North Carolina, a few pairs nested on top of screened chimneys, one of which was capped by an old squirrel nest—but adults exploring for potential nest sites sometimes wind up stuck inside uncapped chimneys.

Wherever they nest, Barred Owls tend to pick the biggest, oldest trees because such specimens are most likely to have sufficiently large cavities. In Alberta, they were most often found nesting in old balsam poplars; in the upper Midwest, in sycamores—which are both the largest hardwoods in the regions, and trees prone to natural cavities. Barred Owls show a remarkable degree of site fidelity, often returning to the same nest location for years, as long as the cavity remains or the platform nest will hold them, since they do nothing to maintain it. Bent and other early ornithologists recorded nest sites and small territories occupied for up to 34 years, although it's highly unlikely that the same individual owls were present that whole time.

A normal clutch is 2 to 3 eggs, with 4 being rare and 5 exceptional. Incubation, by the female alone, lasts 28 to 33 days, and hatching is asynchronous. Chicks start branching by about 4 or 5 weeks of age, and can fly at about 10 weeks. The young are dependent on the adults through early autumn, although not much is known about this period in the Barred Owl's life.

Although biologists assume Barred Owls remain paired for the long term, this too is an area that has been little studied.

BEHAVIOR

"The flight of the barred owl is light, buoyant, and noiseless, with rather slow beats of its spacious wings; it often glides gracefully and skillfully among the intricacies of the forest branches," Bent wrote in 1938.[10] Though primarily nocturnal, Barred Owls are known for being more active by day than most owls; a good imitation of their call may bring in a territorial adult in the middle of the afternoon, and Barred Owls may hunt diurnally when an opportunity presents itself.

Daytime is usually for roosting, though. Like Spotted Owls, they frequently seek out roost sites with cool shade in summer and a sunny southern exposure in winter, usually fairly high off the ground and in thick cover. They can be fairly tame when approached, watching carefully through slitted eyes or boldly bobbing their heads to better triangulate the distance to this two-legged interloper. If the owl flushes, it is liable to find itself mobbed by small birds, a reflection of the very real danger this species poses to larger passerines.

The owls become increasingly restless toward dusk, often beginning their evening hunt early on overcast days. Barred Owls appear to be primarily perch hunters, although they can be surprisingly agile, sometimes snatching smaller owls in mid-flight. Their buoyant flight and wide wingspread account for their tendency to hunt in fairly open habitat.

One peak calling period begins shortly after dusk and lasts roughly 2 hours, when a territorial pair tends to give two-phrase hoots, ascending hoots, and duets. Another peak calling period occurs in the final hours before dawn, when inspection calls and two-phrased hoots are most common.

As with all raptors, home range size is as much a function of prey density as any other factor, and varies widely, although summer ranges tend to be smaller than those used in winter. The ranges of mated pairs overlap significantly, but winter use areas in particular tend be more distinct and separate.

In Minnesota, two studies found average home range sizes of 1,413 and 566 acres (572 and 229 hectares), while in Michigan, home range size was 697 acres (282 hectares). Near the northern edge of the species's range, in Saskatchewan, territory size was 2,399 acres (971 hectares), while in Washington, a study that looked at annual home range size (instead of just that used during the breeding season) found the average territory encompassed 1,782 acres (781 hectares).

Males tend to roam over wider areas than females do; in a different study in Washington, the average male territory was 712 acres (288 hectares) versus 479 acres (194 hectares) for females. One male there moved 17 mi. (27 km) between his summer and winter ranges. Those in suburban North Carolina had smaller ranges than elsewhere in North America, probably reflecting greater resources—an average of 279 acres (118 hectares) for males and 212 acres (86 hectares) for females.

STATUS

The twentieth century was very good to the Barred Owl, and the twenty-first is shaping up swimmingly, too. In addition to nearly doubling the land area of its range by colonizing much of western Canada and the Pacific Northwest, Barred Owl numbers have grown in much of the species's traditional range in the East.

The Breeding Bird Survey, while not ideal for tracking nocturnal birds, showed a continent-wide increase since 1966. A better reflection of the state of Barred Owl populations may be the periodic breeding bird atlas projects in many states. In Maryland, for example, Barred Owls were detected in 19 percent more survey blocks in the early 2000s, compared with those in the first atlas 20 years earlier. In Pennsylvania, the increase over the same period was 17 percent, and in New York, 43 percent—

Blue Jays do their best to make life miserable for a Barred Owl caught out in the open—payback for the significant level of predation these owls inflict on smaller birds at night. *(Texas. Greg Lasley)*

while in Massachusetts, Barred Owls were found in triple the number of blocks.

The continuing maturation of eastern forests, and the Barred Owl's increasing ease with residential neighborhoods and suburbia, appear to be factors in all of these increases. Interestingly, Barred Owls did not show the sort of declines seen among Eastern Screech-Owls and Great Horned Owls in some areas, which were at least partially ascribed to West Nile virus. There is some evidence that sensitivity to West Nile is significantly less acute in those owls, like the Barred Owl, with a primarily southern distribution.

The continuing expansion of the Barred Owl's range in the West should slow, given that the species already occupies much of the best habitat (although in many areas it remains rare to uncommon, and those populations may increase with time). But it seems likely that Barred Owls will move farther north through the coastal rain forests of south-central Alaska and adjacent Yukon, perhaps to the Kenai Peninsula, and fully occupy the islands of the southeastern Alaskan and British Columbian archipelago. A southeastern expansion through much of Idaho may eventually extend into northwestern Wyoming and south through appropriate habitat in the central Rockies.

Recent records from eastern and central Quebec and coastal Labrador suggest that a northeastern expansion from the Gulf of Saint Lawrence into the fringe of the boreal zone is occurring as well.

Barred Owls on the California coast should also eventually cross San Francisco Bay to the south, bringing them into contact with the already declining coastal population of the California Spotted Owl—likely to the detriment of that subspecies, and exacerbating existing conflicts with Spotted Owls as a whole. As noted in the Spotted Owl account, wildlife managers in the Pacific Northwest have undertaken an experimental removal of Barred Owls from Northern Spotted Owl territories in a last-ditch attempt to reduce competition with that federally listed population.

Too little is known about the Mexican race of the Barred Owl to make more than a guess about its status. The subspecies is listed as "threatened" by the Mexican government, and rampant logging is almost certainly having a detrimental effect, especially through the loss of mature trees with large cavities. Mexican populations are likely to be even more fragmented than a range map would suggest, but only targeted surveys will tell. DNA evidence suggesting that this race warrants species recognition makes its status all the more concerning.

Threats to the northern subspecies appear to be minimal. Habitat fragmentation from logging, and the loss of older balsam poplars for nesting, could be a danger to those at the limit of the species's range in Alberta, where fragmentation might favor Great Horned Owls. In the East, the continuing loss of eastern hemlocks to an introduced pest may have unknown consequences; atlas data in Pennsylvania showed that, of the seven species of owls in the state, Barred Owls had the closest association with the presence of hemlock. Anticoagulant rodenticides, especially so-called "second-generation" poisons, have shown up increasingly in the tissues of many raptors, including Barred Owls, and this species's growing tendency to live close to humans may heighten that risk.

NOTES

1. K. M. Mazur and P. C. James. 2000. Barred owl (*Strix varia*). In *The Birds of North America*, no. 508, ed. A. Poole and F. Gill. Philadelphia: Birds of North America.

2. Earhart and Johnson 1970.

3. Craighead and Craighead 1956.

4. R. Bierregaard, pers. comm.

5. Hartman 1955.

6. Hartman 1961.

7. Forbush 1927, p. 204.

8. Odom 2009.

9. Bent 1938, p. 182.

10. Ibid., p. 191.

BIBLIOGRAPHY

Barrowclough, G. F., J. G. Groth, K. J. Odom, and J. E. Lai. 2011. Phylogeography of the barred owl (*Strix varia*): Species limits, multiple refugia, and range expansion. *Auk* 128:696–706.

Beedy and Pandolfino 2013.

Bosakowski and Smith 1997.

Cauble, L. C. 2008. "The diets of rural and suburban barred owls *Strix varia* in Mecklenburg County, North Carolina." MS thesis, University of North Carolina at Charlotte.

Dykstra, C. R., M. M. Simon, F. B. Daniel, and J. L. Hays. 2012. Habitats of suburban barred owls (*Strix varia*) and red-shouldered hawks (*Buteo lineatus*) in southwestern Ohio. *Journal of Raptor Research* 46:190–200.

Eckert 2005.

Ellison, W. G. 2010. Barred owl. In *2nd Atlas of the Breeding Birds of Maryland and the District of Columbia*, ed. W. G. Ellison. Baltimore, MD: Johns Hopkins University Press.

Enríque-Rocha, Rangel-Salazar, and Holt 1993.

Talons poised, a Barred Owl readies for the kill. *(Ontario. Glenn Bartley/VIREO)*

Freeman, P. L. 2000. Identification of individual barred owls using spectrogram analysis and auditory cues. *Journal of Raptor Research* 34:85–92.

Gancz, A. Y., I. K. Barker, R. Lindsay, A. Dibernardo, K. McKeever, and B. Hunter. 2004. West Nile virus outbreak in North American owls, Ontario, 2002. *Emerging Infectious Diseases* 10:2135–2142.

Graham, S. A. 2012. "Diet composition, niche and geographic characteristics, and prey size preference of barred owls (*Strix varia*) in the Pacific Northwest." MS thesis, Boise State University.

Hamer, Forsman, and Glenn 2007.

Harrold, E. S. 2003. "Barred owl (*Strix varia*) nesting ecology in the southern Piedmont of North Carolina." MS thesis, University of North Carolina at Charlotte.

Holt, D. W., and C. Bitter. 2007. Barred owl winter diet and pellet dimensions in western Montana. *Northwestern Naturalist* 88:7–11.

Kapfer, J. M., D. E. Gammon, and J. D. Graves. 2011. Carrion-feeding by barred owls (*Strix varia*). *Wilson Journal of Ornithology* 123:646–649.

Leberman, R. C. 2012. Barred owl. In *Second Atlas of Breeding Birds in Pennsylvania*, ed. A. M. Wilson, D. W. Brauning, and R. S. Mulvihill. University Park, PA: Pennsylvania State University Press.

Livezey, K. B. 2009a. Range expansion of barred owls, part I: Chronology and distribution. *American Midland Naturalist* 161:49–56.

———. 2009b. Range expansion of barred owls, part II: Facilitating ecological changes. *American Midland Naturalist* 161:323–349.

Livezey, K. B., M. F. Elderkin, P. A. Cott, J. Hobbs, and J. P. Hudson. 2008. Barred owls eating worms and slugs: The advantage of not being a picky eater. *Northwestern Naturalist* 89:185–190.

Livezey, K. B., T. L. Root, S. A. Gremel, and C. Johnson. 2008. Natural range expansion of barred owls? A critique of Monahan and Hijmans (2007). *Auk* 125:230–232.

Marks, J. S., D. P. Hendricks, and V. S. Marks. 1984. Winter food habits of barred owls in western Montana. *Murrelet* 65:27–28.

Mason, J. S. 2004. "The reproductive success, survival, and natal dispersal of barred owls (*Strix varia*) in rural versus urban habitats in and around Charlotte, North Carolina." MS thesis, University of North Carolina.

McGowan, K. J. 2008. Barred owl. In *The Second Atlas of Breeding Birds of New York State*, ed. K. J. McGowan and K. Corwin. Ithaca, NY: Cornell University Press.

Monahan, W. B., and R. J. Hijmans. 2007. Distributional dynamics of invasion and hybridization by *Strix* spp. in western North America. *Ornithological Monographs* 63:55–66.

Navarro-Sigüenza, A. G., and A. T. Peterson. 2007. *Strix varia* (búho listado) residencia permanente distribución potencial. In *Mapas de las Aves de México Basados en WWW*, ed. A. G. Navarro and A. T. Peterson. Final report, SNIB-CONABIO project no. CE015. México DF.

Odom, K. J. 2009. "Vocalizations, vocal behaviour, and geographic variation in the calls, duets, and duetting behaviour of a nonpasserine, the barred owl (*Strix varia*)." PhD diss., University of Windsor.

Odom, K. J., and D. J. Mennill. 2012. Inconsistent geographic variation in the calls and duets of barred owls (*Strix varia*) across an area of genetic introgression. *Auk* 129:387–398.

———. 2010. A quantitative description of the vocalizations and vocal activity of the barred owl. *Condor* 112:549–560.

———. 2009. Vocal duets in a nonpasserine: An examination of territory defence and neighbour-stranger discrimination in a neighbourhood of barred owls. *Behaviour* 147:619–639.

Priestley, L. T. 2004. The barred owl, *Strix varia*, in Alberta: Distribution and status. *Canadian Field-Naturalist* 118:215–224.

Retter, M. 2012. "Mexican barred-owl: A split too far?" ABA Blog, May 30, http://blog.aba.org/2012/05/barred-owl-futures.html.

Schmelzer, I., and F. Phillips. 2004. First record of a barred owl, *Strix varia*, in Labrador. *Canadian Field-Naturalist* 118:273–276.

Singleton, P. H., J. F. Lehmkuhl, W. L. Gaines, and S. A. Graham. 2010. Barred owl space use and habitat selection in the eastern Cascades, Washington. *Journal of Wildlife Management* 74:285–294.

Weins 2012.

Whiklo, T. M., and J. R. Duncan. 2012. Occurrences of wing clapping behavior in barred owls (*Strix varia*). *Journal of Raptor Research* 46:413–416.

Winton, B. R., and D. M. Leslie Jr. 2004. Density and habitat associations of barred owls at the edge of their range in Oklahoma. *Southeastern Naturalist* 3:475–482.

FULVOUS OWL
Strix fulvescens
Alpha code: FUOW

LENGTH: About 17 in. (44 cm)

WINGSPAN: No information

MASS: No information. Linear dimensions, including wing chord and overall length of prepared skins, roughly 10–20 percent smaller than Mexican Barred Owl, *S. v. sartorii.*

LONGEVITY: No information

One of the least-known and poorly studied owls in Mesoamerica, the Fulvous Owl is essentially a flying question mark. Besides a penchant for cool, damp mountain forests, most of its ecology, life history, even exactly what it eats and where it nests come down to little more than guesswork, based on what is known of its relatives in the genus *Strix.* Recently the Fulvous Owl has been found hundreds of miles beyond what had been considered the limits of its range, an example of how little we know about this mysterious forest raptor.

SYSTEMATICS, TAXONOMY, AND ETYMOLOGY

Monotypic. The Fulvous Owl has sometimes been lumped with the Barred Owl but is generally recognized as a separate species because of its distinct vocalizations, which more closely resemble those of the Spotted Owl (and with which, along with the Barred Owl, it may form a superspecies). Recent discoveries of this bird in Oaxaca mean it is sympatric with the Mexican subspecies of the Barred Owl, strengthening the case for distinct status.

ETYMOLOGY: For the derivation of the genus name, see "Spotted Owl." The common and specific names both derive from the Latin *fulvus,* meaning "tawny" or "buffy," a reference to its color.
> SPANISH: *Búho leonado, lechuzón, lechuza, tecolote listado guatemalteco*
> MAYAN: *T'ukul* (Tzotzil, Chiapas)

DISTRIBUTION

BREEDING SEASON: Resident. Restricted to southern Mexico and northern Central America. Long known from the highlands of Chiapas, but specimens reportedly taken in 1942 in Totontepec, Oaxaca, had been discredited because of the unreliability of the collector's records. In 2009, however, Fulvous Owls were confirmed at Santa Maria Pápalo, Oaxaca, about 62 mi. (100 km) northwest of

Almost nothing is known about the Fulvous Owl, including definitive details about the nesting, diet, and behavior of this highland forest owl. *(Chiapas. Greg Lasley)*

Totontepec, and the following year in Cerro San Felipe in southern Oaxaca, roughly the same distance to the southeast. This suggests the Fulvous Owl may inhabit much of the Oaxacan highlands and, at a minimum, extends its range almost 220 mi. (350 km) to the northwest, well beyond the Isthmus of

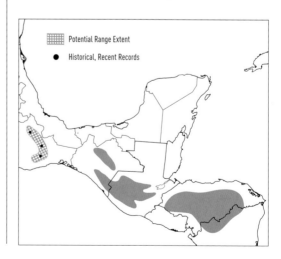

Potential Range Extent

Historical, Recent Records

Long assumed to occur only from Chiapas and northern Central America, the Fulvous Owl has recently been documented almost 220 mi. (350 km) to the northwest, in Oaxaca—evidence of how little is known about this mysterious owl. *(Guatemala. Knut Eisermann)*

Tehuantepec, which had been considered its northern limit.

MIGRATION AND MOVEMENTS: None known

POST-FLEDGING DISPERSAL: No information

DISTRIBUTION OUTSIDE THE COVERAGE AREA: South and east through Guatemala, Honduras, and El Salvador.

DESCRIPTION AND IDENTIFICATION

Similar in build, appearance, and general pattern to the larger Barred Owl, the Fulvous Owl has plumage infused with rich, rusty brown and tawny tones, especially noticeable on the undersides.

BASIC (ADULT) PLUMAGE: Sexes similar. Head and upperparts dark rusty brown, with tawny-buff or whitish barring on the head and upper back, spots becoming whitish on the lower back, scapulars, and upperwing coverts. Flight feathers dark brown above, grayish below, with light brown barring. Tail dark rusty brown with three or four buffy bars.

Facial disk gray to gray-brown, with a few indistinct dark concentric rings, and contrasting with the browner head. Facial disk ruff blackish and pronounced. Eyebrows and rictal bristles gray; brows indistinct. Underparts washed with tawny-buff, especially on the sides and upper chest. Like the Barred Owl, the upper chest has a band of horizontal dark brown barring, darkest along the lower margin. The belly is marked with tapered, vertical brown streaks, wider at the bottom than the top. Undertail coverts are unmarked. Irises dark brown, bill and toes light yellow.

JUVENAL PLUMAGE: Mesoptile down tawny-buff with indistinct barring, and darker facial disk.

SIMILAR SPECIES: Smaller and more richly colored than the grayer Barred Owl, with a tawny wash to the undersides and to the markings on the head, back, and wings. Vertical belly streaking in the Mexican Barred Owl is less tapered and blacker, and the contrast between the facial disk and the dark facial disk ruff is less pronounced in the Barred Owl. Mottled Owl is smaller, with a proportionately smaller head, heavily mottled upper chest, and solidly dark back with a broad whitish bar ("suspenders") along the edge of the scapulars, not the horizontal buff-white barring of the Fulvous Owl.

VOCALIZATIONS

Main call consists of five or six notes with a muted whooping quality, the first three or four notes bisyllabic and rapid, and the pace faltering toward the end. The final note is low and quiet, sometimes absent or inaudible: *a'woo a'WOO-WOO, a'WOO, WOO-ooo*. Both sexes give this call, and they duet in the manner of Barred Owls, but little is known about the behavioral context or other vocalizations in this species. It appears the female's voice is higher-pitched than the male's. A rising, two-noted scream has been recorded from what was presumed to be an adult female.

HABITAT AND NICHE

Fulvous Owls inhabit highland pine-oak, montane evergreen, and cloud forests, usually between 3,940 and 10,170 ft. (1,200 and 3,100 m). In Guatemala, they occur in cloud forests between 6,500 and 7,500 ft. (1,980 and 2,286 m) in the Sierra de las Minas, while in El Salvador they are found between 7,220 and 10,170 ft. (2,200 and 3,100 m), and in Honduras in cloud forests above 3,940 ft. (1,200 m). Beyond basic habitat and altitude information, little is known about their ecology.

DIET: Largely unknown. The Fulvous Owl reportedly feeds on small vertebrates (including mammals, birds, reptiles, and amphibians) as well as insects, but little field research has been published on its diet.

NESTING AND BREEDING

Largely unknown. It is said to nest in tree cavities, as do other *Strix,* and clutch size is reportedly 2 to 5 eggs, with chicks in May.

BEHAVIOR

Nocturnal and presumably a perch hunter like its relatives, but essentially unknown.

STATUS

As with most everything else related to this bird, the Fulvous Owl's status is poorly understood. It is listed as "least concern" with a decreasing population trend by IUCN/BirdLife and was ranked as uncommon throughout its range, with high sensitivity to disturbance, in a regional analysis of Neotropical birds.[1] Reported in "moderate" numbers at El Trufino, Chiapas, where up to seven have been heard calling in a small area. This is a species crying out for fieldwork, and it is hoped that the discovery of Fulvous Owls in Oaxaca, significantly extending its range, may prompt more research and attention.

NOTE

1. Stotz et al. 1996.

BIBLIOGRAPHY

Binford 1989.

BirdLife International. 2015. *Strix fulvescens.* In The IUCN Red List of Threatened Species, version 2014.3, http://www.iucnredlist.org/details/22689097/0.

Enríquez-Rocha, Rangel-Salazar, and Holt 1993.

Gómez-de Silva, H., F. Gonzalez-Gárcia, and M. P. Casillas-Trejo. 1999. Birds of the upper cloud forest of El Triunfo, Chiapas, Mexico. *Neotropical Ornithology* 10:1–26.

Land, H. C. 1962. A collection of birds from the Sierra de las Minas, Guatemala. *Wilson Bulletin* 74:267–283.

Monroe 1968.

Navarro-Sigüenza, A. G., and A. T. Peterson. 2007. *Strix fulvescens* (búho leonado) residencia permanente distribución potencial. In *Mapas de las Aves de México Basados en WWW,* ed. A. G. Navarro and A. T. Peterson. Final report, SNIB-CONABIO project no. CE015. México DF.

The Fulvous Owl is similar to the Barred Owl but somewhat smaller and more richly colored, with a tawny wash. The similarity between the two species may have masked the true extent of the Fulvous Owl's range. *(Guatemala. Knut Eisermann)*

Ramirez-Julían, R., F. González-García, and G. Reyes-Macedo. 2011. Record of the fulvous owl *Strix fulvescens* in the state of Oaxaca, Mexico. *Revista Mexicana de Biodiversidad* 82:727–730.

Ridgway 1914.

Serrano Gonzalez, R., F. Guerrero Martínez, and R. Serrano Velázquez. 2011. Animales medicinales y agoreros entre tzotziles y tojolabales. *Estudios Mesoamericanos* 11:29–42.

Stotz et al. 1996.

GREAT GRAY OWL
Strix nebulosa
Alpha code: GGOW

LENGTH: 25–33 in. (63.5–84 cm)

WINGSPAN: 54–60 in. (137–152 cm)

MASS: Average, male: 30.9 oz. (875 g); range 29–37 oz. (825–1,050 g). Average, female: 44 oz. (1,250 g); range 36–60 oz. (1,025–1,700 g).[1] Average, females only: 38.2 oz. (1,084 g).[2]

LONGEVITY: Average age of banded birds at re-encounter, 2.7 years. Longevity record, a bird banded in Alberta and hit by a car there at 18 years 9 months of age. Other notable records, 12 years 9 months (found dead, Alberta); 10 years 11 months (banded in Minnesota, retrapped and released in Manitoba); 5 years 6 months (banded and later hit by a vehicle in Manitoba).

The largest member of the genus *Strix* in the world, and the only member of its genus to occur across the Northern Hemisphere, the Great Gray Owl is, for most birders, a ghost from the north—huge, silent, and more than a little mysterious, appearing unexpectedly in irruptions that can number in the thousands.

In terms of overall size, this is the biggest owl in the Americas, standing almost 3 ft. (.83 m) tall, with a wingspan of up to 5 ft. (1.5 m). But all that size is mostly fluff; the Great Gray is the most extravagantly feathered owl in our region, and at its core is a body that weighs barely more than the heaviest Barred Owl. Great Horned Owls (especially the big northern races) and Snowy Owls both outweigh the Great Gray by a good bit.

Great Gray Owls are inhabitants of the boreal zone from central Canada west, and montane forests as far south as the Sierra Nevada, where a disjunct subspecies exists in small numbers.

SYSTEMATICS, TAXONOMY, AND ETYMOLOGY

The Great Gray Owl is traditionally divided into two subspecies: *S. n. lapponica* in Eurasia, and the slightly smaller, darker, more heavily mottled *S. n. nebulosa* occupying the entire North American range.

In 2014, however, the small Sierra Nevada population, centered on Yosemite National Park in California, was described as a new subspecies, *S. n. yosemitensis*, primarily on the basis of significant differences in mitochondrial and nuclear microsatellite DNA. Because of the small (roughly half a dozen) number of specimens available, the scientists involved were able to make only a preliminary assessment of how this new race differed from the nominate subspecies in appearance, but the Yosemite owls appear to be grayer, with a more muted facial disk pattern; young Yosemite birds may also have a brighter "necklace" of light feathers along the lower facial disk than *nebulosa,* but more study is needed. The molecular differences suggest the Sierra Nevada race split off from the main population about 26,700 years ago, with no evidence of gene flow since that time.

ETYMOLOGY: For the genus name, see "Spotted Owl." The specific name comes from the Latin *nebulosus,* "clouded," or "misty/foggy," a reference (as is the common name) to the gray, mottled plumage.
>   **FRENCH:** *Chouette lapone*
>   **IÑUPIATUN:** *Naataq*

DISTRIBUTION

BREEDING SEASON: *S. n. nebulosa:* Western Quebec and Ontario north to James and Hudson Bays; northern Minnesota (one recent breeding record from the Upper Peninsula of Michigan, and occasional nesting in northern Wisconson). Breeds in boreal forest zones of Manitoba, central and northern Saskatchewan, Alberta (absent from southeast and south-central), and British Columbia (absent from southwestern coast and islands). North through Yukon and Alaska (uncommon in coastal southeast) to the lower Mackenzie River and Brooks Range and west to the Yukon River valley. Western Washington into northeastern Oregon (Blue and Wallowa Mountains) and south through the Cascades to the northern edge of the Klamath Basin. Northern Idaho and western Montana south into northwestern Wyoming; very rare in the Bighorn Mountains. Occasional summer reports from northern Utah (Uinta Mountains). There are historical

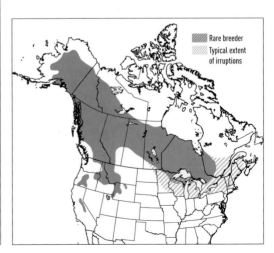

Rare breeder
Typical extent of irruptions

Though not the heaviest or most powerful owl, the Great Gray Owl is the most imposing in North America, standing up to 33 in. (84 cm) tall, with a 60-in. (152 cm) wingspan. Yet it's mostly fluff; a large Barred Owl weighs as much. (*Alberta. Gerrit Vyn*)

reports of extralimital breeding in Connecticut (1885), New Hampshire (1889), and southeastern Ontario (1911), presumably after winter irruptions.

S. v. yosemitensis: Central Sierra Nevada of California and bordering areas of west-central Nevada, from Plumas County, CA, in the north to Tulare County in the south. Found primarily on the western slope. Separated by the Klamath Basin from the most southerly population of *S. n. nebulosa* in the eastern Cascades. Generally found between 2,460 and 8,850 ft. (750 and 2,700 m).

NONBREEDING SEASON: Generally resident, but some irruptive migration, especially in the eastern half of its range, and altitudinal migration in the Sierra Nevadas. Irregular winter movements into the eastern Great Lakes, Saint Lawrence Valley and Canadian Maritimes, New England and New York, northern Michigan, Wisconsin, and, most notably, Minnesota (see "Migration and Movements," p. 240). Exceptionally, south to Pennsylvania (three records), Ohio (two records), Indiana (one 1890s record), Iowa (six or seven records), South Dakota (two records), Nebraska (one record from the winter of 1978–1979; several unconfirmed from the 1890s), northern Utah (nine records since 1949).

MIGRATION AND MOVEMENTS: Great Gray Owls in the Sierra Nevada population, recently described as a distinct subspecies (see "Systematics, Taxonomy, and Etymology," p. 238) are facultative altitudinal migrants in winter, moving to lower elevations only when deep or crusted snow seals off their prey at higher elevations. *S. n. nebulosa* in parts of the Cascades and Rockies also exhibit a variable degree of altitudinal migration, but for the most part stay fairly close to their breeding territories year-round.

Irruptive winter flights occur primarily from Manitoba east, with the main movement east-southeast rather than directly south, and generally remaining within about 300 mi. (500 km) of the southern edge of the normal breeding range. Some individual owls will move 450 to 500 mi. (about 700 to 800 km) between breeding and wintering sites.

With its circumboreal distribution, the Great Gray Owl is found from eastern Canada to Alaska, and across northern Eurasia. Irruptions involving Great Gray Owls, as with Northern Hawk Owls and Boreal Owls, are generally sparked by a collapse of prey populations on the breeding grounds. *(Ontario. Luke Seitz)*

Especially in the eastern half of its range, the Great Gray Owl is prone to major irruptions, such as one epic event in 2004–2005 that brought more than 5,000 of the huge owls to Minnesota. *(Minnesota. Paul Bannick/VIREO)*

Both the frequency and intensity of Great Gray Owl irruptions appear to be increasing, even accounting for the greater number of birders eagerly searching for these dramatic raptors. From the 1890s through the 1970s, irruptions usually involved reports of roughly 20 to 50 Great Gray Owls each time, spread out over southeastern Canada and the northern United States. In the late 1970s, however, flights of up to several hundred Great Grays began occurring regularly, including in 1977–1978, 1978–1979, 1983–1984, 1991–1992, 1995–1996, and 1996–1997.

By far the largest irruption ever recorded in North America occurred in 2004–2005, however, when thousands of Great Gray Owls spread out from Alberta to New England and as far south as Iowa. Many areas saw record numbers, including Quebec, where more than 600 were counted, and Ontario.

Minnesota was at the epicenter, though, with more than 5,200 Great Grays reported in that state, eclipsing the previous record of 394 owls just 4 years earlier. The Christmas Bird Count encompassing Sax-Zim Bog (a traditional hotspot for the species) tallied 70 of the big owls, a North American record, while later in the winter, one group of birders counted 256 Great Grays in just 100 mi. (161 km) of driving. More than 200 were found in the city limits of Duluth alone. Although a lifetime thrill for many humans, the irruption's toll on the owls was great; more than 830 were found dead, almost two-thirds from vehicle collisions. Necropsies showed that fewer than 10 percent starved to death.

Unlike Northern Saw-whet Owls (and, in many cases, Snowy Owls), whose major flights are the result of burgeoning prey supplies and a fruitful nesting season, Great Gray Owls perform true irruptions, driven by collapsing food resources. Small mammal populations in much of Alberta, Manitoba, and Ontario were at low or record low levels prior to the 2004–2005 irruption, and nesting success was low or nonexistent in some areas prior to the flight. The low number of starving owls in 2004–2005, however, suggests that the common belief that irrupting Great Grays are usually food-stressed may be false, or at least overstated.

No irruption has been as closely studied as this 2004–2005 event in Minnesota. The first migrants were detected as early as Aug., and lingering owls remained through the following summer. (Contrary to expectations, none stayed behind to breed outside of the normal range in northeastern Minnesota.) During the course of the winter, birders tracked significant and rapid movements of large numbers of Great Grays, apparently shifting en masse because of weather, snow conditions, and perhaps prey availability.

POST-FLEDGING DISPERSAL: Fairly limited information. In northeastern Oregon, juveniles dispersed an average of 10 to 18 mi. (16 to 29 km) within their first year. In the weeks after fledging, the chicks roost progressively higher and in sites progressively less accessible to predators, as they get older.

DISTRIBUTION OUTSIDE THE COVERAGE AREA: Eurasian boreal forests from Norway, Sweden, and Finland south to Poland and Ukraine, east across Russia to the Gulf of Anadyr in Siberia, and south to northern China, Mongolia, and Kazakhstan.

DESCRIPTION AND IDENTIFICATION

Immense, spellbinding, captivating—a Great Gray Owl, huge and regal, is able to transfix a viewer with its glowering yellow gaze. A Snowy Owl may outweigh this species, but no other owl has the Great Gray's sheer, breathtaking presence. The enormous head and long tail are unlike any other owl in our region.

BASIC (ADULT) PLUMAGE: Sexes similar, but females may average a little buffier and have a darker throat patch than males. Base color is pale silvery gray. Head and upperparts intricately mottled with dark gray, black, gray-brown, and white. Flight feathers and tail gray-brown (fading to brown with age), widely barred with paler, mottled grayish bands. Underwing coverts densely barred in dark gray-brown. Head proportionately huge; facial disk gray with pronounced concentric rings and distinct blackish brown ruff. Eyebrows and rictal bristles gray. Throat and lower margin of facial disk white

As with many owls, complete replacement of the flight feathers takes several years in Great Gray Owls, and older birds often show multiple annual generations of feathers—most obvious in the secondaries of this bird, likely in its second winter. *(Ontario. Tom Johnson)*

with black central chin spot, creating "bowtie" effect. Upper chest marked with broad, diffuse vertical grayish streaks; on lower chest, belly, and flanks, transverse barring on the streaks creates a mottled appearance. Legs and toes feathered, densely barred, and mottled in dark grayish. Eyes pale yellow, bill yellow to yellow-green.

A number of aberrant plumages have been recorded in Great Gray Owls, including "sooty" melanistic birds and leucistic individuals with very pale, washed-out plumage.

JUVENAL PLUMAGE: Natal down white. Mesoptile down grayish, barred with diffuse dark gray; facial disk dark gray marked with thin, contrasting white rim. Adult plumage emerges through mesoptile down beginning at about 30 days of age. First-winter owls show distinctly pointed tail feathers and have pale-tipped primaries, versus plain dark primaries in adults.

SIMILAR SPECIES: No other owl in the Western Hemisphere is larger or has such proportionately small, yellow eyes relative to the great size of its head. The Barred Owl is somewhat similar in general shape and color but is far smaller, with dark eyes and vertically streaked (not darkly mottled) undersides. The large northern races of the Great Horned Owl may be pale and grayish, and their ear tufts may be difficult to see at times, but even they are smaller than the Great Gray and lack its white "bowtie" collar below the throat.

VOCALIZATIONS

The territorial call is a string of deep, rhythmic hoots, often beginning or ending with a quieter note: *wu WUuu WUuu WUuu WUuu WUuu wuu,* at an interval of roughly 1 or 2 per second, generally lasting 6 to 8 seconds. As in most owls, the female is higher-pitched than the smaller male. Although the song sounds powerful at close range, it is a fairly quiet call, given the size of the owl, without a great deal of carrying strength.

Both sexes give a bisyllabic contact call at roughly 1-second intervals: *doo-it doo-it doo-it.* Pairs sometimes duet using the contact call.

Females give a somewhat nasal, ascending "whoop" call when soliciting food from the male: *yeeEET,* and either adult may give a chittering call

The fluffy tips of its mesoptile down cling to the emerging adultlike contour feathers on a young Great Gray Owl. *(Manitoba. Christian Artuso)*

A Great Gray Owl fledgling screams for food, giving its discordant, begging call: a sharp, ascending screech that drops abruptly at the end. *(Alberta. Gerrit Vyn)*

when delivering prey. The juvenile begging call is a sharp, ascending screech that drops abruptly at the end: *eeeeEEEE-eck*.

Typical of many owls, Great Grays use bill-snaps and hisses when agitated.

HABITAT AND NICHE

Great Grays are birds of the boreal zone, and while they aren't fussy about the composition of the forest they inhabit, they do require a very particular mix— stands of conifers or mixed woods interspersed with natural openings like bogs, muskeg, sedge meadows, and other wetlands in lowland areas, and montane meadows at higher elevations. The first nesting pair in Michigan used an area that was 60 percent tamarack, spruce, and red and jack pine, with a variety of wetland habitat and a large open upland nearby—a fairly typical mosaic for this species.

The exact forest communities Great Gray Owls use vary across the species's wide range. In Minnesota they tend to nest in damp hardwood stands of ash, elm, and basswood, while in Saskatchewan, black spruce and tamarack are the dominant species. Spruce and tamarack were also important in one Manitoba study, while researchers in western Manitoba and Alberta found that mixed stands of aspen, birch, spruce, and fir were most often used. Farther west, the owls chose Douglas-fir and lodgepole pine mixed with aspen in British Columbia, and white spruce and balsam poplar with oxbow meadows in Alaska.

In the Rockies, lodgepole pine, Douglas-fir, and aspen were found to be the most important trees in

nesting territories, while in the Cascades, Douglas-fir, grand fir, and lodgepole pine were most common. In the Sierra Nevada, Great Grays are found primarily in old-growth pine-fir forests (ponderosa pine, Douglas-fir, white fir, and sugar pine) or red fir forests, and (more rarely) in pine-oak stands at lower elevations.

The huge birds depend on open areas for hunting, however, and almost all nesting territories are within several hundred yards of grassy openings,

During the breeding season, Great Gray Owls are birds of coniferous or conifer-hardwood forests sprinkled with natural openings like bogs, meadows, and muskeg. In winter, they use a wider variety of habitats, including hardwood forests along the edges of fields. *(Ontario. Gerrit Vyn)*

With a freshly captured vole in its bill, a Great Gray flaps back to its perch on immense wings. These owls are small-mammal specialists, with meadow voles making up 80 percent of their diets on a continental scale. *(Manitoba. Christian Artuso)*

tact forest provided for the nests. They also hunt in open forests with dense grassy groundcover.

In winter, the owls seek out a similar mosaic of habitats but are somewhat more likely to be found in fairly open areas, away from dense forest cover. In the western mountains they may move downslope in search of thinner snowpack, sometimes into more hardwood-dominated areas.

DIET: Great Grays are mammal specialists, and despite their apparent large size (something of an illusion, thanks to their incredibly thick plumage), they stick mostly to small mammals, avoiding hares and other large prey that a Great Horned or Snowy Owl wouldn't hesitate to attack. Although there are records of them taking birds as big as Sharp-shinned Hawks, smaller owls, and Spruce Grouse, birds make up a very small percentage of their diet in most studies.

In the Sierra Nevada, Cascades, and northern Rockies, pocket gophers can be an important prey item; one study in Idaho and Wyoming found that they made up almost 60 percent of the diet, and in Oregon, they comprised more than two-thirds of the biomass. Pocket gophers are important to the Sierra Nevada population as well. But overall, voles—especially meadow voles—are the single most important prey item across the Great Gray

bogs, or meadows. In one study in the mountains of western Wyoming, eight out of ten Great Gray Owl calling locations were within 330 ft. (100 m) of a wet meadow, but a breeding-season study in Manitoba found that Great Grays actually avoided cleared areas, perhaps because of the greater security that in-

An adult Great Gray Owl delivers a pocket gopher—an important prey species in the western mountains—to its fledgling. *(Oregon. Paul Bannick/VIREO)*

Owl's range. By one estimate, meadow voles make up more than 80 percent of the owl's diet on a continental scale. Similar results have been reported from Eurasia, where voles make up some 90 percent of the owl's diet, with shrews comprising much of the rest. In Michigan, star-nosed moles—a wetland species—made up almost a quarter of one pair's diet, the remainder being mostly voles.

NESTING AND BREEDING

Generally monogamous; possibly polygynous in rare circumstances. Pair formation begins in earnest in late winter, with calling and courtship feeding of dead rodents by the male to the female, which begs and gives "whoop" calls. Young birds generally do not attempt to breed until their third year. Where prey is abundant, Great Gray Owls can nest in close proximity to one another, as near as a third of a mile (.5 km) apart.

Across most of their range, Great Gray Owls depend primarily on the old nests of large raptors and corvids, especially Red-tailed Hawks and Northern Goshawks, but also including American Crows and Broad-winged Hawks; the nests may be used for several years in a row but eventually fall apart. To a lesser extent Great Grays adopt broken-off snags in large trees, and the matted conifer branches known as "witches' brooms," caused by infestations of dwarf mistletoe.

The use of snag nests is rare in the northern portions of the Great Gray's range, and progressively more common to the south—as few as 1 in 20 nests in Canada, 1 to 2.5 in Oregon, and exclusively snags among the Sierra Nevada subspecies. Snag nests studied in the northern Rockies were more stable and productive than stick nests.

Well before the winter snow has begun to melt, the earliest females to nest are settling down on eggs. Incubation begins with the first egg, and clutch size varies with the local prey base; 2 or 3 eggs is average in California, and 3 elsewhere, but up to 5 eggs have been reported in rare cases. Average clutch size has been poorly studied in North America, but appears to be smaller than European averages.

The onset of egg-laying appears to be tied to snow depth, coming earlier in seasons and locations where the snowpack is thinner, and later where deep snow lingers. In Oregon, egg-laying takes place from mid-Mar. to mid-Apr., while the average first-egg date in the northern Rockies is May 5, with some as early as Apr. 19 or as late as May 23. A study of seven nests in Manitoba found that egg-laying occurred between Apr. 1 and 28. In Alberta, complete clutches have been reported by the end of Mar., but most egg-laying is complete by mid-Apr. Incubation begins with the first egg and lasts 30 or 31 days, with eggs laid at 2- to 4-day intervals, hatching asynchronously. The female broods the nestlings until they are about 3 weeks old, feeding the chicks while the male does all the hunting.

Fledging occurs at 26 to 30 days, even though the chicks can't fly for another 2 weeks or so. They scramble into the surrounding trees and shrubs, clambering with their feet, flailing wings, and gripping with their beaks, and often end up quite some distance from the nest. Most females eventually abandon care of the fledglings to the male.

Multiple clutches (up to three) have been reported in vole boom years in northern Eurasia.

BEHAVIOR

Great Gray Owls, like many northern species, are famously naive around humans. Birders and photographers can often approach them closely (sometimes too closely; an out-of-range Great Gray can attract thousands of birders over the course of a winter). Scientists have been known to catch them for banding by casting a toy mouse with a fishing rod, reeling in the owl—firmly grasping the mouse

Realizing that the ground isn't the safest place to be, a Great Gray Owl fledgling leaps back to the safety of the trees. (Oregon. Paul Bannick/VIREO)

Great Gray Owls usurp the nests of corvids and large raptors like goshawks, or use "witches' brooms," the matted branches of conifers infested with dwarf mistletoe, as in this case. *(Alaska. Paul Bannick/VIREO)*

ber of owls have asymmetrical ear openings, usually as a result of differences in the structure of the external ear, the bony ear openings in a Great Gray Owl's skull are dramatically asymmetrical. This allows pinpoint accuracy in locating the kind of quiet sounds a small mammal makes. This sharp hearing is further accentuated by the owl's enormous facial disk, the dense ruff of it serving to focus and concentrate sound waves, by some estimates increasing the sound reaching the ear openings tenfold.

The result is a raptor that can hear a vole or shrew moving under several feet of snow, and the reason Great Gray Owls can succeed in one of their most impressive hunting techniques—plunging feetfirst into deep, powdery drifts and coming up with dinner. It's not unusual for an owl to all but disappear beneath the snow—much like an Osprey going underwater for a fish—only to rise with a rodent in its feet.

As placid and approachable as Great Grays are most of the time, they have a well-deserved reputation for aggressively defending their nests, and more than one photographer and scientist have lost blood—and occasionally an eye—to the attack of a

The species name for the Great Gray Owl, *nebulosa,* means "clouded" or "foggy," a reference to its delicately mottled gray plumage. *(Wyoming. Kevin Loughlin/Wildside Nature Tours)*

the whole way back—then clapping a landing net over it.

Great Grays are significantly diurnal, especially during the northern summer when nights are short, but also during midwinter, making it all the easier to observe them. Some scientists have speculated that the proportionately small eyes in the Great Gray are a reflection of this more diurnal lifestyle, but most of the year they are primarily nocturnal. In both California and Sweden, Great Gray Owls call most actively an hour or two before midnight and again an hour or two after, with a significant drop-off in between.

Whether hunting in the dark or pursuing voles beneath a deep blanket of snow, Great Gray Owls depend on their extraordinary hearing. While a num-

When chasing prey hidden by darkness or beneath a thick cover of snow, a Great Gray Owl depends on its keen hearing. Its bony ear openings are asymmetrical, allowing for pinpoint accuracy, and the enormous facial disk focuses and concentrates sound waves. *(Ontario. Gerrit Vyn)*

Using its extraordinary hearing to detect the muffled sounds of a vole beneath the snowpack, a Great Gray Owl drops in for the kill. *(Ontario. Gerrit Vyn)*

furious adult owl. But sometimes guile works better than violence. The Great Gray Owl is one of the few owls that have been observed performing a distraction display, with the female (and sometimes both adults) feigning injury to lure an intruder away from the nest.

There is limited information about home range size in North America. The home ranges of adult Great Grays in Oregon averaged 26 sq. mi. (67.3 sq. km) but ranged from 1.5 to 120 sq. mi. (4 to 312 sq. km). Even when not irrupting, Great Gray Owls will move to areas with shallower snowpack; the Oregon birds moved an average maximum of about 8 mi. (13 km) in the nonbreeding season. Juveniles occupied extensive home ranges, averaging 60 sq. mi. (157 sq. km) in their first year, then appeared to settle down in their second, using much smaller ranges (average of 5 sq. mi. / 13 sq. km) in their second.

The difference between breeding and nonbreeding range is stark. In California, the summer home ranges of Great Gray Owls averaged 152 acres (61.5 hectares) for females and 49 acres (20 hectares) for males—but in winter, they were 9.5 sq. mi. (24.6 sq. km) and 8.2 sq. mi. (21.1 sq. km), respectively, a roughly tenfold increase.

STATUS

Although the Great Gray Owl occupies a wide range, its density is fairly thin on the landscape; Partners in Flight has estimated the North American population at about 31,000 birds. Although listed range-wide as "least concern" by IUCN/BirdLife, regional populations at the edges of its occurrence are of more significant concern. The owl is listed as "vulnerable" in Montana and "imperiled" in Wyoming.

The newly described Sierra Nevada subspecies, which probably numbers only 100 to 200 breeding adults, is listed as "endangered" by the state of California, and conservationists are concerned that continuing development of lower-elevation habitat, into which the owls move during winter, poses a growing threat. So do vehicle collisions and the risk from West Nile virus, to which Great Grays appear unusually sensitive. Inbreeding is also a concern with such a small population, if its numbers drop too low; given its genetically unique makeup, simply bringing in additional owls from other populations would be inappropriate.

To have the least effect on Great Gray Owls, forest management should mimic natural mosaic patterns with clear-cuts smaller than 25 acres (10 hectares). Preventing the loss of snags and large trees,

The rhythmic hoots of the Great Gray Owl may sound powerful at close range, but despite the bird's large size, the call has little carrying power. (Ontario. Gerrit Vyn)

which can provide nest sites, is especially important. Great Grays readily accept artificial nest platforms, suggesting that a lack of natural nest sites is a limiting factor even in many undisturbed areas. One successful design features a shallow, 18-by-24-in. (45-by-60-cm) box, 10 in. (25 cm) deep and sloping inward, mounted about 50 ft. (15 m) from the ground on the side of a tree. They will also use stick nests assembled by humans.

What effect climate change may have on boreal rodent populations—and thus the breeding success of Great Gray Owls—is unknown, but the better-studied European race may hold some clues. In northern Sweden, the number of voles has dropped with warming temperatures since the 1970s, along with a reduction in brood size among Great Gray Owls, especially at the low point in the 3-year vole cycle.

Paradoxically, however, the range of Great Gray Owls in Scandinavia and Europe has been expanding dramatically south and west. In part this reflects a recolonization of areas from which it had been extirpated, like Estonia, but they now breed in Poland and northern Ukraine, and some observers wonder if they will eventually reach the large conifer forests of Germany. Interestingly, similar southward expansions have not been seen in North America or Russia.

NOTES

1. E. L. Bull and J. R. Duncan. 1993. Great gray owl (*Strix nebulosa*). In *The Birds of North America*, no. 41, ed. A. Poole and F. Gill. Philadelphia: Academy of Natural Sciences, and Washington, DC: American Ornithologists' Union.

2. Craighead and Craighead 1956.

BIBLIOGRAPHY

Alaja, P., and H. Mikkola. 1997. Albinism in the great gray owl (*Strix nebulosa*) and other owls. In *Biology and Conservation of Owls of the Northern Hemisphere*, ed. J. R. Duncan, D. H. Johnson, and T. H. Nicholls. Saint Paul, MN: U.S. Forest Gen. Tech. Rep. NC-190.

Anderson and Clark 2002.

Blancher et al. 2013.

Bull, E. L., and M. G. Henjum. 1990. *Ecology of the Great Gray Owl*. Portland, OR: U.S. Forest Gen. Tech. Rep. PNW-GTR-265.

Canterbury, J. L., P. A. Johnsgard, and H.F. Downing. 2013. *Birds and Birding in Wyoming's Bighorn Mountains Region*. Lincoln, NE: Zea Books.

Cheveau et al. 2004.

Collins, K. M. 1980. "Aspects of the biology of the great gray owl, *Strix neulosa* Forster." MS thesis, University of Manitoba.

Great Gray Owls are widespread but uncommon, with an estimated North American population of only about 31,000 individuals. Land management that preserves a mosaic of habitats, and large trees for nesting, is critical for its protection. *(Ontario. Tom Johnson)*

Corace, R. G. III, B. Lundrigan, and P. Myers. 2006. Nest site habitat and prey use of a breeding pair of great gray owls in the Upper Peninsula of Michigan. *Passenger Pigeon* 68:353–360.

Duncan, J. R. 1997. Great gray owls (*Strix nebulosa nebulosa*) and forest management in North America: A review and recommendations. *Journal of Raptor Research* 31:160–166.

Eckert 2005.

Franklin, A. B. 1988. Breeding biology of the great gray owl in southeastern Idaho and northwestern Wyoming. *Condor* 90:689–696.

Hayward and Verner 1994.

Hertzel, A. X. 2006. The 2004–2005 influx of northern owls, part IV: Unusual coloration in great gray owls. *Loon* 78:3–11.

Hinam and Duncan 2002.

Hipkiss, T., O. Stefansson, and B. Hörnfeldt. 2008. Effect of cyclic and declining food supply on great grey owls in boreal Sweden. *Canadian Journal of Zoology* 86:1426–1431.

Hull, J. M., A. Englis Jr., J. R. Medley, E. P. Jepsen, J. R. Duncan, H. B. Ernest, and J. J. Keane. 2014. A new subspecies of great gray owl (*Strix nebulosa*) in the Sierra Nevada of California, U.S.A. *Journal of Raptor Research* 48:68–77.

Hull, J. M., J. J. Keane, W. K. Savage, S. A. Godwin, J. A. Shafer, E. P. Jepsen, R. Gerhardt, C. Stemer, and H. B. Ernest. 2010. Range-wide genetic differentiation among North American great gray owls (*Strix nebulosa*) reveals a distinct lineage restricted to the Sierra Nevada, California. *Molecular Phylogenetics and Evolution* 56:212–221.

Jepsen, E. P. B., J. J. Keane, and H. B. Ernest. 2011. Winter distribution and conservation status of the Sierra Nevada great gray owl. *Journal of Wildlife Management* 75:1678–1687.

Mikkola, H. 2014. Global warming and the great gray owl. *Tyto* 3:7–8.

Nero, R. W. 1980. *The Great Gray Owl*. Washington, DC: Smithsonian Institution.

Peeters 2007.

Pittaway, R., and J. Iron. 2005. Aging and variation of great gray owls. *Ontario Birds* 23:138–146.

Sears, C. L. 2006. "Assessing distribution, habitat suitability, and site occupancy of great gray owls (*Strix nebulosa*) in California." MS thesis, University of California, Davis.

Svingen, P. H., and J. W. Lind. 2005. The 2004–2005 influx of northern owls part II: Great gray owl. *Loon* 77:194–208.

Thogmartin, W. E., F. P. Howe, F. C. James, D. H. Johnson, E. T. Reed, J. R. Sauer, and F. R. Thompson III. 2006. A review of the population estimation approach of the North American Landbird Conservation Plan. *Auk* 123:892–904.

Van Riper, C. III, and J. van Wagtendonk. 2006. Home range characteristics of great gray owls in Yosemite National Park, California. *Journal of Raptor Research* 40:130–141.

Walker 1993.

Long-eared Owls inhabit two worlds—roosting and nesting in dense forests but hunting open meadows and marshes after dark. *(California. Matt Brady)*

LONG-EARED OWL
Asio otus
Alpha code: LEOW

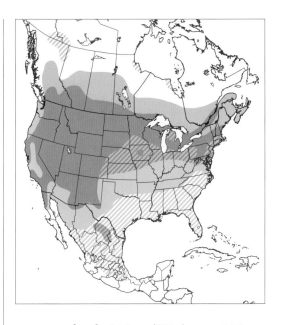

LENGTH: 14–16 in. (35–40 cm)

WINGSPAN: 35–40 in. (90–100 cm)

MASS: Weak reversed size dimorphism. Range-wide: Average, male: 8.6 oz. (245 g). Average, female: 9.8 oz. (279 g).[1]

A. o. wilsonianus: Minnesota (presumed *wilsonianus*): Average, unsexed adult migrants: 9.9 oz. (281 g); range 7.7–13.2 oz. (218–376 g).[2] Michigan (presumed *wilsonianus*): Average, male 9.2 oz. (261g); range 7.4–11.6 oz. (211–329 g). Average, female 10.9 oz. (309g); range 8.6–14 oz. (245–396 g).[3] Source region unspecified: Average, male: 8.6 oz. (245 g); range 6.3–11.1 oz. (178–314 g). Average, female: 9.8 oz. (279 g); range 7.4–12.1 oz. (210–342 g).[4]

A. o. tuftsi: Montana: Average, male: 9.2 oz. (261 g); range 7.9–10.7 oz. (223–304 g). Av-erage, female: 11.9 oz. (337 g); range 10.2–14.4 oz. (289–409 g).[2] Idaho: Average, male: 8.2 oz. (232 g); range 7.2–8.8 oz. (204–249 g). Average, female: 10.1 oz. (288 g); range 8.9–11.4 oz. (252–323 g).[2]

LONGEVITY: Average age at re-encounter for banded birds, 2.1 years. Longevity records, 12 years 1 month (an adult bird banded in New York and found dead in Ontario) and 9 years (an adult banded and later found dead in Ontario). A Long-eared Owl reportedly killed by another raptor in Nebraska, where it had been banded 15 years and 8 or 9 months earlier, lacks full details but appears to be valid. An analysis of 105 band encounters by Houston (2005) found 63 percent lived up to 1 year; 16 percent 1 to 2 years; 8 percent 2 to 3 years; and 8.6 percent from 3 to 7 years.

Slender and secretive, the Long-eared Owl leads a double life—hiding (and usually nesting) in dense forest, the habitat with which birders most often associate it, but doing almost all of its hunting under the cover of darkness in open meadows, marshes, sagebrush, and grassland, coursing back and forth like a harrier to hunt small mammals. Among the most heavily studied owls in Europe, the Long-eared Owl has received relatively scant attention from researchers in North America. The majority of studies here have focused on the winter diets of owls using communal roosts, aggregations that may total up to 100 birds.

Nowhere common, Long-eared Owls appear to be most secure in the western United States and Canada, while their range and abundance seem to have contracted, sometimes dramatically, in parts of the East, Midwest, and California. One of the

There are two weakly differentiated subspecies of Long-eared Owl in North America—the more richly pigmented *A. o. wilsonianus* found west through the Great Plains, and the paler and grayer *A. o. tuftsi* found farther west. (Manitoba. Christian Artuso)

biggest mysteries is its status and distribution (especially as a breeding bird) in Mexico. The Long-eared Owl's apparent nomadism further complicates its distribution picture, as it may irrupt into areas with high rodent populations, breed for a year or so, then disappear again.

SYSTEMATICS, TAXONOMY, AND ETYMOLOGY

Two subspecies are generally recognized in our region, but the plumage differences are clinal and size differences are minor, with the degree of apparent nomadism in this species further calling into question the validity of these two races.

- *A. o. wilsonianus:* Breeds from Nova Scotia west to Manitoba, and south through the central Appalachians and Oklahoma. Averages larger than *tuftsi,* darker and richer brown with indistinct tail barring.
- *A. o. tuftsi:* Breeds from southwestern Manitoba north to southern Yukon, and south to western Texas and northern Mexico. Smaller than *wilsonianus,* paler and grayer, with distinct tail barring.

ETYMOLOGY: The genus name *Asio,* like the specific name for the Eastern Screech-Owl, comes from the Latin writings of Pliny, meaning "a horned owl." Coues believed the derivation was originally Hebrew, of unknown meaning. The specific name

Long-eared Owl populations appear to have contracted dramatically in parts of the East, Midwest, and California, but the owl is difficult to detect, and its distribution is complicated by its habit of irrupting into areas with high rodent populations, breeding for a short while, and then vanishing again. (Manitoba. Christian Artuso)

is from the Greek *otos,* also meaning "a horned owl." (*Otus* was previously also the generic name for the screech-owls now in the genus *Megascops.*) The common name refers to the unusually long ear tufts.

SPANISH: *Búho cornudo caricafé, búho cara café, lechuza caricafé, lechuza barranquera*
FRENCH: *Hibou moyen-duc*

DISTRIBUTION

BREEDING SEASON: The Long-eared Owl is perhaps the most poorly understood of any North American owl, and its complex distribution is clouded by its extreme secretiveness, partial migratory behavior, apparently nomadic tendencies, and significant range contractions over many decades. Breeding birds may expand both north and south in response to rodent population crests, resulting in temporary range extensions. And they may simply be overlooked, especially because they call less insistently, and for a shorter period in spring, than most owls. In southern Quebec, where targeted surveys for vocal nestlings are conducted, the owls have proven to be fairly common (see "Status," p. 259). There is much to be learned about where this owl is found and when.

Breeds from Cape Breton Island and the Gaspé Peninsula west across southern Quebec, Ontario, and Manitoba (rare breeder, possibly irruptive along western James Bay and Cape Churchill), southern and central Saskatchewan, southern Alberta and British Columbia; rare and possibly irruptive to southwestern Northwest Territories (Fort Simpson) and southern Yukon. South through Pacific Northwest and California (largely absent from Central Valley; rare and local in southeastern deserts). Breeds (now rarely?) in northern Baja. Southern limits of normal breeding range extend through central Arizona and New Mexico, including the Madrean Sky Island ranges and possibly including northern Chihuahua and Sonora, and at least rarely into the Davis Mountains, Texas. North and east through Colorado, central Nebraska, central Iowa, southern Wisconsin, and Michigan, and in the central Appalachians into Pennsylvania and western Maryland. Largely absent from the Mid-Atlantic Piedmont and southern New England.

Irregularly detected and even more rarely confirmed breeding roughly from southeastern Colorado across lower Midwest into the Mid-Atlantic. A 1972 nest record in a pine forest in Nuevo León (plumage matching *wilsonianus*) suggests potentially wider breeding distribution in appropriate habitat in northern Mexico, but based on dates, almost all other Mexican records are likely wintering migrants.

Although Long-eared Owls are some of the most thoroughly studied raptors in Europe, they have received little attention in North America, and most of what is known about them relates to their diet. *(California. Gerrit Vyn)*

NONBREEDING SEASON: Winters regularly from southern Ontario and Quebec through the upper Midwest, South Dakota, and Montana into southern British Columbia, and south to northern Mexico (Baja, Sonora, Chihuahua, Coahuila), northern and western Texas, and Oklahoma, east across Arkansas, Tennessee, Virginia, and North Carolina. Irregular and rare south to Georgia, northern Florida, and the Gulf Coast, and in Mexico south to Oaxaca. One record of a Long-eared Owl 71 mi. (114 km) south of the Alabama coast in the Gulf of Mexico.

MIGRATION AND MOVEMENTS: The migratory ecology of Long-eared Owls is poorly understood but seems to include both regular migration and irruptive or nomadic movements. Owls from the northern edge of the range show a great deal of variation in their wintering areas, with some migrating deep into Mexico while others remain north to winter relatively close to their banding sites. Some birds in the western mountains show downslope movements in winter.

Among the more-unusual records is a Long-eared Owl banded in 1934 in California that was shot less than 6 months later in Ontario, 1,950 mi. (3,135 km) away. Others have moved in unexpected directions, including owls originally marked as nestlings that were recovered up to 997 mi. (1,605 km) north of their banding locations.

Long-eared Owls appear to be at least partially nomadic, moving into areas beyond their typical breeding range when prey numbers (especially cyclic vole populations) are at a peak, and may vanish almost completely from those areas when rodent numbers crash. Vole booms in Saskatchewan in 1960, 1969, and 1997 brought large numbers of nesting Long-eared Owls (along with Short-eared Owls and Northern Harriers), while virtually no Long-eared Owls were reported there in the low-vole years of 1970, 1979, 1981, 1982, and 1986. Banded Long-eared Owls have been found to move as much as 280 mi. (450 km) between breeding seasons.

Migration timing has been studied to any degree only in the Great Lakes region and near the Atlantic Coast, where large numbers concentrate. Netting data from New York suggest Long-eared Owls migrate most heavily early in the evening, with a secondary capture pulse just before dawn, perhaps as birds were seeking day roosts—but when the owls are netted is not necessarily when they are most actively migrating.

The complex migration of Long-eared Owls involves both regular migration and irruptive or nomadic movements in ways still not fully understood by researchers. *(Ontario. Gerrit Vyn)*

AUTUMN MIGRATION:

Immature owls appear to migrate earlier than adults, with peak flights in mid- and late Oct., respectively, in Minnesota, and Oct. and early Nov., respectively, in New Jersey. In Michigan, migration overall occurs from early Sept. to mid-Nov., with the peak in Oct.

SPRING MIGRATION:

A mist-netting study in New York found that northward migration took place primarily between mid-Mar. and mid-Apr. and was less weather-dependent than that of Northern Saw-whet Owls. Peak migration in Michigan generally occurs in mid-Apr. through mid-May but has peaked as early as the end of Mar. in some years.

POST-FLEDGING DISPERSAL: Very little information, perhaps because long-distance dispersal makes tracking tagged individuals difficult. In one study, tagged juveniles moved 45 to 52 mi. (73 to 84 km) from their nest site in a matter of days.

DISTRIBUTION OUTSIDE THE COVERAGE AREA: British Isles south to Morocco and east across Eurasia to Siberia (Sakhalin) and Japan, wintering south to Pakistan and southern China.

DESCRIPTION AND IDENTIFICATION

At a glance, a Long-eared Owl looks like a smaller version of a Great Horned Owl that's been stretched like taffy. A slender raptor under any circumstances, with especially prominent and very vertical ear tufts, a Long-eared Owl often assumes a cryptic posture when alarmed by an approaching human. Standing erect, compressing its plumage (including the bright rufous facial disk) and raising its tufts, the owl thus looks even more branchlike than usual. North American birds have yellow eyes, rufous facial disks, and dark underside markings, versus orange eyes, buff facial disks, and less prominent barring in Old World forms.

BASIC (ADULT) PLUMAGE: Description applies to *wilsonianus;* the western *tuftsi* is generally somewhat grayer. Sexes are similar; females tend to be darker, with tawny (versus silvery or pale buff) underwing coverts and more heavily streaked plumage than males.

Forehead and crown finely mottled black and white with buffy undertones; back and upperparts, including upperwing coverts, washed with tawny and intricately mottled with black, dark brown, and white. Scapular feathers broadly marked with off-white to buff, forming distinct bar along the top of the folded wing when perched. Primary feathers rufous with broad dark brown barring, which becomes more heavily mottled on the secondaries; when in flight, the unmarked rufous at the base of the primaries forms a noticeable pale patch. From below, flight feathers are tawny or silvery with neat dark barring, and it has unmarked underwing coverts. Dark carpal patch at the bend of each wing is present on both surfaces, but especially distinct on the underwing. Tail tawny at base, becoming gray, with 7 to 10 broad, dark gray bars.

Facial disk bright rufous, encircled by a salt-and-pepper ruff with heavy black patches at the lower corners. Rictal bristles, chin, and eyebrows gray-white and prominent. Throat mottled black. Ear tufts long and black, broadly edged with rufous and buff. Undersides buffy white to pale rufous. Upper chest indistinctly mottled with blackish brown, merging with dark vertical streaks and horizontal barring. Legs and feet feathered and buffy. Eyes yellow, bill black.

JUVENAL PLUMAGE: Natal down white. Mesoptile plumage, which replaces natal down by 14 days of age, is buffy or gray-buff with narrow, indistinct barring. Facial disk dark brown and distinctly narrower at the top than the bottom, which, with the small, incipient ear tufts (by 19 days of age) give the owl's head a distinctly triangular appearance. Flight feathers erupt from sheaths at 16 days. Eyes brownish. Juvenal plumage resembles that of adults, although downy feather tips may be retained into autumn.

SIMILAR SPECIES: Great Horned Owl is larger, bulkier, with more horizontal and widely placed ear tufts; often (depending on region) lacks the Long-eared's bright rufous facial disk. In flight, most closely resembles the Short-eared Owl in size, shape, and presence of dark carpal patches at the bends of the wings; the latter species is more dis-

tinctly marked above, versus the Long-eared Owl's more solidly grayish upperparts. The ear tufts of a Long-eared Owl are not easily visible when the owl is flying, but when it is perched, they are generally noticeable even when not fully erect. A flying Long-eared Owl can also be mistaken for a Barn Owl, which lacks the distinct carpal patch and is much lighter on the head and undersides.

HYBRIDS: One record of an apparent wild Long-eared × Short-eared Owl hybrid in Ontario, with almost exactly intermediate plumage and measurements.

VOCALIZATIONS

The male advertisement call is a prolonged series of deep, flat *hoos,* about 2.5 to 3 seconds apart, which have the hollow quality of someone blowing across the neck of a large bottle. Long-eared Owls sing for a fairly restricted period of spring—roughly the month of Apr. in Quebec.

The female's primary vocalization, known as a "nest call" (even though it is not always given at the nest), is a nasal bleat, like a short *toot* on a cheap kazoo; others have likened it to blowing through a comb wrapped in tissue paper. The juvenile begging call is a high, piercing screech, lasting about 1 second and falling off slightly in pitch at the end like a squeaking wheel. It is loud, carrying up to a mile on a quiet night.

The alarm call is a quick, slightly ascending bark, *wACK wACK wACK,* higher and faster in the female. As the agitation level increases, so does the duration, pitch, and intensity of the call, which becomes a drawn-out, catlike wail, usually punctuated with bill-popping.

Both sexes, although primarily males, make a loud, sharp snap by clapping the wings together in an exaggerated downstroke while in flight. This is often part of the male's zigzagging courtship flight, but it also accompanies threat displays and agitation calls when an intruder is near the nest.

HABITAT AND NICHE

Long-eared Owls are usually considered woodland raptors, but they actually depend on two very different suites of habitat—dense forest for roosting and nesting, and open grassland after dark, to hunt for the small rodents that make up almost all of their diet.

Beyond those basic requirements, the details don't seem to matter; one can find Long-eared Owls nesting in spruce forests in the northern Rockies, isolated woodlots and wooded hedgerows in the northern prairies, mixed conifer-hardwood stands in New England, pinyon-juniper woods in New Mexico, and stands of old-growth fir in the

Long-eared Owls often congregate in communal winter roosts of anywhere from 2 or 3 birds to nearly 100, usually in dense forest cover. (Pennsylvania. Howard Eskin)

stands mature and thin out, the owls may abandon them for thicker quarters—often about the time they become open enough for visiting humans to discover.)

Despite a relative paucity of records, it appears that in Mexico Long-eared Owls are found primarily in pine-oak habitat. Adults and one juvenile collected in Nuevo León were at about 9,000 ft. (2,743 m) in pastureland with pockets of sparse pine, yucca, and agave.

DIET: No other aspect of Long-eared Owl ecology has been as thoroughly studied in North America as their diet—although this is largely true of communal winter roosts, not during the breeding season. Every study paints the same picture, however: Long-eared Owls are small-mammal specialists, with voles and mice (notably *Peromyscus,* the deer and white-footed mice) making up more than 80 percent of their total prey. Voles are especially important, and in some local studies, they made up all but a few percent of the food eaten by Long-eared Owls. One researcher, pooling dozens of studies from across North America, found that meadow voles alone made up a quarter of the species's diet.

There are regional differences, of course, and although Long-eared Owls are more restricted in their diets than many raptors, they are opportunists and will take whatever small mammal is most readily available. In the West and Southwest, pocket mice, harvest mice, and kangaroo rats are often caught. An examination of pellets at communal roosts in Texas found that cotton rats, harvest mice, deer mice, and pygmy mice were the main prey, with the cotton rats providing 80 percent of the biomass.

Several studies from Kansas show how Long-eared Owl diets vary with the habitat—and how they don't always take what is most readily available. Deer mice, harvest mice, and prairie voles, all common in dry grassland habitat, made up almost 80 percent of the remains found in Long-eared Owl pellets from mixed-grass prairies in north-central Kansas. Hispid cotton rats, on the other hand, were the dominant prey found at an urban roost in Wichita.

Scientists studying a winter roost in native tallgrass prairie in eastern Kansas found that harvest mice comprised more than half of the diet of Long-eared Owls there—even though trapping showed they were far less common than deer mice, which made up three-quarters of the small-mammal population but only a quarter of the remains in the owl pellets. Prey choice may also vary seasonally. In Idaho Long-eareds took mostly deer mice and kangaroo rats in winter, voles in spring, and pocket mice in summer.

Northwest. Along the California coast they often nest in live oak or in blue oak–gray pine forests in the foothills, while in the Mojave Desert they seek out riparian corridors or the lonely pockets of trees around ranch houses. They'll hunt weedy old pastures, sagebrush flats, boggy meadows, desert grasslands, and marshes. Because they don't build their own nests, they need a local population of hawks or corvids whose old nests they can usurp.

Winter roosts in the East are almost always in thick conifer stands, often plantations, and shelterbelts of pine, spruce, or redcedar. In the West and Southwest the owls also use dense salt cedar (tamarisk), willow thickets, palo verde—any tree cover that provides the requisite density of vegetation. (Few birders appreciate the impenetrability of cover that Long-eared Owls often seek out for winter roosts—the kind of tangle that ensnares you in its thorny, vining, poison-ivy embrace. As such

Some European studies found Long-eared Owls taking a high percentage of birds, but avian prey is rare in North America. That said, the heaviest documented prey on record for this species were two Ruffed Grouse, likely killed by the same owl in Pennsylvania in the 1920s, which probably outweighed their attacker roughly two-to-one.

Most Long-eared Owls need 1.4 to 2.1 oz. (40 to 60 g) of food per day—roughly one to three small mammals, depending on what species they're catching.

NESTING AND BREEDING

Long-eared Owls appear to form new pair bonds each season. The males begin calling in late winter, often while part of communal roosts, performing a zigzagging display flight interspersed with wing-claps; they may duet, hooting with females that give the so-called "nest call." But major singing activity takes place in a fairly restricted period, peaking in Quebec in mid-Apr.

Long-eareds almost always take over old raptor, squirrel, and especially corvid nests, although they occasionally use cliff ledges, "witches' broom"

Long-eared Owls are not fussy about habitat and can be found nesting or roosting in mountain spruce forests, desert riparian woodlands, northern hardwood stands, coastal oaks in California, and shelterbelt thickets in the Plains. *(Ontario. Gerrit Vyn)*

mistletoe mats in conifers, and even more rarely will nest in cavities or directly on the ground. In much of the West, where the breeding ecology of this owl has been most carefully studied, stick nests from magpies, crows, and ravens are most commonly used. Of 130 nests in Idaho, for example, 91 were built by magpies and 38 by American Crows; in Alberta, 16 of 26 nests were built by magpies. Old Red-tailed, Red-shouldered, Broad-winged, Swainson's, and Cooper's Hawk nests are also commonly appropriated. In a few cases, biologists have found the eggs of the previous owner mixed with the owl's clutch.

Not only do Long-eared Owls winter in groups, they also sometimes nest in loose colonies, at times only a few dozen yards apart. DNA tests on chicks and adults in Montana found no evidence of extra-pair copulations, but the same researchers later documented a female that raised two broods with different mates in the same year. They also used DNA to detect a case in which a male who was related to the female but was not her mate was helping to bring food to the nest. The helper male may have been the nesting female's brother, or a son from a previous clutch.

The average clutch size is 4.5 eggs, but clutch size increases to the north and west of the owl's range, and in Alberta, the average is almost 5 eggs per nest. Egg-laying begins as early as Mar. 1 in California, peaking there in late Mar. and early Apr. In the Mid-Atlantic and New England, the peak period is mid-Mar. through mid-Apr., and early to mid-May in southeastern Canada. In central Alberta, egg-laying occurred from Apr. 11 to June 11, with the average date May 7. Incubation (by the female alone) begins with the first egg and lasts 26 to 28 days, with asynchronous hatching.

The chicks branch out of the nest at about 21 or 22 days of age, by which time they begin using concealment and threat postures, although they are not able to fly for another 2 weeks. Initially, brancher-stage chicks roost alone, high in trees, but once they are able to fly they roost lower and in groups. In the Alberta study, fledging took place from May 30 through July 30, with the average date June 25. In all, the chicks are dependent on the adults for about 11 weeks.

Almost nothing is known about the breeding ecology of the Long-eared Owl in Mexico. Outside of the small northern Baja population, apparently only one nest is known—a juvenile found in a cavity in a large yucca in Nuevo León in early May 1972, in pine-yucca forest at 9,000 ft. (2,743 m).

BEHAVIOR

Strictly nocturnal, except at the northern edges of its range, where long summer days and the demands of nestlings require some diurnal activity.

Wings flared in a threat display, a young Long-eared Owl tries to make itself as large and intimidating as possible. *(Washington. Paul Bannick/VIREO)*

Long-eared Owls can be remarkably tolerant of a close approach by humans, who generally encounter these raptors on their daytime roosts. Not that the owl is unconcerned; under such circumstances, a Long-eared Owl's usual response is to assume a cryptic, camouflaging posture and hope to be overlooked, remaining motionless even after its cover is blown.

In this posture—very straight and erect, usually turned side-on to the person—the owl's ear tufts are extended, its facial disk narrowed, and its body plumage compressed so that the whole bird may be only 3 or 4 in. (7.6 or 10 cm) in diameter—a reflection of how much of the Long-eared's apparent mass is feathers. An owl roosting well overhead may forego the concealment charade and simply glare at the person below.

Long-eared Owls often congregate in communal winter roosts of anywhere from 2 or 3 birds to nearly 100, although 5 to 30 is more typical. The roosts are usually close to good hunting locations, although it's not clear if the owls choose roost sites based on the degree of cover (and perhaps the thermal protection it offers), or proximity to prime hunting sites. Short-eared Owls have been known to join Long-eared Owl roosts, although only rarely and in small numbers.

Long-eared Owls are active hunters, coursing back and forth low over the ground in the man-

ner of other open-country raptors like Short-eared Owls, Northern Harriers, and Barn Owls. They are light, graceful, and somewhat mothlike on the wing, occasionally hovering. Possessing asymmetrical external ear openings, they appear to depend on sound to locate prey to a greater degree than, say, Great Horned Owls.

Adult Long-eared Owls are usually vocal but not highly aggressive near their nests, though they may take a swipe at the unprotected head of a biologist climbing up to band their chicks. This is one of the few raptors that performs a distraction display when a predator gets too close. A. C. Bent described a female Long-eared Owl that "dropped to the ground, as if wounded, and fluttered along, crying piteously or mewing like a cat; by this ruse, she succeeded in tolling my companion some distance away before she flew."[5] Mikkola described the same trick in the European subspecies: "The bird flies directly at the intruder and, when only three or four metres away, tumbles to the foot of the nest tree and beats its wings and legs feebly before dragging itself a metre or two, then flying off."[6]

Adults and juveniles both perform a dramatic threat display. Leaning forward and wailing its alarm call, the owl opens its wings, flaring the upper surfaces toward the intruder to create an enormous fan, its body feathers fluffed to maximum size and for maximum effect. One early naturalist described a Long-eared Owl in this display as looking like "some impish, malformed creature half beside itself with rage."[7] While juveniles of some other species (notably Great Horned, Short-eared, and Snowy Owls) flare their wings similarly when approached, few produce the same riveting, wholehearted spectacle as the Long-eared Owl.

There appears to be little, if any, fidelity to nesting sites in this owl, although they more often return to the same winter roost in successive years. Adults and juveniles both appear to make abrupt, long-distance movements from the nest area—the adult female first, while the male continues to provision the chicks, then the fledglings and the male. Radio-tagged owls in Idaho moved between 48 and 78 mi. (72 and 125 km) from sagebrush desert to forested mountains following nesting; others disap-

The concealment posture of the Long-eared Owl exaggerates this bird's already slender build. Compressing its feathers and raising its ear tufts, the nervous owl does not look much bigger than a tree branch. *(Quebec. C. Nadeau/VIREO)*

peared completely from a 59-sq.-mi. (150-sq.-km) study area.

There is little information about home range size in North America. In one of the few such studies, two female Long-eared Owls nesting in riparian cottonwoods in Idaho sagebrush desert rarely strayed outside 22-acre (8.8-hectare) grids that included the nests while the chicks were small, then more than doubled their activity range as the nestlings became more independent. Male activity ranges seemed to contract as the chicks aged, but most of the time the males were outside the limited area being monitored. In southern Quebec, Long-eared Owls have been found nesting at a rate of one pair per 2.7 to 7 sq. mi. (7 to 18 sq. km).

STATUS

The same secretiveness, apparent nomadism, and lack of information that clouds much of our understanding of the range and ecology of Long-eared Owls also makes assessing their status difficult. It seems clear, however, that this species has undergone significant range contractions since the early twentieth century, especially in the East, Midwest, and parts of California.

Although listed as "least concern," IUCN/Bird-Life believes the Long-eared Owl shows a declining population trend globally. While not listed federally in the United States, the Long-eared Owl has special status in more than a dozen states. It is listed as "endangered" or "critically imperiled" in Connecticut, Virginia, South Carolina, and Kentucky; "threatened" or "imperiled" in New Jersey, Pennsylvania, Michigan, and Arizona; "special concern" or a related rank in Vermont, Massachusetts, Rhode Island, Ohio, and California. Maryland lists it as possibly extirpated (although there is one recent nesting record from western Maryland), and Missouri lists it as unrankable because of lack of information. Long-eared Owls are not listed at the federal or provincial level in Canada or in Mexico. Partners in Flight estimates the owls' North American population at just 15,000, but notes that the confidence in that estimate is low.

Christmas Bird Counts, conducted every winter across the country, have shown steep declines in Long-eared Owl numbers in some regions. Breeding bird atlases, while not ideal for monitoring owl populations, also give some insight into the changing fortunes of the Long-eared Owl in states that have conducted multiple such surveys.

In Massachusetts, where this species was described as fairly common in the early twentieth century, it had by the 1980s contracted to a few locations, mostly on Cape Cod, and by the 2000s had essentially vanished from the state as a breeding species. In New York, the owl was widely but thinly

Because they call only for a short while early in the breeding season, Long-eared Owls are often overlooked by birders and scientists alike. One survey technique that has proven successful is listening instead for the harsh, grating cries of fledglings in late summer, which carry long distances at twilight. *(California. B. Steele/ VIREO)*

distributed in the 1980s, but two decades later had disappeared from many locales; blocks in which it was found in the Adirondacks dropped from 23 to 5, for example.

In Pennsylvania, where the Long-eared was already rare in the 1980s, 5 years of intensive owl surveys located just four breeding pairs in the 2000s, while only a single pair was found in Maryland. In Michigan, on the other hand, a decline in Long-eared Owls in the southern Lower Peninsula was somewhat offset by an increase in the Upper Peninsula.

Quebec offers an interesting contrast, however. There, birders have adopted a technique (common in Europe) of listening for the loud food-begging calls of nestlings, which carry up to a mile, instead of for adult hooting. Surveys are conducted shortly after dark in late July and early Aug., when the chicks are most vocal. Since the mid-1990s Long-eared Owls have proven to be common in areas of southern Quebec where damp spruce, tamarack, and mixed-wood forest is interspersed with pastures. (They appear rare in intensively cropped areas of the Saint Lawrence Valley, however.) Whether similar surveys elsewhere would produce the same results is an intriguing question.

At a continental scale, capture rates at banding stations in the upper Midwest suggest long, continuing declines in Long-eared Owl numbers mi-grating from Canada, while in much of the West, what little trend data there are suggest populations are fairly stable.

The reasons for regional declines are unclear. In California, the loss of up to 97 percent of riparian habitat in the Central Valley and southern coast undoubtedly underlie major population contractions there and may play a role more widely. In the Northeast, reforestation of open meadows, and conversion of grasslands to row crops, may rob the owls of foraging habitat.

No one knows if a lack of suitable nest sites may be a factor in some regional declines, but Long-eared Owls will accept artificial nest platforms, a technique that has been tried more widely in Europe. Long-eared Owls are known to be susceptible to West Nile virus, which may also reduce the population of corvids, whose nests they tend to use disproportionately. The threat from powerful new anticoagulant rodenticides is also unknown.

NOTES

1. Snyder and Wiley 1976.

2. J. S. Marks, D. L. Evans, and D. W. Holt. 1994. Long-eared owl (*Asio otus*). In *The Birds of North America*, no. 133, ed. A. Poole and F. Gill. Philadelphia: Academy of Natural Sciences, and Washington, DC: American Ornithologists' Union.

3. C. Neri and N. Mackentley, pers. comm.

4. Earhart and Johnson 1970.

5. Bent 1938, p. 162.

6. Mikkola 1983, p. 220.

7. W. Brewster. 1925. The birds of the Lake Umbagog region of Maine. *Bulletin of the Museum of Comparative Zoology at Harvard*, vol. 66, p. 369.

BIBLIOGRAPHY

Anderson and Clark 2002.

BirdLife International. 2015. *Asio otus.* The IUCN Red List of Threatened Species, version 2014.3 http://www.iucnredlist.org/details/22689507/0.

Birrer, S. 2009. Synthesis of 312 studies on the diet of the long-eared owl *Asio otus. Ardea* 97:615–624.

Blancher et al. 2013.

Coues 1882.

Craig, E. H., T. H. Craig, and L. R. Powers. 1988. Activity patterns and home-range use of nesting long-eared owls. *Wilson Bulletin* 100:204–213.

Duncan, R. A., L. Duncan, and L. Kaufmann. 2008. Long-eared owl in the western panhandle of Florida. *Florida Field Naturalist* 36:62–63.

Ellison, W. G. 2010. Long-eared owl *Asio otus.* In *2nd Atlas of the Breeding Birds of Maryland and the District of Columbia,* ed. W. G. Ellison. Baltimore: Johns Hopkins University Press.

Flesch, A. D. 2008. Distribution and status of breeding landbirds in northern Sonora Mexico. *Studies in Avian Biology* 37:28–45.

Gosselin, M., and K. Keyes. 2009. A long-eared owl × short-eared owl (*Asio otus × A. flammeus*) specimen from Ontario. *Ontario Birds* 27:23–29.

Holt, D. W. 1997. The long-eared owl (*Asio otus*) and forest management: A review of the literature. *Journal of Raptor Research* 31:175–186.

Houston, C. S. 2005. Long-eared owls, *Asio otus:* A review of North American banding. *Canadian Field-Naturalist* 119:395–402.

Howell et al. 2001.

Hubbard and Crossin 1974.

Hunting, K. 2008. Long-eared owl (*Asio otus*). In *California Bird Species of Special Concern.* Studies of Western Birds 1. Camarillo and Sacramento, CA: Western Field Ornithologists and California Department of Fish and Game.

Kaufman, D. W., G. A. Kaufman, and D. E. Brillhart. 2010. Small mammals as winter prey of long-eared owls in Kansas. *Transactions of the Kansas Academy of Science* 113:217–222.

Maccarone, A. D., and P. Janzen. 2005. Winter diet of long-eared owls (*Asio otus*) at an urban roost in Wichita, Kansas. *Transactions of the Kansas Academy of Science* 108:116–120.

Maples, M. T., D. W. Holt, and R. W. Campbell. 1995. Ground-nesting long-eared owls. *Wilson Bulletin* 107:563–565.

Marks, J. S. 1999. Genetic monogamy in long-eared owls. *Condor* 101:854–859.

Marks, J. S., J. L. Dickinson, and J. Haydock. 2002. Serial polyandry and alloparenting in long-eared owls. *Condor* 104:202–204.

Marti, C. D. 1976. A review of prey selection by the long-eared owl. *Condor* 78:331–336.

Medler, M. D. 2008. Long-eared owl *Asio otus.* In *The Second Atlas of Breeding Birds in New York State,* ed. K. J. McGowan and K. Corwin. Ithaca, NY: Cornell University Press.

Navarro-Sigüenza, A. G., and A. T. Peterson. 2007. *Asio otus* (búho cara café) residencia permanente distribución potencial. In *Mapas de las Aves de México Basados en WWW,* ed. A. G. Navarro and A. T. Peterson. Final report, SNIB-CONABIO project no. CE015. México DF.

Neri, C., and N. Mackentley. 2011. Long-eared owl. Michigan Breeding Bird Atlas II, http://www.mibirdatlas.org/Portals/12/MBA2010/LEOWaccount.pdf.

Nolan, R. L., T. C. Maxwell, and R. C. Dowler. 2013. Food habits of long-eared owls (*Asio otus*) at a winter communal roost in Texas. *Southwestern Naturalist* 58:245–247.

Peeters 2007.

Priestley, L. T., and C. Priestley. 2013. Long-eared owl nesting phenology and habitat in central Alberta. *Blue Jay* 71:124–131.

Savard, M., B. Dumont, and C. Girard. 1995. L'insaisissable hibou moyen-duc au grand jour. *Québec Oiseaux* 6:12–15.

Siedensticker, M. T., D. T. T. Flockhart, D. W. Holt, and K. Grya. 2006. Growth and plumage development of nestling long-eared owls. *Condor* 108:981–985.

Slack, R. S., and C. B. Slack. 1987. Spring migration of long-eared owls and northern saw-whet owls at Nine Mile Point, New York. *Wilson Bulletin* 99:480–485.

Sutton G. M. 1926. Long-eared owl capturing ruffed grouse. *Auk* 43:236–237.

Ulmschneider, H. 1990. "Post-nesting ecology of the long-eared owl (*Asio otus*) in southwestern Idaho." MS thesis, Boise State University.

Young, E. A., M. N. Harding, M. Rader, and L. Wilgers. 2005. Notes on food habits of wintering long-eared owls in north-central Kansas. *Kansas Ornithological Society Bulletin* 56:25–29.

STYGIAN OWL
Asio stygius
Alpha code: STOW

LENGTH: 16–18 in. (41–46 cm)

WINGSPAN: No information

MASS: Very limited information; degree of reversed size dimorphism unknown. Average of six individuals from Cuba and South America (both sexes): 19.9 oz. (565 g); range 14.4–23.8 oz. (408–675 g),[1] the largest being an *A. s. robustus* female from Colombia.[2]

LONGEVITY: No information

Striking and more than a little eerie, with its sooty plumage and dramatic tangerine eyes, the Stygian Owl resembles a wraith in more ways than one. Although found from Mexico to Argentina, as well as two islands in the Greater Antilles, it is nowhere common, and its presence is often more a case of rumor and conjecture than hard fact. Unlike the other members of its genus around the world, which are rodent specialists, the Stygian Owl appears to feed primarily on birds and bats. Most of the details of its life, including its breeding biology, are only slowly coming to light. Deforestation is a significant threat, and the Hispaniolan race is considered critically endangered.

SYSTEMATICS, TAXONOMY, AND ETYMOLOGY

Four subspecies are generally recognized in our region, although some authorities have questioned the validity of *lambi* and *noctipetens*:

A. s. lambi: Western Mexico from Sonora, Sinaloa, southwestern Chihuahua, and Du-

As black as their name implies, the Stygian Owls of northwestern Mexico, *A. s. lambi*, are especially sooty, as well as being larger than the other mainland and island populations. *(Sonora. Dean LaTray)*

rango to Jalisco. Larger and much darker than *robustus,* with blackish brown instead of chocolate brown markings, little or no mottling on back.

A. s. robustus: Veracruz and Guerrero through Oaxaca and Chiapas, south to Nicaragua and northwest South America. Smaller and browner than *lambi;* flanks and undertail coverts white with a faint buff wash.

A. s. noctipetens: Hispaniola (including Île de la Gonâve). Similarly dark to *lambi,* but with browner (not blackish) markings, and lower belly, flanks, and undertail coverts with bright buffy wash.

A. s. siguapa: Cuba (including Isla de Juventud / Isle of Pines). Grayer overall than *robustus* and *lambi,* with a paler facial disk and whiter markings.

ETYMOLOGY: For the genus name, see "Long-eared Owl." The specific and English names both come from the Latin *stygius*, "dismal," a reference to the blackish plumage.

SPANISH: *Búho cornudo oscuro, búho cara oscura, tecolote fusco, lechuza estigia, lechuza oscura* (Mexico); *siguapa* (Cuba and Dominican Republic); *cu-chi, la lechuza orejita* (Dominican Republic)

FRENCH: *Maître-bois, mèt bwa, chouette*

DISTRIBUTION

Widespread but with a highly disjunct distribution, the Stygian Owl is secretive, quiet, and (apparently) rare enough that the patchiness in its range could be genuine, but is more likely the result of having been missed in many areas. Recent discoveries at several sites in Tamaulipas and South Texas, for example, could represent a northward expansion, but a Tamaulipas record from 1911 suggests there has been a long-overlooked population in northeastern Mexico.

BREEDING SEASON: Resident

Mexico: Generally oak-pine and cloud forests. Vagrant to South Texas (two records, potentially the same individual). Based on habitat, distribution is likely to prove continuous from northern Sonora to Jalisco and Colima, and from Guerrero to Oaxaca, as well as east across the Transvolcanic Belt, and along the eastern Sierra Madre from Coahuila to Oaxaca.

Currently known from Sonora, southern Chihuahua, northeastern Sinaloa, and western Durango south through Guerrero and Oaxaca in the west, and in the east in central Tamaulipas and from Veracruz and Puebla to Oaxaca. Range in Chiapas uncertain except for extreme southern Chiapas on Guatemalan border. Breeding reports from Mexican Yucatán apparently in error, although present in southern Belize (Mountain Pine Ridge district). Opinions differ on whether Stygian Owls on Cozumel Island are casual visitors or residents, perhaps of the Caribbean race *noctipetens*.

Caribbean: Thick deciduous, semi-deciduous, and pine forests from sea level to mountain ridges. Hispaniola, including Île de la Gonâve, and Cuba, including Isla de la Juventud (Isle of Pines).

MIGRATION AND MOVEMENTS: None known. Vagrant to South Texas (two records, 1994 and 1996, potentially the same bird), possibly Cozumel.

POST-FLEDGING DISPERSAL: No information

DISTRIBUTION OUTSIDE THE COVERAGE AREA: Several disjunct populations: Central America from Guate-

mala and Belize to Nicaragua; the Andes from western Venezuela to northern Peru; and broadly across South America east of the Andes from southern Venezuela and northern Brazil to Bolivia, Paraguay, and northern Argentina.

DESCRIPTION AND IDENTIFICATION

Like a big, stocky Long-eared Owl dunked in soot. Prominent black ear tufts and silvery, spearhead-shaped forehead patch are diagnostic. Overall coloration blacker in western Mexico and Caribbean, browner in eastern Mexico.

BASIC (ADULT) PLUMAGE: Upperparts dark brown or blackish brown. Forehead and eyebrows freckled with white, creating a diamond-shaped patch above eyes. Head and upper back blackish brown, lightly to moderately mottled with buffy white; lower back, upperwing coverts, and dorsal surface of flight

Stygian Owls have a disjunct distribution across Central and South America, as well as several islands in the Caribbean. This is *A. s. siguapa*, the subspecies found on Cuba, which is grayer with a paler facial disk than the other races. *(Cuba. Rick Collins)*

feathers lightly to heavily mottled and barred with gray-white or buff-white. Scapulars lightly edged with gray-white or buff. Flight feathers indistinctly barred above, dark gray below with a few grayish bars; underwing coverts grayish with irregular dark mottling. Tail dark brown with gray-buff bars.

Facial disk sooty brown with black rim, with variably broad ruff of whitish speckles, and distinct triangular white markings on either side of the dark chin. Rictal bristles and eyebrows blackish. Ear tufts long, prominent, and black, with white inner edges. Upper chest heavily mottled in sooty brown. Underparts gray-white to tawny, with heavy blackish or dark brown vertical streaks and lateral barring. Iris yellow-orange, bill blackish. Eyeshine reddish orange.

JUVENAL PLUMAGE: Dusky brown to grayish (sometimes darker above than below) with narrow, distinct, dusky barring. Facial disk blackish, speckled with white, with small ear tufts. Eyes yellow, bill blue-black.

SIMILAR SPECIES: Larger and darker than Long-eared Owl, with blackish (not rufous) facial disk. Smaller, slimmer, and darker than Great Horned Owl, with closely spaced, vertical ear tufts.

VOCALIZATIONS

Varies regionally, but little is known about the vocal repertoire of the Stygian Owl or how vocal differences may align with subspecies divisions. Basic male call is a repeated, hollow *huu,* more sharp and forceful in Mexican birds than in the Belizean population, but in all areas soft and fairly quiet compared with most owls. Males produce sharp wing-claps in the manner of other *Asio* owls, likened to a small-caliber gunshot, both in courtship flights and as a threat display. Females give a high-pitched *neik* or screaming *quick, quick, quick,* sometimes duetting with males.

HABITAT AND NICHE

Usually considered a bird of thick, montane forests in our region, the Stygian Owl may be more flexible in its habitat requirements than generally acknowledged. It can be found from near sea level to mountaintops in both Mexico and the Caribbean, and the South American races inhabit a wide variety of lowland habitats.

Most records in Mexico are from cloud forests or oak-pine stands, generally between 4,820 and 9,850 ft. (1,500 and 3,000 m), but recent records in Tamaulipas have occurred as low as 1,060 ft. (325 m) in a heavily planted urban garden near some remnant forest, and in Texas in dry thorn-scrub forests just above sea level. In Chihuahua, Stygian

Stygian Owls are generally found in oak-pine and cloud forests on the mainland, and semi-deciduous and pine forests in the Caribbean. *(Sinaloa. Pete Morris)*

Owls have been found in oak-pine forests at about 5,600 ft. (1,700 m), while in northwestern Durango and northeastern Sinaloa, they have been collected between 6,000 and 6,500 ft. (1,828 and 1,981 m). There is a specimen record from Chiapas (Volcán Tacaná) that came from 10,000 ft. (3,050 m), but the record has been questioned.

The Belize population, the only one to be studied in any depth, is found from sea level to 2,625 ft. (800 m). Although primarily found roosting in montane pine forests, a radio-tagged male left the pine woods to hunt in broadleaf forest and farmland, suggesting greater habitat flexibility in that population.

On Hispaniola, where the Stygian Owl is critically endangered, it was reported in the past from pine forests, cacao plantations, and swampy forests at a variety of elevations. Wetmore and Swales (1931) reported that it roosted in wooded ravines and rain forests, and it hunted plantations and open pine forests. In Cuba, where it is somewhat more common, it is found in remnant semi-deciduous and pine forests from sea level to the mountains, using open areas and coastline when hunting.

DIET: Unlike all other *Asio* owls, the Stygian Owl appears to specialize in flying prey, especially birds but also bats, along with significant numbers of large insects, especially beetles.

In Belize, pellets collected from roosting adults yielded year-round totals of 62 percent birds, 19 percent bats, 12 percent beetles, and 6 percent lizards. Consumption of birds peaked at 81 percent during the first two-thirds of the dry season, from Nov. to Feb., when wintering songbirds were most common, dropping to 37 percent in June through Aug., when bats made up 32 percent of the owls' diet, and beetles 28 percent. Most birds taken were passerines, but a Least Bittern was also captured.

In Cuba, pellets collected from the subspecies *A. s. siguapa* contained only the bones of fruit- and flower-eating bats (61 percent) and birds (39 percent), the latter as large as White-crowned Pigeons. Pellets collected from three or four Stygian Owls in Brazil over the course of 2 years showed that birds (mostly finches) comprised 84 to 91 percent of the diet year-round, and bats 6 or 7 percent. Consumption of insects, mostly beetles and grasshoppers, peaked during the wet season at 9 percent.

NESTING AND BREEDING

Only a handful of nests of this species have been found anywhere in its range, and very few in our region. They appear to nest both on the ground and in stick nests in trees. In Cuba, 2 eggs were found in a ground scrape lined with a few scraps of palm leaves and placed in the middle of a clump of low palms. And in Belize, a nest with a single young was found on the ground in a large clump of ferns. Ground nests have also been found in Brazil.

On the other hand, a female was collected after flushing from a stick nest high in a pine in Chihuahua, and while the nest contained no eggs, an examination of the owl's gonads suggested she was close to laying. In Cuba, guides in the Zapata Swamp, where the Stygian Owl is modestly common, have observed it using tree nests as well as cavities. A nest, possibly from this owl, was found 15 to 20 ft. (4.5 to 6 m) up in a palm. Some authorities have suggested that Stygian Owls may sometimes build a nest themselves, which would be extraordinary, as no other owl in the world is known to build its own stick nest.

The nesting season in Cuba is reportedly Jan. to Apr., with one record from Dec. In Belize, an approximately two-week-old chick was found at the end of Mar., and the Hispaniolan race is believed to breed in Apr. and May. As many as three chicks have been found in a Brazilian nest, but the average clutch size, incubation period, and other details of its nesting and breeding remain a mystery.

BEHAVIOR

Nocturnal, so far as is known—which isn't very far, although the ongoing study in Belize should yield new insights. Stygian Owls roost in fairly dense cover, where they can be difficult to detect, but when found they are often trusting and easily approached.

In Cuba, males and females often roost close together, becoming active around dusk, leaving and returning to their roost sites together. Both members of the pair respond vocally to recordings of a Stygian Owl call, and the male makes wing-claps while in flight. Activity is greatest on dark-moon nights and limited on bright-moon evenings, with calling restricted to a few hours before dawn.

How a nocturnal raptor finds so many diurnal passerines is an intriguing question. Presumably they locate the smaller birds on their nighttime roosts, and such behavior targeting doves has been observed in Colombia. But the high proportion of bats in their diet paints a picture of a skilled aerial hunter. In Cuba, Stygian Owls are often observed flying straight up into the night sky from their perches, presumably in pursuit of bats or beetles, and it's possible that small birds are taken while

The recent discovery of Stygian Owls in Tamaulipas and southern Texas, as well as a 1911 record from the area, suggest there is a long-overlooked population of this rarely seen raptor in northeastern Mexico. *(Sinaloa. Pete Morris)*

active at dusk or dawn or when migrating at night. One radio-tagged male in Belize moved up to 9 mi. (15 km) from its roost site to hunting areas.

STATUS

It's hard to gauge the status of a bird so seldom observed and poorly studied. Estimates of abundance range from common to fairly common in northwestern Mexico, to rare in Veracruz and Belize, but sightings are so few and locations where it has been detected so widely scattered it is difficult to feel much confidence in such assessments.

IUCN/BirdLife ranks the Stygian Owl as "least concern" with a declining population, but it is listed as "threatened" in Mexico, with special protection. The populations at greatest risk are the two Caribbean subspecies. *A. s. noctipetens* on Hispaniola and Île de la Gonâve is critically endangered and appears restricted to a few ruggedly mountainous areas and protected forests on the northeast coast of the Dominican Republic; its status in Haiti is unknown. *A. s. siguapa* is found in low numbers at a few widely scattered locations in Cuba, where it is considered vulnerable.

Across its range, deforestation and habitat loss are the biggest threats, although the owl has been observed in managed, second-growth pine-oak forests in Chihuahua and may not be as dependent on mature pine forests as once assumed. In the Caribbean, habitat loss has been especially acute, compounded by the loss and extirpation of small mammals because of mongoose introductions. There is also a persistent rural belief, especially on Hispaniola, that Stygian Owls are witches that drink the blood of unbaptized babies, leaving the bird open to targeted persecution.

NOTES

1. Dunning 2007.

2. A. H. Miller. 1954. Supplementary data on the tropical avifauna of the arid upper Magdalena Valley of Colombia. *Auk* 69:450–457.

BIBLIOGRAPHY

Arizmendi, M. C., C. Rodríguez-Flores, C. Soberanes-González, and T. S. Schulenberg. 2010. Stygian Owl (*Asio stygius*), In Neotropical Birds Online, ed. T. S. Schulenberg. Ithaca, NY: Cornell Lab of Ornithology, http://neotropical.birds.cornell.edu/portal/species/overview?p_p_spp=214936.

Barbour, T. 1923. The birds of Cuba. *Memoirs of the Nuttall Ornithological Club* 6:1–145.

BirdLife International. 2015. Species factsheet: *Asio stygius*, http://www.birdlife.org/datazone/speciesfactsheet.php?id=2317.

Bond, J. 1942. Notes on the devil owl. *Auk* 59:308–309.

Cooksey, M. 1998. A pre-1996 North American record of stygian owl. *Field Notes* 52:265–266.

Dod, A. S. 1983. The stygian owl (*Asio stygius noctipetens*) in the Dominican Republic. *American Birds* 37:266–267.

Dunning 2007.

Franz, M. 1991. Field observations on the stygian owl *Asio stygius* in Belize, Central America (abstract). *Journal of Raptor Research* 25:163.

Kelso, L. 1934. A new stygian owl. *Auk* 51:522–523.

Kirkconnell, A., D. F. Stotz, and J. M. Shopland. 2005. *Cuba: Peninsula de Zapata.* Rapid Biological Inventories Report 07. Chicago: The Field Museum.

Kirkconnell, A., D. Weschler, and C. Bush. 1999. Notes on the stygian owl (*Asio stygius siguapa*) in Cuba. *El Piterre* 12:1–3.

Latta et al. 2006.

Lopes, L. E., R. Goes, S. Souza, and R. de Melo Ferreira. 2004. Observations on a nest of the stygian owl (*Asio stygius*) in the central Brazilian cerrado. *Ornithologica Neotropical* 15:423–427.

Marini, M. A., J. C. Motta-Junior, L. A. S. Vasconcellos, and R. B. Cavalcanti. 1997. Avian body masses from the Cerrado region of central Brazil. *Ornithologica Neotropical* 8:93–99.

Miller, A. M., and C. L. Chambers. 2007. Birds of harvested and unharvested pine-oak forests, Chihuahua, Mexico. *Southwestern Naturalist* 52:271–283.

Motta-Junior, J. C., and V. A. Taddei. 1992. Bats are prey of stygian owls in southeastern Brazil. *Journal of Raptor Research* 26:259–260.

Navarro-Sigüenza, A. G., and A. T. Peterson. 2007. *Asio stygius* (búho cara oscura) residencia permanente distribución potencial. In *Mapas de las Aves de México Basados en WWW,* ed. A. G. Navarro and A. T. Peterson. Final report, SNIB-CONABIO project no. CE015. México DF.

Phillips, R. 2011. Studying the stygian owl *Asio stygius robustus* in Mountain Pine Ridge, Belize. *Spizaetus* 12:2–6.

Rodríguez-Ruíz, E. R., and J. R. Herrera-Herrera. 2009. A un siglo del registro del búho cara oscura (*Asio stygius*) en el centro de Tamaulipas y notas sobre su distribución en México y los Estados Unidos de América. *Huitzil* 10:56–60.

Stager, K. F. 1954. Birds of the Barranca de Cobre region of southwestern Chihuahua, Mexico. *Condor* 56:21–32.

Wetmore and Swales 1931.

Wright, J. S., and P. C. Wright. 1997. Stygian owl in Texas. *Field Notes* 51:950–952.

SHORT-EARED OWL
Asio flammeus
Alpha code: SEOW

LENGTH: 14.5–15 in. (37–38 cm)

WINGSPAN: 36–39 in. (91.5–99 cm)

MASS: Continental population exhibits moderate reversed size dimorphism; there appears to be little gender difference in mass in the Caribbean populations.

> *A. f. flammeus:* Average, male: 11.1 oz. (315 g); range 7.25–13 oz. (206–368 g). Average, female: 13.4 oz. (378 g); range 10–16.75 oz. (284–475 g).[1] Incubating females (Montana): Average 14.5 oz. (412 g); range 11.75–19.5 oz. (333–553 g).[2]

> *A. f. domingensis:* Cuba: Average, male: 9.9 oz. (280 g); range 9.2–10.5 oz. (260–299 g). Average, female: 9.9 oz. (281 g); range 9.7–10.5 oz. (274–288 g).[3]

LONGEVITY: Limited information; fewer than 60 band recoveries in North America. Long-standing longevity record is 4 years 4 months, banded as a young bird in British Columbia and shot in California in 1970. Average age on re-encounter for banded birds, 1.1 years. In Europe, where the species has been more thoroughly studied, longevity in wild birds is known to exceed 12 years.

Pale as the dead prairie grass or winter marsh over which it flies, the Short-eared Owl is a spectral—and increasingly uncommon—presence over much

The ear tufts of a Short-eared Owl are normally hidden and invisible, unless it is agitated or nervous. *(New York. Gerrit Vyn)*

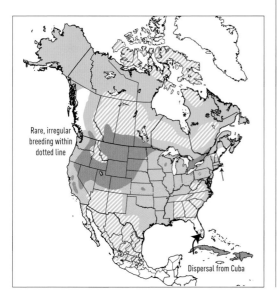

Rare, irregular breeding within dotted line

Dispersal from Cuba

of North America. More likely to hunt in daylight than all but a few other owls, it is often seen toward dusk, coursing low over grasslands, wetlands, or tundra in pursuit of meadow voles and other small mammals, which almost exclusively comprise its prey. The tiny ear tufts for which it is named are almost never visible, except at close range when the owl is agitated or alarmed.

The largest populations of Short-eared Owls nest in the Arctic and subarctic and in the remaining large tracts of prairie, shrub-steppe, and marsh in the West. In the East and Midwest, where healthy grasslands are all but gone, so is the Short-eared Owl, and it is listed as a species of conservation concern in more than half the states and provinces. The Caribbean population, on the other hand, has experienced a population boom in places like Cuba, and these Antillean birds now invade South Florida on a regular basis.

SYSTEMATICS, TAXONOMY, AND ETYMOLOGY

A powerful flier, the Short-eared Owl is one of the most widespread raptors in the world, with populations across most of the Northern Hemisphere,

The nominate race of the Short-eared Owl, *A. f. flammeus,* is the largest and palest of the Western Hemisphere subspecies and is the same subspecies found throughout Eurasia. *(Pennsylvania. Alan Richard)*

South America, and island groups as far-flung as Hawaii, the Galapagos, and Micronesia. Gene flow has maintained a single subspecies across the entire continental Holarctic region, but the taxonomy of the insular Caribbean forms is open for debate and clouded by confusing nomenclature. Two Caribbean subspecies are generally recognized, but the "Antillean" Short-eared Owl was originally considered specifically distinct and was lumped with the continental form without apparent justification in 1936. An argument has been put forward to restore full species rank, with separate subspecies in Puerto Rico and Cuba. What follows is the currently accepted taxonomy.

A. f. flammeus: The nominate race breeds across northern and western North America and winters south to the Gulf and (more rarely) into Mexico. The same subspecies is found in Eurasia (see "Distribution Outside the Coverage Area," p. 269). Largest and lightest-colored of the regional subspecies.

A. f. domingensis: Hispaniola and Cuba. Hoffman, Woolfenden, and Smith (1999) recommended subsuming *portoricensis* into this subspecies, while Garrido (2007) elevated this race (using the original spelling, *dominguensis*) to species level and described a new subspecies within it, *cubensis,* from Cuba.

A. f. portoricensis: Puerto Rico

Caribbean birds are significantly smaller than *A. f. flammeus,* with a larger tarsus and bill; darker and more heavily marked overall, with buffier underparts and little streaking on the lower chest and belly.

ETYMOLOGY: For the genus name, see "Long-eared Owl." The species name is Latin, *flammeus,* "flame-colored" or "fiery," a reference to the tawny tones in the plumage. The common name refers to the short ear tufts.

SPANISH: *Búho orejicorto, tecolote orejas cortas, mochuelo, lechuza llanera* (Mexico); *cárabo* (Cuba); *lechuza de sabana* (Dominican Republic)
FRENCH: *Hibou des marais; chat-haunt, chwèt savann* (Haiti)
IÑUPIATUN: *Nipaiḷuktaq*

DISTRIBUTION

As with its cousin the Long-eared Owl, the Short-eared Owl's distribution is complex, with irregular or irruptive breeding into areas with high rodent populations, followed by long absences, and a tendency to wander far in winter, appearing well beyond the normal core wintering range. There is considerable overlap between breeding and wintering areas in the middle latitudes of North America. It has undergone long-term declines in some areas—especially the Northeast and Midwest, where it now breeds very rarely and in widely scattered locations—

Some experts have argued that the Short-eared Owl subspecies of the Caribbean should be split into a distinct species, the "Antillean" (or "Arawak") Owl. The Caribbean birds are smaller, darker, and more heavily marked than the mainland race. *(Florida. Adrian Binns)*

As twilight falls, Short-eared Owls take to the air, coursing low over open country in search of voles and other small rodents, which make up almost their entire diet. *(Pennsylvania. Alan Richard)*

while the Caribbean population has undergone a major expansion (see "Status," p. 273).

BREEDING SEASON: From Newfoundland and Labrador across Canada and all of Alaska, although rare or absent in the boreal forest zone. Status in the Canadian Arctic unclear; generally absent from the Ungava Peninsula, but breeds north at least rarely to Bylot and Banks Islands. Southern edge of normal breeding range extends from the Maritimes and Saint Lawrence Valley along northern edge of the Great Lakes, northwestern Minnesota, and southwest through the central and western Dakotas, western Nebraska, Colorado, northern and central Utah, and Nevada to parts of California. Western extent of the regular breeding is central Oregon, Washington, and British Columbia.

Breeds in small and declining numbers, not always annually, in northern New England, New York, and Pennsylvania west through Ohio, Michigan, Illinois, Iowa, and Kansas.

In the Caribbean, "Antillean" Short-eared Owls are resident on Puerto Rico, Hispaniola (including Île de la Gonâve), and Cuba (including Isla de Juventud / Isle of Pines).

NONBREEDING SEASON: Found year-round (residents and northern migrants) from the Saint Lawrence Valley and southern Ontario west across the southern Canadian prairies to southern British Columbia, and south through the breeding range outlined above. Wintering individuals are found south to northern Florida and the Gulf Coast to central Texas, eastern New Mexico, Colorado, southern Utah, and Nevada, and much of California into northwestern Baja. Uncommon to exceptional in

Mexico as far south as Oaxaca, but more commonly in northwestern Mexico.

"Antillean" Short-eared Owls (sometimes dubbed "Arawak Short-eared Owls") are now almost annual vagrants to the Dry Tortugas and less frequently to the Keys, and several dozen have been reported in southern Florida, usually in spring and summer. The same race has also been reported in recent years in the Cayman Islands and on the northeastern coast of the Yucatán Peninsula. Given this species's rapid expansion throughout the Greater Antilles, it should be looked for more widely in the Caribbean basin.

MIGRATION AND MOVEMENTS: Very poorly understood for so widespread a species. Populations north of approximately 50°N latitude appear to be migratory, but details of regional wintering locations and migratory connectivity remain a mystery, and limited band returns and tracking studies suggest individuals from the same general breeding area may scatter widely in winter. Short-eared Owls satellite-tagged in Alaska, for example, wintered as far north as British Columbia, as far east as Kansas, and as far south as central Mexico. None of the owls subsequently returned to Alaska but remained in the northern Plains, echoing similar nomadic behavior documented in other individuals—and at odds with still other limited studies that found a degree of site fidelity. It seems likely that nomadism and fidelity are both strategies used by Short-eared Owls in different regions or under differing circumstances.

POST-FLEDGING DISPERSAL: Little information. A few individuals banded as nestlings have returned to their natal area in subsequent years, but long-distance movements in the post-fledging period have not been tracked.

DISTRIBUTION OUTSIDE THE COVERAGE AREA: Holarctic, from Iceland and the United Kingdom south to Spain, across northern and central Europe to Kamchatka and the Commander Islands in the north, and northeastern China in the south. Winters south to northern Africa and across mainland Asia. Also found in northeastern South America (Guyana and Venezuela), and from Colombia south along the Andean arc to Bolivia, and widely across the cone of southern South America. Island races (some perhaps warranting species status) are found on the Falkland Islands, Hawaii, the Galapagos, and Pohnpei Island in the Carolines.

DESCRIPTION AND IDENTIFICATION

A sandy-colored, heavily streaked owl with a round head (despite its namesake small ear tufts), usually seen at dusk coursing over marshes or grasslands

The dark carpal patch at the bend of the underwings, and the large, tawny patch on the upper surface of the primaries are good field marks for flying Short-eared Owls. *(Pennsylvania. Tom Johnson)*

with a buoyant, erratic, mothlike flight, gliding with wings held in a slight dihedral. Dark carpal patches at the bend of the wings, most noticeable from below, are shared with the darker, more heavily marked Long-eared Owl.

BASIC (ADULT) PLUMAGE: Males average grayer and less richly colored than females, with whitish (ver-

sus cream or buff) undersides and underwing coverts, but there is considerable overlap.

Description applies to *A. f. flammeus.* Ground color on head and upperparts, including wings, whitish to tawny, heavily streaked and mottled with brown. Primary coverts dark blackish brown above, forming carpal patch; primary feathers heavily barred near tips but unmarked toward base, creating a large buffy patch visible at rest and in flight. Tail cream to buff with five or six brownish bars (mottled heavily on central tail feathers). Below, wings are whitish to buffy, with distinct dark carpal patch and heavily marked outer primary tips. Inner primaries and secondaries are lightly barred on the outer third of the feathers.

Facial disk buffy to tawny, lightly and indistinctly streaked. Eyebrows, extensive rictal bristles, and chin whitish. Eyes starkly framed by blackish triangular markings, like smeared mascara. Facial ruff narrow and dark brown, with whitish inner band that often forms crescents at upper and lower margins. Ear tufts small, usually concealed unless the owl is nervous or agitated. Underparts whitish to tawny, upper chest mottled, and lower chest and belly lightly streaked. Eyes bright yellow, bill black, feet and toes fully feathered.

JUVENAL PLUMAGE: Natal down whitish to buffy. Mesoptile plumage buffy to grayish with fine, dusky barring. Adultlike contour feathers emerge while the

Pale ochre and buff, the Short-eared Owl blends in beautifully with the tundra, grassland, or marsh habitat where it is most commonly found. *(Alaska. Gerrit Vyn)*

chick wears a dramatic and unique facial pattern—a blackish facial disk with wide white crescents at the top and bottom and a white "mustache" and chin.

SIMILAR SPECIES: In flight, can be confused with Long-eared and Barn Owls. Long-eared is heavily mottled on the underside (versus lightly streaked on the belly), with more finely barred primaries, and flies with flatter wings. Barn Owl lacks dark carpal patches and dark primary barring on wings, and is generally unmarked white or cinnamon on undersides.

VOCALIZATIONS

Although male Short-eared Owls hoot during courtship activity, the vocalizations most often heard are bark calls, given year-round by both sexes in a variety of interactions. Barks are nasal and harsh and can be drawn-out, lasting up to 1 second (*eeee-YUURK!*) or short and abrupt, (*YEEarr* or *KEE-ow*) sometimes given in a rapid series: *rik-rik-rik-rik-rik-rik*.

Courtship flight includes bouts of 10 to 20 low, rapid hoots, at a rate of roughly 2 to 4 per second, given by the male. Hoots are often accompanied by loud, sharp wing-claps, often produced in remarkably quick succession as the male passes over or near the female, which responds with barks. The wing-clap, made on the downstroke of flight, can sound as sharp as a cracked whip at close range, but at a distance it more often resembles the sound of wooden blocks rattled together, or a flag snapping in the wind. Males may occasionally call from a perch, standing in a horizontal posture and bobbing the head slightly in time with the call. Wing-clapping is done in low-level flight when challenging an intruder, and high in the air during courtship flight.

Juveniles produce a thin scream that serves as a food-begging call, described by one naturalist as "a whistling, hissing noise, like escaping steam." Begging calls are often accompanied by wing-flapping, which (along with the dramatically contrasting facial pattern) may help the adults locate the widely scattered chicks.

HABITAT AND NICHE

An open-country raptor, the Short-eared Owl is a bird of grasslands, prairies, sagebrush steppes, marshes, and tundra in both summer and the non-breeding season. The Antillean races are likewise found in open habitat, especially fallow fields, abandoned sugarcane plantations, and pastures. They are small-mammal specialists, but will take significant numbers of songbirds and small seabirds, especially in coastal or island environments. The Short-eared Owl and Northern Harrier represent

Short-eared Owls and Northern Harriers are close ecological and behavioral analogs of each other, hunting and nesting in much the same grassland, marsh, and tundra habitat—and sometimes, as here, mixing it up over a freshly caught vole, which the harriers sometimes pirate. *(Pennsylvania. Tom Johnson)*

one of the closest nocturnal/diurnal analogs among raptors, closely mirroring each other's habitat, prey preferences, and even hunting behavior.

DIET: Small mammals—especially meadow voles—form the vast bulk of the Short-eared Owl's diet. In much of their continental range, vole cycles help determine where and to what degree Short-eared Owls successfully nest, as well as where they winter in significant numbers. One review of large dietary studies in the New World found that mammals made up 95 percent of prey remains in all but two studies, and meadow voles comprised 42 to 97 percent of the diet in each population.

That said, Short-eared Owls will take a wide variety of prey under some circumstances, from large insects to juvenile muskrats and cottontails. In shrub-steppe habitat in Idaho, nesting Short-eared Owls preyed primarily on pocket mice, deer mice, kangaroo rats, and mountain voles, with the proportion of prey varying from year to year. In California, nesting is closely tied to cycles in the population of the California vole. Short-eared Owls in coastal and island areas take a higher percentage of passerines, storm-petrels, terns, shorebirds, rails, and other small and medium-size birds. One notable inland exception was a nest described in 1899 in Wisconsin, from which the feathers of more than

50 species of birds were recovered and identified—and not a single bone from a mammal.

Overall (and as with Long-eared Owls), relatively little has been published about the breeding-season diets of these owls, compared with pellet collection at winter roosts, but voles appear to be the dominant prey during that season as well.

NESTING AND BREEDING

Nomadic and keyed to prey outbreaks, Short-eared Owls may nest near communal winter roosts (which are themselves the product of abundant food), or migrate long distances back to the Arctic and subarctic to breed. Attracted by vole outbreaks, they can nest in dense, semi-colonial concentrations of up to one nest per 14 acres (5.5 hectares).

So far as is known, pair bonds do not last through the winter. Males begin courting in late winter, as early as mid-Feb. in the Canadian prairies, performing one of the most dramatic display flights of any owl. Launching himself into the air near a perched or flying female, he flaps upward in tight spirals until he is several hundred feet above the ground, wing-clapping as he ascends, or while swooping toward the ground (see "Vocalizations," p. 271). He may hover briefly while hooting, and end his flight with a rapid descent, rocking back and forth with his wings in a dihedral, punctuated with still more wing-claps. The spirals and descents with wing-claps may be repeated several times, with display bouts lasting more than an hour.

(Sometimes two owls, both stooping and wing-clapping, will lock talons repeatedly and tumble to the ground. Although often construed as courtship behavior, this may also be an aggressive interaction between territorial males. Exaggerated wingbeats, with the wings brought high above the body, and hovering in front of an intruding owl, are also aggressive displays.)

The nest is usually little more than a flattened bowl amid dense marsh or grassland vegetation, sometimes lined with grasses and dead forbs, or with a few feathers; although modest by the efforts of most birds, the Short-eared Owl's nest is notable since this is among the only owls in the world to build any sort of nest at all (although the word "build" may overstate the effort). There are exceptional records of Short-eared Owls in Alaska using a shallow burrow, and a few records from North America and Europe of nests in low shrubs or stumps.

When prey is abundant, a female Short-eared Owl may lay up to 11 eggs, although the average clutch size is more typically 5 or 6, and increases slightly the farther north and west the nest is found. Hatching is asynchronous, with incubation lasting 21 to 31 days, an unusually wide range. The chicks grow rapidly and leave the nest at 12 to 14 days of age, scattering through the surrounding vegetation to foil mammalian predators. The adults will dive-bomb intruders, calling in agitation, and may perform a broken-wing act. Like their close relative the Long-eared Owl, Short-eared Owls (especially chicks) will fan their wings in a dramatic threat display.

Once the chicks can fly, the siblings often reassemble and roost together. In Idaho, a study of fledgling survival found that almost two-thirds of young owls died before leaving their natal territory, killed by mammalian predators, starvation, and vehicle collisions.

BEHAVIOR

Like all raptors nesting at high latitudes, Short-eared Owls are at least seasonally diurnal in their northernmost range, and they are more typically crepuscular overall than almost any other owl, often hunting in the very late afternoon and gathering dusk.

Short-eared Owls hunt much like Northern Harriers, quartering back and forth low to the ground, eyes and ears sharp for the movement of a vole or other small rodent. With their very low wing-loading, they are light and agile on the wing, often performing quick, twisting turns to drop on prey, hovering in a loose, floppy manner while waiting for a vole to reveal itself, or "kiting" motionlessly in the wind like a buteo. They rarely hunt more than about 9 ft. (3 m) above the ground. Short-eared Owl hunting success rates—the percentage of successful pounces—from several regions and times of the year, ranged from 11 to 29 percent.

Short-eareds roost communally in winter, occa-

A Short-eared Owl nest is usually no more than a flattened bowl among grasses or marsh vegetation. Typical clutch size is 5 or 6, but when voles are abundant, up to 11 eggs may be laid. (Manitoba. Christian Artuso)

Two Short-eared Owls, in the midst of diving and wing-clapping, may lock talons and tumble to the ground. This can be courtship between potential mates, or aggression between territorial males. *(Pennsylvania. Alan Richard)*

sionally with Long-eared Owls in trees, but more typically in single-species groups. They roost most often on the ground in high grass or marsh vegetation but may use low thickets or conifer plantations, especially in harsh or snowy weather, and sometimes on manmade structures like junked cars or large haystacks. Roost size usually peaks in midwinter, ranging from three or four birds to many dozens.

Although Short-eared Owls will roost communally, they do appear to defend winter hunting territories, and they often tangle with Northern Harriers as well as other owls. Home ranges studied during the breeding season varied from 25 to 202 acres (10 to 82 hectares). Territory size is especially fluid depending on prey abundance; in Manitoba average home range size was 182 acres (74 hectares) one season, and 524 acres (212 hectares) the following year. While winter roosts may be occupied for many years in a row, it is unknown whether or not the same birds return.

STATUS

Although still widespread, Short-eared Owls have experienced a prolonged and significant decline across most of their North American range in the past half century. Breeding Bird Survey data, while far from ideal for owls, suggest a range-wide decline since the mid-1960s, while Christmas Bird Count results indicate between a 50 and 80 percent drop since the late 1960s. Partners in Flight estimated the North American population at 500,000, of which three-fifths were in Canada, but noted that confidence in the estimate was low.

Although widespread, the mainland population of the Short-eared Owl has suffered a prolonged and significant decline across its range, especially in the East and Midwest. *(Alaska. Gerrit Vyn)*

The Caribbean population of Short-eared Owls has exploded in number and range, with some individuals routinely occurring in southern Florida and the Keys, where breeding is not out of the question. This bird was in the Dry Tortugas, west of the Florida Keys. *(Florida. Adrian Binns)*

The owl is listed in 26 states, including 12 in which it is considered "endangered" or "imperiled," but it is not federally listed in the United States. In Canada the Short-eared Owl is listed as a "special concern" species at the federal level, and six provinces also list it as "threatened," "vulnerable," or "special concern." Mexico includes it on the "special protection" list. Globally, Short-eared Owls are listed as "least concern," with a decreasing population trend by IUCN/BirdLife, but have been listed as highest conservation concern in Europe.

Several factors complicate Short-eared Owl con-

The last thing many a meadow vole ever sees—a Short-eared Owl about to drop. *(Manitoba. Christian Artuso)*

servation. Like many grassland specialists, this owl has suffered most seriously from the loss and degradation of large tracts of high-quality habitat, especially in the more southerly portions of its historic breeding range, where it is now extremely rare or extirpated. Its apparently highly nomadic nature, coupled with its reliance on cyclical vole population explosions to support concentrated breeding, was probably a very successful strategy when habitat was abundant, but it may be far less so now when options are vastly more limited.

The decline has been especially marked in the Northeast, Mid-Atlantic, and Midwest, where Short-eared Owls have all but vanished from many parts of their former range. In New Jersey, they once nested commonly in salt marsh habitat but had disappeared by 1979. In Massachusetts, the small population nesting on the outer islands in the 1970s had dwindled to 20 to 25 pairs by the 1980s, and by 2011 to just a few breeding birds on Tuckernuck Island off Nantucket. Breeding bird atlasers in New York confirmed the species in only four blocks between 2000 and 2005, with overall detections falling a third since the previous atlas in the 1980s.

In Pennsylvania the only historic nesting site, beside Philadelphia International Airport, was destroyed for a new cargo hub in 2005, but a few breeding attempts were documented on reclaimed strip mines in western Pennsylvania. The species was detected in a single block during 2006–2011 field work for Ohio's second atlas, and had vanished from its only location in Vermont by 2007.

In Illinois, nesting is erratic and unpredictable; no nesting attempts were detected from 1973 to 1990, and only two confirmed breeding pairs were found between 1997 and 2006.

While the continental population is of growing conservation concern, the Greater Antillean races appear to be stable or expanding. The endemic Puerto Rican subspecies, almost extinct by the mid-twentieth century as a result of habitat loss and nest predation by rats and mongooses, has responded to the abandonment of hundreds of thousands of acres of sugarcane fields after the 1960s, and now occupies lowland marsh and fallow savanna around the island.

In the Dominican Republic, Short-eared Owls are widely distributed in lowland and upland grasslands and pastures. (Its status in Haiti is unclear.) What had been a tiny remnant population in Cuba has undergone explosive growth, and Short-eared Owls are now found in every province of the country—the likely source of young, dispersing "Antillean" Short-eared Owls that now increasingly appear in Florida, where eventual breeding may be only a matter of time.

NOTES

1. Earhart and Johnson 1970.

2. D. A. Wiggins, D. W. Holt, and S. M. Leasure. 2006. Short-eared owl (*Asio flammeus*). In The Birds of North America Online, ed. A. Poole. Ithaca, NY: Cornell Lab of Ornithology, http://bna.birds.cornell.edu.bnaproxy.birds.cornell.edu/bna/species/062.

3. W. Hoffman, G. E. Woolfenden, and P. W. Smith. 1999. Antillean short-eared owls invade southern Florida. *Wilson Bulletin* 111:303–313.

4. L. Kumlien. 1899. Habits of young short-eared owls. *Osprey* 3:70.

BIBLIOGRAPHY

Andres, B. A. 2006. An Arctic-breeding bird survey on the northwestern Ungava Peninsula, Quebec. *Arctic* 59:311–318.

Barnés, V. Jr. 1947. Additions to the Puerto Rican avifauna with notes on little-known species. *Auk* 64:400–406.

Beske, A., and J. Champion. 1971. Prolific nesting of short-eared owls on Buena Vista Marsh. *Passenger Pigeon* 33:99–103.

Blancher et al. 2013.

Boom, T. L., G. L. Holroyd, M. A. Gahbauer, H. E. Trefry, D. A. Wiggins, D. W. Holt, J. A. Johnson, S. B. Lewis, M. D. Larson, K. L. Keyes, and S. Swengel. 2014. Assessing the status and conservation priorities of the short-eared owl in North America. *Journal of Wildlife Management* 78:1–7.

Clark and Mikkola 1989.

Clark, R. J. 1975. A field study of the short-eared owl, *Asio flammeus* (Pontoppidan), in North America. *Wildlife Monographs* 47:3–67.

Garrido, O. H. 2007. Subespecie nueva de *Asio dominguensis* para Cuba, con comentarios sobre *Asio flammeus* (Aves: Strigidae). *Solenodon* 6:70–78.

———. 1995. A preliminary review of the short-eared owl *Asio flammeus* complex in the Greater Antilles (abstract). *El Pitirre* 8:8.

Hamerstrom, F., F. Hamerstrom, and D. D. Berger. 1961. Nesting of short-eared owls in Wisconsin. *Passenger Pigeon* 23:46–48.

Holt, D. W. 1993. Trophic niche of Nearctic short-eared owls. *Wilson Bulletin* 105:497–503.

McAndrews, A. E., J. E. Montejo-Díaz, and M. Tabasco-Contreras. 2006. First confirmed record of the short-eared owl (*Asio flammeus*) for the state of Yucatan, Mexico. *Huitzil* 7:32–34.

Montejo-Díaz, J. E., A. E. McAndrews, and M. Tabasco-Contreras. 2009. Comments to López de Aquino and Garza de Léon (2008) on the short-eared owl (*Asio flammeus*) in the Yucatan. *Huitzil* 10:61–62.

Mowry, T. 2009. Biologists use satellite transmitters to track down winter homes of Alaska's short-eared owls. *Fairbanks Daily News-Miner*, Nov. 19, http://www.newsminer.com/features/outdoors/biologists-use-satellite-transmitters-to-track-down-winter-homes-of/article_a58fc91c-c61b-5118-a481-05ce4fb370f8.html.

Rivest, T. A. 1998. "Short-eared owl fledgling survival and breeding season diet." MS thesis, Utah State University.

Roberson, D. 2008. Short-eared owl (*Asio flammeus*). In *California Bird Species of Special Concern*, ed. W. D. Shuford and T. Gardali. Camarillo and Sacramento, CA: Western Field Ornithologists and California Department of Fish and Game.

de Schauensee, R. M. 1941. Rare and extinct birds in the collections of the Academy of Natural Sciences of Philadelphia. *Proceedings of the Academy of Natural Sciences of Philadelphia* 93:281–324.

Vukovich, M., and G. Ritchison. 2008. Foraging behavior of short-eared owls and northern harriers on a reclaimed surface mine in Kentucky. *Southeastern Naturalist* 7:1–10.

Walk, J. 2010. Status review and recovery outline for grassland raptors: Northern harrier *Circus cyaneus* and short-eared owl *Asio flammeus*. Illinois Endangered Species Protection Board, http://www.dnr.illinois.gov/ESPB/Documents/Recovery%20Docs/Status%20review%20criteria%20for%20n%20harrier%20and%20short-eared%20owl%20021910.pdf.

Wiggins, D. A. 2008. COSEWIC assessment and update report on the short-eared owl *Asio flammeus* in Canada. Committee on the Status of Endangered Wildlife in Canada.

Wiley 1986a.

Wiley 1986b.

A common Spanish name for the Striped Owl is *búho cara blanca*, "white-faced owl"—a succinct description of this poorly known but widely distributed species. *(Costa Rica. Chris Jimenez)*

STRIPED OWL
Pseudoscops clamator
Alpha code: STRO

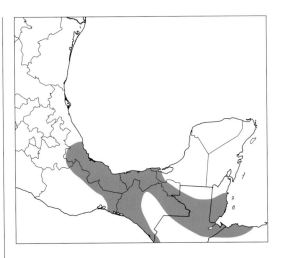

LENGTH: 13–15 in. (33–38 cm)

WINGSPAN: 31–38 in. (78–96.5 cm)

MASS: Strong reversed size dimorphism. Average, male: 14.3 oz. (406 g); range 12.25–17.1 oz. (347–485 g). Average, female: 17.1 oz. (484 g); range 14.1–19.25 oz. (400–546 g).[1]

LONGEVITY: No information on wild populations; up to 10 years in captivity.

A common Spanish name for the Striped Owl is *búho cara blanca*, "white-faced owl," which perfectly captures the most striking feature of this poorly known but widely distributed species. A lowland raptor found throughout Central and South America, the Striped Owl reaches its northern extent in extreme southeastern Mexico, where it inhabits old fields and pastures, savannahs, wetlands, scrubby woodlands, and other open country with scattered trees. It may be more common than usually assumed, based on the paucity of records away from heavily birded locations.

SYSTEMATICS, TAXONOMY, AND ETYMOLOGY

The Striped Owl has bounced around the strigid family tree over the years like a pinball. It was originally classified as *Bubo,* then later moved to the monotypic genus *Rhinoptynx.* In 1983 the AOU moved it to *Asio,* but currently classifies it with the

The Striped Owl has been shuffled around the family tree for years. It is currently classified with the Jamaican Owl in the genus *Pseudoscops*, but DNA suggests it belongs in *Asio*, where most experts place it. *(Costa Rica. Chris Jimenez)*

Jamaican Owl in *Pseudoscops*. Genetic data from Wink et al. (2009), however, placed it in a clade with three *Asio* owls (Long-eared, Short-eared, and African Marsh), although the Jamaican Owl, *Pseudoscops grammicus*, was not included in the analysis. Most authors classify the Striped Owl as an *Asio*, and the AOU South American classification committee has perhaps telegraphed its position by actively soliciting a proposal to move the Striped Owl back to *Asio*.

Four subspecies are generally recognized, only one of which is in our region: *P. c. forbesi*, the range of which extends into southern Central America. It is the smallest race and considerably paler than the nominate in northern South America, with much narrower black streaks, especially on the under-parts.

Striped Owl and Barn Owl have hybridized in captivity, but did not produce viable young.

ETYMOLOGY: The genus name is derived from the Greek *pseudo*, "false," and *skōps*, "a little eared owl." The specific name, *clamator*, is from the Latin *clamare*, "to shout," and also refers to an owl of ill omen in classical natural history. The English name refers to the striped underparts.

SPANISH: *Búho cara clara, búho cornudo cariblanco, búho cara blanca, lechuza cariblanco, tecolote gritón, búho listado*

DISTRIBUTION

BREEDING SEASON: Resident, as far as known. Found from central and southern Veracruz and northern Oaxaca to Chiapas and Tabasco, from sea level to 2,950 ft. (900 m).

MIGRATION AND MOVEMENTS: None known, although there is speculation that southern South American populations may migrate north into Amazonia.

POST-FLEDGING DISPERSAL: No information

DISTRIBUTION OUTSIDE THE COVERAGE AREA: Disjunct populations. Occurs from Belize and Guatemala south through southern Panama, and in South America south to northern Argentina and Uruguay, including both slopes of the Andes in Ecuador and Peru. Apparently rare or absent in the central and eastern Amazon basin, although its distribution in most areas is very poorly known and it may be expanding as a result of deforestation.

Although it is rarely observed, studies of the Striped Owl show it can be surprisingly diurnal. On the other hand, its asymmetrical ear openings suggest a dependence on sharp hearing—a trait common among highly nocturnal owls. *(Costa Rica. Nelson Mena)*

DESCRIPTION AND IDENTIFICATION

An arresting-looking, medium-size owl with creamy plumage, a stark white face with a black rim and large dark eyes, and long black ear tufts—a striking and unmistakable combination.

BASIC (ADULT) PLUMAGE: Sexes similar. Upperparts are cream to golden buff, mottled and densely vermiculated with brown; crown and back broadly streaked with black. Outer webbing of scapular feathers broadly white, forming pale "suspenders" above folded wings. Upperwing coverts mottled brown, buff, and white with broad central dark streaks. Upper surfaces of flight feathers and tail buff to cinnamon, lightly mottled with brown and barred with dark brown.

Facial disk creamy, tinged with buff and boldly rimmed in black. White eyebrows, contrasting with golden brown, heavily streaked forehead. Ric-

The dark facial disk and emergent ear tufts are field marks of the fledgling Striped Owl. (Costa Rica. Nelson Mena)

tal bristles white, chin white or buff. Ear tufts long, broad, and blackish with pale buff inner webbing. Underparts whitish to very pale buff, darker on flanks. Upper chest broadly blotched with blackish brown, lower chest and belly marked with distinct, narrow blackish brown streaks. Underwing coverts white to pale buff with sparse black spots. Legs and toes fully feathered, pale buff. Eyes dark brown, bill black.

JUVENAL PLUMAGE: Natal down white or gray-white. Mesoptile plumage pale buff, darker on the crown and back, developing indistinct, narrowing dusky barring above and contrastingly dark cinnamon facial disk and very short ear tufts, which appear at about 25 days of age. Eyes tawny-rufous.

SIMILAR SPECIES: The combination of white facial disk, dark eyes, and prominent ear tufts make the Striped Owl unlikely to be confused with any other owl in its range. Stygian Owl superficially resembles it in build and shape but is sooty and has a blackish facial disk and yellow eyes. Short-eared Owl (rare in its range and habitat) has yellow eyes and lacks prominent ear tufts.

VOCALIZATIONS

The main vocalization of both sexes is a low, hollow *huuOOOo,* subtly falling off at the end and sometimes given in a rapid pair. Males reportedly have a deeper call than females, as with most owls. Shorter *huu* notes may be given in rapid succession and in duets between a pair.

Adults give a thin, high squeal as a contact call; the contact or begging call of juveniles is a very high squeak, lasting .5 second or so, like an unoiled wheel that's been lightly bumped, or a slightly longer and descending squeal.

HABITAT AND NICHE

A lowland raptor of open woods, reverting farmland and scrub, savannahs, old pastures, grassy openings and river islands, forest light gaps, marshes and field edges, as well as some urban areas, the Striped Owl is found in a variety of open or early successional habitats and seems to avoid dense, unbroken forests. Some research suggests it uses savannah habitat for nesting and sparse woodland for hunting, but so little is known about this species that much more is just guesswork. Nor is much known about its diet.

DIET: Poorly understood, especially in Mexico and Central America. The limited number of pellet-based dietary studies in South America found that the bulk of the Striped Owl's diet was made up of rodents like rice rats and cane rats; small marsupials

Striped Owls are most often found in open or early successional habitats, using savannahs for nesting and open woodlands for hunting *(Costa Rica. Tom Johnson)*

like mouse opossums and rat-tailed opossums; and birds such as doves and woodpeckers. Interestingly, these owls consistently take larger prey—animals weighing more than 3.5 oz. (100 g)—than do similar-size owls, and a study in Brazil found that Striped Owls take prey of larger average size than

The diet of Striped Owls is poorly understood. Rodents, small marsupials, and—as here—birds like doves and woodpeckers make up most of their food. *(Costa Rica. Chris Jimenez)*

four other local species of owls, including the Stygian Owl, which is significantly heavier.

Frogs and insects were taken more frequently during the wet season in Brazil. Striped Owls in an urban environment in Colombia preyed on introduced rats and mice, cockroaches, and crickets, but took no birds, while a pair in a developed area of Brazil preyed heavily on Norway rats. The stomach of a female collected in Veracruz contained a small rodent and a large grasshopper.

NESTING AND BREEDING

Breeding throughout the Striped Owl's range appears to coincide with the dry season—Nov. to Apr. in Central America, Sept. to Nov. in Brazil. Nests with eggs have been found in Dec. in Panama and Jan. and Feb. in El Salvador.

Most Striped Owl nests are on the ground, in dense grass or under shrubs, usually just a small clearing or scrape in which the eggs were laid, sometimes with a tunnel-like entrance and overhanging vegetation. A nest found on a grassy river island in Panama, for instance, was described as "merely a beaten place in the grass on the ground,"[2] although others have been found with a lining of grasses and sticks. There have been reports of nests in palms, in forked tree trunks, and on layers of epiphytes on low branches, but this appears to be less common than ground nests.

Striped Owls usually nest on the ground, in dense grass or under shrubs. Normal clutch size is two or three, as in this case. *(Costa Rica. Nelson Mena)*

The normal clutch size is 2 or 3 eggs, with up to 4 reported in some cases, and 5 in captivity. Incubation is believed to be 30 to 33 days, with asynchronous hatching, although at a nest observed in Brazil, incubation was 28 days, with the male closely guarding the female. The chicks grow rapidly; they begin to assume a raised-wings threat posture at 8 days of age, at 20 days can leave the nest and exercise their wings, and by 26 days they leave the nest and hide in surrounding vegetation. Fledging takes place at about 35 to 38 days of age.

BEHAVIOR

Although usually described as nocturnal or crepuscular, studies of Striped Owls in Central and South America found a surprising degree of diurnal activity, including hunting and feeding chicks—surprising, in part, because this owl is rather seldom observed despite its wide range. Striped Owls hunt with a fluttering, erratic flight similar to that of a Short-eared Owl, often beginning before dark, or they ambush prey from a perch. They are often seen on roadside fenceposts or utility lines after dark. They have asymmetrical external ear structures, an indication of the importance of hearing in their hunting.

"These interesting owls are found in open areas of grass and marshland, where thickets and low trees offer shelter at need," ornithologist Alexander Wetmore wrote of Striped Owls in Panama. "I have seen them at sunset flying low over marshes, quartering the broad expanses of grasses and other floating vegetation. . . . In other areas I found them resting during the day on low perches, sometimes in lines of trees that separate open fields."[3] Other typical roost sites include dense shrubs, thickets, small woodlots, and conifer plantations. They form

Defending its nest, an adult Striped Owl performs a threat display with raised, open wings. *(Costa Rica. Nelson Mena)*

A Striped Owl finishes off a freshly caught bird, of which little but a dangling foot remains. Rodents are more typical prey. *(Costa Rica. Nelson Mena)*

communal roosts in the nonbreeding season, with a dozen or more birds at a single site.

STATUS

Local and rare to uncommon across most of its wide range, the Striped Owl is listed as "threatened" in Mexico, but no one has a clear idea of its true status. For example, it has been described as fairly common in Veracruz, but rare in the Chimalapas region of eastern Oaxaca, one of the most bird-diverse areas in Mexico, and it may well be more common than generally realized. IUCN/BirdLife lists it as "least concern" with a stable population trend, and widespread deforestation may actually be increasing its range, especially in areas like the central Amazon, where it was historically rare or absent in dense rain forests. Its ground-nesting habits place it at risk from humans and dogs, however, and pesticides and rodenticides pose an unknown threat.

NOTES

1. Dunning 2007.

2. F. A. Hartman. 1956. A nest of the striped horned owl. *Condor* 58:73.

3. Wetmore, Pasquier, and Olson 1968.

BIBLIOGRAPHY

Aguiar, K. M. O., and R. H. Naiff. 2009. Aspectos reprodutivos e dieta alimentar dos ninhegos de *Rhinoptynx clamator* (Aves: Strigidae) no campus Marco Zero da Universidade Federal do Amapá, Macapá-AP. *Acta Amazonica* 39:221–224.

Andrle 1967.

BirdLife International. 2015. *Asio clamator.* The IUCN Red List of Threatened Species, version 2014.3, http://www.iucnredlist.org/details/22689522/0.

Delgado-V., C. A., P. C. Pulgarín-R., and D. Calderón-F. 2005. Análisis de egagrópilas del búho rayado (*Asio clamator*) en la cuidad de Medellín. *Ornitología Colombiana* 3:100–103.

Enríquez-Rocha, P. L., and J. L. Rangel. 2008. Ficha téchnica de *Pseudoscops clamator.* In *Fichas Sobre las Especies de Aves Incluidas en el Proyecto de Norma Oficial Mexicana PROY-NOM-ECOL-2000,* pt. 2, ed. P. Escalante-Pliego. México DF: Instituto de Biologia, Universidad Nacional Autónoma de México.

Johnsgard 2002.

Lowery and Dalquest 1951.

Martínez, M. M., J. P. Isaach, and F. Donatti. 1996. Aspectos de la distribucion y biologia reproductiva de *Asio clamator* en la provincia de Buenos Aires, Argentina. *Ornitología Neotropical* 7:157–161.

Motta-Junior, J. C. 2006. Relações tróficas entre cinco Strigiformes simpátricas na região central do Estado de São Paulo, Brasil. *Revista Brasileira de Ornitologia* 14:359–377.

Motta-Junior, J. C., C. J. Rodrigues Alho, and S. C. Silva Belentani. 2004. Food habits of the striped owl *Asio clamator* in south-east Brazil. In *Raptors Worldwide: Proceedings of the VI World Conference on Birds of Prey and Owls,* ed. R. Chancellor and B.-U. Meyburg. Budapest, Hungary: World Working Group on Birds of Prey and Owls, MME BirdLife.

Navarro-Sigüenza, A. G., and A. T. Peterson. 2007. *Pseudoscops clamator* (búho cara clara) residencia permanente distribución potencial. In *Mapas de las Aves de México Basados en WWW,* ed. A. G. Navarro and A. T. Peterson. Final report, SNIB-CONABIO project no. CE015. México DF.

Olson, S. L. 1995. The genera of owls in the Asioninae. *Bulletin of the British Ornithological Club* 115:35–39.

Peterson et al. 2003.

Rudzik, S. M., F. J. Fernández, and J. D. Carrera. 2013. Taphonomic analysis of micromammal remains from striped owl (*Pseudoscops clamator*) pellets in northeastern Buenos Aires Province, Argentina: Implications for archaeological sites formation. *International Journal of Osteoarchaeology* DOI:10.1002/oa.2327.

Thurber, W. A., R. Lohnes, and T. S. Schulenberg. 2009. Striped Owl (*Pseudoscops clamator*), Neotropical Birds Online, ed. T.S. Schulenberg. Ithaca, NY: Cornell Lab of Ornithology. http://neotropical.birds.cornell.edu/portal/species/overview?p_p_spp=36400.

Wink et al. 2009.

JAMAICAN OWL
Pseudoscops grammicus
Alpha code: JAOW

Although fairly common in the woodlands of its island home, the Jamaican Owl is an almost complete mystery, with little concrete information about its diet, breeding ecology, or behavior. (*Jamaica. R. Nussbaumer/VIREO*)

LENGTH: 11–13 in. (28–33 cm)

WINGSPAN: No information

MASS: One specimen, unknown sex: 11.8 oz. (335 g).[1]

LONGEVITY: No information

Although not often encountered, this endemic owl is actually fairly common in most wooded environments on Jamaica, including around homes, farms, and towns. Even more than with many other insular and tropical owls, we have only the sketchiest idea of its basic ecology and biology, however, and while its population appears secure, owls in general on the island still suffer from persecution stemming from superstition—beliefs in ill omens and witchcraft that the Jamaican Owl's weird, otherworldly roar does little to counter.

SYSTEMATICS, TAXONOMY, AND ETYMOLOGY

Monotypic, endemic. If (as many authors contend) the Striped Owl is really a member of *Asio,* then the Jamaican Owl would be the only member of the genus *Pseudoscops.* But the Jamaican Owl was not included in recent molecular analyses, and its relationship with the Striped Owl (and with *Asio,* with which it was once classified) needs clarification.

ETYMOLOGY: For the genus name, see "Striped Owl." The specific name is from the Greek *grammikos,* "linear," and means "lined," or "lettered," a reference to its finely vermiculated plumage. The com-

mon name refers, of course, to this owl's home island.

    JAMAICAN PATOIS: *Patoo* (also applied to Barn Owl and to Common Potoo)

DISTRIBUTION

BREEDING SEASON: Resident on Jamaica. Most common in lower and middle elevations; rarer in mountains.

MIGRATION AND MOVEMENTS: None

POST-FLEDGING DISPERSAL: Unknown

DISTRIBUTION OUTSIDE THE COVERAGE AREA: None

DESCRIPTION AND IDENTIFICATION

A small to medium-size "eared" owl with tawny-brown, intricately vermiculated plumage and dark eyes, unmistakable in its range.

BASIC (ADULT) PLUMAGE: Sexes similar. Overall color rich tawny to cinnamon, more heavily marked with brown on the upper surfaces of the wings but with relatively little contrast. Crown, head, and upperparts with narrow brown streaks and dense brown-black vermiculation. Upper wing coverts with heavier vertical streaks and crossbarring, lightly mottled with buff and brown; primary coverts dark brown with indistinct markings. Tail with 8 to 10 narrow, dark bars and fine vermiculations.

Facial disk, eyebrows, and rictal bristles match overall ground color, with indistinct, slightly darker facial ruff edged with pale buff. Ear tufts moderately long, matching ground color with fine dark vermiculations. Underparts tawny to cinnamon, darkest on upper chest. Chest and belly marked with indistinct, blackish brown streaks, bordered with pale tawny or cinnamon, and with fine horizontal vermiculations. Underwings pale cinnamon, with contrastingly darker outer primary coverts. Undertail pale gray-brown with 8 to 10 narrow dark bars. Legs tawny to buff, unmarked; toes gray, bristled. Iris dark brown, bill gray or yellowish gray.

JUVENAL PLUMAGE: Natal down white. Mesoptile plumage tawny to gray-tawny with very faint dusky horizontal barring; facial disk dark chestnut, fading to tawny at top.

SIMILAR SPECIES: None within its island range. Barn Owl is structurally very different, largely white and lacks ear tufts.

VOCALIZATIONS

Vocal repertoire sketchily understood. Main calls are a coarse, breathy roar lasting about 1 second: *whaaARRrrhh,* and a higher, repeated *who-whooo who-whoo.* Female's voice reportedly lower than male's, which if true is the reverse of what is normal for most owls.

Juvenile begging call is a thin, high screech, sometimes slightly bisyllabic and ascending in pitch.

HABITAT AND NICHE

The Jamaican Owl occupies a variety of forest and edge habitats on the island and appears to be rare or absent only from the highest mountainous areas. Not infrequently found in backyards and gardens as well as field edges, woodlands, and parks. A generalist predator, it takes small mammals, reptiles, amphibians, insects, and at least some birds.

The weird, coarse roar of the Jamaican Owl is a common nocturnal sound in the forests and wooded neighborhoods of the island. *(Jamaica. Dominic Sherony)*

Jamaican Owls, like a number of Caribbean owl species, suffer from direct persecution based on superstition and folklore linking them to death, witchcraft, and the supernatural. *(Jamaica. Rick and Nora Bowers/VIREO)*

DIET: Poorly known. Based on scattered observations, a limited number of pellets, and the examination of a few birds' stomach contents, Jamaican Owls appear to take a variety of small vertebrate and invertebrate prey, but no attempt has been made to quantify their diet. Prey includes introduced black rats and house mice; perhaps bats; geckos, anoles, galliwasps, and other lizards, as well as frogs; crickets, katydids, beetles, and cockroaches; small terrestrial snails; and large spiders. The bones of a Greater Antillean Grackle were found in one pellet, and there are historic reports of them killing domestic Rock Pigeon squabs in dovecotes.

NESTING AND BREEDING

As with much else regarding the Jamaican Owl, its breeding biology is largely unknown. Normal clutch size is 1 or 2 eggs, and it nests in tree cavities, tangles of vines, in tree-trunk crotches, or on dense epiphyte mats on branches amid concealing vegetation. The breeding season appears to coincide with the dry season, roughly between Dec. and Apr., with downy fledglings encountered as late as July, but details are scant.

BEHAVIOR

Nocturnal. No information on hunting behavior. Daytime roosts are generally in dense cover that provides some shelter from midday sun.

STATUS

The Jamaican Owl is fairly common and widespread in lowland and middle elevations of Jamaica, but it is rare or absent from most high-elevation ridges and only infrequently encountered. IUCN/BirdLife lists the species as "least concern" with a decreasing population trend, but not a sufficiently rapid decline to qualify as "vulnerable."

A continuing threat to the Jamaican Owl (and to the island's populations of Barn Owls) is the widespread belief that owls are omens of death and ill fortune, or witches in disguise. Many rural Jamaicans take these beliefs seriously enough that they still routinely stone any owl they find, to such an extent that the national environmental agency has publicly pleaded with Jamaicans to leave the birds in peace.

NOTE

1. Dunning 2007.

BIBLIOGRAPHY

BirdLife International. 2015. *Pseudoscops grammicus*. In The IUCN Red List of Threatened Species, version 2014.3. http://www.iucnredlist.org/details/22689501/0.

Cory, C. B. 1886. The birds of the West Indies, including the Bahama Islands, the Greater and Lesser Antilles, excepting the islands of Tobago and Trinidad. *Auk* 3:454–472.

Cruz, A. 1972. Birds of the Lluidas Vale (Worthy Park) region, Jamaica. *Quarterly Journal of the Florida Academy of Sciences* 35:71–80.

Gosse, P. H. 1847. *The Birds of Jamaica*. London: John Van Voorst.

Graves, G. R. 2007. Prey remains of the Jamaican owl (*Pseudoscops grammicus*). *Journal of Caribbean Ornithology* 20:53–55.

Haynes-Sutton, A., A. Downer, and R. Sutton. 2009. *A Photographic Guide to the Birds of Jamaica*. London: Christopher Helm.

Jamaica Weekly. 2012. Environmental agency wants Jamaicans to stop stoning owls. April 1, http://www. jamaicans.com/news/weeknews/JAMAICANEWSWEEK-LYFortheweekendingApril6th2012-9.shtml.

Pregill, G. K., R. I. Crombie, D. W. Steadman, L. K. Gordon, F. W. Davis, and W. B. Hilgartner. 1991. Living and late Holocene fossil vertebrates, and the vegetation of the Cockpit Country, Jamaica. *Atoll Research Bulletin* 353:1–19.

Raffaele et al. 1998.

Scott, W. E. D. 1892. Observations on the birds of Jamaica, West Indies, II. A list of the birds recorded from the island, with annotations (continued). *Auk* 9:9–15.

Wiley 1986b.

BOREAL OWL
Aegolius funereus
Alpha code: BOOW

LENGTH: 8.25–11 in. (21–28 cm)

WINGSPAN: 21.5–24.5 in. (55–62 cm)

MASS: Strong reversed size dimorphism, second only to the Great Gray Owl among temperate and boreal species. Range-wide: Average, male: 3.6 oz. (101.6 g); range 3–4.2 oz. (85–119 g). Average, female: 4.9 oz. (139.5 g); range 4.3–5.6 oz. (121–160 g).[1] Idaho: Average, male: 4.1 oz. (117 g); range 3.3–4.9 oz. (93–139 g). Average, female: 5.9 oz. (167 g); range 4.6–7.6 oz. (132–215 g).[2]

LONGEVITY: Limited information, with fewer than three dozen re-encounters of banded Boreal Owls. Average age on re-encounter, 2.2 years. The longevity record for a wild Boreal Owl is a recently hatched male banded in Idaho and recaptured 8 years later. Average lifespan in the more intensely studied Eurasian population, 3.5 years.

Boreal owls are common, but only very rarely seen. Inhabiting some of the most remote forests and high mountains in North America, most of them likely spend their lives never encountering a human being—and even if a person does happen to pass close by, the owl's secretive nature means that most folks would walk right past a Boreal Owl sitting, quiet and hidden, among the concealing foliage of a spruce or fir.

So badly overlooked was this species that it wasn't until the latter decades of the twentieth century that ornithologists realized the Boreal Owl nests all the way down the spine of the Rocky Mountains

One of the biggest surprises of recent decades was the discovery that the Boreal Owl, once thought restricted to Canada and Alaska, nests as far south as northern New Mexico in the Rocky Mountains. *(Colorado. Bill Schmoker)*

as far south as northern New Mexico. At least one confirmed nest, and a few tantalizing sightings, show that it breeds at least occasionally in the mountains of New England as well, perhaps after major winter irruptions—another dramatic feature of this nomadic owl's unusual life history.

As with its close relative the Northern Saw-whet Owl, the Boreal Owl's juvenal plumage (carried into early autumn) is dramatically different than the adult's—the young owls being uniformly chocolate brown with a black facial disk and bold white eyebrows and rictal bristles.

SYSTEMATICS, TAXONOMY, AND ETYMOLOGY

The most northerly of the four members of the genus *Aegolius,* the Boreal Owl has seven commonly recognized subspecies, only one of which is found in North America: *A. f. richardsoni,* which is the darkest of the races. The Siberian subspecies *A.*

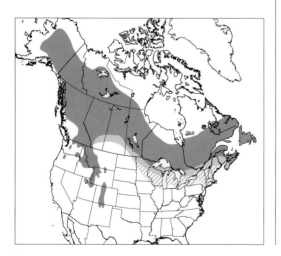

An adult Boreal Owl with a vole in its bill pauses before making a food delivery to its nest. *(Alaska. Paul Bannick/VIREO)*

f. magnus, among the largest and palest races, has been recorded as a vagrant in the Pribilofs.

Even though it is a small raptor dependent on mature forests and has a highly disjunct distribution south of Canada, the Boreal Owl population in North America has a remarkably uniform genetic structure. Scientists think this is a result of their nomadic movements and their ability to disperse across hundreds of miles, as between isolated mountain ranges in the sagebrush plains of Wyoming. Researchers did find significant genetic differences between North American and Eurasian populations, however.

ETYMOLOGY: *Aegolius* is Latin, derived from the Greek *aigolios,* "a bird of ill omen; owl." The specific name is Latin for "funereal," in owls usually a reference to both an unearthly call and the once-unsavory associations with the supernatural. The English name refers to the boreal (northern) forest in which it is found, although in Europe the English name is Tengmalm's Owl.

FRENCH: *Nyctale boréale*
IÑUPIATUN: *Takpiiḷaaġruk*

DISTRIBUTION

BREEDING SEASON: Resident, but nomadic and irruptive. From Newfoundland, southern Labrador, and the northern Maritimes west across central Quebec and Ontario (north to James Bay), along the north shores of Lakes Huron and Superior, including northeastern Minnesota. Northern extent mirrors the northern edge of the boreal zone through Manitoba, southwestern Nunavut, Northwest Territories (north to Great Bear Lake), across northern Yukon, and through interior Alaska south of the Brooks Range (absent from coastal areas and southwestern Alaska).

Southern extent of breeding range from southwestern Manitoba west across southern Saskatchewan, southeastern Alberta, and British Columbia (absent from coastal regions); Washington and Oregon (northern Cascades, Okanogan Highlands, Blue and Wallowa Mountains); northern and eastern Idaho, western and south-central Wyoming, and south through the highest elevations of central Colorado. Reaches the southern extent of its range in high spruce-fir forests of the Sangre de Cristo, San Juan, and Jemez Mountains of northern New Mexico.

The fact that Boreal Owls call very early in spring, when their high-country habitat is still snowbound, may mean that additional populations have yet to be found. Surveys in spruce-fir forests in northern Arizona and the Black Hills of North Dakota have failed to detect them, but the northern Sierra Nevada in California has been suggested as one loca-

tion with appropriate habitat where this species may have been overlooked. There are very rare summer records in New England as far south as Connecticut, including one confirmed breeding record from the White Mountains (Mount Pierce), New Hampshire, in 2001.

The North American and Siberian races have both been found on the Pribilof Islands, Alaska.

NONBREEDING SEASON: Irruptive movements in winter are cyclical and most pronounced from the Great Lakes east. Regular in winter south to the Saint Lawrence River valley, Maritimes, north shores of the Great Lakes, northern Michigan and Wisconsin, and northern Minnesota and northeastern North Dakota. Relatively little movement outside of the breeding range across western Canada, the Rockies,

As their name suggests, Boreal Owls are creatures of the northern coniferous forest, especially spruce, fir, and aspen stands. A single subspecies, *A. f. richardsoni,* is found in North America, from Alaska to Newfoundland. *(Ontario. Gerrit Vyn)*

and Pacific Northwest; some downslope movement into lower elevations in Alaska.

Irregular in winter in New England and New York. Exceptional (usually in heavy irruption years) as far south as New Jersey, Pennsylvania, Ohio, Illinois, Nebraska, and northern California (one heard-only record).

MIGRATION AND MOVEMENTS: As with several other northern owls, the Boreal Owl periodically irrupts south in winter—but unlike Great Gray and Northern Hawk Owls, whose irruptions occur rather erratically, Boreal Owls do so with metronomic regularity, at least in the eastern half of their range. Nomadism in the face of food shortages seems an integral part of their life history.

An analysis of more than three decades' worth of bird records in Quebec found that Boreal Owl irruptions occur there on a very regular, 4-year cycle—one that meshes neatly with the population cycle of red-backed voles in the eastern boreal forest. (Other small mammals in the region do not appear to have a predictable population cycle, making it likely that voles drive this phenomenon.)

Boreal Owl flights generally occur the year after a peak in small rodent populations, when vole numbers have crashed, and the irruptions are made up largely of adult birds that are often in poor physical condition. This hunger-driven movement is the opposite of that in the Boreal Owl's closest relative, the Northern Saw-whet Owl. Among saw-whets, heavy flights are made up largely of plump, well-conditioned juvenile birds, and they occur the same year as a vole peak—the result of a successful breeding season. Boreal Owl irruptions generally occur a year or two later, after the rodent collapse. Such irruptions took place in Quebec in 1996, 2000, and 2004, for example, in each case the year after a very heavy saw-whet flight.

As with Northern Hawk Owl and (particularly) the Great Gray Owl, which have similar continent-wide distributions, the Boreal Owl's irruptions tend to focus on the Great Lakes and Northeast, with limited winter movements into regions south of its western range. Why this is so is unclear, but it could be that the eastern boreal forest experiences more pronounced (or synchronized) rodent cycles, producing more dramatic irruptions—an intriguing, but as-yet-unproven, possibility.

Minnesota has seen some of the largest Boreal Owl irruptions south of Canada. Irruptions took place in the winters of 1995–1996 (214 owls recorded); 1996–1997 (263 owls); 2000–2001 (259 owls); and 2004–2005, the largest incursion on record, with roughly 600 Boreal Owls observed. That largest flight also coincided with a heavy Northern Hawk Owl irruption and by far the largest Great

Boreal Owls are reliably irruptive in the eastern half of their range, moving south into southern Canada and the northern borderlands of the United States every 4 years, when vole populations crash on the breeding grounds. *(Manitoba. Christian Artuso)*

Gray Owl flight ever documented. That year, the first Boreal Owl was seen in mid-Oct., and the last one in early Mar.

Given the limited banding data in North America, little is known about the degree and details of nomadism in the Boreal Owl in this hemisphere. Scientists in Scandinavia have found that females there are more nomadic than males, which tend to remain close to their breeding areas, and that northerly populations are more nomadic than those in central Europe. Molecular studies showing that even the most isolated Rocky Mountain populations exhibit little genetic difference from those in Canada, however, strongly suggest that nomadic behavior is common in North America, continually stirring the pot and spreading genes throughout the bird's range.

POST-FLEDGING DISPERSAL: Little information for North American subspecies. In Finland, juvenile females dispersed an average of 55 mi. (88 km) and up to 398 mi. (640 km), while juvenile males moved an average distance of 13 mi. (21 km) and up to 50 mi. (80 km).

DISTRIBUTION OUTSIDE THE COVERAGE AREA: Holarctic. From northern Scandinavia south to Spain, France, and Italy (Pyrenees and Alps) and east across Eurasia through Russia to northeastern Siberia and Kamchatka. Found south to northern Greece, Belarus, northern Turkey, the Caucauses, northern Kazakhstan, Mongolia, and central China.

DESCRIPTION AND IDENTIFICATION

A small, large-headed, tuftless owl with a whitish facial disk and prominent black ruff framing the face.

BASIC (ADULT) PLUMAGE: Sexes generally similar; female's facial disk tawnier, on average, than male's, but this is not a reliable characteristic.

Forehead and crown blackish, densely flecked with small white spots. Head brown with larger, more diffuse whitish spots, fading to whitish along rear edge of facial ruff. Back and upperparts brown with medium-size whitish spots, most pronounced on the scapulars but not forming distinct "suspenders." Upperwing coverts spotted with white;

The male Boreal Owl's call, given most frequently in late winter and early spring, is a powerful trill that can be heard up to a mile away. *(Manitoba. Christian Artuso)*

As with its close relative the Northern Saw-whet Owl, the juvenile Boreal Owl has a plumage that is dramatically different from the adult—chocolate brown with distinct white facial markings. *(Manitoba. Christian Artuso)*

flight feathers chocolate brown above, with white spots on outer webs of outer primaries, and much-reduced spots on inner primaries and secondaries.

Facial disk gray-white with broad blackish ruff speckled with small white spots; eyebrows white, rictal bristles grayish, chin black. Underparts white with broad, indistinct rust-brown streaks, merging in the upper chest. Eyes yellow, bill pale yellow-gray. Legs and toes fully feathered, mottled gray-brown. When alarmed, capable of creating an ear-tuft–like effect by elongating and erecting the upper ends of the facial disk ruff into triangular points.

JUVENAL PLUMAGE: Natal down white. Striking downy juvenal plumage, acquired at about 21 days of age, entirely dark chocolate brown with little contrast between underparts, head, back, and wing coverts. Facial disk blackish brown, eyebrows and lower face gray-white and initially indistinct, eventually forming a bold X shape. Flight feathers as adult—dark brown with fewer white spots on greater coverts; white spots forming on nape and scapular feathers. Juvenal plumage retained until late summer or early autumn.

SIMILAR SPECIES: Northern Saw-whet Owl is smaller but very similar; face is buffier, and it lacks distinc-

Similar to the more widespread Northern Saw-whet Owl, the Boreal Owl is larger, with a bold, distinct black ruff surrounding the whitish facial disk. *(Manitoba. Christian Artuso)*

tively bold black ruff. Juvenile Northern Saw-whet has buffy to chestnut belly and lower chest; white on face limited to eyebrows.

VOCALIZATIONS

The male advertisement song is a powerful, slightly musical trill of 10 to 20 rapidly repeated whistles, 7 to 8 notes per second and lasting 2 to 3 seconds, quickly increasing in volume but given at a steady pitch. The call has surprising carrying power and can be heard at ranges of more than a mile. Trills are generally repeated every 2 to 6 seconds, often for extended periods; Eurasian birds have been estimated to sing up to 4,000 times a night.

This primary staccato call is given by the male close to a potential nest site; a quieter, less-penetrating version, given when the female is near the cavity, may last 1.5 minutes or longer. Both sexes give a high, squeaky bark, *skiew,* and an ascending, metallic whistle: *mee-EEEik.* Both may function as agitation and contact calls. The juvenile begging call is a short, metallic squeak.

The Boreal Owl's song bears a striking resemblance to sound created by the winnowing display of the Wilson's Snipe. As the snipe dives, air flows through specialized tail feathers that vibrate, creating a weird, quavering *huhuhuhuhuhuhuhuhu.* Because Boreal Owls and snipe are often found in the same muskeg habitat, with snipe heard most frequently after dark, confusion can be an issue. The snipe's sound is hollow and somewhat slurred, usually rising in pitch and intensity before falling off at the end of the dive. The owl's song is crisper and more musical and is fairly steady or rises in pitch only slightly. If the sound is coming from high in the air, it's almost certainly a snipe.

HABITAT AND NICHE

Boreal Owls are, as their name suggests, creatures of the north—the sprawling, mature conifer forests of Canada and Alaska, as well as the high-elevation spruce-fir forests of the western mountains, where the highest peaks mimic the climatic conditions otherwise found far to the north. They feed on small mammals and birds, with voles—especially red-backed voles—making up the bulk of their diet almost wherever they are found.

Across the majority of its Canadian and Alaskan range, the Boreal Owl is most closely associated with black and white spruce, balsam fir, and poplar-aspen stands—a fairly uniform habitat suite, compared with the much wider variety of conifer and hardwood forests it uses in Eurasia. Even so, specific habitats can vary. In the Alaskan interior, for example, Boreal Owls may use mixed spruce-birch-poplar stands, quaking aspen in riparian areas, or pure black spruce forests in upland areas.

In Newfoundland, Boreal Owls were found to

avoid hardwood and mixed-wood habitats for nesting and hunting, but in northern Minnesota they breed in mixed-wood and aspen stands. In Montana, Idaho, and Wyoming, Boreal Owls occur almost exclusively in mature or old-growth stands of Engelmann spruce and subalpine fir above 4,240 ft. (1,292 m). In western Wyoming, they are restricted to elevations between 6,900 and 8,497 ft. (2,103 and 2,590 m) in fairly large, structurally complex spruce-fir stands, and they appear to avoid roads.

A study in Colorado found that Boreal Owls bred most successfully in Engelmann spruce, subalpine fir, and quaking aspen forests dotted with lakes and open meadows. In the mountains of New Mexico, at the southernmost extreme of their range, they are found above 10,000 ft. (3,048 m), again in Engelmann spruce and subalpine fir forests.

Boreal Owls show little difference between summer and winter habitat preferences. They are most common in mature and old-growth forests, although they can persist in younger or early successional forests, such as highly fragmented stands of young balsam fir in western Newfoundland. The Colorado study, however, found a preference for sites with fewer forest openings, fewer aspens, and significantly more old, mature spruce-fir forests— and the most productive Boreal Owl territories were those with the greatest amount of older forest, never less than half the area. Studies in Europe have also found that reproductive success in Boreal Owls increases with the age and size of forests.

DIET: Boreal Owls are vole specialists, although their diet shifts with the boom and bust of rodent populations, and they'll take a variety of small mammals and birds.

Although there have been more than two dozen major studies of the Boreal Owl's diet in Europe, there are only four comparable efforts in North America. But where their diet has been closely

A splash of blood on the snow below it marks a Boreal Owl's recent meal. Voles are the dominant food, but when vole cycles are near their ebb, birds, shrews, small hares and alternate prey take on greater importance. (*Minnesota. Chris Wood*)

studied—in Quebec, the northern Rockies, Alaska, and the Yukon—red-backed voles almost invariably top the list, sometimes comprising nearly 90 percent of the Boreal Owl's diet, with *Microtus* voles, like meadow voles, ranking second. In Quebec, heather voles in the genus *Phenacomys* were also important.

The proportion of each species can ebb and rise dramatically, however, as the vole cycle nears its peak, and alternative prey, like birds and shrews, increases when voles are scarce. In the Yukon, voles made up more than 80 percent of the Boreal Owl's diet one year but dropped to less than 10 percent the following year, when shrews—an odiferous group often shunned by raptors—comprised 73 percent of the hungry owls' diet. They also took more young snowshoe hares when voles were scarce.

Other less commonly taken prey include jumping mice, deer mice, pocket gophers, flying squirrels, shrews, small snowshoe hares, along with a variety of small and midsize passerines, like thrushes, sparrows, finches, and woodpeckers.

NESTING AND BREEDING

Pair bonds last only a single season—a necessity in such a nomadic species—and males find a new mate each spring. Courtship singing by the male begins in midwinter and reaches a peak in late winter and early spring—Feb. and Mar. in Alaska, Mar. and Apr. in the central Rockies. The male will fly back and forth from the female to a potential nest site, singing constantly as well as presenting her with dead voles.

Boreal Owls are obligate secondary cavity users, with excavations by Pileated Woodpeckers and Northern Flickers most commonly adopted—all but 1 of 19 nests in Idaho were created by Pileateds. (Boreal Owls readily accept nest boxes, and most of the nesting studies on this species, especially in Europe, involve owls in artificial nests.) Whether in a natural or manmade cavity, Boreal Owls almost never return to the same hole 2 years in a row.

Paradoxically, the average first-egg date is earlier in Alaska and Minnesota (early Apr.) than in the northern Rockies (early to mid-May), likely because in the latter, owls nest at such high, snowbound elevations. Half of all nests in Idaho were begun by May 1, and half in Colorado by May 10. In Nova Scotia, nesting began as early as the end of Mar., but more typically in May or very early June—however, the numbers were small, and the later nests could have been renesting attempts. In Europe, initiation of nesting and egg-laying varies significantly from year to year, depending on food supplies. In Finland, Boreal Owls may lay eggs as early as mid-Feb. or as late as the end of May.

Clutch size is also closely tied to prey abundance, but also increases south to north, although the information from North America is limited. Boreal Owls in the northern Rockies laid 2 to 4 eggs, with the average clutch size 3.25 eggs, while the average clutch in Alaska was 4.9 eggs—still well below the 5.6-egg average in Finland, at roughly the same latitude.

Eggs are usually laid at 48-hour intervals, with incubation beginning with the second egg, and thus asynchronous hatching after a 26- to 29-day incubation period. In Europe, younger females produce more synchronous hatching, perhaps because they delay the onset of incubation until their clutch is larger.

The male provisions both his mate and the chicks for the first 3 weeks or so, after which the female begins to leave the nest and help to hunt. Fledging takes place at 28 to 36 days of age, and the owlets remain dependent on the adults for another month to month and a half.

Boreal Owls are considered monogamous, but that's being generous: as with most things in this owl's universe, it all depends on the voles. During low-prey years, they hew strictly to one male and one female. But during rodent booms, all manner of bigamy has been documented among well-studied European populations—not only bigamous males with more than one female (which at times may include almost three-quarters of all males) but males with three mates, as well as females abandoning one nest to begin a second with a new male.

Ironically, DNA tests have found no evidence for what scientists call extra-pair copulations—males and females "cheating" on their mates with the neighbors, regardless of their pair (or trio) structure. While such EPCs are common in many groups of birds, they appear to be almost completely absent in owls of any sort.

BEHAVIOR

Nocturnal, at least during periods of seasonal darkness. Daytime roost sites are always well concealed among trees branches, not in cavities, with most sites in conifers. Boreal Owls change roost sites frequently, moving more or less at random throughout their territory, but usually choose sites that will afford cool shade in summer. In winter, these well-insulated birds seem to show little regard for sunny or milder locations. In Newfoundland, researchers found a preference for roosting in mature or old-growth conifer stands, avoiding mixed-wood, scrub, and bog, and they avoided mixed-wood and hardwoods in their home ranges as well.

After dark, Boreal Owls appear to hunt most actively in the hours just after sunset and again a few hours before dawn, moving restlessly from perch to perch through the forest in active search for prey, a pattern similar to their close relative, the Northern Saw-whet Owl—and much like an accipiter, such as a Sharp-shinned Hawk.

Sound plays an outsize role in a Boreal Owl's hunting, as reflected by the profoundly asymmetrical ear openings of this species—among the most asymmetrical of any owl in the world. The Boreal Owl's skull has a bony ear opening on the right side that is high on the skull and angles upward, and one on the left that is low on the skull and angles down. (A similar, slightly less pronounced asymmetry is found in the Northern Saw-whet Owl, as well as in the unrelated Great Gray Owl.)

This asymmetry permits the owl to detect subtle differences in the timing and intensity of both high- and low-frequency sounds, allowing the owl to triangulate the source of very quiet sounds in both the horizontal and vertical planes instantly and simultaneously, without having to move its head.

Boreal Owls are not strongly territorial, except in spring around the nest site—and even then, they may nest within 110 yd. (100 m) of each other in Europe. Breeding population density varies dramatically from year to year based on rodent populations but has not been well studied in North America.

When conditions are good, Boreal Owls (males in particular) will remain close to their territory—but when vole numbers crash, they become more nomadic, moving to new areas with better prospects. This species occupies very large home ranges in both summer and winter. In Newfoundland the average size of a male's breeding-season range was 1,060 acres (429 hectares), with the largest 5,283 acres (2,138 hectares). In Idaho, winter ranges averaged 3,585 acres (1,451 hectares) but were as large as 8,376 acres (3,390 hectares); summer ranges averaged 2,920 acres (1,182 hectares).

STATUS

Although rarely seen, and one of the most sought-after raptors among birders, the Boreal Owl is widespread and perhaps the most common owl in the vast (though lightly inhabited) boreal forest zone, which covers roughly 1.5 billion acres. It is ranked

A Boreal Owl cleans its foot, which—as is typical of owls—is zygodactylous, with two toes facing forward, one to the rear, and one that can pivot in either direction. *(Manitoba. Christian Artuso)*

Nomadism and long-distance dispersal keep the genes flowing among even isolated Boreal Owl populations, scientists have found. How they will fare in the face of climate change, including more intense wildfires in high-elevation Rocky Mountain forests, is less clear. *(Alaska. Paul Bannick/VIREO)*

as "least concern" and stable by IUCN/BirdLife, but on the margins of its range it is listed as "imperiled" in Idaho and Wyoming, "threatened" in New Mexico, and "special concern" in Minnesota.

The presence of nesting Boreal Owls in the southern Rockies wasn't suspected until 1963, when a fledgling was taken in northern Colorado. Since then, intensive surveys have shown that Boreal Owls are found as far south as northern New Mexico—and bones excavated from Pleistocene-era caves and pueblos suggest they are not recent invaders but have been present for thousands of years. Despite frequent searches, however, there are neither recent records nor archaeological evidence for the presence of Boreal Owls in the more-isolated spruce-fir highlands of Arizona.

Only a single nesting record exists for the eastern United States, two juvenal-plumaged birds observed in 2001 on Mount Pierce in the White Mountains of New Hampshire. That same summer, an adult was netted in Vermont, although no evidence of breeding was found.

Boreal Owls will readily accept nest boxes, a common practice in Europe, where in some regions as many as 90 percent of the Boreal Owls now nest in artificial cavities. Because Boreal Owls live where trees often remain small and scrubby, and where large woodpeckers may not be common, availability of nest sites may be a serious limiting factor.

Genetic studies showing extensive gene flow among even isolated Rocky Mountain populations, thanks to this owl's nomadism and long-distance dispersal, are an encouraging discovery, given the ever-more-fragmented condition of the northern forests that comprise most of its range. That suggests the Boreal Owl may be better able to tolerate habitat fragmentation than many mature-forest birds have proven to. Research shows, however, that Boreal Owls respond to logged habitat differently than to natural fire-scarred landscapes, and that their survival rates (in Scandinavia, at least) were affected by timbering. They also need mature trees large enough (at least 13 in. / 33 cm in diameter) for nest cavities. In some frigid, high-elevation regions, trees may require two centuries to grow that big.

Climate change also poses unknown dangers for this species, either directly or through its prey. Scientists in Scandinavia have seen a decline in vole numbers and both a flattening and lengthening of vole cycles since the 1980s because of warmer winters and less-protective snow cover, along with a 75 percent decline in the Boreal Owl breeding population over the same period. No one has detected such changes in North America, but small-mammal populations are not tracked as closely here as they are in Scandinavia. For a nomadic species that has evolved to exploit regular vole highs, the fading of such cycles, if they occur range-wide, may prove challenging to the Boreal Owl.

More directly, catastrophic fires in the Southwest, fueled by a century of fire suppression and a warming, drying climate, pose a profound risk for the most southerly populations of the Boreal Owl. As the climate rapidly changes, there is no guarantee that the spruce-fir forests that now occupy elevations above 10,000 ft. will reestablish themselves in the wake of major blazes, or that they are sustainable in the long term even in the absence of calamitous wildfires.

NOTES

1. Earhart and Johnson 1970.

2. G. D. Hayward and P. H. Hayward. 1993. Boreal owl (*Aegolius funereus*). In *The Birds of North America*, no. 63, ed. A. Poole and F. Gill. Philadelphia: Academy of Natural Sciences, and Washington, DC: American Ornithologists' Union.

BIBLIOGRAPHY

Anderson and Clark 2002.

BirdLife International. 2015. *Aegolius funereus*. In The IUCN Red List of Threatened Species, version 2014.3, http://www.iucnredlist.org/details/22689362/0.

Brasso, R. L., and S. D. Emslie. 2006. Two new late Pleistocene avifaunas from New Mexico. *Condor* 108:721–730.

Buidin, C., Y. Rochepault, and J.-P. L. Savard. 2007. Regime alimentaire de la nyctale de Tengmalm en Minganie durant la nidification. *Le Naturaliste Canadien* 131:28–33.

Among Eurasian Boreal Owls, which have been studied more intensely than those in North America, females are much more nomadic than males, which tend to stay closer to the breeding grounds. *(Minnesota. Chris Wood)*

Canterbury, J. L., P. A. Johnsgard, and H. F. Downing. 2013. *Birds and Birding in Wyoming's Bighorn Mountains Range.* Lincoln, NE: Zea Books.

Cheveau et al. 2004.

Côte et al. 2007.

Doyle, F. I., and J. N. M. Smith. 2001. Raptors and scavengers. In *Ecosystem Dynamics of the Boreal Forest: The Kluane Project,* ed. C. J. Krebs, S. Boutin, and R. Boonstra. Oxford: Oxford University Press.

Eckert 2005.

Ellison, W. G., and N. L. Martin. 2002. New England. *American Birds* 56:28–32.

Given 2004.

Graber, C. S., R. L. Wallen, and K. E. Duffy. 1991. Distribution of boreal owl observation records in Wyoming. *Journal of Raptor Research* 25:120–122.

Hayward, G. D. 1997. Forest management and conservation of boreal owls in North America. *Journal of Raptor Research* 31:114–124.

Hayward, G. D., P. H. Hayward, and E. O. Garton. 1993. Ecology of boreal owls in the northern Rocky Mountains, U.S.A. *Wildlife Monographs* 124:3–59.

Hayward, G. D., P. H. Hayward, E. O. Garton, and R. Escano. 1987. Revised breeding distribution of the boreal owl in the northern Rocky Mountains. *Condor* 89:431–432.

Hayward and Verner 1994.

Herren, V. A. 1994. "Boreal owl mating habitat in Wyoming's Sierra Madres." MS thesis, University of Wyoming.

Hörnfeldt, B., T. Hipkiss, and U. Eklund. 2005. Fading out of vole and predator cycles? *Proceedings of the Royal Society B* 272:2045–2049.

Koopman, M. E., G. D. Hayward, and D. B. McDonald. 2007. High connectivity and minimal genetic structure among North American boreal owl (*Aegolius funereus*) populations, regardless of habitat mix. *Auk* 124:690–704.

Koopman, M. E., D. B. McDonald, and G. D. Hayward. 2007. Microsatellite analysis reveals genetic monogamy among female boreal owls. *Journal of Raptor Research* 41:314–318.

Koopman, M. E., D. B. McDonald, G. D. Hayward, K. Eldegard, G. A. Sonerud, and S. G. Sermach. 2005. Genetic similarity among Eurasian subspecies of boreal owls *Aegolius funereus. Journal of Avian Biology* 36:179–183.

Korpimäki, E., and H. Hakkarainen. 2012. *The Boreal Owl.* New York: Cambridge University Press.

Korpimäki, E., M. Lagerström, and P. Saurola. 1987. Field evidence for nomadism in Tengmalm's owl *Aegolius funereus. Ornis Scandinavica* 18:1–4.

Laaksonen, T., H. Hakkarainen, and E. Korpimäki. 2004. Lifetime reproduction of a forest-dwelling owl increases with age and area of forests. *Proceedings: Biological Sciences* 271:S461–S464.

Lauff, R. F. 2009. First nest records of the boreal owl *Aegolius funereus* in Nova Scotia, Canada. *Ardea* 97:497–502.

Morris, R. 1997. Boreal owl in Rockford: First state record since 1914. *Meadowlark* 6:86.

Munro, K. J. 2012. "Boreal owls in western Newfoundland: Using local field data to assess home range characteristics and test a habitat suitability index model." MS thesis, Memorial University of Newfoundland.

New Mexico Partners in Flight. 2007. Boreal owl. In *New Mexico Bird Conservation Plan* v. 2.1., comp. C. Rustay and S. Norris. Albuquerque, NM: New Mexico Partners in Flight.

Petersen, W. R. 2001. New England. *American Birds* 55:411–415.

Rashid 2009.

Scott, M. K. 2004. "Broad-scale habitat associations of boreal owls (*Aegolius funereus*) in southwestern Colorado." MS thesis, University of Wyoming.

Sleep 2005.

Stahlecker, D. W., and R. B. Duncan. 1996. The boreal owl at the southern terminus of the Rocky Mountains: Undocumented longtime resident or recent arrival? *Condor* 98:153–161.

Stahlecker, D. W., and J. J. Rawinski. 1990. First records for the boreal owl in New Mexico. *Condor* 92:517–519.

Sundell, J., O. Huitu, H. Henttonen, A. Kaikusalo, E. Korpimäki, H. Pietiäinen, P. Saurole, and I. Hanski. 2004. Large-scale spatial dynamics of vole populations in Finland revealed by the breeding success of vole-eating avian predators. *Journal of Animal Ecology* 73:167–178.

Utah Bird Records Committee. 2011. Rare bird sightings in Utah, http://www.utahbirds.org/RecCom/RareBirdsIndex.html.

Whelton, B. D. 1989. Distribution of the boreal owl in Washington and Oregon. *Condor* 91:712–716.

Whitman, J. S. 2008. Post-fledging estimation of annual productivity in boreal owls based on prey detritus mass. *Journal of Raptor Research* 42:58–60.

NORTHERN SAW-WHET OWL
Aegolius acadicus
Alpha code: NSWO

LENGTH: 8–8.5 in. (20.3–21.5 cm)

WINGSPAN: 16–18 in. (40.5–45.5 cm)

MASS: Exhibits strong reversed dimorphism. Females may gain 50 percent in mass during the breeding season.

    A. a. acadicus: (Nonbreeding mass, autumn, Pennsylvania): Average, male: 2.75 oz. (77.8 g); range 2.5–3 oz. (69.9–84.7 g). Average, female: 3.4 oz. (95.4 g); range 2.5–4.25 oz. (70–120.5 g).[1] Average, nesting female (Maryland): 4.5 oz. (126 g); range 3.1–5.7 oz. (86–162 g).[2]

    A. a. brooksi: (Small sample): Average, male: 2.9 oz. (81.3 g). Average, female: 3.3 oz. (93.9 g).[3]

LONGEVITY: The most frequently banded owl in North America, with more than 5,600 encounter records. Average age on re-encounter, 1.9 years. Longevity record 9 years 5 months, an adult owl banded in Ontario in 1999 and recaptured alive in Minnesota. Other notable records: 8 years 3 months, an immature owl banded (in 2001) in California and recaptured alive there; and 7 years 5 months, an immature owl banded in 1977 in Ontario and killed by a vehicle in New Hampshire.

Common in forests across boreal and mountainous North America, the Northern Saw-whet Owl is so secretive that, despite its abundance, it was long considered rare in many regions. Its migrations weren't even suspected until the past century, and their details are only now being unraveled. The Northern Saw-whet is a grail species for many birders—eagerly sought but rarely found—and when they do finally encounter one, birders generally marvel at its naive and trusting nature. Most abundant where humans are rarest, the Northern Saw-whet is so famously approachable that it's often possible to gently pick one up from its daytime perch.

    The unusual name comes from one of its calls, which nineteenth-century naturalists likened to the sharpening, or "whetting," of a saw blade. Strangely, no one today can agree on *which* of this owl's many unowl-like vocalizations is the "saw-whet" call—one more odd footnote to a lovely but still-mysterious raptor.

    Although usually considered a boreal species, the

Continental banding efforts, by independent researchers collaborating through Project Owlnet, have shed light on the annual movements of Northern Saw-whet Owls, which are now the most frequently banded owl in North America. *(Pennsylvania. Scott Weidensaul)*

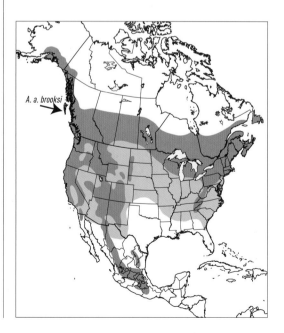

A. a. brooksi

Common but rarely seen, the Northern Saw-whet Owl is, like many northern raptors, trustingly naive around humans and can often be approached closely enough in daytime to be picked up. *(British Columbia. Glenn Bartley)*

Northern Saw-whet is found as far south as Oaxaca in montane pine, oak-pine, and cloud forests. It is replaced east of the Isthmus of Tehuantepec by the closely related Unspotted Saw-whet Owl.

SYSTEMATICS, TAXONOMY, AND ETYMOLOGY

The Northern Saw-whet Owl and its tropical counterpart, the Unspotted Saw-whet Owl (*A. ridgwayi*), form a superspecies, and some scientists argue that they are, in fact, conspecific. Much remains unknown about their genetics and respective ecology.

Two subspecies of the Northern Saw-whet Owl are traditionally recognized—*A. a. acadicus,* found across all of the species's range except for the Queen Charlotte Islands (Haida Gwaii) of British Columbia, where it is replaced with the slightly smaller, darker, and nonmigratory endemic race, *A. a. brooksi.* Even though the mainland subspecies migrates through (and winters in) the island group, recent mitochondrial DNA tests found essentially no evidence of gene flow between the two races. The analysis suggests a separation going back about 16,000 years, just after the peak of the last ice age, when the islands and the surrounding area were an ice-free refugia.

A third subspecies, *A. a. brodkorbi* from Oaxaca, was described in 1954 from a single, possibly immature specimen. It showed reduced spotting on the wings and tail, somewhat intermediate with the *tacanensis* race of the Unspotted Saw-whet, and some authors have assigned it to that species, even though there are no other records of Unspotted Saw-whets west of the Isthmus of Tehuantepec. Most authorities consider *brodkorbi* invalid, especially because the records of the original collector have proven notoriously unreliable.

ETYMOLOGY: For the genus name, see "Boreal Owl." The specific name, *acadicus,* comes from Nova Scotia (Acadia), where the first specimen was collected. The English name refers to the fancied similarity between one of the owl's vocalizations (most likely the raspy *skiew* call) and the whetting, or sharpening, of a saw blade. (Others have pointed to the French colloquial name for an owl without ear tufts, *chouette,* as an alternate explanation.)

SPANISH: *Tecolote abetero norteño, tecolote afilador, lechucita cabezona, tecolotito cabezón*
FRENCH: *Petit nyctale*

DISTRIBUTION

BREEDING SEASON: The Northern Saw-whet Owl is a common and widespread breeding species in northern forests, although its secretive nature makes any attempt to draw the exact boundaries of its range—especially the northern limits—difficult.

Once largely absent from Newfoundland, where the Boreal Owl is the common *Aegolius,* the Northern Saw-whet is becoming more widespread there. Found from the Maritimes and southern Quebec west across northern Ontario (north at least rarely to southern James Bay), west across the boreal forest zone of Manitoba, Saskatchewan, and Alberta, central and southern British Columbia, and the coastal forests of southeastern and south-central Alaska, including the Kenai Peninsula.

Breeds from New England to Pennsylvania (and thence more or less continuously down the Appalachian Mountains to the highlands of North Carolina and Tennessee), west through the upper Midwest, including northern Minnesota. Absent from the Great Plains, but breeding populations have recently been documented in scattered buttes with scrubby forest in the western Dakotas and western Nebraska, in addition to montane forests in the Black Hills.

Widespread in the western and coastal mountains. Common on the Mogollon Rim in Arizona but more sporadic in the Sky Island ranges of southeastern Arizona and southwestern New Mexico; rare breeding records exist for the Guadalupe and (possibly) Davis Mountains of West Texas. Playback surveys have shown they are regular in the mountains of southern California, including the Channel Islands (Santa Cruz and Santa Clara), and in the San Gabriel Mountains, where they are found from 4,300 to 7,500 ft. (1,310 to 2,286 m).

Their Mexican breeding range, although sketchily understood, extends deep into the high elevations of the Sierra Madre Oriental and Occidental and central highlands, south to Oaxaca. It is generally listed as rare everywhere in Mexico, although it may be overlooked more than genuinely uncommon. Found primarily in humid pine, pine-oak, and fir forests between 5,900 and 9,800 ft. (1,800 and 3,000 m). Confirmed in the 1990s in northern Baja (Sierra San Pedro Mártir).

A. a. brooksi on the Queen Charlotte Islands is nonmigratory but may shift to coastal areas in winter, feeding on intertidal invertebrates. It is found from sea level to 4,000 ft. (1,220 m).

NONBREEDING SEASON: Outside the breeding season, Northern Saw-whets are highly secretive and very difficult to locate, factors that have contributed to both the former assumption of their scarcity and to uncertainty about their nonbreeding range. Most frequently encountered in winter from southern Canada through the Mid-Atlantic states, Midwest, and western mountains, Northern Saw-whet Owls may turn up anywhere, including Louisiana, northern Florida, and Sonoran Desert oases in southern California, especially in years with major invasion flights.

The extent of their winter range in the South

and Southeast remains unclear. Recent banding efforts have shown them to be regular in northern Alabama, and their winter range may not be as variable from year to year as once believed, although the number of owls (and thus their detectability) may vary greatly because of population cycles (see "Autumn Migration," p. 302). The degree to which western migrants penetrate Mexico, overlapping with residents, is completely unknown.

Many Northern Saw-whets remain on or near the breeding grounds in winter, and there is some banding evidence to suggest that, as with Boreal Owls, adult males may be generally nonmigratory.

MIGRATION AND MOVEMENTS: While much still remains to be discovered about its movements, the broad outlines of the Northern Saw-whet's migratory behavior is becoming clear. Most of this information has come from a network of more than 120 banding operations, most small-scale and run by avocational researchers, working collaboratively through Project Owlnet (www.projectowlnet.

org)—a powerful example of the ability of citizen-scientists to peel back some of the mystery that still surrounds the movements of even common and widespread species.

The picture emerging from this research suggests a species in which some individuals migrate hundreds of miles, while others may remain on or near the breeding grounds. Broad migration routes have been delineated in the East and Midwest, while much remains to be learned about Northern Saw-whet movements through the West.

Early naturalists considered the Northern Saw-whet Owl a widespread but sedentary species, probably misinterpreting the presence of migrants in the South as evidence of breeding there. (Audubon—whether by mistake or fabrication—claimed to have found the Northern Saw-whet Owl breeding in Louisiana and Mississippi.)

Highly secretive and rarely seen in daylight, it is easily overlooked during migration and the nonbreeding season. By the late nineteenth century a few ornithologists thought the owl might be

Although considered a boreal species, Northern Saw-whet Owls are found as far south as Oaxaca in high-elevation pine, oak-pine, and cloud forests. *(British Columbia. Glenn Bartley)*

Although they lack ear tufts, Northern Saw-whet Owls can compress the facial disk and raise the disk ruff to create the same effect, helping to break up their outline. *(Washington. Gerrit Vyn)*

migratory at the northern extremes of its range, but not until the early years of the twentieth century was the extent of the Saw-whet's migratory nature suspected.

Two incidents, both occurring on Lake Huron, crystallized the realization that this owl was migratory. In 1903, a steamboat crossing the lake reported a flock of "small owls" that landed on its decks, and three years later, a storm over the lake killed thousands of migrating birds, including two dozen Northern Saw-whet Owls collected by naturalists.

Despite this evidence, some authorities argued into the 1960s that Northern Saw-whets were generally permanent residents. That changed with the advent of targeted banding operations in the 1960s, and especially with the development in the 1980s of an audiolure designed to play the *toot* vocalization of the male owl. Combined with mist nets, this technique quickly demonstrated that Northern Saw-whet Owls were abundant migrants in the upper Midwest, Northeast, and Mid-Atlantic regions, where the bulk of the banding was conducted. More recent pioneering work in the West, Pacific Northwest, and Alaska has also shown significant migration in those regions as well, and even some movement across the Great Plains.

Saw-whets appear to have a migratory strategy similar to that of Boreal Owls, in which females (and to an extent immature males) are migratory, while adult males remain on or near the breeding grounds, either holding or seeking out territories with high prey numbers.

AUTUMN MIGRATION:

Migration generally appears to take place across a broad front, with banding locations capturing migrant owls in sites, such as agricultural valleys, far from suitable habitat. But Northern Saw-whets do follow major topographical features like lake and ocean coastlines or ridge systems, the latter perhaps because they provide the security of forested corridors. In the very broadest sense, there are major migration routes south along the Atlantic Coast (including water crossings over the Gulf of Maine, and Delaware and Chesapeake Bays), down the ridges of the Appalachian Mountains, across and around the Great Lakes, along the Rocky Mountain Front, and the Pacific Coast and inland mountain ranges. As with southbound passerines, Northern Saw-whets are concentrated at migrant "traps" like Prince Edward Point and Long Point, Ontario, the Cape May peninsula in New Jersey, and the northwest shore of Lake Superior.

While these owls may adhere to broad regional flyways, significant long-distance movements have also been documented, like an adult owl banded one fall in Montana, then recaptured the following year near Boston, some 1,864 mi. (3,322 km) to the east.

What follows applies primarily to the upper Midwest and East, where most of the banding work has been done. Autumn migration commences in early to mid-Sept. in central Quebec and Ontario, peaking there in late Sept. and early Oct.; the slow-moving wave appears to coincide with hardwood leaf-drop, reaching central Pennsylvania around the end of Oct., Cape May in mid-Nov., and the southern Delmarva Peninsula in mid- to late Nov. At the presumed southern end of the migration route, Northern Saw-whets have been netted in Alabama as early as mid-Oct., but the bulk of the flight appears to arrive there in Nov. and early Dec.

Because Northern Saw-whets are so difficult to detect away from established banding sites, an absence of records should not be assumed to mean an absence of owls. Banding operations in Alabama and Kentucky, to take two recent examples, have shown the species is a regular migrant and wintering bird in those states, despite few previous observations in either.

The timing and routes of Northern Saw-whet migration in the West are less well understood and are complicated by altitudinal movements, but increased banding there is shining a light on this region as well. Autumn migration peaks in mid-Sept. and early Oct. in northern Montana; in late Sept. and mid-Oct. in southwest Saskatchewan and southwestern Idaho; the first week of Oct. in central Alberta and Vancouver Island, British Columbia; and late Oct. in northern California.

An analysis of more than 80,000 banding records showed that, despite evidence of nomadism in the breeding season, Northern Saw-whets exhibit a high degree of fidelity to their regional migration route. It also revealed that they are languid migrants, averaging just 6.5 mi. (10.5 km) per night, while radiotelemetry studies have shown that they undergo relatively long (about 7- to 10-day) periods of stopover between bouts of active migration.

The number of migrant Northern Saw-whet Owls fluctuates dramatically from year to year, especially in the East, where an every-other-year cycle is punctuated with major flights roughly every 3 to 5 years. This is almost certainly tied to population cycles in their rodent prey, especially red-backed voles; the majority of migrants in invasion years is made up of juvenile (hatching-year) owls, the result of higher productivity made possible by an abundant prey base.

Although these flight years are often termed "irruptions," such cyclical peaks in Northern Saw-whets are simply a reflection of higher annual populations in a regular migrant, with none of the unpredictability of a true irruptive migration. Major invasions may occur across large portions of the owl's range; a major flight in 1999 resulted in a 2.5-fold increase over captures the following year in Pennsylvania, and a 6-fold increase in Idaho compared with the following 2 years.

SPRING MIGRATION:

The timing and routes of spring migration are much more poorly documented, even in the East. Peak northward movement may vary from year to year depending on snow cover, but in the latitude of Pennsylvania it appears to fall in early to mid-Mar., and in southern Ontario from late Mar. to mid-Apr. At Whitefish Point, Michigan—a major bottleneck for northbound owls, and the site of a long-running banding program—spring migration for this species peaks in late Mar. and early Apr. In Saskatchewan, spring netting suggests a northbound peak in early Apr.

POST-FLEDGING DISPERSAL: No information. Large numbers of juvenile Northern Saw-whets are captured in late summer each year on the Upper Peninsula of Michigan, which forms a natural migrant trap.

DISTRIBUTION OUTSIDE THE COVERAGE AREA: None

DESCRIPTION AND IDENTIFICATION

The Northern Saw-whet Owl is a small, chunky, round-headed raptor with a body mass roughly that of a jay. It is the smallest owl in the East, but in the West it is larger than the pygmy-owls, and more than twice the mass of the Elf Owl. Northern Saw-whets exhibit significant reversed size dimorphism, with females outweighing males by about 25 percent, although overlap between the genders can make even in-hand sexing impossible. Like those of the Boreal Owl, the enlarged external ear openings of the Northern Saw-whet Owl's skull have a pronounced asymmetry, with the right opening high on the head and facing up, while the left ear is low on the skull and angled down. This presumably aids in pinpointing sounds in the dark.

BASIC (ADULT) PLUMAGE: No sexual differences.

A. a. acadicus: Upperparts rich dark brown suffused with rufous. Fine white streaks on the forehead and crown, and diffuse white mottling forming a broad band across the nape. Outer half of scapular feathers white, creating rows of large spots, although usually only the outermost row is visible, forming "suspender" markings. Smaller white spots on the greater and median coverts. Upper surfaces of flight feathers dark brown, with four or five white spots on the outer primaries. Tail dark brown with two or three narrow white bars.

Young Northern Saw-whet Owls wear a distinct juvenal plumage for several months after leaving the nest, with chocolate upperparts and a buffy belly. *(British Columbia. Laure Neish/VIREO)*

Facial disk buffy with dark streaks, fading to white below the eyes, narrowly edged with a ruff of brown with abundant white flecks. Prominent white eyebrows. No ear tufts, although an agitated Northern Saw-whet may raise two low "bumps" at the upper edges of the facial disc. Underparts white with broad vertical chestnut streaks. Underwing coverts silvery gray to buffy, unmarked. Ventral surfaces of flight feathers gray-brown with four or five rows of white spots. Underside of tail gray-brown with three narrow white bars. Eyes yellow or yellow-orange. Tarsi densely feathered and buffy, bill black.

A. a. brooksi: Similar, except that underparts, facial disk, and throat are suffused with rich rufous-buff tones, and white spots on the upperparts are likewise buffy. Rufous overtones above largely restricted to the head and nape; back and upperwing coverts gray-brown, matching the ground color of the flight feathers.

JUVENAL PLUMAGE: Dramatically different from adult. Natal down white. Fledgling is dark brown and unspotted, except for a few white flecks on the forehead and for small white spots at the ends of the greater coverts. Facial disk dark brown, with large white triangle formed by prominent eyebrows. Chest and belly buff. Iris yellow. At 2 to 4 months of age, the owl begins a rapid molt into adult (basic) plumage. By Sept., only a few immature Northern Saw-whets still retain any vestige of juvenal plumage other than their flight feathers, which are retained.

Juveniles of *A. a. brooksi* are even darker overall than those on the mainland, almost sooty black-brown on the head and more richly colored below.

SIMILAR SPECIES: Boreal Owl is larger, with a whitish, distinctly black-edged facial disc, and underparts spotted more than streaked; back evenly spotted, without white "suspenders." Northern Saw-whet may be confused with screech-owls and Flammulated Owls (which may flatten their ear tufts to present a round-headed profile), but Northern Saw-whets lack the vermiculation and black-brown streaking on their underparts. Note dark eyes of Flammulated. Northern Pygmy-Owl appears smaller-headed with a longer tail.

Juvenile Boreal Owl is dark brown overall with only slightly paler underparts, with sparse white eyebrows and rictal bristles forming X shape, versus bold white forehead marking. Unspotted Saw-whet

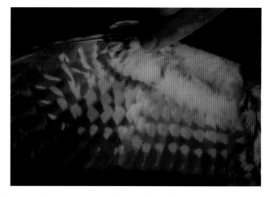

Almost all owls incorporate a group of reddish brown pigments known as porphyrins in their feathers—pigments that fluoresce under ultraviolet light. Because the pigment degrades with time, banders use this phenomenon to help age Northern Saw-whets and other owls—in this case, a second-year owl that has retained many of its older, more faded juvenal flight feathers. *(Pennsylvania. Scott Weidensaul)*

Owl does not overlap in range; similar to juvenal-plumaged Northern Saw-whet, but lacks the latter's wing and scapular spots.

VOCALIZATIONS

Given that this species was named for its call, there is actually a surprising lack of consensus about which of its many vocalizations is the "saw-whet" cry.

Researchers have distinguished at least nine vocalizations, including juvenile food-begging calls. The most commonly heard vocalization is the male advertisement call, a steady repetition of loud, me-

The strange name of the Northern Saw-whet Owl comes from the fancied resemblance of one of its calls to the sound of someone whetting, or sharpening, a saw blade. *(Manitoba. Christian Artuso)*

chanical *toot*s spaced about .5 second apart; females may occasionally respond with a quieter, higher-pitched version, and an agitated or aroused male will give a rapid four- or five-notes-per-second advertisement call. The *toot* call is given most often during the breeding season, with some males singing well into the morning—and into the summer. (As with many songbirds, unmated male Northern Saw-whets will sing longer and more persistently into the summer than paired males.) Advertising males will sometimes sing from a potential nest cavity while trying to attract a mate.

Outside the breeding season, the most common vocalizations, especially in response to recordings, are a series of sharp, two-syllabled barks or chirps, often rendered as *skiew, skiew, skiew* or *skriegh-aw, skriegh-aw, skriegh-aw,* and an eerie, ascending wail lasting about 2 seconds, increasing in pitch and volume before falling off abruptly. Like the *toot* call, the *skiew* call has been credited with the origin of the "saw-whet" name. Presumably made by both sexes, *skiew* and wails are often given in apparent agitation.

Northern Saw-whet Owls sometimes make a high-pitched twittering, especially when in physical discomfort or great distress. Researchers have heard them twittering when being attacked by Barred Owls, for instance, although they will also occasionally give the vocalization while being quietly held.

The "Queen Charlotte" subspecies, *A. a. brooksi,* is said to have higher-pitched vocalizations than the mainland race.

HABITAT AND NICHE

A forest owl that preys heavily—at times almost exclusively—on small rodents, the Northern Saw-whet has traditionally been associated with conifers. Birders may exaggerate the importance of this

Like most small owls, the Northern Saw-whet depends on old woodpecker cavities for most of its nest sites—although few have multiple entrances, as these chicks have found. *(Washington. Paul Bannick/VIREO)*

pine or red fir, and least often in forests dominated by white fir. Elsewhere in California, depending on elevation, Northern Saw-whets may also use montane ponderosa or gray pine and oak forests, or coastal redwood–oak and oak-bay forests. In San Gabriel Mountains, found in mixed forests of bigcone Douglas-fir, Jeffrey and ponderosa pine, white fir, incense cedar, and California black oak. In winter, owls in the Sierra Nevada foothills roost almost exclusively in toyon and canyon live oak. The small resident population on the Channel Islands uses pine, oak, and eucalyptus woodlands. Limited information for Mexico, where its presence is most often detected in montane pine, pine-oak, and fir forests.

During autumn migration in the East, daytime roosts are frequently in large hardwood trees, although after leaf-fall Northern Saw-whets switch to conifers or to dense tangles of evergreen shrubs and vines, like American holly, Japanese honeysuckle, greenbrier, bayberry (along Atlantic Coast), mountain laurel, and rosebay rhododendron. Throughout the year, vegetative density and structural complexity, especially the presence of subcanopy layers, appear to be more important than any particular species composition.

A breeding survey in Pennsylvania found a strong correlation between territorial male Northern Saw-whet Owls and the presence of singing frogs and toads, suggesting a preference for riparian areas with open water.

DIET: Small mammals make up the vast bulk of the Northern Saw-whet's diet, especially white-footed and deer mice and red-backed and microtine voles, although most studies are from the northern and eastern regions. In California, almost half of the diet of wintering Northern Saw-whet Owls was western harvest mice. Small birds and insects are also taken, but rarely comprise a significant portion of the diet. This single-minded focus on rodents is not shared by the "Queen Charlotte" subspecies, which feeds on a wide variety of nonmammalian prey, including intertidal invertebrates like amphipods and isopods; one roadkilled female had 156 marine amphipods in her stomach. The owls frequently take seaweed flies, as well as toads, bats, and the downy chicks of Ancient Murrelets—seabirds that, when grown, weigh almost twice as much as the owl.

Because of their size, Northern Saw-whet Owls fall prey to larger owl species, with Barred Owls showing a particular tendency to respond to recordings of this species. Long-eared, Great Horned, and Eastern Screech-Owls have also been known to attack netted Northern Saw-whets, although less frequently; the degree of predation by these species in the wild is unknown.

relationship to coniferous woods, however, and the species is found in a wide variety of forested habitats, especially in winter and during migration.

The core of the Northern Saw-whet's breeding range certainly corresponds with the vast boreal forests of northern North America, including stands of white, red, and black spruce; balsam fir; tamarack; and northern white cedar. Farther south, important conifers include red pine, eastern white pine, and eastern hemlock, while the breeding range in the southern Appalachians is primarily within high-elevation red spruce–Fraser fir forests.

In south-central Canada, riparian forests of white spruce, aspen, and balsam poplar are said to be the primary nesting habitat, while in western mountains, riparian and low- to mid-elevation forests of Douglas-fir, western red cedar, and ponderosa pine are most important. In the central Sierra Nevada, surveys found them most often in stands of Jeffery

An adult Northern Saw-whet clutches a vole—which belongs to a group that, along with deer and white-footed mice, dominates this small owl's diet. *(Minnesota. Brian E. Small/VIREO)*

NESTING AND BREEDING

Calling males begin soliciting mates in late winter, singing the *toot* call repeatedly, sometimes from potential nest cavities, although the female makes the final selection of the nest site. Egg-laying dates range from late Feb., even in some northern areas, to early July, with the peak probably falling in Mar. and Apr. across most parts of its range. Because snow and ice often deter observers early in the nesting season, and because spontaneous calling often ends during the nestling stage, Northern Saw-whets are often overlooked unless specifically targeted. In Pennsylvania, where they were once considered rare breeders, two seasons of playback surveys showed Northern Saw-whet Owls were present on nearly half of all randomly selected routes in forested mountains.

Dependent on secondary cavities (primarily old woodpecker nests) for nesting; egg collectors believed that Northern Flicker cavities were preferred because of entrance hole size. There are nineteenth-century records of this species using stick nests, but these are generally discounted. Northern Saw-whets will accept a standard nest box with an entrance hole of 3 in. (7.5 cm), mounted 10 to 15 ft. (3 to 4.5 m) high in appropriate habitat. The box should have several inches of dry wood shavings in the bottom and be cleaned prior to Mar.

Clutch size is highly variable (4 to 9 eggs, average 5 or 6), and probably depends on prey abundance. In high-rodent years, some females are suspected of abandoning nests of half-grown nestlings to their father and starting a second nest with a new male, as is known for Boreal Owls. Incubation begins with the first egg and lasts 27 to 29 days.

There is some evidence to suggest that Northern Saw-whet Owls may be nomadic between breeding seasons, shifting territories in response to local prey cycles and abundance, as is well documented for Boreal Owls. A female saw-whet tagged with a geolocator in Pennsylvania nested in southern Canada, Pennsylvania, and New York in successive summers, shifting from southwestern Pennsylvania to the Adirondacks in New York in the same season after an apparent nest failure.[1]

Only a few nests of the nonmigratory *A. a. brooksi* race in British Columbia have been described, all in cavities cut by Northern Flickers or Hairy Woodpeckers in Sitka spruce or western hemlocks. Nests ranged in height from 30 to 82 ft. (9 to 25 m). There

Like most owls, Northern Saw-whets begin incubating with the first egg, so that the age disparity between the oldest and youngest chick in a clutch can be dramatic—as was the case with these two siblings from the same nest. *(Colorado. Scott Rashid)*

Like many cavity-nesting owls, Northern Saw-whets will readily accept nest boxes. These chicks are close to fledging. *(Colorado. Scott Rashid)*

appears to be no difference in nest-season timing compared with the mainland subspecies.

BEHAVIOR

Strictly nocturnal. Like most owls, the Northern Saw-whet is a wait-and-see hunter, dropping on prey from low perches, although recent telemetry suggests a more active hunting pattern, with frequent perch changes and movements over a wide area, than was once suspected—again, similar to that known for Boreal Owls.

Little is known about duration of pair bonds, but they probably last only a single season. Primarily monogamous, but polygyny is known, and sequential polyandry is suspected.

Roosts in trees, thick vegetation, and (less often) tangled blowdowns, ranging in height from on the ground to more than 100 ft. (30 m). Except for the nesting female, it rarely roosts in cavities. Excess prey is cached in cavities or on branches.

Based on radiotelemetry studies of migrant and wintering Northern Saw-whets in Pennsylvania, the owl leaves its roost at or shortly after dusk and begins several hours of active hunting, flying from spot to spot until it detects prey. This is followed by a period of inactivity (presumably after making a kill) that may last for 2 or 3 hours, then a second period of active hunting prior to dawn. Daytime roosts may change daily and may be reused repeatedly over a period of weeks or months. Saw-whets may fly up to 3.5 mi. (9 km) and 1,000 ft. (300 m) in elevation each way from daytime roost to nocturnal hunting area and back.

Early naturalists commented on the Northern Saw-whet Owl's naiveté around humans, describ-

Its head cocked, a Northern Saw-whet listens for a slight rustle to betray the presence of a small mammal. Like other highly nocturnal owls, this species has asymmetrical bony ear openings (inset), which allows it to localize very quiet noises on both a vertical and a horizontal axis. *(Owl: Manitoba. Christian Artuso. Skull: Pennsylvania. Scott Weidensaul)*

Cyclical fluctuations in vole populations drive chick production among Northern Saw-whet Owls. In boom years, a single female may lay up to 9 eggs and will sometimes start a second clutch before the first is fledged. *(Alberta. Gerrit Vyn)*

ing it as tameness or stupidity. Discovered on a day roost, a Northern Saw-whet will usually remain still, often with its eyes closed to slits; it may slowly turn sideways to an intruder, raising the bend of the folded wing and compressing its feathers in a concealment posture. It's not unusual for a person, moving carefully, to be able to pick one up. (At night, except when dazzled by artificial lights, a Northern Saw-whet is considerably less likely to allow a close approach.)

Limited information on home range size. In the southern Appalachians, breeding adults used areas from 148 to 943 acres (60 to 382 hectares), and averaging 479 acres (194 hectares). No home range studies on *A. a. brooksi,* but it is assumed to be the same as for the mainland subspecies. Because male calls are individually identifiable, a researcher in British Columbia was able to determine that male *brooksi* owls showed some degree of site fidelity from year to year—the opposite of the mainland subspecies, which almost never remains in the same territory two breeding seasons in a row.

STATUS

Given its secretive nature and the limited work (besides migration netting) targeting it, little can be said with any assurance about the population and status of the Northern Saw-whet Owl. Based on assumed breeding densities across available habitat, the global population has been estimated at 100,000 to 300,000, in line with estimates based on genetic studies (about 270,000 individuals). No informa-

tion available regarding trends; year-to-year comparisons of long-term banding results are difficult because of cyclical changes.

With an estimated population of 1,900 and ongoing habitat loss due to logging, the island endemic race *A. a. brooksi* is listed as "threatened" by the Canadian government, with an apparent large population decrease since about 1970.

The Northern Saw-whet Owl is a species of conservation concern in states at the southern fringes of its breeding range, although such listings may reflect a lack of information more than actual rarity. The owl was delisted as a special-concern species in Pennsylvania, for instance, after targeted surveys revealed that it was widespread. It is increasing in Newfoundland, perhaps because of the accidental introduction of its primary prey species, the red-backed vole.

The small southern Appalachian breeding population, however, is at particular risk because of its narrow range, limited numbers, and the effects of climate change, which threaten the high-elevation spruce-fir forests in which it breeds. This population is listed as "highly rare" in Maryland, "imperiled" in West Virginia, "extremely rare" in Virginia, "threatened" in North Carolina, "critically imperiled" in Tennessee, and of "special concern" in South Carolina. The southern Appalachian population is listed on the Red Watch List of distinct population units. Elsewhere, it is listed as "special concern" in Connecticut and Rhode Island, of "special interest" in Ohio, and "rare" in South Dakota.

NOTES

1. S. Weidensaul, unpub. data.

2. D. Brinker, pers. comm.

3. J. L. Rasmussen, S. G. Sealy, and R. J. Cannings. 2008. Northern Saw-whet Owl (*Aegolius acadicus*). In The Birds of North America Online, ed. A. Poole. Ithaca, NY: Cornell Lab of Ornithology, http://bna.birds.cornell.edu.bnaproxy.birds.cornell.edu/bna/species/042doi:10.2173/bna.42.

BIBLIOGRAPHY

American Ornithologists' Union. 1998. *Check-list of North American Birds,* 7th ed. Washington, DC: American Ornithologists' Union.

Beckett, S. R., and G. A. Proudfoot. 2011. Large-scale movement and migration of northern saw-whet owls in eastern North America. *Wilson Journal of Ornithology* 123:521–535.

Bendire, Charles. 1892. *Life Histories of North American Birds.* Washington, DC: Smithsonian Institution.

Bent 1938.

Binford 1989.

Bowman, J., D. S. Badzinski, and R. J. Brooks. 2009. The numerical response of breeding northern saw-whet owls *Aegolius acadicus* suggests nomadism. *Journal of Ornithology* 151:499–506.

Briggs 1954.

Buidin, C., Y. Rochepault, M. Savard, and J.-P. L. Savard. 2006. Breeding range extension of the northern saw-whet owl in Quebec. *Wilson Journal of Ornithology* 118:411–413.

Cannings, R. J. 2004. "Queen Charlotte" northern saw-whet owl. In *Accounts and Measures for Managing Identified Wildlife,* v. 2004. Victoria, BC: Ministry of Water, Land and Air Protection.

Catling, P. M. 1971. Spring migration of saw-whet owls at Toronto, Canada. *Bird-Banding* 42:110–114.

Coues, E. 1874. *Birds of the Northwest.* Washington, DC: U.S. Geological Survey of the Territories.

De Ruyck, C. C., J. Duncan, and N. Koper. 2012. Northern saw-whet owl (*Aegolisu acadicus*) migratory behavior, demographics, and population trends in Manitoba. *Journal of Raptor Research* 46:84–97.

Enríquez-Rocha, Rangel-Salazar, and Holt 1993.

Environment Canada. 2011. Northern saw-whet owl *brooksi* subspecies. Status of Birds in Canada, http://www.ec.gc.ca/soc-sbc/oiseau-bird-eng.aspx?sL=e&sY=2011&sB=NSWO_BRO&sM=p1.

Erickson, R. A., and T. E. Wurster. 1998. Confirmation of nesting in Mexico of four bird species from the Sierra San Pedro Mártir, Baja California. *Wilson Bulletin* 110:118–120.

Fleming, J. H. 1916. The saw-whet owl of the Queen Charlotte Islands. *Auk* 33:420–423.

Freye, G. G. 2012. Autumn migration ecology of the northern saw-whet owl (*Aegolius acadicus*) in northern Montana. *Journal of Raptor Research* 46:177–183.

Friedman, Griscom, and Moore 1950.

Groce, J. E., and M. L. Morrison. 2010. Habitat use by saw-whet owls in the Sierra Nevada. *Journal of Wildlife Management* 74:1523–1532.

Hobson, K. A., and S. G. Sealy. 1991. Marine protein contributions to the diet of northern saw-whet owls on the Queen Charlotte Islands: A stable-isotope approach. *Auk* 108:437–440.

Holroyd, G. L., and J. G. Woods. 1975. Migration of the saw-whet owl in eastern North America. *Bird-Banding* 46:101–105.

Holschuh, C. I. 2006. *COSEWIC Assessment and Status Report on the Northern Saw-whet Owl* brooksi *Subspecies in Canada.* Ottawa, ON: Committee on the Status of Endangered Wildlife in Canada.

——. 2001. "Monitoring habitat quality and condition of Queen Charlotte saw-whet owls (*Aegolius acadicus brooksi*) using vocal individuality." MS thesis, University of Northern British Columbia.

Howell et al. 2001.

Johnson, J. W. 1999. "Abundance and distribution of saw-whet owls (*Aegolius acadicus*) on Santa Cruz Island." MS thesis, California State University.

Marks, J. S., and J. H. Doremus. 2000. Are northern saw-whet owls nomadic? *Journal of Raptor Research* 34:299–304.

Marks, J. S., J. H. Doremus, and R. J. Cannings. 1989. Polygyny in the northern saw-whet owl. *Auk* 106:732–734.

Navarro-Sigüenza, A. G., and A. T. Peterson. 2007. *Aegolius acadicus* (tecolote afilador) residencia permanente distribución potencial. In *Mapas de las Aves de México Basados en WWW,* ed. A. G. Navarro and A. T. Peterson. Final report, SNIB-CONABIO project no. CE015. México DF.

Peeters 2007.

Saunders, W. E. 1907. Migration disaster in western Ontario. *Auk* 24:108–110.

Sealy, S. G. 1999. Further data on food items of the northern saw-whet owls (*Aegolius acadicus brooksi*) on the Queen Charlotte Islands, British Columbia. *Western Birds* 30:200–205.

Shaw, J. 2014. "Winter ecology of northern saw-whet owls (*Aegolius acadicus*) in the Sierra Nevada foothills of California." MS thesis, California State University, Chico.

Tarver, C. 2001. Northern saw-whet owl nest on East Limestone Island. In *Laskeek Bay Research 11,* ed. A. J. Gaston. Queen Charlotte City, BC: Laskeek Bay Conservation Society.

Taverner, P. A., and B. H. Swales. 1911. Notes on the migration of the saw-whet owl. *Auk* 28:329–334.

Withrow, P. J., S. G. Sealy, and K. Winker. 2014. Genetics of divergence in the northern saw-whet owl (*Aegolius acadicus*). *Auk* 131:73–85.

UNSPOTTED SAW-WHET OWL
Aegolius ridgwayi
Alpha code: USWO

Solidly brown upperparts and a plain, cinnamon belly distinguish the Unspotted Saw-whet Owl, an endemic of southern Mexico and Central America, from its northern congener. *(Guatemala. Knut Eisermann)*

LENGTH: 7–8.5 in. (17.8–21.6 cm)

WINGSPAN: Unknown

MASS: Limited data. Mexico: Range 3.1–3.25 oz. (89–92 g).[1] Costa Rica: Male, range 3–3.2 oz. (85–90 g). Female, range 3.6–3.8 oz. (101–108 g).[2] A lack of data makes it difficult to assess the degree of reversed size dimorphism in this species. Mass and wing chord measurements from Costa Rica (male 139–142 mm, female 152–155 mm) suggest a similar or somewhat greater degree of dimorphism than shown by the Northern Saw-whet Owl.[2, 3]

LONGEVITY: Unknown

The endemic tropical counterpart of the Northern Saw-whet Owl, the Unspotted Saw-whet inhabits a disjunct range of montane and cloud forests in southern Central America, although its exact taxonomic status needs clarification. Almost nothing is known about its ecology, life history, or behavior, and its nest and eggs have not been convincingly described.

Its plumage, which is brown and unmarked above and cinnamon-buff below, superficially resembles the Northern Saw-whet Owl's juvenal plumage. This once led some experts to suggest this species exhibited neoteny—the persistence of juvenile characteristics into adulthood, in which the Unspotted Saw-whet lacked an adult plumage. Closer study showed that the owl does, in fact, attain adult plumage—just one that looks like a young Northern Saw-whet.

SYSTEMATICS, TAXONOMY, AND ETYMOLOGY

This little-known owl forms a superspecies with the far more widespread Northern Saw-whet Owl, and some authorities argue it is conspecific with it. Besides the nominate race from Costa Rica and Panama, two poorly differentiated subspecies have been described: *A. r. tacanensis* from Chiapas, and *A. r. rostratus* from Guatemala, Honduras, and El Salvador. Both were described on the basis of single specimens, and because they are intermediate in character with the Northern Saw-whet Owl, they may (as some have argued) simply represent hybrids with that species, which reaches the southern limit of its range just northwest of the Isthmus of Tehuantepec. Regardless of their current relationship, it seems plausible that the Unspotted

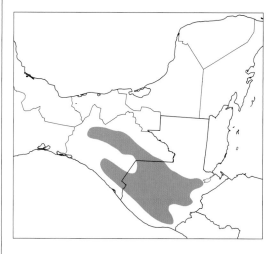

Saw-whet originated with migratory Northern Saw-whets that penetrated across the isthmus and became isolated.

An inhabitant of montane zones, the Unspotted Saw-whet Owl is so poorly known that its nest and eggs have yet to be well described. Little is known about its diet or other aspects of its life history. *(Costa Rica. Ernesto Carman)*

ETYMOLOGY: For the genus name, see "Boreal Owl." The species name commemorates Robert Ridgway, the curator of birds at the Smithsonian Institution for almost 50 years in the late nineteenth and early twentieth centuries; it was named in 1905 by the director of the Costa Rica National Museum, Anastasio Alfaro, "in honor of Professor Robert Ridgway, as a 'souvenir' of his recent explorations of Costa Rica."[4] The common name refers to the lack of spotting on the back in comparison with the Northern Saw-whet Owl. (For the etymology of "saw-whet," see that section under "Northern Saw-whet Owl," p. 300.)

> SPANISH: *Tecolote canelo, tecolotito volcanero, tecolote-abetero sureño, mochuelo moreno, lechucita inmaculada; tecolotito serrano* (Chiapas)

DISTRIBUTION

BREEDING SEASON: Resident. In our region, restricted to montane forests in Chiapas.*

MIGRATION AND MOVEMENTS: No seasonal movements known.

---

*A questionable subspecies of the Northern Saw-whet Owl, *A. acadicus brodkorbi*, was described from a single specimen purportedly taken in Oaxaca in 1949. This putative race has been assigned by some authors to the Unspotted Saw-whet, but there is no evidence that the latter species occurs west and north of the Isthmus of Tehuantepec, and the locale given for the *"brodkorbi"* specimen is highly suspect as well, given abundant errors in the collector's records.

POST-FLEDGING DISPERSAL: No information

DISTRIBUTION OUTSIDE THE COVERAGE AREA: Central highlands and Pacific slope of Guatemala, northeastern El Salvador (current status there uncertain), Volcánica Central, and Talamanca cordilleras of Costa Rica to western Panama.

DESCRIPTION AND IDENTIFICATION

Like all *Aegolius* owls, the Unspotted Saw-whet is plump and round-headed, its plumage resembling that of a dull-colored juvenile Northern Saw-whet, with solid gray-brown upperparts and no white spotting.

BASIC (ADULT) PLUMAGE: Females show more white in face, around eyes and bill. Basic plumage superficially resembles juvenal plumage in the Northern Saw-whet Owl. Head uniformly warm brown, forehead unmarked or with a few buffy streaks. Back and upperwing coverts uniformly gray-brown without white spots, tinged with rust. Wings and tail gray-brown and unmarked, except for diffuse whitish spots on the inner webbing of the inner secondaries; occasionally a hint of white barring in tail. Intensity of rufous tones may vary.

Facial disk warm brown, darker along the lower edge, with a pale disk ruff. Rictal bristles black; chin brown. Eyebrows whitish and limited. No ear tufts. Underparts dark cinnamon-buff or light brown on upper chest, fading to buff (sometimes mixed with white) on lower chest and belly. Legs feathered, buffy; toes partially bare. Underwing coverts buff or buff-brown. Undersides of flight feathers gray-brown, unmarked. Iris color often described as yellow to tawny, but some individuals exhibit dark buff-brown or yellow-brown eyes.

JUVENAL PLUMAGE: Contrasting chestnut upper breast and creamy yellow lower breast.

SIMILAR SPECIES: Lacks the bold white spotting and barring on the head, upperparts, and tail of the Northern Saw-whet Owl, which is present (if reduced) even in juveniles. Facial disk browner; underwing coverts brown or buff, not white. Eye color is darker than Northern Saw-whet's, and, while not a field characteristic, the wings are shorter and rounder than those of the Northern Saw-whet Owl, which is typical of the difference between a nonmigratory and migratory species.

VOCALIZATIONS

The vocalizations of the Unspotted Saw-whet Owl are similar to the Northern Saw-whet's, although the male advertisement song may be subtly lower in pitch and more clipped in natural situations (higher and more insistent in birds responding to playback). The advertisement call is a series of 4 to 80 (sometimes 100 or more) *toots*, which, as in the Northern Saw-whet Owl, sometimes starts quietly and rapidly, then slows to a rhythmic pace of about 3 *toots* per second (4 to 5 per second when agitated) for the remainder of the song.

The agitation call is a thin, ascending whine lasting about a second, shorter and higher-pitched than the corresponding call of the Northern Saw-whet. Juvenile begging call is a burst of 1 to 12 chirring notes; the incubating female gives a similar "high-pitched, insect-like" call from in the nest cavity in response to the approaching male's rapid *toots*.[5]

Three species—two owls and one frog—in our region make vocalizations that are confusingly similar to the Unspotted Saw-whet Owl's.

The "Guatemalan" subspecies of the Northern Pygmy-Owl (*Glaucidium gnoma cobanense*) occurs in the same highland forests as the Unspotted Saw-whet, from Chiapas to Honduras, and can on occasion give a territorial call of evenly spaced *toots* that is only slightly higher-pitched than the saw-whet's. Eisermann (2013), the first to describe the Unspotted Saw-whet's vocalizations in detail, indicates the pygmy-owl usually relapses to its typical double-

Based on its restricted range, Mexico has listed the Unspotted Saw-whet Owl as endangered, but its true status is unknown. *(Costa Rica. Ernesto Carman)*

The *toot* call of the Unspotted Saw-whet Owl is similar to that of its northern relative, and can be easily confused with vocalizations of several other small highland owls in its range. *(Costa Rica. Ernesto Carman)*

or even triple-noted hoot pattern in long singing bouts, easily distinguishing it from the saw-whet, but short, evenly spaced *toot*s are very similar. Each saw-whet note is down-slurred, while each pygmy-owl note slurs up, then down. At a distance, the saw-whet's call is more nasal, but the difference is less noticeable at close range.

The Whiskered Screech-Owl, which occurs with the Unspotted Saw-whet and the "Guatemalan" Northern Pygmy-Owl, may give a series of evenly spaced hoots instead of its more recognizable "telegraphic trill," but these notes are significantly lower-pitched and more hollow than those of the saw-whet.

The spiny-headed tree frog (*Anotheca spinosa*) is found in humid montane forests from Veracruz to Panama. Its repetitive *boop boop boop* call has been described as "amazingly owl-like," and responsible

for low-elevation reports of Unspotted Saw-whet Owl in Costa Rica.[6]

HABITAT AND NICHE

Found from 5,450 to 9,850 ft. (1,660 to 3,000 m) in Mexico, although it has been recorded as low as 4,600 ft. (1,400 m) in arid tropical forests in Guatemala, and is found at generally higher elevations (7,218 to 11,400 feet / 2,200 to 3,475 m) in Costa Rica and Panama. The number of records for Chiapas is fairly limited; it has been collected in cloud forests, pine, and pine-oak–sweet gum forest, as well as field edges and borders.

The Unspotted Saw-whet Owl has traditionally been described as a montane and cloud forest raptor, but researchers working in Costa Rica have rarely found it in woodland. Instead, almost all encounters have been in fields with sparse trees or small groves, with the highest densities above about 9,200 ft. (2,800 m) in pastures and agricultural fields interspersed with small, dense trees such as oaks, *Buddleja*, and *Escallonia*.

It is also found in páramo and subpáramo habitat, where high rodent populations coincide with seeding bamboo.[2]

DIET: In Costa Rica, it was observed catching small mammals by dropping from low (10–15 ft. / 3–5 m) perches, and catching katydids, moths, and beetles on the wing.[2]

NESTING AND BREEDING

Again, there is little solid information on this aspect of the Unspotted Saw-Whet Owl's life history. It is a cavity-nester, but no definitive description of the nest and eggs has been published. Calling intensity peaks in Mar. in Chiapas, and territorial songs stop completely by Apr., suggesting the end of egg-laying and the beginning of incubation and the nestling period. In the Guatemalan highlands, nesting occurs Nov. to Feb. Singing is concentrated between Sept. and Dec. in Costa Rica, peaking in Nov.[2]

BEHAVIOR

Nocturnal. To what degree its behavior resembles that of Northern Saw-whet Owls, which move frequently from perch to perch after dark searching for food, is unknown. Roost sites in Costa Rica were most often in short trees among dense tangles of epiphytic heaths (Ericaceae). At times up to three or four individuals can be heard calling, separated by 550 to 650 yds. (500 to 600 m) between owls.[2] There is a record of an Unspotted Saw-whet roosting in the attic of a thatched hut where corn was being stored.

STATUS

Based on its restricted range and the extensive fragmentation of montane forest habitat within it, Mexico has listed this species as "endangered." IUCN/BirdLife lists its conservation status as "least concern" and assumes a stable population. Partners in Flight estimated the global population at fewer than 50,000 individuals, but hard information on this owl is almost completely lacking. Recent fieldwork in Costa Rica documenting it at highest densities in agricultural fields with scattered trees, however, suggests that concerns about forest fragmentation may be overstated.

NOTES

1. P. L. Enríquez, M. C. Arizmendi, C. Rodríguez-Flores, and C. Soberanes-González. 2012. Unspotted Saw-whet Owl (*Aegolius ridgwayi*), Neotropical Birds Online, ed. T. S. Schulenberg. Ithaca, NY: Cornell Lab of Ornithology, http://neotropical.birds.cornell.edu/portal/species/overview?p_p_spp=215576.

2. E. Carman, pers. comm.

3. Wetmore, Pasquier, and Olson 1968.

4. A. Alfaro. 1905. A new owl from Costa Rica. *Proceedings of the Biological Society of Washington* 18:217.

5. Eisermann 2013, p. 11.

6. Stiles and Skutch 1989, p. 196.

BIBLIOGRAPHY

Baepler, D. H. 1962. The avifauna of the Soloma region in Huehuetenango, Guatemala. *Condor* 64:140–153.

Binford 1989.

BirdLife International. 2015. *Aegolius ridgwayi*. In IUCN Red List of Threatened Species, version 2014.3, http://www.iucnredlist.org/details/22689371/0.

Blancher et al. 2013.

Briggs 1954.

Butchart, S., and J. Ekstrom. Southern saw-whet owl *Aegolius ridgwayi*. BirdLife International (2013) Species factsheet: *Aegolius ridgwayi,* Downloaded from http://www.birdlife.org on 06/02/2013.

Eisermann 2013.

Enríquez-Rocha, Eisermann, and Mikkola 2012.

Enríquez-Rocha, Rangel-Salazar, and Holt 1993.

Foster and Johnson 1974.

Griscom, L. 1930. Studies from the Dwight collection of Guatemala birds III. *American Museum Novitates* 438:1–18.

Hernandez, L. R. 2011. "Composición y abundancia de aves rapaces nocturnas en bosques secundarios a lo largo de un gradiente altitudinal de la Vertiente Pacífica de Costa Rica." MS thesis, Instituto de Biociências da Universidade de São Paulo.

Hunn 1973.

Leck, C. F. 1980. Establishment of new population centers with changes in migration patterns. *Journal of Field Ornithology* 51:168–173.

Marshall, J. T. Jr. 1943. Additional information concerning the birds of El Salvador. *Condor* 45:21–33.

Martínez-Ortega, J. A. 2010. "Distribución, abundancia y asociaciones ambientales de un ensamble de búhos en un bosque de montaña en los Altos de Chiapas." BS thesis, Benemérita Universidad Autónoma de Puebla.

Moore 1947.

Navarro-Sigüenza, A. G., and A. T. Peterson. 2007. *Aegolius ridgwayi* (tecolote canelo) residencia permanente distribución potencial. In *Mapas de las Aves de México Basados en WWW,* ed. A. G. Navarro and A. T. Peterson. Final report, SNIB-CONABIO project no. CE015. México DF.

Stiles and Skutch 1989.

ACKNOWLEDGMENTS

The guts of this book are built on the observations and research of thousands of dedicated individuals, professionals and amateurs alike, who have spent uncountable hours studying the lives, behavior, and ecology of owls. They are diurnal primates studying nocturnal raptors, which calls for even more fortitude and tenacity than is typical in scientific research.

Special thanks to Danny Bystrak and Jo Anna Lutmerding at the federal Bird Banding Laboratory for assistance with lifespan and longevity data; Glenn A. Proudfoot, Vassar College, and Dennis Abbate, Arizona Game and Fish Department, for Ferruginous Pygmy-Owl data; Peter Vickery in Maine and Jim Wilson and Stuart Tingley in New Brunswick for information on Eastern Screech-Owl ranges; Brian A. Millsap, national raptor coordinator for the U.S. Fish and Wildlife Service; Steve Lewis, raptor specialist with the U.S. Fish and Wildlife Service in Alaska; Christian Artuso, Bird Studies Canada in Manitoba; David Johnson, Global Owl Project; Jean-François Therrien of Hawk Mountain Sanctuary, Eugene Potapov, Tom McDonald, and Norman Smith of Massachusetts Audubon for help with Snowy Owls; James R. Duncan, Manitoba Conservation and Water Stewardship; Greg Budney, curator, and Matthew A. Young, collections management leader, both of the Macaulay Library at the Cornell Lab of Ornithology; Angelika Nelson, curator of the Borror Laboratory of Bioacoustics at Ohio State University; Rob Bierregaard and Nate Rice at the Academy of Natural Sciences of Drexel University; Louis Imbeau, Université du Québec en Abitibi-Témiscamingue; Marcel Gahbauer, McGill University; Leo Douglas, Birds Caribbean; Ann Haynes-Sutton, Jamaica; Knut Eisermann, Guatemala; Stephen Schabel and Jim Elliott, Center for Birds of Prey; Gareth Morgan, African Lion Safari; Mary and Nick Freeman; Robert W. Dickerman and Andrew Johnson, Museum of Southwestern Biology regarding Great Horned Owl subspecies. Ernesto Carman generously provided unpublished morphological data and habitat, dietary, and behavior observations on the Unspotted Saw-whet Owl.

Deepest thanks to my editor at Houghton Mifflin Harcourt, Lisa White, for steering this book so handily, and to production editor Beth Burleigh Fuller and copyeditor Kate Davis for their keen eyes and sure sense. Special thanks to my friend and colleague Tom Johnson for sourcing the photographs, often while leading a birding trip to some exotic locale, or via satellite phone from a NOAA survey vessel far at sea. It was a further pleasure working with Larry Rosche to create the range maps. My agent, Peter Matson, has been a bulwark for many years. I'm indebted to the many photographers whose work illustrates this book and makes it such a visual delight. Owl photography is, for all the obvious reasons, an especially challenging field, beyond which lie the special obstacles of working in tropical environments, where many of these species live.

I cannot convey how privileged I have been to work for almost 20 years with such a superb crew of banders and volunteers through the Ned Smith Center for Nature and Art's owl-research program, which is citizen-science at its best. Particular thanks to my friends and colleagues Sandy Lockerman and Gary Shimmel, who have worked closely with me to build that program, and to David F. Brinker and Steve Huy, with whom I codirect Project Owlnet and Project SNOWstorm, studying Northern Saw-whet Owls and Snowy Owls, respectively.

Finally, and most of all, thanks to my wife, Amy. She puts up with a lot, and I'm not sure she knew what she was getting into, but so far the owls haven't been a deal breaker.

GLOSSARY

accipiter. Fast, agile forest hawks of the genus *Accipiter,* including Sharp-shinned and Cooper's Hawks.

adult. A fully mature bird, having attained basic (definitive) plumage.

AOU. American Ornithologists' Union, the oldest professional ornithological group in North America and the arbiter of the official checklist of Western Hemisphere birds.

asynchronous hatching. A clutch of eggs that hatches in the same order as they were laid, instead of all at once.

basic plumage. Among owls, which lack seasonal changes in appearance, essentially equates with definitive or "adult" plumage. It is preceded by the prebasic molt, in which juvenal plumage is replaced, a process that, in the case of the primaries and secondaries, may take several years.

bigamy. Maintaining more than one mate at a time, regardless of gender. See **polyandry** and **polygyny.**

biomass. The total mass of organisms; in reference to diet, the mass (weight) of prey consumed.

boreal (forest, zone). Associated with the cold, largely coniferous forests of Canada and Alaska.

Breeding Bird Survey. A continent-wide survey of breeding North American birds, initiated in 1966 and conducted annually by the USGS Patuxent Wildlife Research Center and Canadian Wildlife Service.

carpal patch. An area of darkly pigmented feathers at the bend of the wing.

clade. An evolutionary group consisting of an ancestor and all of its descendants.

cline/clinal. Among organisms, a gradation of characteristics between geographic populations.

contour feathers. Vaned feathers that comprise the outer shell of a bird's plumage, including the flight feathers.

COSEWIC. Committee on the Status of Endangered Wildlife in Canada, a panel charged with overseeing rare and endangered wildlife protection.

coverts. Small contour feathers that overlap, like shingles, tracts of flight feathers on the wings and base of the tail.

crepuscular. Active at dawn and dusk.

definitive plumage. Plumage that does not change seasonally or with time. Among owls, essentially the same as adult plumage.

dimorphic. Occurring in two distinct forms, either in color, appearance, or size (see **polymorphic**). May or may not be associated with gender.

dispersal. Movement from one area to another, but distinct from seasonal migration. Juvenile dispersal refers to the movement of young birds away from their parents' territory.

diurnal. Active in daylight.

ESA. Endangered Species Act, a U.S. federal environmental law passed in 1973.

etymology. The origin of words and how their meaning has changed.

eyespots. Dark pigmented patches of feathers on the back of a bird's head, sometimes rimmed in white, which resemble eyes.

extirpated. Eliminated from a particular area or region.

facial disk. The semicircular arrangement of feathers surrounding the eyes of an owl; also the underlying structures of the external ear, which permit the owl to collect and direct sound waves for better hearing.

facultative. Occurring in response to conditions. In facultative migration, individuals move different distances in different years depending on climate and prey conditions.

family. A taxonomic unit that encompasses more than one genus. There are two families of owls, the Tytonidae (barn owls) and the Strigidae (typical owls).

fire regime. The frequency and intensity of wildfires, either naturally occurring or caused by humans.

fledge/fledging/fledgling. Strictly speaking, "fledging" refers to a nestling's departure from the nest and first flight, at which point it is considered a "fledgling." Among owls, which may leave the nest weeks before they are capable of flight, "fledging" refers specifically to the onset of the ability to fly. Young birds are considered fledglings while they remain dependent on their parents.

haplotype. A set of DNA sequences (alleles) that are inherited together.

holarctic. Occuring throughout the Arctic region.

home range. The area in which an animal lives. Only a portion of the home range may be actively defended (territory).

immature. Referring to a young bird no longer dependent on its parents but not fully adult or capable of breeding.

irruption. To enter forcefully (as opposed to an exploding out, i.e., eruption). In ornithology, an irruption is the unpredictable movement of an otherwise sedentary species, usually as the result of changes in its food supply.

IUCN. International Union for Conservation of Nature, keeper of the Red List of Threatened Species.

juvenile/juvenal. "Juvenile" refers to a young bird that has not yet attained basic (definitive) plumage. The plumage stage worn by a juvenile bird is known as "juvenal" plumage.

Madrean. Of the Sierra Madre Occidental; used here to refer to the northernmost mountains of this range in northern Mexico and extreme southern Arizona and New Mexico. (See **Sky Islands.**)

mesoptile. The second coat of down grown by owl chicks, replacing the neoptile (natal) down.

monogamous. Referring to a mating system in which a male and female are exclusively paired.

monomorphic. Occurring in one form—in the case of owls, without color morphs.

monotypic. In taxonomy, referring to a species with no recognized subspecies, or a genus containing only one species.

morph. Among owls, an alternate and permanent base-plumage coloration. Replaces the obsolete term "phase," which suggests change with time.

natal down. A chick's first downy plumage; the neoptile coat.

neoptile. Referring to an owl chick's first downy plumage; natal down.

neotony. Exhibiting the characteristics of a juvenile into adulthood.

Neotropical. Associated with the New World tropics.

nomadic/nomadism. Referring to unpredictable movements between breeding or nonbreeding sites within a species's normal range.

nominate. A subspecies given the same trinomial name as the species to which it belongs, e.g., *Aegolius acadicus acadicus*.

nocturnal. Active by night.

order. A taxonomic unit encompassing one or more families. All owls are members of the order Strigiformes.

passerine. A member of the order Passeriformes; a songbird.

pectinate. Toothlike, as in a comb.

pellet. A compact mass of fur, bones, and other undigestible prey remains, regurgitated by owls and several other groups of birds.

pishing. A technique for attracting small birds by making a *spish-spish-spish* sound with the lips.

polyandry. A mating system in which a female has two mates at the same time.

polygyny. A mating system in which a male has two mates at the same time.

polymorphic. Occurring in two or more forms; in the case of owls, two or more color morphs.

polytypic. In taxonomy, referring to a species with multiple subspecies, or a genus containing more than one species.

primaries. The large flight feathers attached to the outer (hand) portion of the wing.

race. See **subspecies.**

reversed sexual dimorphism or **reversed size dimorphism (RSD).** The tendency for females to average larger (in linear measurements or mass) than males of the same species.

rictal bristles. Specialized feathers surrounding the bill.

SARA. Species at Risk Act, a Canadian law encompassing endangered species protection.

scapulars. Feathers attached to the humerus, which overlap and partially cover the folded wing.

secondaries. Flight feathers attached to the forearm (ulna).

siblicide. The killing of one sibling by another, either directly or by depriving the younger, smaller sibling of food.

Sky Islands. The isolated mountain ranges of southeastern Arizona and southwestern New Mexico that form the northernmost extent of the Sierra Madre Occidental (may also refer to corresponding ranges south of the Mexico border).

stoop. A dive, usually in pursuit of prey, by a raptor.

subspecies. A geographically distinct taxonomic category below species, distinguished by physical, vocal, genetic, or behavioral characteristics. Subspecies freely interbreed and often intergrade on a cline. Also known informally as a "race." Subspecies are identified by a trinomial name, e.g., *Bubo virginianus subarcticus*.

supercilium. A contrastingly pigmented plumage stripe above the eye; in owls, informally referred to as the "eyebrow."

superspecies. Two or more similar, closely related species with a common, recent ancestor; sometimes referred to as *sister species* or a *species complex*.

sympatric. Referring to two or more species with overlapping distributions.

sympatry. Occupying overlapping ranges; the opposite of *allopatry*.

systematics. The branch of biology that studies the evolutionary relationships between organisms.

tarsus (pl.: **tarsi**). Informal reference to the tarsometatarsus, the long bone of the lower leg in birds.

tertials. The innermost secondary feathers, which overlap the closed wing at rest.

vermiculated. Marked with intricate, sinuous, and closely spaced lines.

Watch List. Early warning list of rare or declining species of birds, maintained by the North American Bird Conservation Initiative. The Red Watch List includes species at highest risk of extinction; the Yellow Watch List includes those at somewhat lesser risk. Not related to the Red List of Threatened Species, maintained by the International Union for the Conservation of Nature.

wing-loading. A measure of body weight as supported by wing area. Owls generally have low wing-loading, with relatively low mass and relatively large wing area.

xeric. Dry or arid.

zygodactyl. An avian foot with two toes facing front and two behind.

GENERAL BIBLIOGRAPHY

Anderson, S. H., and K. A. Clark. 2002. Comparative habitat use by owls in a high-altitude (1,700–3,000 m) Rocky Mountain forest. In *Ecology and Conservation of Owls,* ed. I. Newton, R. Kavanagh, J. Olsen, and I. Taylor. Victoria, Australia: CSIRO Publishing.

Andrle, R. F. 1967. Birds of the Sierra de Tuxtla in Veracruz, Mexico. *Wilson Bulletin* 79:163–187.

Arredondo, O. 1972. Nueva especie de ave fósil (Strigiformes: Tytonidae) del Pleistoceno Superior de Cuba. *Boletin de la Sociedad Venezolana Ciencias Naturales* 29:415–431.

Arredondo, O., and S. L. Olson. 1994. A new species of owl of the genus *Bubo* from the Pleistocene of Cuba (Aves: Strigiformes). *Proceedings of the Biological Society of Washington* 107:436–444.

Arredondo, O. 1976. The great predatory birds of the Pleistocene of Cuba. In *Collected papers in avian paleontology honoring the 90th birthday of Alexander Wetmore,* ed. S. L. Olson. *Smithsonian Contributions to Paleobiology* 27:169–187.

Banks, R. C., C. Cicero, J. L. Dunn, A. W. Kratter, I. J. Lovette, P. C. Rassmussen, J. V. Remsen Jr., J. D. Rising, and D. F. Stotz. 2003. Forty-fourth supplement to the American Ornithologists' Union Check-list of North American Birds. *Auk* 120 (3): 923–931.

Banks, R. C., J. W. Fitzpatrick, T. R. Howell, N. K. Johnson, B. L. Monroe Jr., H. Ouellet, J. V. Remsen Jr., and R. W. Storer. Forty-first supplement to the American Ornithologists' Union Check-list of North American Birds. *Auk* 114:542–552.

Basakowski, T., and D. G. Smith. 1997. Distribution and species richness of a forest raptor community in relation to urbanization. *Journal of Raptor Research* 31:26–31.

Beedy, E. C., and E. R. Pandolfino. 2013. *Birds of the Sierra Nevada.* Berkeley and Los Angeles: University of California Press.

Bent, A. C. 1938. *Life Histories of North American Birds of Prey,* pt. 2. Washington, DC: Smithsonian Institution.

Binford, L. C. 1989. Distributional survey of the birds of the Mexican state of Oaxaca. Ornithological Monographs 43, Washington, DC: American Ornithologists' Union.

Birkenstein, L. R., and R. E. Tomlinson. 1981. *Native Names of Mexican Birds.* Washington, DC: U.S. Fish and Wildlife Service.

Blancher, P. J., K. V. Rosenberg, A. O. Panjabi, B. Altman, A. R. Couturier, W. E. Thogmartin, and the Partners in Flight Science Committee. 2013. *Handbook to the Partners in Flight Population Estimates Database,* v. 2.0. PIF Technical Series no. 6, http://rmbo.org/pifpopestimates/downloads/Handbook%20to%20the%20PIF%20Population%20Estimates%20Database%20Version%202.0.pdf.

Bond, J. 1993. *Birds of the West Indies,* 5th ed. Boston: Houghton Mifflin.

———. 1934. A partial list of birds observed in Haiti and the Dominican Republic. *Auk* 51:500–502.

———. 1928. The distribution and habits of the birds of the Republic of Haiti. *Proceedings of the Academy of Natural Sciences* 80:483–521.

Bosakowski, T., and D. G. Smith. 1997. Distribution and species richness of a forest raptor community in relation to urbanization. *Journal of Raptor Research* 31:26–33.

Briggs, M. A. 1954. Apparent neoteny in the saw-whet owls of Mexico and Central America. *Proceedings of the Biological Society of Washington* 67:179–182.

Brodkorb, P. 1968. An extinct Pleistocene owl from Cuba. *Quarterly Journal of the Florida Academy of Sciences* 31:112–114.

———. 1959. Pleistocene birds from New Providence Island, Bahamas. *Bulletin of the Florida State Museum* 4:349–371.

Buchanan, O. M. 1964. The Mexican races of the least pygmy-owl. *Condor* 66:103–112.

Ceballos, G., and L. Márquez Valdelamar. 2000. *Las Ave de México en Peligro de Extinción.* México DF: Universidad Nacional Autónoma de México, Instituto de Ecología, Comisión Nacional para el Conocimiento and Uso de la Biodiversidad.

Chesser, R. T., R. C. Banks, C. Cicero, J. L. Dunn, A. W. Kratter, I. J. Lovette, A. G. Navarro-Sigüenza, P. C. Rassmussen, J. V. Remsen Jr., J. D. Rising, D. F. Stotz, and K. Winker. 2014. Fifty-fifth supplement to the American Ornithologists' Union Check-list of North American Birds. *Auk* 131 (4): CSi-CSxv.

Chesser, R. T., R. C. Banks, F. K. Barker, C. Cicero, J. L. Dunn, A. W. Kratter, I. J. Lovette, P. C. Rassmussen, J. V. Remsen Jr., J. D. Rising, D. F. Stotz, and K. Winker. 2013. Fifty-fourth supplement to the American Ornithologists' Union Check-list of North American Birds. *Auk* 130 (3): 558–571.

Cheveau, M., P. Drapeau, L. Imbeau, and Y. Bergeron. 2004. Owl winter irruptions as an indicator of small mammal population cycles in the boreal forest of eastern North America. *Oikos* 107:190–198.

Choate, E. A. 1985. *The Dictionary of American Bird Names,* rev. ed. Boston: Harvard Common Press.

Clark, R. J., and H. Mikkola. 1989. A preliminary revision of threatened and near-threatened nocturnal birds of prey of the world. In *Raptors in the Modern World,* ed. B.-U. Meyburg and R. D. Chancellor. Berlin, London, and Paris: World Working Group on Birds of Prey.

Corman, T. E., and C. Wise-Gervais, eds. 2005. *Arizona Breeding Bird Atlas.* Albuquerque, NM: University of New Mexico Press.

Côte, M., J. Ibarzabal, M.-H. St-Laurent, J. Ferron, and R. Gagnon. 2007. Age-dependent response of migrant and resident *Aegolius* species to small rodent population fluctuations in the eastern Canadian boreal forest. *Journal of Raptor Research* 41:16–25.

Coues, E. 1882. *The Coues Check List of North American Birds,* 2nd ed. Boston: Estes and Lauriat.

Craighead, J. J., and F. C. Craighead Jr. 1956. *Hawks, Owls and Wildlife.* Harrisburg, PA: Stackpole.

Dickinson, E. C., and J. V. Remsen Jr., eds. 2013. *The Howard and Moore Complete Checklist of the Birds of the World,* 4th ed., vol. 1. Eastbourne, UK: Aves Press.

Dunn, E. H., A. D. Brewer, A. W. Diamond, E. J. Woodsworth, and B. T. Collins. 2009. *Canadian Atlas of Banding,* vol. 3. Environment Canada, http://www.ec.gc.ca/aobc-cabb/index.aspx?nav=overview_survol3&lang=en.

Dunning, J. B. Jr. 2007. *CRC Handbook of Avian Body Masses,* 2nd ed. Boca Raton, FL: CRC Press.

———. 1985. Owl weights in the literature: A review. *Raptor Research* 19 (4): 113–121.

Earhart, C. M., and N. K. Johnson. 1970. Size dimorphism and food habits of North American owls. *Condor* 72 (3): 251–264.

Eckert, A. W., and K. E. Karalus. 1973. *The Owls of North America.* New York: Crown.

Eckert, K. R. 2005. The winter 2004–2005 influx of northern owls: An overview. *Loon* 77:123–132.

Ellison, W. G., ed. 2010. *2nd Atlas of the Breeding Birds of Maryland and the District of Columbia.* Baltimore: Johns Hopkins University Press.

Eisermann, K. 2013. Vocal field marks of unspotted saw-whet owl and Guatemalan pygmy owl. *Neotropical Birding* 13:8–13.

Enríquez-Rocha, P., K. Eisermann, and H. Mikkola. 2012. Los búhos de México y centroamérica: Necesidades en investigación y conservación. *Ornithologia Neotropical* 23:251–264.

Enríquez-Rocha, P., and J. L. Rangel-Salazar. 1995. Owl occurrence and calling behavior in a tropical rain forest. *Journal of Raptor Research* 35:107–114.

Enríquez-Rocha, P., J. L. Rangel-Salazar, and D. W. Holt. 1993. Presence and distribution of Mexican owls: A review. *Journal of Raptor Research* 27 (3): 154–160.

Ericson, P. G. P., C. L. Anderson, T. Britton, A. Elzanowski, U. S. Johansson, M. Källersjö, J. I. Ohlson, T. J. Parsons, D. Zuccon, and G. Mayr. 2006. Diversification of Neoaves: Integration of molecular sequence data and fossils. *Biology Letters* 2:543–547.

Flesch, A. D., C. Beardmore, and R. Mesta. 2008. Distribution and status of birds of conservation interest and identification of important bird areas in Sonora, Mexico. Report to U.S. Fish and Wildlife Service. Tucson, AZ: Sonoran Joint Venture.

Forbush, E. H. 1927. *Birds of Massachusetts and Other New England States,* vol. 2. Norwood, MA: Norwood Press.

Foster, M. S., and N. K. Johnson. 1974. Notes on birds of Costa Rica. *Wilson Bulletin* 86:58–63.

Friedman, H., L. Griscom, and R. T. Moore. 1950. *Distributional Check-list of the Birds of Mexico,* pt. 1. Berkeley, CA: Cooper Ornithological Club.

Gerhardt, R. P., N. Bonilla-González, D. M. Gerhardt, and C. J. Flatten. 1994 a. Breeding biology and home range of two *Ciccaba* owls. *Wilson Bulletin* 106:629–639.

Gerhardt, R. P., D. M. Gerhardt, C. J. Flatten, and N. Bonilla González. 1994b. The food habits of sympatric *Ciccaba* owls in northern Guatemala. *Journal of Field Ornithology* 65:258–264.

Given, B. 2004. *Surveys for Rare Owl Species in the Black Hills.* Denver, CO: Western Wildlife Institute.

Gómez Navarrete, J. A. 2009. *Diccionario Introducto: Español-Maya / Maya-Español.* Chetumal, Quintana Roo: Universidad de Quintana Roo.

Hackett, S. J., R. T. Kimball, S. Reddy, R. C. K. Bowie, E. L. Braun, M. J. Braun, J. L. Chojnowski, W. A. Cox, K.-L. Han, J. Harshman, C. J. Huddleston, B. D. Marks, K. J. Miglia, W. S. Moore, F. H. Sheldon, D. W. Steadman, C. C. Witt, and T. Yuri. 2008. A phylogenomic study of birds reveals their evolutionary history. *Science* 320:1763–1767.

Hamer, T. E., E. D. Forsman, and E. M. Glenn. 2007. Home range attributes and habitat selection of barred owls and spotted owls in an area of sympatry. *Condor* 109:750–768.

Hartman, F. A. 1961. *Locomotor Mechanisms of Birds.* Smithsonian Misc. Coll. 143. Washington, DC: Smithsonian Institution.

———. 1955. Heart weights in birds. *Condor* 57:221–238.

Hekstra, G. P. 1982. Description of twenty-four new subspecies of American *Otus* (Aves Strigidae). *Bulletin Zoologish Museum* 9 (7): 49–63.

Hayward, G. D., and J. Verner, eds. 1994. Flammulated, boreal, and great gray owls in the United States: A technical conservation assessment. Gen. Tech. Rep. RM-253. Fort Collins, CO: U.S. Department of Agriculture, Forest Service, Rocky Mountain Forest and Range Experiment Station.

Hinam, H. L., and J. R. Duncan. 2002. Effects of habitat fragmentation and slope on the distribution of three owl species in the Manitoba Escarpment, Canada—A preliminary analysis. In *Ecology and Conservation of Owls,* ed. I. Newton, R. Kavanagh, J. Olsen, and I. Taylor. Victoria, Australia: CSIRO Publishing.

Howell, S. N. G. 2010. *Molt in North American Birds.* Boston: Houghton Mifflin Harcourt.

Howell, S. N. G., R. A. Erickson, R. A. Hamilton, and M. A. Patten. 2001. An annotated checklist of the birds of Baja California and Baja California Sur. *Monographs in Field Ornithology* 3:171–203.

Howell, S. N. G., I. Lewington, and W. Russell. 2014. *Rare Birds of North America.* Princeton, NJ: Princeton University Press.

Howell, S. N. G., and M. B. Robbins. 1995. Species limits of the least pygmy-owl (*Glaucidium minutissimum*) complex. *Wilson Bulletin* 107:7–25.

Howell, S. N. G., and S. Webb. 1995. *A Guide to the Birds of Mexico and Northern Central America.* London and New York: Oxford University Press.

Hubbard, J. P., and R. S. Crossin. 1974. Notes on northern Mexican birds: An expedition report. *Nemouria* 14:1–41.

Hume, J. P., and M. Walters. 2012. *Extinct Birds.* London: T & AD Poyser.

Hunn, E. 1975. Words for owls in North American Indian languages. *International Journal of American Linguistics* 41:237–239.

———. 1973. Noteworthy bird observations from Chiapas, Mexico. *Condor* 75:483.

Jobling, J. A. 1991. *A Dictionary of Scientific Bird Names.* Oxford and New York: Oxford University Press.

Johnsgard, P. A. 2002. *North American Owls,* 2nd ed. Washington, DC: Smithsonian Institution Press.

Keith, A. R., J. T. Wiley, S. C. Latta, and J. A. Ottenwalder. 2005. The birds of Hispaniola. *Auk* 122:1016–1018.

König, C., and F. Weick. 2008. *Owls of the World,* 2nd ed. New Haven, CT, and London: Yale University Press.

Krüger, O. 2005. The evolution of reversed sexual size dimorphism in hawks, falcons and owls: A comparative study. *Evolutionary Ecology* 19:467–486.

Latta, S., C. Rimmer, A. Keith, J. Wiley, H. Raffaele, K. McFarland, and E. Fernandez. 2006. *Birds of the Dominican Republic and Haiti.* Princeton, NJ: Princeton University Press.

Lever, C. 2005. *Naturalised Birds of the World.* London: T & A D Poyser.

Lin, W. L., S. M. Lin, and H. Y. Tseng. 2014. Colour morphs in the collared pygmy owl *Glaucidium brodiei* are age-related, not a polymorphism. *Ardea* 102:95–99.

Lockwood, M. W., and B. Freeman. 2014. *The Texas Ornithological Society Handbook of Texas Birds,* 2nd ed. College Station, TX: Texas A&M University Press.

Lowery, G. H., and W. W. Dalquest. 1951. Birds from the state of Veracruz, Mexico. *University of Kansas Public Museum of Natural History* 3:531–649.

Marks, J. S., R. J. Cannings, and H. Mikkola. 1999. Family Strigidae (typical owls). In *Handbook of Birds of the World,* vol. 5. Barcelona: Lynx Edicions.

Marshall, J. T. 1967. *Parallel Variation in North and Middle American Screech-owls.* Los Angeles: Western Foundation of Vertebrate Zoology.

McCarthy, E. M. 2006. *Handbook of Avian Hybrids of the World.* New York: Oxford University Press.

McGowan, K. J., and K. Corwin, eds. 2008. *The Second Atlas of Breeding Birds in New York State.* Ithaca, NY: Cornell University Press.

Mikkola, H. 2012. *Owls of the World.* Buffalo, NY, and Richmond Hill, ON: Firefly Books.

———. 1983. *Owls of Europe.* Vermillion, SD: Buteo Books.

Monroe, B. L. Jr. 1968. A distributional survey of the birds of Honduras. Ornithological Monographs 7, Washington, DC: American Ornithologists' Union.

Monterrubio-Rico, T. C., and P. Escalante-Pliego. 2006. Richness, distribution and conservation status of cavity nesting birds in Mexico. *Biological Conservation* 128:67–78.

Moore, R. T. 1947. Two new owls, a swift and a poorwill from Mexico. *Proceedings of the Biological Society of Washington* 60:141–148.

Moore, R. T., and J. L. Peters. 1939. The genus *Otus* in Mexico and Central America. *Auk* 56 (1): 38–56.

Navarro, A. G. and A.T. Peterson. 2007. *Mapas de las aves de México basados.* Museo de Zoología, Facultad de Ciencias, UNAM and University of Kansas Museum of Natural History.

Norberg, R. A. 2002. Independent evolution of outer ear asymmetry among five owl lineages; morphology, function and selection. In *Ecology and Conservation of Owls,* ed. I. Newton, R. Kavanagh, J. Olsen, and I. Taylor. Victoria, Australia: CSIRO Publishing.

Nunavut Department of Culture, Language, Elders and Youth. *Inuktitut Living Dictionary.* http://www.livingdictionary.com.

Olson, S. L. 2012. A new species of small owl of the genus *Aegolius* (Aves: Strigidae) from Quaternary deposits on Bermuda. *Proceedings of the Biological Society of Washington* 125:97–105.

———. 1978. A paleontological perspective of West Indian birds and mammals. In *Zoogeography in the Caribbean,* ed. F. B. Gill. Philadelphia: Academy of Natural Sciences.

Olson, S. L., and D. W. Steadman. 1977. A new genus of flightless ibis (Threskiornithidae) and other fossil birds from cave deposits in Jamaica. *Proceedings of the Biological Society of Washington* 90:447–457.

Patten, M. A., H. G. de Silva, A. C. Ibarra, and B. D. Patten-Smith. 2011. An annotated checklist of the avifauna of Palenque, Chiapas. *Revista Mexicana de Biodiversidad* 82:515–537.

Paynter, R. A. Jr. 1955. Ornithogeography of the Yucatán Peninsula. *Bulletin of the Peabody Museum of Natural History* 9:1–347.

Peeters, H. 2007. *Field Guide to Owls of California and the West.* Berkeley and Los Angeles: University of California Press.

Penhallurick, J. M. 2002. The taxonomy and conservation status of the owls of the world: A review. In *Ecology and Conservation of Owls,* ed. I. Newton, R. Kavanagh, J. Olsen, and I. Taylor, pp. 343–354. Victoria, Australia: CSIRO Publishing.

Peterson, A. T., A. G. Navarro-Sigüenza, B. E. Hernández-Baños, G. Escalona-Segura, F. Rebón-Gallardo, E. Rodríguez-Ayala, E. M. Figueroa-Esquivel, and L. Cabrera-Garciá. 2003. The Chimalapas region, Oaxaca, Mexico: A high-priority region for bird conservation in Mesoamerica. *Bird Conservation International* 13:227–253.

Proudfoot, G. A., F. R. Gelbach, and R. L. Honeycutt. 2007. Mitochondrial DNA variation and phylogeography of the eastern and western screech-owl. *Condor* 109:617–627.

Pyle, P. 1997. *Identification Guide to North American Birds*, pt. 1. Bolinas, CA: Slate Creek Press.

Pyle, P., and D. F. DeSante. 2014. Four-letter (English name) and six-letter (scientific name) alpha codes for 2098 bird species (and 98 non-species taxa) in accordance with the 55th AOU supplement (2014), sorted taxonomically. Institute for Bird Populations, http://www.birdpop.org/DownloadDocuments/Alpha_codes_tax.pdf.

———. 2005. Updates to four-letter and six-letter alpha codes based on revisions by the American Ornithologists' Union. *North American Bird Bander* 30:70–72.

———. 2003. Four-letter and six-letter alpha codes for birds recorded from the American Ornithologists' Union Check-list area. *North American Bird Bander* 28:64–79.

Raffaele, H., J. Wiley, O. Garrido, A. Keith, and J. Raffaele. 1998. *A Guide to the Birds of the West Indies.* Princeton, NJ: Princeton University Press.

Rashid, S. 2009. *Small Mountain Owls.* Atglen, PA: Schiffer Publishing.

Ridgway, R. 1914. *The Birds of North and Middle America,* pt. 6. Washington, DC: United States National Museum.

Rosenberg, K. V., D. Pashley, B. Andres, P. J. Blancher, G. S. Butcher, W. C. Hunter, D. Mehlman, A. O. Panjabi, M. Parr, G. Wallace, and D. Wiedenfeld. 2014. *The State of the Birds 2014 Watch List.* Washington, DC: North American Bird Conservation Initiative, U.S. Committee, http://www.stateofthebirds.org/extinctions/watchlist.pdf.

Schaldach, W. J. Jr. 2003. A Partially Annotated and Taxonomic Checklist of the Birds of the State of Veracruz, Mexico, http://www.catemaco.info/docs/schaldach/annotated.html.

Schaldach, W. J. Jr. 1963. Avifauna of Colima and adjacent Jalisco. *Proceedings of the Western Foundation for Vertebrate Zoology* 1:1–100.

Schaldach, W. J. Jr., B. P. Escalante, and K. Winker. 1997. Further notes on the avifauna of Oaxaca, Mexico. *Anales del Instituto de Biologia Universidad Nacional Autónoma de México* 68:91–135.

Seiler, W. A. 2012. *Iñupiatun Eskimo Dictionary.* Dallas, TX: SIL International.

Sibley, D. 2014. *The Sibley Guide to Birds,* 2nd ed. New York: Alfred A. Knopf.

Sleep, D. J. H. 2005. "Responses of boreal forest owls to landscape patterns originating from fire and timber harvest." PhD diss., University of Guelph.

Smelcer, J. E., J. Kari, and M. Buck. 2011. *Ahtna Noun Dictionary,* 2nd ed. Glenallen, AK: Ahtna Heritage Foundation.

Snyder, N. F. R., and J. W. Wiley. 1976. *Sexual Size Dimorphism in Hawks and Owls of North America.* Ornithological Monographs, 20, Washington, DC: American Ornithologists' Union.

Steadman, D. W., and W. B. Hilgartner. 1999. A new species of extinct barn owl (Aves: *Tyto*) from Barbuda, Less Antilles. *Smithsonian Contributions to Paleontology* 89:75–83.

Stiles, F. G., and A. F. Skutch. 1989. *A Guide to the Birds of Costa Rica.* Ithaca, NY: Comstock.

Stotz, D. F., J. W. Fitzpatrick, T. A. Parker III, and D. K. Moskovits. 1996. *Neotropical Birds: Ecology and Conservation.* Chicago and London: University of Chicago Press.

Voous, K. H. 1988. *Owls of the Northern Hemisphere.* London: William Collins Sons.

Walker, L. W. 1993. *The Book of Owls.* Austin, TX: University of Texas Press.

Webster, D. H., and W. Zibell. 1970. *Iñupiat Eskimo Dictionary.* Fairbanks, AK: Summer Institute of Linguistics.

Weick, F. 2006. *Owls (Strigiformes): An Annotated and Illustrated Checklist.* Berlin: Springer-Verlag.

Weidensaul, S., M. Stoffel, M. S. Monroe, D. Okines, B. Lane, J. and S. Gregoire, and T. Kita. 2015. Plumage aberrations in northern saw-whet owls (Aegolius acadicus). *Journal of Raptor Research,* 49:84–88.

Weins, J. D. 2012. "Competitive interactions and resource partitioning between northern spotted owls and barred owls in western Oregon." PhD diss., Oregon State University.

Wetmore, A., R. F. Pasquier, and S. L. Olson. 1968. *The Birds of the Republic of Panama,* pt. 2. Washington, DC: Smithsonian Institution.

Wetmore, A., and B. H. Swales. 1931. *Birds of Haiti and the Dominican Republic.* Washington, DC: Smithsonian Institution Bulletin 155.

Weyden, W. J. van der. 1975. Scops and screech owls: Vocal evidence for a basic subdivision of the genus *Otus. Ardea* 63:65–77.

Whitacre, D. F., ed. 2012. *Neotropical Birds of Prey.* Ithaca, NY: Cornell University Press.

White, C. M., and L. F. Kiff. 2000. Biodiversity, island raptors and species concepts. In *Raptors at Risk,* ed. R. D. Chancellor and B.-U. Meyburg. Berlin: World Working Group on Birds of Prey and Blaine, WA: Hancock House.

Wiley, J. W. 1986a. Habitat change and its effects on Puerto Rican raptors. *Birds of Prey Bulletin* 3:51–56.

———. 1986b. Status and conservation of raptors in the West Indies. *Birds of Prey Bulletin* 3:57–70.

Wilson, A. M., D. W. Brauning, and R. S. Mulvihill. 2012. *Second Atlas of Breeding Birds of Pennsylvania.* State College, PA: Pennsylvania University Press.

Wink, M., A. El-Sayed, H. Sauer-Gürth, and J. Gonzalez. 2009. Molecular phylogeny of owls (Strigiformes) inferred from DNA sequences of the mitochondrial cyctochrome b and the nuclear RAG-1 gene. *Ardea* 97 (4): 581–591.

INDEX

Index pages in **bold** refer to photographs, maps, or captions.

PETERSON FIELD GUIDES®

Roger Tory Peterson's innovative format uses accurate, detailed drawings to pinpoint key field marks for quick recognition of species and easy comparison of confusing look-alikes.

BIRDS

Birds of North America

Birds of Eastern and Central North America

Western Birds

Eastern Birds

Feeder Birds of Eastern North America

Hawks of North America

Hummingbirds of North America

Warblers

Eastern Birds' Nests

PLANTS AND ECOLOGY

Eastern and Central Edible Wild Plants

Eastern and Central Medicinal Plants and Herbs

Western Medicinal Plants and Herbs

Eastern Forests

Eastern Trees

Western Trees

Eastern Trees and Shrubs

Ferns of Northeastern and Central North America

Mushrooms

North American Prairie

Venomous Animals and Poisonous Plants

Wildflowers of Northeastern and North-Central North America

MAMMALS

Animal Tracks

Mammals

Finding Mammals

INSECTS

Insects

Eastern Butterflies

Moths of Northeastern North America

REPTILES AND AMPHIBIANS

Eastern Reptiles and Amphibians

Western Reptiles and Amphibians

FISHES

Freshwater Fishes

SPACE

Stars and Planets

GEOLOGY

Rocks and Minerals

PETERSON FIRST GUIDES®

The first books the beginning naturalist needs, whether young or old. Simplified versions of the full-size guides, they make it easy to get started in the field, and feature the most commonly seen natural life.

Astronomy

Birds

Butterflies and Moths

Caterpillars

Clouds and Weather

Fishes

Insects

Mammals

Reptiles and Amphibians

Rocks and Minerals

Seashores

Shells

Trees

Urban Wildlife

Wildflowers

PETERSON FIELD GUIDES
FOR YOUNG NATURALISTS

This series is designed with young readers ages eight to twelve in mind, featuring the original artwork of the celebrated naturalist Roger Tory Peterson.

Backyard Birds

Birds of Prey

Songbirds

Butterflies

Caterpillars

PETERSON FIELD GUIDES® COLORING BOOKS®

Fun for kids ages eight to twelve, these color-your-own field guides include color stickers and are suitable for use with pencils or paint.

Birds

Butterflies

Dinosaurs

Reptiles and Amphibians

Wildflowers

Seashores

Shells

Mammals

PETERSON REFERENCE GUIDES®

Reference Guides provide in-depth information on groups of birds and topics beyond identification.

Behavior of North American Mammals

Birding by Impression

Molt in North American Birds

Owls of North America and the Caribbean

Seawatching: Eastern Waterbirds in Flight

PETERSON AUDIO GUIDES

Birding by Ear: Eastern/Central

Bird Songs: Eastern/Central

PETERSON FIELD GUIDE / *BIRD WATCHER'S DIGEST* BACKYARD BIRD GUIDES

Identifying and Feeding Birds

Hummingbirds and Butterflies

Bird Homes and Habitats

The Young Birder's Guide to Birds of North America

The New Birder's Guide to Birds of North America

DIGITAL

App available for Apple and Android.

Peterson Birds of North America

E-books

Birds of Arizona

Birds of California

Birds of Florida

Birds of Massachusetts

Birds of Minnesota

Birds of New Jersey

Birds of New York

Birds of Ohio

Birds of Pennsylvania

Birds of Texas